OPEN SOURCE FOR
WINDOWS ADMINISTRATORS

OPEN SOURCE FOR WINDOWS ADMINISTRATORS

CHRISTIAN GROSS

CHARLES RIVER MEDIA, INC.
Hingham, Massachusetts

Editor: David Pallai
Cover Design: Tyler Creative

CHARLES RIVER MEDIA, INC.
10 Downer Avenue
Hingham, Massachusetts 02043
781-740-0400
781-740-8816 (FAX)
info@charlesriver.com
www.charlesriver.com

This book is printed on acid-free paper.

Christian Gross. *Open Source for Windows Administrators.*
ISBN: 1-58450-347-5

All brand names and product names mentioned in this book are trademarks or service marks of their respective companies. Any omission or misuse (of any kind) of service marks or trademarks should not be regarded as intent to infringe on the property of others. The publisher recognizes and respects all marks used by companies, manufacturers, and developers as a means to distinguish their products.

Library of Congress Cataloging-in-Publication Data
Gross, Christian.
   Open source for Windows administrators / Christian Gross.
      p. cm.
   Includes bibliographical references and index.
   ISBN 1-58450-347-5 (pbk. with dvd-rom : alk. paper)
   1. Operating systems (Computers) 2. Client/server computing. I. Title.
   QA76.76.O63G7679 2005
   005.4'3—dc22
                              2005004608

05 7 6 5 4 3 2 First Edition

CHARLES RIVER MEDIA titles are available for site license or bulk purchase by institutions, user groups, corporations, etc. For additional information, please contact the Special Sales Department at 781-740-0400.

Printed in Canada

Contents

1 Introduction to Open Source

ABOUT THIS BOOK

This book is about using Open Source on a Microsoft® Windows® operating system. Whether you're an administrator managing a computer network or a power user running a small home/office network, this book is for you. The material presented is entirely based on Open Source software and how it can be used to solve specific problems on the Windows platform. For many people, Open Source is associated with the Linux and FreeBSD™ operating systems. However, the Windows operating system is not excluded from using Open Source software. In fact, a very large part of Open Source applications work on multiple operating systems, including Windows.

The purpose of this book is not to overhaul your "operational routine," nor convert you to the world of Open Source software because that would be misleading about the strengths and benefits of Open Source. This book is about providing a set of tools that can be used to complement your current operational routine. Open Source sometimes becomes necessary for two notable reasons: budget restrictions and the need for an individual solution that solves the immediate problem as opposed to an all-encompassing transformation.

As for the first reason, closed source software is most often packaged with a price tag and budgets may not have room for additional spending. Money is commonly a limitation. Open Source is free software, accessible to anyone.

The second reason refers to the situations when a problem arises that does not require an application overhaul, yet the closed source application doesn't have the capability to adequately manage the problem. Alternatively, a proposed solution might require changes in the operation of currently running applications.

Open Source is flexible and allows you to choose and implement specific tools to solve individual problems, such as Web servers, file servers, or mail client applications. For example, suppose that your network is running smoothly until a user asks you to install a SPAM filter to get rid of the user's SPAM e-mails. You suddenly realize you have a problem and need a piece of software. Searching the Internet, you find plenty of client-installed SPAM filters or e-mail servers that include SPAM filters. The objective is to filter e-mails, without interrupting the operations of a fully functional mail server. In Chapter 9, "Processing E-mail," the application Anti-Spam SMTP Proxy (ASSP) can be installed as a preprocessor and is essentially plug and play. The ASSP application does not, for example, manage security; it just manages SPAM, which is the problem that required a solution.

Because this book covers a wide swath of ever-evolving applications, there will be updates, changes, etc. to the individual applications as time goes on. To keep you up to date on the latest changes, a wiki has been setup at the following URL: *http://www.devspace.com/Wikka/wikka.php?wakka=BookOSSForWinAdmin.*

THE ORIGINS OF OPEN SOURCE

Why does Open Source exist? The answer can be best summarized with a quote from Eric Raymond.

> Every good work of software starts by scratching a developer's personal itch. Perhaps this should have been obvious (it's long been proverbial that "Necessity is the mother of invention"), but too often software developers spend their days grinding away for pay at programs they neither need nor love. But not in the Linux world—which may explain why the average quality of software originated in the Linux community is so high.
> —Eric Raymond (*The Cathedral and the Bazaar*)

People in the Open Source market develop software to scratch an itch, as Eric Raymond put it. The developers of Open Source software aren't motivated by profit, as their reward lies in creating a solution that is used for the common good. The problem may be related to Web sites, e-mail, or business processes. Regardless of the context, the result is an assembled group of developers who share a common itch to scratch. Instead of competing against each other, they cooperate and create solutions that may be used by everyone. Think of Open Source as an open community whose purpose is to advance a common good.

The widespread assumption is that Open Source evolved during the last decade. The truth, however, indicates that Open Source has existed since the time computers became accessible to the public. In the early seventies, Open Source was called public domain software. A significant change occurred in the nineties, when Open Source became an official term.

There are two definitions for Open Source, distinguished by lowercase or uppercase letters. A lowercase *open source* indicates that a program's source code can be viewed and modified by other users and developers, generally without restrictions. Licensing, however, does apply and will be discussed later in this chapter.

An uppercase *Open Source* defines a certification owned by the Open Source Initiative (OSI, *http://www.opensource.org*). Software is considered Open Source when it uses a license approved by the OSI. The OSI started as a response to concern in the nineties about ownership of intellectual property. As a result, the OSI has approved certain open source licenses as being Open Source.

The Three Cs

At an O'Reilly Conference keynote, Tim O'Reilly talked about Open Source and its impact on the industry. In that talk, he mentioned the three C's of Open Source:

- **Commodization** of software
- User-**customizable** systems and architectures
- Network-enabled **collaboration**

Commodization of Software

Software is quickly becoming a commodity, with Open Source software leading the way because it is available and plentiful. In the age of the Internet, software is easy to come by and its price value is dropping. This trend does not imply the market's indifference toward software, but its knowledge of the availability and abundance of software.

As software becomes a commodity, it will become plug and play compatible with other pieces of software—similar to a TV and a satellite receiver. A satellite receiver can be connected to a TV with a generic cable, and when both are powered, the picture received by the satellite is displayed on the TV. Nobody purchases a specific satellite receiver for a specific TV. The assumption is that the two pieces of hardware will automatically work together.

Software and, particularly Open Source, are starting to behave like a satellite receiver and TV, which means that other software vendors have to adapt or potentially suffer the consequence of losing market share and income. The outcome of commodization is downward pressure on the price of software.

User-Customizable Systems and Architectures

In the past, closed source software was traditionally extended by using an application programming interface (API). The API limits the scope of the functionality that an extension can offer. Often, an API won't change for years at a time, and when a change does occur, it's usually extensive and causes working extensions to stop functioning. Anyone using an extension is then caught in a bind: to get updates to the main application, the extensions have to be updated as well. To gain more functionality, the application is extended using APIs, which causes more dependence on the entire solution of application and extensions. This result is a potentially very expensive and difficult upgrade path.

In contrast, Open Source rests on a paradigm of solving problems using individual applications that change constantly.

Do not interpret this paradigm as meaning that the user must constantly update the individual applications. The best way to interpret Open Source is to understand that applications can be upgraded when necessary. By using modular and generic programming techniques, Open Source creates solutions that can be assembled like a puzzle. Old components never die in Open Source; they get bug fixes and new components run alongside old components. There is no forced upgrade. The administrator glues applications together to create the solutions that are required.

Network-Enabled Collaboration

Usenet and the Internet made Open Source possible. Open Source developers are similar to traditional developers in that they have requirements and specific problems to solve. Using the Internet, developers can collaborate virtually and can get a project started with a minimum of bureaucratic effort. Traditionally, to start and execute a new project, developers had to set up meetings and make phone calls, which generally revolved around the topic of how to proceed. In the Open Source community, discussions are carried out using Internet chat, e-mail, and Usenet newsgroups—communication mechanisms that are lightweight and flexible. The result is that making something happen in the Open Source community is simpler and more efficient then making things happen using traditional means.

Furthermore, the Open Source development model is neither chaotic nor unstructured. All applications are developed using a coding style, code pieces are peer reviewed, and structure is defined in the overall application development environment. The Open Source development model is entirely virtual, which makes it much simpler to shift resources when necessary.

Should an Administrator Care About Open Source?

At the end of the day, should an administrator care about Open Source? Let's look at different sides of the argument.

Open Source may be harder to understand than many closed source applications. In the long run, however, both Open Source and closed source require the same amount of administrative knowledge. With many closed source applications, it is simple to install and start the application. Closed source applications may solve most of the user's worries, but not all of them. The problems that remain are usually difficult to solve, and require extensive understanding of the closed source application. Open Source, on the other hand, is often not as simple to install and get running, and requires initial, and possibly, upfront understanding of the application. As the user becomes familiar with the application, solutions to problems are easier to find. The point is that knowledge is requisite, regardless of whether the application is Open Source or closed source.

Open Source is flexible, so it is easier to fine tune and tweak. Open Source is a component technology for administrators. Administrators use protocols and de facto APIs to glue individual generic programs together to create a specific solution. The advantage of the gluing approach is that it allows an administrator to pick and choose when to use Open Source and when to use closed source or binary products. Open Source administrators control which pieces go into the overall solution, which is typically "run and forget." The administrator finds the components, pieces them together, and lets the application run. At that point, only patches and little updates are necessary.

Open Source is not a silver bullet. Open Source is a step-by-step solution infrastructure that appears over time. No *one* complete solution with all the bells and whistles appears in a day. For example, if an administrator is currently using a closed source Web server and database engine, simultaneously replacing both products is the wrong approach. A possible Open Source approach would be to replace the Web server and then the database, or to replace the database and leave the rest of the infrastructure as is. The point is that the administrator controls updates, patches, and replacements. Administrators are in control with flexibility on their side.

Understanding the Open Source Licenses

You've seen the short explanation of Open Source, but now a more in-depth explanation is necessary due to the individual licenses that are involved. In contrast to software released using the public domain license, Open Source software has explicit licensing terms.

For the administrator, the different Open Source licenses are generally unimportant because the administrator and other users are considered consumers. Open Source licenses are important, however, when an administrator modifies the source code and then attempts to distribute those modifications. At that point, the modifications are subject to the terms of the Open Source license distributed with the unmodified source(s). The following sections explain the main Open Sources and closed source licenses and their ramifications.

GNU

The GNU license (a play on words that stands for "GNU is Not Unix") or free software movement is the result of the work of Richard Stallman, considered the founder of Open Source. The free software movement started because of his frustrations with a buggy printer driver. He wanted the sources to a printer driver so that the bugs could be fixed, but the company balked.

The GNU or free software movement is not about free software as in free beer. The GNU movement is about free software as in free speech. GNU does not say that software should be free and does recognize that software has an associated cost. However, restricting access to the sources of software is against the GNU philosophy. Many people consider such a notion strictly idealist, because not paying for software kills motivation to develop it. Neither does the free software movement provide the answer to solve the dilemma. The result is that many consider the GNU movement to be unprofitable and the GNU license viral. However, there are companies that have built successful business models from free software. The philosophical debate of the GNU movement is beyond the scope and purposes of this book.

If you are interested in further information, search for the phrases "Eric Raymond" or "Free Software Foundation" on the Web. The search results should give you insight into the meaning of Open Source within a larger picture.

The following sections describe the license types and their ramifications.

Binary

Binary is a closed source license with which the user has the right to use the application, but cannot extend it using programmatic methods unless hooks are provided. The software's creator can impose restrictions on how the software is installed and used. Typically, binary licenses are accompanied by an EULA (End User's License Agreement).

Public Domain

Public domain is a license that is virtually unused these days. Public domain refers to software that may be used for any purpose. The user does not have to inform the software's creator concerning how the software is being used. It is the most liberal and least complicated of all licenses.

GPL (General Public License)

The GPL is an official Open Source license that is frequently used by commercial companies when open sourcing their previously binary licensed products. As an Open Source license, any changes to the source(s) must be published under the same terms as the GPL. For example, if a company develops a product and decides to Open Source it, another company could see the product, make some changes, compile the new source code, and sell the application without sharing the changed source code. The original developer would be unhappy about their work being incorporated into another product without paying the original developers a license fee or giving the changes back to the original developers. The GPL stops such actions, because it requires that all modifications be shared.

The GPL is sometimes considered viral because if a program links into GPL software, then the program must make its sources available. The GPL does not apply if the application uses a neutral technology or external process to call the GPL program. For example, the database MySQL™ is licensed as GPL, but it is possible to access the MySQL database using ODBC (Open Database Connectivity). In theory, if a program connected to the MySQL database using ODBC, the program would have to be licensed using the GPL because the program is "linking" to the MySQL database and therefore subject to GPL. However, the reality is different, because the application using the ODBC connection is not relying specifically on the MySQL database. The application using the ODBC connection could use another ODBC compatible database. If the program had accessed the MySQL database using MySQL APIs, then the GPL could be enforced because the program is dependent on the MySQL database. Further details of the GPL are beyond the scope of this book. (If you need more information, you might consider seeking legal counsel as well.)

Mozilla, LGPL (Lesser General Public License)

This license is similar to the GPL, but without the viral nature. An LGPL or Mozilla licensed program can be combined with another program without having to relicense the other program. However, if the LGPL or Mozilla licensed program is changed, the modifications must be distributed like a GPL. When an LGPL licensed program is combined with another program, a shared or dynamic library must be used. Doing otherwise violates the LGPL or Mozilla licenses and constitutes a GPL integration.

Apache™, Perl, BSD™, MIT™

These types of licenses are liberal in terms of usage, but strict in terms of copyrights. The license terms are liberal because a program written using this type of license can be combined with other programs using other types of licenses without having to change the license type.

Using these types of licenses, it is possible to tweak and modify an already existing application and keep those changes for yourself. However, keep in mind one restriction: the modified program cannot be called the same program, nor the person who modified the program be given credit for the original work. For example, if you modify the sources of Apache, the final package cannot be called Apache. The final package must be called something else, and it must reference that Apache was used to create the final package.

For this licensing category, sometimes the original sources must be distributed alongside the modified application in source code or binary format.

Shared Source

The shared source type of license is not an Open Source license at all, but is mentioned here because some applications may use this license. This license allows the end developer to look at what is underneath the hood, but not use it in a commercial environment. An administrator needs to be very wary of this license because the terms of how the software may be used in a production setting are often defined.

When selecting Open Source software, you should always investigate the nature of the license. In most cases, as an administrator there are no legal issues, but ignorance of the license's details is not a legal defense.

What Hardware and Software Should an Administrator Use?

In Open Source, the configuration of the administrator's computer is not relevant to the overall solution. The administrator's operating system does not have to be the same as the operating system running on other network computers. This is a bold and interesting statement because, traditionally, closed source companies have restrictions on which platforms are supported for the administrator. In Open Source, for example, the administrator can use an Apple® Mac® OSX client to administer a Windows server. The tools the administrator needs are typically not operating system specific.

The tools are often based on Unix®. Many Windows administrators might equate Unix with a cryptic and esoteric past. However, it's important to note that there is a traditional Unix and a modern Unix. Traditional Unix refers to using editors such as vi and Emacs™, and a console. Modern Unix, on the other hand, means using visual editors and GUI toolkits. In modern Unix, the traditional files and batch scripts still exist, but tools that manipulate the traditional files and batch scripts often hide them. In other words, modern Unix is the blending of traditional Unix and GUIs.

I referred to vi, Emacs, and console applications as traditional and not modern to illustrate that modern Unix is a combination of both console and GUI applications. In fact, I regularly use the vi (or vim) editor and explain its use in Chapter 2 "Writing Scripts Using a Shell and Its Associated Tools."

Attempting to distinguish between modern and traditional Unix in a book is difficult because every time "Unix" is referenced, it would have to be accompanied by "modern" or "traditional." A better terminology is reached by defining the different modern Unix operating systems. Modern Unix's refer to operating systems such as FreeBSD, Linux, OpenDarwin/OSX, and so on. Because this book is about Open Source, we'll consider the Linux/BSD operating systems and GNU/OSI (Open System Interconnection) tools that are available on Linux/BSD or the Windows operating system.

TIP

GNU/OSI applications are, traditionally, console-based applications, but higher-level GUI applications that mask the console complexities are available.

Table 1.1 defines the typical software and hardware configurations that an administrator could use to manage GNU/OSI applications.

As you can see in Table 1.1, using Open Source does not mean you are bound to one platform. In theory, an administrator could design the infrastructure using multiple platforms. However, this book is aimed at the Windows administrator and, therefore, we'll discuss the Windows operating system. (The exception to this rule is the use of Linux for one task in this book. Linux was chosen because of licensing terms and not because Windows is inferior or problematic.)

UNDERSTANDING OPEN SOURCE PACKAGES

When confronted with Open Source software for the first time, the combinations and permutations of Open Source software can be mind numbing. It may seem that Open Source software is chaotic and random, which is far from the truth.

In Open Source, there is no concept of an identifier for a released software application. For example, the software used to write this document is OpenOffice 1.1 and Office 2000. Both software packages were executed on a Windows XP operating system. All the mentioned software products (OpenOffice, Office, and Windows) had an explicit reference to a version of software. Sometimes the reference was a numeric identifier; other times it was an alphabetic acronym.

Open Source uses long version numbers to identify the state of the software application. Generally, these version numbers are not easy to remember, as illustrated by the released versions of the Apache Web Server (2.0.52) and Jakarta Tomcat Web Server (5.5.53). Complicating the entire situation, there are also released packages for the versions: 3.2, 3.3, 4.0, 4.1 and 5.0 on the Tomcat Web site.

TABLE 1.1 Typical Administrator Hardware and Software Configurations

Hardware and Software	Required Core Installation
Windows (2000 or XP) should be professional running on an x86 compatible computer	Cygwin™ full installation, Perl, Python™, Java™ VM full installations. Microsoft Terminal client. For the other applications, binary installation files are typically available.
Linux (Preferably Red Hat®, SuSE™, Mandrake™, or Knoppix, but any other Linux would be compatible with installation of extra pieces of software) running on an x86 compatible computer	Most Linux distributions have all the pieces required to administer a Windows Open Source network. For some missing pieces, binary installation files are available. Ideally, CrossOffice for Linux should be installed so that some Windows-only applications can be run.
Apple hardware running OSX	Perl, Python, Java VM full installation. Other tools are available, but typically need to be compiled and installed on the machine. In most cases, there are no compilation problems, but they may occur. Although the Apple hardware running OSX is extremely user friendly and powerful, it is a different platform and requires learning yet another platform.
FreeBSD running on x86-compatible computer	Perl, Python, Java VM full installation. Other tools are available, but typically need to be compiled and installed on the machine. Although there are no compilation problems, FreeBSD does require administrators who are experienced with modern Unix.
Linux running on a non-x86-compatible computer	Using Linux on a non-x86 is, generally, not a recommended option for a novice Windows Open Source administrator. The exception is using Apple hardware running a distribution such as Yellow Dog Linux (YDL). Even with YDL, however, some modern Unix experience is required.
Other Unix type operating system (Solaris™, HPUX™, and so on)	Unknown, many Open Source packages may or may not compile.

In Open Source, version numbers are structured and each part of the version number is significant. Version numbers in Open Source tend to be based on major and minor numbers. It is often difficult to figure out if software is an alpha, beta, or released version. For example, for Linux, odd minor numbers (e.g., 2.5, 2.3) are considered developer unstable releases, whereas even numbers (2.4, 2.6) are considered stable builds. Version numbers in Open Source are considered attained milestones, indicating which major and minor features have been implemented.

It is important to realize that even though there are multiple versions of a particular software, it does not mean that the latest version is the most appropriate to install. Open Source often has parallel versions of the same piece of software. Newer versions will have added features, but often older pieces of software are good enough because the features of the newest versions are of no interest to you. Traditionally, having an older version meant not having access to the newest patches and security fixes. Open Source even with older versions will apply patches and security features.

Version numbers are structured as follows:

Major build number: In the case of Apache Web Server 2.0.52, the major build number is 2. The number 2 represents a major version of the software application. With respect to the Apache Web Server 1.3.28, it is expected that there are major changes and there may not be a simple upgrade possibility.

Minor build number: In the case of Apache Web Server 2.0.52, the minor build number is 0. The number 0 is a minor version of the software application. Differing minor build numbers indicate minor changes and do not require major upgrades.

Patch build number: In the case of Apache Web Server 2.0.52 the patch build number is 52. In other words, the number 52 is a patch version of the software application. This number is used to indicate that fixes and changes were introduced, but the configuration of the application has not changed.

Different major build numbers denote major differences in architecture. Essentially, an Open Source program with two different numbers can be equated to two different programs. For example, Apache HTTP server 1.3.x and 2.x are in many respects identical, but entirely different in other ways. An administrator, when confronted with such an upgrade, must take the time to analyze the differences. The administrator needs to read the included change logs and features to understand the ramifications of the new version. Important to remember is that both versions of Apache HTTP can be executed on the same computer. Running two versions concurrently can simplify the upgrade path and allow an administrator to slowly move to the new version.

When upgrading and patching systems, it is very important to read the change log file that is distributed with every Open Source program. The change log contains descriptions of all the changes made for a particular version. By comparing the version numbers of the installed application and the upgraded version, you can understand changes in terms of functionality.

The different Open Source programs use the following terms to describe the state of the program:

Stable, Release: Software that can be used in a production context and is comparable to released closed source software. Note: because there are no time deadlines, a stable piece of Open Source software is, generally, very robust.

Unstable: Software that probably compiles and possibly executes. If the software executes, then problems are to be expected. Typically, unstable software contains newer features and is comparable to beta closed source software.

Nightly, Daily: Software downloaded from the version control system and used to create a daily or nightly build. This kind of software may compile, and most likely will not execute well. Typically, this version of software is important for the developer to continue adding features. The latest and greatest changes are included in this build of the software.

Milestone: Software that represents the inclusion of specific features. The software may be stable, but most likely is not. The version number is increased because specific features are added that distinguishes the milestone version from a previous version.

Demo: Software that represents a specific state of the software to execute a specific task. The software may or may not be stable. Typically, demo software is hacked to run a specific task and will not run any other task.

Knowing the terms to describe the state of the software and the version numbers makes it simpler for you to know which piece of Open Source software to download. All Open Source software uses the terminology described. For most cases, the administrator would download a stable or release build. To help test a piece of software, the administrator would download an unstable version. Usually, however, an administrator will never download nightly or snapshot builds because those releases are intended for developers.

In Open Source, patches are different from how they exist in the closed source context. For any piece of software, there can be multiple stable builds. In the case of Jakarta Tomcat, versions 4.1.18 and 4.1.24 are stable builds. Version 4.1.24 can be considered a patch for version 4.1.18, which means that an administrator who wants to apply a patch, needs to separate the executable files from the configuration files. Open Source software, like Apache, often does that automatically. There is no single patch, but a series of patches, which may seem daunting until the administrator has gone through one patch cycle. The process then becomes simple as most Open Source programs behave the same way. In most cases, an upgrade requires the administrator to stop the program, copy the application files, and restart the program.

SUMMARY

Open Source software is not a single piece of software that is installed to solve all problems. Open Source software is a technology that is used to solve individual problems that are potentially part of a bigger problem.

The purpose of this book is to present some of the best the Open Source software out there to solve a specific problem. There are various choices available for a specific task, but this book discusses the options that are useful, easy to use from a Windows administrator perspective, and cross-platform compatible. Each chapter in this book defines a specific set of related problems, and the individual Open Source programs that can be used to solve those problems. Each Open Source program is explained using a Program Identifier, Short Description, Reference Table of Critical Information, Impatient Installation, Deployment, and Solution Techniques.

A short description of each chapter is given as follows:

Chapter 2 "Writing Scripts Using a Shell and Its Associated Tools": Explains how to write shell scripts using BASH and its associated text-processing tools. Using the information presented in this chapter, you'll learn how to write automation scripts to manage other programs.

Chapter 3 "Using Python to Write Scripts": Explains the Python programming language to write scripts. This second programming language is introduced because Python is a more sophisticated language that can be used for more complex administrative scripts.

Chapter 4 "Managing Security Using Encryption and Privacy Tools": Focuses on using encryption to secure data and communications between two computers.

Chapter 5 "Running Tasks on a Local Computer": Focuses on using tools installed on a local computer that processes information which controls the computer, manages its files, and runs administrative scripts.

Chapter 6 "Authentication and Managing Files": Focuses on storing data using the Light Weight Directory Access Protocol (LDAP) data store and Windows-compatible File Server SAMBA. Both data stores can be used for providing user authentication services.

Chapter 7 "Managing Data Stores": Explains the management of a relational database. The relational database programming language, Structured Query Language (SQL), is not discussed at length and covered only for administrative purposes.

Chapter 8 "Generating Web Content": Focuses on how to manage a Web server.

Chapter 9 "Processing E-mail": Focuses on how to process e-mail, send, receive, and filter e-mail.

Chapter 10 "Productivity Applications": Focuses on how to install and manage productivity applications, such as an e-mail client or Office software package.

2 Writing Scripts Using a Shell and Its Associated Tools

ABOUT THIS CHAPTER

The focus in this chapter is to show you how to write shell scripts in the context of the Windows operating system. Shell scripting is a powerful way to process files, read directories, and perform administrative tasks. Shell scripting is common on Unix or Linux/BSD operating systems. Windows has a cut down shell-scripting environment called Windows batch files, but these batch files make it difficult to write sophisticated scripts as they only contain a subset of the functionality that a full shell script contains.

Recently, however, Windows offered a dual approach by making it possible to write scripts using the Windows Scripting Host. The Windows Scripting Host shouldn't be confused with shell scripts because they are not the same. A Windows scripting host manipulates objects to automate some tasks. A Windows Script is complicated to use when automating tasks that you would normally perform on the command line. This is especially apparent when manipulating text blocks or directories. To create a directory using Windows Scripting Host, an object has to be instantiated, and the appropriate method has to be called. Using shell scripting, a directory is created by using the `mkdir` command, just like the command line.

The following technologies are specifically covered in this chapter:

Windows Shell: The Windows shell is not just about Windows batch files, but includes how processes are executed, how environment variables are manipulated, and how to store or retrieve data from the Windows registry. When writing shell scripts using the Cygwin toolkit, it's necessary to learn about the Windows shell.

Cygwin: The Cygwin toolkit and environment is used as a Unix compatibility layer on Windows allowing an administrator to write scripts using Unix tools. This chapter covers the details of how to install Cygwin for deployment and individual installations.

Vi: Many editors can be used to edit files, and Vi (Vim) is one of the oldest and still very popular. This chapter explains the keystroke details for using Vi.

BASH, awk, etc.: Unix administrators use many tools. This chapter covers BASH (a scripting environment), awk (a line processor), and many others. Multiple scripts will be illustrated that show how to manipulate directories and write scripts using programmatic techniques.

Even though the focus in this book is on the Cygwin toolkit, the Msys and GNUWin32 tools also offer similar functionalities. You might use those tools for performance reasons or because you only need one or two utilities and don't want to install the Cygwin toolkit.

UNDERSTANDING THE WINDOWS SHELL

The biggest difference between Windows and any Linux/BSD operating system is the filesystem. When an application, or utility, executes on Windows or Linux/BSD, that same application or utility will appear identical. The operating system to a large degree has become irrelevant. In much earlier times, when an application ran on one platform, it was very difficult if not impossible to make the application run on another platform. However, today those problems have largely been solved because toolkits such as Cygwin have reasonable solutions.

Filesystems

The one difference that remains between Windows and Linux/BSD operating systems is the structure of the filesystem. On Windows, the filesystem is based on the premise that drive letters are associated with devices as shown in Figure 2.1.

In Figure 2.1, Windows Explorer has been started, which allows any Windows user to navigate the drives (devices) and inspect the content that the drives contain. Figure 2.1 shows the A (floppy drive), C, D, E (CD-ROM drive), and F drives. On a Linux/BSD operating system in contrast, there are no A, C, or D drives. There is only the root, which is a single slash (/) and devices are attached to the directory

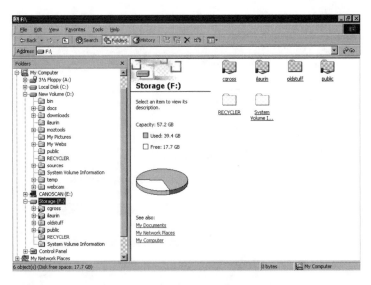

FIGURE 2.1 Windows Explorer showing the various devices on a specific computer.

tree as other directories. For example, on a Linux/BSD operating system, you could create the directories /A, /C, /D, and so on and attach the various hard disk and floppy drive devices to those directories. A Linux/BSD operating system doesn't define the devices with letters to indicate the device type. A typical Linux/BSD operating system mounts the devices in specific directories such as /mnt/floppy for the floppy drive. When writing Unix scripting utilities, the directory structure difference must be carefully considered.

Mounting a Device in a Directory

Windows 2000 and later operating systems have the capability to mount a storage device in a particular directory. To do that, you can follow these steps:

1. Start the Computer Management application, which is located in the Administrative part of the Control Panel.
2. Select the tree control node Storage → Disk Management.
3. From the listbox on the righthand side, select a volume and right-click to open the shortcut menu as shown in Figure 2.2.
4. In Figure 2.2, select Change Drive Letter and Path from the context menu. The Change Drive Letter dialog box appears.
5. Click on the Add button and the Add New Drive Letter or Path dialog box appears as shown in Figure 2.3.

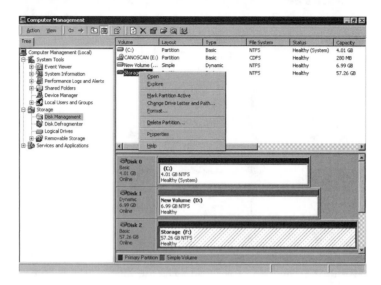

FIGURE 2.2 Selecting a hard disk volume that will be mapped to a directory.

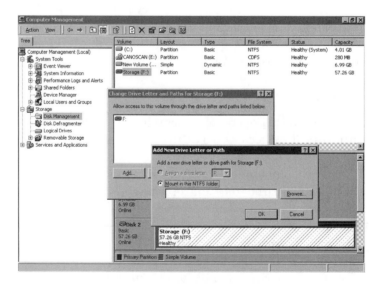

FIGURE 2.3 Assigning the directory that the hard disk volume will be assigned to.

6. In Figure 2.3, the Mount in this NTFS Folder radio button is preselected in the Add New Drive Letter or Path dialog box. You can also click on the Browse button to select a directory for where the device will be mounted. When a hard disk volume is mounted this way, it's entirely identical to a Linux/BSD operating system.

Modern File Management in Windows

Being able to mount a device within a directory makes it simpler to manage a filesystem as one contiguous directory space. You still need to create at least one drive letter, which is typically the drive letter C. That difference aside, it's possible to navigate the directory structure and create scripts that function similarly on Windows and Linux/BSD operating systems. As an example, Figure 2.4 shows the user drive F from Figure 2.2 mounted as the Cygwin user's home directory.

A major problem when manipulating files within a shell script are slashes (e.g., c:\somedirectory). Sometimes is necessary to use the forward slash (/), instead of the backward slash (\ ). The Windows operating system typically uses the backward slash and the Windows console requires it. Using the forward slash, which is often required by Cygwin, can cause problems with some Windows-supplied utilities. For example, the command xcopy will not work using the forward slash.

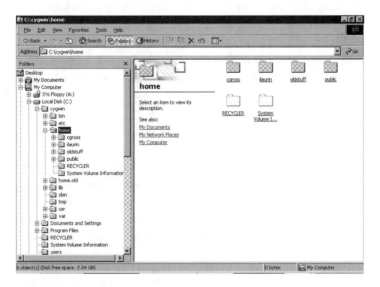

FIGURE 2.4 Mapping a hard disk volume to the Cygwin user home directory.

The problem with the backward slash is that GNU/OSI applications recognize a single backward slash as an escape sequence character. To make a GNU/OSI application recognize a backward slash as a backward slash, you must use a double slash (e.g., `c:\\somedirectory`). If there are spaces in the path, then you must use either quotes around the path (e.g., `"c:\\some directory"`) or an escape sequence (e.g., `c:/some\ directory`). The rules are generally not necessary when writing Windows batch files, where the only exception is the quotes for paths with spaces. GNU/OSI applications and scripts require that the administrator is very careful with their slashes and spaces. With time and practice, it will become obvious when to use each slash.

Windows Shell and Environment

The current Windows shell is a leftover from the DOS era. With Windows NT, the `.bat` extension has been replaced with the `.cmd` extension. The `.cmd` extension should be used instead of `.bat` because it invokes a newer version of the shell command `cmd.exe`. Regardless of which extension is used, remember that the Windows shell is a wrapper-oriented programming language.

Wrappers are shell scripts used to start other programs, set up paths, make operating system environment decisions, and update the operating system environment. A wrapper programming language is generally not considered a full-fledged scripting language. Windows batch files are considered a wrapper programming language because they are unable to handle complex tasks.

Essentially Windows batch files allow the definition of environment variables, make simple decisions, select applications, and execute a specific application. You can do more using additional tools, but that is beyond the scope of this book. To write a more sophisticated script that adds users or manipulates a log, the scripting languages BASH or Python should be used. BASH is discussed later in this chapter, and Python is discussed in Chapter 3.

Managing Environment Variables

Even though Windows batch files are less sophisticated, they are still useful. A batch file can be used to define environment variables before running an application. Using a batch file in this context is called writing a wrapper script. Wrapper scripts can be written very quickly because they are simple. Following is an example wrapper script used to run the Ant build tool, which runs on the Java Virtual Machine (JVM):

```
@echo off
REM   Copyright (c) 2001-2002 The Apache Software Foundation.
All rights
```

```
REM   reserved.
if "%OS%"=="Windows_NT" @setlocal
if ""%1""=="""" goto runCommand
rem Change drive and directory to %1
if "%OS%"=="Windows_NT" cd /d ""%1""
if not "%OS%"=="Windows_NT" cd ""%1""
shift
REM Slurp the command line arguments. This loop allows for
an unlimited number
REM of arguments (up to the command line limit, anyway).
set ANT_RUN_CMD=%1
if ""%1""=="""" goto runCommand
shift
:loop
if ""%1""=="""" goto runCommand
set ANT_RUN_CMD=%ANT_RUN_CMD% %1
shift
goto loop
:runCommand
REM echo %ANT_RUN_CMD%
%ANT_RUN_CMD%
if "%OS%"=="Windows_NT" @endlocal
```

In the example, the environment variables are OS, and ANT_RUN_CMD. The OS environment variable is from the operating system, whereas the ANT_RUN_CMD environment variable is dynamically created in the batch file. The command REM should be ignored because it is a comment. The example code checks the operating system type and then executes a program appropriate for the operating system.

The reference to the environment variable %1 is not an environment variable, but a command-line option. The variable %1 references the first command-line option as shown by the following sample command line:

```
antrun otherapp.exe
```

The command antrun is the wrapper script to execute. The second argument otherapp.exe is the environment variable %1. It's important to remember that the first command-line argument (zeroth index) is always the program or script that is executing.

In the example wrapper script, the environment variable OS is referenced using the %OS% notation where the percentage characters are delimiters. The environment variable OS is one of many environment variables defined by default in Windows. The Control Panel shows all the environment variables defined on the local computer. In

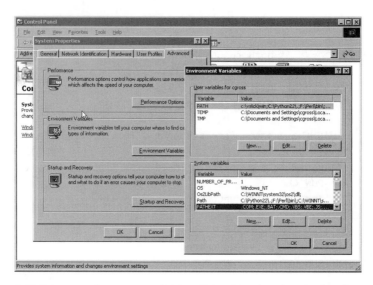

FIGURE 2.5 Environment Variables dialog box showing the locally defined environment variables.

the Control Panel, double-clicking the System icon opens the System Properties dialog box. From there, you click the Advanced tab and then click the Environment Variables button. The resulting dialog box should appear similar to Figure 2.5.

In Figure 2.5, there are two listboxes shown in the Environment Variables dialog box. The upper listbox represents the user environment variables and the lower listbox represents the system environment variables. In Windows, a user environment variable is a variable defined specific to an individual user. This means when other users log on, they do not see the environment variables of the other user. This allows an administrator to define individual environment variables for each user. System environment variables define environment variables that all users share and are shared by Windows Services.

Environment variables are not case-sensitive on the Windows platforms. When writing scripts that will execute on multiple platforms, be consistent regarding the case used.

TIP

In Figure 2.5, the environment variable path exists in both the user and system listbox. When this happens, the value of the environment variable in the user listbox overrides the value of the environment variable in the system listbox. By defining an environment variable in the system listbox, a default value is defined that can be refined by a user. There is only one exception to the rule. The user listbox value of the environment variable path does not override the system listbox value, but concatenates the two values due to the special nature of the path environment variable. The path environment variable defines the search path of where to find applications. It would make logical sense to concatenate the user local paths and the system paths when attempting to find an application.

Integration: Registry

On the Windows platform instead of using configuration files, Microsoft urges software vendors to use the registry. The *registry* is a type of giant file that contains settings about the computer and the installed software. To interact with the registry, there are a set of APIs. Open Source applications typically make very limited use of the registry. If an Open Source application does make use of the registry, usually it's to bootstrap an application. Figure 2.6 shows the structure of the registry as viewed from the Registry Editor application.

Bootstrapping an application is a way of providing an initial reference point from a central location where the application can get more detailed configuration information. Let's say that an application is started as a Windows Service. Most Windows Services do not start with predefined command-line parameters. This means that when the Windows Service starts, the application does not know where to get its configuration information. One solution is for the program to expect a file to exist at a certain location. The problem with this approach is that the administrator must always ensure that the file and path exists. The administrator is locked into a solution that is not typical on the Windows operating system. The better approach is for the application to define a central directory that is predefined by the operating system. Windows used this approach in the past when storing configuration information in

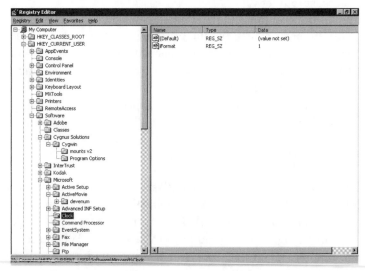

FIGURE 2.6 Registry Editor showing the structure of the registry.

.ini files. Microsoft then upgraded.ini files to use the registry. So while an Open Source application might not make excessive use of the registry, the Windows administrator must interact with the registry for some tasks.

Using Reg.exe from the Command Line

When it's necessary to create scripts that interact with the registry, a console-based program must be used. Shell script languages such as BASH interact entirely with the console and therefore the registry manipulation program must interact with the console. The program reg.exe (reg) solves the console problem and is downloaded from the Microsoft site at *ftp://ftp.microsoft.com/bussys/winnt/winnt-public/reskit/nt40/i386/reg_x86.exe.* Alternatively, you can get the program by installing the Support Toolkit that ships with the Windows Operating System CD or the Windows Resource Toolkit that is appropriate for the operating system. The free version from the Internet is an older version that works on newer operating systems, but has different command-line arguments.

TIP

If for some reason you cannot install, find, or use the reg.exe *program, the Cygwin toolkit provides a program called* regtool.exe, *which is similar to* reg.exe *but has different command-line arguments.* reg.exe *was chosen as a tool for this book because it is from Microsoft and can be used in any shell scripting language. For example, this means those individuals who use MSYS can use* reg.exe *as well.*

The reg.exe program has a command-line structure similar to the following:

```
reg command options
```

The option command can be one of following values: query, add, delete, copy, save, restore, load, unload, compare, export, or import. The option options identifier represents the options specific to the command. Next, each of the commands and its associated options are explained.

The query command is used to find a specific key. Following is an example query to search within the Software key for all child keys and values:

```
reg query HKCU\\Software
```

Notice in the example that double slashes are used because the command reg is executed in the context of a BASH shell. Were reg executed in the context of a Windows batch file or Windows shell, then the double slash would not be necessary, and only a single slash would need to be written. When the reg command is executed, content similar to the following is generated:

```
HKCU\Software key information
! REG.EXE VERSION 2.0
HKEY_CURRENT_USER\Software
HKEY_CURRENT_USER\Software\Adobe
HKEY_CURRENT_USER\Software\Cygnus Solutions
HKEY_CURRENT_USER\Software\InterTrust
HKEY_CURRENT_USER\Software\Kodak
HKEY_CURRENT_USER\Software\Microsoft
HKEY_CURRENT_USER\Software\Netscape
HKEY_CURRENT_USER\Software\Nico Mak Computing
HKEY_CURRENT_USER\Software\Policies
HKEY_CURRENT_USER\Software\Qualcomm
HKEY_CURRENT_USER\Software\VB and VBA Program Settings
HKEY_CURRENT_USER\Software\WinZip Computing
HKEY_CURRENT_USER\Software\Classes
```

In the generated output, the key HKCU is an abbreviation for the root registry key HKEY_CURRENT_USER. Following is an enumeration of all valid abbreviations that can be used to define a root registry key:

HKLM: HKEY_LOCAL_MACHINE contains all the settings specific to the local machine. Typically, system-wide software configuration items are stored within the SOFTWARE child key.

HKCU: HKEY_CURRENT_USER contains all the settings specific to a user on the local machine. User-specific software configuration items are stored within the SOFTWARE child key.

HKCR: HKEY_CLASSES_ROOT contains all the settings specific to the objects registered on the machine. Typically an object is a Component Object Model (COM) library.

HKU: HKEY_USERS contains all the users registered on the machine.

HKCC: HKEY_CURRENT_CONFIG contains all the settings specific to the current configuration of the machine.

Following is an example query that retrieves the value of a registry value:

```
reg query HKCU\\Software\\Microsoft\\Clock /v iFormat
```

Executing the example query, the following output is generated:

```
HKEY_CURRENT_USER\Software\Microsoft\Clock
    iFormat    REG_SZ  1
```

In the generated output, the value of the registry value `iFormat` is output in a format that includes the parent key, value identifier, and the type of the value.

Following is an example query that lists and/or enumerates all descendent keys and values:

```
reg query "HKCU\\Software\\Cygnus Solutions" /s
```

Adding a key or value to the registry is a bit more complicated because there are more command-line options. When adding a key or value, only a single key or value can be added for each execution of `reg.exe`.

Following is an example of how to add a key to the registry:

```
reg add HKCU\\Software\\Devspace
```

TIP

The add *command automatically creates keys if they do not exist. For example, imagine that the key is* HKCU\\Sofwares\\key *and the identifier* Softwares *is a typo that should have been* Software. *The* add *command creates the key* Softwares *and hence creates an incorrect registry tree without any feedback. Therefore, check key spelling before running lengthy scripts. You should also invest in a utility or a script that rolls back the registry, when registry scripts are being tested.*

Following is an example of how to add a value to the registry:

```
reg add HKCU\\Software\\Devspace /v strValue /t REG_SZ /d hello
```

The command `reg` uses four options that are needed to add a value to the registry. The purpose of each of the four options is described in Table 2.1

Following is an example of adding a DWORD value using a hexadecimal notation:

```
reg add HKCU\\Software\\Devspace /v dwVal /t REG_DWORD /d 0x04d2
```

Following is an example of adding a DWORD value using decimal notation:

```
reg add HKCU\\Software\\Devspace /v dwVal2 /t REG_DWORD /d 42
```

The difference between the two previous examples is that the first example uses a 0x notation to indicate that the number to be added is encoded in hexadecimal.

TABLE 2.1 Description of Options

Option	Description
`HKCU\\Software\\Devspace`	Registry key that will be the parent of the value.
`/v strValue`	Name of the value that is added to the registry.
`/t REG_SZ`	Type of the value that is added. Can be one of the following:
	`REG_SZ`: A variable length string value type.
	`REG_MULTI_SZ`: A multiple variable length string value type.
	`REG_DWORD_BIG_ENDIAN`: A 32-bit Big Endian number value type (such as `REG_DWORD`).
	`REG_DWORD`: A 32-bit number value type.
	`REG_BINARY`: A binary value type.
	`REG_DWORD_LITTLE_ENDIAN`: A 32-bit number value type.
	`REG_NONE`: A no specific datatype value.
	`REG_EXPAND_SZ`: A variable length string that contains references to environment variables. The value is expanded when the registry key is read using a specific Windows API.
`/d hello`	The data that is saved to the value. If binary data is required as for the type `REG_DWORD`, it's in hexadecimal format.

TIP

Hexadecimal encoding is counting using base 16. By default, humans count to base 10 (0,1,2,3,4,5,6,7,8,9). After the digit nine comes a zero, and then a one is carried to the next decimal place to create 10. The same occurs in hexadecimal, except the numbers are counted 0,1,2,3,4,5,6,7,8,9,a,b,c,d,e,f, and after the f is 10.

Following is an example of saving a value in binary format:

```
reg add HKCU\\Software\\Devspace /v binaryValue /t REG_BINARY
/d 61626364655A
```

In the example, the string of hexadecimal numbers is a piece of binary data. A 0x is not prefixed before the hexadecimal number because it is implied. The binary data could in theory be as long as required. The reality is that the console command line can only accept so many characters. A way of getting around this restriction in a shell script is to use a variable to reference the data. By referencing a variable, the shell script copies the data and the command line can handle a much larger data set.

Deleting registry keys and values is simple and straightforward. In the following example, a registry key and all its descendant keys and values are deleted:

```
reg query HKCU\\Software\\Devspace
```

The command will delete each item, but a command prompt will ask if the key or value should be deleted. In an automated scripting context, this will lead to problems because there may be no one to react to the command prompt.

The following command-line example does not prompt for confirmation when deleting keys or values:

```
reg query HKCU\\Software\\Devspace /f
```

Following is an example where only the immediate child values are deleted:

```
reg delete HKCU\\Software\\Devspace\\Another /va
```

The command option copy is used to copy keys and values from one location of the registry to another location. Copying is useful when creating default values that are used as a basis for custom values. An example that copies the values below the key orig to the location dest is as follows:

```
reg copy HKCU\\Software\\Devspace\\orig HKCU\\Software\\Devspace\\dest
```

If in the process of copying, a key or value already exists, then a command prompt appears asking if the key or value can be overwritten. The following example executes the reg command that does not prompt to ask if a key or value can be overwritten:

```
reg copy HKCU\\Software\\Devspace\\orig
HKCU\\Software\\Devspace\\dest /f
```

Following is an example that copies all descendant keys and values:

```
reg copy HKCU\\Software\\Devspace\\orig
HKCU\\Software\\Devspace\\dest /s
```

Using the command compare, you can compare two registry keys, their descendent keys, and their values. The output results of the comparison can be defined to display the elements that are different or that match. The following example is a comparison between two registry keys:

```
reg compare HKCU\\Software\\Devspace\\branch1
HKCU\\Software\\Devspace\\branch2
```

When the previous example is executed, the following output is generated:

```
< Value:  HKEY_CURRENT_USER\Software\Devspace\branch1
dwordValue  REG_DWORD  0x4d2
> Value:  HKEY_CURRENT_USER\Software\Devspace\branch2
dwordValue  REG_DWORD  0x4d3
< Value:  HKEY_CURRENT_USER\Software\Devspace\branch1
expanded  REG_EXPAND_SZ  c:\something;%path%
> Value:  HKEY_CURRENT_USER\Software\Devspace\branch2
expandeddiff  REG_EXPAND_SZ  c:\something;%path%
Result Compared:  Different
```

In sample output, each line that is output follows a pattern. For each line, the first character can be a <, >, or =. If the first character is a < character, then the value displayed is less than the compared value. If the first character is a > character, then the value displayed is greater than the compared value. When the < or the > characters are displayed, the lines in the output are always in pairs.

In the sample output, the first line is less than the second line, and the second line is greater than the first line. The third line is less than the fourth line and the fourth line is greater than the third line. The = character indicates that the identifier value equals the other identifier value.

Following is an example where the comparison includes the keys and values and descendant keys and values:

```
reg compare HKCU\\Software\\Devspace\\branch1
HKCU\\Software\\Devspace\\branch2 /s
```

When the command reg is executed, the following matched keys and values are generated:

```
reg compare HKCU\\Software\\Devspace\\branch1
HKCU\\Software\\Devspace\\branch2 /s /os
```

The flag /os (and its three other variations) is used to filter the generated output resulting from a compare action. The four filtering options are defined as follows:

/**oa**: Output all elements that are different and equal.

/**od**: Output all elements that are different.

/**os**: Output all elements that are equal.

/**on**: Do not output anything.

The option /on is puzzling because when it's executed using the reg command, no results are generated. This option is useful when only a test of equality or inequality needs to be executed. The output of the equality test is generated by a returned value that is generated by reg.exe when it exits. Following is a list of return codes:

0: The application returned successfully and the compared registry values are equal.

1: The application failed.

2: The application returned successfully and the compared registry values are unequal.

The three commands save, export, and unload function in a similar manner. All three commands save the state of the registry key and its descendents to a file. The difference between the three commands is the format of the saved data. The actions of the three save commands are listed here:

save: Saves a key and its descendents to a binary formatted file called a hive (.hiv).

export: Saves a key and its descendents to a text formatted file called a registry file (.reg).

unload: Saves a key and its descendents to a binary formatted file called a hive. Regardless of which command is used to save some registry information, only those keys that have as an ultimate parent the keys HKLM and HKU can be saved.

Following is an example that saves a registry key and its descendents to the file devspace.hiv:

```
reg save HKCU\\Software\\Devspace devspace.hiv
```

The three commands restore, import, load function in a similar manner and load into the registry keys and values. The difference between the three commands is the format of the file that is loaded into the registry. What each of the three commands does is defined as follows:

restore: Loads some keys and values stored in a binary hive file (.hiv) into the registry.

import: Loads some keys and values stored in a registry file (.reg) into the registry.

load: Loads a number of registry entries, such as the restore command, except that the ultimate parent of the loaded keys must be either HKLM or HKU.

Following is an example that loads a hive file into the registry at the specified registry key path:

```
reg restore HKCU\\Software\\Devspace devspace.hiv
```

The restore command requires an additional option, which specifies the path in the registry where the hive will be restored. In the example that means the hive devspace.hiv will be restored under the registry key HKCU\\Software\\Devspace. If the registry key does not exist, then an error will be generated.

Following is an example of importing registry settings using a registry file:

```
reg import devspace.reg
```

Notice that when importing into the registry using the import option, a registry key path is not used. The reason is because a hive stores registry keys and values using relative paths, and registry files stores registry keys and values using absolute paths.

Managing the Path and Environment Variables

Managing the path and environment variables in a runtime scenario using scripts can be challenging because a shell script that changes an environment variable is not a permanent change. A permanent change is a change that is visible in the Environment Variables dialog box shown previously in Figure 2.5. To make a permanent change, there are two free utilities available from the Microsoft Web site that makes things simpler: setx.exe and pathman.exe.

On the Windows platform, changes in the execution environment of a process may or may not be reflected in the child process. This means when changing the value of an environment variable, the change has been made permanently in the registry directly. When you use setx.exe, the changes made to environment variables are permanent. This is useful for scripts that will be executed in different processes.

Following is an example where an environment variable is set:

```
setx testvariable "something else"
```

There are a couple of catches when using the `setx` program. First, the environment variable is written to the environment, which is the registry. The value of the environment variable is not stored in the currently executing console session or process. A new console session has to be started. Second, if the environment variable is referenced from within a batch script or a shell script that is case sensitive, then the environment variable must be referenced in the other scripts with all letters in uppercase. This is a requirement even if the environment variable is defined using lowercase letters.

By default, when the `setx` command is executed, the environment variable is written to the user environment variables list. Following is an example where the environment variable is written to the system environment variable list:

```
setx testvariable "something else" -m
```

Another way to assign and retrieve environment variables is to manipulate the registry values located under `HKCU\Environment` for the user environment variable list or `HKLM\SYSTEM\CurrentControlSet\Control\SessionManager\Environment` for the system environment variable list. By using the `reg.exe` program and the techniques described in the previous section, you can manipulate environment variables. The only downside to manipulating the registry directly is that it's a discovered hack and could potentially change in the next version of Windows. Just as in `setx.exe`, the environment variable changes will only be activated when the next console session is started.

The application `pathman.exe` is a program that can add or remove directory locations to the environment variable `PATH`. You can do the same thing manually using the registry. The advantage of `pathman.exe` is that you don't have to search the registry key value for the existence of a path. Following is an example that adds the Cygwin `bin` directory to the path:

```
pathman /au "c:\\My Cygwin\\bin"
```

The directory `c:\\My Cygwin\\bin` is enclosed in quotes because there is a space between the words `My Cygwin`. If multiple directory locations are to be added or removed from the path, then each directory location has to be separated by a semicolon. The command line option `/au` is one of four options that manipulates the `PATH` environment variable:

/as: Adds a path(s) to the system path.

/au: Adds a path(s) to the user path.

/rs: Removes a path(s) from the system path.

/ru: Removes a path(s) from the user path.

PROJECT: CYGWIN

Cygwin is a Linux/BSD compatibility layer for the Windows operating system. When Windows NT was created, Microsoft created a POSIX compatibility layer. POSIX is a neutral version of Unix. The Windows POSIX layer implemented the basics, but not enough to accomplish most tasks. As a result, companies developed Unix compatibility layers and sold them as products. Microsoft eventually bought one of the software companies that created a Unix compatibility layer, and has freely provided the product as *Microsoft Windows Services for Unix.*

The product Microsoft provides is excellent, but geared toward traditional Unix. Cygwin is intended to be a Linux/BSD compatibility layer and distributes various open source packages. An example is the inclusion by Microsoft of a native NFS (Network File System) driver, which allows Windows computers to connect to Unix computers. NFS is used in the Open Source community, but also used is Common Internet File System (CIFS). If a computer network consists solely of Unix computers, traditionally NFS is used. Cygwin cannot connect to an NFS server because Cygwin does not provide an NFS driver. The Windows Services for Unix does provide an NFS client driver and server. Microsoft uses the CIFS protocol, implemented by Samba for Linux/BSD, to communicate when serving files or managing domains between Windows computers.

There are two parts to the Cygwin toolkit; a dynamic link library (DLL) and a set of tools that are very similar to the Linux/BSD environment. Cygwin provides a set of tools that can be used to compile Linux/BSD applications that will execute on a Windows operating system. For the administrator, the Cygwin toolkit can be used to manage a Windows computer. Programming languages are included, such as Python and Perl, as well as shell environments such as BASH and the Z Shell (ZSH). For the scope of this book BASH and Python are used manage the Windows computer.

The Cygwin toolkit tools are split into two subparts. One part is the console application part, which is the traditional Cygwin toolkit. The other part is a fairly recent inclusion of the X-Server toolkit derived from the XFree sources. In Linux/BSD speak, X-Server is a GUI toolkit. Unlike Windows, the X-Server toolkit is based on a server and client. This allows a user to remotely log on to an X-Server. The X-Server included with Cygwin can run X-Windows applications natively, or can connect to another Unix or Linux/BSD computer and use its resources. X-Server is similar to Terminal Services for Unix and Linux/BSD operating systems. Figure 2.7 is an example snapshot of the Cygwin toolkit running the console BASH shell and the X-Server based BASH shell.

For the Windows administrator and user, the native X-Server functionality is not that useful because Cygwin X-Server native applications are not that popular. What is important is the capability to use the Cygwin X-Server to log on to another

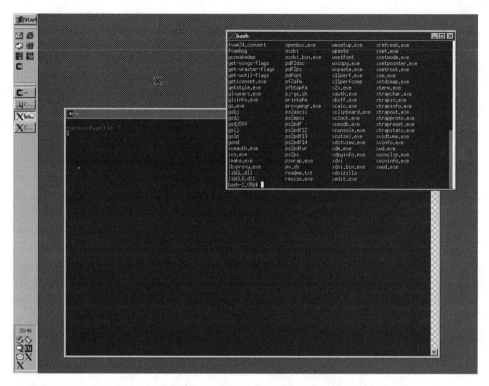

FIGURE 2.7 Snapshot of running a console window and X-Server application.

Unix or Linux/BSD computer and execute Unix or Linux/BSD applications. Table 2.2 lists the reference information for the Cygwin toolkit.

Additional Notes

The Cygwin toolkit's documentation is adequate. The individual packages that make up the toolkit are not documentated. The user is encouraged to seek documentation for the individual packages elsewhere. What is well documented are the runtime issues of the Cygwin library as documented in *Cygwin Users Guide*. You should download and read this as either an HTML document or PDF document. Another option is to read the mailing list when there are particular problems.

The mailing lists offered by the Cygwin team are comprehensive. There are the following mailing lists:

cygwin: A mailing list that discusses how to use the Cygwin toolkit. Often the topics discussed deal with the packages included with Cygwin.

cygwin-xfree: A mailing list that discusses the X-Server implementation for Cygwin. The X-Server implementation used is based off XFree.

TABLE 2.2 Reference Information for the Cygwin Toolkit

Item	Description
Home page	*http://sources.redhat.com/cygwin*
Installation	The default installation procedure is to download an application that then downloads the other packages.
	http://sources.redhat.com/cygwin/setup.exe
Documentation	There are several pieces of documentation, but for administrators the most important one is *Cygwin Users Guide.* Be sure to read the document because although the most important details are covered in this book, some details are not.
	http://cygwin.com/docs.html
Versions	Versions of the Cygwin toolkit is a misnomer because the toolkit contains many applications, each of which has its own version. By default, any version of Cygwin that is downloaded using the setup application is a released version and considered stable.
Mailing Lists	Although there are several mailing lists, the three mailing lists of particular interest to administrators are cygwin, cywin-announce, and cygwin-apps.
	http://cygwin.com/lists.html
Impatient Installation Time Required	Setup program: 20 minutes to select and post install packages not including download time.
	Bytes Downloaded: Setup program ~500 KB. Package downloads range from 100 MB to 300 MB depending on what is selected.
DVD Location	The Cygwin toolkit is located under the directory `cygwin`. To do a fresh install of the program from the DVD, run the program `setup.exe` located under the DVD directory `cygwin`.

cygwin-announce: A mailing list that announces releases of the Cygwin toolkit. Included in the announcements are releases relating to new packages that make up the Cygwin toolkit.

cygwin-announce-xfree: A mailing list that announces releases of the Cygwin X-Server toolkit. Included in the announcements are applications that execute within the X-Server.

cygwin-apps: A mailing list intended for those who want to submit packages to the Cygwin package or those who want to build and modify the `setup.exe` application.

cywin-patches: A mailing list used to submit patches for the Cygwin DLL.

cygwin-developers: A closed and by approval mailing list intended for those who want to modify and help build the Cygwin toolkit. This mailing list is very low level in nature and tends to discuss obscure issues needed for the Cygwin toolkit.

cygwin-cvs: A mailing list that receives Concurrent Versions System (CVS) updates.

cygwin-apps-cvs: A mailing list that receives CVS updates for the applications that are distributed with Cygwin.

The mailing lists can be download as Unix mail-formatted files. Applications such as Mozilla or Thunderbird can read Unix mail files natively. The search facility offered by the Cygwin mailing lists is acceptable, and you can use it to find an answer to a problem. When searching, use different combinations of search terms and be prepared to browse the results to find the answer you are looking for. For more detailed searches, download the mailing list files, import them into a mail reader, and then perform a search. If you cannot find an answer, you might consider subscribing to a mailing list so you can post your question.

Impatient Installation

The simplest way to install Cygwin is to install the setup application referenced on the Cygwin Web site (*http://sources.redhat.com/cygwin/*). Go to the site and then follow these steps:

1. Find the Install or update now! link. The link references the application `setup.exe`, which when downloaded and started will start the Cygwin installation process. The application `setup.exe` bootstraps the Cygwin installation that installs multiple other applications such as Apache.
2. Click the link to open the Cygwin Setup dialog box as shown in Figure 2.8.
3. The only options are to cancel the installation or click on the Next button. Click Next to open the Choose Installation Type dialog box (see Figure 2.9).

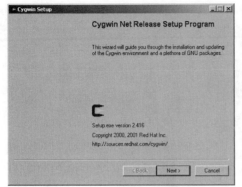

FIGURE 2.8 Initial Cygwin installation dialog box.

FIGURE 2.9 Dialog box used to install Cygwin using three different options.

4. You have three choices for how to install the Cygwin toolkit:

   - **Install from Internet**: The individual programs are downloaded from the Internet, stored in a temporary directory, and then installed.
   - **Download from Internet**: The individual programs are downloaded from the Internet, and stored in a user-defined local area network (LAN) directory.
   - **Install from Local Directory**: The individual programs are installed from a user-defined LAN directory.

   For the initial bootstrap install, choose Install from Internet to create a working Cygwin toolkit installation.

5. Click the Next to go to the next dialog box (see Figure 2.10).

6. The Choose Installation Directory dialog box has three major sections. In the Root Directory section at the top of the dialog box, the installation directory of Cygwin is defined. The default choice is the c:\cygwin directory, so leave it selected. In the Install For section, you should also leave the default All Users selected. (This book assumes each user of the computer has access to the Cygwin installed programs.) In the Default Text File Type section, you can define how Cygwin interprets files. The option you choose here is important when building Unix applications from their sources.

   The difference between the DOS and Unix options is how Cygwin interprets a carriage return and line feed combination. File interpretation details are discussed further in Chapter 3 "Using Python to Write Scripts." The default is to consider the individual files as Unix; if the Unix option does not work, then try reinstalling using the DOS option. The worst-case scenario is that the building of some Unix applications will fail.

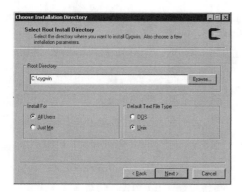

FIGURE 2.10 Dialog box used to define where and how Cygwin is installed.

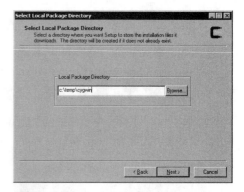

FIGURE 2.11 Dialog box used to define the temporary directory used to store the downloaded Cygwin packages.

7. Click the Next button to open the Select Local Package Directory dialog box similar to Figure 2.11.
8. When you chose the Install from Internet option in Step 4 and clicked the Next button, the dialog box in Figure 2.11 appeared because when the individual Cygwin toolkit packages are downloaded, a location is required for installation. The dialog box is used to define that location. The Cygwin setup application installs the Cygwin toolkit in two steps: downloading all packages and then installing all packages. For reference purposes, it is possible to use the location where the packages were downloaded as a location to install Cygwin onto another computer. Click Next to open the Select Connection Type dialog box as shown in Figure 2.12.

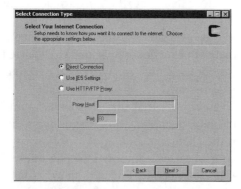

FIGURE 2.12 Dialog box that defines the Internet connection used to download the Cygwin toolkit files.

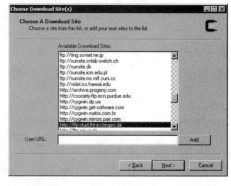

FIGURE 2.13 Dialog box used to select a Cygwin mirror from where the Cygwin toolkit will be downloaded.

9. This dialog box enables you to choose the type of Internet connection to use when the Cygwin setup application downloads the individual applications. The choice depends on the type of Internet connection the computer has. The first and third options are self-explanatory. The second option Use IE5 Settings is a Windows-specific option. In Windows, it is possible to define a reference on how a computer connects to the Internet. The reference information is stored at the operating system level and other applications can query and use that information when connecting to the Internet. The option that you choose depends on how your network is configured. For the purposes of this book, choose Direct Connection. Click Next to open the Choose Download Site(s) dialog box as shown in Figure 2.13.

10. The Available Download Sites listbox contains a list of all servers that mirror the Cygwin toolkit. Choose the server that is located physically closest to where the toolkit is being downloaded. To get a hint of how close the server may be, look at the extension of the URL. Some servers are listed multiple times because those servers can be accessed using different protocols.

   The three protocols that can be used to access a server are FTP, HTTP, and rsync. The best choice is to use HTTP because ftp connections time out frequently. A timeout typically occurs when selecting the packages to download on a slow computer. The process of selecting and checking the dependencies requires too much computing time and causes the waiting ftp connection to time out. After a timeout has occurred, the entire Cygwin setup process has to be started again. It seems like the timeout problems do not occur as frequently and often downloads are quicker with HTTP, but that assertion is not proven by any statistics. Click the Next button to open the Select Packages dialog box as shown in Figure 2.14.

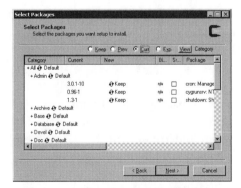

FIGURE 2.14 Dialog box that shows all the Cygwin applications that can be selected, downloaded, and installed.

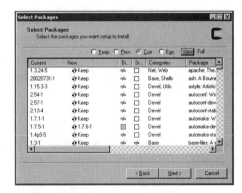

FIGURE 2.15 Dialog box showing the Full style view listing all packages that can be installed.

The contents in the main listbox of the Select Packages dialog box change depending on which packages you choose and which radio buttons you select. Figure 2.14, for example, shows the contents of the main listbox after selecting a package type and then expanding that node to expose the included packages. The View button above the listbox is used to toggle between the styles of views that are displayed. In Figure 2.14 the default style view called Category is displayed. Figure 2.15 shows the listbox in Full package view.

11. For a slow machine, select packages in Full view (it's faster than using the default Category view). The radio buttons across the top of the listbox define which packages will be shown. When doing a fresh install, choose any of these radio buttons because it doesn't make a difference:

Keep: Do not upgrade any of the packages and keep the old packages.

Prev: Downgrade the package with a previous version. Unless of course the current package is not up-to-date and is the downgraded package.

Curr: Upgrade the packages to the most recent package.

Exp: If there are experimental packages, then download those.

After you select one of the four options, the package list is updated. You can select a package by checking on the checkbox in the third column. If there is no checkbox in the third column, the package is already installed. You can click the second column to modify the status of the package defined in the first column. There are four states that can be applied to the second column:

[**Version number**]: Either updates or downgrades the package to the shown version number. The leftmost version number represents the currently installed version of the package.

Keep: The package is not upgraded and the current package is kept.

Uninstall: The package is removed from the Cygwin installation.

Reinstall: The current package is reinstalled. This is a good option if one package has been corrupted.

12. For the initial install, select every package (see the following Note first). This might take a moment or two to accomplish, but is simpler than having to constantly add packages to the installation. The Cygwin toolkit then takes about 1 GB of hard disk space.

TIP

You might want to reconsider installing Perl and Python interpreters when you install all packages. The Cygwin toolkit includes both of these interpreters that can conflict with the native Windows API-compiled Python and Perl interpreters. Either do not install the interpreters, or when installed, rename them to something else.

13. Click the Next button to download and install the packages. Depending on the speed of the Internet connection, this could take a few minutes or a few hours.

14. After all packages have been downloaded and installed, a final dialog box appears asking whether shortcuts should be created. Allow the shortcuts to be installed.

15. After the install, start the default BASH shell from the menu as shown in Figure 2.16.

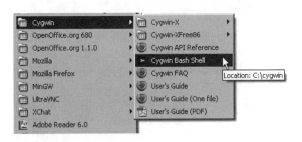

FIGURE 2.16 Menu shortcut used to start the Cygwin BASH shell.

Notice in Figure 2.16 that shortcuts have been created for the X-Server applications.

Deployment: File Server Variant

The way Cygwin was installed in the "Impatient Installation" section is recommended for a first-time installation. For deployment, however, you shouldn't use the Cygwin setup.exe program as outlined in the "Impatient Installation" section. Allowing each user to download a version of the Cygwin toolkit is an administrative nightmare and costs an unnecessary amount of Internet bandwidth.

TIP

Automating the Cygwin toolkit deployment is not that simple because the setup.exe *program was not optimized for automated deployment and there are too many independent packages. The* setup.exe *program can be run in unattended mode using some command-line switches; however, when the application runs, a dialog box still appears. This makes it more difficult to run the setup application as a service because the service must interact with the desktop. Complicating the situation is that the Cygwin command-line options do not allow individual selection of the packages. '*

For deployment purposes, installing the Cygwin toolkit using a file server saves the network Internet bandwidth. When using the file server variation, you can install Cygwin on a user's desktop in two steps. The first step is to download the packages, and the second step is to have each user install the packages from the downloaded location. In the second step, the user goes through all the steps listed in the "Impatient Installation" section, and the source of the packages to install is the file server.

To download the applications to a file server, you execute the `setup.exe` program and select options for the dialog boxes just as you did in the "Impatient Installation" section. Where the file server installation is different is when the Choose Installation Type dialog box appears as shown earlier in Figure 2.9. For the file server deployment variation, you choose Download from Internet and click Next to open the Select Local Package Directory dialog box shown in Figure 2.17.

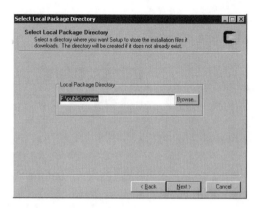

FIGURE 2.17 Dialog box used to define the directory where the packages are downloaded.

Figure 2.17 is identical to the earlier Figure 2.11, but their purposes are different. In Figure 2.11, the directory where the packages are downloaded is considered temporary, but in Figure 2.17 the directory is permanent. The permanent directory should be on a file server accessible by all users. The rest of the installation should be the same as the steps defined in the "Impatient Installation" section. After the files have been downloaded, the Cygwin setup program exits. Note that no toolkit files are installed.

The second step in the file server installation variation is to have the user install the packages to his computer. Again, start `start.exe`. This time when the user reaches the Choose Installation Type dialog box shown in Figure 2.9, the user selects the option Install from Local Directory. The next set of dialog boxes are identical to the dialog boxes in the "Impatient Installation" section. When the Select Local Package Directory dialog box (refer to Figure 2.11) appears, the directory of the local packages is the shared location defined in Figure 2.17. From that point on, the dialog boxes are the same as the "Impatient Installation" section. There will be an intermediate step where the Cygwin setup program checks the validity of the individual packages before installing the packages. After the packages have been installed, the Cygwin BASH shell can be used as shown earlier in Figure 2.16.

Using the file server variation of the Cygwin installation, the administrator can mostly control the packages that are deployed on the Internet. Where this approach fails is when the user does not remember to choose the option Install from Local Directory. The default is the option to Install from the Internet, and a user could potentially install packages that the administrator does not want installed. Installing Cygwin using a file server is the best approach for nonmanaged machines. A non-managed machine is a machine that is tweaked and managed by an individual user such as developers or other administrators. The reason a nonmanaged installation is a good idea is because users who manage their own machines want full control of that machine.

Deployment: Automated Installation of Cygwin

For computers that are fully managed by the administrator, the Cygwin toolkit needs to be installed fully automated. For the fully automated deployment, there is a file server that contains all the packages. Ideally, the Cygwin toolkit is installed when a user logs on to his computer and script tests whether a Cygwin deployment exists or needs updating. The user does not interact with the installation and the installation happens transparently. When deploying Cygwin fully automated, you need to know some additional Windows operating system techniques. These additional techniques concern the automated execution of scripts in a specific context, which is discussed in Chapter 5 "Running Tasks on a Local Computer."

Regardless of the technique used to execute the script, a batch file has to be created that runs the Cygwin `setup.exe` program. The batch file is created, not a BASH script, because the setup program might be installing the Cygwin toolkit for the first time there is no BASH interpreter. As a side note the batch file that runs the Cygwin setup program might also be used to update other programs such as an e-mail or Web server. The simplest batch file that will run the Cygwin `setup.exe` application is as follows:

```
START /WAIT \\APOLLO\public\cygwin\setup.exe
```

The simplest batch file executes the application `setup.exe` that is located on a remote server using a UNC path reference. In a batch script, using the START command is the preferred way to start an application. The START command executes the program in another window and starts applications associated with extensions other than `.exe`. The option `/WAIT` causes the login script to wait until the program being executed is finished. The simplest batch file is a simple way to start the Cygwin setup program, but it also forces the user to guide the installation as you saw in the "Impatient Installation" section.

The next step is to control the installation program using the correct command-line arguments. The program `setup.exe` has the following command-line options:

`testoption` (**Boolean**): An example option that does nothing useful.

`help` (**Boolean**): The help option that is supposed to output a help phrase, but displays nothing.

`quiet-mode` (**Boolean**): This option is used to run the setup in unattended mode. The dialog boxes will not appear. For the login script, this option simplifies the login.

`override-registry-name` (**String**): Changes the name of the registry key that Cygwin uses to store registry information.

`root` (**String**): Directory where the Cygwin toolkit is installed.

`site` (**String**): The name of the site used to download the individual Cygwin packages from.

`download` (**Boolean**): The default Cygwin installation mode is to Install from the Internet, but setting this option to true will only download the Cygwin toolkit, and not install anything.

`local-install` (**Boolean**): The default Cygwin installation mode is to Install from Internet, but setting this option installs the toolkit from the local directory.

`disable-buggy-antivirus` (**Boolean**): This option disables antivirus software that may conflict with the installation of the Cygwin toolkit. At the time of this writing, the option checks for the McAfee Service. If the service exists, the service is stopped.

`no-shortcuts` (**Boolean**): Does not create the shortcuts when the installation has completed.

`no-startmenu` (**Boolean**): Does not create the start menu entry when the installation has completed.

`no-desktop` (**Boolean**): Does not create the desktop shortcut when the installation has completed.

`no-md5` (**Boolean**): When installing Cygwin as a local install, the individual packages are verified using an MD5 signature. This process can take a long time especially on a slow computer. In an intranet scenario, skipping the MD5 signature verification might be okay. The reason for the signature verification is to ensure that the packages have not been infected with a virus.

`no-replaceonreboot` (**Boolean**): Does not replace files on reboot. If the user is using any of the tools while an installation is being carried out, those files are replaced on reboot. Generally, you shouldn't use this flag because in the worst-case scenario, Cygwin toolkit inconsistencies may result.

Following is a rewritten version of the simplest batch file that will install or update a Cygwin toolkit installation:

```
mkdir C:\cygwin\etc\setup
echo \\Apollo\public\cygwin> C:\cygwin\etc\setup\last-cache
START /WAIT \\APOLLO\public\cygwin\setup.exe --local-install
--root=c:\cygwin --no-md5 --quiet-mode
```

The rewritten batch file uses a trick to make the setup.exe program believe it is doing an update. The Cygwin toolkit installs by default in the directory c:\cygwin. In a subdirectory c:\cygwin\etc\setup, the file last-cache is overwritten with the contents of the remote location of the Cygwin file server. If the file last-cache is not overwritten when the setup program is executed, it will search for the packages in the local directory or where the setup application is executed from.

The only problem that still exists is that if a new installation is performed, then the package selection used in the rewritten batch file is the absolute minimum and will probably not include all the packages that you want. You cannot define which packages are installed from the command line without any user interaction. After the setup application has run its course, the Cygwin toolkit is installed.

The package selection is a manual step that cannot be automated. Having selected a package list, the automation scripts automatically update the selected packages. Package selection is not automated because Cygwin has a large number of toolkits that are added and removed over time.

When the Cygwin toolkit is installed for the first time, the file [Cygwin root installation]/etc/setup/installed.db is created. The file installed.db contains the packages and the versions that are installed. The administrator could perform an initial manual package installation and then copy the installed.db file to all the clients.

Using the files installed.db, last-cache, *or* last-mirror *as references for an automatic deployment is an undocumented functionality. The files could change from one day to the next and old scripts that worked at one time will no longer work. As per the Cygwin mailing lists and site, it seems the only way to be safe is to manually install and update Cygwin.*

The file installed.db should not be created manually. The administrator should download and install the desired packages and let setup.exe generate the installed.db file. When the client Cygwin setup scripts execute, they will reference the same installed.db file as was created in the initial installation in "Impatient Installation." Following is a modified Windows batch setup script that copies the package list before running the setup program:

```
mkdir C:\cygwin\etc\setup
echo \\Apollo\public\cygwin> C:\cygwin\etc\setup\last-cache
copy \\APOLLO\public\cygwin\installed.db
c:\cygwin\etc\setup\installed.db
START /WAIT \\APOLLO\public\cygwin\cygwinsetup.exe --local-install
--root=c:\cygwin --no-md5 --quiet-mode
```

Remember, installing the Cygwin toolkit is both a manual and automated process. The manual process is used to discover new packages and determine which packages should be downloaded and installed. The automated process is used to download updates of the already existing packages. The automation process could be triggered every day, whereas the manual process could be performed every week. That decision is up to you. Following is an example script that downloads the updated packages to a local directory:

```
#!/bin/bash
echo $PACKAGE_CYGWIN>/etc/setup/last-cache
$PACKAGE_CYGWIN/cygwinsetup.exe --download
--site=http://ftp-stud.fht-esslingen.de --no-md5 --quiet-mode
```

The script downloads the latest packages. Notice the use of the site command-line option to specify a server to download the sources from. The same server shouldn't always be used for the downloading.

TIP

If for some reason a package needs to be reinstalled, the installed.db *file can be manipulated to automatically reinstall a package. This solution is undocumented and may not work at a later point in time. Consider the following sample line from an* installed.db *file:*

```
agetty agetty-2.1.1.tar.bz2 0
```

This could be updated to the previous version number:

```
agetty agetty-2.0.tar.bz2 0
```

This change causes setup.exe *to download the latest version of the agetty package, thus overwriting any previous change.*

Deployment: Tweaking the Environment

If Cygwin tools are used outside the BASH shell, then the Cygwin toolkit needs some additional tweaks. It is possible to use the Cygwin toolkit packages from within a Windows batch file. To use Cygwin applications outside of Cygwin, the Cygwin toolkit binary directory has to be added to the PATH environment variable. If the Cygwin toolkit were installed in the directory c:\cygwin, then the directory location to add to the path is c:\cygwin\bin.

You also must add the ability to execute a BASH script automatically like a Windows batch file. Consider the following example BASH shell script:

```
#!/bin/bash
echo "hello world"
```

The example BASH shell script is stored as the hello.sh, where the extension .sh denotes a BASH script. Running the script from a console like an executable file results in an error and additional configuration is required to make the script run automatically because Windows does not know about the .sh extension and how to interpret it properly. When attempting to run the script from the console, an error similar to Figure 2.18 is generated.

```
hello.sh.
```

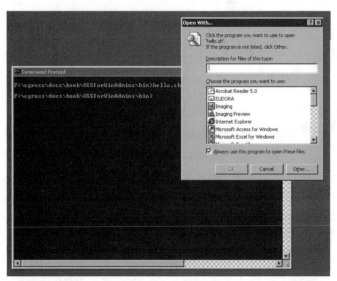

FIGURE 2.18 A Windows-generated dialog box asking how to process the script.

In Figure 2.18, Windows generated a dialog box because the .sh extension is not registered with the Windows operating system as executable content. From the dialog box, you can automatically configure Windows to process shell scripts. However, for the scope of this book, do not configure the .sh extension using the generated dialog box as that can cause other problems.

The better way to is to configure the extension manually and associate the extension with an action:

1. Open the Windows Control Panel and double-click on the Folder Options icon. The Folder Options dialog box appears with the File Types tab selected (see Figure 2.19).

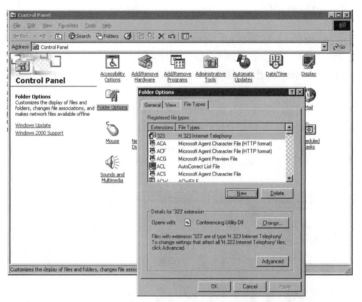

FIGURE 2.19 File extension configuration in the Folder Options dialog box.

2. The Registered File Types listbox contains all the known extensions that have associated actions. Because .sh is a new extension, click the New button.
3. A dialog box appears asking for the extension name. Type **sh** into the text box and then click OK.
4. The Registered File Types listbox now includes the extension SH with some extra text (e.g., FT000002) as its description at the top of the listbox. Select the SH extension and click on the Advanced button.
5. In the Edit File Type dialog box that appears, click on the New button and the Editing Action for Type: Bash Shell Script dialog box appears. The three dialog boxes used to define the action of the extensions are shown in Figure 2.20.

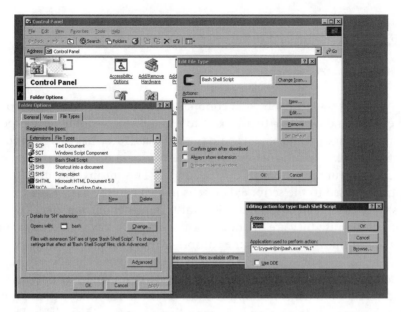

FIGURE 2.20 Dialog boxes used to configure an action for the `.sh` extension.

In Figure 2.20 the three dialog boxes show how the operating system attempts to determine the correct action for an extension. When a user clicks on a file, the system searches the Registered File Types listbox of the Folder Options dialog box. If the extension is found, the system searches the Actions listbox in the Edit File Type dialog box for the Open action. If the system finds the Open action, it executes the associated action definition shown in the Editing Action for Type: Bash Shell Script dialog box. Note that the task of creating an action or the entire process of updating the actions for an extension has to be executed by the administrator or someone with administrative rights.

6. In the Editing Action for Type: Bash Shell Script dialog box, enter the following in the Application Used... text box :

```
"C:\cygwin\bin\bash.exe" "%1"
```

The text says that whenever a file with the extension `.sh` is being executed, the BASH shell executable (`bash.exe`) will be called. The `%1` is a command-line argument that represents the file being executed. If a console program executes the filename `hello.sh` as illustrated earlier in Figure 2.18, then the Windows operating system would replace the `%1` with the `hello.sh` script.

A problem arises if a user executes the `hello.sh` script from the console with some command-line arguments as follows:

```
hello.sh "Hello world"
```

The text `"Hello World"` is a command-line option being passed to the script. The command `bash.exe` that is used to run a BASH script has only specified one command-line parameter (`%1`), and the script `hello.sh` has a command-line parameter as well. From the perspective of the Windows operating system, `hello.sh` is an alias for running the `bash.exe` executable. This means that any command-line options passed to the script `hello.sh` is invisible to the `bash.exe` executable. The `bash.exe` executable also does not want to know about the extra command-line options because they are intended for the script. A way is needed to blindly pass command-line options from the console to the script.

The Action command text needs to be changed and the additional parameters need to be passed blindly to the script. To pass command-line options blindly, the wildcard `%*` command-line option must be used. The wildcard `%*` command-line option passes all remaining command-line options as one block. Following is a rewritten Action command text:

```
"C:\cygwin\bin\bash.exe" "%1" %*
```

When associating the `.sh` file extension with the BASH executable, be sure to add the Cygwin toolkit to the path; otherwise, some utilities may not work as expected.

The final step to take to ensure that BASH scripts are automatically executed is to add the `.sh` extension as a recognized extension. The `.sh` extension is appended to the environment variable PATHEXT as shown in Figure 2.21.

Normally any executable content you are running from within a BASH console that also exists in the current directory should be executed as follows:

```
./hello.sh "Hello World"
```

By default, Linux/BSD systems do not include the current directory in the path of executable content; hence the need to prefix the characters `./`.

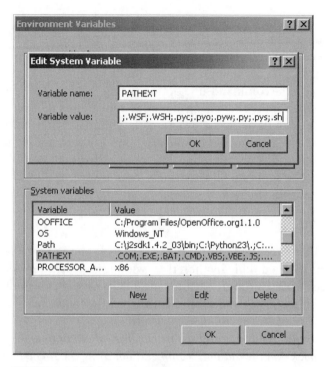

FIGURE 2.21 Dialog box used to append the `.sh` extension to the `PATHEXT` environment variable.

Technique: Understanding Command-Line Applications

Command-line options are used extensively by the Cygwin toolkit. Many people hate command-line options because they are cryptic and difficult to understand. Generally this is true, but times have changed. The following examples show how the console-based `tar` program, which includes some command-line options, is executed.

```
tar -cvf file.tar directories
```

The command line written in such a form means absolutely nothing to somebody who has never used the `tar` program. Now consider a rewritten modern version of the same command line:

```
tar --create --verbose --file=file.tar directories
```

This time the command line is self-explanatory, and says that the program `tar` is going to create something in a verbose mode using the file `file.tar` for some reference. The only definition that is missing is what `tar` does. `Tar` is a program that archives a set of files or directories into a destination. Combining the definition of `tar` with the command-line options using `tar` does not seem as cryptic.

Open Source has changed how administrators interact and manage computers. In the example of the `tar` program, the command-line options have been simplified to the point that using console programs is not that difficult.

The available command-line options for each console program are not evident. The command line option `--help` is used to display the available options as shown by the following example:

```
tar --help
```

The generated output of this example shows that there are many more options with a double hyphen than with a single hyphen. The single hyphen references classic command-line options, whereas the double hyphen represents newer, easier-to-understand command-line options.

Some people may still use the single hyphen command-line option notation. This book and the author recommend not using the single hyphen notation. The double hyphen command-line options are longer to type out, but leads to maintainable and easier to read scripts. Easier to read scripts mean that debugging a problematic script becomes simpler and less frustrating.

Technique: Managing Files and Directories

The problem of the slashes was already mentioned earlier, but there are more considerations. On a Linux/BSD operating system, files can be linked and directories can be mounted. Windows does not support linked files and mounted directories in the Unix sense. In several scripts, the directory `/etc` was referenced. For all vanilla Windows distributions, there is no `/etc` directory. Cygwin has mounted the directory `[Cygwin installation directory]/etc` as `/etc..` To see all the mounted virtual drives, start a BASH shell and type in the `mount` command:

```
cgross@zeus ~/book/OSSforWinAdmins/bin
$ mount
C:\cygwin\usr\X11R6\lib\X11\fonts on /usr/X11R6/lib/X11/fonts
type system (binmode)
c:\cygwin\bin on /usr/bin type system (binmode)
c:\cygwin\lib on /usr/lib type system (binmode)
c:\cygwin on / type system (binmode)
c: on /cygdrive/c type user (binmode,noumount)
e: on /cygdrive/e type user (binmode,noumount)
```

In the first line of the BASH shell, there is a tilde character followed by some directory information. The tilde is a shortcut used to identify a user's home directory. In the case of Cygwin and the user `cgross`, the Windows absolute path would be `c:\cyg-win\home\cgross`. Looking at the third line from bottom of the BASH shell, the drive `c:\cygwin` is mounted to the directory `/`, which is the root drive of the Cygwin toolkit. All other drives and devices are virtually mapped below that directory. For example the c drive is mapped as `/cygdrive/c`, and the e drive is mapped as `/cygdrive/e`.

To mount other drives below directories on the c drive, you should use the Windows mounting technique. Allowing the user to mount drives virtually makes it simpler to port scripts to different operating systems. For example, it's better to write a script that uses the directory `/cygdrive/c/some/directory` than the directory `c:/some/directory`. The use of the leading drive letter would confuse a script on any Linux/BSD operating system. However, the ability to virtually mount devices and drives does make it more confusing to know where a file is located. A Windows batch file and BASH script may reference entirely different locations. The prefix `cygdrive` can be changed to something else by changing the value in the registry: `HKEY_LOCAL_MA-CHINE\SOFTWARE\Cygnus Solutions\Cygwin\mounts v2\cygdrive prefix`.

When working with the Cygwin toolkit, the mount tables and directory definitions only matter when you are using BASH scripts. BASH scripts should use the Cygwin way of referencing drives and directories. Scripts will work better because some Cygwin tools still have problems with drive letters, especially from the root of a drive.

Technique: Running the Shell

Although we've referenced the BASH shell many times and shown a few scripts, we haven't formally introduced the BASH shell. BASH is short for Bourne-again shell. The Bourne shell was a standard shell with traditional Unix systems. BASH has become a de facto standard among Linux/BSD operating systems. BASH is case sensitive, unlike Windows batch files or the Windows Scripting Host. Figure 2.22 shows the default BASH console.

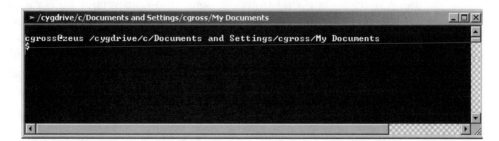

FIGURE 2.22 Menu item used to start the BASH shell.

The BASH shell can execute commands such as ls (directory Listing), mv (move file), pwd (present working directory), and so on. The power of the shell is not the script language that BASH supports, but the additional tools such as ls, mv, and pwd that perform tasks. If you are uncomfortable with the BASH shell, have a large number of already written files, or the BASH shell does not work to your expectations, the additional tools will function as any other console executables.

When the BASH shell is started, two files are processed in sequential order, first /etc/profile and then ~/.bash_profile. The file /etc/profile is a login script executed the first time a user starts a BASH script. The script ~./.bash_profile is located in the home directory of the user, which in the case of the user cgross would be the /home/cgross directory. The file contains personal settings that relate to environment variables. The defined environment variables are only visible in the scope of the BASH environment. This means if an environment variable is defined dynamically by BASH, it is not visible to native Windows API compiled applications. The only way around this is to use the setx.exe application to define the environment variable on a permanent basis. Following is an example .bash_profile file:

```
# ~/.bash_profile: executed by bash for login shells.
if [ -e /etc/bash.bashrc ] ; then
  source /etc/bash.bashrc
fi
if [ -e ~/.bashrc ] ; then
  source ~/.bashrc
fi
BOOKHOME=~/docs/book/OSSforWinAdmins
BOOKBIN=$BOOKHOME/bin
PACKAGE_CYGWIN=f:/public/cygwin
export BOOKHOME BOOKBIN PACKAGE_CYGWIN
```

A .bash_profile file is defined so that the user has certain command aliases and environment variables specific to the user.

Technique: Getting Help Using man

In the previous section, "Understanding Command-Line Applications," you saw how to get help from the command-line options for a console program by using the command-line option --help. For additional and more detailed help, you can also use the command man. On Linux/BSD operating systems, man is the Windows shell equivalent of help. The man command is used in the same way as the help command in a Windows console. An example of using man to describe the command ls is as follows.

```
man ls
```

When man is executed, if a help file for the topic exists, the console changes and a document appears. You can navigate the document using the keyboard directional keys. To view the next and previous pages, press the Page Down and Page Up keys. To view the next and previous lines of text, press the Down Arrow and Up Arrow keys. The text (END) appears at the bottom of the document. To search and perform other instructions, vi (pronounced vie) commands are used. *Vi* is a console editor that has special processing commands (vi is discussed in the next section). To exit the man program, use the q key.

Technique: Editing Files with VI (VIM)

You can use multiple console editors—such as Emacs, vi, or nano—with the Cygwin toolkit. Nano is a very simple editor similar to Notepad but with some extra bells and whistles. Emacs is a sophisticated editor that has a host of features. Emacs is a useful tool for those developers that are adept at using multiple keystroke shortcuts. Vi on the other hand is a much simpler editor that does not require as many keystrokes to perform operations. Many people use vi as a programmer's editor, whereas others use vi for quick file editing. Vi is not an Integrated Development Environment (IDE). When developing larger scripts or programs, vi is lacking because you cannot easily manage a collection of documents. Table 2.3 contains some of the reference information about vi.

TABLE 2.3 Reference Information for Vi

Item	Description
Home page	*http://www.vim.org*
Installation	Part of the Cygwin installation.
Documentation	*http://www.vim.org/docs.php*
	The URL provides several references for more detailed VIM editing information. The default Cygwin installation lacks many of the add-ons that are available at the VIM home page. These add-ons must be installed manually.
Mailing Lists	*http://www.vim.org/maillist.php*
	There are several mailing lists, with none specifically geared toward the administrator. Of most interest is the vim mailing list, which is for general users.
Impatient Installation Time Required	Included with Cygwin.
	OR
	Fresh Install takes a few minutes.
	Bytes Downloaded: 6 MB

Simple File Edit

Starting with the simple, this section shows how to use vi to edit a file that contains several lines. Note that not all features of vi are shown in this book, just the features necessary to edit a file. To edit the file hello.sh, the command is shown as follows:

```
vi hello.sh
```

If the file hello.sh does not exist, vi creates an empty buffer, which means a file of length zero.

Sometimes it is necessary to create empty files, which means a file with a length of zero. Many editors have problems with zero-length files, but vi does not. Vi is also very useful with files that have no names, and only extensions need to be edited. For example, the filename .unison has no filename, and only an extension.

Figure 2.23 is an example of vi having loaded the contents of a file and displaying it in a buffer.

```
➤ ~/docs/book/OSSforWinAdmins/bin
#!/bin/bash
# Just a simple BASH script
echo "Hello"
echo $1
~
~
~
~
~
~
~
~
```

FIGURE 2.23 Vi editing the contents of a file.

In Figure 2.23, there are four lines of text. After those four lines are a number of lines with a single tilde that serve as placeholders for nonexistent empty lines. Attempting to edit the content right after the file has been loaded by using the keyboard will most likely result in errors or beeps indicating errors because vi is operating in *command mode*. In command mode, you can move the cursor, delete lines, and move blocks of code. Command mode operations allow you to manipulate the overall structure of the buffer, but to edit the individual letters and numbers of the buffer, vi has be to be switched into *edit mode*. Typing the letter **i** switches vi into edit mode. (Be sure to use the lowercase **i**.) Once in edit mode, you can add, delete, and manipulate text using the keyboard just as you can in Notepad. Vi has an additional mode called the status line mode, which is like command mode except that the commands entered can be more detailed.

Vi Command Mode

While in command mode, you can move the cursor to different rows or columns in two ways. The traditional method is to use the keyboard keys:

h: Moves the cursor left one column.

j: Moves the cursor down one row.

k: Moves the cursor up one row.

l: Moves the cursor right one column.

The Cygwin toolkit release of vi has implemented the second method of moving a cursor, which is a keymapping that uses the keyboard cursor. The **h, j, k,** and **l** keys are only useful when using a Telnet or remote console session that does not support the escape sequences of the keyboard cursor keys.

When working in vi, there are two common ways of deleting text: deleting one text character and deleting one line of text. Following are the keys you can press in command mode and their associated actions:

x: Deletes one character at a time. Move the cursor to the character to be deleted and press **x**. Any text after the deleted character is automatically moved backward.

d: Deletes one line of text. Move the cursor to the line of text to be deleted and press the **d** key twice.

Shift+s: Replaces one line of text with an empty line of text. The overall buffer is not collapsed. Move the cursor to the line that is being deleted, and then press the **Shift+s** key combination. The line is removed and the cursor switches into edit mode at the beginning of the empty line. The deletions that are preformed are not permanent until the file is saved.

u: Undoes the last change made to the buffer.

Input Mode

When vi is in edit mode, you can manipulate the text using the text and numeric keys, including backspaces, deletes, and carriage returns. The cursor keys can be used to position the cursor for further editing. Following are the keys and their associated actions:

esc: Exits input mode and switches back to command mode.

a: When in command mode, pressing the **a** key moves the cursor one position to the right from the current location, and enters into edit mode. Any text that is after the cursor is automatically shifted toward the righthand side of the document.

o: When in command mode, pressing the **o** key inserts a line at the current cursor location. After the line has been inserted, the current cursor position is changed to be the beginning of the newly added line. After the cursor position changes, vi switches into edit mode at the beginning of the new line.

Shift+o: Does the same thing as pressing the **o** key, except the line is inserted above the current cursor location. Vi then switches into edit mode at the beginning of the new line.

Shift+a: When in command mode, pressing the Shift+a key combination shifts the current cursor position to the end of the line and switches vi into edit mode.

Status Mode

Status mode is useful saving, reading, or searching files. The keys :, /, or **?** switch vi into status mode. After the status mode command has executed, vi switches back to command mode. Status mode operations are started by typing in the : key and one of the following keys:

w: Saves a file. The filename used to save the file is the same used when vi loads an already existing file. To complete the save command, press the Enter key. If you want to rename the file, instead of pressing the Enter key, press the spacebar, enter the new name, and press Enter again. At that point, the identifier of the buffer is the new filename.

wq: Saves the file and exits vi.

q: Exits vi if no changes have been made to the document.

q!: Exits vi and discards any changes made to the document.

e [filename]: Discards the contents of the current document and loads a new document. If the new document does not exist, then an empty document is created.

You can also search for text in status mode. Searches can be performed forward or backward from the current cursor location.

/[query]: Perform a forward search and find text that matches the query characters.

/: Perform a forward search and find text that corresponds to the last query characters. This type of search can be considered a "find again" search.

?[query]: Perform a backward search and find text that matches the query characters.

?: Perform a backward search and find text that corresponds to the last query characters. This type of search can be considered a "find again" search.

With all search modes, when the search reaches the end or the beginning of the document, vi generates a notice at the bottom of the editor window. If you perform multiple searches and reach the bottom of the document, the search restarts at the top of the document.

Technique: Writing BASH Scripts

If you're a Windows administrator, you may be asking yourself why you should program in BASH. The answer is that BASH is capable of many tasks without having to learn all the ins and outs of a major programming language. Windows Scripting Host is similar to shell programming, but it's not shell programming. The Windows Scripting Host uses Visual Basic scripting and JavaScript. Both of these are programming languages, not shell scripts. The Windows Scripting Host interacts with its environment like a programming language does in that it requires someone to have written an object. A shell scripting language interacts with its environment as if it's part of the environment. For example, it's very simple to process text using a shell script language.

BASH should be used in place of Windows batch files. BASH should also be used to perform wrapper script type operations. A BASH script should not attempt to mimic a programming language such as Visual Basic, JavaScript, or Python. A BASH script should not be used to implement complex business processes. BASH scripting should be used to maintain program installations, perform user maintenance, generate log statistics, and do things an administrator would expect to be done automatically.

Complex implementations should be processed using a more sophisticated programming language. In this book, the chosen programming language is Python because it's an easy to learn and clean programming language that is ideally suited for an administrator. Table 2.4 contains the reference information for BASH.

Although BASH appears to be like a programming language, it is not. BASH can execute commands, redirect content, and manage pipes. BASH requires a console program for everything, including the addition of numbers. This is a major difference between a programming language and a shell scripting language.

TABLE 2.4 Reference Information for BASH

Item	Description
Home page	*http://www.gnu.org/software/bash/bash.html*
Installation	Part of the Cygwin installation.
Documentation	Online documentation exists and is easily found. Specifically of interest are the following URLS:
	http://www.gnu.org/manual/bash/index.html: The reference documentation for the BASH shell.
	http://www.tldp.org/HOWTO/BASH-Prog-Intro-HOWTO.html: An introduction to programming with BASH.
	http://www.tldp.org/LDP/abs/html/: A more advanced online documentation that answers many advanced questions.
Mailing Lists	There are not many useful BASH mailing lists. For BASH support, the best place to ask questions is on the *gnu.bash* newsgroup. The Web site *http://www.dejanews.com* has a large archive of past postings and should be the first place to search for answers.
Impatient Installation Time Required	Part of Cygwin installation.

Writing a Simple Script

Keeping with the tradition of using the Hello World example to illustrate a language, following is the BASH variant of Hello World:

```
echo "Hello World"
```

The source code should be saved as the file `hello.sh`. For the Windows platform, the file can be executed directly because the file extension associations have been set. On a Linux/BSD operating system, the file could not be executed because the file has no execute privileges and there is no concept of file extension association. This only matters with Cygwin when scripts are calling other scripts. Following is an example that sets the executable flag on the same script:

```
chmod a+x hello.sh
```

The command chmod is used to assign rights to a file or directory. Before we explore the details of chmod, a quick explanation of Linux/BSD security privileges is necessary.

Linux/BSD security and rights are based on the traditional Unix security model. Windows (NT, 2000, or XP) security is based on an access control list (ACL). An ACL allows the user to manage individual security flags on every object. This type of security allows for more fine-tuning, but sometimes it makes the security model more complicated than it needs to be. Linux/BSD security is not as complicated and fulfills all expectations required of it.

Linux/BSD Security in One Sentence

In Linux/BSD security, the user root can do anything it wants. The other users exist, but their rights are limited. The previous sentence explains everything about Linux/BSD security. The root is akin to the Windows Administrator account. A root user can do whatever he wants. This rule applies regardless of how you set the security bits of the individual files, directories, and processes. This means if a hacker gains access to the root account, he can bring down the entire system. However, Linux/BSD systems have adapted in that gaining access to the root account has been restricted to only specific situations. It is possible to act on behalf of the root account, without becoming the root account.

There are three levels of security:

owner: The owner of an object is typically the user that created the object initially.

group: Defines an entity that contains multiple users. There can only be one group per object.

everybody: This is everybody else and could be considered as a guest in Windows security terms.

For each security level, there are three types of accesses:

read: Allows reading of the object.

write: Allows writing of the object.

execute: Allows execution of the object.

The security level is combined with an access right to define the security privileges of an object such as a file or directory.

Modifying Security Privileges

When the command chmod was first introduced, there were two command-line options: a+x and the file hello.sh. The somewhat cryptic command-line option a+x assigns execute access to all security levels. A security privilege is the combination of security level and access, and is a sequential combination of three parts. The first part, the letter a, stands for all and defines the security level. The second part is the plus sign that says to add the access level defined in the third part to the security level defined in the first part. Instead of the plus sign, the minus sign could have been used, which means to remove the access level from the security level. The last part is the letter x, which is the access level.

The possible characters that can be used for each of the three parts are defined as follows (note that each of the letters can be added side by side, e.g., part one could be gou):

First part: g - group, o - others "everyone else," u - user "owner," a - a simple letter that is the same as gou.

Second part: - take these rights away, + adds these rights, = assigns these rights ignoring whatever has been assigned thus far.

Third part: l - locks the object during access, r - allows read, s - sets user or group id, t - sets the sticky bit, w - allows write, x - allows execution of a file.

NOTE

The security privileges that Cygwin exposes clash with the Windows security privileges and are provided for compatibility reasons. If security is important to your scripts, then use Windows security and console programs that are native to Windows and typically not part of the Cygwin toolkit. Typically these programs are available as Windows support files or as part of a Windows Resource Toolkit. The Windows Resource Toolkit requires a small fee. The Web site at http://gnuwin32.sourceforge.net has a number of native Windows-compiled tools that could be used instead of Cygwin. Another source of free or low-priced commercial tools is Systools (http://www.sysinternals.com).

Adding a Comment

Comments in a BASH script are defined using the hash character as shown in the following example:

```
# My Hello World Bash Script
echo "Hello world"
```

Comments can be located anywhere in a BASH script. All text after the hash character will be ignored until an end-of-line character or a new line character is encountered. Following is an example of adding a comment after the echo command:

```
echo "Hello world" # My Hello World Bash Script
```

Specifying a Shell

We know that on the Windows platform, a BASH shell script is a BASH shell script because of the file extension. However, within the BASH shell, you can define an interpreter that will be used to process the script. To execute the correct shell interpreter, a script descriptor is defined. The script descriptor is a special notation put at the top of any script file. The script descriptor is used to define the script interpreter and extra command-line options. A modified version of the hello.sh script with a script descriptor is shown as follows:

```
#!/bin/bash
echo "hello world"
```

In the example, the first line is a combination of hash character and exclamation mark. That combination when on the first line and only on the first line is a special token used to associate the interpreter with the script. In the case of the hello.sh script, the interpreter to use is /bin/bash or the BASH executable.

You can define other interpreters using Windows absolute paths such as c:/cygwin/bin/bash.exe. By correctly defining the script descriptor, you can target a specific interpreter when multiple interpreters are installed. For example, you could install the Python interpreter from both the company ActiveState and Cygwin. When using absolute paths, it's important to use the same installation path of the script interpreter on different computers.

Using Variables

Variables serve the same purpose as environment variables, but are usually only used in the script to be executed. You can define variables with BASH. All environment variables defined in Windows are BASH variables. The difference between an environment variable defined in Windows and a BASH-defined variable is scope. An environment variable is active even when the BASH script ends. However, the BASH script-defined variable is only available during the execution of the script. By using the `export` keyword, you can define a variable that is exposed to any child-executed BASH script. Following is an example in which a variable is assigned:

```
variable1="Hello World"
```

The variable assignment looks deceptively simple, but there is an important catch. The equals character or assignment does not have any spaces to the left or right of it. An error would be generated if space were included. The following example shows how to output the value of a variable:

```
echo $variable1
```

Prefixing the dollar character in front of the identifier `variable` creates a variable reference for output purposes.

It was previously mentioned how a BASH script-defined variable does not exist beyond the scope of the BASH script. Yet child BASH scripts have the capability to see BASH-defined variables defined by another process. This is a special feature of the Cygwin environment. This means if you were to run a Cygwin BASH script that executes the Python interpreter from `ActiveState` *that executes a Cygwin BASH script, then the variables from the first BASH script will not be present in the second BASH script.*

Quotes in a BASH script have special meanings. So far, all examples have used the double quote character. The single quote and the backquote can also be used. When using the double quote to bound buffers, embedded variables are automatically expanded. Following is an example that uses double quotes to define some variables, which are then included in the definition of another variable:

```
answer="yes"
question="Is another variable included?  Answer: $answer"
echo $question
```

When the example is executed, the generated result is as follows:

```
Is another variable included?  Answer: yes
```

When double quotes are used, any embedded variable reference is expanded when the buffer is assigned or generated.

A buffer is expanded dynamically before the assignment is made. If the value of a variable changes, then the variable that was assigned with the value of the original variable will not be updated. For example, were the variable question *to be assigned with the variable* answer, *then when the variable* answer *is updated, the variable* question *would not be updated. The variable* question *would still contain the old value of the variable* answer.

Following is a similar example to the double quote example, except single quotes are used to bound the buffer:

```
answer="yes"
question='Is another variable included?  Answer: $answer'
echo $question
```

When the example is executed, the generated result is as follows:

```
Is another variable included?  Answer: $answer
```

Using the single quote does not expand the variable answer into the output buffer. When using double quotes to enclose a buffer, the same effect of not expanding embedded variables is achieved by escaping the dollar character using the backward slash character as shown in the following example:

```
answer="yes"
question="Is another variable included?  Answer: \$answer"
echo $question
```

Another quote character that can be used to perform some action is the backquote. The backquote character expands an entire buffer as if it was a command. Following is an example that executes a directory listing and then outputs the result of the command. Note that the command ls is used in place of the Windows dir command.

```
strcommand=`ls -alt`
echo $strcommand
```

The backquote can be applied to a variable, except in that case the contents of the variable is the buffer to be executed.

```
command="lst -alt"
commandresult=`$command`
echo $commandresult
```

BASH has a number of special variables that are reserved in their functionality. Some of the special variables are predefined to contain specific pieces of information, and others relate to command-line options.

Command-line options are variables identified using a number. For example, the following example illustrates a command line where some script is to be executed, followed by three command-line options.

```
./parameters.sh option1 option2 option3
```

The passed in command-line options can be output using the following script.

```
echo $0
echo $1
echo $2
echo $3
```

The variables 0, 1, 2, 3 refer to command-line options. The command-line option index starts at zero, and can continue on for as many command-line options as necessary. The zeroth command-line option is the script filename. Running the example script with three command-line options the following output is generated:

```
./parameters.sh
option1
option2
option3
```

Notice in the output that the zeroth index is the script that is executing.

Referencing the tenth command-line parameter is a problem with scripts because of the way that BASH escapes variables. For example the script

```
echo "$10"
```

generates the following output:

```
option10
```

This happens because the trailing zero is considered part of the buffer and not the variable identifier $1. The following example shows how to properly escape the tenth command-line option or any variable references that can be confused as the buffer reference:

```
echo "${10}"
```

The curly brackets in the example delimit the identifier; otherwise, the script will escape the first command-line option and append a zero.

Some other predefined variables are defined as follows:

$*: All the command-line parameters returned as one string.

$@: All the command-line parameters returned as individually quoted strings.

$#: The total number of parameters not including the command.

$$: The PID (Process Identifier) of the current process. Often used to generate temporary files.

$!: The PID of the most recent process.

$?: The exit status of the last process that was called. When a script executes a child process, the exit status refers to the child process when it has exited.

There are some special considerations concerning command-line options. The first concerns command-line options that include spaces. The simple solution is to use double quotes; however, there is another issue, and it relates to processing command-line options with spaces.

A command-line option is considered such because it is an identifier separated by spaces. If an identifier is a sentence that has spaces, then a set of double quotes has to be used to make the sentence appear as a command-line option. Following is an example that illustrates a sentence:

```
./parameters.sh "option1 option2" option3
```

In the example, the buffer that contains the text option1 option2 is considered a single command-line option. The example would generate the following output:

```
./parameters.sh
option1 option2
option3
```

The generated output does not have a missing line feed, but the output is problematic because of the space between option1 and option2. To understand the problem, consider if the script parameters.sh were to call another script, as shown in the following example:

```
./someotherscript.sh $1 $2
```

When someotherscript.sh is called with the double quote enclosed buffer, the expanded command line would look like this:

```
./someotherscript.sh option1 option2 option3
```

If you look closely at the expanded command line, you'll see a subtle error. What was one command-line option (`option1 option2`) will be interpreted again as two command-line options because of the missing double quotes. The result is that the script `someotherscript.sh` is called with three command-line options. The correct way to call the script `someotherscript.sh` is:

```
./someotherscript.sh "$1" "$2"
```

Wrapping variable references using double quotes ensures that a variable containing spaces will not inadvertently be mistaken as multiple command-line options. Therefore, a general rule to follow is to always use double quotes.

A problem with using quotes and variable references occurs when multiple commands are called. Consider the following example script (don't worry about the commands being executed as they are explained later in the chapter):

```
ps | awk '$1 < $1 { print $1; }'
```

The problem with the example is the buffer enclosed by the single quotes. In the buffer there are three references to the `$1` variable, where two references relate to the command `awk`, and the remaining one relates to the script command-line option. The problem is that neither you nor the BASH script knows which reference is which. To remove the obscurity, the quotes have to be repositioned as shown by the following example:

```
ps | awk '$1 < '$1' { print $1; }'
```

The second `$1` reference is enclosed by two single quote-enclosed buffers, which are concatenated. You don't have to use double quotes to enclose the script referenced command-line option because everything is being concatenated.

Variable Scope

BASH shell variables in the simplest case have a script scope, which means referencing the same variable from another script results in an empty value. Consider the following scripts:

```
#!/bin/bash
# child-output-parent-defined.sh
echo "VARIABLE value is: ${VARIABLE}"

#!/bin/bash
# parent-define.sh
VARIABLE="Defined in parent"
```

```
./child-output-parent-defined.ksh
```

When the `parent-define.sh` script is executed, the output will be similar to the following:

```
$ ./parent.sh
VARIABLE value is:
```

The variable `VARIABLE` has an empty value because `VARIABLE` is only defined in the local scope of the file `parent-define.sh`. To extend the scope, the `export` intrinsic command is used. The file `parent-define.sh` would be rewritten to the following:

```
#!/bin/sh
# parent-define.sh
VARIABLE="Defined in parent"
export VARIABLE
./child-output-parent-defined.sh
```

The `export` keyword is used to globally define the variable `$VARIABLE` before calling the child script. When exporting a variable, the scope of the variable is from parent to child, and not from child to parent. This means if a child declares a variable, the parent will not see it. Alternatively, if the child modifies an exported variable, then the parent will not see the modified value. For a child-defined variable to be exported back to the parent, the . operator has to be used as shown in the following example:

```
#!/bin/ksh
# parent-define.sh
VARIABLE="Defined in parent"
export VARIABLE
. ./child-output-parent-defined.sh
```

The . operator exposes variables even if a child of a child script is executed. The only requirement is that each child script is executed with the . operator.

Array Variables

Arrays can be created in BASH by using square brackets as shown in the following example:

```
a[1]=something
a[2]=another
a[10]=more
```

```
echo "All: (${a[*]}) a[1]: (${a[1]}) a[10]: (${a[10]})"
```

When the script is executed, the following output is generated:

```
$ ./variables.sh
All: (something another more) a[1]: (something) a[10]: (more)
```

Arrays can be dynamically created by assigning values to an array index. The array index is any integer greater than or equal to zero. Notice how there are no spaces between the variable identifiers and square brackets. You can also assign an array using the type command, but this method isn't covered in this book.

When extracting a value from an array, the variable should be referenced using curly brackets. Although optional, using curly brackets ensures that the array index is properly identified. The asterisk (*) is an array index that is used to return all array elements. Alternatively, the @ character can be used to return all elements. If the variable is referenced without any array index, then the zeroth element is being referenced.

The length of the array is returned using the following script:

```
echo "Length: (${#a[*]})"
```

When the hash character is added in front of a variable identifier, it returns the length of the variable. This works with or without the square brackets. The hash character can also be used on string buffers to retrieve the length of the buffer. When the variable is an array, be sure to add the square brackets and the asterisk character; otherwise, the length of an individual array element is returned. Remember, when the length of the array is retrieved, the actual length is used, not the array indices. In the array sample, the tenth index of the variable a was assigned, which could have created an array length of 11 elements. As array a has been defined, the length of the array would be 3.

To get a slice of an array, which is a subset of an array, the following example is used:

```
${variables[*]:1:2}
```

The example is interpreted as: retrieve all the array elements in the variables array, and then return two elements starting at the first index (1). You can leave off the number of elements to return. The difference is that all elements starting from the first index are returned. A string buffer can be slicing like an array because a string buffer is an array of characters.

Variable Assignment Decision Sequences

Often when writing BASH scripts, a variable has to be assigned. Another variable might be used to assign the original variable. A problem arises if the other variable has no value. In that case, it's necessary to assign the variable a default value. To implement such logic, a decision test must be implemented. BASH makes it simpler by using a combination statement that combines test and assignment in one line. Following is an example of assigning a default value:

```
myvar=${1:-"default value"}
```

When using combination statements, the curly brackets are required and the colon/hyphen combination separating the number 1 and buffer is the decision. The logic is that if the first command-line option (1) contains a value of some type, the variable myvar will be assigned the first command-line option. Otherwise, if the first command-line option is not defined or contains an empty buffer, the buffer default value is assigned to the variable myvar.

Following are the different combination statements that can be used when assigning a variable:

alen=${#a}: Assigns the variable alen the length of the variable a.

c=${a:-b}: Assigns the variable c the value a if a is not empty or not defined; otherwise, assigns the variable c the value b.

c=${a-b}: Assigns the variable c the value a if a is not defined; otherwise, assigns the variable c the value of b.

c=${a:=b}: Assigns the variable c the value a if a is defined and not empty; otherwise, assigns the variable c the value b. Note that the variable a has to be defined or an error will be generated.

c=${a=b}: Assigns the variable c the value a if a is defined even when empty; otherwise, assigns the variable c the value of b.

c=${a:+b}: Assigns the variable c the value a if a is defined and not empty; otherwise, assigns the variable c the value b.

c=${a#b}: Assigns the variable c the value a, where a is the smallest part of the lefthand side matched of b deleted. For example, ${00010001#0*0} would return 01001.

c=${a##b}: Assigns the variable c the value a, where a is the largest part of the lefthand side matched of b deleted. For example, ${00010001##0*0} would return 1.

c=${a%b}: Assigns the variable c the value a, where a is the smallest part of the righthand side matched of b deleted. For example, ${10001000%0*0} would return 100010.

c=${a%%b}: Assigns the variable c the value a, where a is the largest part of the righthand side matched of b deleted. For example, ${10001000%%0*0} would return 1.

c=${a:?}: Assigns variable c the value a if a is defined and not empty; otherwise, generates an error.

c=${a:?b}: Assigns variable c the value a if a is defined and not empty; otherwise, assigns the variable c with the variable b and then exits the script.

c=${!a*}: Lists all variables whose names begin with a.

Doing Mathematics

Sometimes, adding numbers is necessary, and most programming languages offer this capability. BASH offers limited mathematical capabilities. For example, you would use double brackets to multiply two numbers as illustrated in the following example:

```
echo "Multiplication of two numbers $((3 * 3))"
```

Another way to perform a mathematical operation is to use the let statement as shown in the following example:

```
let "3 + 3"
```

The difference between the let and (( )) commands is that the (( )) returns a result and must be assigned or passed to another command or variable. The example illustrates the multiplication of two integers, but floating-point numbers can be used as well.

When using math, you often need to use numbers instead of string buffers because adding two string buffers results in a concatenation. The following example illustrates how to declare an integer variable:

```
declare -i variable
```

When a variable is declared as an integer, operations such as addition (+=) will increase the value by one and not append data to the end of the buffer. You can also declare a floating-point value as shown by the following example:

```
declare -r variable
```

The BASH shell supports the following operators:

!: Logical negation.

-: Unary minus.

~: Bitwise negation.

*: Multiplication.

/: Division.

%: Remainder.

+: Addition.

-: Subtraction.

<<, >>: Left shift, right shift.

<=, >=, <>, ==, !=: Comparison.

&: Bitwise AND.

^: Bitwise exclusive OR.

|: Bitwise OR.

&& : Logical AND.

||: Logical OR.

=, &=, <,<=, >,>=, &=, ^=, |=: Assignment.

Streams

Streams and pipes redirect content from an input to an output, or vice versa. When a script uses the echo command, the content is automatically piped to the output stream. Shell scripts can control the content flow of data using pipes and streams. *Pipe* is a special term with respect to a script in that it is used to move data from a source to a destination.

There are two types of streams: an input stream and an output stream. An input stream could be a script reading a file and then processing the data. An output stream could be the saving of processed data to a file. However, for most cases, a stream is the reading or writing of a file. Following is a simple example of generating and streaming some content:

```
ls > Listing.txt
cat Listing.txt
```

The command ls performs a directory listing in the local directory where the generated list is piped using the output stream and saves the content to the file Listing.txt. The > character is the output stream operator. Putting the > character between the command ls and the file Listing.txt streams the content from the command to the destination. If the file Listing.txt already existed, it would be overwritten with new content. The command `cat` is used to read the file `List-ing.txt`, and then stream it directly to the console.

The problem with the previous example is that it overwrites the file, which is not always a good idea. BASH can be forced not to overwrite a file; if an overwrite is attempted, an error is generated. Following is an example that shows how to stop a file from being overwritten:

```
set -o noclobber
ls > Listing.txt
cat Listing.txt
```

It is still possible to overwrite a file even if file protection is in place. You might want to do this when you are resetting an environment for a specific application. Following is an example that shows how to override the protection:

```
set -o noclobber
ls >! Listing.txt
cat Listing.txt
```

The ! beside the > character overrides the overwrite protection mechanism and will overwrite an existing file.

Often when generating logging events, overwriting a file is a bad idea because old events are deleted. Instead, you would append content to a file. Using the >> characters, as in the following example, appends the generated content onto the end of the file:

```
ls >> Listing.txt
```

When the example is executed, the output of the directory listing is appended to the file `Listing.txt`. If the file `Listing.txt` does not exist, it is created.

When many open source console applications generate errors, they do so on the error stream. The *error stream* is a form of output stream, but it can be distinguished from the generic output stream. The output stream and error stream are not the same streams. You should capture each stream in different files to keep further processing of the text files simpler. The following example shows how the output stream is captured in a file and the error stream is captured in another file or both streams are captured in one file.

```
command.sh > output1.txt 2> output2.txt
command.sh &> both_output.txt
```

On the first line, the 2 in front of the second output stream redirects the error second stream to the file `output2.txt`. The second line where the & is before the output stream generator combines both the error and standard output streams. Capturing the error stream means that no messages are lost. For example, when running a Windows Service, the console has no meaning, and hence error messages might be lost.

The other type of stream is the input stream, which usually is a file. Reading a script that reads content from an input stream is a bit puzzling because of the notation. In action terms, a script reads the content of a file, which is sent to the input stream, and then finally sent to a command. When the `ls` command executes, the generated list is unsorted. By using the `sort` command and the input stream, you can sort the contents as shown by the following example:

```
ls > Listing.txt
sort --ignore-case < Listing.txt
```

The input stream is defined by the < character sign. The commands of the second line indicate that the `sort` command is executed before the reading of the file `Listing.txt`. However, BASH interprets the second line as a reading operation and reads the file `Listing.txt` before executing the `sort` command. After the list has been sorted, it is output to the standard output stream. This is because there are no output stream operators that would redirect the content to a file. The following example illustrates how to capture the sorted content and send it to the file:

```
ls > Listing.txt
sort --ignore-case < Listing.txt > sorted.txt
cat sorted.txt
```

The second line of the example is confusing because the input and output streams seem to be surrounding the filename `Listing.txt`. The confusion stems from how to interpret the second line. First the file `Listing.txt` is read, and then the command `sort` organizes the data, which is then saved to the file `sorted.txt`.

Sometimes when one file or stream is being read, another file or stream needs to be read or written to as well. The problem is that the default input or output streams are for a single item. This means reading from one input stream, and then from another input stream will cause the original input stream to be closed. BASH makes opening multiple streams possible by opening temporary streams and reassigning them as shown by the following example:

```
exec 3<&0
exec < temp2.image.file
while read line
do
    echo " $line" >> binary.ldif
```

```
done
exec <&3
exec 3<&-
```

The default input stream 0 is stored to the stream identifier 3 using the `exec` command. The default input stream 0 can be redirected to read another stream, which in the case of the example is the file `temp2.image.file`. After the stream has been read, the stream identifier 3 is assigned to the original stream 0 again using the `exec <&3` statement. To make sure there are no dangling open streams, the temporary stream 3 is closed using the `&-` statement.

The default input stream is not well suited for reading interactive console input. If interactive input is required, then the command `read` can be used to read in a line of text from the command line as shown in the following example:

```
read alineoftext
echo $alineoftext
```

When the example is executed, the input stream waits for the user to type in some content. The command keeps reading the keyboard content until the user presses the Enter key. When the user presses Enter, the typed-in content is saved to the variable `alineoftext`. The command `echo` is used to display the contents of the variable.

Pipes

You can use a pipe to process contents in memory instead of reading or writing contents from a file. A pipe is used to send the data from an output stream of one source to the input stream of another source. The vertical split bar character (|) represents the pipe character. The following example is a sorted directory listing that uses pipes instead of the streams used previously:

```
ls | sort --ignore-case
```

The pipe character is the vertical bar between the command `ls` and the command `sort`. The command `ls` is executed and the content is piped to the command `sort`. After the command `sort` has sorted the data, the results are piped to the output stream, which is the console. The output stream character could have been added after the `sort` command to send the sorted results to a file. The command `sort` is part of a set of commands called filters. *Filters* consume a stream of data, manipulate the data, and then output the data. The difference between the pipe and standard streams is that a pipe processes data in memory.

Pipes are meant to send content from one stream to another. This is useful when stringing together a series of commands to process data. Some commands, such as sort, are known as filters because they only process data that need to be part of a pipe. For example, the results of the directory listing could be assigned to a variable, where the variable could be manipulated at a later point in the script. A potential solution to save the listing to a variable is shown in the following example:

```
ls | var
echo $var
```

The problem with the example is that it does not work. The content from a directory listing cannot be piped directly into a variable. Another solution would be to use another command to read the piped content that converts the content into a variable, as shown in following example:

```
ls | read var
echo $var
```

The example does not work either, but it is correct. The read command does not work because it executes in the context of another process. This means the data will be read and stored in the variable var, but var is created and destroyed in the child process. Remember that child variables are not visible in the parent process. The problem to solve is that the variable needs to be exposed to the parent process, as follows:

```
ls | (read var; echo $var)
echo $var
```

The example works and displays the value of the variable var; however, the contents of the variable are dumped to the console, which defeats the original task of storing the data in a variable. Following is the final and correct solution to storing the variable problem:

```
var=$(ls | sort --ignore-case)
echo $var
```

The way to solve the problem is not to pipe the content to a variable, but to stream the resulting data to a variable. The solution is to assign the end result from the piped content to a variable. The way to do this is to use the $(and) characters to convert the piped content into an assignable buffer. After the piped content has been assigned to the variable var, that data can be used for other purposes.

Some shell scripts do very impressive data processing. The problem with this impressive work is that it is difficult to read and maintain. If scripts take too long to

TIP

write or do not work as desired, you should use Python. Usually at that point, the script contains too much processing logic that is much simpler to express in Python.

Decision Making Using `if`

When writing scripts, often you need to perform one set of actions based on some decision, such as the existence of a file or command-line option. Decisions are possible using the `if` statement. Following is a pseudo-code example of a decision:

```
if COMMANDS
then
     EXECUTE-COMMANDS-TRUE
elif OTHER-COMMANDS
then
     EXECUTE-COMMANDS-TRUE-2
else
     EXECUTE-COMMANDS-FALSE
fi
```

In the pseudo-code example, the COMMANDS are executed. If the COMMANDS return a 0 value, then the commands EXECUTE-COMMANDS-TRUE are executed. If a nonzero value is returned, then the OTHER-COMMANDS are executed because the `elif` is the second test in the `if` statement block. If OTHER-COMMANDS returns a 0 value, then the commands EXECUTE-COMMANDS-TRUE-2 are executed. Otherwise, if everything tested returns a nonzero value, then the commands EXECUTE-COMMANDS-FALSE are executed. Following is an example script that executes some command depending on the value of a command-line option:

```
if [[ $1 = "greet" ]]
then
    echo "You are friendly"
else
    echo "You are grouchy"
fi
```

The COMMANDS are surrounded by a set of square brackets. The purpose of the square brackets is to execute a test on the resulting value of the commands within the brackets. The commands within the brackets do not need to use any Boolean operators. The commands only need to generate some output that will be assessed as `true` or `false`. The spacing of the square brackets is important: a space appears to the left and right of each bracket set. A single set of brackets can also be used.

In the previous code example, if the first command-line option has a value of `greet`, then the command `echo` outputs the string `"You are friendly"`. Otherwise, the string `"You are grouchy"` is output.

The following list defines the other test operators:

`=`: Are the two values equal?

`!=`: Are the two values not equal?

For numeric values the following operators can be used:

`-eq`: Are the two values equal?

`-ne`: Are the two values not equal?

`-lt`: Is the first value less than the second value?

`-le`: Is the first value less than or equal to the second value?

`-gt`: Is the first value greater than the second value?

`-ge`: Is the first value greater than or equal to the second value?

Some other operators can be used in place of `-le` or `-gt` as shown by the following list:

`-a file`: Returns true if the file exists.

`-b file`: Returns true if the file exists and is a block special file.

`-c file`: Returns true if the file exists and is a character special file.

`-d file`: Returns true if the directory exists.

`-e file`: Returns true if the file exists.

`-f file`: Returns true if the file exists and is a regular file.

`-g file`: Returns true if the file exists and the `set-group-id` bit is set in the file privileges.

`-G file`: Returns true if the file exists and is owned by the currently running group, which is a bit of a problem on Windows as the group idea is not portable.

`-h file`: Returns true if the symbolic link exists.

`-L file`: Returns true if the file is a symbolic link.

`-n string`: Returns true if the string length is nonzero.

`-N file`: Returns true if the file has been modified since it was last read.

`-O file`: Returns true if the file exists and is owned by the currently running user id.

-p `file`: Returns true if a named pipe exists.

-r `file`: Returns true if the file exists and is readable, and not locked by some other process.

-s `file`: Returns true if the file exists and has a length greater than zero.

-S `file`: Returns true if the identifier is a socket.

-u `file`: Returns true if the file exists and its `set-user-id` bit is set.

-w `file`: Returns true if the file exists and can be written to.

-x `file`: Returns true if the file exists and is executable. This option is tricky on Windows as any file could be executable and hence might be very problematic to function consistently.

-z `string`: Returns true if the string has a length of zero.

`file1` **-nt** `file2`: Returns true if the file modification date of `file1` is newer than `file2`.

`file1` **-ot** `file2`: Returns true if the file modification date of `file1` is older than `file2`.

`file1` **-ef** `file2`: Returns true if `file1` and `file2` reference the same file location on the hard disk.

Decision Making Using `select` and `case`

Another way of making a decision is to use `case`. In contrast to the `if` statement, the `case` statement uses a word pattern match to decide which set of commands to execute. Following is a description of the `case` statement using pseudo-code:

```
case WORD in
PATTERN1 | PATTERN2 )
    COMMAND
    ;;
PATTERN2 | PATTERN3 )
    COMMAND2
    ;;
esac
```

In the pseudo-code example, WORD could be a variable, or it could be a command where the results are converted into a buffer. Enclosing a variable name in double quotes can also create a buffer. After the buffer has been generated, it is tested against the individual patterns (PATTERN1, PATTERN2, and so on) for potential matches. The patterns are separated by a vertical bar and terminated by a closing bracket. If a pattern matches the buffer, then the associated command is executed

(COMMAND1 or COMMAND2). A double semicolon terminates the commands and separates the individual pattern blocks. Following is a case code example:

```
varGreet="greet"
case $1 in
    $varGreet)
        echo "You are friendly"
        ;;
    *)
        echo "You are grouchy"
        ;;
esac
```

In the code example, the asterisk is used as a catchall to be executed if none of the other patterns match. The asterisk is special because it illustrates the use of special characters to match a pattern, and the asterisk matches everything. Pattern matching is a type of regular expression that can match individual characters of a buffer. Following is a list of example expressions and their associated matches:

[a][b]: Match a buffer ab that is two characters long.

[a-z][b]: Match a two-character buffer that starts with a lowercase letter and has a b as the second character.

[!ab][b]: Match a two-character buffer that does not start with the letters a or b and has b as the second character.

[a-zA-Z][1-4]: Match a two-character buffer that starts with either an uppercase or lowercase letter and has a number between one and four as the second character.

*[a][b]: Match a buffer that has somewhere a letter a followed by the letter b.

[a]*[b]: Match a buffer that starts with the letter a and ends with the letter b.

"": Match an empty buffer.

One additional twist that can be added to the case statement is to encapsulate the case in a select statement. The purpose of the select statement is to present a menu of options to the console. The user chooses one of the options from the menu, which serves as the option for the case statement. The advantage of using the select statement is that it creates a menu and only allows the user to choose a specified option. Following is a select code example:

```
select greeting in greet other
do
    case $greeting in
```

```
            greet)
                echo "You are friendly"
                break
                ;;
            *)
                echo "You are grouchy"
                exit
                ;;
        esac
done
```

In the example, the `select` statement is combined with a loop created by the command `do`. Executing the `select` statement presents the options `greet` and `other` as shown in the following output:

```
cgross@apollo ~/code.ksh
$ ./select.ksh
1) greet
2) other
#?
```

After the user has selected one of the presented options, the selection is saved to the variable `greeting`. The `do` command is used in combination with `select` to create a loop that constantly repeats itself. The only way to exit the loop is to select the default pattern. The default pattern command subblock includes the command `exit`, which breaks out of the loop and continues the script.

Looping Using `while` and `until`

In the `select` command example, a menu-based loop was shown. You can also create generic loops using the `while` or `until` statements. A loop is useful when it is necessary to perform an iteration of some buffer or directory. Following is a description of both looping constructs using pseudo-code:

```
while TEST-COMMANDS
do
        COMMANDS
done

until TEST-COMMANDS
do
        COMMANDS
done
```

In the pseudo-code, the TEST-COMMANDS are tests as in the if statement case. The while loop continues while the TEST-COMMANDS returns a zero value. The until loop continues while TEST-COMMANDS returns a nonzero value. The loop is started with the command do, and when the done command is reached, the script loops back and starts processing after the do command.

Following is an example script that shows both loop types and counts every time the loop is executed:

```
typeset -i counter=0
while [[ $counter -le 10 ]]
do
    echo "Counter is $counter"
    counter=$(($counter + 1))
done

counter=0
until [[ $counter = 11 ]]
do
    echo "Counter is $counter"
    counter=$(($counter + 1))
done
```

In the code listing, the first line declares the variable counter to be an integer type. When looping and using a variable as a counter, this is necessary for the additions to function properly. Then within the while and until commands are two tests that trigger an exit condition after the variable counter reaches 11. For each iteration of the loop, the echo statement outputs the value of the variable counter.

Looping Using for and for-in

Another way of looping is to use the for and for-in commands. The command for is used to iterate the command-line parameters. The command for-in is used to iterate a list of values. Following is a description of both looping constructs using pseudo-code:

```
for VARIABLE
do
    COMMANDS
done

for VARIABLE in ITEM1 ITEM2 ITEM3
do
```

```
      COMMANDS
done
```

The previous example shows the two variants of `for` loops. The first variant of the `for` loop references a VARIABLE. When the first variant executes, the command-line options are iterated and stored in the variable VARIABLE. When the second variant executes, the values ITEM1, ITEM2, and ITEM3 are iterated and stored in the variable VARIABLE. Iterating hardcoded variables (ITEM1, ITEM2, ITEM3) may seem pointless, but is valuable when you have a variable that contains a buffer of space-separated identifiers that will be iterated. Remember that BASH will expand the variable before executing the `for` loop.

The following is a simple example of iterating the command-line options and displaying them:

```
for commandline
do
    echo $commandline
done
```

Another simple example of iterating a number of values in a list is shown as follows:

```
list="something another"
for data in $list
do
  echo $data
done
```

A `for` loop is very powerful because many different buffers can be iterated. Following is an example where the directory is iterated for all shell scripts:

```
for filename in *.sh
do
  echo $filename
done
```

In the example, the local directory is iterated for all files that end with an `.sh` extension. The variable `filename` references the short version of the filename without the prefixed directory identifier. To retrieve the name of the directory where the script is currently executing, the command `pwd` is used. When iterating a directory using this technique, it is always useful to change the current working directory to the directory being iterated.

You can also iterate text, where each identifier is separated by a space as shown here:

```
for filename in $(ls | sort --ignore-case)
do
    echo $filename
done
```

In the example, the ls command performs a directory listing and pipes the result into the sort command. The sort command organizes the directory listing, which is then converted into a buffer using the $( ) characters. The for loop iterates the buffer, which contains the individual filenames.

The notation of converting an output into a buffer using the characters $( ) is a powerful one. Often it is the only way to convert a stream into a buffer.

Function Declaration

No scripting language or programming language would be complete without having the capability to define and call functions. In BASH, defining a function is like defining a command. A BASH function is a command and the command-line option variables ($1, $2, and so on) are the parameters used to call the function. This means if a script has command-line options, then calling a function changes the values of the command-line option variables. This change is only present for the duration of the function call. Following is an example of declaring and then calling a function:

```
myFunction() {
    echo "Scope test: $scopedvar"
    echo "Function parameter: $1"
}
scopedvar="Global scope"
echo "Script parameter: $1"
myFunction "Hello world"
```

In the example, the function myFunction assumes there is one parameter, which is referenced using the $1 notation. The variable scopedvar is a global variable in the context of a script that can be referenced by the function.

Another notation in BASH can be used to declare a function:

```
function myFunction {
    echo "Scope test: $scopedvar"
```

```
      echo "Function parameter: $1"
}
scopedvar="Global scope"
echo "Script parameter: $1"
myFunction "Hello world"
```

The difference between the two notations is that using the `function` command creates a new environment and can be used for recursive calls. However, practice has shown that there is no difference. Any variable created within a function is defined within the scope of the file. When using a `return` statement, a value and exit code of the function is returned, and not a value that can be assigned to a variable.

Execution-Related Functions

Process context is a valuable feature. By using a child process, you can manipulate variable values from a parent process and those values are not altered in the parent process. Calling other scripts is useful when embedding larger pieces of functionality. There are additional commands that make it simpler to call other commands or child processes dynamically. An example of a dynamic script execution has been shown using the backquote. The command `eval` executes a buffer as if it were another script as shown here:

```
commandstring="ls | sort--ignore-case"
eval $commandstring
```

When the example script is executed, the command `eval` is run in the context of the current shell instance. If you want to create a new process, then the command `exec` is used. A reason for using `eval` or `exec` is to escape variables before the command is executed.

Another way to execute a set of commands in another shell is to use a pair of brackets as shown in the following example:

```
variable="original value"
( echo "in subshell before ($variable)" ;
  variable="modified value" ;
  echo "in subshell after ($variable)")
echo "Value after subshell execution ($variable)"
```

When the script is executed, the following output is generated:

```
$ ./function-scope.ksh
in subshell before (original value)
in subshell after (modified value)
```

```
Value after subshell execution (original value)
```

To have the commands execute in the context of the current shell, a pair of curly brackets are used. That would result in a behavior similar to executing the commands without the curly brackets, but in the local script.

Another useful functionality is the ability to execute a command on the dependency of another command returning a success error code. For example, imagine wanting to generate an event, but before that event can be sent an FTP update has to be accomplished. With BASH that is possible, as shown here:

```
firstcommand && secondcommandifsuccess
```

The double ampersand defines an AND operator and is used to join the scripts firstcommand and secondcommandifsuccess. In the example, the command firstcommand is executed, and if that application is successful, the command secondcommandifsuccess is executed. Note that a success is defined when a script returns a success error code.

Another possible operator is the OR operator shown as follows:

```
firstcommand  || secondcommand
```

The OR operator is very clever in that secondcommand will only execute if firstcommand failed. If firstcommand returns a success, then secondcommand will not be executed.

Handling Errors and Exit Codes

Good scripts always know how to handle errors and return proper codes. Not writing scripts that handle errors might lead to strange results. It is good practice to return an error code. Following is an example of returning a success error code:

```
ls -l
exit 0
```

The exit command is responsible for returning an error code. By calling the exit command, it is possible for other scripts to use a script and expect proper result codes. Good result codes mean that scripts will act in a predictable manner. For example, the AND or OR operator illustrated a few paragraphs ago expects proper exit codes.

A script can capture errors by using the trap command. By trapping an error code, the script can process the error and potentially provide a workaround. The BASH interpreter sends signals when specific events occur, such as the program exiting. The following example shows how to trap the exit event and do some additional processing such as deleting files:

```
myhandler() {
    echo "caught the exit"
}
trap myhandler EXIT
echo "program running"
exit 0
```

The command `trap` has two parameters. The first parameter is the name of the function that will be caught when an error signal is generated. The second parameter is the error signal to be caught, which is the signal `EXIT`. To get all available signals that can be trapped, the `kill` command executed is shown as follows (also shown are the results):

```
cgross@zeus ~
$ kill -l
 1) SIGHUP        2) SIGINT        3) SIGQUIT       4) SIGILL
 5) SIGTRAP       6) SIGABRT       7) SIGEMT        8) SIGFPE
 9) SIGKILL      10) SIGBUS       11) SIGSEGV      12) SIGSYS
13) SIGPIPE      14) SIGALRM      15) SIGTERM      16) SIGURG
17) SIGSTOP      18) SIGTSTP      19) SIGCONT      20) SIGCHLD
21) SIGTTIN      22) SIGTTOU      23) SIGIO        24) SIGXCPU
25) SIGXFSZ      26) SIGVTALRM    27) SIGPROF      28) SIGWINCH
29) SIGLOST      30) SIGUSR1      31) SIGUSR2
```

In the generated list, each of the signals is associated with a number, which can be used in place of the identifier. The `EXIT` error signal code is not shown, but it has a value of 0 indicating a successful exit. To know what each of the error signals mean, it is best to run the command shown as follows:

```
man kill
```

As you page down the help file, there is a description of what each error signal means, and an example listing is shown as follows:

```
SIGHUP     1    hangup
SIGINT     2    interrupt
SIGQUIT    3    quit
SIGILL     4    illegal instruction (not reset when caught)
SIGTRAP    5    trace trap (not reset when caught)
SIGABRT    6    used by abort
SIGEMT     7    EMT instruction
SIGFPE     8    floating point exception
SIGKILL    9    kill (cannot be caught or ignored)
```

```
SIGBUS       10    bus error
SIGSEGV      11    segmentation violation
SIGSYS       12    bad argument to system call
SIGPIPE      13    write on a pipe with no one to read it
SIGALRM      14    alarm clock
SIGTERM      15    software termination signal from kill
SIGURG       16    urgent condition on IO channel
SIGSTOP      17    sendable stop signal not from tty
SIGTSTP      18    stop signal from tty
SIGCONT      19    continue a stopped process
SIGCHLD      20    to parent on child stop or exit
SIGTTIN      21    to readers pgrp upon background tty read
SIGTTOU      22    like TTIN for output if (tp->t_local&LTOSTOP)
SIGPOLL      23    System V name for SIGIO
SIGXCPU      24    exceeded CPU time limit
SIGXFSZ      25    exceeded file size limit
SIGVTALRM    26    virtual time alarm
SIGPROF      27    profiling time alarm
SIGWINCH     28    window changed
SIGLOST      29    resource lost (eg, record-lock lost)
SIGUSR1      30    user defined signal 1
SIGUSR2      31    user defined signal 2
```

Technique: Using Regular Expressions

When writing scripts, an administrator needs to understand regular expressions. The earlier "Decision Making Using `Select` and `Case`" section briefly introduced regular expressions. The regular expressions topic could fill an entire book, but this section presents the essentials of writing your own regular expressions.

TIP

If you want to become a regular expression master, read Master Regular Expressions *from O'Reilly after reading this book.*

BASH Shell String Command Operators

Within BASH shell, you can search string buffers and extract substrings or replace substrings. All these operations are geared toward the manipulation of directories and filenames. The BASH shell regular expressions are similar to the standard regular expressions. The four base search regular expressions are defined as follows:

*(exp): 0 or more occurrences of exp.

+(exp): 1 or more occurrences of exp.

?(exp): 0 or 1 occurrences of exp.

!(exp): Anything that doesn't match exp.

For example, to match `buffer` at least once, the regular expression would be `+(buffer)`. To match `buffer` or `something` at least once, the regular expression would be `+(buffer|something)` where the `|` character is an `OR` operator.

The base search expressions are then added to a variable output reference to match the beginning or ending of a buffer. The exact definitions are:

${variable#pattern}: If the pattern matches the beginning of the variable's value, delete the shortest match and return the rest.

${variable##pattern}: If the pattern matches the beginning of the variable's value, delete the longest match and return the rest.

${variable%pattern}: If the pattern matches the end of the variable's value, delete the shortest match and return the rest.

${variable%%pattern}: If the pattern matches the end of the variable's value, delete the longest match and return the rest.

To understand how the operators work, it's best to consider some examples. For reference purposes, the path used for searching is as follows:

```
/Users/cgross/active/CYGWIN/software/bin/sh
```

To return the filename (`sh`), the following regular expression is used:

```
echo "Filename (${dirlocation##/*/})"
```

The regular expression is saying "find the longest buffer that matches two slashes, and return whatever is left over."

To return the path, the following regular expression is used:

```
echo "Directory (${dirlocation%/*})"
```

The regular expression is saying "start searching from the rear of the buffer and the first time a slash is matched, return the remaining buffer."

Remember that when a regular expression match is made, the `#` means to start searching from the front of the buffer, and the `%` means to start searching from the rear of the buffer.

To match any subdirectory underneath the `software` directory, the following regular expression is used:

```
echo "Software subdir (${dirlocation##/*/software})"
```

Notice how the trailing slash is not added so that the returned subdirectory leads with a slash.

To match any subdirectory underneath the software or bin directory, the following regular expressions are used:

```
echo "Software or bin subdir (${dirlocation##/*/+(software|bin)})"
echo "Software or bin subdir (${dirlocation#/*/+(software|bin)})"
```

This search is a bit of trick example because the path has both the expression software and bin. The correct path that is returned depends on whether a single # or double # is used. For each case, a different answer will be returned. The correct answer depends on which directory is of interest to the administrator. The trick example is not intended to confuse, but highlight that sometimes a regular expression will not select what you want.

Instead of searching for a substring, you can match and replace a buffer segment. Following is a list of the different expression syntaxes that are supported:

${variable/pattern/repl}: If the pattern matches anywhere in the variable's value, replace it with repl and then stop matching any further patterns.

${variable//pattern/repl}: If the pattern matches anywhere in the variable's value, replace it with repl and continue replacing any further matches.

${variable/pattern}: If the pattern matches anywhere in the variable's value, delete the pattern and stop matching any further patterns.

${variable//pattern}: If the pattern matches anywhere in the variable's value, delete the pattern and continue deleting any further matches.

${variable/#pattern/repl}: If the pattern matches the beginning of the variable's value, replace it with repl.

${variable/%pattern/repl}: If the pattern matches the ending of the variable's value, replace it with repl.

For example, to replace the hyphens in the path with underscores, the following regular expression is used:

```
echo "_ replaces first - (${dirlocation//-/_})"
```

To switch forward slashes with backward slashes, the following regular expression is used:

```
echo "bslash replaces fslash (${dirlocation//\//\\})"
```

The example with the different slashes is another trick example that illustrates how some slashes are used to escape other slashes. Specifically the / character is used to escape the other slashes.

Using Regular Expressions

The most commonly used regular expressions are used to find text within a buffer or a file. A regular expression can be used to filter mail as SPAM, or to recognize a hacker in a log file. Regular expressions are both useful and frustrating to write because of their syntax. For the purpose of showing regular expressions, the grep command is used. The grep command can be used to find data within a text file by performing a line-by-line search. Following is an example of using grep to search files for the identifier text.

```
grep 'text' *
```

The grep command has two command-line options: the text to search for ('text') and the files to search (*). When using grep, the text to search for is bounded in single quotes. The single quotes are not necessary, but added for convention because a text to search may include spaces. The files to search is also a regular expression and the wildcard character includes all files. Used in this context, grep searches all the files in the current directory for the text text.

Searching the current directory is not as useful as it could be, because it requires the administrator to navigate the directory structure. It is possible with grep to search the various directories recursively. To search for content in subdirectories the --recursive tag has to be used as shown in the following example:

```
grep --recursive --include=*.txt 'text' *
```

The search parameters mean something slightly different and a recursive directory search is not as logical as doing a search within the current directory. The search in the example says to search in all subdirectories for files that contain the content text and the files that have an extension of .txt. The last parameter, which is the file identifier when doing a search in the current directory, has to be an asterisk because the example is carrying out a search with two levels of filtering.

When the --recursive option is used, the files to search option (*) becomes a directory and file to search option. For example, if the files to search option were the value *.txt, then only directories that match *.txt would be included in the recursive search. Of course, directories are rarely identified with a *.txt identifier and hence no subdirectories are searched. By using the wildcard character, all the files and subdirectories are collected into a set, which is then filtered by the --include option. The --include option then looks at the identifier of all files and only includes those that fulfill the regular expression. You can also use the `--exclude` option to search all files except those that match the `--exclude` regular expression.

The `egrep` and `fgrep` commands are also available for use. The difference with `egrep` and `fgrep` is the regular expression syntax that is supported. The command `egrep` supports an enhanced set of regular expressions. Note that `egrep` and `fgrep` are often aliased to `grep -E` and `grep -F`, respectively.

The simplest regular expression is to use the identifier itself. In previous examples, the identifier `text` was used to match some data within the buffer that is being searched. If the search were executed, `usertext`, `usertexts`, and `text` would be matched. `Text` would not be matched because regular expressions are case sensitive. A case-insensitive search can be performed if the `grep` option `--ignore-case` is used. A case-insensitive search can also be carried out by searching for both cases as shown in the following example:

```
grep '[Tt][Ee][Xx][Tt]' *
```

What should be apparent is that the regular expression syntax of the previous example is identical to the pattern-matching examples illustrated when explaining the `select` and `case` statements. The square brackets represent a single character to match, which can be one of the letters within the square brackets.

When `grep` searches the files for the identifier `text`, the identifier can be located anywhere in the file, but the individual lines are searched. So when the identifier is found, the entire line that contains the identifier is output. As `grep` searches on a line per line basis, it is possible within the regular expression to identify the beginning or end of the line. The beginning of the line is identified in the regular expression using the ^ character and the end of the line is identified using the $ character. The ^ character is always prefixed to the front of the buffer, and the $ character is always appended to the rear of the buffer. Following is an example that shows how to find the text identifier on a line by itself:

```
grep '^text$' *
```

Because the ^ and $ character are used in the same query, the only possible match is a single line with the identifier `text`. Following is an example that shows how to query for a line that starts with the identifier `text` and ends with the identifier `text`:

```
grep '^text*text$' *
```

By adding the wildcard character (*) in between the two text identifiers, any text in between is matched. As a rule, the wildcard character matches anything that is encountered. It is also possible to match the whole word text by limiting it using the characters \< and \> as shown in the following example:

```
grep '\<text\>' *
```

In the example, the identifiers usertext and texts will not match. It is also possible to use only a single \< or \> to indicate matching the beginning or ending of a word. Do realize, however, if the text is part of a buffer, such as text/xml, the example regular expression will still match. The regular expression only applies to alphanumeric values.

If the ^ character is used in the context of a character class descriptor, meaning in between two square brackets, then the matches found are those that do not match the regular expression as shown in the following example:

```
grep '[^t]ext' *
```

The regular expression in the example would match Text, next, and Next, but not text because the ^ character matches everything except the letter t. It is possible to match two initial letters using a notation defined in the following example:

```
grep --extended-regexp '(T|N)ext' *
```

The brackets define a grouping that allows the definition of a list, and the | character defines an option that allows matching of data using an OR operator. This explains regular expressions in a nutshell for searching. There are other operations, but those operations are used with respect to a specific utility. Based on these simple operators, you can define very sophisticated queries.

Technique: Some Additional Commands

When writing shell scripts, a problem for the administrator is to know which commands to use because there are so many. There are commands to manipulate directories, and many commands are called filter commands. Filter commands process data and then send the processed data to another filter command. A filter command does not generate data itself. The administrator needs to know the most common filter commands because they provide the basis of writing shell scripts and using the pipe. Note that grep and sort, which have already been discussed, are considered filter commands.

Command: expr

The command expr makes it possible to perform mathematical operations. Previously the declare command was used to declare an integer datatype used for incrementing a counter. The purpose of the command `expr` is to evaluate an expression such as addition or comparison. It is possible to do many of the operations supported by `expr` in BASH directly, but `expr` makes sure that there is no ambiguity when performing math operations. One of the simplest purposes would be to use `expr` to increment a counter as shown here:

```
counter="10"
while [ $counter != "20" ]
do
    ./dosomething.sh "$counter"
    counter=$(expr $counter + 1)
done
```

The `counter` variable is assigned a string value of 10, which has not been declared as an integer type, but is a string buffer. The `while` loop iterates and checks to make sure the value of the counter variable does not reach the value 20. Within the `do` loop, the `counter` is incremented using the `expr` command. When `expr` executes, even though the variable `counter` is a string buffer, it is considered a command-line option for `expr`. The generated output from `expr` is assigned to the variable counter. It is important to realize that the operation performed by `expr` is mathematical from the perspective of the administrator. From the perspective of BASH, the script is just a call to some command that generates some text.

The comparison (`$counter != "20"`) used to check if the loop should continue looping is problematic in that it is comparing a string value to a numeric value. This is problematic because it might not be doing the correct comparison, even if the script behaves as desired. That is why it is important to use whenever possible the declare statement to define an integer or floating numeric value. By using the `expr` command, you can test if the `counter` variable has a value less than 20 as shown in the following example:

```
counter="10"
while [ $(expr $counter "<" 20) = "1" ]
do
    ./dosomething.sh "$counter"
    counter=$(expr $counter + 1)
done
```

The operator < is wrapped in a set of double quotes because otherwise the BASH shell interpreter would interpret the < operator as a stream operator. You can also use the backward slash (\) to escape the < character. The result of the `expr` command is saved to the string buffer, which is then tested for equaling the value of 1, which means that the `expr` command has proven true. When the `expr` command returns a 0, then the comparison is false.

Not all operators of `expr` have been shown, but you can inspect them by using the Cygwin manpages. `expr` is an effective way to accurately perform numeric or numeric comparison operations when all you have are string buffers.

Filter: sed

Often when processing text, it is desirable to modify a stream by replacing some text with other text. The simplest example is the parsing of a Unix text file for carriage return and line feeds because Windows uses a different notation. You can process a stream buffer using the BASH shell, but that would be complicated. It is simpler to process a stream using the `sed`. With `sed`, the purpose is to parse a stream blindly looking for text that matches a regular expression. If the regular expression is matched, then the text is modified.

A `sed` command is very cryptic and although some logic is involved, the best advice is to simply remember a few `sed` scripts and reuse them. A rule of thumb is to use `sed` as a command in the context of a BASH script. One of the simplest scripts for `sed` is to replace found text items as shown in the following example:

```
sed s/'^Find text'/'Replace text'/g
```

There are four items to remember in this example. The first is the letter `s`, which is defined as the substitute command. Then the regular expression after the first forward slash is the text to match. The identifier after the second forward slash is the replacement text. The letter `g` at the end of the buffer is a flag to indicate that all found instances should be replaced. It is possible to replace the flag `g` with a numeric identifier, meaning that the n'th find should be replaced. Remember, however, that the n'th find is not the n'th find in the stream, but the n'th find within a found line.

Another purpose of `sed` is to delete lines that match a pattern with an example shown as follows:

```
sed /'^Find text'/d
```

The letter `d` at the end of the buffer is the command used to delete a line. `sed` is most useful for doing inline replacements that are not field bound. The problem with `sed` is that it is too cryptic and complicated. Common `sed` recipes are given at these Web sites: *http://www.student.northpark.edu/pemente/sed/sed1line.txt* or *http://www.cornerstonemag.com/sed/sed1line.txt*. `sed` can be added to a filter such as `awk`, which will be discussed later in this chapter.

Filtering Commands

The sort and grep (partially) commands are filter commands used to filter data sent to it via a pipe. There are more filter commands, which are defined as follows:

comm: This command is used to compare two files. You can check whether a file changed in comparison to another file. The generated result is a list of lines that is unique to either file.

cut: This command is used to remove sections in stream. The cut is based on character positions in a line or field positions in a line. The field position counter starts at index 1 and not 0.

expand / unexpand: The two commands are a pair used to convert tabs to spaces (expand) or spaces to tabs (unexpand).

find: This command is used to find files according to some filter restrictions.

fold: This command breaks a long line into multiple smaller lines. For example, if a line is 150 characters long and the line length should only be 70 characters, then the command fold creates two lines of 70 and one line of 10 characters.

grep: This command is a very powerful way of filtering lines of text that is described in more detail in the "Regular Expression" section. For now, grep 'item' will find the item in the data stream.

head: This command outputs the first n lines or bytes of a file.

join: This more sophisticated command allows the merging of two streams into a single stream based on some index. For example, if two files have lines that start with an identifier field1value, then the merged stream will contain a single line that references the fields of field1value from the two files. You can define the index for the join command so that a field value in one file must match a field value in another file.

sort: This command is used to sort data according to an index in the field data. The sorting parameters can be fine-tuned, and you should take some time to investigate all the possibilities.

split: This command splits a file into multiple smaller files based on the number of lines or bytes.

tail: This command outputs the last n lines or bytes of a file. The tail command is useful when looking at the last number of lines of a log file for further inspection.

tr: This command is used to translate characters much like the sed command. However, tr is much simpler and not as sophisticated as sed. For most of your stream processing, tr is adequate.

uuencode / **uudecode** / **gzip** / **bzip2** / **bunzip2** / **zip** / **unzip:** These commands are used to convert a stream into another type of stream, such as a compressed stream or a text-based stream. For example, OpenOffice stores its files as compressed archives. By using the zip and unzip commands, a script can uncompress an OpenOffice file, manipulate the contents, and then create the zip archive again.

uniq: This command is used to filter out repeated lines.

wc: This command prints the lines or bytes in a file. By default the wc command is not that useful on its own, but it is useful in conjunction with other commands. For example, by getting the line count of a file, a script could dynamically stream out the last n percent of a file using the tail command.

Following is an example of using a filter to combine the commands ps and grep to find a specific process:

```
centaur:~ cgross$ ps -ax | grep 'stunnel'
  PID  TT  STAT      TIME COMMAND
  217  ??  Ss     8:34.98 /System/Library/...
```

The awk command is useful when the data being filtered is made up of records and fields. Log files meet this criteria. Awk is a script environment in its own right, but often is used in shell scripts as a way of iterating data.

Technique: Using awk to Process Data

Often an administrator has the task of searching log files, configuration files, or text files. The awk command is useful because it allows the iteration of a file, which can then be filtered. awk often is used as a command as part of a pipe in BASH, but awk is a full-blown scripting environment. awk uses its own scripting language.

awk Theory

The theory of awk is relatively simple in that awk requires two inputs: a script and data. The script can be defined on the awk command line or can be defined in the form of a script. The data can be a file or the result of a pipe or stream. Following is an example where awk reads both inputs from two files:

```
awk -f script.awk file.data
```

Following is an example where awk receives the data stream from a pipe:

```
ls | awk -f script.awk
```

Following is an example where awk receives the data stream from a pipe and the script to execute from the command line:

```
ls | awk '{print $1 $2}'
```

An awk script in generic terms is defined as follows:

```
BEGIN { ...commands... }
optional match { ...commands...}
END { ...commands...}
```

Each of the lines defined in the example represents a block of code. A block of code is not restricted to a single line, but is defined by a set of curly brackets. Within the curly brackets, there can be multiple lines. The order of events is as follows:

1. awk is started and the input script is parsed.
2. All blocks of code that begin with the BEGIN identifier are executed.
3. A line of text is read from the input data. The end of line in the default case is defined as a carriage return or line feed.
4. The line of text is chopped in a set of blocks, where each block is defined by a delineator. In the default case, the delineator is the space character.
5. The script's optional match blocks of code are iterated and tested against the line of text. If a match occurs, then the block of code is executed.
6. The remaining lines of text are iterated until an end-of-file condition is reached.
7. All blocks of code that begin with the END identifier are executed.

Searching and Transforming Data

The best way to illustrate how to use awk is to create a normal scenario. When using Windows, the network administrator distributes patches for each machine. A server computer contains directories for each client computer that hold the patches that need to be applied. On the client side, a script executes and contacts the server looking for its patches. If the patches exist, they are downloaded and installed.

An administrator when identifying the patches to download from the client does not want to hardcode the identifier of the computer in the script. The best solution is to create a script that identifies the identifier of the computer. The command net config workstation returns a description of the local computer that contains the identifier of the computer. Following is a sample output from the net command:

```
Computer name                            \\ZEUS
Full Computer name                       zeus
User name                                cgross

Workstation active on
NetbiosSmb (000000000000)
NetBT_Tcpip_{9781554A-0913-4BD9-AD23-7D52243435C5} (00022D8DAB6F)

Software version                         Windows 2002

Workstation domain                       DEVSPACE
Workstation Domain DNS Name              (null)
Logon domain                             ZEUS

COM Open Timeout (sec)                    0
COM Send Count (byte)                     16
COM Send Timeout (msec)                   250
The command completed successfully.
```

In the example output, the local computer identifier is in the first line, but for the purposes of the script, assume that the identifier could exist anywhere in the output. We want to be able to extract the identifier ZEUS, without the backward slashes. To get the desired result, the commands in the following example are used:

```
net config workstation | grep '^Computer name' | awk '{print $3}'
| tr--delete '\\'
```

The purpose of each command is explained in the following list:

net config workstation: The command that is used to generate the content that contains the workstation identifier.

grep '^Computer name': The command that is used to find the line that contains the workstation identifier. The regular expression matches the front of the line with the identifier Computer name. The content after the grep will be whittled down to one line.

awk '{print $3}': The command used to filter the third record of the input line, but it could be multiple lines. After this command has run, only the text \\ZEUS results.

tr-delete '\\': This command is used to remove the backward slashes from the input buffer. After the command has executed, the output will only contain the workstation identifier ZEUS.

In a big picture sense, the example demonstrates that a script slices the data multiple times. Trying to find the exact data using a single magical command is too difficult.

An awk script matches lines of text and then performs some filtering. awk does not require scripts to match data; everything awk does is optional. For example, awk could be used to replace grep. Following is an example awk script that would match the same records as the grep command in the computer identifier script excerpt:

```
awk '/^Computer name/'
```

Following is a modified listing that does not use the grep command:

```
net config workstation | awk '/^Computer name/ {print $3}' |
  tr --delete '\\'
```

In the example, an awk procedure is enclosed by a set of curly brackets. Within the curly brackets are instructions used to output fields that are from the selected record. The variable $3 means to select the third field. For awk, a field is separated by a space or tab. Going back to the sample output, the identifier \\ZEUS is the third word, meaning that awk considers the identifier \\ZEUS as the third field.

It is possible to use awk to reverse the order of the fields as shown by the following example:

```
awk '/^Computer name/ {print $3,$2,$1}'
```

Instead of matching to any data in the field, comparisons can be executed on the fields themselves as shown in the following example:

```
$7 !~ /^\"zoe*/ && $6 !~ /"LOCAL"/ {print $0}
```

The awk command is saying "if the seventh field does not match the regular expression /^\"zoe*/ and the sixth field does not match the regular expression /"LOCAL"/, then print out the entire line."

When writing optional match conditions, regular expressions can be used, but some additional operators can be used to create more sophisticated match patterns.

==: Equal, but not an assignment.

!=: Not equal.

<: Less than.

>: Greater than.

<=: Less than and equal to.

>=: Greater than and equal to.

~: Matches the regular expression.

!~: Does not match the regular expression.

( ): Grouping of comparisons.

/regex/: Definition of a regular expression.

&&: Logical AND.

||: Logical OR.

!: Logical negation.

It is very important to realize that awk is not space sensitive and does not use escaping as a BASH script. For example, to print a concatenated string, the following example is used:

```
{ print $1"buffer"$2"another buffer" }
{ print $1,$2,$3 }
```

Performing Arithmetic Calculations

Like the BASH shell, awk has the capability to perform mathematical operations on values or variables. For example, you can multiply two fields and return the value as shown by the following example:

```
{ print $1, $2, ($1 * $2)}
```

The following mathematical operators are supported:

+, +=: Addition, and add and assignment.

-, -=: Subtraction, and subtract and assign.

*, *=: Multiplication, and multiply and assign.

/, /=: Division, and divide and assign.

%, %=: Remainder, and remainder and assign.

^, ^=: Exponentiation, and exponentiation and assign.

++: Increment.

–: Decrement.

awk also supports a number of mathematical functions: atan2, cos, exp, int, log, rand, sin, sqrt, and srand.

Variables

Variables in awk can be assigned and manipulated like a shell script. Typically, however, a variable is initialized in the BEGIN section and manipulated in a found record. The following example counts how many records are in a datafile.

```
BEGIN { count=0 }
{ count+= 1}
END { print "There were " count " records"}
```

In the example, where there is no optional match condition, it means that the block of code will be executed for every line of text.

awk defines the following global variables. (Note that the variables defined depends on the implementation of awk and is best found out by using the man awk command.)

ARGC: Argument count used to start awk.

ARGV: Array of arguments used to start awk.

ENVIRON: Array of environment variables, where the subscript is the name of the environment variable (e.g., ENVIRON["PATH"]).

FILENAME: Current filename.

FNR: Ordinal value of the current record in the current file. This is different from the NR because awk can filter and FNR references the original line number before the filtering.

FS: Field separator used by awk to distinguish a separator between two fields. The default value is a space.

NF: Number of fields in current record.

NR: Number of current record.

OFMT, CONVFMT: Format used when output numbers and when converting a number to a string.

OFS: Buffer used when outputting a field separator. The default value is a space.

ORS: Buffer used when outputting a record separator. The default value is a newline character.

RS: Record separator used by awk to distinguish two records. The default value is a newline character.

$0: The entire current record.

$n: The n'th field of the current record.

There is a problem when embedding awk scripts within a BASH script. Consider the following problem:

```
ls | awk ' $1 ~ /$1/ { print $1 }'
```

In the example, the $1 refers to both the first field in the select script, and the first positional parameter. Neither awk nor BASH knows who manages the parameters.

Looping and Decision Making Using Control Structures

The awk shell has the capability to add programmatic constructs such as loops and decision blocks. Following is an example that illustrates the three different looping constructs that can be used in awk:

```
for (i = 2; i <= NF; ++i)
    grades[i-1] = $I
while (! file) {
    printf "Enter a filename: "
    getline < "-"
}
do {
    printf "Enter a filename: "
    getline < "-"
} while (! file)
```

The expressions used to match a true or false in either the while or for loop are the same as the conditions used to match a record in the optional match section. In effect, it is possible to iterate the lines of text using a block of code or using a loop. The for loop has a special notation that allows the iteration of an array as shown in the following example:

```
for( data in grades) {
    print item
}
```

Using the in keyword creates an iterator of the array grades that on each loop assigns the current index value to the variable data.

Following is an example decision block using an if statement:

```
if (file !~ /^\//) {
    "pwd" | getline
    close("pwd")
    file = $0 "/" file
}
```

The `if` statement is not complicated to understand. What is new, however, is the additional line `"pwd" | getline`. This is a special notation used to execute a command within `awk`, and then read data while processing another data stream. It is useful when processing data that might need further processing. Using loops and decision blocks, fields of certain values can trigger other processing actions.

Storing Data in Arrays

`awk` can manipulate arrays, which are created dynamically, usually initialized in the `BEGIN` section, manipulated by each field, and then processed in the `END` section. An example is the manipulation of a bitmap field is shown here:

```
BEGIN {
    FS = ","
    WIDTH = 12
    HEIGHT = 12
    for (i = 1; i <= WIDTH; ++i)
        for (j = 1; j <= HEIGHT; ++j)
            bitmap[i, j] = "O"
}
{
    bitmap[$1, $2] = "X"
}
END {
    for (i = 1; i <= WIDTH; ++i){
        for (j = 1; j <= HEIGHT; ++j)
            printf("%s", bitmap[i, j] )
            printf("\n")
    }
}
```

In the code example, the array is the variable `bitmap` with two dimensions. The array is defined using square brackets, and the individual dimensions are separated using a comma. The value of an item in an array does not need to be preallocated, but can be assigned. Using loops, it is possible to iterate a multidimensional array.

Searching Multiline Records

A line, which is a record in `awk`, is defined by the record separator (RS) by default. Being creative and clever with the record separator makes it is possible to read multiple lines that are separated by some other character. However, do realize that when altering the record separator, the newline character is recognized as a field.

Another solution is to use the function `getline`. The function `getline` can be used in multiple contexts. One example has already been shown where `getline` is used as part of loop to read an entire file. The command `getline` can be used in the context of blocks of code, which then reads the next line of text as illustrated by the following example:

```
{
    print FNR, $0
    getline
}
```

When the `getline` command is executed, the global variables (e.g., $0, $n) are updated and filled with the contents of the new record. The example awk script reads every other line. Because the `getline` syntax can be odd, it is best to put the command on its own line or enclose it in brackets. Otherwise, the awk script may exhibit odd behavior.

awk - Provided Functions

awk has a number of provided functions that are defined as follows. (Note that not all functions are outlined, just the most interesting ones. To get a complete listing use the man awk command.)

gsub(r, s, [t]): Using the regular expression r, replace the matched text in t with the buffer s. If t is not given, use $0.

length(s): Return the length of the string.

match(s, r): Match the regular expression pattern r in s. Returned is the starting position of the match, or 0 if no match is found.

split(s, a, [fs]): Split the string s into the array a, using the optionally provided field separator. This function is useful when fields need to be subdivided.

sub(r, s, [t]): Like the function gsub, except only the first match is replaced.

substr(s, p, [n]): Return the substring of s starting at the position p and optionally the length of n.

tolower(s): Convert the string buffer s to all lowercase letters.

toupper(s): Convert the string buffer s to all uppercase letters.

Using Custom Functions

Custom functions make it possible to encapsulate logic in a separate location. Following is an example definition of a custom function:

```
function hello( param, localvar) {
    print "hello " param
}
```

In `awk`, a function usually has more parameters than the caller sends. For the function `hello`, there are two parameters: `param` and `localvar`. `param` is a parameter, and the parameter `localvar` is a local variable. The difference between a local variable and parameter is nomenclature, not any type of checking that `awk` does. The reason for creating local variables as parameters is to enable a function to be called recursively.

Parameters are passed by value, but arrays are passed by reference. This means if a function changes the array, the original array is modified. Using the `return` statement, the function can return a value to the caller of the function.

The following example calls the function `hello`:

```
{
    print FNR, $0
    hello("variable")
    getline
}
```

When calling the function, there must be no spaces between the function identifier and the opening bracket. Otherwise, `awk` will misinterpret the command.

Usually custom `awk` functions are included in the `awk` script. You can define a function in another script and include the function on the command line as the following example shows:

```
cat network.data | awk -f function.awk -f sample-multi.awk
```

There are no restrictions on the number of times the `-f` option is used to reference a script. In the case of the example, the main script is in `sample-multi.awk` and the external function is in the file `function.awk`.

Formatting Output Using `Printf`

The output command `print` used thus far is relatively simple and did not include any formatting. The command `printf` allows more complex formatting of individual fields. Following is an example that inserts a fixed-length string within another buffer creating a fixed-width table:

```
{ printf "%-10s \n", $1}
```

The `printf` command at a minimum accepts one parameter, but at least two parameters are typical. The first parameter is a string buffer that contains escape sequences, which are defined by a leading `%` character. Each escape sequence is associated with a parameter. The first escape sequence is associated with the second parameter, second escape sequence is associated with the third parameter, and so on. When `printf` executes, the escape sequence defines how the parameter will be inserted into the output buffer.

The generic notation of the escape sequence is defined as follows:

```
%[flag][width][.precision][control letter]
```

The control letter is the base type of the insertion:

`c`: ASCII character.

`i`, `d`: Decimal character.

`e`, `E`, `f`: Floating-point format.

`g`, `G`: e or f conversion, with trailing zeros removed.

`o`: Unsigned octal value.

`s`: String.

`u`: Unsigned decimal value.

`x`, `X`: Unsigned hexadecimal number.

The different flag values are defined as follows:

`-`: Left justify the formatted value within the field.

`space`: Prefix the positive values with a space and negative values with a minus.

`+`: Always prefix numeric values with a sign.

`0`: Pad output with zeros and not spaces.

SUMMARY

The purpose of this chapter was to introduce the concept of a shell and shell programming language. A shell implies command-line console, which implies a difficult and hard to learn application. In the old days, Unix shell scripting was difficult and used cryptic commands. With the introduction of Open Source and the Linux/BSD operating system, the command-line console is not as difficult. More commands are available and the names of commands are not as cryptic. The command-line console when used properly represents powerful scripts that can automate grunt work.

The chapter started out with the simple Windows batch file. The Windows batch file is not very powerful and is generally used as a wrapper script. BASH, which has more expressions, can manage very complex scripts. With BASH, the administrator has a very powerful text-processing and filtering tool. This chapter showed the essentials of BASH shell programming to carry out most tasks. There are many more tricks and tips, so be sure to investigate the links provided on the DVD in the directory */packages/Shell/links*.

3 Using Python to Write Scripts

ABOUT THIS CHAPTER

The focus of this chapter is to enable you to write scripts that are too difficult to write using BASH and its associated tools. BASH is a powerful scripting language, but some things are too complicated to express in a shell script. Python is a simple language that can be used to write powerful programs. Note, however, that writing a Python script is not akin to writing a shell script. Python is a full-fledged programmatic language and BASH is a shell scripting environment.

The advantage of Python is that it is part programming language and part scripting language. The Python purist might argue that Python is a first class object-oriented language; however, Python can be used as an effective scripting language and can be used in place of BASH if so desired. The ease of Python is its simple syntax and consistency in contrast to other programming languages.

The following is a list of Python programming topics covered in this chapter:

- Understanding Python
- Deploying Python
- Learning the essentials of Python language semantics
- Writing scripts that interact with the hard disk and other resources
- Creating scripts that can interact with BASH scripts
- Deploying scripts for production use

PROJECT: PYTHON

Python started out as an idea in December 1989 by Guido Van Rossum, a big *Monty Python* fan who was looking for a hobby programming language to experiment with. Python has grown in popularity and has attracted many people who admire the language.

Python is a good programming language because it reminds a programmer of the old days of BASIC. This is not to say that Python is like the BASIC programming language, which is not even close to the truth. In the early programming days, BASIC was considered an easy to learn language that allowed programmers to quickly put together solutions. Bill Gates himself was a huge BASIC fan. Python is a fresh way to put together solutions that uses modern concepts such as objects and classes.

One of the biggest improvements that Python incorporates is its use of spaces to define scope. Although many people consider this a weakness, using spaces is a strength because no arguments occur regarding the best place to put the curly bracket. Python code is written to one consistent standard, which makes it easier for programmers to exchange code. Table 3.1 contains the reference information for Python.

TABLE 3.1 Reference Information for Python

Item	Description
Home page	http://www.python.org
Installation	Following is a list of different Python distributions (details of each distribution are given after the table):
	Cygwin Python: The Python distribution that is within Cygwin.
	ActivePython: ActiveState corporation's easy to install and use Python distribution that integrates into Windows.
	Python.org: The main distribution is from the Web site *http://www.python.org*. An additional download is the win32all, which adds Windows-specific functionality.

$\longrightarrow$

Item	Description
Versions	The version number was 2.4.0 for all the distributions.
Documentation	Python generally has one set of documentation that is centrally located at *http://www.python.org*. The documentation contains information for both the developer and administrator.
	Other distributions have documentation that is an extension of the original documentation or a repackaged form of the original documentation.
Mailing Lists	Python has many mailing lists distributed across the Internet. The three best sources for the Windows programmer and administrator are:
	http://www.python.org/dev/lists.html: Main mailing lists from the central Python Web site.
	http://aspn.activestate.com/ASPN/Mail/: Mailing lists and archives for various Python-related mailing lists. The mailing lists for the ActivePython is located at this URL as well.
	news://comp.lang.python: A newsgroup that discusses Python language problems. The Web site *http://www.dejanews.com* has an archive of past posts.
Impatient Installation Time Required	Cygwin Python: Is included when selected in Cygwin installation.
	ActivePython: Installation time is a few minutes. Download size is ~17 MB.
	Python.org: Installation time is a few minutes when both installers are run. Download size for Python is ~9MB and Win32 extensions is ~4MB.
DVD Location	The directory `/packages/python` contains the Python.org distributions and links to the ActiveState distributions.

Additional Notes

Three different Python distributions can be used to write scripts:

Cygwin Python: When Cygwin is installed, you can install the Python scripting environment. This distribution of Python is specific to the Cygwin toolkit and cannot be optimized for the Windows environment. This distribution of Python is easy to install and configure because no additional installation steps are necessary. The downside is that this installation is not tuned for the Windows platform and excludes many extensions that are useful on the Windows platform.

ActivePython: ActivePython is a distribution that is installed as a Microsoft installation file (.msi). The advantage of this distribution is that Python Windows extensions are included. The disadvantage of this distribution is that it trails the main Python distribution when brand new versions of Python appear.

Python.org: The main Python distribution is located at *http://www.python.org*. The Windows distribution is a Windows native installation distributed as an executable. The Windows extensions are a separate download as a package called Win32All. The Win32All package can be downloaded from *http://starship.python.net/crew/mhammond/*. The two packages combined make up the ActivePython distribution.

When writing GUI applications, the default toolkit is Tkinter, which is based on the Tcl/Tk toolkit. Using Tkinter does not require learning Tcl, but does require learning Tk's way of building GUIs. For Windows, the recommended way of building GUI tools is to use the wxPython. The wxPython toolkit gives any Python application the Windows look and feel because the underlying wxWindows toolkit uses the native Windows GUI toolkit. To create wxPython GUI applications, the GUI designer Boa Constructor should be used. The information at *http://www.awaretek.com/toolkits.html*, outlines and compares the different Python GUI toolkits.

Impatient Installation

For the most impatient developers who want to quickly install Python and start developing solutions, the ActivePython distribution is the best. ActivePython is usually a bit behind the curve with respect to the latest features, but that is only a time delay of maybe one or two months. The advantage of installing the ActivePython distribution is that after installation completes, the developer is ready to write scripts. The ActivePython installer associates the Python extensions properly, as was shown in Chapter 2, and the BASH extension .sh.

Characteristics of the ActivePython Installation

ActivePython is a painless and simple installation of a Windows .msi file, which integrates fully into the Windows architecture. This means an easy install today could be converted into a more complex install tomorrow. An administrator could experiment with Python, and then update the .msi file to include any necessary changes.

The simplest way to update the .msi install file is to use a free (not Open Source) program such as WinINSTALL LE edition (*http://www.ondemandsoftware.com/*). This editor opens the ActivePython install file and enables an administrator to tweak and update the settings and files. Basing the installation on msi files is good from a Windows perspective, but it requires that you learn about the Windows installation architecture.

Characteristics of the Python.org Installation

The Python.org installation is simple, but in newer releases (>2.4), the Windows Installer is used. The difference with this distribution and the ActiveState distribution is that no Windows32 extensions are installed.

Experimenting with Python

After Python has been installed, you can start writing Python code. You should use the PythonWin editor that is installed when the Python for Windows extensions, or ActiveState distribution, is installed. Figure 3.1 shows where in the menu structure

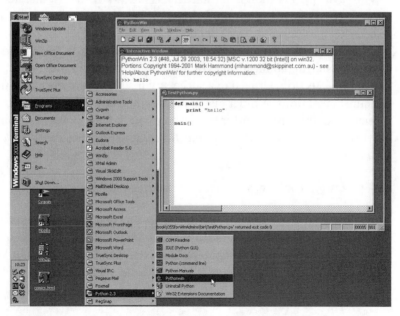

FIGURE 3.1 Desktop image showing where the PythonWin menu is located and a running instance of the PythonWin application.

the PythonWin application is installed, if the Python.org and Win32 extensions distributions have been installed. If the ActivePython installation is used, then Python-Win will appear as a choice under the ActivePython menu item, not under the Python 2.3 menu item.

Under the menu in Figure 3.1 is an instance of PythonWin running. The PythonWin application is a GUI that wraps the Python interpreter. PythonWin includes an editor and debugger. PythonWin is almost a full IDE, except that there are no project-management capabilities. Each file has to be manually opened and edited.

If you have multiple files to edit and you want an IDE, it's best to use an IDE such as ActiveState's Komodo (*http://www.activestate.com*). Komodo is not free, but runs on both Windows and Linux, and is a full-blown IDE. Another potential IDE choice is Visual SlickEdit®, but SlickEdit (*http://www.slickedit.com*) does not have an integrated Python debugger like Komodo does. Overall, however, Python-Win is a good choice because the focus of this book is administrative tasks in which Python scripts are wired together using a shell environment.

Deployment: Simple Python Distribution

If you just need to get a Python installation onto the individual machines, then the Active State installation is the best choice. You can use the WinINSTALL LE application to modify and update the installation. The problem with using the WinINSTALL LE toolkit is that the Windows MSI installer technology is extremely complicated. This book does not delve into any details of the Windows Installer technologies.

The ActivePython installer can easily be installed in quiet mode, using a login script or startup application as defined in Chapter 5 in the "Automated Execution of Scripts" section. Crucial to a successful installation is the use of the proper command-line options. A quiet install can be run using the following command. (Note details like this are found in the ActiveState release notes distributed on the ActiveState Web site *http://aspn.activestate.com/ASPN/docs/ActivePython/2.4/rel-notes.html.*)

```
ActivePython-<version>.msi /i
```

This default installation does not show any dialog boxes. When running the example from a DOS console, the installer automatically starts because the .msi file extension has been properly registered with the Windows registry. If Windows brings up a dialog box asking what to do with the file, then the Windows Installer has not been installed. The best bet to solve this problem and other potential problems is to read the content at *http://www.microsoft.com/windows2000/community/centers/management/msi_faq.mspx*. If the URL does not work, search the Microsoft site using the words `Windows Installer FAQ`. The following example shows how to control the directory where the Python runtime files are installed:

```
ActivePython-<version>.msi /i INSTALLDIR=c:\python
```

Added to the command line is the variable `INSTALLDIR`, which is the installation directory used to install Python. The only problem with using the variable is that there cannot be a space in the path. Even if double or single quotes are used, the installer has problems with the directory name. The following example shows how to install specific features of the installer:

```
ActivePython-<version>.msi /i INSTALLDIR=c:\python
ADDLOCAL=core,pywin32
```

The features to be installed are `core` and `documentation`. These modules are part of a hierarchy that is installed. The feature hierarchy is simpler to understand if the `/i` option is ignored and the installation is manually driven until the features dialog box appears as shown in Figure 3.2.

In Figure 3.2, a tree control contains a number of nodes, where each node represents a feature. At the root of the tree control is the feature ActivePython. Below the root are two child nodes: Python for Windows Extensions, and Documentation. In Figure 3.2, the Documentation feature is not installed because it was not defined in the command line when specific features were installed.

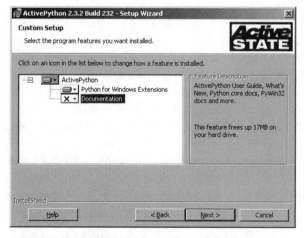

FIGURE 3.2 Installable features available with ActivePython distribution.

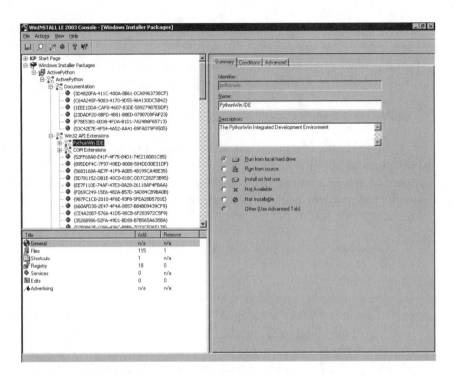

FIGURE 3.3 WinINSTALL LE view of the ActivePython 2.2 installation program.

The features that are installed and the features that are defined in the installation program might not be the same identifiers. To figure out the identifiers, you can use the freeware .msi installer tool WinINSTALL LE. Figure 3.3 shows the loaded MSI from the ActiveState 2.2 installation and the PythonWin IDE feature.

In Figure 3.3, the tree control in the upper-left corner displays all the features in the install file. The identifier of the features is found in the righthand pane in the grayed out Identifier text box. The value of the identifier is equal to pythonwin, which is a feature identifier that can be used from the command line.

This does not mean that for every installation, the administrator has to use WinINSTALL LE to figure out the feature identifiers. In its release notes, Active State has identified all the features exposed by the appropriate ActivePython installer. Following is a list of available features for the 2.4 installer:

core: The core runtime files used to make Python scripts run.

pywin32: Extensions to Python intended for use on the Windows platform.

documentation: Documentation about Python and the ActivePython distribution.

register: Registers the ActiveState Python installation as the default installation.

An installer can have dependencies as shown previously by the tree control in Figure 3.2. When a feature is installed, so are its dependencies. The difference is that dependencies work in reverse in that a child feature installs all the parent features that include the child feature. For example, installing the core feature does not imply installation of the other features. The core feature is not dependent on the documentation feature. Installing the pywin32 feature does imply installing the feature core, but not documentation. The dependency is from the bottom of the tree control upward. The default installation for the installer is to install all features.

Deployment: Python.org Distribution

Installing the Python.org as an automated installation is the same as the ActiveState installation. The advantage of the Python.org installation is as a plain vanilla installation, it can be used by cross-platform scripts. The ActiveState Python installation is the combination of the default Python.org installation and the Python Windows Extensions installation.

It might be tempting to create a custom Python extension; however, because of the complexities involved in creating a custom Python distribution, it is not discussed further in this book. The only reason to create a custom Python distribution is to be able to add some extra Python modules. Deploying custom Python modules is a separate issue, which is well documented and understood. Therefore, the deployment strategy is to use ActiveState and then deploy the modules. A ZIP file of the Python runtime distribution is not enough to deploy Python because the Python runtime installs a few files in the Windows System directory and manipulates the Windows registry.

Deployment: External Python Modules

A programmer writes Python code to create an application, and then the administrator deploys the code to all machines that need to use the application. When deploying applications, an administrator is typically deploying Python modules. When deploying Python modules, there are three issues to consider: creating the distribution, installing the distribution, and structuring the application in the distribution.

If you want to write Python code, you can skip forward to the "Technique: Writing Python Code" section. Deployment is covered first because some of you may be Perl, VBScript, or JavaScript administrators. Those administrators have no interest in programming Python code and are more interested in how to deploy Python modules.

Responsibility of the Programmer

Let's say that a team of developers wrote a huge Python application that is ready to deploy. The question is does the administrator write the installation or does the programmer write the installation? The administrator always writes the installation program because it allows the administrator to control which files are deployed to which location. To help the administrator write the installations scripts, the Python programmer needs to provide the items in Table 3.2.

Structuring a Python Application

A Python application is based on the concept of files and directories. For example, if a developer creates a function in a file called `myfile.py`, then the function would be located in module `myfile`. The following example shows the file `myfile.py` with a single method:

```
def Greeting() :
    print "Hello world"
```

The next example shows how another module could use the function `Greeting` defined in the previous listing:

```
import myfile
def Main() :
    myfile.Greeting()
```

The `import` statement binds the reference of `Greeting` to the module that has defined the `Greeting` function. Python finds modules by searching for the module in one of the Python library paths. To find out the current available library paths, the `sys.path` method is executed as shown in the following example:

```
>>> import sys
>>> sys.path
'E:\\book\\OSSforWinAdmins\\src\\pythonmodules\\simplemodule',
'E:\\book\\OSSforWinAdmins\\src\\pythonmodules\\modules',
'C:\\Python22\\Lib\\site-packages\\Pythonwin',
'C:\\Python22\\Lib\\site-packages\\win32',
'C:\\Python22\\Lib\\site-packages\\win32\\lib',
'C:\\Python22\\Lib\\site-packages',
'C:\\Python22\\DLLs', 'C:\\Python22\\lib',
'C:\\Python22\\lib\\lib-tk', 'C:\\Python22']
```

TABLE 3.2 Items a Programmer Should Provide to the Administrator

Item	Description
Zip file	A ZIP file that contains all the Python modules that make up the application. The Python modules can be source-code based files or already precompiled files.
List of Python Extension Dependencies	Many Python applications rely on external modules that may or may not be installed in the Python runtime. Regardless of whether the module exists in the Python runtime deployment, it must be added to a list. The version number and URL where the extension could be downloaded if necessary should be included. IMPORTANT: The programmer should not give the administrator a ZIP file that contains extension files because a programmer might have tweaked the installation or sources. A URL allows the administrator to download a clean copy of the extension for proper installation.
Preconditions	A list of preconditions that must be met before the application can be installed. Included are database connections, network software installations, and so on. *http://cygwin.com/docs.html*
Configurations	A detailed list of the files and registry settings that are used to configure the application. This includes configuration of the Python extensions and preconditions.
Post Install	A detailed list of steps that need to be taken after the files have been copied to the destination computer. This does not include configuration parameters. It does include the execution of programs that generate default configuration information.

In the generated output, the first line with the >>> characters is the Python shell displaying a command prompt. Python is not only a programming language, but also a shell like BASH. Using the Python shell it is possible to interactively perform operations such as directory creation and deletion. The Python shell can be executed by running the application Python.exe or IDLE.

In the generated output below the line >>> sys.path is a listing of the individual paths where Python modules can be found. The first directory listed is the current execution directory that is always added by default by the Python Interpreter. The second directory listed is a programmatic path added for custom modules. The remaining paths listed are Python default paths.

A path can be added to the Python library path using the following techniques:

- Define the Python environment variable PYTHONPATH and add the path to the value of the environment variable.
- Create a filename with a pth extension. Within the file are paths that should be added to the Python library path, with each path on its own line. The file is stored in the root directory of the Python installation. For example, if the Python installation directory is c:\Python24, then the file is stored as c:\Python24\myextrapaths.pth. The filename given to the file is not important.
- In the Python runtime, add the path to the sys.path list. This solution is dynamic, and requires the programmer to add the paths using programmatic techniques. Ideally, this solution should be used for an application server framework and as a general solution. An exception to the rule is for installation scripts that temporarily need access to other custom modules.

Directories are package identifiers for modules. Shown in the following example is an example Python application directory structure:

```
- modules
    - pkg
        - _ _init_ _.py
        - myfile.py
```

The example directory structure shows that the file myfile.py resides in the directory pkg. The directory pkg resides in the directory modules, which is added to the Python library path. To reference the module myfile, the notation pkg.myfile is used. To convert the directory pkg into a true Python package, the file _ _init_ _.py needs to be present. The file does not need to contain any code because it is both a placeholder and location for global package operations. When a module is loaded from the package pkg, or in any descendent packages, the file _ _init_ _.py is compiled and executed.

When the programmer delivers a set of Python files for deployment, the application should have a directory structure with only one root directory for deployment purposes. A good directory structure makes it simpler to deploy a complex Python application. In the example Python application structure, the directory pkg acts as a root package descriptor. Of course, externally developed modules are not included in this rule.

Simple Python Package Deployment

For the example Python application directory structure, the package deployment requires the creation of a ZIP file. When executing a deployment, the created ZIP file is copied to another directory and expanded. The directory where the ZIP file is expanded is added to the search path in the form of a .pth file. The BASH script to deploy the ZIP file is illustrated in the following example:

```
#!/bin/bash
sharedfolder=\\\\Pluto\\packages\\pythonmodules\\dist
pythoninst=/cygdrive/c/Python22
mkdir $1
cp "$sharedfolder\\$2" "$1\\$2"
unzip "$1\\$2" -d $1
rm "$1\\$2"
echo "$1" >> "$pythoninst\\$2.pth"
```

To run the BASH script, two command-line arguments are expected. An example of calling the BASH script is shown as follows:

```
simplepythondeploy.sh /cygdrive/c/apps functions-1.0.zip
```

The first command-line argument is the destination directory where the Python application is installed. Notice that the calling of the script uses a Cygwin directory reference, which only works if the Cygwin Python interpreter is used. The second argument is the name of the application, which is the ZIP file that will be installed.

In the BASH script used to deploy the application, the fourth line (mkdir $1) creates the application directory and the line thereafter copies the archive to the application directory. Notice the use of quoted string buffers to expand the variables into full-fledged pathnames. The sixth line references the command unzip, which decompresses and copies the files within the ZIP archive to the destination directory. After the archive has been expanded, the archive is deleted.

The last line of the previous BASH script creates a .pth file in the root directory of the Python installation. The .pth file has only the application directory added to it. Now whenever Python starts, the directory of the newly deployed Python application will be added to the Python library directory and Python can start the application from the command line. In the previous listing, two variables are defined: sharedfolder and pythoninst. Those variables are defined in the script, but could have just as easily been defined as general environment variables for each computer.

Defining various globally required variables as environment variables is a good idea. For example, the value for a global file share of all packages should be an environment variable. When the administrator deploys a Python package, the script depends on a variable definition and not a hardcoded path. As a general deployment rule, the administrator should create a list of environment variables that every computer will define. Using that list, administrators can write scripts that will work on different computer configurations. The previous listing showed an example of how not to define global variables, but the hardcode path definition was created for illustration purposes.

Python-Based Package Deployment

The other type of deployment is when a Python setup script is written. A Python setup script installs the library as a package in the directory where the Python runtime is installed. The advantage of this approach is that it does not require an administrator to manipulate the Python library path. When using this approach, the modules are installed into a directory that has explicitly been designated as a place to store third-party applications and packages.

The following is an example directory structure that represents a potential Python setup application:

```
- application
    - myapplication.py
    - setup.py
```

The directory application contains two files: myapplication.py and setup.py. For the creation of the Python setup application, the directory application does not need to be part of the Python library path. The file myapplication.py is a single file application. The file setup.py is a Python script that will create a Python setup application. An argument could be made that even though the application is a single file, a package should be created underneath the application directory. Always creating a package descriptor in a corporate setting is a good rule to follow.

The following example shows the sources in the file `setup.py`:

```
#!c:/python24/python.exe
from distutils.core import setup

setup(name="myapplication",
      version="1.0",
      description="Example application",
      py_modules=["myapplication"])
```

The example is in essence the entire Python setup application. The first line imports the method `setup` from the module `distutils.core`. The method `setup` defines the structure of the Python application that will be installed. The parameters to the `setup` method are defined as follows:

name: The name of the application that will be installed. This is a required parameter.

version: The version of the application that is installed. This is a required parameter.

description: The description of the application being installed. The description should be something that people can easily understand.

py_modules: A list of modules that are to be installed. The modules are filenames with the `py` extension and are relative to the location of the directory where the setup application is being executed. The square brackets define a list, where the individual modules are a number of double- or single-quoted comma-separated buffers. To create a distribution, the file `setup.py` is executed as shown here:

```
setup.py sdist
```

If any errors occurred when running the example command, then most likely it is because of a missing Python interpreter (`python.exe`). If the script being executed is running in the context of a BASH shell, then consider adding a script descriptor. Otherwise, run the script directly with the following command:

```
python.exe setup.py sdist
```

The command-line parameter `sdist` is used to create a distribution. The other possible options are defined as follows:

sdist: Creates a generic archive that is manipulated and managed using the Python setup routines.

install: Installs the package created using the sdist installer.

register: Registers the package with PyPi, which is the public Python Package Index. If the package is private, do not execute this option.

bdist: Creates a binary installer that has different archive file formats. The default format used by the sdist option is the ZIP file.

To generate an output of all the supported formats, use the command:

```
setup.py bdist --helpformats
```

The executed command outputs the following formats: rpm, gztar, bztar, tar, wininst, and zip. For the Windows platform, the only formats of interest are wininst and zip. The wininst format creates a GUI-driven executable that installs the modules into the correct directory. The zip format creates a ZIP file that can be directly unzipped from the root directory. For the zip format, it is assumed that the Python directory structure on the machine that creates the ZIP file and the destination machine are identical. To following command executes the installer builder:

```
setup.py bdist --formats=wininst
```

The deployment includes both Python applications and modules. A sample package directory structure is the following:

```
- directory
    - pkg
        - _ _init_ _.py
        - myfile.py
    - setup.py
```

The package pkg has one module called myfile. To create a setup package where the pkg directory is part of the directory structure, the following Python setup source code is shown:

```
from distutils.core import setup

setup(name="functions",
      version="1.0",
      description="Example functions that can be imported",
      packages=['pkg']
      )
```

In setup source code, the parameter `packages` has been replaced by the parameter `py_modules`. When the parameter `packages` is specified, it is telling the setup routine to gather all the modules contained within a package. In the case of the sample package directory structure, it means that the files `_ _init_ _.py` and `myfile.py` are made part of the `pkg` package.

Now consider the following directory structure:

```
- directory
    - pkg
        - _ _init_ _.py
        - myfile.py
    - main.py
    - setup.py
```

The directory structure contains a main module (`main.py`) and a package (`pkg`) containing other modules. In a software-development context, the main module is used to execute the program logic contained within the package modules. The application is properly structured, but it is improperly structured for a deployment. The file `main.py` is a generic name, and a deployment would potentially create a scenario where a main module overrides another main module. The directory has to be restructured and would appear similar to the following:

```
- directory
    - app
        - main.py
        - pkg
            - _ _init_ _.py
            - myfile.py
    - setup.py
```

The overall directory structure has been redefined and the directory `app` has been added. Within the `app` directory is the package `pkg` subdirectory. The purpose of the `app` directory is to define a root directory of the application. The problem with this solution is that the setup program will consider the new root directory `app` as a package directory. The `app` directory is only a placeholder to define a root for an application. You might want to define multiple applications, for example, if you have directories `app1`, `app2`, and so on. The solution is to add an alias in the setup procedure that recognizes the `app` directory as the root directory. Following is an example setup implementation:

```
from distutils.core import setup
```

```
setup(name="Application",
      version="1.0",
      description="Example Application",
      packages=['', 'pkg'],
      package_dir = { '': 'app'}
      )
```

In the example setup implementation, the parameter `package_dir` is a dictionary variable that is an alias of a path. The alias works by recognizing certain directory identifiers and replacing them with prefixes defined by the dictionary. A *dictionary* is a key value pair separated by a colon, and commas separate multiple key value pairs. For the parameter `package_dir`, the key is an empty buffer and the value is app.

When the `setup` method is executing, the requested directories are iterated and found files are added to the deployment package. If a directory is found that matches a defined alias, then the directory identifier is replaced with the alias. This means that the directory app is recognized by the parameter `package_dir` as a root directory. When a match of app is made, then the value in the directory, which is the key and root, is replaced. When the package is expanded, the reverse occurs and the files are prefixed with the dictionary value. The result is that the root package is located in the relative directory app and the package pkg is located in the relative directory app/pkg.

Administrators might need to deploy Python scripts that interact with shell scripts. A Python shell script is like a BASH script and has as its first line a script descriptor to the Python runtime (e.g., `#!c:/python24/python.exe`). When using the `scripts` parameter, the path of the scripts installed is automatically added to the Python runtime. Following is an example of using the `scripts` parameter:

```
from distutils.core import setup

setup(name="scripts",
      version="1.0",
      description="Example Scripts",
      scripts=['script1.py', 'directory/scripts2.py']
      )
```

Files that are neither Python shell or script files can be added to an installation and are treated as direct copy from one location to another location. Any type of file can be copied, including configuration files or DLLs. Following is an example of how to copy a regular file:

```
from distutils.core import setup
```

```
setup(name="scripts",
      version="1.0",
      description="Example Scripts",
      data_files=[('config', ['dir1/item1', 'dir/item2']),
('log', ['dir3/item6', 'dir/item7'])]
      )
```

The parameter data_files is used to define the files that are copied to the archive when the setup installation is created, and then copied to the destination when the installation is being executed. The files that are copied to the setup archive can be anywhere and do not reflect how the files will be copied to the destination. The parameter data_files is a tuple list that contains a list of items to copy. The regular brackets are used to define a *tuple*. The first item in the tuple 'config' defines the destination directory. The list after the first tuple item contains files that will be copied to the destination directory config.

When copying files, typically relative directory paths are used. When the setup application executes and installs the files, the relative paths are converted into an absolute path. The absolute path is a concatenation of the sys.prefix value and the relative directory identifier.

When files are being added and extracted to and from a setup archive, it is not possible to alter the name of the file. This means whatever the name of the file was during creation of the setup archive will be the name of file after extraction from the setup archive.

You can also add files to a Python setup archive by using a MANIFEST.in template file. When the setup archive is created, the Python setup routines generate a file called MANIFEST. The MANIFEST file contains a list of files that belong to an archive. You can add extra content to the MANIFEST file by creating the file MANIFEST.in in the same directory as the setup.py file. Within the MANIFEST.in file can be instructions to select a number of files that are included in the installation file. Following is an example MANIFEST.in file:

```
include app\main.py
include app\pkg\*.py
```

Each file(s) in the MANIFEST.in to be included is defined by a command and a descriptor that reference the file(s). Regular expressions that include wildcards such as the asterisk can be used to select multiple files. Following is a list of supported regular expressions used to select files:

[a][b].py: Match a Python file called ab.py.

[a-z][b].py: Match a Python filename that starts with a lowercase letter and has a b as the second filename character.

[!ab][b].py: Match a Python filename that does not start with the letters a or b and has b as the second character.

[a-zA-Z][1-4].py: Match a Python filename that starts with either an uppercase or lowercase letter and has a number between one and four as the second character.

?[a][b]?.py: Match a Python filename that is four characters in length, where the first and last character can be anything, but the second and third must be the letters a and b, respectively.

[a]*[b].py: Match a Python filename buffer that starts with the letter a and ends with the letter b.

Commands can also be used to select files that will be included in the setup archive. Following are the supported commands:

include pattern(s)…: Include all the files specified by the pattern(s).

exclude patterns(s)…: Exclude all the files specified by the patterns(s).

recursive-include directory pattern(s)…: Include all the files specified by the pattern(s) in the directory specified and any of the descendent directories.

recursive-exclude directory pattern(s)…: Exclude all the files specified by the pattern(s) in the directory specified and any of the descendent directories.

global-include patterns(s): Include all the files found in the source tree.

global-exclude patterns(s): Exclude all the files found in the source tree.

prune directory: Exclude all the files found within the directory and its descendent directories.

graft directory: Include all the files found within the directory and its descendent directories.

When using the sdist option to create the setup archive, a MANIFEST file is created if it does not exist. The MANIFEST file is created when the setup method call processes the file list. If an administrator attempts for the second time to create the setup archive using the sdist option, then the already created MANIFEST file will not be overwritten. The problem is that if the administrator changed the MANIFEST.in, the setup creation routines will not pick up the latest changes. The created setup archive will reference the old files. The trick in a code, debug, and test scenario is to delete the MANIFEST file before each debug and test cycle.

The setup function has been referenced multiple times, but the function has not been explicitly defined. Following is a list of parameters that can be used:

name: The name of the application that will be installed. This is a required parameter.

version: The version of the application that is installed. This is a required parameter.

author: The author of the package.

author_email: The e-mail address of the author.

maintainer: The name of the maintainer of the installation package.

maintainer_email: The e-mail address of the maintainer.

url: The URL for the home page of the package.

description: The description of the package being installed. The description should be something that people can easily understand.

long_description: A lengthy and more explanatory description of the package that is being installed.

download_url: The URL where the package can be downloaded.

classifiers: A list of classifiers used by PyPi to index the package.

The optional parameters, such as download_url, are known as metadata. The metadata is generally used only for registering modules with the Python Index, but should be added for descriptive purposes.

When the setup function is executed, the files are by default added to the directory site-packages, which in a default Python 2.4 installation would be the directory c:\Python24\Lib\site-packages. The directory site-packages is the default directory for all third-party Python packages.

The Python package installer has the capability to automatically compile and link Python extensions. Python extensions are libraries written using C, C++, or another compiled language. The Python extensions have the file extension pyd, and are treated like pure Python script files when referenced and manipulated. For the scope of this book, we won't discuss how to use setup to compile and link the Python extensions because administrators should not have to learn how to compile and link C or C++ files—that's the job of the developer.

The purpose of the automatic compilation of an extension was to facilitate cross-platform deployment.

After the Python setup archive has been created, it can be deployed. Deployment can be manual or automatic. A manual deployment requires expanding the archive and executing the setup script. An automatic deployment involves the following steps:

1. The archive is stored on a common network share.
2. A temporary network connection is made to the common network share.
3. The archive is copied to a local temporary directory location.
4. The archive is expanded.
5. Python setup script is executed.
6. Temporary directories are deleted.
7. Temporary network connections are removed.

Following is a BASH script that uses this strategy:

```
#!/bin/bash
tempdir="/cygwin/c/temp/pythonunzip"
sharedcomputer="pluto"
net use z: "\\\\$sharedcomputer\\packages"
shareddrive="/cygwin/z"
rm -r -f "$tempdir"
mkdir --parent "$tempdir"
cp "$shareddrive/pythonmodules/$1.tar.gz" "$tempdir/$1.tar.gz"
cd "$tempdir"
#me=`whoami`
me="$HOSTNAME"
path="$shareddrive/pythonmodules/$me/$1"
mkdir --parent "$path"
date > "$path/success.log"
date > "$path/error.log"
gzip -d "$tempdir/$1.tar.gz" >> "$path/success.log"
2>> "$path/error.log"
tar xvf "$tempdir/$1.tar" >> "$path/success.log" 2>> "$path/error.log"
cd "$1"
python setup2.py install >> "$path/success.log" 2>> "$path/error.log"
cd "../.."
rm -r -f "$tempdir"
net use z: "/DELETE"
```

In the BASH script, there are four variables, two of which (tempdir and shared-computer) could be considered environment variables. In the BASH script, the simple package was stored in a common shared directory. The problem with this approach is that a user could potentially browse the directories and install or delete something that should not be installed or deleted. Therefore, instead of allowing the user to browse the directory, a temporary network connection is made using the command net. The temporary network connection is necessary because Cygwin tools cannot cope with a UNC directory description. The common network share needs to be represented as a drive letter, which is the letter z. Notice also that the variable shared-drive points to a cygwin-defined mounted directory instead of x:/. This notation is used to keep to the Cygwin notation of referencing directory locations.

After the common network share has been established, the commands gzip, tar, cd, rmdir, and mkdir are used to copy and expand the remote located archive. The command-line option –parent is necessary for the command mkdir. The additional command-line option is necessary because mkdir can create multiple directories with only a single call to the command. After the archive has been expanded, the Python interpreter can be called and used to install the module.

The variable me is assigned twice, and one assignment has been commented out. The purpose of the variables path and me is to define a place where the output of the different operations is dumped. For example, when the Python deploy script is running most likely as a background process, it would be good to capture the output of the Python deploy script to verify if everything went well. The output is written to the shared package directory under the directory of the package name and the variable me.

The variable me references the $HOSTNAME (name of the computer running the script) environment variable, which means that there will be output files stored for each install of the package on the individual computers. Writing the output files to the package file server makes it easy for a logging routine to figure out which installations worked and which did not. The commented out assignment uses the command whoami, which returns the name of the user that is currently logged on. This is useful when the Python module package is installed for a specific user. The output is piped to the output stream and the error stream. The file success.log is for the general output and the file error.log is for any errors that occur.

Technique: Learning the Python Shell

Python is a programming language similar to BASIC in the sense that Python enables you to write programs using a simple syntax. In Python, whitespace and line feeds are deliminators. The following example illustrates a Hello World Python script:

```
def main ():
    print "hello world"
main()
```

The first two lines are part of a function declaration. The last line calls the function. The keyword def is used to define a function. The identifier following the def keyword is the name of the function and the brackets are used to define parameters. In the case of the function main, there are no function parameters. After the closing bracket there is a colon, which represents the definition of a subblock. The defined subblock is a function declaration, so anything indented will be associated with the function declaration. It is important to keep the indenting consistent.

In the example, the second line is a subblock that belongs to the method `main`. The indent of the second line gives an indication that the second line belongs to a parent. Specifically, the indent of one line must be farther to the right than another line to establish a parent subblock relationship. All lines that want to be part of the function `main` need the same amount of indenting as the second line.

In the example, the third line is not part of the function because the indenting of the line matches the declaration of the function declaration. The Python interpreter then knows to consider the third line as another piece of source code that belongs to some other block. The third line belongs to the global space source and is used to execute the function `main`.

Consistent indenting is important. For example, if you are indenting using four spaces, then each part of the subblock must be indented four spaces. Most editors perform indentation automatically, so this is generally not an issue. The only time it can be an issue is if one editor sets up its indentation to use tabs, and another editor uses spaces. This confuses Python and causes errors.

NOTE

The use of whitespace to define blocks of code is unique among programming languages. Some programmers consider this a fault of Python, but other programmers consider this a blessing. The problem with languages such as Java, JavaScript, C, and C++ is that the formatting of the code becomes a battle of where to put the curly brackets. There are many code formats from which to choose. Forcing a consistent code format means that code is easier to read even though the person reading the code and the person writing the code might not be the same person. It is easier to maintain and extend Python code when the code is consistent.

The Hello World example can be typed in directly in the Python shell as shown in Figure 3.4.

In Figure 3.4, the Python shell is an application that is composed of Python-Win, the IDLE shell, and the console program Python. The command line of the Python shell is a series of three > characters. In Figure 3.4, the first line typed in is the `main` function definition. After you enter the colon and press Enter, the Python shell displays three dots. The three dots represent a change in mode of the Python shell indicating that a user could add additional commands. The second line (`print "hello"`) belongs to the `main` function declaration. After you typed it in and press Enter, the three dots appear again. Another line of code belonging to the subblock can be added. To exit the subblock, press the Enter key and a command line of three > characters appears. After the mode changes, the function declaration is complete and the function can be called as if were some command. When the function is called, the result appears similar to Figure 3.4.

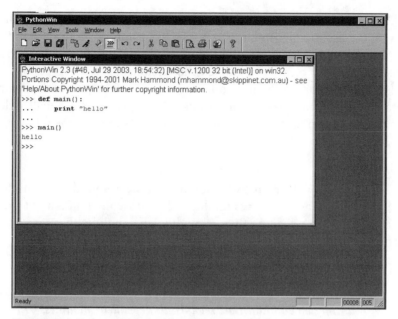

FIGURE 3.4 Python shell showing the coding of the Hello World example.

For some developers or administrators, the Python shell is useful because it can be started from the command line. However, the developer or administrator must exit the console shell to continue to do something else. The Python shell is exited using the pressing Ctrl+Z and then pressing the Enter key. This key sequence only works on Windows and not Unix. For Unix, pressCtrl+D. Pressing Ctrl+Z on Unix freezes the Python task and puts it into the background. If the Ctrl key sequences do not work, then use the following code to exit the Python shell:

```
import sys; sys.exit()
```

The interactive example shown in Figure 3.4 uses the Python shell from the PythonWin IDE. When running Python scripts as console applications, the Python shell does not run. Instead the Python interpreter simply executes the Python script, and after the script has completed, the Python interpreter exits.

Modules are extensions that define additional Python code functionality. Modules are loaded in Python using the `import` statement:

```
import sys
```

When the `import` function is called, the module `sys` is loaded. The module `sys` is converted into the filename `sys.py`. The Python interpreter searches the system paths and attempts to find the file `sys.py`. When found, the file `sys.py` is compiled and then loaded into the execution space of the Python interpreter. The compiled `sys.py` file has the filename `sys.pyc`. The extension `pyc` is used to indicate a byte code compiled version of a Python source code file. If the compiled version of a file exists, it is loaded before the source code version.

When developing Python code, source code changes are often not reloaded into the Python interpreter. This means a developer has to manually reload the file for recompilation using the `reload` command as shown in the following example:

```
reload( sys)
```

The method `reload` drops the instance of the sys module from memory, and loads a new instance of the sys module. The `reload` method is a not a deep reload. This means when reloading the sys module, the modules that sys depends on are not reloaded.

At the http://www.idyll.org/~n8gray/code/ *Web site is a Python script called* `deep_reload.py`. *The module* `deep_reload` *replaces the default* `reload` *function with an implementation that reloads all dependent modules. This is useful for writing, debugging, and testing complex Python applications.*

Technique: Writing Python Code

Python is a powerful language because of its simplicity; for example, the Python shell can be used as a calculator. The reference to the calculator is to illustrate that Python does not require a large amount of learning if someone just wants to add two numbers. Following is an example that shows the simple addition of two numbers:

```
>>> a = 12
>>> b = 23
>>> a + b
35
>>>
```

In the first line, the variable a is being assigned the value of 12. The variable a is an object, which is referencing a numeric value. The variable b is also an object referencing a numeric value. The third line adds the two objects, which is the addition of two numeric values that results in the value of 35. In Python, everything is an object, including primitives such as numbers.

Although everything is an object, not everything can be added or multiplied. For example, including a string value complicates the addition of two numbers:

```
>>> c = "1234"
>>> a + c
Traceback (most recent call last):
  File "<interactive input>", line 1, in ?
TypeError: unsupported operand types for +: 'int' and 'str'
>>>
```

The variable c references a string value. Attempting to add the variables a and c results in an error as shown by lines three to six. Specifically, line five says that Python does not know how to add an int (numeric value) to a str (string value). From a logical point of view, this makes sense because the outcome of adding a numeric and string value cannot be reliably determined. Python variables are not typed, but after they are assigned, they are type safe.

Many people consider dynamic languages with no data type declarations a problem. Programmers groan at not knowing the data types because it is never known what kind of object something is by looking at the code, which can cause problems at runtime. Python is different in that it is dynamic, but strongly typed. This means when assigning a variable as string, then attempting to retrieve the value as type integer might not be compatible. Python will not perform the task if it cannot be performed safely and will generate an error. Python does not want to guess at what the result might be.

The correct solution is to convert the string to an integer and then add the integer to the variable:

```
>>> import string
>>> a + string.atoi( c)
1246
>>>
```

The string module is imported and the function atoi is used to convert the string into a numeric value, which makes the addition legal again. Maybe instead of adding two integers, you want to concatenate two buffers:

```
>>> str(a) + c
'121234'
```

Using the function str converts the variable a that is of type integer to a string and concatenates the two buffers.

The only time when a mathematical operation might seem not so obvious is when the multiplication operator is used as shown in the following example:

```
>>> c * 8
'12341234123412341234123412341234'
```

The variable c, which is referencing a string buffer, is multiplied by 8. You would think that means multiplying the number 1234 by 8. Because the variable c is a string buffer, however, the Python definition of a string multiplication means creating a new string buffer that contains eight copies of the original buffer. This answer is logical, but most programmers are not used to it because of the traditional nature of the multiplication sign.

Python has the unique capability to use extremely large numbers. For example, the following is a very large number that is exponentiated with another large number:

```
>>> 100000000000000L ** 1000L
10000000000000000000000000000000000...
```

The triple dots indicate that many more zeros are available for display, which would have been displayed in the Python shell. However, to keep from showing all those zeros in the book the triple dots are used. The point is that Python can manipulate large numbers without rounding them off, which can be useful when dealing with currencies.

The numeric value types support by Python are:

Integers: 32-bit signed integer values.

Long Integers: Numeric values that can be as long as necessary. It is possible to perform long integer math. When defining a long number, the L needs to appended to the rear of the number similar to the following number: 12345678901234567890L.

Hexadecimal: Defines a number that is base 16 instead of base 10 and includes the letters a, b, c, d, e, f to represents the six extra digits. An example of a hexadecimal number would be 0xa34, which is the integer value 2612. The characters 0x begin a hexadecimal number declaration.

Octadecimal: Defines a number that is base 8 instead of base 10 and does not include the numbers eight and nine. An example of an octadecimal number is 0123, which is the integer value 83. The character 0 begins an octadecimal number declaration.

Floats: Defines a number that is floating point, and the length depends on the Python runtime.

Complex Numbers: Defines a complex number type that is defined similar to the following: (3 + 2j).

Using Arrays, Lists, and Tuples

Multiple pieces of data, which are considered as arrays in a BASH script, are stored as a Python list. Following is an example that illustrates a simple list:

```
alist = ["item", 2, 'another']
```

In the example, a pair of square brackets defines the list. Between the square brackets are the list elements, with a comma separating each item. To reference a list element, the variable name is combined with a set of square brackets as shown in the following example:

```
alist[ 2]
```

Between the square brackets is an index that references the element of the list, where zero is the first element. In the example, the element referenced would be the value another.

Lists can embed other lists as shown in the following example:

```
blist = ["item", [1, 2, 3], 'another']
```

The length of a list can be found using the len function as follows:

```
len( alist)
```

The len function returns a value of 3 for the list variable alist because there are three elements. To get the length of an embedded list variable such as blist, the array index is used:

```
len(blist[ 1])
```

There is a catch involved in retrieving the length of a list. Consider the following example where a list contains a combination of different data types:

```
>>> blist=["item", [1, 2, 3], 'another']
>>> len(blist[ 1])
3
>>> len(blist[ 2])
7
>>>
```

In the example, the list blist contains three elements. Using the len function on the second item (blist[1]) returns the value of 3. The value 3 is correct because the second element of the list is an embedded list with three elements. The returned value from the length of the last item (`blist[2]`) in the variable `blist` is 7. The returned value of 7 is a bit odd because it doesn't seem correct. The value is correct because the function `len` is not object specific. The function `len` produces different results depending on the type of object. The second item in `blist` is an object of the type `list`. The third item in `blist` is an object of the type `string`. Taking the length of the string results in the correct answer of seven characters.

You can also address an element in a list using a negative index value. A negative index means that the index starts counting from the right toward the left or from the end to the beginning. The following example illustrates how to use the `-1` index of the list `alist`:

```
>>> alist = ["item", 2, 'another']
>>> alist[ -1]
'another'
>>>
```

In contrast to referencing the elements from the left to the right, when using negative numbers the zeroth element on the right is `-1`.

To extract a subset of a list, the list must be sliced. *Slicing* is the process of copying some items from a list. The following example shows how to copy the middle element from `alist`:

```
>>> alist[1:2]
[2]
>>>
```

The two numbers inside the square brackets separated by a colon define the slice. The number to the left of the colon is the starting index of the slice. The number to the right of the colon is the index that defines the end of the slice, but does not include the defined index. You can also use negative indices for the slice. However, the resulting slice will still order the list elements from the left to the right. If either the lefthand or righthand number is not given, then the slice starts at the beginning of the list or ends at the end of the list, respectively. Omitting either of the numbers will copy the entire list.

Assigning elements in a list can be both simple and dangerous. The next example shows how to append elements to the previously defined `alist` list variable:

```
>>> alist[2] = ["added", "more"]
>>> alist
['item', 2, ['added', 'more']]
>>>
```

In theory, the `alist` assignment could be thought of as replacing the `alist[2]` element with `"added"` and appending to the list `alist` the identifier `"more"`. However, when the contents of the variable `alist` are retrieved, the output shows that the assigned list has been embedded and not appended. To append the list, the following solution is used:

```
>>> alist[2:] = ["added", "more"]
>>> alist
['item', 2, 'added', 'more']
>>>
```

The assignment of `alist` is a bit peculiar in that a slice of the array is defined. While appending the list worked, the third list element was removed. The slice is performing a list resize, so the third element is removed from the list. When using a slice notation to append list elements, Python interprets the command as the creation of a slice that cuts at the specified index and removes everything after that. Had the starting index of the slice been the second element instead of the third, then the second element and every element thereafter would have been cut from the list. The presented solution is not incorrect, and is a good solution, even though it did not work properly. The reason the solution did not work is because of the index used to reference the list insertion point. The correct solution used to append a list to the rear or front of a list respectively is shown as follows:

```
alist[len(alist):] = ["appended", "rear"]
alist[:0] = ["appended", "front"]
```

To remove the middle list element:

```
alist[1:2] = []
```

To insert data into a specific index in a list:

```
alist[1:1] = ["data", "added"]
```

The trick in this solution is that when an element is referenced using the same number to the left and right of the colon, an empty element is specified. This results in no list items being deleted, and the assignment automatically inserting the list at the array position defined by the lefthand number.

Other functions that can manipulate a list include `insert`, `del`, `remove`, `index`, `min`, and `max`.

When using list elements, a copy is not always a copy. Consider the following example, which creates a `"copy"` to an embedded list and then redefines the value:

```
>>> blist=["item", [1, 2, 3], 'another']
>>> clist = blist[ 1]
>>> clist
[1, 2, 3]
>>> clist[ 1] = "changed"
>>> blist
['item', [1, 'changed', 3], 'another']
>>>
```

The first line in the example is the definition of the variable blist, which contains an embedded list. The variable clist is assigned the second item from the variable blist, which is the embedded list. When clist is displayed, the list contains the same data as the embedded list from the variable blist. The question is if the data referenced by clist is a copy or a reference to the embedded list. If the data is a copy, then a modification of the data in the clist variable will not affect the embedded list. If the data is a reference, then a modification of the data in the clist variable will also modify the embedded list.

The proof that the variable clist is a reference lies when clist[1] element is modified to the value changed. When the blist variable is output, the embedded list has been altered. This means that the clist variable is a reference to the embedded list. This is a problem because it means that when one routine receives the reference, it might assume the data to be unique and not part of another list. A change will change the list, which may or may not be a desired behavior. The programmer needs to be aware of the problem.

If instead of a reference, you want a unique value, then the list must be copied. A simple copy cannot be used, and the following example shows a deep copy:

```
>>> import copy
>>> dlist = copy.deepcopy( blist[ 1])
>>> dlist
[1, 'changed', 3]
>>> dlist[ 1] = "changed"
>>> blist
['item', [1, 2, 3], 'another']
>>>
```

The module copy is imported; instead of doing an assignment, the function copy.deepcopy is used. When changing an element in dlist, the original embedded list in the variable blist is not changed.

The lists illustrated so far can be modified after they are assigned. In Python, you can create a tuple, in which the individual elements of a list cannot be modified. The following example shows how to create a tuple:

```
atuple = ("item", 2, 'another')
```

A tuple value can be read using the same notation as a reading list. Where an array and tuple differ is that a tuple cannot be modified. Attempting to alter the contents of a tuple will result in an error. A list can be converted into a tuple, which can then be converted back into a list as shown in the following example:

```
atuple = tuple(alist)
alist = list(atuple)
```

One side effect of using the `list` function is that the function can be used to split apart a string buffer as shown in the following example:

```
>>> alist = list("world")
>>> alist
['w', 'o', 'r', 'l', 'd']
>>>
```

Decision Making

Making a decision in Python involves using an `if` statement. The `if` statement makes it possible to choose a next action depending on the result of a condition. The `if` statement requires a `true` or `false` value. The decision can be based on calling a function, running a mathematical comparison, or using some other operation that generates a `true`, `false`, zero, or nonzero value.

In Python, a null or empty result is a `None`. A comparison involving a `None` is `None` and `not None`. The following example shows how to use `None` and `not None` in a comparison:

```
if not None :
    print "should display"
if None :
    print "should not display"
```

The first `if` statement should print `"should display"` because using the `not` operator on the `None` produces a `not None` value or the number 1. The second `if` statement will not print because the `None` value results in the number 0. The following example shows a more useful demonstration of the `if` statement:

```
a = 10
b = 20
if a < b :
    print "a is less than b"
```

```
elif a == b :
    print "a = b"
else:
    print "a is greater than b"
```

The variables a and b have been declared and assigned a value. The first if statement does a less than comparison. Variable a is less than b and the comparison results in a value of 1. The value of 1 executes the subblock that belongs to the if statement. The elif and else in this are ignored because the first if statement returned a nonzero value. Had the first if returned a zero value, then the elif would have been tested. If the elif returned a zero value, then the subblock part of the else statement would be executed. The else statement is a catchall if nothing matches.

In Python, the following comparison operators can be used:

<: Is the lefthand value less than the righthand value?

<=: Is the lefthand value less than or equal to the righthand value?

>: Is the lefthand value greater than the righthand value?

>=: Is the lefthand value greater than or equal to the righthand value?

==: Is the lefthand value equal to the righthand value?

!=, <>: Same way of expressing the comparison that the lefthand value and righthand values are not equal to each other.

is: Compares whether two objects are the same. The comparison will return a value of true if the object identities are the same or if the object values are the same. The is object value comparison will only work successfully on simple objects such as numbers or strings.

is not: The inverse of the is comparison.

in: Compares a simple value and checks whether the simple value is in the list or a tuple.

not in: Compares a simple value and checks whether the simple value is not in the list or tuple.

and: Performs a logical AND comparison.

not: Performs a logical NOT comparison.

or: Performs a logical OR comparison.

All the comparison operators are fairly obvious except in and is. The following example illustrates how the is comparison operator can be used:

```
astr = "hello"
```

```
bstr = "hello"
if astr is bstr :
    print "the strings are the same"

alist = ["hello", "bye"]
blist = ["hello", "bye"]
clist = alist
if alist is blist :
    print "the lists are the same is not output"
if alist is clist :
    print "the list identifiers are the same is output"
```

The following example illustrates how the in comparison operator can be used:

```
buffer = ("hello world", "hello")
if "hello" in buffer :
    print "hello is found"
```

Looping

Looping is the process of repeatedly executing the same piece of code multiple times. The purpose of a loop can be to iterate a list or generate a data series. The simplest loop is the while statement:

```
a = 0
while a < 10 :
    a = a + 1
    print "Iteration: (" + str( a) + ")"
    if a == 3 :
        print "clean exit version 1"
        break
else:
    print "clean exit version 2"
```

The while loop keeps going while the value of a is less than 5. The while statement uses the same comparison operators as the if statement. Within the while subblock, any other Python statement can be added.

Notice that the while statement has an associated else statement. The best way to explain the else statement is to consider a potential scenario. Imagine writing an application that polls five serial ports. The loop is intended to poll the serial ports and see which port is available. If there are no available serial ports, then an alternate action must be taken. If there is an available port, then some action is taken and the loop is exited. If the else statement did not exist, the same logic would be much harder to express as is shown in the following example:

```
foundavailable = false
while a < 5 :
    if portavailable( a) :
            clearflag( a)
            foundavailable = true
            break
    a = a + 5
if not foundavailable :
    noportavailable()
```

The flag foundavailable must be added to indicate whether an available serial port has been found. If a serial port has been found, then the if statement in the while subblock must set it. Outside of the while loop, an additional if statement has to be added to check whether a serial port has been found or not. Overall this loop has become less readable and more complicated. The foundavailable flag has to be set and reset, which are extra programming steps that could potentially make the code more difficult to maintain and extend. Using the else statement, the double-check if is not required and a loop can be written as follows:

```
while a < 5 :
    if portavailable( a) :
            clearflag( a)
            break
    a = a + 5
else :
    noportavailable()
```

The rewritten loop using the else statement is simpler and has fewer lines. The logic is that if the loop can iterate through all the numbers, then there must not be a port available. When Python has iterated all the elements, it will call the statements contained within the else subblock. If the break statement is used within the loop, then the else subblock is not called.

Another way to iterate data is to use the for loop. The for loop is generally used for iterating over a list, as shown in the following example:

```
alist = ["item", 2, 'another']
for item in alist :
    print item
else :
    print "finished list"
```

The variable alist refers to a list of three items. The for keyword expects two variables separated by the keyword in. The variable alist that is part of the for

statement is the list that will be iterated. For every iteration of the loop, the variable
`item` contains a reference to an element from the list. In the example, the subblock
that is part of the `for` statement will print out each element. The downside to using
the `for` loop is that during the iteration, the subblock does not know the index in
the list that the variable `item` is referring to. There is no index definition.

The `else` keyword can be applied as outlined for the `while` keyword. To iterate
the indices instead, the following example is shown as a solution:

```
for item in range( len( alist)) :
    print alist[ item]
```

The clever part in this solution is that a list of indices is iterated. When the
`range` function is executed on the length of the `alist` list, the result is shown as follows:

```
[0,1,2]
```

Combining the range function with the `for` loop will iterate a list of counters
that can then be used to specify a list element. This same approach could be used in
a `while` loop, except the `while` loop would involve the use of a variable that contains
a counter.

Programming with Strings

Strings such as lists and tuples are extremely important in Python. A string in
Python is similar to a tuple in that strings are immutable after they are created, they
cannot be altered. To alter a string, therefore, a new string has to be created.

A Python string can be read using an array notation as shown in the following
example:

```
buffer="hello"
print "second character is " + buffer[ 1]
```

A string is sliced like a list is sliced, and the same listings that worked on a list will
work on a string. Although a string is not a list, it has all the functionality of a list.

In Python, it's important to remember when creating buffers that some characters might need to be escaped. Character escaping is similar to using double slashes
as you saw in Chapter 2, "Writing Scripts Using a Shell and Its Associated Tools."
For example, the following illustrates an attempt to insert a quote in a buffer:

```
buffer = "A quote " will be added to the buffer"
```

The example is not correct because the second double quote terminates the buffer started by the first double quote. The characters after the second double quote are free hanging characters that will cause interpretation problems. The second double quote needs to be escaped, which is a term used to denote that a special character should not be considered a special character, but a normal character. For example, escaping the second double quote means to translate the second double quote as a double quote. Escaping the second double quote fixes that problem and is the reason why escape sequences are needed. Python uses the following escape sequences:

\': Escape the single quote.

\": Escape the double quote.

\\: Escape the slash, because the slash is an escape sequence starting character.

\a: Escape the bell character.

\b: Escape a backspace character.

\f: Escape the form feed character.

\r: Escape the carriage return character, which sometimes is needed when writing files or outputting data.

\n: Escape the newline return character, which does the same as the carriage return escape, but is not the same.

\t: Escape the tab sequence.

\v: Escape the vertical tab character.

Another way of escaping and adding special characters is to use hexadecimal values such as \x6D. Escaping is generally only used for specific cases such as new line feeds or slashes when defining Windows paths.

When manipulating strings, the string module is very useful. Within the string module are a number of routines that can manipulate a string. For example, the function string.uppercase converts all the characters of the string to uppercase. If you want to swap the case of the strings, you can use the function string.swapcase. You can trim whitespace using the function string.rtrim. Regardless, it's useful to peek into the string.py file, located in the lib directory of a Python distribution.

Python can tokenize or assemble strings using the string.split and string.join functions. Pulling strings together and taking them apart is especially important when manipulating filenames, directories, or UNC definitions. The function string.split will tokenize a buffer based on a defined deliminator. For example, the following source code tokenizes the string using the space character:

```
>>> abuffer="hello world how are you doing"
>>> string.split( abuffer, " ")
['hello', 'world', 'how', 'are', 'you', 'doing']
>>>
```

The function `split` has two parameters. The first parameter is the buffer itself. The second parameter is the deliminator that the `split` function uses to tokenize the buffer. The result is a list of the tokenized words. The function `string.join` can be used to assemble the list back into a buffer:

```
>>> abuffer="hello world how are you doing"
>>> string.join( string.split( abuffer, " "))
'hello world how are you doing'
>>>
```

The output is the same as the variable `abuffer`. Essentially the example broke apart a buffer, and then reassembled it. Considering the result of the example, you might erroneously conclude that `split` and `join` are used together to do opposite actions. This is not correct because the `split` function can split on different deliminators, but the `join` function can only insert spaces between the individual list items.

The `string` module contains functions that can convert strings to numbers as defined by the following list:

string.atof: Converts a string to a floating-point number.

string.atol: Converts a string to a long integer.

string.atoi: Converts a string to an integer.

Function Declarations

You've already seen a few examples of using a function declaration. In each of the examples, the function declaration had no parameters. You can define functions with parameters as shown in the following example:

```
def singleParameter( item) :
    print "You wrote (" + item + ")"
```

The function `singleParameter` has one parameter that is output using the function `print`. If a Python script wanted to call the function `singleParameter`, the calling script would have to pass a parameter. An example calling the function `singleParameter` is shown here:

```
singleParameter( "hello world")
```

Parameters can have default values allowing the caller of the function to optionally pass in a parameter. Optional parameters are useful for creating default conditions when an application environment is being created. In the following example, the function singleParameter is rewritten to have a single default parameter:

```
def singleParameter( item = "default value") :
    print "You wrote (" + item + ")"
```

The function singleParameter can be called without specifying a parameter:

```
singleParameter()
```

Because the method call singleParameter passes no parameter, the function assigns the default value to the parameter item.

Multiple parameters can be defined for a function, where a comma separates the parameters. When a function declaration contains both default and regular parameters, the default parameters must follow the last regular parameters. The following example shows how to create functions with multiple parameters where some parameters have default values:

```
def somefunc(param1,param2,param3="default value",param4=3) :
    print "some function"
```

The somefunc function declaration illustrates that first the parameter without defaults (param3) is declared after the last regular parameter param2.

To return a value, the function uses the return keyword and returns some object or value as shown in the following example:

```
def somefunc( input) :
    return input
```

The function somefunc has one parameter. The parameter is not processed, but returned to the caller. The caller of the function could store the return value by assigning it to a variable, or use it as a value for another function call. The following example shows how to store the return value to a variable:

```
var = somefunc( "hello world")
```

Functions can be assigned to variables like other variables, except the data referenced by the variable is a function and not a value. Function variables are powerful because they allow the administrator to write generic code that has a specific implementation when the script is executing. Following is an example of assigning a function variable and then calling the function:

```
otherfunc = singleParameter
otherfunc( "hello world")
```

The variable otherfunc is declared and assigned the function reference singleParameter. The variable otherfunc can be called as if the variable were a function reference.

Programming with Dictionaries

Lists and tuples are useful when you know what element to reference in a list. To find an element in a list or tuple, it must be iterated, which can be very inefficient for large lists. *Dictionaries* are Python data types that store data using key value pairs. The major difference is that instead of using an index to reference a list value, a key is used to reference a dictionary value. The following example shows how to use a dictionary to define hot and cold temperature values (in degrees Celsius):

```
aDictionary = { "hot":35, "cold":15}
```

The key value pairs are separated by a colon. The item to the left of the colon is the key, and to the right is the value. A comma separates each key value pair. To retrieve a value from the dictionary, a key is specified. The following example shows how to display the value associated with the key cold:

```
aDictionary["cold"]
```

In the example, one thing you cannot do is reference the dictionary value with an index value of two, as would be the case for a list. To manipulate a dictionary, the dictionary methods must be used. The following example shows how to generate a list of all keys contained within a dictionary:

```
>>> aDictionary.keys()
['hot', 'cold']
>>>
```

The next example shows how to generate a list of all values contained within a dictionary:

```
>>> aDictionary.values()
[35, 15]
>>>
```

Following is an example that shows how to generate a list with all elements in the dictionary:

```
>>> aDictionary.items()
[('hot', 35), ('cold', 15)]
>>>
```

Notice that the data is a generated list with embedded tuples. This form of dictionary is an export operation only. You cannot import a dictionary using the same format. Python generates an error if this is attempted. Python uses this format because it's easier to iterate the individual values of the dictionary.

Sorting Lists

Lists are useful, but unsorted lists are less useful because searching the list can be more resource intensive. Sorting with Python is a useful functionality because after processing a list, in many scenarios, sorting the data improves readability. Following is an example list:

```
aList = [1, 5, 7, 2, 6, 0]
```

To sort the list, the sort function is used:

```
>>> aList.sort()
>>> aList
[0, 1, 2, 5, 6, 7]
>>>
```

When the sort function is called, the data is sorted in place. To sort the list but keep the order of the original list intact, the list must be copied to another list. The sorting routines are fairly generic and almost any type of object, string, and so on can be sorted. For those lists that contain complex objects, a custom sorting definition can be defined. Consider the following list definition:

```
aList = [[4, "value"], [2, "other"], [1, "data"]]
```

To sort the list according to the first element of each embedded list, a comparison function has to be written. The way custom sorting works is that the Python runtime manages the list, but the application needs to provide a comparison function that indicates which element has a higher precedence than another. Following is an example comparison function to sort the example list definition:

```
def embeddedListSort( item1, item2) :
    if item1[ 0] < item2[ 0] :
        return -1
    elif item1[ 0] > item2[ 0] :
        return 1
    else :
        return 0
```

The function `embeddedListSort` has two parameters: `item1` and `item2`. The purpose of the function is to compare the two parameters and return a value that indicates the sorting order of the two parameters. The comparison used is privy to the function itself, and the Python runtime doing the sort doesn't care how the result is found. This means a comparison function could retrieve additional information from a database to help decide the sorting order. For the function `embeddedListSort`, it is assumed that the variables `item1` and `item2` are structured like the elements of the variable `alist`. The sorting is based on the comparison of the first element of the parameters.

After a comparison has been performed, the function has the option of returning one of three values:

-1: The parameter `item1` is less than the parameter `item2`.

1: The parameter `item1` is greater than the parameter `item2`.

0: The parameter `item1` is equal to the parameter `item2`.

The sorting function can be passed as a parameter to the function `sort`, as shown in the following example:

```
aList.sort( embeddedListSort)
```

Technique: Interacting with the Environment

When using Python in an administrative context, the most important task is to interact with the operating system. Because this book is focusing on the Windows operating system, there are four environment interactions: files, registry, processes, and COM objects.

Manipulating Files

Open Source projects use logging files, configuration files, and other sorts of files. Open Source projects like to use files to drive every aspect of the application. This is not a bad thing, but it does require an administrator to know how to read and write files from Python.

Reading and writing a file in Python is simple and only requires a few function calls. Following is an example of how to open a file, read a line, and then close the file again:

```
fileobject = open( "C:\\bin\\SimpleHello.py", "r")
print fileobject.readline()
fileobject.close()
```

The function `open` has two parameters. The first parameter is the file to be opened, and the second parameter is the mode to use to open the file. The file `SimpleHello.py` is opened in read-only mode as defined by the letter `r`. The file is assumed to be text encoded. A file handle is returned and assigned to the variable `fileobject`. The file handle represents a reference to a file that can be used for further file operations. The method `readline` is used to read a single line of text that is terminated by a carriage return or newline feed. After performing all the necessary operations, the file is closed using the function `close`.

Assuming that the file could be opened, a typical operation would be to parse the file, line by line. Python has a module called `xreadlines` to do that automatically:

```
import xreadlines
fileobject = open( "C:\\bin\\SimpleHello.py", "r")
for line in xreadlines.xreadlines(fileobject):
        print line
fileobject.close()
```

The module `xreadlines` is imported. The function `xreadlines` is used in the `for` loop. The function `xreadlines` requires one parameter, which is the file handle reference `fileobject`. Then for each loop, the `xreadlines` module reads one line of the file. Reading a file using the function `readline` would have worked as well, but would not be as simple.

TIP

The xreadlines *module isn't necessary anymore because the functionality has been added directly into the Python runtime. In fact, using a runtime that doesn't need the functionality will generate a deprecated warning message.*

Files can be written by opening the file in write mode. Special write methods are then used to write content to the file. Following is an example that opens a file and writes some text:

```
fileobject = open( "c:\\test.txt", "w")
fileobject.write( "hello world")
fileobject.close()
```

The second parameter for the function open is the letter w, which says to open the file for write access. If the file exists, the contents will be overwritten. The method write is used to write data to the file and has one parameter, which is the string to write. Like the reading of the file example, after all writing is complete, the file must be closed using the close function. Closing the file is especially important when writing content because a file close will flush all the data.

Another way to write a file is to use the function writelines, which writes a list of strings. Following is an example of using writelines:

```
fileobject = open( "c:\\test.txt", "w")
aList = ["hello", "world"]
fileobject.writelines( aList)
fileobject.close()
```

The list aList references two strings that are written using the function writelines. Regardless of whether the function write or writelines is used in either case, the written data in the file will appear similar to the following:

```
helloworld
```

The generated content does not contain any spaces, nor does it contain any new lines. By default, the file write routines in Python do not add the line feed, carriage return characters, or spaces between items written. The application has to add those characters.

If instead of overwriting the file, you want to append to a file, then the second parameter (w) of the open function is replaced with the letter a. The letter a opens the file in append mode, meaning any writes are automatically added to the end of the file.

When reading and writing files in text mode, the carriage return and line feed characters are converted to a standard format. For example, in Windows the end of a line is usually a combination of the carriage return and line feed characters. When text mode is used to read a file, the end-of-line character will be a line feed only. If there are carriage return and line feed problems, then opening the file in binary mode might be the solution. In binary mode, the carriage return or line feed characters are not altered.

Python is not as well geared to reading and writing binary files as the C programming language because Python is a higher-level language than C. For example, the storage of Python objects and structures is accomplished using pickling. *Pickling* is an automatic functionality, and the Python script writer does not deal with the low-level bits and bytes. More details about binary files are beyond the scope of this book.

Handling Errors and Exceptions

Thus far, all the examples assume that the applications work, files exist, and so on. Often that is not the case, and the application will encounter an error. For example, if the function opens a file that does not exist, an error will be generated. Generating an error is good, but the default handling of the error is bad. The problem is that the default error-handling mechanism causes the Python runtime to abort execution of the application. The following example shows the text of the error that is generated when the file does not exist:

```
Traceback (most recent call last):
  File "C:\Python24\Lib\site-
packages\Pythonwin\pywin\framework\scriptutils.py",
line 301, in RunScript
    exec codeObject in _ _main_ _._ _dict_ _
  File "C:\docs\cgross\book\OSSforWinAdmins\bin\testXReadLines.py",
line 13, in ?
    testFile()
  File "C:\docs\cgross\book\OSSforWinAdmins\bin\testXReadLines.py",
line 5, in testFile
    fileobject = open(
"C:\\ssdocs\\cgross\\book\\OSSforWinAdmins\\bin\\SimpleHello.py",
"r")
IOError: [Errno 2] No such file or directory:
'C:\\ssdocs\\cgross\\book\\OSSforWinAdmins\\bin\\SimpleHello.py'
>>>
```

The text generated in the example is a bit puzzling and not user friendly. By using the Python exception-handling mechanism, you can gracefully handle errors. Exception handling is a Python mechanism used to catch errors as they occur. With exception handling, the Python program can gracefully exit or try something else. For example, if a script needs to read a configuration file but the configuration file can have four different names, the standard error-handling mechanism would cause the application to exit on trying to open the first file it could not find. By implementing exception handlers, the loop would catch the exception and allow the program to continue processing. Following is an example that is written using an exception handler:

```
try :
    fileobject = open( "C:\\bins\\SimpleHello.py", "r")
    for line in fileobject:
        print line
    fileobject.close()
except Exception, (errno, strerror) :
    print "Error: ", strerror
```

The keyword `try` defines a protected subblock. It is protected in the sense that if any error is generated, the error will be caught by the `except` keyword. After the `except` keyword is the exception type to catch and the variables where the exception details will be stored. In this example, the `Exception` type is caught, which is also the base exception type that catches all types of errors. The variables `errno` and `strerror` are part of a tuple that represents the runtime error. In the `except` subblock, the error is written to the standard output.

For administrative tasks, catching exceptions is not complicated. The exception-handling mechanism defined in previous examples is as complex as the code should be. You can refine the error-handling mechanisms, but that is beyond the scope of this book.

Some Common File and Directory Functions

Python has various modules that can be used to perform operations that manipulate a directory or file. Specifically within the `os` module, there are many useful functions that perform operating system tasks. Table 3.3 highlights the methods that would be the most useful for an administrator.

TABLE 3.3 Commonly Used Methods within the `os` Module

Function	Description
chdir(path)	Changes the current working directory to the directory specified. The current working directory is used when relative file and directory operations are carried out.
getcwd()	Retrieves the current working directory of the Python script currently executing.
listdir(path)	Returns a list of all items in the path, including files and directories. The list does not distinguish between a file and a directory.
mkdir(path)	Creates a directory as specified by the path. Directories have to be created incrementally. This means if the directory to be created is c:/something/another/more, then the directory another has to already exist.

$\rightarrow$

Function	Description
makedirs(path)	Creates a directory such as mkdir, but also creates any parent directory that does not exist.
remove(path)	Removes a file specified by the path. A directory cannot be removed.
removedirs(path)	Removes a directory and any subdirectories contained.
rename(source, destination)	Renames a source file or directory to the destination file or directory.
rmdir(path)	Removes a directory.
stat(path)	Retrieves the status of a file or directory. A tuple is returned that contains multiple integer values that correspond sequentially to the following: **st_mode**: Protection bits. **st_ino**: Inode number. **st_device**: Device. **st_nlink**: Number of hard links (Unix). **st_uid**: Owner of the file or directory. **st_guid**: Group owner of the file or directory. **st_size**: Size of the file. **st_atime**: Last time the file or directory was accessed. **st_mtime**: Last time the file or directory was modified. st_ctime: The time when the file or directory was created. More details about how to manipulate this tuple are given in the walking the directory example.
system(command)	Executes a command. More details are given in the process execution example.
sep	A useful variable that defines what the separator is when manipulating files and directories.

Within the `tempfile` module are many useful functions that can be used to manage temporary files and directories. Table 3.4 highlights the methods that are the most useful for an administrator.

Function	Description
`mktemp( prefix)`	Generates the name of a temporary file using an absolute path.
`tempdir`	A variable that can be set. When set, this path will be used by the function mktemp to generate temporary filenames.

TABLE 3.4 Commonly Used Methods within the `tempfile` Module

Within the `shutil` module are many useful functions that can be used to copy or perform other higher-level operations on a file. Table 3.5 highlights the methods that are the most useful for an administrator.

Function	Description
`copyfile( source, destination)`	Copies the contents of a file from the source location to a destination location.
`copytree( source, destination)`	Copies recursively the file or directory and descendent files to the destination.
`rmtree( path)`	Deletes an entire directory tree as specified by the path.

TABLE 3.5 Commonly Used Methods within the `shutil` Module

Walking a Directory Tree

When manipulating files, often you won't know the name of the file while writing the script. You will known the directory where the file is located. For example, when processing XMail server log files, a log file is generated for each day. Therefore, when processing the server logs all the files have to be processed. The task is to have the script dynamically iterate the directory for files and other subdirectories. Following is a sample script that iterates a directory and displays the name of the file by using a callback. Note that the code example is very similar to the directory walker code example provided in the Python.org tutorial.

```
def walkdirectories(dir, callback):
    for f in os.listdir(dir):
        pathname = '%s/%s' % (dir, f)
        mode = os.stat(pathname)[ST_MODE]
        if S_ISDIR(mode):
            walktree(pathname, callback)
        elif S_ISREG(mode):
            callback(pathname)
        else:
            # Unknown file type, print a message
            print 'Skipping %s' % pathname

def dosomethingwithfile(file):
    print 'visiting', file

walkdirectories ( "c:\\program files", dosomethingwithfile)
```

The function `dosomethingwithfile` is a callback function that is called whenever a file is found. The function `dosomethingwithfile` could add the found file to a list, copy the file, or do whatever is necessary in the script. The function `walkdirectories` has two parameters: the first is the directory and the second is the callback.

In the code example, it's important to note that the `stat` function is used to figure out if the pathname is a file or directory. The function `S_ISDIR` is part of the `stat` module, but is automatically included when the `os` module is imported. Using the function `S_ISDIR`, it is possible to see whether the path is a directory or a filename. For the scope of this book and the Windows operating system, the code example illustrates using the two most important functions (`S_ISDIR` and `S_ISREG`). The other available functions are more useful for Unix administrators.

Executing Another Process

When running a script, it is useful to execute other processes that perform other tasks such as using commands from the Cygwin toolkit. You can start another process by using the `os.system` method call. The following example shows how to start the Notepad application:

```
os.system( "notepad.exe")
```

When the `os.system` method executes, the `notepad.exe` application will start. The Python interpreter will at that moment freeze and wait for the Notepad application to finish. The following example shows how to start Notepad and open a specific document:

```
filename="hello.txt"
os.system( "notepad.exe %s" % (filename))
```

In the code example for the method call os.system, formatted buffers are used as dynamic command-line parameters. Within the buffer is the %s character sequence, which is the dynamic part of the buffer. This character sequence is an escape that is filled with the value of a variable defined after the buffer. The % character is used to separate the buffer to create with the variables to fill the buffer. After the % character, there needs to be a tuple that contains the same number of items as escapes in the buffer. Python will then take apart the tuple and insert it into the buffer string.

The advantage of using this approach is that it is possible to dynamically build commands without having to use the join function. Using the join function is not that difficult, but using character sequences is simpler.

Manipulating the Registry

Python can manipulate the registry as shown in Chapter 2. The registry routines are located in two modules: win32api and _winreg. The module we'll examine is _winreg because it's close to how registry keys and values were manipulated in Chapter 2. Table 3.6 lists the methods available in the module _winreg. It's important to realize that most methods return a key handle that represents a connection to a specific key.

Manipulating COM objects

.NET is a technology that has largely replaced existing technologies for writing native Windows applications. In the past and today, there are a large number of already existing applications called COM objects. *COM objects* implement functionality such as connecting to a database or editing a document. Python can consume COM objects and does so using the IDispatch interface. In COM terms, the IDispatch interface uses late binding and dynamic method calls. For example, to call a COM object that acts as a calculator, the PROGID needs to be given when instantiating the object. The following example adds two numbers together:

```
import win32com.client
calc = win32com.client.Dispatch("devspace.calculator")
result = calc.Add( 3, 4)
cal.mode = "scientific"
```

TABLE 3.6 Registry Methods Available in Module `_winreg`

Function	Description
`CloseKey( hKey)`	Closes the open registry key handle.
`ConnectRegistry( computer, key)`	Connects to a remote registry, where the `computer` is a name using UNC formatting (e.g., `\\Computer`), and the key that is to be opened.
`CreateKey( key, subkey)`	Creates or opens a registry key based on a root key and a subpath key. When a key is open for the first time, the key must be one of the root keys. For the `_winreg` module, the following are the root key definitions, with associations from Chapter 2 section "Integration Registry."
	`HKEY_CLASSES_ROOT` is HKCR.
	`HKEY_CURRENT_CONFIG` does not have a counterpart.
	`HKEY_CURRENT_USER` is HKCU.
	`HKEY_DYN_DATA` does not have a counterpart.
	`HKEY_LOCAL_MACHINE` is HKLM.
	`HKEY_PERFORMANCE_DATA` does not have a counterpart.
	`HKEY_USERS` is HKU.
	An example of opening the registry key software is shown as follows:
	`rootkey = winreg.CreateKey( _winreg.HKEY_CURRENT_USER, "Software")`
	The variable `rootkey` could then be used as the first parameter to open or create a child path.
`DeleteKey( key, subkey)`	Deletes a key defined by the two parameters. The parameters follow the same usage convention as in the function `CreateKey`.
`DeleteValue( key, value)`	Deletes the value associated with a specific key. The key value should be created with the function `CreateKey`.

$\longrightarrow$

Function	Description
EnumKey(key, index)	Allows the enumeration of the descendent keys pointed to by the parameter key. The parameter index is a numeric index that retrieves the name of the key at that index.
EnumValue(key, index)	Allows the enumeration of the child values pointed to by the parameter key. The parameter index is a numeric index that retrieves the contents of the value at that index. Returned is a tuple that contains three items: • Identifier of the value • Data managed by the value • Type of data managed by the value
FlushKey(key)	Writes all the data associated with the key to the registry. This function should only be called as a safeguard to make sure that the registry has the right data.
RegLoadKey(key, subkey, filename)	Loads a registry into the location pointed to by the key and subkey from the file filename. The file format is the hive registry.
OpenKey(key, subkey)	Opens a registry key based on the key and subkey.
QueryInfoKey(key)	Returns a tuple of information about the registry key reference by the key. The tuple contains the following information: • Number of subkeys the key has • Number of values the key has • Long integer of the time when key was last modified
QueryValue(key, subkey)	Retrieves the unnamed value for a path defined by the key and subkey.

$\longrightarrow$

Function	Description
QueryValueEx(key, value)	Retrieves a tuple that describes the value defined by the key and value. The tuple contains two pieces of information: • Value of registry value • Data type of registry value
SetValue(key, subkey, type, value)	Assigns the default value associated with the location pointed to by the key and subkey. The type must be registry data type, and the value is the data to be stored in the registry value. The registry types must be one of the following. (Note the types are identical to the types identified in Chapter 2 section "Integration Registry." REG_BINARY: Binary data in any form. REG_DWORD: A 32-bit number. REG_DWORD_LITTLE_ENDIAN: A 32-bit number in Little-Endian format. REG_DWORD_BIG_ENDIAN: A 32-bit number in Big-Endian format. REG_EXPAND_SZ: Null-terminated string containing references to environment variables ("%PATH%"). REG_LINK: A Unicode symbolic link. REG_MULTI_SZ: A sequence of null-terminated strings terminated by two null characters. (Python handles this termination automatically.) REG_NONE: No defined value type. REG_RESOURCE_LIST: A device-driver resource list. REG_SZ: A null-terminated string.
SetValueEx(key, valuename, reserved, type, value)	This function is identical in functionality as SetValue, except that the value is not the default value associated with a key, but by the parameter valuename.

The sample shows how to create a COM object and then call various methods on the COM object. It's all fairly simple and straightforward, which is why this is the shortest section in the book.

COM is a legacy technology because Microsoft has put all its energy into .NET, which is an evolution of the COM technologies. Therefore, putting large amounts of development time into creating Python-based COM servers is futile. Consuming COM is not futile because for a long time to come there will always be certain tools that can be controlled using COM interfaces.

Technique: Integrating with BASH Scripts

All the material shown thus far is assuming that Python is the scripting language in control. As was shown in Chapter 2, BASH can be used to accomplish some power-ful tasks. Python can be integrated into BASH by the way of the pipe. The following example shows a simple BASH script that pipes the output into a Python script:

```
#!/bin/bash
ls | ./piped.py
```

The output of ls is piped into the Python script. The Python script needs to in-teract with the BASH shell by reading the input and output streams. The Python script piped.py is implemented as follows:

```
#! c:/python24/python.exe
import sys
for line in sys.stdin:
    sys.stdout.write( line)
```

The module sys is imported and the variable stdin is referenced. The variable stdin is like a file handle descriptor, except that a stream of data is referenced. The for loop will then chop up the stream and feed it one line at a time. The data is then output to the standard output using the method sys.stdout.write. It is important to realize that the script uses the standard input (stdin) and output (stdout) streams. This makes the Python script act like a filter command and do things that a BASH script would expect. If an error is to be written to the stream, then variable sys.error should be used.

It is possible for the script to process command-line options using the sys.argv variable as shown in the following example:

```
#! c:/python24/python.exe
import sys
def main ():
```

```
        print sys.argv
main()
```

The previously defined Python script can be executed; the following command line shows an execution and the associated results:

```
cgross@zeus ~/book/OSSforWinAdmins/bin
$ ./SimpleHello.py first second third
hello world
['./SimpleHello.py', 'first', 'second', 'third']
```

The variable `sys.argv` references a list that contains the arguments passed to the script. The first item in the list is the name of the script. The other items are the command-line arguments. A program would manipulate this list and do what is expected.

If a script is run in the context of a pipe, then there may or may not be command-line arguments depending on how the script is called. There is no rule that says if the script is run in the context of a pipe, there cannot be command-line arguments and vice versa. The script needs to check the streams and command-line arguments and make sure which context the script is being executed in.

SUMMARY

Python is a great programming language for administrators. Python is as powerful as BASH, but has a programming ease that BASH does not. What Python does lack is the breadth of what BASH can do. BASH programmers are capable of truly amazing techniques; however, BASH scripts can very quickly become hard to maintain and decipher. Python, on the other hand, can be used for more complex tasks and is still easy to read and maintain. Additionally Python is capable of manipulating files, running processes, and interacting with the operating system.

However, having said all that, there is no one best solution. It is largely up to the administrator. For example, a BASH script was used when deploying the Python modules. This is because it was simpler and faster to write a BASH Script, even though Python could have been used. In the end, however, when the BASH script becomes too complicated, it's time to use Python. Maybe when the task is a few lines of code, BASH is the better choice. You should experiment and see which language fits you best in which context. Maybe after the experiment, you might say that all scripts have to be written in Python. There is nothing wrong with that rule and you will not regret such a decision.

In either case, you'll have to learn the available libraries and commands of BASH or Python. In terms of being able to learn the commands, Python is simpler because it is consistent. BASH has some commands that are fairly cryptic and hard to figure out. The best part is that when writing scripts, you have two good choices: BASH and Python.

4 Managing Security Using Encryption and Privacy Tools

ABOUT THIS CHAPTER

The focus of this chapter is to show some techniques to make your computer secure, and to explain software that will make your daily communication and data secure. When users log in to a computer, they are using a form of security called user authentication. *User authentication* enables only certain people to gain access to certain resources.

Security that relates to privacy is woefully underused even though the software exists. We expect user authentication to be good enough security, but it is not. Consider this, only a car key can start a car, so the car is considered secure. However, a crook can still pick up the car with a forklift and drive away with it. Sure the thief cannot easily get access to the car, but the car is still lost and a driver waving a key in the sunset is not going to bring the car back. The purpose of this chapter is to introduce privacy so that even if the car is stolen (that is, your system is compromised), the crook can do nothing with the car (no serious damage will be done).

User authentication security that relates to Windows has been well covered by Microsoft and elsewhere, so this chapter instead focuses on security that relates to communications. Typically, that type of security covers topics such as encryption and privacy.

This chapter will cover the following topics:

Securing a Windows Computer: The administrator can activate changes that will make Windows secure. The chapter covers some of the details that are available to the administrator to lock down a Windows computer and make it more hacker resistant.

GNU Privacy Guard (GPG) and Windows Privacy Tray: Encryption involves using an algorithm to make data unreadable to all those who do not possess a key. A third party cannot easily read encrypted communications or data, which is what you want. However, there are third parties that want to be able to snoop or individuals that want to recover their old encrypted data. Without the key, neither is possible, which makes many people angry. GPG can be used to encrypt and sign e-mails or documents that can only be decrypted by a specific person.

OpenPGP Public Key Server: To make GPG work effectively, public key encryption is used, which requires keys to be exchanged. Using the OpenPGP Public Key Server, you can define a central location where public keys are stored for retrieval.

STunnel, OpenVPN, and OpenSSL: Another form of encryption is the encryption of communications across the Web and e-mail. Communication encryption involves similar encryption techniques as document encryption, but uses a different protocol. OpenSSL is the basic toolkit used to perform encryption for both STunnel and OpenVPN. You can use OpenSSL to create or delete the keys. STunnel is a tool used to encrypt a single socket port such as Web or e-mail. OpenVPN is an encryption tool used to encrypt general network communications. With OpenVPN, you can communicate with a remote network as if it was local. During all the communications to the remote network, the data is encrypted.

SECURING A WINDOWS COMPUTER

Some people consider Windows computers to be one of the most insecure operating systems because there is a seemingly never-ending prevalence of viruses and worms. However, very often Windows has been dealt an unfair hand because Windows by virtue is secure if the proper precautions are taken. The job of the administrator is to figure out how to secure a Windows computer appropriately for the context.

Managing a Windows Computer Security Policy

The security of a Windows computer can be fine-tuned using the Local Security Policy, which is located in the Administrative Tools section of the Windows Control Panel as shown in Figure 4.1. Click on the Local Security Policy icon to open the Local Security Settings dialog box shown in Figure 4.2.

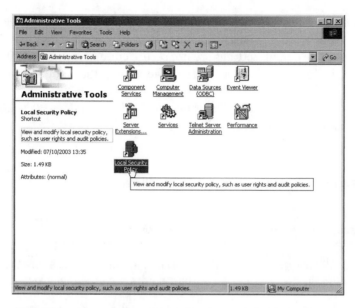

FIGURE 4.1 The Local Security Policy icon used to tune the security policies of the local computer.

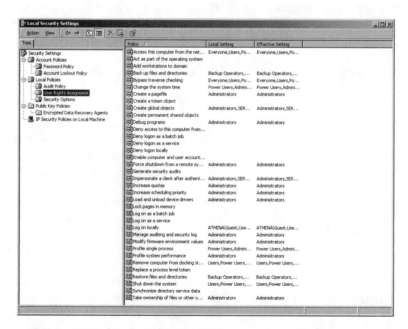

FIGURE 4.2 Local Security Settings dialog box used to set the security policies.

The Local Security Settings dialog box is a Microsoft Management Console (MMC) snap-in that makes it possible for you to tweak the security policies of the computer. The default settings are not secure enough if the computer has to interact with the Internet. Table 4.1 defines the settings that should be altered.

The security setting identifier is not identical on Windows 2000, 2003 Server, and Windows XP, but they are similar.

TABLE 4.1 Security Settings that Need to Be Altered

Security Setting Identifier	Description
Password Policy/Enforce Password History	Activate this policy to make sure that the same password is not used multiple times.
Password Policy/Maximum Password Age	This setting defines how long a particular password can be used before having to change it. A good password age is a year.
Password Policy/Minimum Password Length	This setting defines how long a password should be. A longer password is harder to crack. A good password minimum length is 12 characters.
Password Policy/Password Must Meet Complexity Requirements	This Boolean setting defines how complex a password should be and if it should be enabled.
Account Lockout Policy/Account Lockout Duration	This setting defines how long an account should remain locked out after a lockout has occurred. A good timeout is one to two hours.
Account Lockout Policy/Account Lockout Threshold	This defines how many times someone can enter the wrong password before the account is locked out. A good value is four times, because three times is a value often hit by many people.
Account Lockout Policy/Reset Account Lockout Counter After	This defines that when a locked out account is reset, the lockout counter should be reset as well. A good timeout value should be the same period as the account lockout duration.

$\longrightarrow$

Security Setting Identifier	Description
Audit Policy/Audit Account Logon Events	This defines whether to audit the logon of a remote user to the computer. This value should be enabled so that remote logon attempts can be monitored.
Audit Policy/Audit Account Management	This defines whether to audit if anyone or any program is attempting to change the characteristics of the account. This should be monitored to see if anyone is attempting to give more or less rights to a specific user.
Audit Policy/Audit Logon Events	This defines whether to audit the logon of a local user to the computer. This value should be enabled to see if anyone is attempting to access the computer that should not be.
Security Options/Additional Restrictions for Anonymous Connections	On Windows XP, this setting is two different settings, but similar. Essentially this option restricts what an anonymous user can see. Assign the Do Not Allow Enumeration of SAM Accounts and Shares value. This way an anonymous connection cannot see the available accounts or shares (worms also attempt access in this way).
Security Options/Digitally Sign Client Communication (Always)	This setting is used to digitally sign communications that a client makes. Enable this option to prevent man-in-the-middle attacks. This type of attack is explained a bit later in this chapter.
Security Options/Digitally Sign Server Communication (Always)	This setting is used to digitally sign communications that a server makes. Enable this option to prevent man-in-the-middle attacks.
Security Options/Rename Administrator Account	This setting renames the administrator account to another name. Enable this option and rename the administrator account.

→

Security Setting Identifier	Description
Security Options/Rename Guest Account	This setting renames the guest account to another name. Enable this option and rename the guest account.
Security Options/Shutdown Down System Immediately If Unable to Log Security Events	This option shuts down the computer immediately if the security log cannot be written to. Enable this option to ensure that no log events will be missed in case of a hacker attack.

Table 4.1 only highlights settings that should be changed immediately. Exposing the server to the Internet with these settings changed will ensure that any hacker will have a harder time accessing your computer.

Setting the expiration of a password to a year might seem extremely long. However, because people tire very quickly when having to constantly change the password, they often choose passwords that are similar, such as password1, password2, and so on. Even worse, a user might write down the password on paper or in a file on the computer. A better strategy is to create long, complex passwords, such as "Gretzky 99 was the great one" which when combined with an account lockout policy makes it extremely hard to guess. Even though the password is obvious, meaning that it will not need to be written down, it is not obvious to the hacker. The chances of a hacker guessing the password correctly in a few tries are extremely remote, and, of course, the administrator should be constantly monitoring the event logs to see if any hacker is attempting to gain access.

The settings described are only some of the possible settings that can be manipulated. To find out what a settings does, do a Google search for Rename Administrator Account. Within the search results are multiple pages, but the best one is the URL http://www.windowsnetworking.com/kbase/WindowsTips/WindowsXP/AdminTips/Security/RenameTheAdministratorAccount.html.

Managing Updates

Another security policy is to update the computer regularly with the latest security updates by using the Windows Update Service. The purpose of the Windows Update Service is to communicate to Microsoft and determine whether any patches are available. The Windows Update Service checks for Windows operating system, software, and hardware driver updates.

Activating the Windows Update Service

Windows XP and Windows Server 2003 have the Windows Update Service installed by default. Windows 2000 and other Windows operating systems need to install the latest service pack to have the Windows Update Service installed. For Windows XP, when you log in, a balloon appears on the Windows task bar asking about starting the Windows Update Service. Figure 4.3 shows the Automatic Updates icon in the Control Panel and the Automatic Updates dialog box.

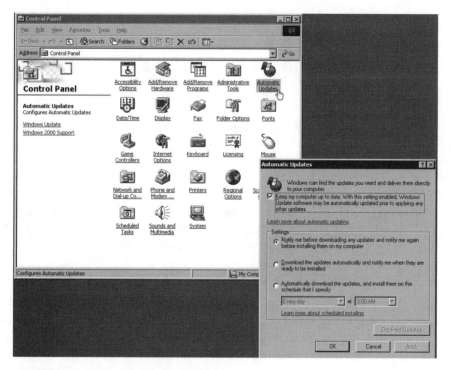

FIGURE 4.3 Windows Update Service.

In Figure 4.3, the Windows Update Service is configured using the Automatic Updates dialog box. To open this dialog box, double-click the Automatic Updates icon in the Control Panel. The Automatic Updates dialog box can be configured to perform automatic updates. The Keep My Computer Up to Date… checkbox performs automatic update checks. Within the Settings group box are three options:

Notify me before…: This option communicates with the Microsoft servers and asks which updates would be applicable and should be downloaded.

Download the updates…: This option automatically downloads any update, but notifies the administrator before installing them.

Automatically download…: This option automatically downloads any updates, and notifies the administrator for immediate installation; otherwise, the installation will occur at the specified time.

After the update service has been activated, from time to time users who are part of the administrator's group will see a message balloon icon in the icon tray when they log in (see Figure 4.4).

FIGURE 4.4 Updates balloon showing the availability of updates.

The balloon indicates that new updates are ready to download. The origin of the balloon is a little icon that looks like a globe with a Microsoft Windows flag. To activate the installation or download the updates, the user double-clicks the icon to open a dialog box that contains the updates the user can choose from. The user can then proceed to the next step to download or install the updates.

Manually Installing the Updates

The administrator will most likely allow updates to be installed automatically and will allow the Windows Update Service to query the Microsoft server network. The network communications overhead for one or two client machines is not a problem. The network communications bandwidth overhead becomes a problem, however, when the administrator is managing more than two or three computers. The problem is that the same patch file will be downloaded from the same resource multiple times. There are two solutions to this problem: use a proxy or perform a manual install using the Windows Update Catalog and script.

The Windows Update Service uses HTTP to communicate to the Microsoft servers. By using a proxy, you can manage the content so that only one computer has to download the patch that will be used by all the other computers.

Using a proxy solves the problem of having the same file downloaded multiple times. To have the updates install automatically, select the Automatically Download… option as shown earlier in Figure 4.3. Choose a time to install the updates that is not a busy time for the computer because the computer might be rebooted

TIP

automatically. When using the Automatically Download... option, it is imperative that everything happens automatically and that there are scripts to restart all processes and services.

Another solution to the network download problem is to use the Windows Update Catalog. The *Windows Update Catalog* contains all updates and patches available for download. The advantage of using the Windows Update Catalog is that the administrator has full control over what is and is not installed. The administrator is free to test a patch before applying it across an entire network of computers. When developing a process for applying patches for the Windows operating system, you can also apply application patches for applications that are not from Microsoft.

When using the manual approach, the Windows Update Service has to be disabled using the Automatic Updates dialog box as shown earlier in Figure 4.3. After the Windows Update Service has been disabled, the administrator needs to access the Windows Update Service Web site using a browser. The simplest way to access the catalog of updates is to start Windows Update from the Start menu. A browser will be created, but there will be no Windows Update Catalog reference. To access the Windows Update Catalog, the Windows Update listbox has to be updated by clicking on the *Personalize Windows Update* link (see Figure 4.5.

On Windows XP computer systems, the Start menu contains a Windows Catalog icon that is not the same thing as the Windows Update Catalog. The Windows Catalog icon refers to Windows products that can be purchased.

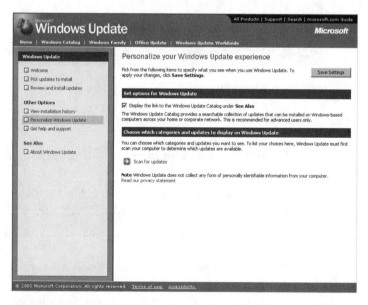

FIGURE 4.5 Browser window that displays the Windows Update Service Web site.

In the main window, the Display the Link to the Windows Update Catalog... checkbox is used to display the Windows Update Catalog option. After you check this checkbox, click the Save Settings button. The *Windows Update Catalog* link now appears below the listbox item See Also on the left side of the window. Clicking the *Windows Update Catalog* link changes the appearance of the Windows Update window as shown in Figure 4.6.

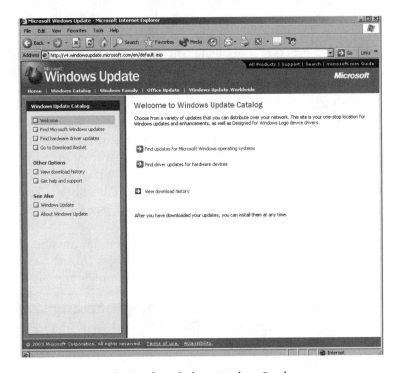

FIGURE 4.6 Introducing the Windows Update Catalog.

The main window shows three choices denoted by small icons:

Find Updates for Microsoft Windows Operating Systems: Find updates for a specific operating system.

Find Driver Updates for Hardware Devices: Find updates of specific third-party drivers that are hosted on the Microsoft Web site.

View Download History: View which updates have been previously downloaded.

Select the link *Find Updates for Microsoft Windows Operating Systems* and the main window changes (see Figure 4.7).

In Figure 4.7, the Operating System listbox contains a list of operating systems. Some operating systems are repeated multiple times because they refer to the operating

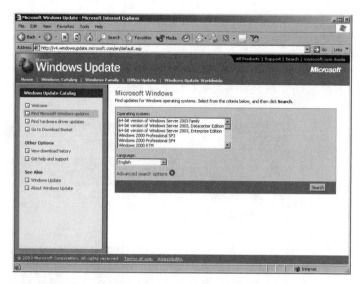

FIGURE 4.7 Windows Update allows you to choose the operating system used to find available patches.

system with a service pack applied. To find all updates related to a particular type of operating system, select the operating system and the language from the Language listbox and then click on the Search button. For example, if you chose Windows XP SP1 English language edition, the main window looks like Figure 4.8.

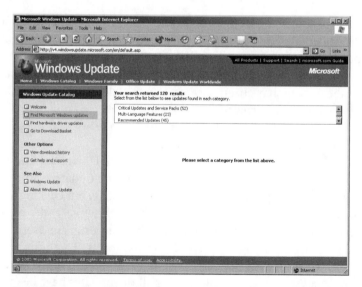

FIGURE 4.8 List of found updates that can be applied for a particular operating system.

In Figure 4.8 the search results are displayed in a listbox and the updates are grouped according to the nature of the update. Updates that are part of the Critical Updates and Service Packs grouping should be installed. The other update types are optional and do not need to be installed. The items in the listbox are links; click on the *Critical Updates and Service Packs* link to open the main window shown in Figure 4.9.

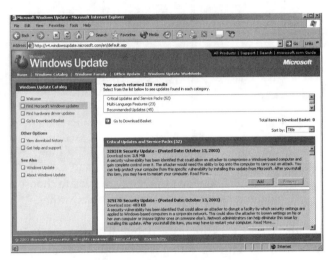

FIGURE 4.9 Listed details of the Critical Updates and Services Packs patches.

The lower part of the window has been replaced by a list of updates that can be downloaded. The individual updates can be added to a shopping cart and then downloaded as a group when the administrator checks out. Note that even though a shopping cart mechanism is used, there is no cost to download the updates. After all the updates have been selected, you can click on the *Go to Download Basket* link beside the green arrow to download all the selected updates. When you have added at least one update and clicked on the *Go to Download Basket* link, the main windows changes as shown in Figure 4.10.

In Figure 4.10, the Type or Browse to the Download Location of Your Choice text box allows you to input a path where the updates should be downloaded. In Figure 4.10, the path has been defined manually, but clicking the Browse button allows the administrator to select a path. In either case, the path specified must already exist. Clicking on the Download button results in a series of dialog boxes that asks if you are willing to accept the license terms. To physically download the files, you must accept the license terms. After the license terms have been accepted, the download starts and completes after all the updates have been downloaded.

After downloading has completed, a WU directory is created as a subdirectory in the path defined in the text box of Figure 4.10. The WU directory is a sort of top-level

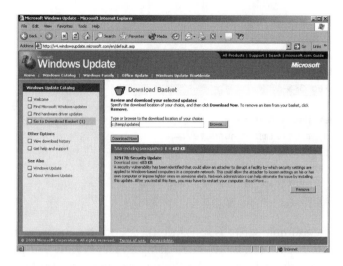

FIGURE 4.10 Downloading updates.

directory for all updates. The administrator should go through the individual directories and inspect the individual updates. The directory structure is simple and associated with each update is an HTML page shortcut that explains the purpose of the update. Each update is distributed as an executable that can be executed directly. To install the update for a particular computer, the administrator would double-click on the update on the particular computer.

For a network of computers, a script is used to apply the updates. The strategy of the script is to create a share to the computer that contains the updates downloaded by the administrator. After connecting to the share, the script would search for any updates that need to be executed. An example update script is shown here:

```
#!/bin/bash
rm -r -f /tmp/runupdate.tmp
computerid=$(net config workstation | grep '^Computer name'
| awk '{print $3}')
net use x: \\\\pluto\\shared
mkdir /tmp/runupdate.tmp

c:/bin/scripts/getfilenames.py "x:/updates/$computerid"
| grep '.exe' > /tmp/runupdate.tmp/found
didUpdate ="false"
exec 3<&0
exec < /tmp/runupdate.tmp/found
while read line
do
    filename=$(basename "$line")
    mv "$line" "/tmp/runupdate.tmp/"
```

```
        `"/tmp/runupdate.tmp/$filename" -q -f -n`
        didUpdate="true"
done
exec <&3
exec 3<&-

net use x: /delete
rm -r -f /tmp/runupdate.tmp
if [ $didUpdate = "true" ]
then
    shutdown —force —reboot now
fi
```

The example script is split into three code blocks: preparation, execution, and cleanup. Each block is separated using an empty line. The preparation code block starts with the deletion of the temporary directory /tmp/runupdate.tmp using the command rm. The temporary directory /tmp/runupdate.tmp will be recreated, but is initially deleted to make sure all temporary files used previously are removed. The variable computerid is the name of the computer where the script is running. To get the name of the computer, the command net config workstation is used and generates a verbose output that is trimmed by the commands grep and awk. The command net use is used to connect the computer to the share storing the updates. In the example, there is no username or password specified, which is a problem the administrator can solve for his own specific context. The last preparation command is mkdir, which creates the temporary directory.

The first execution step is to execute the Python script gefilenames.py that iterates a given directory and returns a list of all the files contained in the directory. The found files list is piped to the grep command and filters all the executables. The found executable files are piped to the file /tmp/runupdate.tmp/found. The file /tmp/runupdate.tmp/found is iterated and each file is moved manually from the shared location to a local temporary location. The command basename extracts the name of the file, which is then executed with the flags -q -z -n. Those flags will be explained a bit later in this section. The loop is continued until all updates have been applied.

In the cleanup block, the network share and the local temporary directory are deleted. The last step is to reboot the computer in case there were updates that require a reboot. The shutdown command only reboots the computer if any updates have been applied. The computer reboot is sometimes optional, but having the script always reboot ensures that the computer is in a stable state.

In the execution code block, the flags -q -f -n control how the update program executes. All the updates have flags that will control how the update is applied on the computer. The available flags are output using the -h command-line option. An individual update program accepts the following command-line options:

-u: Runs the program in unattended mode and expects an answer file to answer any questions that arise. In the case of updates, this is not necessary because there are generally no questions to answer. If this option is used, then a file called unattend.txt must be saved in the same location as the update executable.

-f: Forces the computer to shut down all processes when a reboot is required.

-n: Does not back up the removed files making it impossible to uninstall the update. In an automated situation, this option should be used because it reduces space. The administrator would have tested the update on another machine before installation to understand the potential ramifications.

-o: Does not allow OEM files to be overwritten without prompting. This option is used in the context of installing updated drivers. The administrator creates an answer file.

-z: Does not restart the computer after the installation even if it is required. This option is useful when attempting to install multiple updates. However, it may then become necessary to reboot the machine after the script. The reboot would have to be done manually using the shutdown command.

-q: Makes no user interaction required in a scripting context.

-1: Lists all the installed hotfixes.

The discussed example script can be executed when the computer starts up by assigning it to the startup event. The Group Policy Editor can be used to assign the script to the startup event. The details of the Group Policy Editor are discussed in the "Automated Script Execution" section in Chapter 5.

With the release of Windows XP Service Pack 2, major changes have been introduced in the protection of a PC. Be sure to activate those changes to help protect against hackers and other malware. The previous explanation of how to apply updates hasn't changed even though the dialog boxes may look a little different.

PROJECT: GNU PRIVACY GUARD AND WINDOWS PRIVACY TRAY

The GNU Privacy Guard (GnuPG) application makes it possible for anyone to use encryption. *Encryption* is a technique in which a person takes some data and converts it into some other data that resembles noise. The noise can be sent to someone else who would convert the noise to the original data again. The two parties have a secret or public password that is used to convert the data to the noise and back again. The strength of encryption is that no one can decipher the noise because it looks like gibberish and possesses no structure.

Most of GnuPG is written in Germany due to German federal funding. The GnuPG project has become a de facto encryption standard in the community and is a full encryption implementation. There is another encryption suite called Pretty Good Privacy (PGP), but due to recent events involving corporate PGP origin, the Open Source nature of the product and the availability of sources is in jeopardy. GnuPG is a full implementation of the PGP suite, but does not use the patented encryption algorithms. This does not mean GnuPG is less valuable, however, as many patent-free algorithms work equally well.

The following encryption algorithms are supported: ElGamal (signature and encryption), DSA, RSA, AES, 3DES, Blowfish, Twofish, CAST5, MD5, SHA-1, RIPE-MD-160, and TIGER. Different spoken languages are also widely supported. Table 4.2 contains more details about the GnuPG tool.

The GnuPG tools are console-based applications. The command line is useful when used in context of a script. However, for everyday usage, the command line can be tedious. The Windows Privacy Tray (WinPT) application provides an easy-to-use interface for the GnuPG tools. The WinPT application executes as either a Windows tray application or within the context of a mail application. When operating in the context of a mailing application, you can sign e-mails or encrypt sent e-mails. Table 4.3 contains reference information about WinPT.

TABLE 4.2 Reference Information for GnuPG

Item	Description
Home page	*http://www.gnupg.org/*
Version	At the time of this writing, the version is 1.4.0.
Installation	The GnuPG tools are installed when Cygwin is installed with all tools. Otherwise, a manual installation is undertaken using a ZIP archive.
Dependencies	GnuPG tools have no dependencies, other then a network connection when distributing keys for public consumption.
Documentation	The documentation for the GnuPG application is located at *http://www.gnupg.org/(en)/documentation/index.html*. There is also an associated FAQ at *http://www.gnupg.org/(en)/documentation/faqs.html*. The documentation is acceptable for general reference purposes. Also useful is a beginners guide to PGP located at *http://www.glump.net /archive/000060.php*.

$\rightarrow$

Item	Description
Mailing Lists	The mailing lists are located at *http://www.gnupg.org/(en)/documentation/ma iling-lists.html.* For the administrator, the mailing lists gnupg-announce and gnupg-users is of most interest.
Impatient Installation Time Required	Download size: 1.5 MB Installation time: 5-10 minutes
DVD Location	Due to legal issues, the DVD does not contain any files.

TABLE 4.3 Reference Information for the WinPT

Item	Description
Home page	*http://winpt.sourceforge.net/en/*
Version	At the time of this writing, the version number is 1.0.
Installation	The WinPT application is installed using a Windows installation program that includes all programs, or each program can be individually downloaded.
Dependencies	No dependencies, even though GnuPG is a dependency. The WinPT installer with all programs includes a GnuPG version. However, when individual programs are downloaded, the GnuPG program must be downloaded separately. $\longrightarrow$

Item	*Description*
Documentation	The WinPT program has a user's handbook that can be downloaded at *http://winpt.sourceforge.net/en/download.php*. There is also an FAQ at *http://help.helpem.com/help/winpt/faq.html*.
Mailing Lists	The WinPT program has several mailing lists located at *http://help.helpem.com/display.html?ref=more_info_winpt&uid=winpt*. For the administrator, the most important are *winpt-users* and *winpt-announce*.
Impatient Installation Time Required	Download size: Maximum 3 MB if the installer with all applications is downloaded. Installation time: 5-10 minutes, including key chain configuration.
DVD Location	Due to legal issues, the DVD does not contain any files.

Additional Notes

Encryption is a touchy subject because governments have laws on how encryption can be used. This makes it extremely important to look at your own situation and how encryption will be used. A slightly dated link on the various encryption laws is located at *http://rechten.uvt.nl/koops/cryptolaw/index.htm*. Be sure to understand it because ignorance is not an excuse.

As a general rule of thumb, if you can get legal access to the software in your country, then you can use it throughout your country. Where the law becomes delicate is if you decide to export the encryption software from your country to another country. Another rule of thumb is that Canada and the United States are considered one block, and so is the European Union. That means encryption software can be exchanged within the block, but is restricted between blocks. Exchanging encrypted data between blocks is not a problem and does not tend to cause legal issues. Of course, this presupposes that you can get the software from the block to communicate across blocks.

Another issue with encryption is that many of the toolkits are not distributed as precompiled executables. You might be able to find these precompiled executables on some Web sites if you do some searching. This means you'll need access to a C++ compiler so you can compile your own programs and shared libraries.

Not everybody has access to a Windows C++ compiler or knows how to use a Windows C++ compiler. If you cannot access a compiler, send an e-mail to osswin-binaries@devspace.com *that includes your location and your binary request. (Note that encryption binaries will not be sent free e-mail address accounts, such as Yahoo, Hotmail, and so on.). If your location and e-mail address qualify, you should receive the binaries in a week or so.*

Do not attempt to run the Cygwin GnuPG and native GnuPG distribution side by side. The Cygwin shell scripts will not see the native GnuPG distribution. The best solution is to either remove or not install the Cygwin GnuPG installation when attempting to use the native GnuPG distribution.

Impatient Installation

There are two ways to impatiently install GnuPG: Cygwin or WinPT. When the Cygwin toolkit was installed in Chapter 2, the GnuPG tools would have been installed by default and therefore no further installation is necessary.

The main distribution of WinPT is an installation program that can be used to install both the WinPT and GnuPG program. In the default case, WinPT will use the GnuPG that is distributed with the WinPT distribution. To download and install WinPT, follow these steps:

1. Download WinPT - Windows Privacy Tools from the WinPT Web site.
2. Double-click the downloaded file and a dialog box appears asking which language should be used to install.
3. Choose the English language, unless of course you would prefer another language.
4. Follow through the individual dialog boxes leaving all the default choices. At the end of the installation, the WinPT application will be started.

When the WinPT application starts, a dialog appears that seems to indicate a bad installation (see Figure 4.11). The installation was successful, but the keyrings do not yet exist and GnuPG requires a set of keyrings.

The error in Figure 4.11 is not actually an error, but a condition indicating an initial install. Clicking on the Yes button will configure WinPT and GnuPG. The next dialog box is a choice that allows you to generate a keyring (see Figure 4.12).

FIGURE 4.11 WinPT dialog box that indicates the GPG keyrings are missing.

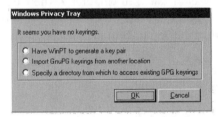

FIGURE 4.12 WinPT dialog box that gives you a choice on how to create the initial keyring.

Choose the Have WinPT to Generate a Key Pair option, and then click OK to have WinPT initialize everything correctly.

The next dialog box is used to define an initial public/private key. Figure 4.13 shows the Key Generation dialog box.

The text boxes in the Key Generation dialog box should all be filled in with meaningful data. The Key Type combo box default value is okay, but the value for the Sub-key Size in Bits text box might need tweaking. The key size can vary between 1,024 and 4,096 bits, and the initial reaction is to use the 4,096 bit size. The result would be a big

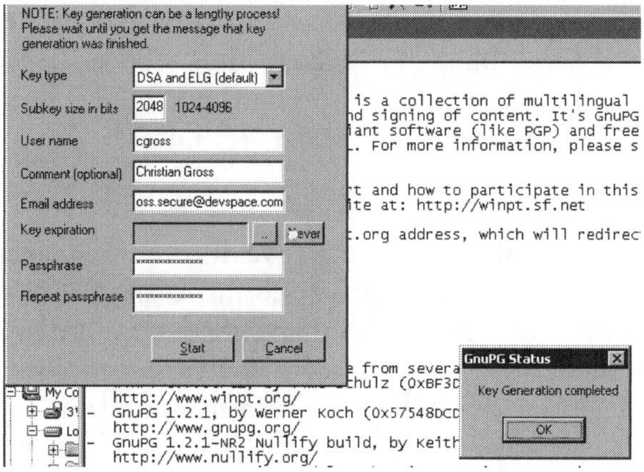

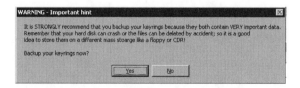

FIGURE 4.13 Dialog box used to generate a public/private key.

key that would make encryption communications hard to decrypt in contrast to a key size of 1,024. The downside is that it would take a longer time to encrypt and decrypt data. The value of 2,048 as chosen in Figure 4.13 is adequate for most communications.

After you've filled in all the text boxes, the key will be generated. The GnuPG Status dialog box appears indicating that the key has been successfully generated. The key generation could take several minutes. Click OK and the Warning dialog box shown in Figure 4.14 appears.

The dialog box asks to back up the generated public and private key. Click Yes to back up the generated keys. Accept the backup command and save the files in a safe location. After the files have been saved, the installation is complete and you are ready to encrypt and decrypt files.

FIGURE 4.14 Dialog box warning the user to back up the generated keys.

Deployment

Deploying GnuPG and/or WinPT within a script is more complicated and the steps must be followed very closely. The GnuPG application is relatively easy to install manually, but the WinPT applications are more complicated because the WinPT applications integrate with the Windows shell. When deploying WinPT, GnuPG must be deployed first.

The GnuPG application is a console application; the WinPT application is a GUI application. Although you can't write scripts using WinPT because of the GUI limitation, you can write scripts using GnuPG. All console applications, however, have a direct counterpart in the GUI of WinPT.

Installing GnuPG

Installing the GnuPG Windows native distribution makes sense if you don't have Cygwin installed if you want the performance of a natively compiled Windows application, or if you want the latest and greatest feature set.

The GnuPG Windows native distribution is downloaded from the GnuPG Web site. A binary for the Windows platform is available in a ZIP archive. The ZIP archive can be downloaded to a local directory. When expanding the ZIP archive, the expansion must be performed in a subdirectory where only the GnuPG application resides. Unlike most archives, the GnuPG archive does not create a subdirectory that contains the individual applications. For example, the subdirectory c:/bin/gnupg could be created where the ZIP archive is expanded.

After the archive has been expanded, the GnuPG application can be executed without any further installation steps, but some additional configuration is necessary to make GnuPG work properly. To make the GnuPG executables available from any location in a console, the PATH environment variable has to be updated to include the GnuPG path (e.g., c:/bin/gnupg).

Some registry keys and values are created that reference the location of GnuPG applications and GnuPG keys. The GnuPG directory contains the Windows registry file gnupg-w32.reg. The file can be executed directly, but must be altered before execution to reflect the location of the actual GnuPG installation. The following listing shows the contents of the gnupg-w32.reg file with correct paths assuming GnuPG is installed in the directory c:/bin/gnupg:

```
REGEDIT4

[HKEY_LOCAL_MACHINE\Software\GNU]
[HKEY_LOCAL_MACHINE\Software\GNU\GNUPG]
[HKEY_LOCAL_MACHINE\Software\GNU\GNUPG]
"HomeDir"="C:\\bin\\gnupg"
"gpgProgram"="C:\\bin\\gnupg\\gpg.exe"
```

The contents of the gnupg-w32.reg file are added to the registry by either double-clicking it from the Windows Explorer or by executing it from the Windows console as shown in following example. Note that due to problems with the Cygwin BASH console and how it treats Windows registry files, do not execute the following command from a Cygwin BASH console; instead, use a DOS console.

```
start gnupg-w32.reg
```

The settings that are registered in the file gnupg-w32.reg relate to a local computer installation of GnuPG and do not relate to an individual user. Each user of GnuPG needs to add some registry settings that tell the GnuPG applications where to read and write items, such as a GnuPG key. The following registry example shows how to define the registry keys and values for the user osswin:

```
Windows Registry Editor Version 5.00

[HKEY_CURRENT_USER\Software\GNU]
[HKEY_CURRENT_USER\Software\GNU\GnuPG]
"HomeDir"="C:\\Documents and Settings\\osswin\\Application Data\\GnuPG"
"gpgProgram"="C:\\bin\\gnupg\\gpg.exe"

[HKEY_CURRENT_USER\Software\GNU\OpenCDK]
"pubring"="C:\\Documents and
Settings\\osswin\\Application Data\\GnuPG\\pubring.gpg"
"secring"="C:\\Documents and
Settings\\osswin\\Application Data\\GnuPG\\secring.gpg"

[HKEY_CURRENT_USER\Control Panel\Mingw32]
[HKEY_CURRENT_USER\Control Panel\Mingw32\NLS]
[HKEY_CURRENT_USER\Control Panel\Mingw32\NLS]
"MODir"="C:\\bin\\gnupg\\Locale"
```

The key HomeDir represents a directory where the configuration file gpg.conf is found. A configuration is defined in the gpg.conf file. The configuration file can be empty, but it must exist for GnuPG to execute properly. The registry key's pubring, and secring refer to the user's public and secret keyrings. These keyring files can be precreated by the administrator and can hold as many keys as needed. When installing GnuPG, the administrator could save time for the user and precreate the keyring files automatically. If the installation is an upgrade, then the administrator should back up the keyring files regularly so that those files will be copied to the new installation.

When backing up the keyring files for reference purposes, back up the files referenced by the registry settings pubring *(public keys) and* secring *(secret keys). The more important file to back up is the one containing the secret keys. Losing the secret key files means forever losing access to any files encrypted with the secret keys.*

Installing WinPT

In the impatient installation of WinPT, all the applications were installed. The WinPT application as a whole is a combination of a number of smaller applications. Each smaller application does one thing as follows:

Eudora Plug-in: This application enables the Eudora mail client to make use of GnuPG.

Explorer Extensions: This application enables Windows Explorer to encrypt and decrypt files using a context-sensitive menu.

Outlook Express Plug-in: This application enables the Outlook Express mail client to make use of GnuPG.

Passphrase Agent: This application enables WinPT to cache passphrases when using GnuPG. Passphrases are used in encryption to enable the use of certain keys.

Tray: This application is the overall bigger application that resides in the Windows Tray and enables a user to encrypt and decrypt files from the clipboard and other sources. In general, this application is always installed if WinPT is installed.

The installation of the Eudora and Outlook Express plug-ins are beyond the scope of this book. If you are interested in installing these plug-ins, read the WinPT Handbook, Appendix B "Manual Installation."

The tray application is an important application to install because it provides a quick and comfortable way of interacting with the GnuPG application. Installing the tray application is required if any other WinPT application is used. The WinPT Tray application file is downloaded from the WinPT - Individual Applications Downloads section of the WinPT Web site. The downloaded file is a ZIP archive that contains two files: PTD.dll and WinPT.exe. These two files can be installed in a subdirectory, potentially even the GnuPG directory.

To install the tray application, double-click the WinPT.exe file. Some dialog boxes will appear that are similar to the sequence shown earlier in Figures 4.12, 4.13, and 4.14. To get WinPT.exe to start automatically when the computer starts, you can add a WinPT.exe shortcut to the Startup menu.

When running Windows Explorer, WinPT has an application called Explorer Extensions that makes it possible to perform GnuPG operations from within Windows Explorer. From the WinPT Web site, the file WinPT Explorer Extensions application is downloaded from the WinPT - Individual Applications Downloads section. The downloaded file is a ZIP archive that contains several files. The files need to be stored in the same location as the WinPT.exe files.

When configuring the WinPT Explorer Extensions, the user registry script used to install GnuPG will be needed by the WinPT Explorer Extensions. Specifically needed are the OPENCDK settings that describe where the keyrings are located. The files WinPTEE.dll and OpenCDK.DLL need to be copied to the Windows System directory (e.g., System32 or System).

To activate the WinPT Explorer Extensions, another registry file located in the expanded archive needs to be executed. If the operating system is Windows 95, 98, or Me, then the file install-win9x.reg is executed. If the operating system is Windows NT, 2000, XP, or 2003, then the file install-winNT2K.reg is executed. Regardless of which file is executed, the registry file should be inspected to make sure that the path defined by the key @ in the section InProcServer32 is correct. A reboot will activate the new extensions.

The WinPT Passphrase Agent application is optional and used to cache passwords used by the user in a session. From the WinPT Web site, the file WinPT Passphrase Agent application is downloaded from the WinPT - Individual Applications Downloads section. The downloaded file is a ZIP archive that contains several files. The files need to be stored in the same location as the WinPT.exe files. There are no WinPT Passphrase Agent registry settings or configuration items. The only additional extra step is to add the line use-agent in the gpg.conf file.

Technique: Trusting Content Using PKI

The classical use of encryption technology is to encrypt a file, send the file to someone, and have the receiver decrypt the file. Between the sender and receiver, the classical solution used to encrypt and decrypt the file would be a password that both the sender and receiver know. The trust that is created when an encrypted file is sent from one person to another is based on the fact that only the sender and receiver know the magic password.

Trust is not that simple because sometimes users might want to send files to multiple people. In this context, it would mean that each receiver needs a password. To send each person a password becomes a problem. Sending passwords for each user would be an administrative nightmare; worse yet, how is the password sent to each user? You cannot use a password because the other user needs the password. The only option is to physically go to the people and tell them your password. You could use the telephone, but if your data is important enough, somebody might be listening. The problem with traditional encryption is that the trust used relies on technologies that are inherently weak because people are involved. People will tell passwords when they should not, or they will use easy-to-guess passwords. Security needs to be human proof.

GnuPG implements an encryption technology called public key infrastructure (PKI). Using public keys, two people can exchange information without having to exchange a password. When WinPT was installed in the Impatient Installation, a public/private key was defined. The key that was created has a public key and a private key. Each and every user would create their own public key and private key.

The two keys are related, but it isn't possible to deduce the private key from the public key, nor deduce the public key from the private key. Therefore it is important that you lose neither the public, nor the private key.

The public key as its name implies is distributed publicly and the private key is kept private. When two people want to communicate with each other, they exchange public keys and encrypt the message to the other person using the public key from the other person. The encrypted message can then only be decrypted using the private key from the person. By encrypting with a private key, a person can send a message to another person and prove that the message is authentic by decrypting it using the public key. The other person would decrypt the message and have verified that the message is from the correct person.

For example, imagine Bob and Mary want to exchange messages. Bob would send Mary his public key, and Mary would send Bob her public key. Bob writes his message and encrypts it using Mary's public key, and then encrypts the content using his private key. The message is sent to Mary; she uses Bob's public key to verify that the message is from Bob and then uses her private key to decrypt the contents of the message.

The magic of PKI is the public and private keys. Encryption works on a logical level with no human interaction to mismanage the process. Of course, this does not preclude humans accidentally sending their private keys. The only downside to PKI is that encrypting and decrypting can take longer than using secret password encryption. PKI does not preclude secret password encryption, which is also known as passphrase or symmetric encryption. They very often complement each other and are used in specific contexts.

Technique: Creating and Deleting Keys

After GnuPG has been installed, you need to manage the public keys and private keys locally. For example, your associates might send a public key or you might want to create multiple private/public keys. That could mean exporting a public key, importing a public key, or generating new key pairs. To create a key, the command gpg in the following console session example is executed and the generated steps are followed (underlined text should be entered by the user):

```
$ gpg --gen-key
gpg (GnuPG) 1.4.0; Copyright (C) 2004 Free Software Foundation, Inc.
This program comes with ABSOLUTELY NO WARRANTY.
This is free software, and you are welcome to redistribute it
under certain conditions. See the file COPYING for details.

Please select what kind of key you want:
   (1) DSA and ElGamal (default)
```

```
   (2) DSA (sign only)
   (5) RSA (sign only)
Your selection? 1
DSA keypair will have 1024 bits.
About to generate a new ELG-E keypair.
              minimum keysize is  768 bits
              default keysize is 1024 bits
    highest suggested keysize is 2048 bits
What keysize do you want? (1024) 2048
Requested keysize is 2048 bits
Please specify how long the key should be valid.
        0 = key does not expire
      <n>  = key expires in n days
      <n>w = key expires in n weeks
      <n>m = key expires in n months
      <n>y = key expires in n years
Key is valid for? (0) 2y
Key expires at 11/02/05 14:01:13
Is this correct (y/n)? y


You need a User-ID to identify your key; the software constructs the
user id
from Real Name, Comment and Email Address in this form:
    "Heinrich Heine (Der Dichter) <heinrichh@duesseldorf.de>"


Real name: Christian Gross
Email address: chg@devspace.com
Comment: Christian Gross
You selected this USER-ID:
    "Christian Gross (Christian Gross) <chg@devspace.com>"


Change (N)ame, (C)omment, (E)mail or (O)kay/(Q)uit? O
You need a Passphrase to protect your secret key.

passphrase not correctly repeated; try again.
We need to generate a lot of random bytes. It is a good idea to perform
some other action (type on the keyboard, move the mouse, utilize the
disks) during the prime generation; this gives the random number
generator a better chance to gain enough entropy.
.+++++.+++++.++++++++++++++..++++++++++++++++++++++++++++++++++++++
++++++++++++++++.++++++++++..+
+++.++++++++++++++++++++++++.+++++.+++++>.++++++++++.>+++++.......
+++++
We need to generate a lot of random bytes. It is a good idea to perform
```

```
some other action (type on the keyboard, move the mouse, utilize the
disks) during the prime generation; this gives the random number
generator a better chance to gain enough entropy.
+++++..++++++++++...+++++..++++++++++.++++++++++++++++++++.++++++++++
++++++++++++++++++++.+++++++++
+++++++++++++++..+++++.+++++.+++++++++++++++.+++++.........+++++.+++++
>.+++++..+++++>.+++++....>+++
+.................................................................
................................
................<+++++...........>+++++..............................
................................
.+++++^^^
public and secret key created and signed.
key marked as ultimately trusted.

pub   1024D/374D2BF3 2003-11-03 Christian Gross (Christian Gross)
<mailing@devspace.com>
      Key fingerprint = 771E 6C1B 4BB6 BCD1 8628  59EB 2C4C 1D54
374D 2BF3
sub   2048g/51C16A00 2003-11-03 [expires: 2005-11-02]
```

The questions in the console session example should have been very similar to the questions presented in Figure 4.13 because they both generate a set of keys. After gpg has exited and returned control to the command line, a new public/private key pair will have been generated.

You should always set an expiration of the keys so that users will regularly replace their keys and reduce the ramifications of a key compromise. When a key is compromised, an intruder can decrypt all the files encrypted with the compromised key.

To list the keys in your key chain, the following command is executed as shown in the following console session output:

```
$ gpg --list-keys
C:/Documents and Settings/cgross/Application Data/GnuPG\pubring.gpg
---------------------------------------------------------------
pub   1024D/1E0FE2F0 2003-11-03 cgross (Christian Gross)
<cgross.secure@devspace.com>
sub   2048g/E1CC8ABA 2003-11-03 [expires: 2006-01-01]

pub   1024D/39458621 2003-11-03 Christian Gross (Christian Gross)
 <christianhgross@yahoo.ca>
sub   2048g/6275C370 2003-11-03 [expires: 2003-11-17]
```

```
pub  1024D/FCA09AAE 2003-11-03 Serpent Mage (Test User)
<christianhgross@yahoo.ca>
sub  1024g/3A136F54 2003-11-03 [expires: 2003-11-17]
```

The generated result is a table of keys. The keys listed are for the users `cgross`, `Christian Gross`, and `Serpent Mage`. When manipulating individual keys for the command line, the user identifiers are used as the unique descriptor of the key.

A public key is shared with others, and for maximum visibility, the public key should be submitted to a key server. A *key server* is a public repository of public keys that can be searched and retrieved. Anyone can upload a key and give the key whatever identifier they wish on a public key server because it's nothing more than a public repository. The following example shows how to publish a key to a key server:

```
gpg --keyserver wwwkeys.ch.pgp.net --send-key "Serpent Mage"
```

There are two command-line options: `--keyserver` and `--send-key`. The option `--keyserver` is used to define the name of the server that will receive the public key of the `Serpent Mage` key. The `--send-key` option is used to define the name of the key that will be published. Notice the use of quotes to correctly define the name of the key.

The key server (`wwwkeys.ch.pgp.net`) used in the previous example is one of the publicly available key servers taken from the following list:

```
http://wwwkeys.nl.pgp.net
http://wwwkeys.pl.pgp.net
http://wwwkeys.at.pgp.net
http://wwwkeys.ch.pgp.net
http://wwwkeys.de.pgp.net
http://wwwkeys.dk.pgp.net
http://wwwkeys.cz.pgp.net
http://wwwkeys.es.pgp.net
http://wwwkeys.eu.pgp.net
http://wwwkeys.uk.pgp.net
http://wwwkeys.us.pgp.net
```

Any of the key servers in the list can be used to submit your own key. You can also manage your own key server as shown in the "Project: OpenPGP Public Key Server" section later in this chapter.

When a key has been published, everyone has access to the key and can use it to encrypt messages or prove the authenticity of a message. Remember, however, that it is a public key and cannot be used to encrypt data that someone else will want to decrypt. However, imagine crackers have compromised a key or the private key has been illegally distributed. In either case, the public key might need to be deleted so that no one in the future will use the compromised key. In encryption terms, to delete a public key is to revoke it. It is not necessary to revoke a private key, as a private key is not distributed. To revoke a private key, it is deleted from the hard disk. To revoke a public key, the commands in the following example are used (underlined text should be entered by the user):

```
$ gpg --gen-revoke "Serpent Mage"

sec  1024D/FCA09AAE 2003-11-03   Serpent Mage (Test User)
<christianhgross@yahoo.ca>

Create a revocation certificate for this key? y
Please select the reason for the revocation:
  0 = No reason specified
  1 = Key has been compromised
  2 = Key is superseded
  3 = Key is no longer used
  Q = Cancel
(Probably you want to select 1 here)
Your decision? 3
Enter an optional description; end it with an empty line:
> Testing revoke rights
>
Reason for revocation: Key is no longer used
Testing revoke rights
Is this okay? y

You need a passphrase to unlock the secret key for
user: "Serpent Mage (Test User) <christianhgross@yahoo.ca>"
1024-bit DSA key, ID FCA09AAE, created 2003-11-03

ASCII armored output forced.
Revocation certificate created.

Please move it to a medium which you can hide away; if Mallory gets
access to this certificate he can use it to make your key unusable.
It is smart to print this certificate and store it away, just in case
your media become unreadable.  But have some caution:
The print system of
your machine might store the data and make it available to others!
---BEGIN PGP PUBLIC KEY BLOCK---
```

```
Version: GnuPG v1.2.1 (MingW32)
Comment: A revocation certificate should follow

iF4EIBECAB4FAj+madUXHQNUZXNOaW5nIHJldm9rZSByaWdodHMACgkQk9DSG/yg
mq7EOgCdFs91cpzCAB5/woFt6GDKGdsFSKgAmwYaUHJyGfzF7NEjglH/wyD47wj/
=4UP1
---END PGP PUBLIC KEY BLOCK---
```

The revoked key is generated at the end of the example text between the text --BEGIN... and --END.... When cutting and pasting the generated text, include the text with the dashes. Another way to generate the revoked key is by using the command-line option --output to generate a file shown as follows:

```
gpg --output "revoked.asc" -gen-revoke "Serpent Mage"
```

The generated revoked key is revoked with respect to the file only. To revoke the key publicly, the key needs to be imported into the local key chain so that the revoked key is also revoked locally. After the key has been revoked locally, it is revoked globally, by sending the revoked key to the public key server. To import a key to the local keyring, the following command is used:

```
gpg --import "revoked.asc"
```

After the revoked key has been imported, it is exported to the public key servers as was done previously. Then when doing a key search, the revoked key will be displayed similar to the following:

```
$ gpg --keyserver wwwkeys.ch.pgp.net --search-keys "Test User"
gpg: searching for "Test User" from HKP server wwwkeys.ch.pgp.net
gpg: DBG: increasing temp iobuf from 8192 to 16384
Keys 1-10 of 138 for "Test User"
(1)     Serpent Mage (Test User) <christianhgross@yahoo.ca> (revoked)
          1024 bit DSA key FCA09AAE, created 2003-11-02
```

To perform a search, the option --search-keys is used with the name of the user. In actuality, there will be many more keys returned as many people use similar identities. For sake of simplicity, only the Serpent Mage key is shown in the result.

To remove a key from a local key chain, the key has to be deleted. However, it is not as simple to delete a key because if the key has an associated private key it must be deleted first. GnuPG purposefully differentiates between a public key and a private key. The reasoning is that most likely you will interact with public keys and not the private keys. The following command shows how to delete a private key and a public key:

```
gpg --delete-secret-keys "Test User"
gpg --delete-keys "Test User"
```

Besides importing a key, you will also want to export a key. By default, an export will only export a public key. The idea is that private keys should be kept private. To specify the private key, a different command-line option has to be used. The following command example shows how to export a public key to the console in ASCII format:

```
gpg --armor --export "Test user"
```

To have the key output generated to a file, the --output command-line option can be used. The command-line option --export is used to export the key, and if the option is used by itself, all public keys in the keyring are exported. To know which key to export, an associated quote-enclosed buffer with the identifier of the user is defined. The command-line option --armor generates the exported key as base64-encoded ASCII data. Not using the command-line option --armor generates a binary encoded buffer that needs to be directly saved to a file. If the binary-encoded buffer is not saved to a buffer and allowed to be output to console, strange characters and noises will be generated.

Technique: Encrypting and Decrypting Content

Files can be encrypted using GnuPG, but you must be clear on how you want to encrypt the files. The traditional encryption method is to associate a password with a file. The other method is to use a public key. Using traditional encryption, the file can be encrypted without having to find the public key of the recipient. One of the most difficult things to find is a private key that has been safely stored away to decrypt a five-year-old file. Hence, password encryption of privately kept files is sometimes not a bad idea.

To encrypt a file using a password, the following command is used:

```
gpg --symmetric file.txt
```

When executing the command, a prompt will appear asking for the passphrase or password used to encrypt the file. That passphrase will need to be repeated, and if the passphrases match, the file is encrypted. Because the option –output is not specified, the encrypted file will assume the filename of the file with the extension .gpg. The following command shows how to decrypt the file that was encrypted:

```
gpg --decrypt file.gpg
```

The command is used to decrypt files that have been encrypted using either a passphrase or a public key. The decryption routines figures out which encryption technique was used and then decrypts the file. When the decryption routines execute, the commands will ask for the passphrase used to encrypt the file.

If using a public key is okay or if the file will be sent to someone with a public key, then public key encryption can be used. Use the following command to encrypt a file using a public key of a person that is found in the local key chain:

```
gpg --recipient "Another User" --encrypt file.txt
```

The command-line option `--recipient` and the associated buffer `"Another User"` represents the name of the public key used to encrypt the file. The command-line option `--encrypt` and associated buffer `file.txt` represents the name of the file that is encrypted. The encrypted file is saved in the same manner as in the passphrase example, where the extension of the encrypted file is `.gpg`. Just by looking at the file extension does not indicate whether the file was encrypted using a passphrase or a public key. When the file is decrypted, GnuPG does know which encryption technique was used.

Technique: Passing the Passphrase on the Console

Using the command line does pose a problem with respect to the passphrase. In Figure 4.13 shown earlier, a passphrase is required to encrypt the key. A passphrase is similar in concept to a password. A passphrase needs to be given manually when the GnuPG tools are executed. For example, whenever an encryption operation happens, a user must manually enter the correct passphrase. If this operation were to occur on a Web server, the Web server would grind to a halt waiting for someone to enter the passphrase. Manually entering a passphrase is not useful in a server-execution context. To get around this problem, GnuPG can have the password passed to it using a pipe as shown in the following example:

```
echo $PASSPHRASE | gpg --passphrase-fd [options]
```

The command `echo` outputs a passphrase that has been saved as an environment variable. The passphrase is piped to the program `gpg`. For `gpg` to know that a password is being piped to it, the command-line option `--passphrase-fd` must be used. Of course, you shouldn't store a passphrase as an environment variable, but it's shown here to illustrate how to pipe a password. Storing the passphrase as a file would be better, but even then there are security issues because the file needs to have the proper permissions. There is no simple way to store a password without some type of security issue.

Technique: Signing Documents

Signing a document is putting your signature on a specific piece of data. Essentially the signature says that the piece of data originated from you and has not been tampered with. You would sign a document if you wanted to prove that you wrote the document. This is often important when writing e-mails. To ensure that at some later point in time nobody misrepresents your comments, the e-mails could be signed. A signed e-mail cannot be altered in any way. Three command-line options can be used to sign a document:

--sign: Sign the document, attach the signature to the document, and save all data in binary file format with the extension `.gpg`.

--clearsign: Sign the document, attach the signature to the document in ASCII text format, and save all data in a file with the extension `.asc`. This option only makes sense if the file to be signed is in ASCII text format as well (e.g., e-mail).

--detach-sign: Sign the document, but do not attach the signature; instead, place it in separate file. The separate file has the extension `.sig`.

To sign a document the following command is used:

```
gpg --detach-sign file.txt
```

When the command is executed, the file is signed using the first private key in the key chain (the first private key available in the list when the keys are listed using `--list-keys`). To specify a specific private key, the command-line option `--local-user` is used as shown in the following example:

```
gpg --local-user "Another User" --detach-sign file.txt
```

To verify a signed document, the following command is executed:

```
gpg --verify file.sig
```

If the command is executed and the public key of the signer exists in the key chain, then the verification will succeed; otherwise, an error will be generated. If there is an error, then it is necessary to retrieve the public key of the user who sent the file. The simplest solution is to ask the sender of the document to send you their public key.

Signing a document is important because anyone could send you a document and claim it. Let's say you are awaiting an e-mail from someone who encrypts the document with your public key. It is possible for someone else to intercept the e-mail and replace the e-mail with another document. Note that the actual contents cannot be replaced, just that the interceptor could send you a similar document if the interceptor knew what the document was about. When you receive the document, you would decrypt the document and assume it is from the original sender.

This is called a man-in-the-middle attack. One way to solve this problem is to sign the document. If the document is signed, then the interceptor cannot replace the document because they would need the private key of the sender to sign the document. If the interceptor attempts to use his own private key to sign the document, it will become obvious who the sender is. The only remaining issue is to ensure that you get the correct public key. The interceptor could send you his public key and make it appear he is the sender. Therefore, be sure to verify public keys before verifying documents.

The following command shows how to encrypt a file using a public key and then sign the encrypted document:

```
gpg --local-user "Another User" --recipient "Remote User"
--clearsign --encrypt file.txt
```

The document is signed with the private key of Another User, and encrypted using the public key of the Remote User. When the command is executed, the file file.asc is produced, which is an ASCII text file. The receiver of the document Remote User can decrypt the file file.asc; during decryption, a verification of the document occurs. If anything is not correct, an error will be generated.

Technique: I Lost My Public or Private Key, Help!

One of the biggest potential problems with public key encryption is the loss of the private key. Users must carefully manage their private keys.

Losing a private key is a problem because there is no way to recreate the private key. The only solution is to create a new private and public key and inform everyone that there is a new public key.

Losing a public key, on the other hand, is not that important because most likely a public key can be retrieved from a public key server. A public key can also be retrieved from the private key because the GnuPG system stores the public key within the private key. The following command shows how to retrieve the public key from the private key:

```
gpgsplit --no-split --secret-to-public secret.pgp > publickey.gpg
```

The commands will automatically generate the public keys to the console, and then save them to a generic public key file. The command-line option --no-split should be used so that the keys aren't broken apart and only the public keys are extracted.

Technique: Using WinPT

The command line is useful for scripts, but less useful for daily tasks. Every technique illustrated so far with GnuPG can be carried out using WinPT. WinPT is a user-friendly interface to GnuPG. WinPT is a tray application that is activated by right-clicking and choosing the Key Manager option from the menu as shown in Figure 4.15.

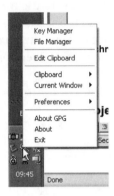

FIGURE 4.15 WinPT context-sensitive menu.

The menu contains the following options:

Key Manager: Opens the Key Manager dialog box.

File Manager: Opens the File Manager dialog box.

Edit Clipboard: Opens the Clipboard Editor dialog box. The Clipboard Editor is used to edit the contents of the Windows clipboard using ASCII text. The Windows clipboard can be loaded or saved. Essentially it allows you to cut, copy, and paste text that needs to be processed using some type of encryption or decryption.

Clipboard: Used to encrypt, decrypt, or verify the contents of the clipboard. For example, you receive an e-mail or a document that is encrypted and needs to be decrypted. You simply need to copy the contents to the clipboard and then use this menu option to process the data. The format of the clipboard data could be binary or ASCII text.

Current Window: Used to process the text of the current window. This feature works on plain ASCII text windows only and hence is not that useful.

Preferences: Sets the configuration options of WinPT and the GnuPG. By using either configuration option, you can fine-tune which keyrings are used and how to automatically do certain steps using a keyboard sequence.

About GPG, About: Displays an About dialog box.

Exit: Exits the WinPT application.

The Key Manager dialog box is a user-friendly dialog box used to manage the keys in the key chain as shown in Figure 4.16.

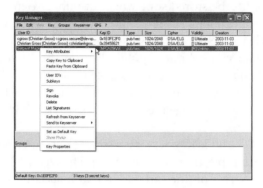

FIGURE 4.16 Key Manager dialog box.

In Figure 4.16, the Key Manager dialog box contains a listbox that has loaded the keys in the local keyring. When a key has been selected, the context-sensitive menu that applies to the key is shown in Figure 4.16. The main concept of the Key Manager dialog box is to allow you to perform all possible key operations, including publishing, searching, signing, exporting, and revoking keys. When a script is not required or desired, it's faster to use the WinPT Key Manager dialog box to manage the keys. The exception to this rule is if you have to perform key management operations that involve thousands of keys.

To perform encryption or decryption, the File Manager dialog box is used as shown in Figure 4.17.

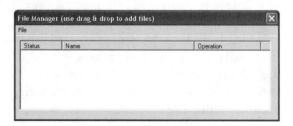

FIGURE 4.17 File Manager dialog box.

The File Manager dialog box is used by dragging and dropping files to add them. The File menu item is then used to encrypt, decrypt, or verify the dropped files.

The File Manager dialog box is a bit awkward, and should only be used if operations need to be performed that the WinPT Windows Explorer Extensions cannot handle. The Windows Explorer Extension can perform the same operations in the Windows Explorer.

TIP

PROJECT: OPENPGP PUBLIC KEY SERVER

Public keys need to be stored somewhere in public. Generally people store their public keys on some public key server for future reference. In many cases, it is perfectly acceptable to use the key servers on the Internet. However, there are no restrictions on who can submit a public key on the Internet-based key servers. Anyone can submit a key, so it isn't possible to control the identity of the key. For those situations when a corporation wants to roll out a PKI infrastructure, the company will want to manage the public keys so that only valid keys are available on its own Intranet.

The OpenPGP Public Key Server is a simple key server. Some things are not implemented, for example, user authentication. The OpenPGP Public Key Server acts like a public key server on the Internet in that it accepts any key and does not attempt to distinguish between different keys. However, some configuration settings make a key server act in certain ways so that the administrator has control over which keys can be read and added. Table 4.4 contains the reference information for the OpenPGP Public Key Server project.

Impatient Installation

There is no impatient installation for the Open PGP Public Key Server. The administrator has to use the formal deployment procedure to deploy a distribution.

Deployment

To deploy the key server, the sources have to be compiled using the Cygwin toolkit, and then the compiled applications need to be manually installed. You can download the sources using CVS, but for the scope of this book, it is assumed a stable released version is downloaded from *http://pks.sourceforge.net/downloads.html*. The sources are packaged as a tarred gzip file, which needs to be expanded. After the sources have been expanded, a subdirectory will exist with the name `pks-[version number]`.

To compile the sources, open a BASH console and navigate to the `pks-[version number]` subdirectory. Within the subdirectory, execute the `configure` command:

```
./configure
```

The `configure` command can be extended by including the `--prefix` command-line option to specify where to install the key server. However, because the key server will be deployed manually and all the configuration options manually defined, it is not necessary to provide a prefix. The purpose of the `configure` command is to define a configuration used to compile the application. After the

TABLE 4.4 Reference Information for OpenPGP Public Key Server

Item	*Description*
Home page	*http://pks.sourceforge.net/*
Version	At the time of this writing, the version was 0.9.6.
Installation	The OpenPGP Public Key Server must be installed manually and there are no quick installations.
Dependencies	The OpenPGP Public Key Server requires that Cygwin be fully installed because the server has to be compiled using the Cygwin toolkit.
Documentation	There is virtually no documentation, other than this book and the README file that is distributed with the OpenPGP server. You can also run the generated files with the command-line option `--help` to return the options available with the tool.
Mailing Lists	For any questions, send e-mails to the mailing lists located at *http://pks.sourceforge.net/lists.html.*
Impatient Installation Time Required	Download size: 0.5 MB Installation and configuration time: 30-60 minutes.
Port	
DVD Location	The sources are located in the directory `/packages/pks.`

configuration has completed, it is necessary to compile and link the sources using the `make` command:

```
make
```

When the `make` command has completed, the entire server components will have been compiled and you can deploy the key server. The executable applications `pksclient.exe`, `pksd.exe`, and `pksdctl.exe` should be placed somewhere in the path so that they are visible to any console application.

Before the key server can be executed, the database and configuration file have to be prepared. To prepare a database, the command `pksclient.exe` is used:

```
pksclient /usr/local/var/db create
```

The command `pksclient` has two options: the path `/usr/local/var/db` and the command `create`. The first option is a path that must exist and is the place where the key database is stored. Notice that the path is specified using a LINUX/FreeBSD notation and not a Windows shell notation. This is because the key server has been compiled as a Cygwin application and hence interprets paths using the LINUX/BSD notation. The second option `create` is the create action to initialize a database.

Within the sources of the application, there is the configuration file `pksd.conf`. The configuration file can be copied to any location desired. After the file has been copied, any configuration changes should be made to the copied file. Following is an example of starting the key server using the copied configuration file:

```
pksd.exe /usr/local/etc/pksf.conf
```

The command will continue executing until it is told to stop processing key requests. To shut down the key server, the following command from another BASH console is used:

```
pksdctl.exe shutdown
```

Technique: Adding Keys to the Key Server

The key server as it is deployed does nothing because the database is empty and no one can add data. This configuration is useful if the key server is to be used as a read-only database. There are two ways to add keys: by adding to the key server as was shown using the GnuPG command line or by adding the keys using a script.

When the key server does not accept a request to add a key, the key server is acting as a read-only key server. This is useful if the administrator wants to control which public keys are available. In an intranet scenario, this is extremely useful because managing the exposure of the public keys and private keys can partially control the identity of the users.

When the administrator wants to add a key, it is added manually using the `pksclient` command:

```
pksclient /usr/local/var/db add keys.pgp
```

The command to add a set of keys is very similar to initializing the database. The first option `/usr/local/var/db` is the path of the key server database. The second option `add` is the command to add data to the database. The third option `keys.pgp` is a public key file, just like the public key file used by GnuPG.

In a scripting context, when an administrator creates the public and private keys for the individual users, the administrator could also add a script that uses the `pksclient` application to add the public keys to the key server database. By using a scripting approach, the administrator also could at the same time back up the private keys in case the users lose their own private keys.

If instead the administrator wants to run a key server where people can add, revoke, and update their own keys, then the configuration file `pksd.conf` has to be updated to include the options defined as follows:

```
www_readonly 0
max_last_reply_keys -1
max_reply_keys -1
```

The command options in the configuration file enable a key server to accept key adds (`www_readonly`) and to accept searches that return as many keys as necessary (`max_last_reply_keys`, and `max_reply_keys`).

Technique: Deleting Keys from the Key Server

To delete keys when the key server accepts keys, the same procedure is used as described in the "Technique: Creating and Deleting Keys" section. If the administrator needs to delete keys manually, however, then the following command is used:

```
pksclient /usr/local/var/db delete 0x1E0FE2F0
```

The third command-line option represents the key ID of the key to be deleted.

PROJECT: STUNNEL AND OPENSSL

Many projects use SSL, most notably any Web server. Netscape®'s SSL makes it possible to encrypt communications between a client and a server. SSL is a combination of public key and passphrase encryption. The combination is used because using public key encryption for all communications is too computationally intensive for a server.

The technique that SSL uses is a combination of a handshake and key exchange. To start the process, the client requests the public key from the server. Using that public key, the client encrypts a random passphrase and sends the encrypted data to the server. The server receives the package, decrypts the data, and reads the passphrase. When the client and server communicate, they use passphrase symmetric encryption. During the communication, the client and server may coordinate to use a different passphrase to make it more complicated for a hacker to figure out the contents of the data.

The OpenSSL toolkit is based on the SSLeay library that was originally developed in Australia. The SSLeay toolkit made it possible for non-American and non-Canadian companies to use strong encryption for their Web servers. With the relaxation of encryption rules in the United States and the expiration of the RSA patent, the OpenSSL toolkit has been created. The OpenSSL toolkit provides a foundation for many other applications (e.g., Web servers, mail servers, and so on).

For the scope of this chapter, techniques of using OpenSSL are not shown because OpenSSL is a library. Instead, this chapter shows how to use the OpenSSL toolkit in conjunction with the STunnel application to encrypt communications and create secure channels and potentially even provide an SSL frontend to a Web server without modifying the server. The STunnel application is an application that uses OpenSSL to encrypt communications between a client and a server. It is useful when the administrator wants to encrypt communications that should not be captured by any party in-between, for example, communications between wireless networks or between home workers and a corporate network.

Table 4.5 provides reference information for the OpenSSL toolkit, and Table 4.6 provides reference information for the STunnel application.

TABLE 4.5 Reference Information for OpenSSL Toolkit

Item	Description
Home page	*http://www.openssl.org/*
Version	At the time of this writing, the version is 0.9.7e. $\longrightarrow$

Item	*Description*
Installation	The OpenSSL toolkit is generally provided only in source code format and must be manually compiled. Binaries are available on the Internet, but you must search for them. If you have access to a Visual C++ compiler, you can compile your own binaries. Do not use the Cygwin distributed SSL libraries as they are not as performance oriented as a natively compiled library.
Dependencies	The OpenSSL toolkit has no dependencies if downloaded in binary form. If, however, the sources are compiled using the Visual C++ compiler, then it is necessary to install the Perl interpreter from ActiveState.
Documentation	The documentation associated with using the OpenSSL toolkit is minimal as the toolkit is often used in other applications. Applications that use the OpenSSL toolkit usually provides the documentation necessary to deploy OpenSSL. For example, to use SSL with Apache, the module `mod_ssl` is used, and there is extensive documentation on how to use `mod_ssl`.
Mailing Lists	There are mailing lists on how to use OpenSSL, however, it is not entirely advisable to ask about SSL issues in other applications. For example, an OpenSSL toolkit programmer might be interested in the mailing lists. Questions can be asked about the several applications that are distributed with the OpenSSL toolkit. The mailing lists are found at *http://www.openssl.org/support/*, and the mailing list `openssl-users` would be of interest for administrators.
Impatient Installation Time Required	Download size: 3.0 MB OpenSSL toolkit, 20 KB OpenSSL VC++ projects.
	Installation and configuration time: 30-60 minutes.
DVD Location	Due to legal issues, the DVD does not contain any files.

TABLE 4.6 Reference Information for STunnel Toolkit

Item	Description
Home page	*http://www.stunnel.org/*
Version	At the time of this writing, the version is 4.0.7.
Installation	The STunnel application is extremely simply to install because it is a single executable with the name `stunnel-[version number].exe`.
Dependencies	The STunnel application relies on the OpenSSL toolkit libraries.
Documentation	The documentation associated with the STunnel application is rather sparse, due to the fact that the application only does one or two things. You should read the usage examples located at *http://www.stunnel.org/examples/*.
Mailing Lists	There are mailing lists on how to use STunnel located at *http://www.stunnel.org/support/*. For the administrator, the useful mailing lists are `STunnel-announce` and `STunnel-Users`.
Impatient Installation Time Required	Download size: STunnel 54 KB. Installation and configuration time: 10-15 minutes.
Firewall Port	STunnel can use any port that is required and is not limited to a specific port.
DVD Location	Due to legal issues, the DVD does not contain any files.

Impatient Installation

If the binaries do not exist for the OpenSSL library, then there is no impatient installation possible. If the binaries do exist, then installation of OpenSSL and STunnel is simple because the DLLs need to be copied to a location in the PATH environment variable. In particular, the following files are needed: `libeay32.dll`, `SSLeay32.dll`, and `stunnel-[version number].exe`.

Often many applications complain that the file `libssl32.dll` does not exist. That is okay, because the file `SSLeay32.dll` is `libssl32.dll`. The simplest solution is to copy and rename the file `SSLLeay32.dll` to `libssl32.dll`.

If you do not have any SSL certificates, then you will need to compile OpenSSL and its various executable applications. Those applications can be used to generate SSL certificates. More information about the executable files will be given in the next "Deployment" section of this chapter.

Deployment

In most cases, the OpenSSL library will not be precompiled and it is necessary to compile the toolkit. Compilation requires the installation of either Visual C++ 6.0 or later. The OpenSSL toolkit can be downloaded from *http://www.openssl.org/source/*. The latest stable release is highlighted in red. The toolkit is downloaded as an archive that has been gziped and tarred. When the archive is expanded, the subdirectory `openssl-[version number]`.

```
Building OpenSSL
```

You also need to download the Microsoft Dev Studio® workspace for OpenSSL, which can be found at *http://www.openssl.org/related/*. Clicking on the associated link will load a Web page that includes a number of links to OpenSSL associated workspaces. For example, if you downloaded OpenSSL version 0.9.7e, then you'll need the 0.9.7 Dev Studio workspaces. The downloaded archive is also a gzipped tar file, which when expanded will generate the directory `Msvc097`. The directory `Msvc097` needs to be moved to become a subdirectory of the `openssl-[version number]` subdirectory.

To be able to load the Microsoft Dev Studio project files a couple of console applications have to be executed. These console applications depend on the installation of the Perl interpreter from ActiveState. It is not recommended to use the Cygwin-included Perl interpreter as it might cause errors. If the Cygwin-included Perl interpreter exists, it should be renamed. The ActiveState Perl interpreter can be downloaded from *http://www.activestate.com/Solutions/Programmer/Perl.plex*. After the Perl interpreter has been installed, the OpenSSL toolkit can be compiled.

Open a console window, change the current directory to the OpenSSL toolkit subdirectory, and execute the following command:

```
perl Configure VC-WIN32
```

The command will configure the build environment to use the Visual C++ development environment. The next step is to run a batch file that will initialize all the build directories. The following two commands are executed in successive order:

```
ms/do_ms.bat
perl msvc087/doinc.pl
```

After the two commands have been executed, you can load the Microsoft Dev Studio workspace located in the directory `openssl-[version number]/msvc097/openssl.dsw` using Microsoft Visual Studio®.

After the workspace has fully loaded in Microsoft Visual Studio, there will be about 40+ projects. The simplest way to build all projects is to do a batch build of all projects. The Batch Build command is found under the Build menu. A dialog box will appear with all projects selected, and you just need to click on the OK button. The compile will take at least 10 minutes.

After a full compilation, all the programs and libraries are located in the directory `openssl-[version number]/out32dll/Release`. The following files should be copied to a directory in the path: `libeay32.dll`, `SSLeay32.dll`, `ca.exe`, `ciphers.exe`, `crl.exe`, `dh.exe`, `dhparam.exe`, `dsaparam.exe`, `enc.exe`, `engine.exe`, `errstr.exe`, `gendh.exe`, `openssl.exe`, `passwd.exe`, `pkcs7.exe`, `pkcs8.exe`, `pkcs12.exe`, `rand.exe`, `rsa.exe`, `s_client.exe`, `s_server.exe`, `s_time.exe`, `sess_id.exe`, `smime.exe`, `speed.exe`, `spkac.exe`, `verify.exe`, `version.exe`, and `x509.exe`.

TIP

The easiest way to copy all the correct files is to copy all files with the extension `.dll`*, and all executable filenames that do not contain the word* `test`*.*

Downloading STunnel

The STunnel application can be downloaded from the STunnel Web site AT *http://www.stunnel.org/download/binaries.html*. The downloaded file is an executable that can be executed directly, but requires a compiled OpenSSL library.

If you want to install STunnel as a service, execute the following command:

```
stunnel.exe -install
```

To remove the service, execute the following command:

```
stunnel.exe -uninstall
```

In an Open Source book, the question that arises is why use the Visual C++ compiler and not the gcc or mingw gcc compiler? The answer is simply that the Visual C++ compiler generates the fastest binaries. Although most packages can be downloaded as binary only, many packages when downloaded in source code format will compile only against the Visual C++ compiler. It would be possible to adapt the project workspace to use the mingw gcc compiler, but that can be a lot of work.

Technique: Generating a Server Certificate

By default, OpenSSL and STunnel distribute a file called stunnel.pem. This is the server certificate that contains the public and private keys of the server. The public and private keys serve the exact same purpose as discussed previously in the GnuPG PKI "Technique: Trusting Content Using PKI" section. The difference being that the certificate is intended for a server and not an end user.

The default stunnel.pem file should not used because it is a generic certificate. Practically, a hacker can easily get access to the private and public key of stunnel.pem. You need to generate your own certificate to identify yourself to the end user. To do that, you need the openssl.exe application and a configuration file formatted in Public-Key Cryptography Standards 10 (PKCS10) format. PKCS10 is a specific format that includes a number of required key value pairs. The following text block is a sample configuration file used to generate a certificate:

```
RANDFILE = stunnel.rnd

[ req ]
default_bits = 1024
encrypt_key = yes
distinguished_name = req_dn
x509_extensions = cert_type

[ req_dn ]
countryName = Country Name (2 letter code)
countryName_default              = CH
countryName_min                  = 2
countryName_max                  = 2

stateOrProvinceName              = Zurich
stateOrProvinceName_default      = ZH

localityName                     = Stallikon
```

```
O.organizationName                 = devspace.com
O.organizationName_default         = devspace.com

organizationalUnitName             = NA
#organizationalUnitName_default =

O.commonName                       = neptune
O.commonName_default               = localhost

# To create a certificate for more than one name uncomment:
# 1.commonName                     = DNS alias of your server
# 2.commonName                     = DNS alias of your server
# ...

[ cert_type ]
nsCertType = server
```

The key value pairs in the configuration file are relatively self-explanatory. Essentially the configuration file defines the context of the generated public/private key. The key default_bits defines how many bits are used to encrypt the data and should be changed to a larger value for a stronger key. The other values that will be changed are all the key values in the req_dn section. These key values define the default certificate identifiers.

The important part for the certificate is that the keys 0.commonName, 1.commmonName, and so on refer to the DNS identifiers of the appropriate servers. If the key to be generated is intended for a Web server, then identify the DNS address of the Web server. When a client loads a certificate, it will attempt to identify the certificate with the DNS name of the server. If that name does not correspond, an error message will be generated. There can be multiple servers associated with a certificate.

After the configuration file has been defined, it can be used to generate a certificate:

```
openssl req -new -x509 -days 365 -nodes -config stunnel.cnf
-out stunnel.pem -keyout stunnel.pem
```

The command-line options are explained as follows:

req: Generates or processes PKCS10 formatted certificates, and can be used to create certificates for use as a root Certificate Authenticator (CA).

-new: Generates a new certificate.

-x509: Generates the certificate signed by itself, trusted by itself. Note that usually certificates are generated and associated with a trusted CA, such as the Thawte Corporation. When generating a certificate trusted by yourself, you are saying that you are who you are, but are not letting another party verify who you are. A self-trusted certificate can be used on the Internet, however, a warning message will be generated.

-days: Generates a certificate that is valid for a number of days, which in the example is 365 days or a year.

-nodes: Specifies that if the private key is generated, it will not be encrypted.

-config: Specifies the name of the configuration file.

-out: Specifies the name of the file where the data is written to.

-keyout: Specifies the filename of where to generate the private key, which for the previous example is the same name of the -out option. This is done for simplicity.

When the openssl command is executed, a number of questions will be asked. These questions are a repeat of the definitions in the configuration file. This is because the configuration values are default values that could be tweaked. You should either use the default value or enter new values. After the questions have all been answered, the certificate file stunnel.pem will be generated. The newly generated certificate can be used for secure communications. To view the values in the certificate, use the following command:

```
openssl x509 -noout -text -in stunnel.pem
```

Technique: Signing a Certificate By a CA

The certificate generated in the previous technique is a self-signed certificate. Although legitimate, it always generates an error when the certificate is loaded for the first time in a browser. The certificate is not faulty or bad, the browser is simply indicating that the certificate has not been validated by any other authority. A user can save the certificate to avoid getting the error in the future. The user might not trust it and avoid loading the certificate, thus making it impossible to provide a secure communications channel.

The best solution is to not have the warning in the first place. To do that, the certificate has to be signed by some authority that will vouch for your identity. Note that most authorities on the Internet, such as Thawte, require a passport or other legal documentation to verify who you are before signing a certificate. After the information is verified, the signing authority signs the certificate and it is considered as authentic. Think of it like this: A passport is only legal because a country issued the passport. If you decided to create your own passport with your own data, the passport would be rejected because the data could not be verified. Just as a country verifies your passport, a signing authority verifies your certificate.

The signing of a certificate involves the following steps:

1. Client generates a separate private key and public key.
2. Client sends generated public key to a signing authority.
3. Signing authority receives the public key, encrypts it with the signing authority private key, and returns the encrypted public key to the client.
4. Client combines the private key with the newly encrypted public key in a new certificate.
5. User requests access to client and receives the encrypted public key. Using the public key of the authority decrypts the public key and verifies that the public key is acceptable.

The way this works in Web browsers is that most browsers distribute a number of public keys of accredited signing authorities. Public keys signed by an accepted authority will generate no warnings or errors.

To generate a certificate that will be signed by an authority, execute the following command:

```
openssl req -new -days 365 -nodes -config stunnel.conf
-out certreq.pem -keyout stunnel.pem
```

The command to generate a certificate as a signing authority is not that much different from the command to generate a general certificate. The only difference is that command-line options -out and -keyout reference different files. This occurs on purpose because the permanent certificate file is stunnel.pem, but the public key still needs to be signed. The file certreq.pem contains your public key, and it should be sent to a signing authority.

After the private/public keys have been generated, remember to immediately back up your private key file. The signing authority will sign your generated public key. Your public key is related to the private key and losing your private key file means you will have to go through the entire process again. Going through the entire process costs money and time. The exception to this rule is if you are your own signing authority.

After the public key has been signed and returned, the contents defined by the BEGIN CERTIFICATE and END CERTIFICATE sections shown as follows need to be appended to the original private key file stunnel.pem:

```
Certificate:
    Data:
        Version: 1 (0x0)
```

```
...
---BEGIN CERTIFICATE---
...
---END CERTIFICATE---
```

When copying the data, remember to include the BEGIN... and END... boundary definitions. The contents of the `stunnel.pem` file should resemble the following example file:

```
---BEGIN RSA PRIVATE KEY---
...
---END RSA PRIVATE KEY---
---BEGIN CERTIFICATE---
...
---END CERTIFICATE---
```

After the `stunnel.pem` file has been updated, it should be backed up immediately and can be used anywhere that you need to enable SSL encryption.

Technique: Becoming a Signing Authority

Becoming a signing authority is easy. The hard part is getting people to trust you. To become a trusted signing authority, the client has to accept your signing authority certificate. The signing authority certificate is the public key used to verify keys signed by your signing authority.

To generate a signing authority certificate, a private key that has an associated passphrase needs to be created. The following command shows how to create a private key:

```
openssl genrsa -des3 -out ca.key 1024
```

The options used by the command are explained as follows:

genrsa: Generates an RSA private key.

-des3: Specifies the algorithm to use when generating the key. The -des3 option is triple DES encryption. It is also possible to use the IDEA algorithm (-idea), but be forewarned that it is under patent protection and requires a valid license to use commercially.

-out: Specifies the name of the output key.

1024: Specifies the length of the key.

After the private key has been generated, it is necessary to generate a server certificate using the correct format. The following command shows how to generate the correct signing authority certificate:

```
openssl req -new -x509 -days 365 -config stunnel.conf
 -key ca.key -out ca.crt
```

The command looks similar to creating a certificate, and in fact it is. This goes back to the original statement regarding the signing process in that a signing authority is nothing more than a public key that you trust, which is why it is technically easy to become a signing authority, but difficult to get people to trust you.

To begin signing certificates, an OpenSSL configuration file has to be created that defines the characteristics of how public keys will be signed. The following text block shows an example openssl.conf file:

```
[ca ]
default_ca      = CA_default

[CA_default ]
dir             = c:/bin/certificates
database        = $dir/index.txt
new_certs_dir   = $dir/newcerts

certificate     = $dir/ca.crt
serial          = $dir/serial.txt
private_key     = $dir/ca.key
RANDFILE        = $dir/openssl.rnd

default_days    = 365
default_crl_days= 30
default_md      = md5

policy          = policy_any
email_in_dn     = no

nameopt         = ca_default
certopt         = ca_default
copy_extensions = none

[policy_any ]
countryName             = supplied
stateOrProvinceName     = optional
organizationName        = optional
organizationalUnitName  = optional
```

```
commonName              = supplied
emailAddress            = optional
```

In the example `openssl.conf` file, many defaults can be kept as they are. However, what needs to be manually defined is explained as follows:

default_ca: Defines the section that is used when signing public keys.

dir: Defines the root directory where all the appropriate files are stored.

database: Defines a file that is used as an index file to manage all the signed public keys. The index file references files in the directory defined by the key `new_certs_dir`. This file can initially be empty, but must exist.

new_certs_dir: Defines a directory where all signed public keys are stored.

certificate: Defines the filename of the public key signing authority.

serial: Defines a file that contains a serial number. The serial number file is a single line file that on the single line references some long hexadecimal number. You can randomly create the file and add a serial number.

private_key: Defines the filename of the private key signing authority.

default_days: Defines the number of days that the signed public key should be valid.

The keys defined in the `policy_any` section of the `openssl.conf` file determine which pieces of the to-be-signed public key must be present. For example, the `countryName` must be provided, but the organization name is optional. For an Internet scenario, changing all the `optional` values to the value `supplied` might be better because then there is no confusion concerning the identity of the public key.

To sign a public key, use the following command:

```
openssl ca -config openssl.conf -in certreq.pem -out signed.cert
```

The command-line options are explained as follows:

ca: Executes the signing authority service.

-config: Specifies the name of the OpenSSL configuration file, which should be similar to the `openssl.conf` file.

-in: Specifies the filename of the key to be signed.

-out: Specifies the identifier of the filename that will contain the signed public key.

After the public key of the user has been signed, the signed public key can be incorporated into the original server certificate as discussed in the previous "Technique: Signing a Certificate By a CA" section.

The next step is to get the client to trust the signing authority and automatically accept all signed public keys. To get the client to trust the signing authority it has to be added as a trusted certificate. In Windows, the signing authority public key is added via the Internet security options. Open the Control Panel, and click the Internet Options icon to open the Internet Properties dialog box (see Figure 4.18).

Next, click the Content tab. Click the Certificates button in the Certificates group box to open the Certificates dialog box shown in Figure 4.19.

FIGURE 4.18 Internet Options dialog box.

FIGURE 4.19 Certificates dialog box used to add a signing authority public key.

The dialog box in Figure 4.19 contains all the certificates from signing authorities that are trusted by the local computer. The different tabs relate to the types of certificates and their intended purposes. Importing a signing authority public key using the Certificates dialog box is only useful if the Internet applications use the Windows Internet API. For example, if Mozilla is used as a Web browser, the same process of importing the signing authority certificate has to be used. To add a signing authority certificate, click the Trusted Root Certification Authorities tab and then click the Import button. A wizard starts asking which certificate to import. The file is the public key of the signing authority, which is the file generated using the -out command-line option. After going through a number of steps and verifications, the certificate will be incorporated.

After the import, any SSL certificates signed by your local signing authority will be considered trusted. This process is very useful when you want to distribute content in an intranet because the administrator can control the client and server.

Take a step back and consider the signing authority process again. Microsoft software uses trusted certificates for many pieces of Windows. An administrator could use signed pieces of software to ensure that only valid software is installed and used. This form of security complements user security and can be effectively used in an overall security policy.

Technique: Enabling SSL on a Non-SSL Enabled Application

Many applications can speak SSL, e.g., Web browsers, mail clients, and so on. Your local Web server or mail server might not be able to speak SSL. STunnel can be used to provide SSL services when none exist. The client communicates to STunnel using the SSL protocol and STunnel communicates to the server using the clear text protocol. Usually it's wise to ensure in this configuration that both STunnel and the server are on the same LAN, and if possible on the same server.

When the STunnel application is executed, it expects to find in the same directory the configuration file stunnel.conf. If that file is not found, then some command-line arguments need to be provided that can replace the configuration file. The simplest is to use the stunnel.conf file, which has a format that is essentially identical to a Windows .ini file. A configuration file has a global section and a number of service subsections. The global section configures how STunnel will generally react, and the subsections are used to declare port redirections. Following is an example configuration that exposes a secure HTTP port for a Web server that does not support secure connections:

```
cert = c:/bin/stunnel.pem

[https]
```

```
accept  = 443
connect = pluto:80
TIMEOUTclose = 0
```

The global section is where the key cert is defined. The key cert refers to a certificate that has been generated using the OpenSSL techniques described previously. For STunnel, the private key and public key have to reside in the same file on the server side; otherwise, errors will be generated.

The identifier https defines a service level section where an encrypted connection provided by STunnel will connect to some service that is not encrypted. Secure HTTP requires that the encrypted port accepts connections on port 443 and redirects the communications to the nonencrypted port 80. The encrypted listen port is defined by the key accept. The unencrypted connection is defined by the key connect. The connect key is a combination of server name and port identifier. In the example, it means that Web server is located on the computer pluto and is listening to port 80. The key TIMEOUTclose is used to identify when the connection to the browser should be closed. The value of 0 for TIMEOUTclose should be added because there are some issues with some versions of Internet Explorer.

The following command example illustrates how to start the STunnel application:

```
./STunnel-[version number].exe
```

After the STunnel application has started, the log output and tray icon should appear similar to Figure 4.20.

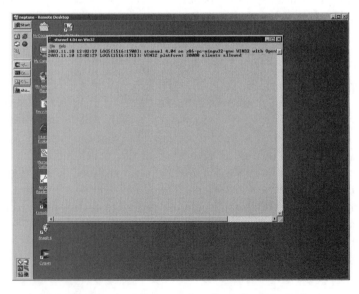

FIGURE 4.20 A successfully started and running STunnel application.

If the STunnel application did not start successfully, a dialog box with an error will appear. The user should then look at the log window that is activated by double-clicking the STunnel tray icon located in the lower-right corner of the Windows Tray in Figure 4.20.

Technique: Redirecting a Port

Another usage of STunnel is to provide secure communications between a client and server when neither the client nor the server are capable of communicating using SSL. Imagine wanting to receive your e-mail across the Internet. The default POP3 protocol sends the username and password using clear text. Some e-mail servers support digest authentication, but the data still travels as clear text across the Internet. It is not desirable to have any e-mail data travel across the Internet without encryption. STunnel can help by providing a secure channel on the client and server. Note that using STunnel in this configuration requires installing the STunnel application on the client and server.

The client and server STunnel application work together to provide a transparent encrypted connection. The configuration of the server is similar to the `stunnel.conf` configuration file. The difference is that instead of exposing STunnel for HTTPS communications, the administrator can define the encrypted port to be any number. An example configuration is shown as follows:

```
cert = c:/bin/stunnel.pem

[pop-proxy]
accept  = 12345
connect = pluto:110
```

The server listens to port 12345, which is a random number because unlike the secure HTTP (HTTPS) example, a predetermined port identifier is not required. When a request arrives on port 12345, it is redirected to the server `Pluto` and port 110, which is the POP server port.

STunnel needs to be running on the client side, and the configuration file is defined so that STunnel operates in client mode. The following text block is an example configuration file:

```
client=yes

[pop-proxy]
accept = 110
connect = neptune:12345
```

The global configuration key `client` puts the STunnel application into client mode. In client mode, the `accept` connection is unencrypted and the `connect` connection is encrypted. That is the inverse of when the STunnel application is running in server mode. Notice that the local port is 110, which is the POP port, and the remote connection port is 12345.

To finish the infrastructure, the client e-mail program is configured to retrieve its e-mail from the "local" e-mail server. The "local" e-mail server is a redirect to an encrypted connection, and is then redirected to the POP3 server. This configuration solves the problem of having other people potentially intercept any POP messages.

This configuration works, but there are a few issues to resolve. The first issue is that STunnel can only accept TCP-based protocols. For example, DNS cannot be redirected. The second issue is that each port has to be remapped, and there is no general way to remap a series of ports. The last issue is that this configuration stops people from intercepting your communications, but it does not stop people from creating their own SSL connection to attempt to hack into the system. The first and second issues are solved by a VPN, which is discussed later in the "Project: Open-VPN" section. Using client certificates can solve the last issue.

Technique: Port Redirection and Authentication

When using STunnel to create a transparent connection between client and server, the communication is encrypted, but any client can connect. By default, STunnel does not provide user authentication, but a form of user authentication can be added. STunnel provides a form of user authentication by defining a certificate that is present on the server and the client. To do that, the server-side and client-side configuration files have to be slightly altered. The following text block is a modified client-side configuration file:

```
cert = c:/bin/client.pem
client=yes

[pop-proxy]
accept = 110
connect = neptune:12345
```

Added to this client-side configuration file is the cert key. When the cert key is used in conjunction with a client-side STunnel instance, it provides an identity that is sent to the server for further verification in an encrypted communication link. The client.pem file contains both a private and public key, generated by the techniques defined in the section "Technique: Generating a Server Certificate."

On the server side, the configuration file has to be slightly modified to something similar to this:

```
cert = c:/bin/stunnel.pem
verify = 2
CApath = c:/bin/certificates
```

```
CAfile = c:/bin/certificates.pem

[proxy]
accept  = 12345
connect = pluto:110
```

In the server configuration file, there are three additional keys: verify, CApath, and CAfile. The key verify is used to assign the authentication level. When the authentication level is set to 2, it means all communications must be authenticated; otherwise, all communications must be rejected. If the verification level is set to 3, then it means verify the signature of the certificate. To do that, the public key of the signing authority has to be installed.

The key CApath refers to a directory where the individual certificates are installed. The client-side configuration file referenced the file client.pem, which must be located in the directory specified by the key CApath. When the client.pem is added to the server, the filename identifier of the certificate is the hash value of the certificate. The hash values are computed using the following command:

```
openssl x509 -hash -noout -in client.pem
```

When the command is executed, a hexadecimal number is generated. That hexadecimal number is appended with a .0 and represents the name of the client certificate that is stored in the directory of the key CApath.

Another way of adding certificates is to store the certificate data within the file defined by the key CAfile. An example certificate file is shown as follows:

```
---BEGIN CERTIFICATE---
...
---END CERTIFICATE---
---BEGIN CERTIFICATE---
...
---END CERTIFICATE---
---BEGIN CERTIFICATE---
...
---END CERTIFICATE---
```

In the example certificate file, each boundary (BEGIN CERTIFICATE, END CERTIFICATE) represents one certificate. The data that is copied from client.pem is added in between a boundary. Using either the single file or a directory to manage the client certificates on the server is acceptable; there is no real advantage either way. This choice is up to the administrator and should be scripted to make maintenance simpler.

After both the client and server configuration files have been defined, any communications attempted will involve exchanging certificates and authentication information. The entire process is transparent to the calling application and happens automatically.

If for some reason the authentication does not work or STunnel is not working, then a trace can be added. A trace is useful because it generates a log file that may contain some additional information that can be used to figure out the problem. A trace is added by defining a debugging flag. By adding the debugging flag in the configuration file, more information is output to the log window. The following text block sets `debug` key as the highest level of debug output. The `debug` key is put in the global section of the configuration file:

```
debug = 7
```

PROJECT: OPENVPN

Security and privacy over the Internet can be very difficult to achieve. Security and privacy is a must for those people who work "on the road" and need to access their networks at the company. At one time, the Internet was relatively safe, but with the popularization of the technology, the Internet has become akin to the Wild West. Many people think creating stronger and tougher laws will help "clean up" the Internet. The reality is that regulation has its limits on the Internet, so preventative measures are necessary for a company to protect itself.

VPNs are networks where people that may not be on the same physical network can virtually share the same workspace. For example, a worker might log on to the corporate network while working on the road. Using a VPN, the user can securely log into the corporate network and interact with the corporate network computers without anyone else being able to log in. VPNs are very secure when implemented properly. VPNs are about the most difficult type of networks to hack into.

OpenVPN is a project that originally started as a simple way to create secure networks. OpenVPN does not use IPSEC and is not a kernel-level modification to the TCP/IP stack. The entire OpenVPN application executes within the user space of the operating system so that the OpenVPN application can be portable across operating systems. A VPN can be created with OpenVPN in different configurations and using different encryption algorithms. The reference information for the OpenVPN project is defined in Table 4.7.

TABLE 4.7 Reference Information for OpenVPN

Item	*Description*
Home page	*http://openvpn.sourceforge.net/*
Version	At the time of this writing, the version is 2.0.
Installation	The OpenVPN project has a compressed archive, and a Windows installation file.
Dependencies	The OpenVPN tools are self-contained, but they do depend on the OpenSSL libraries. If another application requires the OpenSSL libraries, be careful not to mix versions, as it could have undesired consequences.
	The OpenVPN tools *only* work on Windows NT, 2000, and XP operating systems (including Server editions). The OpenVPN tools *will not* work on Windows 95, 98, or Me.
Documentation	The documentation for the OpenVPN project is acceptable if OpenVPN is executing on Linux/FreeBSD operating systems. For the Windows operating system, the documentation is entirely incomplete.
Mailing Lists	The mailing lists that are available are located at *http://sourceforge.net/mail/?group_id=48978*. The mailing list of most use to the administrator is openvpn-users. If you need help with OpenVPN, use the mailing list.
Impatient Installation Time Required	Download size: 1.8 MB.
	Installation time: 30-45 minutes. The main issue in setting up OpenVPN is being able to set up the environment.
Firewall Port	5000, but the port can be defined to whatever the administrator wants.
DVD Location	Due to legal issues, the DVD does not contain any files.

Additional Notes

Installing the OpenVPN application on Windows is simple. The problem is getting OpenVPN to do something useful. The context is that OpenVPN is very easy to install and run simple demos. The hard part is making OpenVPN interact with the network on both ends. It isn't impossible, but it can be tricky. The Windows administrator needs to understand network routing principles because an effective OpenVPN installation requires it.

Deployment and Impatient Installation

There is no impatient installation because the impatient installation requires knowledge about network routing and about how various pieces of the network fit together. Therefore an impatient installation is a deployment.

For the Windows platform, OpenVPN is distributed as a source distribution, and as an installer. It is highly recommended to use the installer. The OpenVPN program installs itself as a virtual network adaptor, which is very difficult to do manually. The downside to this form of deployment is that every computer will need to have the OpenVPN program installed using the GUI-based installer.

To make matters worse, the computer has to be rebooted after the installation has completed. In other words, when deploying OpenVPN, make sure that you have set aside the necessary time.

The installer can be downloaded from the main page of the OpenVPN Web site. After the installer has been copied to the local hard disk, double-click it. Follow the instructions and leave all the default values. During the installation, a dialog box appears saying that the driver to be installed has not been signed and asking if installation should continue. Click the Continue button to finish the installation. After the installation has completed, the computer will not automatically reboot. You have to do that manually and it's required.

After the computer has rebooted, there will be a disconnected network connection as shown in Figure 4.21.

In Figure 4.21, the Local Area Connection 3 Properties dialog box is the OpenVPN driver. The OpenVPN driver is type TAP-WIN32. After the driver has been installed, the driver is not active, and therefore will generate the error message that the network cable is not plugged in. That is an incorrect message because the TAP-WIN32 driver does not expect a plugged in network cable. The message is generated because the driver does not have a running instance of the OpenVPN program to communicate with. To make the network connection active, either the OpenVPN program has to be started from the console or started as a service.

 Do not attempt to configure the TAP-WIN32 driver or configure the properties (e.g., Internet Protocol [TCP/IP]) because that might require a reboot or cause

CAUTION

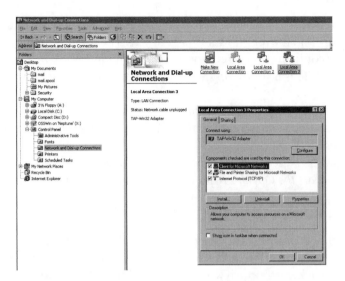

FIGURE 4.21 Network configuration after installing OpenVPN.

*problems in the configuration file. Essentially if items are configured at the driver
level, then the configuration file must not configure those same elements. The simplest way is not to configure anything at the driver level. In client mode, it is usually better to run the OpenVPN as a batch file. However, there is a problem when
running a batch script. It is not possible to dynamically assign using the* ifconfig
*key if the user does not have administrative rights. To get around this problem, the
IP address will have to be set manually on the TAP-WIN32 driver.*

Technique: Installing OpenVPN as a Service

When using the OpenVPN installation program, the OpenVPN service is installed but
not activated. To activate the OpenVPN service, the service must be set to start automatically. The OpenVPN process is bootstrapped by the application openvpnserv.exe.
The application openvpnserv.exe reads the registry for configuration information used
to start the OpenVPN process. The registry information is located under the key
HKEY_LOCAL_MACHINE\SOFTWARE\OpenVPN and contains the following values:

config_dir: Specifies the directory where the configuration files are stored.

config_ext: Specifies the extension used to define an OpenVPN configuration file.

exe_path: Specifies the location for the OpenVPN executables.

log_dir: Specifies the location where the service will output the logging information.

priority: Specifies the priority of the OpenVPN process, which should be left
as is.

When the `openvpnserver.exe` process starts, it reads the registry value `config_dir` and the registry value `config_ext`. The process then iterates each of the files in the configuration directory and starts an OpenVPN process for each configuration file. This is useful on the server side when creating multiple VPNs.

On the client side, using the service is not as simple. You can run the OpenVPN process as a service, except that there are circumstances when the OpenVPN process uses 100 percent of the CPU when the remote network cannot be found. This wastes battery power and slows down other applications. Ideally it would be better to start the OpenVPN process using a batch script, which is activated by the user.

Technique: Creating a Static Key

The power of a VPN is that a client has a difficult time hacking into the network because the network is protected by very strong encryption and secret information that a hacker is not privy to. There are different ways to encrypt the communications between the client and server. The simplest is to use a single secret key. The secret key encrypts the communications between the client and the server, but once connected, the security descriptors are used from the operating system.

When OpenVPN is installed, a menu item is created that autogenerates a static secret key. The Generate a Static OpenVPN Key menu item is shown in Figure 4.22.

Running the command in Figure 4.22 generates a secret key that is stored in the OpenVPN configuration directory. If the default installation is used, then the location of the configuration directory is `c:\Program Files\OpenVPN\config` and the secret filename is `key.txt`.

The secret key can be generated from the command line:

```
openvpn.exe --genkey --secret key.txt
```

The command `openvpn.exe` is located in the directory `c:\Program Files\OpenVPN\bin` and is the main executable for the OpenVPN network. The command-line option `--genkey` is a command to generate a key. The command-line option `--secret` generates a secret key in a file called `key.txt`.

The secret key file is shared on the server by all clients that will be using the same VPN connection. The administrator must be careful to ensure that some hacker does not compromise the private key. The private key solution is used because it is the simplest and does not take long to implement. The problem with using a secret key arises if a hacker manages to steal a computer with a secret key on the machine. At that point the hacker has the ability to gain access to the network regardless of which computer is used. There is no real way around this problem other than using public key authentication.

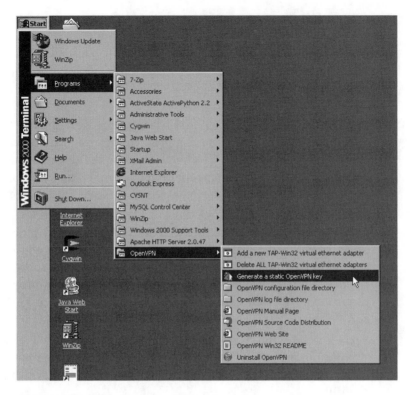

FIGURE 4.22 Generating a secret key from the menu.

Technique: Creating a Peer-to-Peer Network

A VPN is like a network that redirects a port as shown in the earlier section "Technique: Redirecting a Port." The difference with the VPN is that the user does not need to redirect the port manually because the VPN will manage the redirection automatically. VPNs are like SSL tunnels and use the same encryption technologies. The simplest VPN to create is a peer-to-peer VPN where the client sees the server and the server sees the client.

OpenVPN uses a local file and not the registry to configure the VPN. To establish communications between the client and the server, the client and server must have a configuration file. The server waits for a client to connect. The following text is a sample server configuration file:

```
dev tap
ifconfig 10.3.0.1 10.3.0.2
secret key.txt
ping 10
comp-lzo
```

```
verb 3
mute 10
```

The example configuration file defines a minimal server configuration file. The individual keys are explained as follows:

dev: Defines how the connection will be made between the client and the server. The value `tap` creates an Ethernet protocol connection, whereas the value `tun` creates an IP connection. The value must be the same on the client and the server. When the virtual network driver listens, it will listen either at the Ethernet protocol level, or at the higher-level IP level. For the scope of this book, the choice is `tap`.

ifconfig: Defines the IP address that the TAP-WIN32 adaptor will be exposed as, and the IP address of the associated peer. Both of these addresses are the virtual addresses used for VPN communications. If the IP address is assigned in the dialog box shown earlier in Figure 4.20, then using this option will generate an error. It is best to use this option and not assign the TAP-WIN32 adaptor.

secret: Defines the secret key that the client and server will be using for communication purposes. The key should be the same one on both the client and server. Ideally the key should be exchanged on a secure network before using the VPN.

ping: Sends a ping from the client to the server whenever there has been no communication between the server and client. The delay is specified by the value in terms of seconds.

comp-lzo: Uses LZO compression when sending packets over the Internet.

verb: Defines the number of messages that are generated by the application on a scale between 1 and 11. The best level is generally 3 as it displays most messages and errors. The levels 6 and above show debug information.

mute: Suppresses when a certain message is repeatedly output. For example if the same message is output six times and the key value is three, the fourth, fifth, and sixth message are not output.

The client configuration file is almost identical, except the client provides a remote IP address used to connect to the VPN server. The following text is a minimal client configuration file:

```
remote vpn-server.devspace.com
dev tap
ifconfig 10.3.0.2 10.3.0.1
```

```
secret key.txt
ping 10
comp-lzo
verb 3
mute 10
```

The key `remote` references a server that is executing the OpenVPN server process. Also notice that the `ifconfig` key references a different IP address, but is part of the same subnet as the OpenVPN server.

Each configuration file is stored by default within the directory `c:/Program Files/OpenVPN/config`, using the filename `default.ovpn`. This directory is chosen because by default that is where OpenVPN installs into. When the filename has been changed to use the extension `ovpn`, the filename changes icon and is recognized as a registered file type. When you make a context-sensitive click, the icon is added to the menu that starts VPN, per the configuration defined by the icon. For simplicity, you can start a VPN by selecting the menu item. Another way to start the VPN is to use the command line defined as follows:

```
openvpn.exe --config default.ovpn
```

To create the VPN connection, the server is started before the client, and the server is started as follows:

```
openvpn.exe --config vpn-server.conf
```

The client is started as follows:

```
openvpn.exe --config vpn-client.conf
```

On both sides, the generated output should be similar to the following:

```
centaur:~ cgross# openvpn-2.0_beta11/openvpn --config test.conf
Mon Aug 23 10:58:21 2004 OpenVPN 2.0_beta11
[SSL] built on Aug 19 2004
Mon Aug 23 10:58:21 2004 Static Encrypt: Cipher 'BF-CBC' initialized
 with 128 bit key
Mon Aug 23 10:58:21 2004 Static Encrypt: Using 160 bit message hash
'SHA1' for HMAC authentication
Mon Aug 23 10:58:21 2004 Static Decrypt: Cipher 'BF-CBC' initialized
with 128 bit key
Mon Aug 23 10:58:21 2004 Static Decrypt: Using 160 bit message hash
'SHA1' for HMAC authentication
Mon Aug 23 10:58:21 2004 Data Channel MTU parms
```

```
[ L:1544 D:1450 EF:44 EB:0 ET:0 EL:0 ]
Mon Aug 23 10:58:21 2004 Local Options hash (VER=V4): '09bcadc2'
Mon Aug 23 10:58:21 2004 Expected Remote Options hash
(VER=V4): 'd6e09596'
Mon Aug 23 10:58:21 2004 UDPv4 link local (bound): [undef]:5000
Mon Aug 23 10:58:21 2004 UDPv4 link remote: 212.254.35.68:5000
Mon Aug 23 10:58:29 2004 Peer Connection Initiated with
212.254.35.68:5000
Mon Aug 23 10:58:29 2004 Initialization Sequence Completed
```

If everything went well on both the client and the server, the last message states that the connection has completed. At that moment, the client and server see each other. From the client, the command ping is used to test the connection to server:

```
centaur:~ cgross$ ping 10.3.0.1
PING 10.3.0.1 (10.3.0.1): 56 data bytes
64 bytes from 10.3.0.1: icmp_seq=0 ttl=64 time=222.602 ms
64 bytes from 10.3.0.1: icmp_seq=1 ttl=64 time=203.456 ms
```

With a connection, the client can use all the services on the server. There are a couple of issues to consider, however:

- You can only manipulate the resources of the server and not the network that the server is connected to. Routes need to be added to see the rest of the server's network.
- The server can process only one client connection at a time. For more than one connection, more than one server instance has to be running and they each must use a different port.

TIP

When setting up an example, VPN is the safest way to use two entirely different physical networks. For example, people will access the corporate network using public Internet providers. When testing, use a public Internet provider to access the corporate network. Make sure that the server is in a safe zone. Using a public Internet provider makes sure that you do not miss any small implementation detail. Setting up a VPN can be tricky and you will be battling other problems without having to also battle test configuration issues.

Technique: Setting Up a Network

The most complicated part of a VPN is setting up the infrastructure and then properly routing the packets from one machine to the other machine. As an example, a VPN might be set up for both wireless users and Internet users. It is highly recommended to set up a VPN for wireless such as WiFi because wireless networks can be cracked in several hours even if WEP security and MAC address filtering is used. Only a VPN will ensure the maximum amount of security.

The example presented is just a prototype intended to show a simple scenario, using simple tools. A corporate network administrator can easily scale the concepts shown for their own scenario. The example scenario assumes all machines involved are at least Windows 2000 Professional.

For example, to route packets from one computer network adaptor to another, the command route is used. The Windows Server operating system editions support dynamic routing such as Routing Information Protocol (RIP), Open Shortest-Path First Interior Gateway Protocol (OSPF), or even the GUI Routing and Remote Access Service (RRAS). However, using those tools is beyond the scope of this book. The essentials include how the packets need to be routed using static routes put in place by the console-based route command.

Enabling IP Forwarding

To route packets across a computer that has multiple interface adaptors, IP routing must be enabled. In Windows NT, IP forwarding was an option that could be checked, however, with later editions of Windows operating systems, that option has been removed. The option still exists, but it must be activated by using a registry setting. Of course, if you are using any Windows Server operating system, then it can be activated using the routing administrative tools. Figure 4.23 shows the Registry Editor and the highlighted registry value.

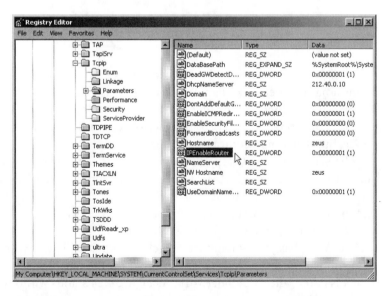

FIGURE 4.23 Registry setting used to activate IP forwarding.

In Figure 4.23, the value `IPEnableRouter` can be found under the key `HKEY_LOCAL_MACHINE\SYSTEM\CurrentControlSet\Services\Tcpip\Parameters`. The default value is 0, which should be changed to 1 as shown earlier in Figure 4.22. After the value has been changed, the computer must be restarted. This feature of activating routing works in Windows XP Professional, and Windows 2000 Professional.

Example Scenario

The example scenario is shown in Figure 4.24.

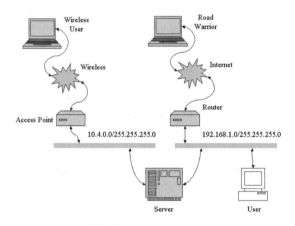

FIGURE 4.24 Example scenario architecture.

In Figure 4.24, the example scenario shows a `Server` that is dual homed, which means it has two network adaptors. The `Server` is connected to two networks with different IP subnets. The `10.4.0.0` subnet is the wireless subnet, and the `192.168.1.0` subnet is the corporate network. A `Router` could have replaced the `Server`, but that would complicate things.

The `Server` has the OpenVPN server process running on it with the `ifconfig` value of `10.3.0.1`. The `Wireless User` connects to the wireless network and is part of the `10.4.0.0` subnet. The `Road Warrior` is part of the Internet. Both want to connect to the `192.168.1.0` subnet and be part of that network. The `Wireless User` and `Road Warrior` do not have to have IP addresses in the `192.168.1.0` subnet.

The VPN has its own subnet, which is `10.3.0.0`. The `Server` has to manage three subnets, and the challenge is to program the network so that the `10.3.0.0` subnet is part of the overall network. As Figure 4.24 stands without any routing information, the `Wireless User` can access the `Server`, but cannot access the `User` and the Road Warrior. The Road Warrior cannot access the Server, the Wireless User, or the User. The Server can access the User and the Wireless User, but not the Road Warrior. So far, the network is relatively secure, with the exception of the Wireless User being able to access the Server, but that will be fixed a bit later in this section.

The server configuration file has to be changed:

```
#local 192.168.1.240

port 5000
proto udp
dev tun0
server 10.3.0.0 255.255.255.0
push "route 192.168.1.0 255.255.255.0"
#push "redirect-gateway"
#client-to-client
secret key.txt
keepalive 10 60
#tls-auth ta.key 0
max-clients 100
status openvpn-status.log
pull
verb 4
mute 20
```

The server configuration has changed quite a bit and the individual identifiers are explained as follows:

client-to-client: Allows clients to see each other and exchange Internet packets.

local: An optional identifier that binds the OpenVPN service to a specific IP when the server is multihomed.

keepalive: Determines when a client connection has gone dead. In the example, a ping is sent every 10 seconds and the server waits 60 seconds. If there is no receiving ping, then the connection is terminated.

max-clients: Controls the maximum number of client connections an Open-VPN server process will manage.

port: Defines the listening port for the OpenVPN service.

proto: Identifies the Internet protocol used to communicate to the client, and should be kept to UDP for efficiency purposes.

pull: A required keyword that instructs the client to retrieve any additional configuration information from the server.

push: Pushes commands from the server to the client, when the client connects. In the example server configuration, there are two sample commands: route and redirect-gateway. The route command defines a route and replaces the up.sh and down.sh commands. The up.sh and down.sh commands were shown to illustrate the use of the route command, and must be used when static OpenVPN IP addresses are used. The server-side route commands must still be added, however, because OpenVPN does not manage that. The redirect-gateway command is a special form of route that makes the OpenVPN connection the default route for all packets.

server: Identifies a subnet that the server will push to the client when a client connects to the server.

status: This identifier outputs the status of current connections and other informational data. The file openvpn-status.log is rewritten every minute.

tls-auth: When exposing port 5000 to the external world, it is possible to get a denial-of-service (DoS) attack. The DoS is a form of hacker attack that can be prevented by using the tls-auth keyword. Using the tls-auth keyword forces a validation based on some secret key defined by the file ta.key. The number 0 indicates that the keyword is used in a server configuration file, and 1 indicates a client configuration file. Note that if the tls-auth keyword is to function it must be present in both a client and server configuration.

Let's focus on the configuration of the Wireless User. The Wireless User starts a VPN process and connects itself to the Server. The configuration files used by the client are different than the peer-to-peer network because there will be multiple users accessing the Server machine. Following is an example configuration file:

```
client
dev tun
proto udp
remote vpn-server.devspace.com 5000
resolv-retry infinite
nobind
verb 4
mute 20
secret key.txt
```

The configuration used is an OpenVPN 2.0 configuration example where the client identifier means that the client connection is being defined. By defining a client configuration, the server can send configuration parameters, such as an IP address, to the client. Also new is the proto identifier, which signals to use the UDP when sending OpenVPN packets. Do not use TCP as it adds unnecessary overhead that OpenVPN already manages. The remote identifier is modified to the number 5000, which means to use port 5000 when connecting to the remote server.

The Wireless User can connect to the server, but any attempt to access the 192.168.1.0 network will fail. The packets will fail because the IP packets have to be routed from one subnet to another subnet. To create the desired route for the packets of 10.3.0.0 subnet to the 192.168.1.0 subnet, the routing table of the Wireless User has to be modified. Using the route command, the routing table is generated and shown as follows (this routing table is for the Wireless User):

```
C:\WINDOWS\system32\drivers\etc>route print
===============================================================
Interface List
0x1 ......................... MS TCP Loopback interface
0x2 ...00 08 74 04 05 56 ......
3Com 3C920 Integrated Fast Ethernet Controller (3C905C-TX Compatible
) - Packet Scheduler Miniport
0x3 ...00 c0 49 bc c5 09 ......
U.S. Robotics 22Mbps Wireless Lan Adapter -
Packet Scheduler Miniport
0x4 ...00 ff 1a 6d 87 4a ......
TAP-Win32 Adapter - Packet Scheduler Miniport
===============================================================
===============================================================
Active Routes:
Network Destination     Netmask        Gateway       Interface      Metric
0.0.0.0            0.0.0.0           10.4.0.1     10.4.0.101    20
10.3.0.0           255.255.255.0     10.3.0.5     4             30
10.3.0.5           255.255.255.255   127.0.0.1    127.0.0.1     30
10.4.0.0           255.255.255.0     10.4.0.101   10.4.0.101    20
10.4.0.101         255.255.255.255   127.0.0.1    127.0.0.1     20
10.255.255.255     255.255.255.255   10.3.0.5     4             30
10.255.255.255     255.255.255.255   10.4.0.101   10.4.0.101    20
127.0.0.0          255.0.0.0         127.0.0.1    127.0.0.1     1
224.0.0.0          240.0.0.0         10.3.0.5     4             30
224.0.0.0          240.0.0.0         10.4.0.101   10.4.0.101    20
255.255.255.255    255.255.255.255   10.3.0.5     2             1
255.255.255.255    255.255.255.255   10.3.0.5     4             1
255.255.255.255    255.255.255.255   10.4.0.101   10.4.0.101    1
Default Gateway:            10.4.0.1
===============================================================
Persistent Routes:
  None
```

The generated output has a bunch of numbers grouped in different columns. A routing table is a simple set of rules that tell what will be done with network packets. Routing is similar to delivering a letter from one person to another. The letter is addressed to a certain person, but how to get to the other person is not known. Most people would use a map and look at the streets that they need to pass and intersections that they need to cross. Things get tricky when you have to use an intersection to go from one street to another. Consider the intersection as the router.

The difference with the Internet and packets is that there is no map. Instead, the packets are instructed on the fly concerning how to reach a destination. The way that the Internet addresses all combinations is to use IP addresses and subnet masks. The routing table generated by the command `route print` contains a bunch of road signs that tell where a packet must be sent.

There are five parts to a route:

`Network Destination`: Defines the place where you want to go. This is used in combination with the `Netmask`.

`Netmask`: Defines the subnet mask that is used with the `Network Destination` to define a subblock of IP addresses.

`Gateway`: Defines the IP address where the packet should be sent if the packet is part of the subblock of IP addresses.

`Interface`: Defines the network adaptor from where the packet should be arriving. This could be an IP address or a simple numeric identifier that references a network adaptor output by the `route print` command.

`Metric`: Defines the importance of the route, which is necessary when a packet could be sent using two different routes.

To fully understand the routing table, it is important to understand IP addresses and subnet mask addressing. A couple of URLs that might be helpful for calculating subnets are *http://www.networkclue.com/routing/tcpip/calculating-masks.php* and *http://www.wundermoosen.com/TMAHelp/pgs/IPmask.htm*.

The problem right now is that the routing table routes all packets (0.0.0.0/0.0.0.0) to the gateway 10.4.0.1, which is incorrect. The VPN should be used to manage all packets and not the physical network. The way to change the routing information is to modify the routing table within the configuration file shown as follows:

```
client
dev tun
proto udp
remote vpn-server.devspace.com 5000
resolv-retry infinite
```

```
nobind
verb 4
mute 20
secret key.txt
up upwirelessnetwork.sh
down upwirelessnetwork.sh
```

Notice in the modified configuration, the use of the keys up and down. The key up is used to run a script when the VPN device has been opened. The key down is used to run a script after the VPN device has been closed. The scripts are used to add the routing information. You can add the route commands into the configuration file, but that will be shown in the server configuration example. If the scripts are used, then it is necessary for the server to give each client a fixed IP.

Following is the up script used to modify the routing of all packets to the VPN adaptor:

```
route change 0.0.0.0 MASK 0.0.0.0 10.3.0.1 METRIC 20
```

Now all the packets not destined for the local machine will be routed to the OpenVPN subnet. The OpenVPN server automatically forwards the IP packets and they arrive at their destination.

Testing this configuration using the command ping will result in lost packets because a problem still exists. The problem that still exists is very common, and has to do with the fact that the configuration is not finished.

Looking back at Figure 4.24, the reply from any machine on the 192.168.1.0 subnet is sent to the router because the routing table of each machine on the 192.168.1.0 will define the router as the gateway. In routing terms, this means if there is a packet not intended for the 192.168.1.0 subnet, the router is sent the packet and the router has to figure it out. The router sees the packet intended for the VPN and sends it to the Internet, which is the incorrect answer and causes the packet to be lost.

The solution is to provide a route back to the machine on the VPN. In that case, it means that the User machine needs to add a route similar to the following:

```
route add 10.3.0.0 MASK 255.255.255.0 192.168.1.240
```

The added route instructs the User computer to send the packet to the Server (192.168.1.240), which is the gateway for the OpenVPN server process. After the OpenVPN server process receives the packet, it knows how to send the packet to the Wireless User.

It is possible to update all the computers on a subnet with the correct route to the VPN. More likely though is that the administrator will add the route to the router so that there is only one place to update the route if in the future the route changes again. To add a route to a router, consult the router documentation.

The purpose of the down key in the modified script is to restore the old routes of the networking card when the VPN is not running. The down script is defined as follows:

```
route add 0.0.0.0 MASK 0.0.0.0 10.4.0.1 METRIC 20
```

Note the add command is used instead of change because when the VPN shuts down, all associated routes are deleted; in other words, the main route is deleted and the computer will have no idea where to send any packets.

The configuration for the Road Warrior who is using the Internet from another provider uses a very similar configuration. In fact, the exact same configuration could be used, other than the value of the remote key. The IP of the remote host would not be 10.4.0.1, but whatever the Router in Figure 4.24 exposes. The downside to this approach is that all packets will be routed via the home network, which for idle Web surfing might not be the most useful. The surfing packets would be routed to the VPN network, then the VPN server, then to the router, and finally to the Internet. The solution is to modify the up script defined previously to the script defined as follows:

```
route add 192.168.1.0 MASK 255.255.255.0 10.3.0.1
```

The down script does not need to exist because when the VPN connection stops so will the route defined to reroute private packets to the home network.

There is one small issue with defining a network using this fashion. The subnet 192.168.0.0 defines a default block used by many routers. Hence the problem could be that the Road Warrior could have an IP address that is part of the subnet block, which also exists in the corporate network. The route command will work and make the correct servers visible. What becomes invisible are the local servers that exist as part of the local subnet. Often this is not a problem, but if it is a problem, then more sophisticated routing is required. The corporate network subnet might even need to be remapped to something other than 192.168.1.0.

Securing the Ports

One of the problems in the architecture shown in Figure 4.24 is that the Wireless User can access the Server. Therefore, it is absolutely imperative that the Server is only a routing server and does not contain any data or applications. There are other ways to secure the network and other configurations, but that is beyond the scope of this book. A firewall could be installed on the `Server` computer that will filter the packets from the `10.4.0.0` subnet.

Technique: Using Certificates for Authentication

The static shared key technique is simple, but not as secure as using OpenSSL certificates. When using OpenSSL certificates in the context of OpenVPN, OpenVPN acts as a trusted signature authority. Any keys used by the client and server must be signed by the trusted signature.

For OpenVPN to become a signing authority, the public and private key certificates have to be created using the following command:

```
openssl req -nodes -new -x509 -config openvpn.conf
-keyout ca.key -out ca.crt -days 3650
```

In the command example, the CA certificate is created and will last 10 years. The configuration file used is similar to those used when creating a generic SSL certificate, except the individual fields are generated for a VPN authority certificate.

The Diffie-Hellman parameters have to be created using the command defined as follows:

```
openssl dhparam -out dh1024.pem 1024
```

The Diffie-Hellman parameters are a way for two hosts to share secret keys without giving the secret keys away. The output file `dh1024.pem` is not used to encrypt communications, but key exchange.

To make the communications work, the client and the server have to generate their own private keys and public keys. For this example, the client will be called `user` and the server `corporate`. To create the `corporate` public keys and have them signed, the following commands are used:

```
openssl req -config openvpn.conf -nodes -new
-keyout corporate.key -out corporate.csr
openssl ca -config openssl.conf -in corporate.csr -out corporate.crt
```

The same commands are executed to generate the `user` certificates, except the identifier `corporate` is replaced with `user`.

The generated files `ca.crt`, `dh1024.pem`, `corporate.key`, and `corporate.crt` are copied to the server configuration directory. The generated files `ca.crt`, `user.crt`, and `user.key` are copied to the client configuration directory. The file `ca.crt` is copied to both the client and server configuration directories because it is the public key of signing authority. When either the client or server is presented with a public key, the client or server tests the key and checks whether the correct authority signed it. This ensures that only keys and users allowed by the administrator will use the VPN.

To make everything work, the client and server configuration files have to be updated. The key `secret` is commented out and replaced with the correct keys. The following server configuration file shows the added keys:

```
tls-server
dh dh1024.pem
ca ca.crt
cert corporate.crt
key corporate.key
```

The added keys are defined as follows:

tls-server: Defines TLS-SSL communications between the client and server.

dh: References the generated Diffie-Hellman parameter file.

ca: Defines the public key of the signing authority.

cert: Defines the local VPN process signed public key.

key: Defines the local VPN process private key.

On the client machine, the `secret` key is also commented out. The following client configuration file shows the added keys:

```
tls-client
ca ca.crt
cert user.crt
key user.key
```

The client configuration keys appear similar to the previously defined server configuration file, but there are a couple of changes. Instead of using `tls-server`, the key `tls-client` is used to indicate a client configuration. The keys `cert` and `key` refer to local VPN process keys. When the client and server OpenVPN services start, they will do a handshake and exchange keys very similarly to the SSL protocol itself. A different client does not need to use the same public/private key combination. The idea with using PKI is that each remote user is given a public/private key.

Technique: Disabling a VPN User

When using PKI to manage the VPN connection, each computer or user will get a public/private key. If the computer is stolen, however, then the administrator can block the computer by revoking the certificate of the stolen computer. In the GnuPG section "Technique: Creating and Deleting Keys," you saw how to revoke a key. Those techniques are similar, but not identical to revoking a key for Open-VPN. What happens is that when SSL certificates are signed, a database is kept. To disable the user, the certificate has to be disabled in the database. The disabled certificate is then copied to the OpenVPN database.

In the "Technique: Becoming a Signing Authority" section, you saw how to configure the openssl.conf configuration file. When managing certificates for OpenVPN, the openssl.conf file needs to be defined so that the database of signed certificates is kept in a central location. Following is a modified openssl.conf configuration file:

```
[ ca ]
default_ca      = CA_default

[ CA_default ]

dir             = c:/bin/certificates
database        = $dir/db/index.txt
new_certs_dir   = $dir/db/newcerts

certificate     = $dir/ca.crt
serial          = $dir/db/serial.txt
private_key     = $dir/ca.key
RANDFILE        = $dir/temp/openssl.rnd

default_days    = 365
default_crl_days= 30
default_md      = md5

policy          = policy_any
email_in_dn     = no

nameopt         = ca_default
certopt         = ca_default
copy_extensions = none

[ policy_any ]
countryName             = supplied
stateOrProvinceName     = optional
```

```
organizationName        = optional
organizationalUnitName  = optional
commonName              = supplied
emailAddress            = optional
```

Notice in the modified configuration file that the directories for the keys `data-base`, `new_certs_dir`, `serial`, and `RANDFILE` have been modified to use subdirectories. This is done so that the generated files do not interfere with the configuration files. A copy of the subdirectory `db` needs to be kept somewhere safe because it contains all keys that have been signed.

The file `index.txt` contains references to all certificates that have been signed. An example `index.txt` file is shown as follows:

```
V 041113131015Z 1238 unknown
    /C=CH/ST=ZH/O=vpn.devspace.com/OU=NA/CN=corporate
V 041113131057Z 1239 unknown
    /C=CH/ST=ZH/O=vpn.devspace.com/OU=NA/CN=user
```

In the example `index.txt` file, two public keys have been signed. The distinguished name of the certificate is given by the last column and is used to figure out which certificate is which. For example, the part `O=vpn.devspace.com` corresponds to the field value `O.organizationName` in modified `openssl.conf` file. The part `CN=corporate` corresponds to the field value `O.commonName`. Notice how the `vpn` organization name, the `devspace.com` domain name, and the common name (`corporate` or `user`) relate to the user or computer identifier.

To revoke the certificate for the user, either use the signed public key that is distributed, or use the file within the `newcerts` directory. The name of the certificate is the third column of the `index.txt` file. The following command shows how to revoke the user certificate:

```
openssl ca -config openssl.conf -revoke 1239.crt
```

After running the command, the user certificate will be recognized as revoked and you can generate a Certificate Revoked Listing (CRL). The OpenVPN process uses the CRL data to reject specific signed public keys. The following command generates a CRL:

```
openssl ca -config openssl.conf -gencrl -out revoked.txt
Finally the CRL file is referenced in the server configuration file:
crl-verify revoked.txt
```

The key `crl-verify` is a list of revoked certificates that is checked whenever a client connects. If the certificate is revoked, then the client will not be able to connect.

SUMMARY

This entire chapter did not discuss how to perform authentication using Windows security because there are two forms of security: user rights and privacy/communication rights. Many people focus on user rights, when in fact privacy rights are just as important.

Privacy rights make it harder for a hacker to hack and get access to your user rights. With privacy rights, the hacker is left solely with a brute force hack attack. Brute force is possible, but choosing the right key length makes a brute force attack not worth the effort. When managing privacy, there are several things to consider. First consider securing the computer. Securing the computer fixes many of the hacking attacks. Part of securing your computer is keeping the computer constantly updated with the latest patches and updates. Nobody writes perfect software, so no software package is hacker proof. The best you can do is keep up to date with the latest patches and updates to make life more complicated for the hacker.

Another key privacy issue is the ability to encrypt communications. There are multiple forms of communications such as documents or applications. Securing communications makes your infrastructure appear like a black box. A black box is harder for hackers to hack and figure out weaknesses.

Putting all the pieces together, a Windows computer becomes very secure and not vulnerable to hackers. The techniques presented do not preclude using other security techniques such as firewalls and Windows security. These techniques are meant to complement a secure computing strategy.

5 Running Tasks on a Local Computer

ABOUT THIS CHAPTER

The focus of this chapter is to illustrate tasks that can be used to simplify the management of a computer's files or resources. Often an administrator wants to solve a simple little problem without raising a big fuss. This chapter tries to solve some of those problems.

The PC became successful because it empowered people and made them more productive. This does not mean that servers are not required, but it does mean that people should be kept empowered. Portable computing devices and people working on the road or from home are also common today, which must be taken into account as you determine how to manage PCs.

The following topics/projects are covered in this chapter:

Script Execution: When managing a computer, it isn't possible to require a user to manually run a script. A script needs to be executed automatically, where the trigger could be starting the computer, shutting down the computer, or some periodic event. The script to be executed could be used to back up data or install patches.

XYNTService: Many scripts and console programs need to run as services. The default Windows Service does not allow the execution of scripts as services. The application XYNTService solves that problem by creating a surrogate service that can be used to start other applications.

VNCServer: Controlling a set of computers was a big issue in the past with Windows. With the release of Windows XP and Windows 2000 or later, terminal services are included that allow a remote client to connect to the computer. This process generally works well. A problem arises, however, when an administrator needs to be in front of the computer to install software or perform some operation. Using VNCServer, you can remotely log in to a computer and act as if you were sitting in front of the computer.

Unison: Copying files is not difficult if only one or two files are copied. The problem arises when one directory needs to be copied to another directory and the other directory contains some files found in the original directory. Copying becomes difficult when decisions have to be made on which file should be copied. Unison is a synchronization tool that can be used to keep two directories up-to-date.

7-Zip: Windows does not include a simple to use and flexible file compression utility. To make up for that void, the 7-Zip application can compress and expand multiple types of archives.

AUTOMATED SCRIPT EXECUTION

One of the most important tasks that an administrator needs to manage is executing scripts. Executing a script from a console is not a challenge. The challenge comes in when you are executing the script when a computer boots or when a user logs in. The administrator might want to execute scripts at those moments to perform upgrades, backups, and other administrative tasks. The Windows operating system allows an administrator to define an automated script in multiple places: computer startup and shutdown, user login and logout, and periodic scripts.

Computer Startup and Shutdown Scripts

A startup or shutdown script is defined using the Group Policy Editor application. The Group Policy Editor is a Microsoft Management Console (MMC) snap-in that is defined, but not referenced, as a menu item or an icon in the Windows operating system. You can start the snap-in by choosing Start and then Run to open the Run dialog box (see Figure 5.1).

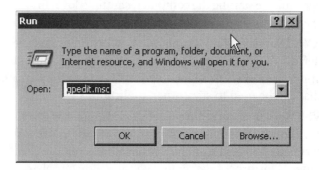

FIGURE 5.1 Dialog box used to run the Group Policy Editor application.

To start the Group Policy Editor, run the application `gpedit.msc` (see Figure 5.2).

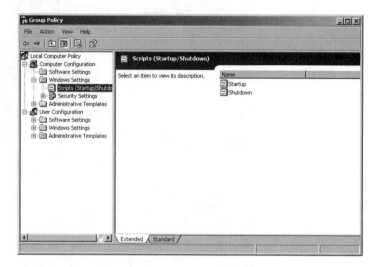

FIGURE 5.2 Group Policy Editor highlighting the startup and shutdown script definitions.

The Group Policy Editor can be used to manage different configuration aspects of the computer including features such as security and user rights when accessing applications. In this section, we'll focus on defining a startup and shutdown script. The entries used to add a startup and shutdown script are located in the Local Computer Policy/Computer Configuration/Windows Settings/Scripts (Startup/Shutdown) directory. Double-click the Startup item to open the Startup Properties dialog box as shown in Figure 5.3.

The Startup Properties dialog box usually contains a number of scripts that can be assigned to when the Windows computer boots. Figure 5.3 shows the default, which is no startup scripts. To add a script, follow these steps:

1. Click the Add button to open the Add a Script dialog box.
2. Define the script that is executed when the startup event is triggered by a booting computer. In Figure 5.3, for example, the script name is the `bash.exe` executable, and the script parameters are a BASH script. Additional command-line parameters could be defined, but that is optional.

You could define an update script with the rebooting of a computer. The problem is is that ideally you do not want your computer to be rebooted. The computer should just continue running. Therefore, for updates it might make more sense to use a periodic task and not run the script on startup or shutdown.

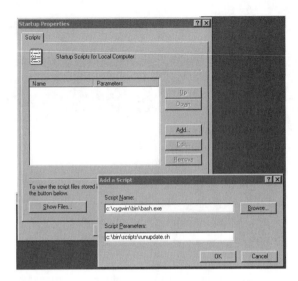

FIGURE 5.3 Startup properties dialog box and dialog box used to add a startup script.

TIP

When a computer starts or stops and a script is executed, the script is not executing in the context of any user. This is extremely important because it can influence the PATH environment variable and the state of the environment. The default is to run under the system account, which does not have a home directory. Therefore, when writing scripts, you shouldn't assume there is a home directory, and if necessary define a command-line parameter that references a file or location that contains the environment settings required.

Profile and Login Scripts

Another way of running scripts involves using a user profile or a login script. When using this approach, the script is executed in the context of an individual user. A profile on a Windows computer represents a number of files and directories that are stored in a single location. Some of the things stored in a profile are menu items or Internet Explorer favorites. A login script has nothing to do with a profile, but is a way of executing a script after someone logs on to a machine. In any case, a script can create network connections or create files. Figure 5.4 shows the user properties dialog box used to assign both a profile and a login script. The dialog box appears when the user is selected from the user list.

In Figure 5.4, the Profile Path text box contains the path where the profile is stored using Windows UNC notation, which contains a server name, network

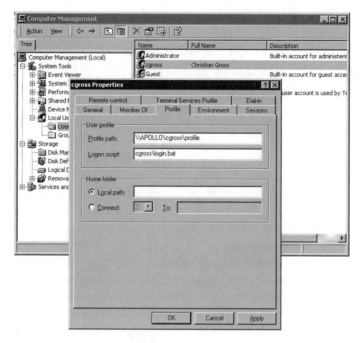

FIGURE 5.4 Dialog box that defines the profile and login script locations.

share, and path. The Login Script text box contains a relative path and a batch file. The batch file should always be a Windows batch file because it reduces complexity and the likelihood that something will go wrong.

TIP

The Profile Path and Login Script text boxes are in the same group box, but that doesn't mean they are related. The two text boxes have nothing to do with each other. Each text box requires a path where the data is stored. The content of the Profile Path text box is absolute and the content of the Login Script text box is always relative. Note that entering an absolute path for the Login Script text box will generate an error.

The profile path is used when a user logs on and logs off. The profile is used to store the settings of an individual user that are loaded and saved each time a user logs on and logs off. In Figure 5.4, the profile path is the UNC location \\APOLLO\cgross\profile. In production if the administrator were to inspect the contents of the profile path with the contents of the directory C:\Documents and Settings\cgross, which is the user's local directory settings, there will be identical files.

The idea of a profile path is that users store their settings on a remote server and when a user logs on any machine, those

settings are downloaded and stored locally. Then regardless of which machine users log on to, they will have the same settings. Of course, this assumes that the various machines users log on to are identical or at least have all the important applications and settings in the same location. If necessary, the administrator can manually manipulate the directories and files, which would have the effect of manipulating the user's desktop. The administrator manipulates the profile files on the server, and then these files are automatically downloaded when the user logs in, thus installing new applications and configuration settings.

The logon script is a bit more complicated. In Figure 5.4, the logon script that is called depends on where the user's credentials are stored. The credentials of the user is the place where the user's security information and group information is stored. If the user's credentials are stored locally, because the user is not part of a Windows domain, then the logon script must be stored locally. If the user logged in to a Windows domain, then the logon script is hosted on the Windows domain controller (DC). The path entered in the Login Script text box is a relative path to where Windows has determined login scripts can be referenced.

To understand the logic, let's consider an example. If a user is in the process of logging in to an account managed by the local computer (Windows XP, NT, or 2000), Windows will search for a local share called `netlogon`. If the share is found, the relative path for the logon script is appended to the share. Using Figure 5.4 as an example, the complete UNC path would be `\\[LOCAL MACHINE]\netlogon\cgross\login.bat`. The script referenced by the UNC path would be executed. As the script executes, files on the network can be referenced, downloaded, and executed. After the logon script has finished, executing the user is logged in.

When the user logs in to an account managed by a Windows DC, the exact same steps occur, except the UNC path is not local, but is determined by the Windows controller. More about the Windows DC is discussed in Chapter 6, "Authentication and Managing Files."

Using the profile approach is not that much different than using a login script approach. The same script is used, but the location of the script differs. The location used is the Startup menu as shown in Figure 5.5.

Going back to Figure 5.4, the profile path was defined to be on the network. Figure 5.5 shows the file server that stores the profile. The profile information is taken from the `c:\Document and Settings\[User]` directory. In Figure 5.5, the directory `Start Menu` corresponds to the Start menu that is used in Windows (2000, XP, and so on). The folders within correspond to menu items that the user sees on the desktop. Windows has a special menu item called the Startup menu. Any file within the Startup menu item is executed when the user logs on the machine. In effect, the Startup menu is like a login script. The difference is that the Startup menu is generally used by applications that are installed on the local computer. A script

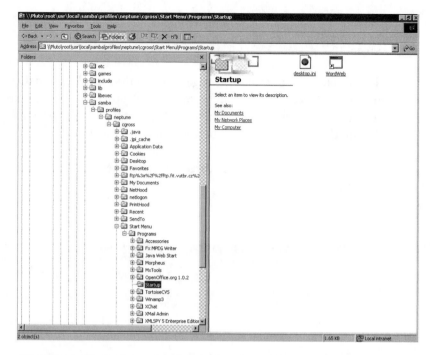

FIGURE 5.5 File Explorer showing the location of the Startup menu item.

could reference files stored in the profile including executable files to perform up-dates or backups. As a convention, the menu items are links to files on the hard disk. That is a convention and not a rule, and there is no reason you shouldn't embed a script in the menu.

Profiles are managed like files. You can manage a profile using the registry, but for the open source administrator, files are preferred. A profile can contain directories as shown in Figure 5.5. The profiles that are stored on the server could be manip-ulated using scripts and could embed executables. The only practical limitation is that the profiles do not embed multimegabyte files, which would cause unnecessary network traffic and potentially create bandwidth problems.

Running Tasks Periodically

Some tasks need to be run periodically, which could be every hour, every day, or every certain time period. For example, a periodic task could be the update of the Cygwin toolkit. Using the Scheduled Task Wizard, periodic tasks can be easily defined. For ex-ample purposes, the following simple script will be executed as a periodic script:

```
#!/bin/bash
echo "hello world"
sleep 10
```

The simple script outputs a message to the console window, and then sleeps for 10 seconds. The `sleep` command is important so that a user can see the output generated by the script. Otherwise, a flash occurs and the user has no idea what happened.

To run the simple script as a periodic task, follow these steps:

1. Click the Control Panel directory, and then click Scheduled Tasks (see Figure 5.6).

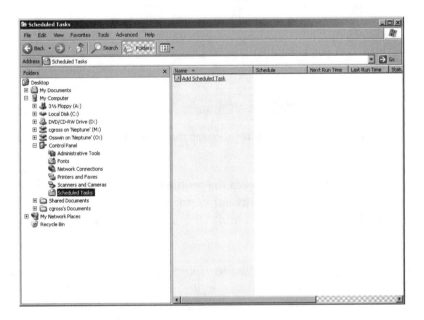

FIGURE 5.6 Scheduled Tasks shown in Windows Explorer.

2. Double-click the Add Scheduled Task icon to open the first Scheduled Task Wizard dialog box as shown in Figure 5.7.
3. Click the Next button to go to the next wizard dialog box as shown in Figure 5.8.

FIGURE 5.7 First dialog box of the Scheduled Task Wizard.

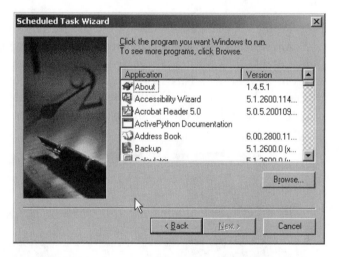

FIGURE 5.8 Dialog box that selects the application to run.

4. At this step select anything, as it does not matter. At a later step, the command line will be refined. Click the Next button to go to the next dialog box as shown in Figure 5.9.

The dialog box in Figure 5.8 is out of place. The purpose of the dialog box is to allow you to select an application to run either from the listbox or by using the Browse button. The problem is that it's not easy to specify exactly what script is executed.

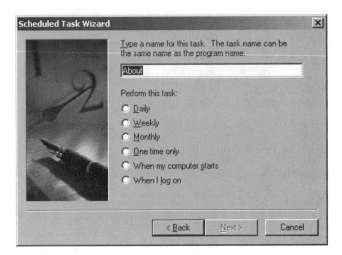

FIGURE 5.9 Dialog box used to define the title and period
of the task.

5. In Figure 5.9, change the name for the task from About to something more meaningful. The default text used as a name is the same as the name of the executable chosen from the dialog box in Figure 5.8.
6. From the Perform This Task list, select one of the periods to use when starting the application (for this example, choose Monthly). Click Next to go to the next dialog box as shown in Figure 5.10.

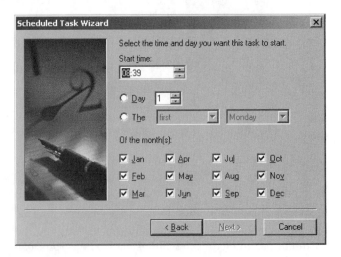

FIGURE 5.10 Dialog box used to define the period specifics
for the monthly time period.

TIP

If you choose the When My Computer Starts radio button, the necessary security privileges will typically require administrative rights.

TIP

The exact look of Figure 5.10 depends on which time period is selected from the dialog box in Figure 5.9. This dialog box enables you to refine the period specifics.

7. Define the months, day of the month, and time when the task will be executed as shown in Figure 5.10. Click Next.
8. The dialog box in Figure 5.11 is very important because it defines the security rights of the task that will be executed. It is important to know if the script will need administrative rights. For example, installing applications for all users will require administrative rights. To complete the task definition, type in the appropriate user and password and click Next. The final dialog box is shown in Figure 5.12.

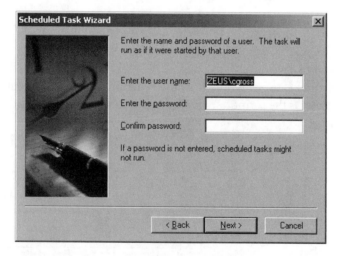

FIGURE 5.11 Dialog box used to define the user and password for script execution.

9. Check the Open Advanced Properties… checkbox so that the script can be properly defined.

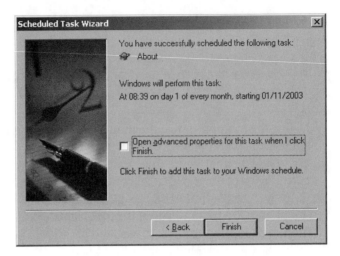

FIGURE 5.12 Final dialog box that is displayed before creating the scheduled task.

10. Click the Finish button to open the About dialog box as shown in Figure 5.13.

In Figure 5.13, the text in the Run text box has been modified to run the script `hello.sh`. Notice how the program `bash.exe` is executed and the first parameter is the script to run. The script name is enclosed in double quotes because

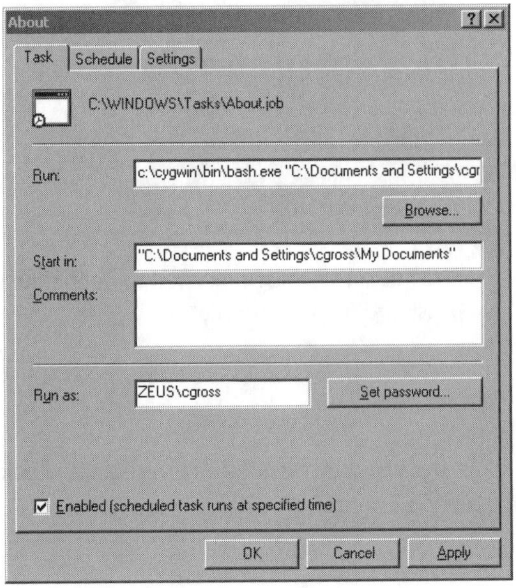

FIGURE 5.13 Modified command line for the scheduled task.

the path has spaces. The Start In text box references the directory where the script resides.

The other two tabs, Schedule and Settings, allow you to refine how the script runs. For example, on the Settings tab you can define that the script only runs when the computer is idle or that it stops the task if it runs to long.

11. After you have finalized the task, click the OK button to add the task to the listbox shown earlier in Figure 5.6. You can right-click the item in the list-box to run and test the script.

PROJECT: XYNTSERVICE

Running a background process on the Windows platform requires running a Windows Service. To run a Windows Service, you must have an application that is Windows Service aware. A BASH script is not Windows Service aware and neither are many console applications. Converting those applications into a Windows Service is not feasible. Without any additional applications, it's very complicated to run a console application as a service. Microsoft distributes with its Resource Toolkit an application that converts a console program into a Windows Service. Unfortunately, the Resource Toolkit is not available free.

A solution that is free, however, is the XYNTService Open Source application, which allows an administrator to define a console program and its options to execute. The XYNTService application is a Windows Service that reads a configuration file to know which applications to run. Table 5.1 contains reference information for the XYNTService project.

TABLE 5.1 Reference Information for XYNTService

Item	Description
Home page	Project home page: *http://www.codeproject .com/system/xyntservice.asp*, and author home page *http://mysite.verizon.net/ XiangYangL/index.htm*.
Version	No version number, but the last update at the time of this writing was made in February 28, 2004.
	$\rightarrow$

Item	Description
Installation	The installation is very easy, and adequately documented on the project home page.
Dependencies	No dependencies.
Documentation	Virtually no documentation, other than this book, and the text on the project home page. The documentation at the project home page is good enough to accomplish all tasks.
Mailing Lists	No mailing lists.
Impatient Installation Time Required	Download size: 28 KB Installation and configuration time: 5-10 minutes
DVD Location	The directory /packages/XYNTService contains the binary distribution; to see an example configuration file surf to the URL *http://www.codeproject.com/system/xyntservice.asp*.

Additional Notes

This Open Source project is not actually a full project, but more of a single solution to a common problem. Although the home page and documentation seem amateur in comparison to other Open Source projects, they really aren't. The developer Xiangyang Liu has managed to develop very professional simple solutions to common problems.

Impatient Installation and Deployment

The impatient installation and deployment are entirely identical. You can download the application XYNTService from the Code Project Web site or from the provided DVD. (Code Project requires a user registration to download the sources and application.)

The downloaded and expanded archive contains a small executable called XYNTService.exe. Copy this executable to a directory that will serve as your XYNTService application directory and then execute the following command to install the service:

```
XYNTService.exe -i
```

The following command removes the service:

```
XYNTService.exe -u
```

When installing the XYNTService application as a Windows service, be sure to run the service in the context of a specific user. Some console applications might need to read user environment variables or files and the local system account does not have those attributes.

Technique: Running a Console Program

The XYNTService is installed, but it's not yet capable of doing anything. On starting XYNTService, the application XYNTService.exe searches the initial execution directory for the file XYNTService.ini. The contents of the file XYNTService.ini are identical to other Windows .ini files. An example configuration file is as follows:

```
[Settings]
ServiceName = XYNTService
ProcCount = 2
CheckProcess = 30
[Process0]
CommandLine = c:\bin\unison.exe -socket 8118
WorkingDir = c:\
PauseStart = 1000
PauseEnd = 1000
UserInterface = No
Restart = Yes
[Process1]
CommandLine = C:\j2sdk1.4.1_05\bin\java.exe -ms1m -cp . scache
WorkingDir = c:\bin\scache
PauseStart = 1000
PauseEnd = 1000
UserInterface = No
Restart = Yes
```

In the example configuration file there are two main section types: Settings and the other sections (Process0 and Process1). The Settings sections contain all the main global definitions related to the XYNTService application. The other sections define the individual processes that will be started when the XYNTService starts. The individual keys of the Settings section are defined as follows:

ServiceName: Sets the service name of the XYNTService. Modifying this value will allow an administrator to install multiple XYNTService instances.

ProcCount: Specifies the number of processes that will be started. The main reason this key exists is for the XYNTService application. It uses the value as a maximum value when iterating all the ProcessX sections. In the example configuration, the value is 2, which means that Process0 and Process1 sections must exist.

CheckProcess: This value specifies how often XYNTService should check to see if the processes started are still alive. If the value is 0, then no checking is done; otherwise, the process is restarted. When this value is active, if the started process has died, it will be restarted if the Restart property of the ProcessX section allows it. Be careful with this property because an incorrectly configured process could be constantly dying and restarting, potentially causing the computer to become inoperable.

For each process, there is a Process[n] section, which from the example configuration file means Process0 and Process1. Each Process section has the following key definitions:

CommandLine: Defines the command line that is executed to start the process. Full paths should be used.

WorkingDir: Defines the working directory of the process that is started.

PauseStart: Specifies the number of milliseconds to wait before the process is considered initialized. Internally within XYNTService, all that occurs is a sleep for the length of time specified by the value.

PauseEnd: Specifies the number of milliseconds to wait before a process is forcibly terminated. When the XYNTService shuts down due to one reason or another, a quit message is sent to the process and the value of PauseEnd causes XYNTService to wait. After the waiting period is done, the process is forcibly shut down.

UserInterface: Specifies whether the XYNTService can interact with the desktop, which only works with the Local System account. Note that there is no My Documents directory when using the Local System account, which could be problematic with some console applications that expect a My Documents directory.

Restart: Specifies whether the process should be restarted if the process dies.

Technique: Restarting the Processes

When running scripts in the context of XYNTService, some problems will arise. For example, imagine a script that runs another process and waits for the process to end. When XYNTService shuts down, it sends a WM_QUIT message. The Cygwin

BASH shell does not trap the WM_QUIT message, so the shell will be killed in a hard fashion. When the XYNTService restarts, old processes will already exist. The problem of not trapping the WM_QUIT message is not isolated to the BASH shell, but Windows batch processes have the same problem.

The solution to the problem is to modify the script to kill off any of the old processes before starting new ones. The following script shows how to find old processes and then kill them using PSTools (*http://www.sysinternals.com/ntw2k/freeware/pstools.shtml*):

```bash
#!/bin/bash
pslist | grep $procIdentifier | awk '{print $2}' > /tmp/pids.txt
exec 3<&0
exec < /tmp/pids.txt
while read line
do
    pskill $line
done
exec <&3
exec 3<&-
rm /tmp/pids.txt
```

In the script, a listing is made of all running processes using the command pslist. That result set is searched using grep for the process ID as identified by the variable $procIdentifier. The grep results are then fed into awk to retrieve the process IDs, which are saved in the file pids.txt. The file pids.txt is loaded and iterated. Each iteration contains the process ID of a found process that needs to be killed using the command pskill. Finally, the file pids.txt is deleted. The script code is a sure way to kill off the old processes. You can also use kill to send a specific signal. Note that the key PauseStart should include the time taken to kill off already existing processes.

Technique: Restarting Services and XYNTService

The executable XYNTService is not just a Windows Service executable, but also a control application that can locally start and stop services, and restart specific XYNTService services. The following command shows how to restart the second ProcessX section shown in the example configuration file:

```
XYNTService.exe -b 2
```

The following command shows how to stop a service named Apache:

```
XYNTService -k Apache
```

The following command shows how to run a service named Apache:

```
XYNTService -r Apache
```

PROJECT: VNC SERVER

Remote logging makes it possible to carry out tasks on a computer without sitting in front of that computer. The advantage of remote logging is not limited to accessing machines remotely, but also extends to managing computers remotely. For example, if a user cannot get a piece of software working, the administrator can remotely log in, diagnose the problem, and potentially fix it.

Logging remotely onto a computer on Windows was only available to Terminal Services enabled operating systems. Typically this meant purchasing a server operating system. With the release of Windows XP Professional, a user can log on and use the resources of another machine. This feature makes it possible for someone to log on remotely to a computer, although another user using the computer being logged on to will be automatically kicked off, albeit their session will be saved. However, Windows 2000, Windows XP Home edition, and other personal Windows operating systems cannot be logged on remotely.

The solution to the remote logon problem is Virtual Network Computing (VNC). VNC is a multiimplementation cross-platform toolkit that can be used to control and share resources. Several VNC implementations are available for the Windows platform: RealVNC, TightVNC, and UltraVNC to name a few. Each of these implementations can communicate with each other, but some offer specific advantages that other implementations do not have. The implementation used for the scope of this book is UltraVNC because it is a Windows-specific implementation and has many extra optimizations that allow UltraVNC to run faster on Windows. Table 5.2 contains reference information for the UltraVNC project.

TABLE 5.2 Reference Information for UltraVNC

Item	Description
Home page	Project home page: *http://ultravnc.sourceforge.net/*
Version	At the time of this writing, Release 1.0 was being distributed.
Installation	The installation can either be carried out using the Windows installation program, or the binary archive with some manual instructions. In either case, a reboot is not necessary.

$\longrightarrow$

Item	Description
Dependencies	No dependencies. However, the VNC protocol is not private. To make the VNC protocol private, *STunnel* must be used as shown in the "Technique: Port Redirection and Authentication" section of Chapter 4.
Documentation	Not a large amount of documentation is available at the UltraVNC Web site. Most of it is specific to UltraVNC. The best documentation is a combination of the documentation from the projects UltraVNC, RealVNC, and TightvNC.
Mailing Lists	The only mailing list is `ultravnc-list`, which is relatively active. All questions should be directed to the mailing list.
Impatient Installation Time Required	Download size: 1.5 MB approximately, depending on the distribution downloaded. Installation and configuration time: 5-20 minutes, depending on the distribution used.
Firewall Port	5900 is the default port used, but UltraVNC allows any port to be used.
DVD Location	`/packages/VNC` contains the self-installing package.

Additional Notes

VNC is not only a remote access tool, but also a training tool and a demonstration tool. You can even use VNC to spy on another computer and watch what someone is doing. This is useful when teaching a user to carry out a task on the computer. You can use the chat feature in UltraVNC to guide a user through the steps without having to do the actual steps.

VNC is cross platform and is commonly used on Linux/BSD systems. For example, to log in remotely using a GUI, a Windows user usually would have to find an X-Server on Windows. With VNC, the administrator has one solution for all platforms.

VNC is also extremely useful on the Windows Server operating system. Often many scripts or applications do not allow themselves to be configured using Windows

Terminal Services. A VNC connection makes it seem as as if the user is using the keyboard in front of the computer and the administrator can perform all the tasks required without having error messages appear.

Impatient Installation

The impatient installation uses the Windows installation program. The Windows installation program can be downloaded from *http://ultravnc.sourceforge.net/download.htm*. The package that should be downloaded is identified as the self-installing package.

After the archive has been downloaded, double-click it to begin the installation process. It will ask which language to use for the installation and you should pick whichever one you are most comfortable with. The following dialog boxes are assigned default values and they should be kept. You'll also have to accept the GPL license agreement. One of the last dialog boxes, Select Additional Tasks (see Figure 5.14), needs further explanation.

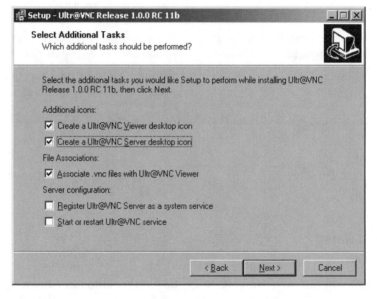

FIGURE 5.14 The UltraVNC Select Additional Tasks dialog box.

The Select Additional Tasks dialog box is used to assign default settings of the UltraVNC application. The default is to not register the UltraVNC application as a service and to not start the service. This assumes that the user will start the UltraVNC server manually. This is a good choice if the computer to be managed is a client that will access another VNC server. It's not such a good choice if the computer to be managed needs VNC server access.

After making the appropriate selection, the next dialog boxes will install the application. The final installation dialog box is another decision dialog box that can automatically start the VNC server. If the computer is primarily a client installation, then it isn't necessary to start the VNC server.

If the VNC server is started, an error will be raised saying that the server does not have a valid password. The Current User Properties dialog box appears, and you can define a password in the Password text box. To activate the server, you click the OK button and a blue and yellow dot icon appears in the system tray.

Deployment

The other distribution that can be downloaded from the main UltraVNC Web site is the binary-only distribution. That distribution is a simple zipped archive file that needs to be expanded in a directory. Note that the distribution does not expand into a subdirectory, and hence you need to create an UltraVNC subdirectory.

Once expanded, the subdirectory contains a number of files and a `driver` subdirectory. The advantage of the UltraVNC distribution is its native kernel driver. The native kernel driver is used on Windows 2000 and Windows XP computers and allows a faster refresh of the desktop on the remote client connection. If the UltraVNC application will be used solely as a client, then the deployment is complete. The only things missing are the shortcuts or menu items. The file `winvnc.exe` is the server portion, and the file `vncviewer.exe` is the client portion of the VNC application.

UltraVNC Server Installation

The UltraVNC server needs some additional settings before it can be used. You can install the server as a service, but you don't need to. For example, the UltraVNC server could be started from a console script. To install the server as a service the following command is executed:

```
winvnc.exe -install
```

To remove the server from the Windows Service list, the following command is executed:

```
winvnc.exe -remove
```

To upgrade or reinstall the UltraVNC service, the following command is executed:

```
winvnc.exe -reinstall
```

Setting up the driver and configuring the registry is the more complicated part of the installation. The driver is installed using the application `setupdrv.exe` and appears similar to Figure 5.15.

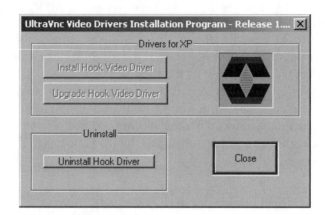

FIGURE 5.15 The Setupdrv.exe application is used to install the kernel driver.

The two grayed-out buttons allow a user to install or upgrade the driver. They are grayed out because the driver has already been installed and there is no new version to upgrade. The button to uninstall the driver is enabled and allows an administrator to force the UltraVNC server to use traditional means to access the computer's resources. Be sure to install the driver to take advantage of a significant performance improvement.

The only problem with the kernel driver is that there is no easy way to manually install the driver. The setupdrv.exe application is not command line enabled so it requires user intervention. A GUI-based macro utility must be used to install the driver automatically.

Setting Up the Registry

The binary installation directory has a file called VNCHooks_Settings.reg, which is a registry file that can be imported for each user and represents some default application settings. The file settings are mainly required for the VNC client application. For the server, the following text block illustrates an abbreviated list of the necessary server registry settings:

```
Windows Registry Editor Version 5.00

[HKEY_LOCAL_MACHINE\SOFTWARE\ORL]
```

```
[HKEY_LOCAL_MACHINE\SOFTWARE\ORL\WinVNC3]
"DebugMode"=dword:00000000
"MSLogonRequired"=dword:00000001

[HKEY_LOCAL_MACHINE\SOFTWARE\ORL\WinVNC3\Default]
"TurboMode"=dword:00000000
"EnableVirtual"=dword:00000000
```

Note the two registry keys: WinVNC3 and Default. The WinVNC3 key is used to define some basic execution settings that cannot be overridden. The Default key is used to define default settings when the server executes. Both keys need to be defined in the registry when doing a manual deployment. Following is a list of all registry values associated with the WinVNC3 key (if not explicitly stated, the value is a DWORD):

DebugMode: Specifies where debug output is generated and can be one of the following values: 1 - debug out, 2 - generated to file WinVNC.log, and 4 - generated to the console.

DebugLevel: A numeric value that can range between 0 and 20, where 20 is the highest level specifying the verbosity of the debug output.

DisableTrayIcon: Specifies whether a tray icon is generated. A value of 1 removes the tray icon, which is useful when wanting only one server process to run, and not allowing a client to modify any settings.

LoopbackOnly: A setting that is either a 0 or 1; when set to 1, it forces the UltraVNC server to only accept local connections.

MSLogonRequired: A setting that is either 0 or 1; when set to 1, it ignores the UltraVNC password and uses the user and password of the computer or domain. This setting should be set to 1 because it ensures that only those with user identifiers and passwords can access the computer.

AllowLoopback: A setting that is either a 0 or 1; when set to 1, it allows the UltraVNC server to accept local connections.

AuthRequired: When set to 1, this setting ensures that there is no empty VNC password.

ConnectPriority: This option specifies how concurrent VNC clients behave when connecting to a single server. The correct value is especially important in a classroom setting because one user might boot off another user. The values this option can have are defined as follows: 0 - disconnect all existing connections, 1 - don't disconnect any existing connection, 2 - refuse the new connection, and 3 - refuse all new connections.

AuthHosts: This option is a string (REG_SZ) of multiple-character blocks that define which remote clients can get access to the server. The string is a wildcard that can be a pattern defined as follows: (Multiple string filters are concatenated using the : character)

+[IP address]: The IP address matched in this form means that the client is allowed access. For example, 192.168.1.1 as an IP address is the same as saying 192.168.*.* where the asterisk matches any block identifier. Using the + character means that the IP address of the client must match the IP address specified by the block.

?[IP address]: The IP address matched with a question mark in front means that the server must first accept the connection.

-[IP Address]: The IP address with a minus in front means that the IP address that matches cannot be allowed access. For example, the string -:+192.168 means "decline all incoming connections except those that start with a 192.168."

The only important settings that should be set to something else other than the default are the keys AuthHosts and MSLogonRequired. These two keys used in combination ensure that the security of your server is at a maximum level. The only missing aspect is the encrypted communications. The encrypted communications is made possible by using a utility such as STunnel. The Default key does not need any values; setting them would be for optimization purposes.

After initializing the registry settings, you can run the UltraVNC server by either starting the service or a batch script.

Technique: Tweaking the Server

When setting up the UltraVNC server, you can assign various settings. The settings are directly related to the registry settings found at *http://ultravnc.sourceforge.net/registrys.htm* and to the WinVNC: Current User Properties dialog box shown in Figure 5.16.

The WinVNC: Current User Properties dialog box in Figure 5.16 is displayed when you right-click on the UltraVNC tray icon and select Properties from the menu.

The following sections describe a number of techniques to use with UltraVNC server.

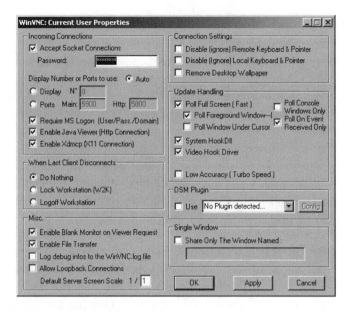

FIGURE 5.16 UltraVNC properties dialog box.

Assigning a Different Port

In Figure 5.16, the Display Number or Ports to Use radio button is part of a group that includes Display and Ports radio buttons as well. The default is to use Auto, which means each server instance of WinVNC will use its own display. A *display* is a screen that a remote user can use when connecting to a server. Each VNC client connects to a display. In Windows, the concept of a display is not meaningful. The exception is with Windows Terminal Services, but the display identifier should not be modified because it could cause other problems.

The best way to understand VNC and displays is to consider that what the remote client sees and manipulates on the desktop is the exact same desktop you would see if you were sitting in front of the computer. This is an important fact because VNC is not like Terminal Services or X-Windows in which a remote desktop is entirely on its own. Overall it makes the term `Display` quite useless and all Ultra-VNC servers on Windows use display zero. The reason the term `Display` is used at all is because by knowing the display number, the port used can be calculated. `Display 0` is on port 5900, `display 1` is port 5901, and so on. Using the Port option allows you to define any port to accept `display 0` client connections.

Using the Port option also enables the Http Connection port, which by default is 5800. The Java client that can be embedded as a Java applet on an HTML page uses the Http Connection port.

Using VNC Server in a Classroom or Support Context

VNC server is commonly used as a classroom tool. For example, the trainer might ask all students to download the client and connect to a server. The trainer could go through the steps and the students would see the steps executed in front of them. Likewise, the trainer could connect to the students and see what they are doing. This setup enables interactive remote learning because the trainer does not have to be in front of the student.

The only problem with this type of setup is that the student could in theory start typing and executing applications on the trainer's computer. Figure 5.16 shows the Connection Settings group box, which contains three options. When the Disable (Ignore) Remote Keyboard & Pointer option is enabled, the student is unable to manipulate the trainer's computer. You should also select the Remove Desktop Wallpaper checkbox because backgrounds are typically bitmaps, which slows down the server and client refresh rate.

Another useful set of features is the chat and file transfer features. The file transfer feature is enabled on the server by checking the Enable File Transfer checkbox in the lower-left corner of Figure 5.16. You don't needs to do anything on the server side to enable the chat feature. To use either the chat or file transfer features, the client initiates the process. Figure 5.17 shows the UltraVNC toolbar that is used by the client.

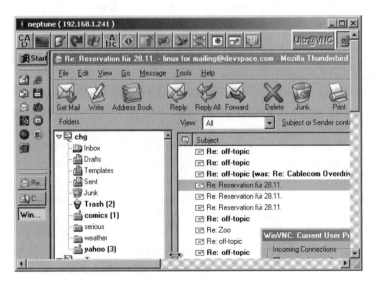

FIGURE 5.17 UltraVNC client window and toolbar.

In Figure 5.17, the buttons below the window title bar make up the UltraVNC client toolbar. The window below the toolbar is the remote client desktop. From the toolbar, the client could start either a file transfer or a chat.

To start a chat, you click the Chat button on the toolbar. On the client side, a dialog box starts in which the client can type in some text. On the server side, a dialog box also appears. When a user on the server side types in some text, it will appear on the client side. Although not the most sophisticated chat program, it works well. The only problem is that if the client kills the chat dialog box, it is automatically killed on the server. This is problematic if the student types some text as a one-way message and then immediately kills the dialog box. The trainer wouldn't have time to read the message.

The file transfer feature is a bit more problematic because it works too well in that everyone can get access to all files on the entire computer of the server. The file transfer feature is activated by clicking the File Transfer button (double green arrows) as shown in Figure 5.17. Clicking this button opens a dialog box that allows the user to transfer any file from the local machine to the remote machine and vice versa.

Controlling the Server from the Client

On the client side, several other features can be used to control the server. Specifically, these tricks fall into the category of sending keystrokes to the server that are generally processed on the client side.

A Ctrl+Alt+Delete key sequence is sent to the server using the CAD toolbar button. A Windows Start key sequence is sent to the server using the Windows flag icon toolbar button. Custom key sequences such as Alt or Ctrl are sent using the ABC toolbar button to the right of the Windows Start toolbar button.

The toolbar button to the right of the CAD toolbar button is used to maximize the client window to the full desktop of the client. The Desktop Refresh toolbar button (single curved arrow) is useful if the server desktop in the client window is messed up and littered with window fragments.

PROJECT: UNISON

When a computer has to be reinstalled or formatted, reconstructing can be problematic because of the data. One approach is to reinstall everything and then reinstall the data. Another approach is to have periodic backups of the computer and reconstruct the computer automatically. Yet another approach is to copy a number of files from one location to the computer that will be formatted.

The point is that there are many ways to reconstruct a computer. The classical answer is to run periodic backups of the computer and then restore the backup. This is a good answer if you have a single computer doing a single task. Take for example a user who has a desktop and a notebook. Using a backup strategy, each computer would have its data backed up. Now imagine a user regularly copies files from the desktop to the notebook and back again. Will the backup have the correct files when restoring to both the desktop and the notebook? If a crash occurs, which computer has the latest data? Will the user have to inspect each file to determine which one is newer? The user is not attempting to back up the data, but to synchronize it.

TABLE 5.3 Reference Information for Unison

Item	Description
Home page	Project home page: *http://www.cis.upenn.edu/~bcpierce/unison/*
Version	At the time of this writing, Release 2.10.2.
Installation	The installation of the program is extremely easy because it's a single executable that is executed directly. The Unison applications are downloaded from the contributed ports page. With recent releases of Cygwin, Unison has been included and therefore it is not necessary to download and install Unison if Cygwin is installed.
Dependencies	No dependencies, except potentially for Gimp Toolkit (GTK) DLLs. The DVD distribution includes the dependent DLLs.
Documentation	The documentation of the project is relatively good even though it is a single document (*http://www.cis.upenn.edu/~bcpierce/unison/manual.html*). Most of the conditions and problems are described; reading the Unison documentation solves most if not all problems.
Mailing Lists	Three mailing lists are mentioned in the documentation; for the administrator, the mailing lists `unison-announce` and `unison-users` are relevant.

$\longrightarrow$

Item	Description
Impatient Installation Time Required	Download size: 800 KB to 3MB depending on whether a GUI version of Unison is downloaded or not.
	Installation and configuration time: 5-15 minutes depending on the distribution used.
Firewall Port	No default port is used because it is defined entirely by the administrator.
DVD Location	`/packages/unison` contains both the GUI and console versions of Unison.

The problem has been transformed from purely backup and restoration to synchronization. Synchronizing data is very different from backing up data, although there are similarities. Synchronization enables data to be in multiple places and be edited in multiple places. Using synchronization, the user can edit a document in one place and have the contents replicated in multiple places. Synchronization and backup solve the same problem in very different ways. The power of synchronization is that the data is strewn across a network, so a new computer can be easily added to the network and loaded with the missing files. Backups can do the same, except backups are focused on a single computer.

The Unison application is a file-synchronization tool. The tool is given two locations and some instructions to synchronize the contents between the two locations. Files can be deleted in one location and Unison propagates those deletions. Files can be added, manipulated, and so on and Unison propagates those changes. Ideally then a backup utility only needs to back up one of the locations and assume the other location will have the most updated data. Table 5.3 contains reference information for the Unison project.

Additional Notes

When downloading Unison, there are two versions: console based (`unison-[version number]-win32-text.exe`) and GUI based (`unison-[version number]-win32-gui.exe`). The console-based version is best for scripts and servers and the GUI-based version is best suited for end users.

Deployment and Impatient Installation

The deployment and impatient installation of Unison are identical, but there is a difference between the server and the client installation. The client and server installation also use different executables. The client uses a GUI-enabled application and the server is console only. However, if so desired the client can use the console application.

For the server side, the executable `unison-[version number]-win32-text.exe` should be copied to a location that is on the PATH environment variable.

For the client side, the executable `unison-[version number]-win32-gui.exe` should be copied to a location that is on the PATH environment variable. Most likely the DLLs required to run GTK are not installed. This means that the file `unison-win32-gui-dlls.zip` has to be downloaded and expanded in the same directory as the GUI version of Unison. After all the files have been copied, you can run Unison.

Technique: Setting Up a Unison Server

There are different ways to set up a Unison server. You don't need to run a Unison server application because Unison can synchronize two directories using file shares and a remote shell. Synchronizing using file shares is not efficient, and using a remote shell is not easy to do on Windows. The solution is to set up the Unison server by using the XYNTService. Communications between the client and server use Unison sockets, and the communications can be transparently encrypted using STunnel that was presented in Chapter 4. For road warriors, the safest method is to use a VPN. Not using any form of encryption will make your server vulnerable to modifications by any user that has access to the server. Unison does not include any form of user authentication or privacy.

The Unison server is started using the command line shown as follows:

```
unison.exe -socket 8118
```

The command-line option `-socket` defines which port the Unison server will accept requests from. The sheer simplicity of the command masks two complications. The first complication is which user context the server process is executing in, and the second complication is the directory from which the application is executing. Both of these attributes are important because Unison references a user's home directory and uses the current execution directory to resolve paths.

When the Unison server process starts and a request is received, the synchronization process starts. If the synchronization is brand new or an update, a database of files synchronized is created or updated. The database is stored in the `.unison` subdirectory in the user's home directory. On Windows that means for the user

Administrator, the `.unison` subdirectory would be created under the directory `c:\Documents and Settings\Administrator`.

When using the XYNTService to execute the Unison process, ensure that the XYNTServer service is executing in the context of a specific user. Otherwise, the `.unison` subdirectory might be stored in an odd location.

The location where the Unison server executes is important because when a client connects and references specific directories, the specific directories are relative to the execution directory. When using the XYNTService to execute the Unison process, make sure that the working directory is assigned to the correct directory.

Ensure that the client and server of Unison are the same version numbers. Otherwise, synchronization errors will result so that the client and server will not communicate.

Technique: Running a Client Process

Unison can be run from the command line or the GUI. In either case, when using Unison as a client, a profile file should exist in the `.unison` subdirectory. A profile file is used for the client to connect to the server and then begin exchanging information.

To illustrate how a client and server synchronizes a set of files, the XYNTService configuration file for a server is illustrated before showing the client profile file. The following text block is an example XYNTService configuration file:

```
[Settings]
ServiceName = XYNTService
ProcCount = 1
CheckProcess = 30
[Process0]
CommandLine = c:\bin\unison.exe -socket 8118
WorkingDir = c:\
PauseStart = 1000
PauseEnd = 1000
UserInterface = No
Restart = Yes
```

The working directory for the Unison server is the c drive root directory. This is done on purpose because the client can synchronize to any directory with respect to the root directory. From an accidental overwrite point of view this is a dangerous setting.

This raises the question of how to define the root directory for synchronization. The way to do this depends on the context of the synchronization. Typically there are two types of synchronization: user and application.

Application synchronization occurs when application settings or configuration files are synchronized. For example, a Web server farm can be synchronized using Unison. One Web server serves as a Unison server and master. The master is connected to periodically by the other Web servers, which act as clients that synchronize the files from the master. For such a case, the Unison directory would be the root directory, or some directory that has been defined as the application directory. If you are running mostly Open Source software, then a directory called /apps is appropriate.

The second type of synchronization is user synchronization, which generally is simpler, but for a multiuser scenario, is more complicated. The first strategy is to define a synchronization point, which would contain subdirectories for all users. The problem with this strategy is that it's very easy to make a mistake and accidentally delete content that should not be deleted. Another solution is to make the user's machine a Unison server and have the main file server periodically connect to the user's machine to synchronize content. The choice of solution depends on the security requirements of the network. If security is required, you can use Cygwin and its SSH facility to create a secure authenticated connection.

On the client side, a profile file is created by creating a filename with the extension prf. The following text block is an example profile file that is saved to the file default.prf and is located in the .unison directory:

```
root = C:/Documents and Settings/cgross/My Documents
root = socket://neptune:8118/Documents and Settings/cgross/My Documents
```

There are two entries with the same key root. The key root defines the root synchronization locations on both the client and the server. The first root definition is the local directory. The second root definition is a remote URL specification. Notice that the second root definition uses the identifier socket to indicate a socket connection. The next part of the URL identifies the server neptune and the port identifier 8118. Both the server and port have to be explicitly identified, as the Unison server has no concept of default server or port identifiers. Then the path after the port identifier is the path that is appended to the execution directory of the server Unison application. By comparing the local and remote paths, Unison attempts to synchronize the contents.

To run Unison, the following command is executed:

```
unison.exe default -silent
```

The command automatically contacts the server and synchronizes the contents. The `-silent` flag stops any interactive input and automatically makes synchronization decisions on behalf of the client.

TIP

Each profile should be saved to its own file in the subdirectory `.unison`. *To use a profile when synchronizing, the identifier is the profile filename without the extension and dot. For example, the file* `default.prf` *has an identifier* `default`.

Technique: How Unison Synchronizes

When Unison synchronizes two separate directories, the data in the two directories will be the same. What is not known is the logic used to synchronize the data in the two directories. For example, if one file is newer than the other, determining which file is copied is an example of logic. Unison uses the concept of a *replica*, which contains information about the files within a directory. If the directories are being synchronized for the first time, then the replica is created. The replica is a state of synchronization when two roots are considered identical.

When Unison synchronization is executing, updates of files are searched. An *update* is when one of the following occurs:

- A file is not identical to the recorded version in the replica.
- A directory and its contents are not identical to the recorded version in the replica.

If an update is necessary, then it is converted into a conflict, which needs to be reconciled. If a directory is new or deleted in one replica, then the contents of the directory is not tested because it would be meaningless.

The synchronization rules are as follows (based on the premise that a replica has already been created):

- If a path (file or directory) does not exist in one root, then it is copied to the other root.
- If a path is deleted from one root, it is deleted from the other root.
- If a path is updated in one root and the same path is not updated in the other root, then the not updated root is updated.
- If one path is updated in one root and the same path is updated in the other root, then a conflict will arise where neither is updated. The end user will then

have to do a manual update, merge, or some other type action. By default, Unison does not attempt to do anything because any decision Unison makes might be the incorrect decision.

Unison by default does most things correctly, but there are situations when Unison needs a helping hand. The problem is when conflicts arise because the same path is updated in two different roots. The conflicts can be guided by defining one root of a higher precedence, or by synchronizing the file that was modified last. The other solution to a conflict is to merge the two different files using a merge utility.

The following command uses the -force command-line option to copy the contents of one root to another root:

```
unison default -silent -force C:/temp
```

The command-line option -force is used to replicate one root to another root. The problem of the force command-line option is that it forces the contents of root onto another root. In the example command, the root C:/temp is the local root and all files on the local root will take priority over the remote root. If a file exists on the remote root and does not exist on the local root, then the file will be automatically deleted. The reason is because the structure of the local root takes priority over the remote root. This means files can be accidentally deleted or overwritten.

The following command uses the force command based on the newer date:

```
unison default -silent -force newer -times
```

The identifier newer when used in conjunction with the command-line option -force means when a conflict occurs, choose the newer version of the path or file. It is also possible to use the identifier older that will choose the older version of the path or file. When using the newer or older keyword, the command-line option -times must also be used.

To merge files that conflict, the command diff3 can be used. The command diff3 is part of the Cygwin toolkit. The only catch is that merges only work well on simple text files such as source code files. Merging XML files or Microsoft Word Document files is not a good idea and will corrupt a file. Following is an example where the merge option is added to the profile file:

```
merge = diff3 -m CURRENT1 OLD CURRENT2 > NEW
```

The identifiers CURRENT1, OLD, CURRENT2, and NEW are defined and replaced by Unison to identify the filenames of the files. They are defined as follows:

CURRENT1: The name of the local file.

CURRENT2: The name of the temporary file that represents the remote file that has been copied to the local computer.

OLD: The name of the backed up old copy of the original version of the file from the local computer.

NEW: The name of the new version of the file based on the merge of the two original documents.

Technique: Selectively Synchronizing Files and Paths

Let's say that a user wants to synchronize the My Documents folder. A Unison best practice is to define a local root at the user's My Documents folder. When both roots are synchronized, the user will have all files available locally and remotely. This is not bad as a strategy, but not optimal.

A blind synchronization is not optimal because not every subdirectory of the root needs to be copied. For example, some users like to create temporary directories, which should not be synchronized. Another example is when an application is being developed. Often compilers used to build applications create temporary build files that are huge and should not be synchronized as that would waste space.

With Unison, you can synchronize only what needs to be synchronized, and files that should not be synchronized can be ignored. The following is an example configuration file that shows how to synchronize explicit paths and ignore other paths or files:

```
root = C:/Documents and Settings/cgross/My Documents
root = socket://neptune:8118/Documents and Settings/cgross/My Documents

path = Background
path = books
path = memorizer
path = MozillaChristian

ignore = Path books/OSSforWinAdmins
ignore = Name MozillaChristian/b90ttvff.slt/Cache/*
ignore = Name MozillaChristian/b90ttvff.slt/Cache.Trash/*
```

In the example configuration file, there are two new keys used: path and ignore. The key path is used to include a directory. It is important to note that when at least one path is defined, the default inclusion logic is inverted and only the defined path is included. The logic is inverted because when no path is specified, all subdirectories are included from the paths specified by the `root` key. The `path` value is converted into an absolute path by appending the value as a subdirectory to the root for both the local and remote locations.

The key `ignore` is used to filter out paths or filenames that should not be synchronized. The key's `ignore` value has a special format, which is an identifier followed by a path. The identifier can either be `Path` or `Name`. If the identifier is `Path`, then the associated path represents a path to ignore. If the identifier is `Name`, then the associated path represents a file to ignore regardless of where it may occur. It is important to realize that if the path is `books/OSSForWinAdmins`, it is appended to the paths specified by the `root` key.

The associated path can also be a very simple regular expression in that you can use the wildcard character to define generic filenames and paths. The following text block shows some wildcard examples:

```
ignore = Name .*
ignore = Name *.o
ignore = Name *~
ignore = Path */debug
ignore = Path */src/*
```

The asterisk is used to match anything. From the example `ignore` statements, the files `.cvspass`, `build.o`, `backup~`, and the path `/build/debug` would be ignored. However, the path `/another/build/debug` would not be ignored. The reason is because the wildcard character does not match the additional `/` character, and in the path `/another/build/debug` there is an additional `/` character. This means only `debug` directories nested one level below the root will be ignored. Using the identifier `Name` does not have the slash problem because the name of the file is matched. It is advisable to always specify files that should be ignored because otherwise the synchronization process might become too resource intensive and be littered with useless information. To solve the problem of the nested paths, regular expressions need to be used. The following example ignores all `debug` subdirectories regardless of where it occurs:

```
ignore = Regex .*/debug/*
```

The path after the `Regex` identifier is a regular expression. Specifically, the characters after the dot character make up a regular expression. Before the dot is an expression that matches the path and file literally. When a regular expression is used, everything must be matched, not just parts of the file or path. So looking at the example, the `.*` says to match everything before `/debug/`, and the trailing `*` matches everything after the `/debug/`. The regular expression used is the same as those defined in the "Technique: Regular Expressions" section of Chapter 2. When using regular expressions, the asterisk character includes the slash character. The slashes are added to the debug identifier so that files like debug.o or directories are not matched.

Unison can reference other files that provide additional definitions or actions to perform using the include key shown as follows:

```
root = C:/Documents and Settings/cgross/My Documents
root = socket://neptune:8118/Documents and Settings/cgross/My Documents

include common.paths
include myspecial.paths
```

The example uses two include keys to load the command paths (file common.paths) and the special paths (file myspecial.paths). The idea is to define a set of generic paths that are used for everyone and special paths that are designed for an individual user. The include key is not only used for paths, but for any Unison configuration directive.

Unison will work on both Windows and Linux/FreeBSD operating systems. However, there is a problem in that Linux/FreeBSD operating systems are case sensitive and Windows is not. Windows ignores case sensitivity and therefore filenames or directories that use different cases for the same identifier will cause problems. If this occurs, then the only safe way to perform synchronization is to use a Samba file share.

TIP

Technique: Backing Up Original Versions of the Files

For the paranoid administrator who wants to make sure that no files are deleted, it is possible to back up replaced files on both the local and remote machine. The backed up files can then be retrieved or deleted at the administrator's discretion. Unison is especially intelligent in that it can keep backups of multiple versions for the same file. For example, it could keep the last and before last copy of the same file. Older versions are automatically pruned from the backup tree. Following is an example abbreviated configuration file that shows how to use backups:

```
maxbackups = 3
backupdir = c:/backups
backup = Name *
```

In an abbreviated configuration, there are three keys that can be used in association with a backup: maxbackups, backupdir, and backup. The only key that is necessary is backup.

The key `maxbackup` when not specified has a value of 2 and represents the number of old backup versions to keep. Each backed up file will be appended with the extension `.n.unibck`, where n represents the backup number. A higher number represents an older version of the file.

The key `backupdir` represents the place where the backup files should be stored. Using a custom backup directory is an easy and clean solution, except that multiple profiles have to have multiple backup directories, or conflicts might arise. This might not be a problem on the client side, but could be a definite problem on the server side where multiple users might be synchronizing their content. For example, specifying a backup directory of `c:/backups` is a bad example of a backup directory because multiple users might be using the same directory. The best solution is not to use the `backupdir` key, which results in the default subdirectory `.unison/backup` being used for backups. The only reason this key should be used is if the partition hosting the `.unison` subdirectory is not large enough.

The key `backup` is used to select the files that should be backed up. The format of the key value is identical to the `ignore` key. Multiple backup keys can be used to select multiple filenames from the list of files that are synchronized. The `backup` example in the previously defined abbreviated configuration file selects all files that are synchronized to be backed up.

The `backups` can also be used to back up files. However, it should not be used because it appends the `.bak` extension to the file being synchronized. The file is not copied to the backup directory, but copied in the directory where the file exists.

PROJECT: 7-ZIP

Archiving files is an important task because it provides a way to store older inactive data. Many open source applications are distributed as compressed archives using tar, gzip, or the zip file format. In general on the Windows platform, the zip file format has become the de facto archive format. The 7-Zip application is an excellent utility for managing manage archives.

The zip file format is not the only compressed and archived file format that exists. There is tar, bzip2, gzip, and others. The tar file format is a traditional Unix file format still used extensively today. The tar file format is not a compressed file format, but a legacy file format used to write a single file for a list of files. That single file was then copied to a tape drive or other device. To save space, programs such as gzip were created that have the capability to compress the tar file. However, programs such as gzip can compress or expand single files as they work in conjunction with programs such as tar.

The 7-Zip application is a file manager, command line, and enhanced functionality utility. Using 7-Zip, a user can expand most compressed and archived file formats. 7-Zip can create archives in these file formats: tar, zip, gzip, tar, bzip2, and 7z. 7-Zip also can create expandable executables that resemble a very simple installation program. Table 5.4 contains reference information for the 7-Zip project.

TABLE 5.4 Reference Information for 7-Zip

Item	Description
Home page	Project home page: *http://www.7-zip.org/*
Version	At the time of this writing, Release 4.13 was being distributed.
Installation	There are three installations: full installation distributed as an executable, console installation, and 7z DLL distribution.
Dependencies	Depending on the distribution, there are either no dependencies or dependencies on 7-Zip distributed DLLs.
Documentation	Documentation is available on the Web site, but also within the distribution in the form of a Windows Help file.
Mailing Lists	No mailing lists are associated with the 7-Zip application. A forum is available that is part of the 7-Zip SourceForge project at *http://sourceforge.net/forum/?group_id=14481*.
Impatient Installation Time Required	Download size: All downloads are less than 1 MB. Installation and configuration time: 2-5 minutes
DVD Location	`/packages/7-Zip` contains the self-installing package.

Additional Notes

Within the Cygwin distribution are the command-line tools Zip and Unzip, which have the ability to read and write ZIP archives. Using Zip and Unzip is acceptable and could be used in place of 7-Zip if you only need to manipulate archives from the console. The 7-Zip application can manipulate different archive formats and can do more complicated things with an archive.

Impatient Installation

The impatient installation uses the Windows self-installing package executable. The latest stable version is available from the main page of the 7-Zip Web site. Download an executable and then double-click to start the installation. After the installer starts, it will ask some questions and you can choose the default answers. When the installation has completed, the application can be used immediately.

TIP

If the 7-Zip application is used from the command line, then the installation directory of the 7-Zip application needs to be added to the path.

Deployment

Deploying the 7-Zip application is not difficult. You do have to decide whether the GUI and console application will be deployed, or only the console application. The GUI application, which is the file manager, is more complicated to distribute because it requires the addition of a small registry change, whereas the console only needs to distribute three files.

Distributing the GUI Application

The simplest way to distribute the 7-Zip file manager is to use the self-installing package distributed by the 7-Zip Web site. If that is not possible, then the 7-Zip self-installing package should be installed on a computer using a manual copy command such as xcopy. You can zip up the 7-Zip application, but then it would need to be expanded. Because the 7-Zip application is used to manage archives, it's hard to expand an archive when the tool to expand the archive does not exist in the first place. This dilemma raises a chicken and egg scenario and therefore the simplest is to distribute an executable that installs 7-Zip.

For simplicity, the 7-Zip application is distributed using the xcopy command. The following script shows how to copy the 7-Zip application from a network share. It is assumed in the script that the package directory on the network share is the directory contents from the 7-Zip installation:

```
#!/bin/bash
sharedcomputer="neptune"
installdir="c:\\bin\\7-Zip"

net use X: "\\\\$sharedcomputer\\osswin"
mkdir $installdir
xcopy x:\\packages\\7-Zip $installdir /E /V *.*
```

```
reg /add HKLM\\SOFTWARE\\7-Zip
reg /add HKLM\\SOFTWARE\\7-Zip /a Path /t REG_SZ /d $installdir
net use X: /DELETE
```

In the script, there is an additional use of the `reg` command to add one registry key used by the 7-Zip applications to define where the application is located.

If the GUI application is installed using this technique, no context menu is added to the Windows File Explorer. Those settings must be added manually.

Distributing the Console Application

The console application is downloaded as a ZIP archive from *http://sourceforge.net/projects/sevenzip/*. The file that should be downloaded is `7za[version number].zip`. The downloaded file can be expanded using another zip program, probably the 7-Zip file manager, which was installed on an administrator's machine. After the archive has been expanded, the expanded files are copied to a server. To install the console-based 7-Zip application on individual computers, a script similar to the following can be executed:

```
#!/bin/bash
sharedcomputer="neptune"
installdir="c:\\bin "

net use X: "\\\\$sharedcomputer\\osswin"
mkdir $installdir
xcopy x:\\packages\\7-Zip-Console $installdir /E /V *.*
net use X: /DELETE
```

The script is very similar to the original 7-Zip installation script, except that there is no need to modify the registry. You do need to make sure that the `$installdir` value is in the PATH environment variable.

Technique: Expanding an Archive from the Console

When downloading open source programs from the Internet, very often the program will be distributed as a file that can be in one of two formats: compressed gzip or bzip with tar, or ZIP file. For either case, 7-Zip can be used to extract the files. 7-Zip can extract the following file formats: 7z (own 7-Zip format), zip, gzip, tar, bzip2, rar, cab, arg, cpio, rpm, deb, and split. To extract a set of files from a ZIP file, the following command is used:

```
7za.exe e myfile.zip
```

Running the command extracts all the files from the archive myfile.zip, except all the files in the archive are expanded into the directory where the command is executed. This happens even if paths are stored in the archive file myfile.zip. The reason is that the command-line option e extracts to the common directory. To generate the subdirectories, the command-line option x has to be used:

```
7za.exe x myfile.zip
```

If there are already files in the location where the archive is being expanded, then the 7-Zip console application will ask questions regarding whether to overwrite the files. To answer yes to all overwrites, the -y option is used as shown in the following example:

```
7za.exe x -y myfile.zip
```

Using the -y option automatically overwrites a file, but you can fine-tune when a file is going to be overwritten. Following are some possible choices other than the option -y:

-aoa: Overwrite all existing files without prompting.

-aos: For already existing files, do not overwrite and skip extracting the file.

-aou: If a file already exists, extract the file and then rename it with an _1 appended to the identifier.

-aot: If a file already exists, extract the file and rename the already existing file identifier with an appended _1.

The following command shows that you can use the -o command-line option to specify the output directory to use instead of the current directory:

```
7za.exe x -y -oc:\temp myfile.zip
```

CAUTION

The extract process works well on all files, except there is a gotcha with gzip or bzip2 encoded files. These files contain a single encoded tar file, so you first need to expand the gzip or bzip2 file and then expand the tar archive. The easiest way to do this is to create a script file that will do both steps in one.

Technique: Creating and Updating an Archive from the Console

The converse of expanding an archive is to create an archive. An archive can be created using the following command:

```
7za.exe a -tzip archive.zip adir\*
```

In the example command, the command-line option a is used to add files to an archive that either exists or is newly created. The option -tzip is actually two options in one. The first part of the option is the -t, and the second part of the option is zip. The first part of the option is to create an archive of a specific type, which is specified by the second part of the option. 7-Zip can create files of the types 7z, zip, gzip, tar, and bzip2. The archive identifier is the command-line option archive.zip and the contents added are all the files under the directory adir.

CAUTION

*Notice in the example how the wildcard * is used instead of *.*. This is because the * selects all files, whereas *.* only selects files that have an extension.*

The following command shows how to add all files within a subdirectory and its subdirectories:

```
7za.exe a -tzip -r archive.zip adir\*
```

The command-line option -r causes the 7-Zip application to iterate each of the subdirectories and adds the files as they are found. The subdirectory structure is recreated in the archive file.

When creating very large archive files, often the problem is that the partition, which is used to create the temporary archive file, does not have enough available disk space. 7-Zip can define a temporary working directory using the -w option:

```
7za.exe -a -tzip -r -wc:\temp adir\*.*
```

Technique: Assigning a Password

When assigning a password to a ZIP archive file, the archive file becomes encrypted using shared password encryption. Using the encryption technique within the 7-Zip application is okay, but a better strategy is to use GNUPG and WinPT as described in Chapter 4. Part of the problem with using the password that is part of the ZIP file format is that it's yet another security strategy. If you will use the security provided by the ZIP file format, then as per the manual the password needs to be at least 14 characters long to provide a semiadequate amount of security.

Technique: Creating a Self-Extracting Archive

A useful feature of 7-Zip is its capability to create a self-extracting archive. By default, the archive is expanded using another application. A self-extracting archive has the extraction code built in to the archive itself. The advantage of a self-extracting archive is that no additional application is needed to expand the archive. There are two ways to create a self-extracting archive, using the Windows batch file `copy` command or using the 7-Zip application.

The `copy` command is a not commonly known way of creating a self-executing archive. Essentially what happens is that three files are appended to each other and the resulting file is an executable. This works because the first file that is appended is an executable. The following command shows how to create a self-installing executable:

```
copy /b 7zS.sfx + config.txt + myarchive.zip application.exe
```

The files `7zS.sfx`, `config.txt`, and `myarchive.zip` are combined into the file `application.exe`. The `/b` command-line option is used to define that the binary flag needs to be used. The magic of using the `copy` command is that the file `7zS.sfx` is actually an executable file used to bootstrap the archive. It is possible to change the filename to `7zS.exe` and execute the file. An error will result, however, because the file is not part of a larger file that has a configuration file and archive embedded within it.

The file `7zS.sfx` is an application that will execute as a Windows application. The file can be found in the root directory of the 7-Zip application when the 7-Zip installer is installed. The purpose of the individual bootstrap files are defined as follows:

7z.sfx: A Windows bootstrap file.

7zC.sfx: A Windows bootstrap file that has been compressed to take up less space.

7zCon.sfx: A console bootstrap file.

7zS.sfx: A Windows version for installer applications.

7zSD.sfx: A Windows version for installer applications that requires the standard C library (`MSVCRT.DLL`). The advantage of this version is that it is smaller.

The configuration file `config.txt` is very simple and contains at a maximum three keys as follows:

```
;!@Install@!UTF-8!
Title = "My Archive"
BeginPrompt = "Proceed with expansion of file"
RunProgram = "MyScript.sh %%T"
;!@InstallEnd@!
```

The configuration file is defined as follows:

Title: This key specifies the name of the self-installing package. Typically this identifier is displayed when the bootstrap file starts.

BeginPrompt: This key's value is a message used within a message that is displayed when the self-installing archive executes. The key is displayed just as the archive is executing and is the last place the user can reject the installation of the archive.

RunProgram: This key's value is a command line that is executed when the self-installable archive has expanded the archive. The script or executable must be part of the archive and the %%T parameter is the root directory of the temporary directory where the archive contents were copied to. The command line could be the start of an installation program or some script that simply copies the contents from the temporary location to a permanent location.

The first and last lines in the config.txt configuration file are used as place markers to indicate the start and end of the installation keys.

Another way to create a self-installable package is to use the 7-Zip application itself as follows:

```
7za.exe -sfx7zs.sfx -r application.exe adir\*
```

The example command combines the creation of the archive and the executable in one step. The disadvantage of this approach is that the self-extracting package does not run any programs and only expands to a specific directory.

TWEAKING YOUR ENVIRONMENT

The Windows Environment and Application Konfigurator (TWEAK) utility is used to tweak the Windows environment. For example, if the administrator needs to configure a user's icons or change the Windows boot loader, then TWEAK is the utility that does the job. TWEAK is very powerful in that applications such as OpenOffice can be tweaked and properly configured. Table 5.5 provides the reference information for TWEAK.

Additional Notes

There is not much to explain with TWEAK because TWEAK changes constantly and is updated with new features. The TWEAK application is started using the TWEAK.BAT file. From there, a console window appears and by selecting the appropriate option something on the computer can be tweaked.

TWEAK is ingenious because all its functionality is based on the execution of some Windows batch files. Therefore, if an administrator wanted to add a tweak to the administration scripts, they would simply find the appropriate batch file and then call it from their scripts.

TABLE 5.5 Reference Information for TWEAK

Item	Description
Home page	Project home page: *http://thegoldenear.org/ tweak/*
Version	At the time of this writing, 0.8.42 was being distributed.
Installation	The application is distributed as a ZIP archive, which is expanded.
Dependencies	There are some dependencies depending on the utilities used: Perl, SetACL, and Associate. More information about the home pages of these tools is given on the TWEAK home page.
Documentation	The main documentation is at the Web site and should be consulted. The documentation is sparse and tends to focus on how to make TWEAK work properly. There is no documentation about the individual features of TWEAK.
Mailing Lists	There are no mailing lists associated with the TWEAK application.
Impatient Installation Time Required	Download size: All downloads are less than 1 MB. Installation and configuration time: 2-5 minutes
DVD Location	/packages/TWEAK contains ZIP archive.

SUMMARY

This chapter covered several projects used to solve many common problems when administering a Windows computer. The idea was not to solve a single large problem, but to solve multiple smaller problems. In the Open Source community, there are oodles of these application types available on the Internet. Therefore, when attempting to solve some problem, first check a Web site such as Freshmeat (*http://www.freshmeat.net*) to see if it has already been done before.

6 Authentication and Managing Files

ABOUT THIS CHAPTER

The focus of this chapter is to illustrate two projects that can be used to provide user identification and file server infrastructure.

User authentication is not the same as user identification. Windows has a user authentication mechanism built in, so only valid users can access a computer. User identification provides an infrastructure to identify who someone is by name, address, e-mail, telephone number, and so on. The Windows operating system can do that as well, but it requires investing in Microsoft Active Directory™.

Windows provides a file server infrastructure; in fact, Microsoft's release of Windows for Workgroups was one of the first operating systems to allow ad-hoc file sharing. This chapter covers Samba on the Linux operating system as an alternative file server.

The following projects are covered in this chapter:

OpenLDAP: OpenLDAP implements the Lightweight Directory.

Access Protocol (LDAP). LDAP makes it possible to do both user authentication and user identification. In fact, OpenLDAP could be viewed as a hierarchical database storage application in which you can store all sorts of information, such as computer and application reference information. This book covers the details of installing OpenLDAP manipulating objects within the LDAP directory.

Samba: On the Linux/BSD platforms, the Samba program provides Windows file services. Samba can function as a Primary Domain Controller (PDC) and file server. This chapter shows how to install and use Samba.

Why Linux?

For this chapter, Linux is required, as Samba only runs on Unix operating systems such as Linux. As a side note, OpenLDAP runs best on Linux. Linux and Samba are used because of the licensing issues that are required when using Windows Server. The Microsoft Product User Rights (PRU) licensing manual explicitly states that whenever Server Software Services are used a Client Access License (CAL) is required, along with a server CAL. The client CAL already exists if you using a Windows client operating system. The tricky bit is the server CAL. The PRU manual states that a license is required whenever server software is executing in the context of an authenticated user. This seems unnerving because it implies that running Apache with authentication requires server CALs. In the glossary section of the Microsoft site, however, the terms CAL and server are defined explicitly as Microsoft-based software, so that leaves Apache clear in the running.

Still, if Samba is used to authenticate SQL Server users, then CALs must be purchased for SQL Server. CALs must also be purchased if Microsoft IIS is used with a Samba authenticator. The inverse is also true. If a Linux client uses Samba to connect to a Windows server, Linux must have a CAL. Finally, licensing often depends on your situation, so please get proper advice that is specific to your situation.

PROJECT: OPENLDAP

LDAP has become a standard for reference information, and is the white pages of the Internet. The main idea is to store large amounts of information for others to reference. LDAP databases are read mostly, which means most of the time when a client interacts with the LDAP database, a query is made. Username and password data is stored on an LDAP database. When a user is authenticated, the application queries the LDAP database to determine whether the submitted information is correct. An e-mail program might use an LDAP database for reference information such as identity and e-mail address.

Often people are nervous to use an LDAP server because LDAP seems complex. LDAP is not so complex that only large enterprises are capable of using it effectively. LDAP is small and lightweight enough that a small home network could use it to store all reference information in a central location. LDAP is focused on doing one thing: storing reference information.

The OpenLDAP project is the de facto Open Source LDAP server available on the Internet. The OpenLDAP project is part of the OpenLDAP foundation, which was established in August of 1998. The foundation has a single task, which is to create an Open Source LDAP server. Table 6.1 contains reference information about the OpenLDAP project.

TABLE 6.1 Reference Information for OpenLDAP

Item	*Description*
Home page	*http://www.openldap.org*
Installation	Installing OpenLDAP requires a compilation of the OpenLDAP server sources. The entire process is not complicated.
Version	Latest stable 2.2.20
Dependencies	Cygwin toolkit with full installation (requires gcc compiler and many of the development tools).
	For the Windows platform, there are Windows-specific compilation instructions. Check the *http://www.devspace.com/osswinadmin* wiki for updates on precompiled Windows binaries.
Documentation	The documentation at the OpenLDAP site answers many of the questions that an administrator would have. The only problem is that OpenLDAP has traditionally been a Linux/BSD exclusive project, which means that Cygwin support is only acceptable.
Mailing Lists	Several mailing lists are offered by the OpenLDAP group. The different mailing lists are defined and explained at *http://www.openldap.org/lists/*. For the administrator, the mailing list `OpenLDAP-Software` is the most useful.
Impatient Installation Time Required	NOTE: A full installation of the Cygwin toolkit is highly recommended.
	Installation time: 2 minutes.
	Compilation: 20-50 minutes depending on the speed of the hardware.
	Download size: 2MB

$\rightarrow$

Item	Description
Firewall Port	Default: 389 SSL: 636
DVD Location	Located on the DVD are the sources in the directory /packages/LDAP.

On the Windows platform, there are two ways to authenticate a user: using an LDAP server or using a Windows Authentication Server. The administrator should choose an LDAP server when most of the applications used are based on Open Source packages. By using an LDAP server, licensing is automatically taken care of because authentication occurs outside of the standard Windows way. The administrator should choose a Windows Authentication Server if the applications are a mixture of Open Source and binary-only applications such as Microsoft IIS, or Microsoft SQL Server.

Impatient Installation

The OpenLDAP project does not distribute any binaries, and requires each administrator to compile and install the program manually. In the Open Source world, if a program is written in either C or C++, then the compilation and installation of the application are separated into four separate steps: downloading, configuring, compiling, and installing.

Downloading

The links for downloading the OpenLDAP sources are located at *http://www.openldap.org/software/download*. The download is structured in a matrix of mirrors and distributions. Choose the mirror that is nearest to your physical location. At each download site, you can choose from various distributions and release sources. Download the file and save it to your hard disk.

The OpenLDAP distribution is distributed as an archive created by the tar command and compressed using the gzip command. To uncompress the archive, use the following commands:

```
gzip --decompress openldap-<version>.tgz
tar --extract --verbose --file=openldap-<version>.tar
```

The individual commands can be combined into one command:

```
tar --extract --verbose --gzip --file=openldap-<version>.tgz
```

After the source code files have been extracted, the OpenLDAP server program needs to be compiled. Compiling the server is a three-step process: configuration, compilation of the dependencies, and compilation. The configuration of the server program is not a configuration in the sense of application execution configuration, but configuration of how the sources will be compiled.

On the Windows platform, there are three ways to compile Open Source applications: Visual C++, MinGW, or Cygwin. Most Open Source applications use Visual C++ and MinGW to develop and compile their applications on Windows. For this project, we recommend you use MinGW. When MingGW is used to compile an Open Source application, the administrator should read the OpenLDAP build documentation, because it contains details on how to fine-tune the compilation of the application.

The other way to compile Open Source applications on Windows is to use the Cygwin toolkit. People use this toolkit because it is very similar to Unix and makes the build work with Cygwin relatively simple. On the Unix platform, compiling an application is very simple and generally only requires the execution of three commands: `configure`, `make`, and `make install`. The command `configure` is a dynamic application that inspects the operating system, adjusts standard library calls, and generates the necessary build files. There are options that can be passed to the `configure` command to adjust specifics such as installation directory. The command `make` calls the generated makefiles to build the application. The command `make install` installs the compiled application ready to be executed.

The following command configures the OpenLDAP server program so that it will compile on Cygwin; however, it is important to be in the local root directory of the OpenLDAP sources:

```
./configure --disable-bdb --enable-ldbm --enable-ldap
--enable-passwd --without-threads
```

The `configure` program has more options, which can be viewed by typing in the command shown as follows:

```
./configure --help
```

The configuration of the program often takes a while because the speed of the command depends on the speed of the computer. After the configuration has completed, the last line of the configure program will say to run the following command:

```
make depend
```

The command builds the dependencies of the OpenLDAP server program. To build the OpenLDAP server program the following command is executed:

```
make
```

The compilation of the OpenLDAP server program takes at least 10 minutes and at most an hour, depending on the processor speed of the computer. When the compilation has been completed, the OpenLDAP application has to be installed using the following command:

```
make install
```

The OpenLDAP server is ready to process LDAP requests, but the configuration file has to be updated. The OpenLDAP configuration file `slapd.conf` is stored in the location `/usr/local/etc/openldap` and should contain the contents as defined here:

```
include      /usr/local/etc/openldap/schema/core.schema
include      /usr/local/etc/openldap/schema/cosine.schema
include      /usr/local/etc/openldap/schema/inetorgperson.schema
pidfile      /usr/local/var/slapd.pid
argsfile     /usr/local/var/slapd.args
database     ldbm
suffix       "dc=<domain>,dc=<extension>"
rootdn       "cn=Manager,dc=<domain>,dc=<extension>"
rootpw       <password>
directory    /usr/local/var/openldap-data
index        objectClass     eq
```

The items enclosed with the < and > brackets need to be updated with values that are defined as follows:

<domain>: The name of the domain that the LDAP server should manage. If the URL is *http://www.mycompany.com*, then the domain is *mycompany*.

<extension>: The name of the domain extension that the LDAP server should manage. If the URL is *http://www.mycompany.com*, then the domain is *com*.

<password>: The root password that is used to access the LDAP server. This password is necessary so that the initial database can be created. For the impatient install, the password is stored in clear text.

After the configuration file has been updated and saved, the OpenLDAP server can be started using the following command:

```
/usr/local/libexec/slapd -d 255
```

The command starts OpenLDAP with full debug output as specified by the -d option. In a production setting, the -d command-line option is not necessary. For the initial installation and execution, the -d option is good to use because if anything is not correct, the error will be displayed in the console window.

To stop the server, the following command must be used or the LDAP backend database might become corrupted:

```
kill -TERM `ps -e | grep 'slapd' | awk '{print $1}'`
```

Note the important differences between the single quote and the backquote. The command is a more complex command that kills the pid that is associated with the slapd program. The kill command is sent to the OpenLDAP server, but the -TERM command-line option is a shutdown request. Starting the slapd server is assumed to be executed in the context of a Cygwin Bash console session.

The OpenLDAP server will be installed and able to execute, but the OpenLDAP server will have no contained data. It is essential to initialize the database before using it. The later-defined techniques "Managing LDAP Database Content Using LDIF Files" and "Structuring an LDAP Database" describe how to initialize and manipulate LDAP data.

The OpenLDAP server that is configured is without full transaction capabilities. When using Cygwin to build the OpenLDAP server, a single threaded application is created. The OpenLDAP is a lighter weight when compiled on Cygwin because the Cygwin toolkit does not support all Unix packages. The bdb library does not work with the Cygwin toolkit, so the light version of the bdb database (ldbm) is used instead, which is acceptable for small corporations.

For a larger installation, you should install and build OpenLDAP on a Linux computer because all features of LDAP are supported on Linux. This is not a problem if the administrator intends to use Samba to manage users. If Samba is not installed, then it's still advisable to get a Linux/BSD computer that will run the OpenLDAP application. The computer doesn't need to be powerful because the computer will be running a dedicated task.

At the time of this writing, Red Hat announced that it plans on open sourcing its acquired Netscape Directory Server. If you need an enterprise-capable LDAP server that executes on Windows, consider looking into that option.

Deployment: OpenLDAP Server

Deploying the OpenLDAP server can be a bit of a challenge because the OpenLDAP server is compiled from the sources. In theory, the easiest way to deploy the Open LDAP server is to compile the server from the sources for each machine. This solution is optimal if the servers are not in similar configurations. The other option is to distribute the application based on the files installed by the command make install. Overall, the problem is that there is no best way to distribute the OpenLDAP server because it is distributed in source code format.

You can copy an OpenLDAP server installation from one computer to another computer. The different computers must have similar operating systems installed and all the dependencies installed. When deploying an OpenLDAP configuration, the data files need to be copied as well.

Configuring an OpenLDAP Server

An OpenLDAP server is configured by a number of files and directories as explained by Table 6.2.

The files and directories referenced assume a default installation from the ./configure *command.*

TABLE 6.2 Files and Directories Used in the OpenLDAP Configuration

Directory/File	Description
/usr/local/slapd.exe	The OpenLDAP server program.
/usr/local/bin/ldap*.exe	A number of command-line programs that are used to manipulate an LDAP server database.
/usr/local/sbin/slapadd.exe	Adds LDAP entries to a SLAPD database using the LDIF (LDAP Data Interchange Format) file format.
/usr/local/sbin/slapcat.exe	Converts a SLAPD database into an LDIF file.
/usr/local/sbin/ slapindex.exe	Converts a SLAPD index into an LDIF file.
/usr/local/sbin/ slappasswd.exe	Used to generate a root password for the SLAPD configuration file.

$\rightarrow$

Directory/File	Description
`/usr/local/etc/openldap/ldap.conf`	A configuration file that is used by client applications to connect to an LDAP server. This file is a global file. A file called `.ldaprc` is stored in the user directory and can specify individual settings. In a Windows context, this file is only useful when using Cygwin applications to access an LDAP server.
`/usr/local/etc/openldap/slapd.conf`	The configuration used by `slap.exe`.
`/usr/local/etc/schema/core.schema`	The core schema file that describes the various objects that can be stored in a SLAPD database.
`/usr/local/etc/schema`	Different schema files that can be used to describe specific attributes and objects in a SLAPD database.

Local Directory Service

An LDAP server can be installed as part of a network or as a single computer. The simplest configuration is a local directory installation. The local directory installation occurs when OpenLDAP is installed on a single server, serving requests for an entire network. In this configuration, the LDAP server will not seek the assistance of other LDAP servers when attempting to resolve a request.

This configuration is ideal when a network does not contain many servers or when the data is application specific in nature. For example, a Web server that wants to manage and validate users on a Web application might use this configuration. The impatient installation installs and configures the OpenLDAP server using this configuration.

Local Directory Service with Referrals

In an enterprise context, there are multiple LDAP servers that are typically chained together in a parent child configuration. Figure 6.1 illustrates an example configuration where a request is redirected to a parent server.

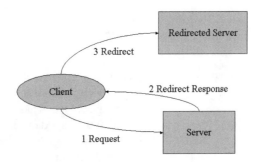

FIGURE 6.1 Example configuration where one
LDAP server is a parent and the other a child.

In Figure 6.1 the main server is the box with the text Server. In a chained con-figuration, when a client makes a request to the main server that the main server cannot fulfill, a redirect response can be sent. The redirect response is an instruc-tion where the main server has indicated that another server could potentially ful-fill the request.

For OpenLDAP, a referral to another LDAP server is an entry that is added to the slapd.conf file:

```
referral ldap://parent.devspace.com
```

The referral entry is a reference to a server that could process an unprocessed request. Most clients will automatically redirect and query the redirected server. The definition of the referral value contains the ldap identifier before the server identifier to indicate that the ldap protocol is used when communicating to the ldap server.

If there are multiple referral entries in the configuration file, the client might process only the first entry, and ignore the other entries. The referral process can start at one server, then redirect to another, which redirects to another server, which can go on indefinitely. It all depends on the nature of the LDAP client implementa-tion. Most clients have built-in intelligence that will catch a loop and stop when a server is about to be queried twice for the same query. When the client is querying a server, it is the responsibility of the client to process all the generated referrals.

Technique: Initializing the OpenLDAP security

When the OpenLDAP server is started for the first time, the database contains no data and has no user information. In other words, there is no security because there are no users. The OpenLDAP database is in a chicken and egg scenario. The prob-lem is that the server has no data, which means no users. To log in to the OpenLDAP server a user is required, but there is no user defined in an empty database. To solve this problem, OpenLDAP defines the `rootdn` and `rootpw` configuration entries in the `slapd.conf` file. Both of these entries refer to a super user that is not subject to the authentication mechanisms used for all the other users. Following is an example of specifying the `rootdn` and `rootpw`:

```
rootdn    "cn=Manager,dc=devspace,dc=com"
rootpw    {SSHA}+bkQipjvmJekw2DQBBVOy9CyPPFCtplo
```

The `rootdn` entry points to the user `Manager` using the X.500 naming notation. The `rootdn` is an identifier that does not need to exist in the local database. However, the `rootdn` descriptor should coincide with the `suffix` configuration entry in the `slapd.conf` file because otherwise the OpenLDAP database might search for the credentials in another repository, which is not desired. In general, if the `rootdn` entry is defined as shown in the previous example, then the `suffix` entry is defined as follows:

```
suffix  "dc=devspace,dc=com"
```

The details of the terms `cn` and `dc` will be explained in the upcoming section "X.500 Notation." It's important to remember that `suffix` contains all the `dc` entries in the same order as the `rootdn` entry.

The `rootpw` entry was prefixed by the descriptor `{SSHA}`, which is an OpenLDAP convention to indicate that the password text following the descriptor is a uuencoded, encrypted hash of the password. Another option is to store the password in clear text. Storing a password in clear text is not a good idea because any user that has read access to the configuration file has access to the root password. Having root access to the OpenLDAP server means the user can do anything on the server. Using a uuencoded hash, the application can read the password in encoded form but does not know what the password is.

The uuencoded buffer is a one-way hash encryption algorithm technique. A one-way hash encrypted buffer is a one-way conversion of some text to "noise." The noise is predictable, but the noise cannot be converted back to the original text. This means when comparing passwords, what is actually compared are the hash codes. A hash code is secure because there is no simple direct relation between the text and hash buffer. The one-way encrypted hash text is generated using the `slappasswd` application shown as follows:

```
cgross@venus /book/files/openldap
$ /usr/local/sbin/slappasswd -s secret
{SSHA}fpQPlaYkeCtOHAqcNilSugL6CCdX4BxJ

cgross@venus /book/files/openldap
```

The -s command-line option defines the password that will be hashed, which for the example is the password secret. When defining your passwords, the password should be more sophisticated than secret. The generated output text (buffer that starts with the descriptor {SSHA}) is then copied and pasted beside the rootpw entry in the slapd.conf file.

Technique: Structuring an LDAP Database

A LDAP database is not useful unless it contains data. The issue with LDAP is that the database cannot contain a free-for-all of information. The LDAP data is structured in a strict hierarchy, similar to a directory structure used by an operating system. As stated previously, the suffix is very important in an LDAP database; it is comparable to a drive letter in a Windows filesystem. The suffix defines the root of the data that is stored on a local computer. In the simplest case, a suffix can be a nothing value:

```
suffix     ""
```

The example implies that the local LDAP server can potentially process all LDAP requests. This is okay if the network or application being managed is a single global LDAP server. In an enterprise scenario, this might not be an optimum solution. Typically a better solution is to define a structure where some server processes a set of data. The following example would be used to describe a root LDAP database in a corporation:

```
suffix     "dc=devspace,dc=com"
```

The example implies that the LDAP server will process all requests being sent to the domain devspace.com. The following example describes an LDAP server that would be a child of the root LDAP database and be specific to a department:

```
suffix     "ou=manufacturing,dc=devspace,dc=com"
```

In the example, the LDAP server manages the department manufacturing. By defining the correct suffix, it is easy to chain multiple LDAP servers together using the referral configuration entry. Typically the local LDAP server will refer to the parent, which means the domain defined by the suffix manufacturing will have a referral key to the server managing the domain devspace.com. A configuration file may contain multiple suffix entries to indicate multiple LDAP domains that will be managed by the local LDAP server.

X.500 Notation

The notations used in the previous examples (e.g., `dc=devspace,dc=com`) are X.500 LDAP references. Converting the X.500 notation `dc=manufacturing`, `dc=devspace`, `dc=com` to a sample directory reference the following path results:

```
\com\devspace\manufacturing
```

The sample path is an accurate conversion, but the letters before the various directory references are lost. In previous examples, the identifier `com` was associated with the identifier `dc`. That extra identifier makes X.500 unique. In X.500, each part of the URL must be a key value pair. The purpose of the key is to give a hint of the purpose of the value. The most commonly used keys in X.500 are defined as follows:

cn: Common name.

dc: Domain component.

l: Locality, city, or village name.

o: Organization name.

ou: Organizational unit name.

c: Country name.

street: Street address.

st: State or province.

uid: User ID.

Let's continue comparing LDAP and directories. In a directory there are subdirectories, and directories can contain files. LDAP is no different in that objects can contain other objects creating LDAP "directories."

Technique: Managing LDAP Database Content Using LDIF Files

When an LDAP database is empty, LDAP objects are created using an LDAP Data Interchange Format (LDIF) formatted file:

```
dn: dc=devspace,dc=com
objectclass: dcObject
objectclass: organization
o: devspace
dc: devspace
```

An LDIF formatted file consists of a number of defined entries grouped into a single section. A single line typically defines each entry, but multiple lines can be used to a single entry. Each entry starts with an identifier followed by the value for the identifier. It is a sort of key value pairing that mirrors the key value nature of X.500.

Each LDIF section consists of three major parts: distinguished name, object class type, and contents. The distinguished name is an entry that starts with the dn identifier, and is a way of identifying the object in the LDAP database. In the example LDIF file, the dn is saying to reference the domain devspace.com.

The second part starts and ends with the lines that begin the identifier object-class. Each time the identifier objectclass is used, an object type is defined that defines the attributes of the distinguished name. In the example, two class types make up the directory devspace.com: dcObject and organization. So whenever the distinguished name references the domain devspace.com, an object that is composed and contains all the attributes of the objects dcObject and organization is also referenced.

The remaining lines of the example LDIF file are the values of attributes defined by the class types dcObject and organization. Not all attributes of the class types have to be defined; at a minimum, only the required attributes of the class types must be defined. Notice that the attribute that starts with the identifier dc coincides with the value of the first dc of the distinguished name. That is not a coincidence and is necessary because some parts of the distinguished name are attributes of the class type.

An empty line separates each section in an LDIF file. There can be as many entries as needed in an LDIF file.

An LDIF entry can span multiple lines when the next associated line of the entry has a single space or tab as the first character of the line. Using that technique, the single entry can span as many lines as necessary.

The example LDIF file is saved to the hard disk that can then be processed by an LDAP server using the program ldapadd shown here. (Note that the command ldapadd can be used on different LDAP servers and is not specific to OpenLDAP.)

```
cgross@venus /book/files/openldap
$ ldapadd -f example.ldif -h localhost
-D "cn=Manager,dc=devspace,dc=com" -x -w something
adding new entry "dc=devspace,dc=com"
cgross@venus /book/files/openldap
$
```

The ldapadd program has five command-line options that cover most of the cases of adding LDIF content to the LDAP server. The five command-line options are described as follows:

-f: LDIF file that will be processed by the LDAP server.

-h: LDAP server hostname that will be contacted.

-D: Defines the distinguished name to bind to the LDAP server, which usually means the user used to access the LDAP server. For the administrator, this would typically be the rootdn distinguished name.

-x: Use simple authentication instead of SASL (Simple Authentication and Security Layer).

-w: Defines the password on the command line.

The LDIF entry defined by the -D option is necessary and must match the distinguished name to the suffix key in the slapd.conf file.

LDIF Distinguished Name Details

An LDIF file is meant to be a textual representation of the data that is stored on the LDAP server. An LDAP client program uploads the LDIF content to the LDAP server, which processes the file and makes the appropriate changes. The general format of an LDIF file is shown here:

```
#comment
dn: <distinguished name>
<attribute description>: <attribute value>
<attribute description>: <attribute value>

dn: <distinguished name>
<attribute description>: <attribute value>
<attribute description>: <attribute value>
```

In the example LDIF file, there are two LDAP object descriptions and a comment. A comment is represented by the first line, which starts with the hash character. This is identical to Bash and Python. Each object is started with a distinguished name descriptor dn. The distinguished name is a unique descriptor that describes the location of the object. The distinguished name must reference an already existing partial or full location in the LDAP database. An example LDIF entry is shown here:

```
dn: mail=mycompany.com,dc=devspace,dc=com
objectclass: dcObject
objectclass: organization
o: mycompany.com
dc: devspace
```

The distinguished name is made up of three keys: mail, dc, and another dc. The key mail is referencing an object that is the child of the object with the dc key, which again is the child of the dc key. The dc references require further consideration. The distinguished name, which is referenced by both dc keys, happens to be the suffix distinguished name. This is done on purpose as an object can only be added if the parent object already exists. This means the suffix object must exist.

Adding the LDAP object defined in the example LDIF entry will result in an error because neither the object class organization nor dcObject recognize the key mail as an attribute that belongs to the object. The attribute mail exists, but is not part of the classes in the example LDIF entry. Even if the attribute were part of the classes used, an error would be generated because the o attribute is defined. The correct distinguished name to use when describing an object would be the following modified example LDIF entry:

```
dn: o=email-contacts,dc=devspace,dc=com
objectclass: dcObject
objectclass: organization
o: email-contacts
dc: devspace
```

In the modified example LDIF entry, the distinguished name contains a key value pair that uses the organization (o) descriptor, which is also referenced as an attribute in the fourth line of the modified example LDIF entry. This is the correct approach because the organization class type exposes the o attribute, which can be used in the distinguished name.

Defining an Object in the LDIF

In an LDIF file, all the objects defined represent some object declared in the LDAP schema. Therefore to create an LDIF with its associated objects, it is necessary to read the gist of an LDAP schema. It is important to read the gist of a schema because the LDIF file is usually hand coded or generated and that means you need to know what objects and attributes are available.

An LDAP server uses the schema as a blueprint to the types of objects and attributes that can be stored in the LDAP database. In OpenLDAP, the schema files are located in the directory schema, which is a child directory of the directory where the configuration file slapd.conf is located. In particular, the schema files of interest to you are core.schema, cosine.schema, and inetorgperson.schema.

When reading the schema file, there are two types of items: attributes and objects. Attributes are key value pairs. Objects are collections of attributes, and can extend another object. The following is an example schema attribute declaration:

```
attributetype ( 2.5.6.3 NAME ( 'cn' 'commonName' )
```

```
DESC 'RFC2256: common name(s) for which entity is known by'
SUP name)
```

The individual parts of the attribute can be dissected as follows:

2.5.6.3: The unique ID that represents the attribute. This number is not important when creating LDIF scripts.

(**'cn'** **'commonName'**): The identifier that is used in the key value pairs of the LDIF file. When there are multiple identifiers, each can be used in place of the other because they all mean the same thing.

SUP name: Defines the base type of the new attribute. Typically this means that when the attribute is being validated, the rules of validation are based on the base type. The SUP identifier is a keyword and the identifier after is the name of the base type.

In the case of the example schema attribute declaration, there is no example of a rule that defines the type's behavior, because the type is a derived from another type (name). Following is an example that shows a more complex definition of an attribute that uses rules to define the data type:

```
attributetype ( 2.5.6.5 NAME 'serialNumber'
    DESC 'RFC2256: serial number of the entity'
    EQUALITY caseIgnoreMatch
    SUBSTR caseIgnoreSubstringsMatch
    SYNTAX 1.3.6.1.6.1.1466.115.121.1.44{64} )
```

The new parts of the attribute can be dissected as follows:

EQUALITY: Rule used when performing search and comparison operations on the attribute. The rule used is the identifier after the EQUALITY keyword.

SUBSTR: Rule used when performing a substring filter operation on the attribute. The rule used is the identifier after the SUBSTR keyword.

SYNTAX: Rule used when the attribute is being transported by LDAP.

ORDERING: A not shown keyword that is used when ordering the LDAP entries. The rule used is the identifier after the ORDERING keyword.

The rules seem a bit odd because they reference operations typically not used. However, the rules are necessary because of the nature of data that is stored in an LDAP server. The following text illustrates the problems partially solved by the rules:

```
Mr. John A. MacDonald
Prof Mr John   A    Mac Donald
```

The identifier of the person is the same on both lines. There are minor differences, such as spacing and periods. Performing a test on both strings for equality using standard comparison routines would return an empty result. Worse yet is trying to find the records as query. For example, imagine using the following identifier as a sample query:

```
John MacDonald
```

The search routines would find nothing because the search routines perform a byte-by-byte comparison. LDAP makes searches more effective by making it possible to ignore certain problematic issues, such as spaces and case. The special rules compensate and make it possible to find identical names that might be written slightly different. The available rules that can be added to a schema are defined in Table 6.3.

TABLE 6.3 LDAP Schema Rules and Their Context

Name	*Attribute*	*Description*
booleanMatch	EQUALITY	Boolean match
objectIdentifierMatch	EQUALITY	OID (object identifier) match
distinguishedNameMatch	EQUALITY	Distinguished name match
uniqueMemberMatch	EQUALITY	Distinguished name match and optional UID (user identifier) match
numbericStringMatch	EQUALITY	Numerical match
numericStringOrderingMatch	ORDERING	Numerical match
numerStringSubstringMatch	SUBSTR	Numerical match
caseIgnoreMatch	EQUALITY	Case insensitive, space insensitive match
caseIgnoreOrderingMatch	ORDERING	Case insensitive, space insensitive match
caseIgnoreSubstringsMatch	SUBSTR	Case insensitive, space insensitive match
caseExactMatch	EQUALITY	Case sensitive, space insensitive match

$\rightarrow$

Name	Attribute	Description
caseExactOrderingMatch	ORDERING	Case sensitive, space insensitive match
caseExactSubstringsMatch	SUBSTR	Case sensitive, space insensitive match
caseIgnoreIA5Match	EQUALITY	Case sensitive, space insensitive match, using the IA5 text encoding or 7-bit ASCII
caseIgnoreOrderingIA5Match	ORDERING	Case insensitive, space insensitive match, using the IA5 text encoding or 7-bit ASCII
caseIgnoreSubstringsIA5Match	SUBSTR	Case insensitive, space insensitive match, using the IA5 text encoding or 7-bit ASCII
caseExactIA5Match	EQUALITY	Case insensitive, space insensitive match, using the IA5 text encoding or 7-bit ASCII
caseExactOrderingIA5Match	ORDERING	Case sensitive, space insensitive match, using the IA5 text encoding or 7-bit ASCII
caseExactSubstringsIA5Match	SUBSTR	Case sensitive, space insensitive match

TIP

When reading schema files of attributes, the important part to remember is the format of the type, and the names used to reference the attribute. The rest is just extra bits that you may need to be aware of, but only as an afterthought.

Attributes are combined as a set into a collection and called an *object*. Objects are more work to define in a schema, but are simpler to understand. Following is the schema definition for the person object:

```
objectclass ( 2.5.6.6 NAME 'person'
    DESC 'RFC2256: a person'
    SUP top STRUCTURAL
```

```
MUST ( sn $ cn )
MAY ( userPassword $ telephoneNumber $ seeAlso $ description ) )
```

In the definition, the individual parts of the object declaration can be dissected as follows:

NAME 'person': The name of the object.

SUP top: The base type of the object. This is identical inheritance used by attributes. When an object uses inheritance, all the fields of the subobject are available in the object. The object top is a generic reference to a root object declaration.

STRUCTURAL: Defines the type of object. The keyword STRUCTURAL means that the object can be instantiated directly. If the keyword ABSTRACT were used instead, then the object cannot be instantiated directly, but a derived object must be used. The other attribute is AUXILIARY, which means that the object defined is a helper object. When declaring an object in an LDIF file, an AUXILIARY can only be used when there is at least one STRUCTURAL object reference. The AUXILIARY object is used to help finish a declaration to another object.

MUST: Defines all the attributes that must be defined when declaring the object. In the case of the person schema definition, the attributes sn and cn must be defined.

MAY: Defines all the attributes that may be defined when declaring the object. In the case of the person schema definition, the attributes userPassword, telephoneNumber, seeAlso, and description may be defined.

Adding Objects

After an LDIF file has been created, the objects defined within the file need to be added to the LDAP database. To add the data to the LDAP database, the data needs to be sent to the LDAP server using one of the following programs:

ldapadd: The same as ldapmodify with the -a command-line option.

ldapmodify: A program used to add or modify entries on an LDAP server.

The command ldapadd is the simplest command used to add an LDIF record to the database. The problem with using the ldapadd command is if any record of the LDIF file causes a problem, the entire LDIF file is not processed any further. A more robust command line that does the same as ldapadd is shown as follows:

```
ldapmodify -c -a -f example.ldif -h localhost
-D "cn=Manager,dc=devspace,dc=com" -x -w something
```

The command `ldapmodify` is the only command necessary to manipulate data on the LDAP server. The command-line options are explained as follows:

-c: Turns on continuous mode, where an LDIF file will process all objects even if some objects cause errors.

-a: Adds the objects defined in the LDIF file. If this option is removed, then objects are assumed to exist in the database and all objects in the LDIF are modification operations.

Modifying Objects

An LDIF file can contain the definitions of objects that represent objects that will be modified on the server. The difference when modifying objects is that the object might not have all fields declared. Following is an example LDIF that adds and modifies an entry in the same processing step:

```
dn: cn=Alison Bury,dc=devspace,dc=com
objectclass: inetOrgPerson
cn: Alison Bury
mail: alisonb@somecompany.co.uk
givenname: Alison
sn: Bury


dn: cn=Alison Bury,dc=devspace,dc=com
mail: alisonb@anothercompany.co.uk
```

Every object that is added and modified is defined by the distinguished name. Both LDIF entries reference the same object, but the two entries serve two entirely different purposes. The first reference to the object adds the object to the LDAP database. The second reference to the object modifies an object in the database. In the second reference of the object, the `mail` attribute is modified. There are limitations on which attributes can and cannot be modified. For example, any part of the distinguished name cannot be changed because that would be defining a new object. In that situation, the only solution is to delete the old object and add a new object.

Generic LDIF scripts

The usual approach to writing a multipurpose LDIF file is to use the `ldapmodify` command shown previously, but within the LDIF file, the action to be taken on the object is specified. Following is an example LDIF file that contains an addition, deletion, and modification:

```
dn: cn=Alison Bury,dc=devspace,dc=com
objectclass: inetOrgPerson
cn: Alison Bury
mail: alisonb@somecompany.co.uk
givenname: Alison
sn: Bury

dn: cn=Alison Bury,dc=devspace,dc=com
changetype:modify
mail: alisonb@anothercompany.co.uk

dn: cn=Alison Bury,dc=devspace,dc=com
changetype:delete
```

In the example LDIF file, the attribute changetype was used twice. The attribute changetype is associated with the object in the LDIF file and represents a command executed by the LDAP server. In the first instance, the key changetype was used with the value modify, which means to modify the object attributes referenced by the distinguished name. In the second instance, the value delete was used, which means to delete the object referenced by the distinguished name. In each instance, the key changetype was the line right after the distinguished name.

You can also manually control the addition, modification, or deletion of each attribute as shown in the following LDIF file:

```
dn: commonName=Alison Bury,o=contacts,dc=devspace,dc=com
changetype: modify
pager: 123
displayName: Alison Bury-Hurry

dn: commonName=Alison Bury,o=contacts,dc=devspace,dc=com
changetype: modify
delete: displayName

dn: commonName=Alison Bury,o=contacts,dc=devspace,dc=com
changetype: modify
delete: pager
```

The first LDIF object declaration, which is a modification changetype, adds the attributes pager and displayname. In the second and third object declarations, the changetype is still a modification, but the third line of each object uses the delete key, where the value is the identifier of the attribute to delete.

Logically in the example LDIF file, the second and third objects could have been folded into one object declaration with two delete keys. The problem is that the ldapmodify tool generates an error. Therefore, whenever deleting an attribute, each attribute must be deleted individually. You can also use the keys replace and add, to replace or add attributes, but in most cases those operations are implied. When the changetype identifier is modify, a replace is implicitly defined if the attribute exists and add is implied if the attribute does not exist.

Adding Binary Data

All the examples shown so far assume that the data in the LDIF file can be expressed in a single line. When binary data is added to an LDAP server, it must be Base64 encoded. Base64 encoding is when binary data is converted into a buffer that is represented by letters and numbers. In most cases, binary-encoded data will result in the creation of a buffer that is large and extends beyond the limits of a single line. For multiple lines, the line continuation LDIF notation is used. Following is an example LDIF file used to add a binary attribute (jpeg image file) to the LDAP database:

```
dn: cn=Alison Bury,o=contacts,dc=devspace,dc=com
changetype: modify
jpegPhoto::  /9j/4AAQSkZJRgABAQEBLAEsAAD/2wBDAAgGBgcGBQgHBwcJC
DBkSEw8UHRofHhOaHBwgJC4nICIsIxwcKDcpLDAxNDQOHyc5P/
```

The last line of the example LDIF file is a continuation of the previous line because the first character is either a space or a tab. The third line uses a double colon notation to indicate that the value data is Base64 encoded. The problem with Base64 encoded data is that it must be cut and pasted into an LDIF file. That is tedious and potentially error prone. Following is a BASH script that automatically generates and adds the binary field to the LDAP database by generating an LDIF file:

```
#!/bin/bash
echo "dn: $3,$2" > binary.ldif
echo "changetype: modify" >> binary.ldif
echo "delete: $4" >> binary.ldif
echo "" >> binary.ldif

echo "dn: $3,$2" >> binary.ldif
echo "changetype: modify" >> binary.ldif
printf "$4:: " >> binary.ldif
```

```
uuencode --base64 $1 /dev/stdout > temp.image.file
imagelc=$(wc --lines temp.image.file | awk '{print $1}')
imagelc=$(expr $imagelc - 1)
tail --lines=$imagelc temp.image.file > temp2.image.file

exec 3<&0
exec < temp2.image.file
while read line
do
    echo " $line" >> binary.ldif
done
exec <&3
exec 3<&-

ldapadd -c -f binary.ldif -h localhost
-D "cn=Manager,dc=devspace,dc=com" -x -w something

rm binary.ldif
rm temp.image.file
rm temp2.image.file
```

The BASH script has been broken into six sections separated by an empty line. Each section has a specific purpose. The BASH script would be executed with the following command-line options:

File (e.g., personal.jpg): The name of the binary file that will be stored in the LDAP database.

Base dn (e.g., dc=devspace,dc=com): The name of the base dn that is the "directory" where the object is located.

Object dn (e.g., cn=Alison Burg): The name of the object.

Attribute (e.g., jpegPhoto): The name of the binary attribute to add to the object.

In the BASH script, the first section outputs an LDIF instruction to delete the attribute that is represented by the fourth command-line option. Not deleting the attribute causes a validation error. The second section of the BASH script is the generation of the text example LDIF file shown before the BASH script, except that the Base64 encoded data has not been generated.

The magic of adding the Base64 encoded data to an LDIF file is illustrated in the third and fourth sections of the BASH script. In the third section, a binary file is converted to an encoded buffer using the command uuencode. The output of uuencode is piped to the file temp.image.file. The problem with the file temp.image.file is that the Base64 encoded data contains an encoding reference in the first line. The idea in the BASH script is to copy the contents of the output content into the LDIF file, but the first line needs to be trimmed. To trim the first line, the command `tail` is used. The command `tail` is used to output the bottom lines of a file, up to including the number of lines specified.

The default the command `tail` displays are 10 lines, but by using the `--lines` command-line option, you can specify a custom number of lines to output. The number of lines to display is the total number of lines in the file minus one, which automatically trims the first line. To get the line count of a file, the command `wc` with the `--lines` option is used. The generated content is piped into the `awk` command, which returns the line count as a single number. The line count is decremented using the command `expr`, which is a command-line calculator that takes two arguments and performs operations such as adding, subtracting, multiplying, or making comparisons.

In the fourth section of the BASH script, the individual lines of the encoded file are iterated and output to the LDIF file. The lines are iterated because each line of the output file must be prefixed with a space before being added to the LDIF file. The iteration uses a trick because the input stream is temporarily stored and assigned the third input stream. The input stream is then assigned the encoded file. When the `while` loop executes, the lines of the encoded file are read. Each line is then output with a leading space to the LDIF file.

In the fifth section of Bash script, the command `ldapadd` is executed to manipulate the objects defined in the LDIF file. The last section deletes the files that have been created. The deletion is important so that no superfluous files remain.

Technique: Manipulating LDAP Data in a Script

LDAP administrators will want to add, manipulate, and search the LDAP server. A previous LDIF script added a user, modified an attribute, and then deleted an attribute. You saw how to perform all types of operations on an LDAP database. When working with LDIF files, a query results in an LDIF file, which could in theory be modified to manipulate the data on the LDAP database. The following script shows the results in an LDIF format, which can be used to add or modify the data in the LDAP database:

```
#!/bin/bash
echo "dn: $3,$2" > binary.ldif
printf "changetype: delete\n\n" >> binary.ldif

ldapsearch -h localhost -b "$2" -LLL "($3)" |
./removefield.py "jpegPhoto" > temp.binary.ldif

uuencode --base64 $1 /dev/stdout > temp.image.file
imagelc=$(wc --lines temp.image.file | awk '{print $1}')
```

```
imagelc=$(expr $imagelc - 1)
tail --lines=$imagelc temp.image.file > temp2.image.file

ldiflc=$(wc --lines temp.binary.ldif | awk '{print $1}')
ldiflc=$(expr $ldiflc - 1)
head —lines=$ldiflc temp.binary.ldif >> binary.ldif

printf "jpegPhoto:: " >> binary.ldif

exec 3<&0
exec < temp2.image.file
while read line
do
    echo " $line" >> binary.ldif
done
exec <&3
exec 3<&-

ldapadd -c -f binary.ldif -h localhost
-D "cn=Manager,dc=devspace,dc=com" -x -w something

rm temp.binary.ldif
rm temp.image.file
rm temp2.image.file
rm binary.ldif
```

In the script there are multiple sections separated by an empty line. The second section is new as the command ldapsearch is used. The output generated by the command ldapsearch is an LDIF file. A search is executed by specifying two parts: the base of the search and the query. The query is specified by the text after the command-line option -LLL. The base of the search is specified by the text after the command-line option -b. The search results are then piped into the Python script removefield.py. A script is used because deciphering the contents of an LDIF file is simpler with Python. The Python script removefield.py has one command-line parameter, which defines the field to remove from the LDIF output. After the Python script has executed, the remaining LDIF data is streamed to the file temp.binary.ldif.

The third section of the script is a line trim as shown in the previous BASH script example of appending the Base64 encoded data. The file needs to be trimmed because the ldapsearch command generates an unnecessary line feed at the end of the file that needs to be removed. This time, however, instead of using the tail command, the head command is used. The head command displays all the lines of a file starting from the top of the file. The rest of the listing appends the binary attribute to the LDIF.

The generated LDIF data is parsed using the Python script:

```
#!c:/python23/python.exe
import os, sys, xreadlines, string

isBinary = False
for line in xreadlines.xreadlines(sys.stdin):
    if string.find( line, sys.argv[ 1]) == -1 :
        if isBinary == True :
            if line[ 0] != ' ' :
                isBinary = False
                sys.stdout.write( line)
        else :
            sys.stdout.write( line)
    else :
        if string.find( line, "::") != -1 :
            isBinary = True
```

The Python script reads the data from the input stream as shown in the Python scripting example. For each line read, the string is scanned to see if the field being searched for is found within it. If the field is found, then a test is made in the else clause to see if the field is binary. If the field is binary, the binary flag isBinary is set. This is necessary because binary fields have a leading space or tab and those lines need to be removed as well. The Python script assumes that the buffer has leading spaces.

The example Python and BASH scripts have shown that it is possible to query for an LDAP object, retrieve it, and then save it again after some small modifications. The tool ldapsearch *is a great utility because the results are LDIF formatted. This provides a consistency necessary when writing scripts that need to read and write LDAP data.*

Technique: Securing the LDAP Server

There are multiple ways of securing an LDAP server, but the two major ways are encrypted communications to the LDAP server and access rights to the LDAP server. In the scripts used so far, all the modifications used the root username and password. In general that is okay for the administrator, but is not okay for other users. Other users should have restrictions in what they can modify and how they can modify the data. OpenLDAP is powerful because it has a flexible authentication mechanism.

One way to authenticate is to use the Simple Authentication and Security Layer (SASL) framework. Using SASL, a user can be authenticated using another security mechanism like Kerberos or Generic Security Services Application Programming Interface (GSSAPI). In all frankness, that defeats the purpose of creating the LDAP server for authentication in the first place. For example, imagine adding all users and their passwords to the LDAP database and then having to go through that procedure one more time for Kerberos. There are situations where that approach might be useful, for example when the LDAP server is a secondary information reference. This book assumes that the LDAP server is the reference point for all information, including usernames and passwords. The exception to this rule for the book is when the Windows PDC is the reference point for all information.

Using the LDAP server as a reference point for all reference information is a good idea because it is not difficult. In this scenario, the LDAP server executes in the context of a simple authentication system as the previous scripts demonstrated. Using simple authentication means that the username and password are communicated across a network in free text, and anyone with a network snooper could see the username and password. That is not a good idea, and needs to be changed. This chapter will not get into that topic because secure communications were covered in Chapter 4.

Specifying a Password for a User

The security presented in this part of the chapter relates to access rights. In the simplest case all users have all rights to the database and can do what they want. Outside of the special case of the root user, all users who want to authenticate against the LDAP server must have a username and password. Following is an example user defined in LDIF format:

```
dn: cn=Christian Gross,o=contacts,dc=devspace,dc=com
objectclass: inetOrgPerson
cn: Christian Gross
mail: christianhgross@yahoo.ca
o: Author
givenname: Christian
sn: Gross
userPassword: {SSHA}kOmBY4W/B8f4dJeYA9bLAmH8eHRJUada
```

The object type declared is `inetOrgPerson`, but the base object type `person` would have sufficed as a declaration. The object `inetOrgPerson` is a distant subclass of the object `person`. The base object `person` has an attribute `userPassword`, which represents the password of the user. The password could be stored in clear text, but a safer approach is to use the `slappasswd` command to generate an encrypted, hash-encoded buffer.

The script to add a password to a user is shown as follows:

```
#!/bin/bash
echo "dn: $2,$1" > binary.ldif
echo "changetype: modify:" >> binary.ldif
echo "delete: userPassword" >> binary.ldif
echo "" >> binary.ldif

echo "dn: $2,$1" >> binary.ldif
echo "changetype: modify" >> binary.ldif
printf "userPassword: " >> binary.ldif

/usr/local/sbin/slappasswd.exe -s $3 >> binary.ldif

ldapadd -c -f binary.ldif -h localhost
-D "cn=Manager,dc=devspace,dc=com" -x -w something

rm binary.ldif
```

The script generates an LDIF file that deletes the old password, and then adds a new password. The contents of the slappasswd are piped to the output LDIF file. Another approach is to use the ldappasswd command, which can change a password on the LDAP server without using an LDIF file.

Specifying Access Rights

Access control rights are specified in the configuration file. The general format of the access rights is outlined in the OpenLDAP administrators guide in the slapd configuration file specification under the heading "Access Control." For fine-tuning access rights, be sure to look at that documentation. This book focuses only on the most common scenarios.

When users log on using credentials from the LDAP database, they are checked against the LDAP database. So in the case of the previously defined user, it is the user cn=Christian Gross,o=contacts,dc=devspace,dc=com. When logging into an LDAP server, the first major difference is that the username is much longer. A script could prefix and append standard data to simplify logging in. When authenticating against the LDAP server, the distinguished name has to be used. The supplied password is verified against the password in the attribute userPassword of the person object. If both username and password match, then the user is considered logged on and the system determines the access rights based on the access rights rules.

The simplest of access rules is to only allow all users read access to the entire database:

```
access to * by * read
```

The keyword access starts an access reference. The parts are defined as follows:

to *: Specifies what objects can be accessed by the rule. The asterisk means all objects.

by *: Specifies the users that this rule applies to. The asterisk means all users.

read: Specifies the access level that the user(s) are allowed in this rule. The read identifier means that the objects can only be read.

Following is a rule that allows a user to modify his own object, but only has read-only access to the rest of the objects.

```
access to *
     by self write
     by anonymous auth
     by * read
```

Notice in the rule that the by keyword can be used multiple times. This means that the selection has multiple modes of access depending on the object that is inspected.

The rules are matched in an order that starts with the object, then the user, and then the access level. To get an idea of what this involves, consider the sample rules defined as follows:

```
access to dn.subtree="o=contacts-email,dc=devspace,dc=com"
     by anonymous auth

access to dn.subtree="dc=com"
     by users read
     by anonymous auth
```

When a user logs onto the LDAP server, he wants to access the object identified by the following distinguished name:

```
dn: cn=Christian Gross,o=contacts,dc=devspace,dc=com
```

The authentication steps that occur are defined by the following steps. The distinguished name is associated with a to rule that is matched first. In the case of the sample rules, that would mean the first rule is bypassed as the distinguished names are different and the second rule applies. The second rule applies because the object's distinguished name falls into the tree defined by the second rule. Notice how the access rules are defined with the most specific location rule first and more generic rules last. This is because the access template uses the first found location rule, not the most specific access location rule.

The status of the user is determined and then the first by part of the second rule is matched. In the case of the sample rules and specifically the second rule, it means the users. The user that is matched is a first match found algorithm.

The access type of the found user is associated with the object, which is read. Second rule, users identifier, means the object defined by the previous distinguished name can only be read and not manipulated.

For the sample rules shown, three new concepts were used: distinguished name identifier, user type, and access type.

Access Rights Details

The distinguished name applied to the to keyword references the part of the LDAP database tree that is described. There are four different tree selectors: base, one, subtree, and children:

dn.base: Selects the object referenced by the distinguished name.

dn.one: Selects all the immediate child objects of the distinguished name.

dn.subtree: Selects all the children objects, including the object referenced by the distinguished name.

dn.children: Selects all the children objects, not including the object referenced by the distinguished name.

The following is an example LDAP database structure:

```
                        dc=devspace,dc=com (1)
              o=contacts,dc=devspace,dc=com (2)
 cn=Christian Gross,o=contacts,dc=devspace,dc=com (3)
     cn=Alison Bury,o=contacts,dc=devspace,dc=com (4)
```

Consider the following distinguished name:

```
dc=devspace,dc=com
```

Applying the different tree selectors to the distinguished name generates the following results:

dn.base: Line 1 from the example LDAP database structure.

dn.one: Line 2 from the example LDAP database structure.

dn.subtree: Lines 1, 2, 3, and 4 from the example LDAP database structure.

dn.children: Lines 2, 3, and 4 from the example LDAP database structure.

After the distinguished name has been matched, a user role is matched. The following list of user roles are ordered from most general to most specific precedence:

`*`: Matches every user, including anonymous and authenticated users.

`anonymous`: Matches a user that has been bound to the LDAP database as anonymous. This is a special mode that many tools use to connect to the LDAP database for quick replies and information.

`users`: Authenticated users.

`self`: The logged on authenticated user.

`dn.[base | one | subtree | children]`: A way of identifying a user that is located in one part of the tree. This way of specifying the user is similar to associating a user to a group. For example, a user that belongs to a tree deemed as administrators could have a higher access than another user.

`domain`: A way of identifying a user belonging to a part of the tree using regular expressions.

Let's go back to the rule where a user can access his own object, but has read-only access to the other objects. Attempting to follow the user match logic, the first rule is a very specific user, and the last rule is a very general user.

After a user has been matched, the role assignment given is defined by the following list ordered from lowest to highest precedence. A higher precedence implies an inheritance of a lower precedence right.

`none`: No access is allowed to the LDAP database.

`auth`: Authorization needed to bind to the server. It is important that this precedence is always added because if not, the client cannot bind to the LDAP server during authentication. The resulting error would seem that the user is typing in the wrong password, which is not the case.

`compare`: Authorization used to compare LDAP entries.

`search`: Authorization used to search LDAP and retrieve LDAP entries.

`read`: Authorization used to read an LDAP entry.

`write`: Authorization used to write an LDAP entry.

Let's consider the sample rules again:

```
access to dn.subtree="o=contacts-email,dc=devspace,dc=com"
    by anonymous auth

access to dn.subtree="dc=com"
```

```
by users read
by anonymous auth
```

Rules 1 and 2 can therefore be explained as follows:

Rule 1: For all the objects below and including the distinguished name "o=con-tacts-email,dc=devspace,dc=com", let them connect to the LDAP database, but they cannot be read by anyone other than the root password.

Rule 2: For all objects below and including, but not including any rules mentioned previously, the distinguished name "dc=com", let all authenticated users be able to read the LDAP entries; the anonymous user can only connect.

Although it might be tempting to use the none *access keyword, its use can cause problems with some LDAP clients. Use* anonymous auth *instead to get the same effect.*

Technique: Replicated Directory Service

With OpenLDAP, you can replicate the content in one OpenLDAP server to another OpenLDAP server. The replication is only from master to slave. This does pose a problem, however, because the LDAP server that is queried may not be the LDAP server that is updated. For example, let's say in the corporation that the master replicates its data to the slave. If the client is appropriated as a slave, then any updates that are made must be made to the master; otherwise, the data might become inconsistent. This can be achieved using an LDAP redirection. The way to do that is to add a redirection to the parent server as shown in a previous section, and to make the slave database read only. OpenLDAP automatically redirects the requests as necessary.

Replication is implemented using a transaction log that is read by the slurpd program and copied to the slaves. Following is the configuration entry added to the slapd.conf file to generate the transaction log:

```
replogfile /usr/local/var/slurpd-data/logfile.txt
```

The configuration item replogfile generates a file that contains all the actions that have occurred on the LDAP server as LDIF instructions. Even without replication, the log file can be used as a transaction log to recreate the LDAP database if an LDAP database becomes corrupted.

Then on the master server, the following defined configuration entry must be added:

```
replica    host=slave:389
```

```
binddn="cn=Manager,dc=devspace,dc=com"
bindmethod=simple
credentials=secret
```

The configuration item `replica` instructs a server to read the generated log file and replicate it to a specific server. There can be multiple replicas to replicate to multiple slaves. The key value pairs are explained as follows:

host: The slave host.

binddn: The username used to log on to the slave machine. This would typically be the `rootdn`.

bindmethod: The way that the master connects to the slave. For the scope of this book, the only `bindmethod` used is `simple`.

credentials: The secret password used to log on to the slave machine. The problem of putting the password into the `slapd.conf file` is to ensure security. Replication using the simple `bindmethod` can be a security risk.

The `replica` configuration item has to be complemented on the slave LDAP server side by an `updatedn` configuration entry shown as follows:

```
updatedn "cn=Manager,dc=devspace,dc=com"
```

The distinguished name referenced by the `updatedn` configuration entry is the name of the user that will make the changes to the slave database when a replication is being executed.

Doing a clean replication involves synchronizing two servers when they may not be synchronized. The best approach to adding a slave LDAP server to a master LDAP server is to carry out the following steps:

1. Take the master offline from the network so that nobody can modify any records, but leave the `slapd` server running.
2. Using the tool `/usr/local/sbin/slapcat,` extract the entire LDAP server contents as an LDIF file.
3. Stop the master.
4. In the configuration of the master, add the configuration entries to generate a log file and to replicate the log file to the associated slave.
5. Take the slave offline from the network, but keep `slapd` running.
6. Empty the entire slave database if necessary, by deleting the root object.

7. Using the tool `/usr/local/sbin/slapadd`, add the generated LDIF file to recreate the slave database.
8. In the configuration of the slave, add the configuration entry for updating the LDAP database. Add an LDAP redirection to the master and make the client database read-only for most users.
9. Stop the slave.
10. Start the master.
11. Start the slave.

After the steps have been completed, replication is available but it will not run because replication is not managed by `slapd`. There is another application that manages replication. More importantly, both the slave and master have been synchronized and there will be no data consistencies problems.

`Slurpd` is the application used for replication; it runs on the master only. Replication does not have to be carried out by `slurpd`. Because the transaction log created is in LDIF, a combination script and the command `ldapmodify` are acceptable. This solution is useful when the slaves are not OpenLDAP servers because replication with `slurpd` only works when both master and slave LDAP servers are OpenLDAP.

The `slurpd` application is not by default compiled using the impatient instructions. `Slurpd` requires threading to be active. In the impatient installation, you can leave off the command-line option `–without-threads`. This is not an option, however, because the threaded version of the Cygwin-compiled `slapd` cannot send the kill signal. This results in potentially corrupting the LDAP database.

The `slapd` server application has to be recompiled using the MinGW compiler or the Visual C++ compiler, which uses native Windows function calls. Compiling the individual applications using this approach has some issues and requires a bit of time to get it right. Assuming that you compiled `slurpd`, use the following command to execute `slurpd`:

```
/usr/local/libexec/slurpd -d 4
-r /usr/local/var/slurpd-data/logfile.txt
```

In the command, the `-d` option is used to output debug messages. The `-r` option references the file where the generated log files are. Note that the directory is specified in Linux/BSD format, which may not work from a script and an absolute path may be required.

Technique: Indexing

When an LDAP database is filled with a large number of objects, searching for a particular object may become slow. Indexing an LDAP database will increase the search speed. An LDAP database can only be indexed by its attributes, not its objects. The indices are created in the slapd.conf file using the index configuration entry shown as follows:

```
index cn, sn, mail    pres,eq,sub
```

The attributes cn, sn, and mail are indexed with the indexing commands pres, eq, and sub. The index configuration entry does not have to reference an indexing command, which means that the default pres and eq is assumed. There can be multiple index configuration entries in a slapd.conf file. The available index command types are defined as follows:

pres: Indexes the attribute using a present index. (Should be used.)

eq: Indexes the attribute using an equality index, which is the entire string or value. (Should be used.)

approx: Indexes the attribute using an approximate index, which makes it simpler to match when doing approximate searches. Approximate searches are similar to wildcard type searches.

sub: Indexes the attribute using a substring index, which makes it easier to match pieces of string buffers.

The indices created depend on the situation and the types of queries executed. Creating too many indices will slow down the add or modification object operation times.

When creating a new index or modifying an existing index, stop the LDAP server using the program /usr/local/sbin/slapdindex to build a new set of indices.

Technique: Some Common Configuration Tips

In the slapd.conf file, there are some common configuration tips that can be used (see Table 6.4). Note if the required configuration tip is not found in the table, it is recommended to reference the administration documentation available at the OpenLDAP Web site.

TABLE 6.4 Common Configuration Information

Item	Description
include [filename]	Instead of defining everything in one file, it is possible to include other files containing configuration information.
idletime [time in seconds]	The amount of time that slapd waits before forcibly closing a client connection.
sizelimit [entries]	The maximum number of objects to display when a search is executed.
timelimit [time in seconds]	The maximum time a request will execute a search. If the time is exceeded a time limit error is returned.
readonly [on | off]	A switch to make the LDAP database read-only or not.
cachesize [number]	An LDBM database configuration entry that defines how much in-memory cache should be used.
dbcachesize [number]	An LDBM database configuration entry that defines how much memory is used by the index file. If a computer has plenty of RAM, this configuration entry can increase performance dramatically.
dbnolocking	An LDBM database configuration entry that prevents locking of the database. This is a risky entry and could corrupt the database.
dbnosync	An LDBM database configuration entry that uses the in-memory cache instead of writing contents straight to the disk.

PROJECT: SAMBA

The Samba server is a file server that runs on the Linux/BSD operating systems. Samba can also be a Primary Domain Controller (PDC) and a Windows Internet Name Service (WINS) server.

The original Samba project, started in December 1991, was used to mount Sun drives on PC computers. The original developer was Andrew Tridgell who released version 1.0 in January 1992. The project was converted into a Linux project on November 1992. In December 1993, the project NetBIOS for Unix was started, which could also be called the starting point for today's Samba. Today's resulting software has become a mainstay among many Linux/BSD enthusiasts. Table 6.5 provides the reference information on Samba. Because an installation of Samba will imply Linux, you need to know about the recommended Linux distribution Knoppix, which is explained in Table 6.6.

TABLE 6.5 Reference Information for Samba

Item	Description
Home page	*http://www.samba.org* provides links to the mirrors that contain the Samba information.
Installation	Installing Samba requires that Linux already be installed. Because this is a Windows book, that is a bit of a challenge. It is advised that the reader read the Impatient Install to show how to get up to speed very quickly using Samba.
Version	Latest stable version 3.0.10, but the Knoppix ISO distributed with DVD is 3.0.
Documentation	The documentation found on the Samba site is very good. The best documentation is found distributed with the sources of Samba. You should download the latest stable release source tree that contains a number of documents in the docs directory. Of specific interest are the files/directories: Samba-HOWTO-Collection.pdf, docs/htmldocs, and docs/htmldocs/using_samba. $\rightarrow$

Item	Description
Mailing Lists	There are several mailing lists offered by the SAMBA group. The different mailing lists are defined and explained at *http://samba.epfl.ch/samba/archives.html*. For the administrator, the mailing list samba would be most interesting.
Impatient Installation Time Required	The impatient installation for Samba including download would take the better part of a morning or afternoon. A broadband connection is assumed when downloading the files. Installation time: 30-50 minutes CD-ROM burn time: 10-30 minutes Download size: 710 MB for Knoppix
Firewall Port	42: WINS replication port and usually not needed for Samba. 135: RPC port used to accept RPC requests (can be blocked, but depends on the context). 137 (UDP): NetBIOS name service used for browsing the server names (can be blocked and used by application nmbd). 138 (UDP): Broadcast port for what shares are available (can be blocked and used by application nmbd). 139 (TCP): File sharing port used to accept connections to shared resources (should not be blocked and used by application smbd). 445: Native "Windows" mode for file sharing when NetBIOS over TCP/IP is disabled (depending on the configuration should not be blocked and used by application smbd).
DVD Location	Part of the Knoppix Linux distribution.

TABLE 6.6 Reference Information for Knoppix

Item	Description
Home page	The main page is located at *http://www.knoppix.org/*. From that page, different language versions can be selected.
Installation	Knoppix is an extremely simple install because it runs from the CD and does not require an installation.
Version	Latest released version 3.7, but distributed with the DVD is 3.4. A 3.4 installation can be upgraded to 3.7 by running the Debian upgrade.
Documentation	The documentation associated with Knoppix is very scant because Knoppix is based on the Debian Linux distribution. For information related to Linux, the Debian site (*http://www.debian.org*) is better suited. Debian is not for the faint of heart; however, Knoppix offers a good forum.
Mailing Lists	There are no mailing lists for Knoppix, but there is an extremely helpful forum located at *http://www.knoppix.net*. Searching the forum will most likely yield answers to most questions. Especially important are those messages in a forum that are sticky notes. These notes contain general information that should be read.
Impatient Installation Time Required	The impatient installation for Knoppix, including download, would take the better part of a morning or afternoon. A broadband connection is assumed when downloading the files. Installation time: 30-50 minutes. CD-ROM burn time: 10-30 minutes. Download size: 710 MB for Knoppix. Computer Requirements: Minimum 4 GB hard disk, 128 MB RAM, and Pentium II CPU.
DVD Location	The ISO image of Knoppix is located in the directory `/packages/knoppix`. You will need software to convert the ISO image into a bootable CD.

Additional Notes

At the time of this writing, the latest released version of Samba was 3.0.10. However, there are some things to consider. The purpose of the Samba software is to integrate Linux/BSD operating systems in a Windows context. This generally works and there are conditions of operations that are defined in Table 6.7. Note that the conditions are sometimes restrictions,

TABLE 6.7 Conditions that a Samba Server Implies

Condition	Description
PDC Controller	A SAMBA server is not a PDC in the complete sense of the word. The best way to describe it is that Samba is a Common Internet Filesystem (CIFS) server, which makes Samba a Windows NT 4 type domain.
No Backup Support	Samba cannot act as Backup Domain Controller (BDC) when the PDC is a Windows Server. Nor can a Windows-based BDC work in conjunction with a Samba server. However, a Samba server can be a BDC to another Samba server.
Not an LDAP or Kerberos Server	Samba is not an LDAP server, nor is it a Kerberos server. However, Samba can be used with an LDAP server and a Kerberos server. One of the very powerful aspects of Samba is that other sources can be used to authenticate the user that attempts to use Samba.
Active Directory Support	Samba can be a member of an Active Directory, and can authenticate using LDAP/Kerberos, but cannot participate in replication or other advanced topics.
Access Control Lists (ACL) Support	With appropriate patches to the Linux/BSD system, Samba can fully supported Windows ACLs.
Other Restrictions	No machine policy files. No group policy objects. No asynchronously executed Active Directory scripts.

sometimes features, depending on how much of the features in a Windows network are used.

Reading all the conditions in Table 6.7 you might get the impression that Samba is not capable of doing much at all. That is a wrong assumption because the focus was on features that do not work, and not the features that do work. Essentially if the condition is not in Table 6.7, then it is possible with Samba, with some notable examples being PDC controller, WINS server, printer server, and of course file server.

When using Samba, consider using it as either the PDC or as a member, and not something in between. It is best to think of Samba as an all-or-nothing scenario where if the Samba is the PDC, then all authentications is carried out by the Samba server. If the authentication occurs elsewhere, then all authentications must happen elsewhere and Samba is solely a participant much like the client workstations are.

Documentation

With Samba, the problem is not lack of documentation, but too much documentation. Very often the problem has been that a new Samba user wants to create a little network where files can be shared, but when the user asks a question, he gets pages and pages of answers on how to do this. Although it is useful to have all the information available, it still does not help the novice user. The best strategy to take is to read this book, do an impatient installation, follow some of the techniques, and then see if there are any necessary extras. After that, reading the Samba Web site documentation and asking intelligent questions will be easier.

Impatient Installation

The impatient installation of Samba is a challenge because it requires installing either Linux or BSD or another Unix. In the Linux world, the challenge is to find a distribution that makes it easy to install and configure Linux and Samba. The distribution recommended by the impatient installation is Knoppix.

Knoppix is not the only Linux distribution that you could use, but the major advantage of Knoppix is that it's a straightforward and simple installation that will either work or not work. The key in installing Linux is to know whether something will work or not work. You do not want to waste time twiddling some bits or configuration flags to find out three weeks later that Linux is not going to solve your problem.

Many people use Knoppix to rescue corrupted machines that do not boot anymore. Other people use Knoppix to rescue files from a hard disk. Administrators

who need a quick way to access a computer to perform some critical repairs are well advised to keep a Knoppix CD handy.

The Linux distribution Knoppix can be downloaded from the Web site *http://www.knoppix.org*. The download is an ISO CD image that can be burned to a CD. Most CD-burning applications know how to transfer an ISO image to a raw CD. The Knoppix download is about 720 MB and depending on the line speed can take some time. Therefore, do the download on a machine that will not be interrupted.

Booting Knoppix

After the Knoppix distribution has been burned onto a raw CD, that CD can be used to boot Linux. The advantage of using the Knoppix CD is that Linux will start from the CD and not touch any of the computer's hard disks. You could first experiment with a live running Linux operating system, and verify that all the computer's peripherals are functioning properly before modifying the hard disks. When the Knoppix CD first boots, it will show a command prompt in the lower-left corner of the computer screen as shown in Figure 6.2.

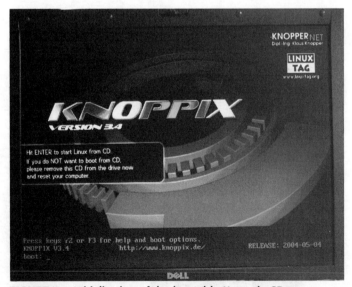

FIGURE 6.2 Initialization of the bootable Knoppix CD.

At the command prompt, you press the Enter key and then Knoppix begins to boot and configure itself, which should look similar to Figure 6.3.

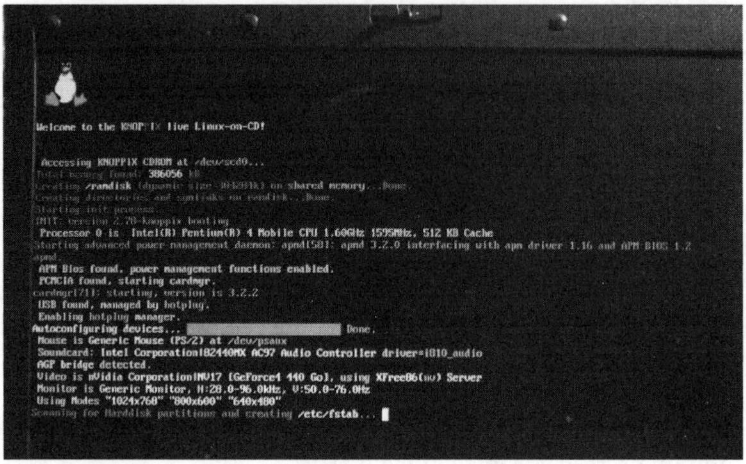

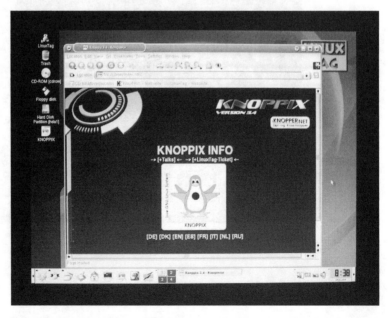

FIGURE 6.3 Knoppix booting up.

When Knoppix has finished booting, a desktop display similar to Figure 6.4 is shown.

FIGURE 6.4 Booted Knoppix Linux Operating System showing desktop.

After Knoppix has booted, it is important to know if the computer has access to a network and Internet. The first check to make is to see whether the computer has a network card, and working network cable plugged into the network card. If either of these conditions are not true, then stop and find a computer that has a network card and live network cable plugged into the network card. Blinking links beside the network adaptor indicate a live network cable.

From the Knoppix desktop, start a console session, which is the clam icon highlighted in the bottom toolbar as shown in Figure 6.5.

FIGURE 6.5 Knoppix desktop showing the started console application.

When the console application has started, type the command sudo ifconfig and press Enter. An application starts that displays the status of any found network adaptors. In Figure 6.5, the output shows that a network card has been found and configured. The desired output should contain some text on the left side of the console that says eth0, eth1, and so on. For the ethX, there should be an associated attribute inet addr that should have a real IP address as shown in Figure 6.5. A real IP address would be a four-digit number not including 127.0.0.1. If there is no ethX entry, then either the network card could not be configured or the computer could not find a network address.

If there is a network adaptor, enter in the console the command traceroute [some server], where [some server] is a known public server. This command only works if the Knoppix computer's network is connected to the Internet. If not, enter the IP address of a computer on the network. Do not use the computer name because the Knoppix computer will not know about that computer name as the name is registered using Windows protocols. If the `traceroute` command works, at least one IP address will appear. If the `traceroute` command fails, then only the asterisk characters will appear or an error will be printed to the console.

Configuring a Network Card

If your computer trace works, you can skip this section or read it as a reference for when the network configuration needs to be modified. When the commands `sudo ifconfig` or `traceroute` return an error, something is wrong with the network card or the configuration. Most likely, there probably was not a Dynamic Host Configuration Protocol (DHCP) server on the network and could not retrieve an IP address. With Knoppix, the network configuration is altered using the script `netcardconfigure`. From the console, enter the command `netcardconfigure`, and press the Enter key. One of the following dialog boxes may appear depending on the decisions made:

Use DHCP Broadcast: Enables you to choose DHCP. Clicking on Yes means you'll use DHCP to retrieve an IP address and associated configuration data automatically. Clicking on Yes also ends the network card configuration process as there is nothing more to do. Clicking on No means retrieving the data manually and further dialog boxes will appear.

Please Enter IP Address for eth0: Defines the IP address for the network adapter. The identifier eth0 means the first network card in the local computer.

Please Enter Network Mask for eth0: Defines the network mask for the network adapter. The default of 255.255.255.0, which is automatically filled, should be acceptable.

Please Enter Broadcast Address for eth0: Defines the broadcast address used, which should be kept as default and not changed.

Please Enter Default Gateway: Defines the default gateway used for the computer when accessing other computers beyond the current subnet defined by the network mask.

Please Enter Nameserver(s): Defines a list of space-separated IP addresses used by the computer to resolve names of computers to IP addresses.

If everything went successfully, the console should appear similar to Figure 6.6.

If there are any problems, such as the network card device driver not available, then those problems will be displayed as errors in the form of a dialog box or a console message.

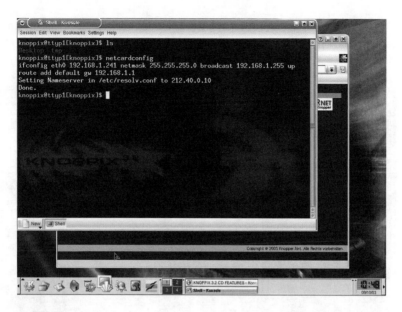

FIGURE 6.6 Console application showing a successfully modified network configuration.

Installing to the Hard Disk

TIP

If anything at all has gone wrong, like not booting properly, no access to the network, or screen driver not working at all, then do not attempt to twiddle with the computer in hopes that it will work. The Knoppix distribution is the simplest and most reliable of all Linux distributions. This means if Knoppix does not work, then the likelihood that Linux can be installed on the computer is fairly remote and not worth the effort. This only affects a small percentage of computers, but it can happen. This is why Knoppix is so useful, because if Linux will not boot or function properly, you've only wasted 10 minutes and not hours or a formatted hard disk.

When the Knoppix Linux distribution is running successfully, Knoppix can be transferred to a hard disk so that instead of booting from the bootable CD-ROM, Knoppix will boot from the hard disk like other operating systems. It is important to realize that Knoppix can be multibooted with other operating systems, and that partitions can be adjusted and manipulated. However, for the impatient install, this is not recommended because it can be problematic and requires more explanations. The simplest approach is to format the computer's hard disks and then install only the Knoppix Linux operating system.

From the Knoppix console, enter the command sudo knoppix-installer and a dialog box will appear similar to Figure 6.7.

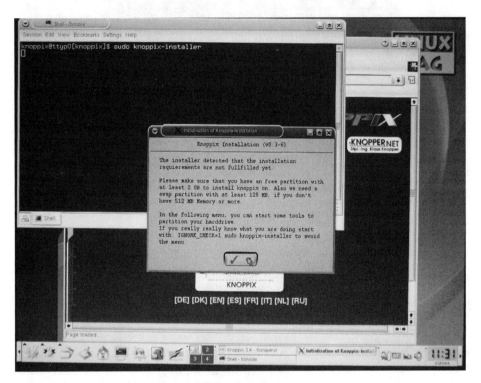

FIGURE 6.7 Starting the Knoppix hard disk installation process.

Click the Yes button to open the Partition Hard Disk dialog box (see Figure 6.8).

In Figure 6.8, a single hard disk is displayed in the tree control because this particular computer only has a single hard disk. If your computer has multiple hard disks, select one of them. The best hard disk choice is the one where the three letter short form below the Disks ends with an a, e.g., sda or hda. The reason for this choice is that the hard disk that ends with the letter a is the first hard disk in the physical configuration of the computer.

In the listbox on the right side of the dialog box, select and delete all partitions on the hard disk. By selecting a partition and then right-clicking, a menu appears allowing you to resize, format, and delete the selected partition. At this stage, all the partitions need to be deleted. After all the partitions are deleted, only one free partition is available. On that partition, use the tool to create a Linux and swap partition.

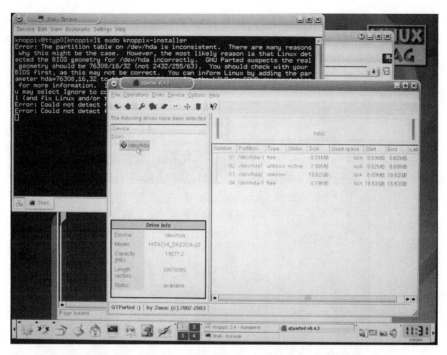

FIGURE 6.8 Dialog box used to select the hard disk on which to install Knoppix Linux.

When creating a partition, the dialog box in Figure 6.9 is displayed.

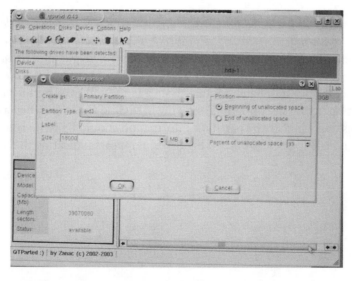

FIGURE 6.9 Creating a Linux partition using the Create Partition dialog box.

You will want to create two partitions: the first is a partition type `ext3` and the second is a swap. The size of the first partition should be the result of the hard disk size minus two times the RAM size. The size of the swap partition should be twice the RAM size and is created using the dialog box shown in Figure 6.10.

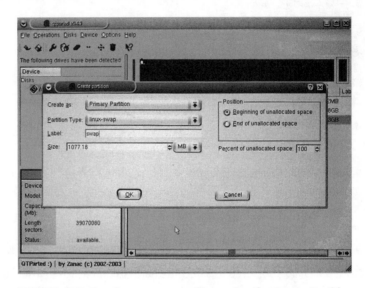

FIGURE 6.10 Creating a swap partition using the Create Partition dialog box.

The hard disk selected for partitioning will be formatted and all data on it will be lost. Remember to back up all important data because you will not be able to retrieve the data after the disk has been repartitioned and formatted.

After the partition table contains both a Linux and swap partition, choose File→ Commit to write the configuration to the hard disk. Click Yes when a dialog box appears asking whether the partition information should be written to the hard disk. A Progress dialog box similar to Figure 6.11 appears indicating the disk operations.

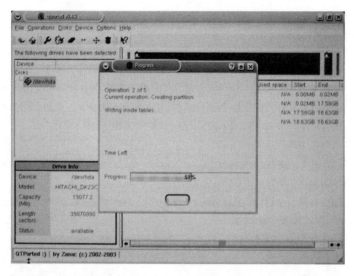

FIGURE 6.11 Dialog box that shows the progress of disk operations.

After the partitioning of the hard disk, a dialog box appears similar to Figure 6.12, which defines the operations that can be carried out.

For an initial installation, choose the item Create a New Configuration. The Choose System Type dialog box shown in Figure 6.13 appears asking which type of installation should be carried out.

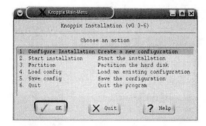

FIGURE 6.12 Knoppix Main-Menu dialog box shows the operations that can be carried out.

FIGURE 6.13 The Choose System Type dialog box asking which type of Knoppix installation should be carried out.

For simplicity, choose the first option (beginner) and the following text boxes appear:

Choose the Partition to Install Knoppix: A listbox appears asking where to install Knoppix. Choose the partition that you just partitioned.

Input Your Whole Name (Name Surname): When Knoppix is installed, a username is created initially. This text box asks for the full name of the initial username.

Input Your Username: You need to define a username for the whole name created initially.

Input Your User-Password: You'll enter the password associated with the initially created user twice.

Input Your Administration Password: This is the password associated with the root user.

Input Your Preferred Hostname: This is the hostname of the computer on which Knoppix is about to be installed.

Choose Where the Boot-Loader (lilo) Shall Be Installed: This defines where the boot files are stored for Knoppix. The default is master boot record (MBR) and should be kept as the default choice. Otherwise, you will need a boot disk.

After the individual dialog boxes have been filled out, the Knoppix Main-Menu dialog box appears again. This time, select the option Start Installation to open the Starting Knoppix Installation dialog box as shown in Figure 6.14.

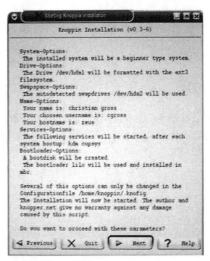

FIGURE 6.14 This dialog box outputs the installation parameters.

If all the parameters are correct, click Next. The next dialog box formats the selected hard disk. After the hard disk has been formatted, the data is copied from the CD to the hard disk.

After the data has been copied, a dialog box appears asking if you want to create a backup floppy boot disk. This is optional and only helps if you want to boot Knoppix from the floppy disk. Note that this is required if you selected to install the boot-loader on the partition and not MBR. After the backup floppy dialog box, a Knoppix installation confirmation dialog box appears. At this point, you can reboot the machine and run Linux.

Log off as the Knoppix user, and the computer will shut down and pop open the CD-ROM drive. Remove the CD, close the CD-ROM drive, and reboot the computer. Linux will now boot from the hard disk, and when the booting is complete, a logging window should appear. At that point, log in using the root username and password given in the dialog boxes of the install to hard disk application.

Knoppix is already serving Samba content because the Samba server will be running. All that remains is the configuration of the Samba server so that the server will integrate into the overall network. However, from an impatient installation point of view everything is done.

To remotely administer the Knoppix Linux computer, from the console type in the command vncserver. *The command* vncserver *will ask for a password twice and start the VNC server application on the first port. More details about the VNC server and ports can be found in Chapter 5.*

Deploying Samba

Deploying the Samba server is very much like the impatient installation because to use Samba, Linux has to be installed. Linux has to be installed manually, or in the more sophisticated case using scripting. The scripting of a Linux installation is beyond the scope of this book because Samba is being used to provide a file server and possibly an authentication server. Samba is also unique in that to get specific features, they have to be compiled into the application. The configuration and compilation of a custom Samba server is also beyond the scope of this book, but can easily be reviewed and implemented by reading the associated documents distributed with the Samba sources. This section focuses on the ability to maintain, upgrade, and install software packages. However, the default installation of Linux and Samba as shown in the impatient installation is adequate.

An Introduction to `apt-get`

On the Knoppix Linux distribution, applications are distributed as packages using the Debian packaging system. The Debian packaging system is a very simple and clever way of installing and maintaining applications on a local machine. Although it is not necessary to generally know about compiling and configuring Samba, it is necessary to know how to use the Debian packaging system. Using the Debian packaging system, the administrator can easily maintain the latest edition of Samba and any other application that has been installed.

The Debian packaging system uses a local and remote database to manage packages that are available and packages that have been installed. When a package is installed from a remote location, everything is installed and configured so that the administrator has nothing to do. For example, Samba can use the OpenLDAP server as a backend user database. Using one command, you can install the OpenLDAP server. The installation of the OpenLDAP server includes a dependency check, which ensures that all required modules are installed so that the application will function properly.

Finding out what is installed on the local computer is very important because the list allows you to figure out the package versions and dependencies. To display all the packages installed locally, the following command is executed (note that for most of these commands, you will have to log in as the root user):

```
dpkg --list
```

The command dpkg is used to operate on the local Debian packages, and the option --list lists all the local packages installed. A sample output listing is shown as follows:

```
ii  ace-of-penguins  1.2-5  Solitaire-games with penguin-look
```

In the sample output listing, there are five fields, even though there are four fields separated by spaces. The first field is the concatenation of two fields, where the first letter i is one field and the second letter i is another field. The purpose of each field is explained as follows:

Status (i): Defines the status of the package installation on the local machine. Can be one of the following identifiers: Not for not installed, Installed for installed, Config-file for configuration files installed, Unpacked for package downloaded, unpacked for not installed, Failed-config for a failed configuration, and Half-installed for an incomplete installed package. Note that the first letter of the status identifier defines the status type.

Error (i): Defines the error status when the status of the package indicates a problem. When the package is installed, the error bit will be the letter i to indicate a successful install. Otherwise, the error bits could be Hold for the package is on hold and not fully installed, Reinst-required for the package needs to be reinstalled because something went wrong, or X= for both the package is on hold and needs to be reinstalled.

Package name (`ace-of-penguins`): The name of the package that is installed. It is important to correctly type this identifier because when packages are installed, upgraded, and removed, this identifier is used as a reference.

Version number (`1.2-5`): The version of the installed package. Note that the version of the package is the same as the version of the application.

Description (`Solitaire...`): The description of the package and its purpose. The text should be clear and evident on the purpose of the package.

When executing the dpkg command, the result set will be fairly large. You can narrow the search by specifying a search string after the --list option:

```
dpkg --list *apache*
```

The identifier apache was prefixed and appended with the asterisk character meaning to search for all packages that have the apache identifier included. Without the asterisk character, a specific package identifier would have been searched for.

To see which files are part of a package, the following command is used:

```
dpkg --listfiles apache
```

The option –listfiles appended with the name of the package results in an output that displays all the files associated with a particular package. The generated output will be a series of files using an absolute path reference.

To go in the opposite direction and find which file belongs in which package, the following command is executed:

```
dpkg --search /etc/default/slapd
```

The option --search is used to search the locally installed package directory. The option after the --search option is the filename using an absolute path. This command takes a bit longer to execute, as the command has to search all the databases and perform a comparison. If anything is found, the generated output should be similar to the following:

```
slapd: /etc/default/slapd
```

In the generated output, the first field is the name of the package where the file is located and the second field is the filename found. The reason the filename is given is because it is possible in the search pattern for the command-line option

`--search` to use wildcards and partial identifiers. The output will then contain whatever could be matched, which might be multiple files.

Before a package can be installed, the reference to the package list must be downloaded locally. The package list needs to be updated regularly so that the latest package identifiers are downloaded. The following command shows how to update the local package database:

```
apt-get update
```

The first thing that you should do with the fresh install of Knoppix is update the package list. Consider using the command apt-get update *as a required task when Knoppix has been installed, and also execute this command once a week.*

The package lists that are downloaded are usually stable builds of the software, which is good because it means your server will be stable.

Another way to search for a package is to use the following command:

```
apt-cache search samba
```

The output from the command will return a listing of all packages that reference the Samba term. Often the result from the search command is a lengthy list and should be investigated carefully because often installing a package like Samba only gives you the essentials and not the added features that make configuring a piece of software simpler.

To get more detailed information about a package the following command is executed:

```
apt-cache show samba
```

The output from the command results in a detailed listing of the package name, its dependencies, description, maintainers, and other pieces of information. For a primarily Windows administrator, the contained applications of the package are important.

Installing a package is simple as shown in the following command:

```
apt-get install slapd
```

The first option (`install`) is the command to execute. The second option is the name of the package to install, which is the OpenLDAP server `slapd`. The Debian packaging system will figure out the dependencies and hard disk space required and present that information from the command line. At that point, you can continue the installation or cancel it. After Debian has downloaded the package, it will be installed and configured, and you simply have to start the application.

The Debian packaging system is really that easy and straightforward. In fact it is so easy that using the Debian packaging system and this book intended for the Windows operating system, a Windows administrator could manage the same open source applications on Linux. The open source applications use the same configuration files, with the only major difference being directory locations.

There are multiple ways to remove a package. The simplest is to use the following command:

```
apt-get remove slapd
```

The first option `remove` is the command to remove the package, and the second option `slapd` is the package to remove. When the `apt-get` program is finished executing, the files associated with the package are deleted. The configuration files associated with the package are not deleted. To remove both the application and configuration files, the following command is used:

```
apt-get --purge remove slapd
```

The addition of the `--purge` option removes the configuration files and the application files. The only problem with using `--purge` is that if a simple `remove` was first executed, the purge will fail as the package does not exist. To purge the configuration files when the package has been deleted, the following command is used:

```
dpkg --purge slapd
```

On a Debian-based operating system, there are two ways of upgrading a package on a computer. The first is to upgrade all the packages on the computer, and the second is to upgrade an individual package. To upgrade an entire computer with new packages, the following command is executed:

```
apt-get upgrade
```

Be careful about running the command as it could take a very long time to upgrade every package on a computer. If all packages are upgraded, you can be confident that you've done all you can to avoid worms and hacker attacks.

Upgrading an entire system is useful, but it can be resource intensive. When you upgrade a system, be sure not to do it during peak operating hours.

To upgrade an individual package, the package is installed again as shown in the `apt-get install` command example. The Debian packaging system will know whether the install is a fresh install or an upgrade. It is important to refresh the global package listing before testing for an upgrade.

Technique: Starting and Restarting Samba

In contrast to a Windows server, one of the great things about Samba is the ability to experiment with configurations. Samba uses only the configuration file to determine how it should behave, which allows a dynamic configuration as a file server, PDC, or other kind of server. Switching configure types using a Windows server often requires a fresh install. There are other solutions when using a Windows server, but they tend not to be as quick as using Samba. On the Knoppix Linux installation, the Samba server is started and stopped automatically whenever the server is booted or rebooted.

To manually stop a server, open a console and type in the following command. (Make sure that you are logged on as root because only an administrator can execute the command.)

```
/etc/init.d/samba stop
```

Within the directory /etc/init.d are a number of scripts that represent services that are started when the computer is started. The samba script is used to start, stop, and restart the Samba server. The Samba server is stopped because the first command-line option is stop.

Following is an example command to start the Samba server:

```
/etc/init.d/samba start
```

Following is a combination command, which stops the Samba server if it is running and then restarts Samba:

```
/etc/init.d/samba restart
```

The Samba server uses a configuration file to determine what shares to expose and how to expose them. When making changes to the configuration files, the safest way to expose those changes is to restart the Samba server. The downside to restarting the Samba server is that any client using the resources exposed by the Samba server will be automatically disconnected. This can cause problems.

There is an exception to the rule of restarting the Samba server in that the Samba server will reread the configuration files every 60 seconds and reconfigure itself if there are changes. The automatic reload only affects data that is not part of a global configuration definition. This means shares can be added, removed, or updated.

Changing the Samba identifier or changing from a server to a PDC requires a reboot of Samba. Most likely when Samba needs to be rebooted, the administrator should wait a few minutes while the entire network gets a broadcast of the changes.

Technique: Guest File Sharing

The simplest of all file-sharing techniques is to create a share on the Samba file server and allow guest access to it. A guest share allows anyone on the network to read and write files to the share. Samba uses a configuration file to determine which shares are made available and who may access it. The Samba configuration file is stored on the Knoppix Linux server in the directory /etc/samba. Within that directory there are two files to manipulate:

smb.conf: Contains the main directives that control how the Samba server will expose itself to the network.

smbpasswd: Contains a number of usernames and passwords that represents the Samba usernames and passwords.

For the guest share, the smb.conf should resemble the following:

```
[global]
        workgroup = DEVSPACE
        netbios name = PLUTO
        encrypt passwords = yes
        map to guest = bad user

[test]
        comment = my first share
        path = /home/temp
        read only = no
        guest ok = yes
```

The smb.conf file is structured like an .ini file used in Windows. In the example Samba configuration, there are two headers: global and test. The purpose of the header is to define a section of key value pairs. In the smb.conf file, the global section is associated with three keys: workgroup, encrypt passwords, and map to guest. global is a reserved section that defines key value pairs that are global definitions. Table 6.8 explains the purpose of each key.

Many books and documentation show how to use the guest account to anonymously share resources. The problem with many of those examples is that they forget the map to guest *key and hence the anonymous guest strategy will not work.*

TABLE 6.8 Key Descriptions for the `global` Section

Key	Description
`workgroup`	A string identifier that defines the workgroup identifier that the Samba server will use to broadcast. The workgroup identifier on a Samba server is identical to the workgroup identifier on a Windows computer.
`net bios name`	A string identifier that defines the NetBIOS name of the server that is broadcast to other clients and servers.
`encrypt passwords`	A yes/no value that encrypts passwords on the Samba server, which is the preferred solution. This option is default yes for Samba 3.0, so it only needs to be set for old Samba installations.
`map to guest`	A not widely known option used to allow the sharing of resources for guests. By default, Samba does not allow access to any user who does not have a Samba user account. There are three possible values: Never: Never allow unknown guests onto the Samba server. Bad User: Allow anonymous guest users to access the Samba server. Bad Password: Allow valid users to map to a guest if they mistype their password. Not a recommended option because it gives a user a false sense of being able to access the Samba server. The only exception is when the server is exposed to the Internet, because a Bad User value will show that the username exists, but the password was wrong. A hacker could use that information for hacking purposes.

In the sample `smb.conf` file, the section `test` defines shared resources accessible by Windows clients. Consider the shared resource as a shared drive on a Windows computer, except that the shared resource information is stored as a section in the `smb.conf` configuration file. Windows clients will see the shared resource with the identifier `test`. Table 6.9 explains the purpose of each key.

In plain English the configuration file says the following: the Samba server will expose itself to the outside world as PLUTO that is part of the workgroup DEVSPACE. The Samba server accepts totally anonymous requests. A shared resource called TEST (UNC name \\PLUTO\TEST) is exposed and it references the local directory `/home/temp`, which anyone can access and manipulate.

TABLE 6.9 Key Descriptions for the `test` Section

Key	Description
comment	A string identifier that describes the purpose of the share. Useful when the user is browsing the shares offered by the server.
path	A string identifier that references a path that will be shared on the network.
read only	A yes/no key value that determines whether or not the share is read only. If the value is yes then the share is read only regardless of the security descriptors. If the value is no, then the share in theory can be read and written to.
guest ok	A yes/no key value that determines whether or not guests can access the share. This key is used in combination with the map to guest key.

Technique: Sharing Files Using File-Based Security

In most cases, the file server should implement some type of user authentication security policy. An example security policy could be to let everyone read the contents of a directory, but only allow specific people to update the contents. Samba allows administrators to implement security, but not in the Windows Object Policy sense. Samba attempts to map a Windows user to a Unix user.

Let's revisit the `smb.conf` configuration file shown previously and make it secure:

```
[global]
        workgroup = DEVSPACE
        netbios name = PLUTO
        encrypt passwords = yes
        map to guest = bad user
        guest account = nobody

[test]
        comment = my first share
        path = /home/temp
        read only = no
        guest ok = yes
```

The key guest account has been added, which says that if someone wants to access the server, then they are granted the rights of the nobody user. In Linux terms, the user nobody is like the guest account on a Windows computer.

If you are familiar with Samba, you are probably cringing at the thought that the smb.conf file defined in the configuration file is considered secure because the share test might not be entirely secure. The amount of security depends on the security descriptors of the directory /home/temp. For example, if all files are owned by the guest account nobody, then there is no security.

In plain security English, the configuration file is saying to allow access to anyone to the share test. If the user is a Samba user, then let that user use those credentials; otherwise, the guest user will be given the same credentials as the nobody.

The credentials assigned to the user depend on whether or not that user has been recognized as a Samba user. As the configuration stands right now, every user accessing the shared folder test will be recognized as the user nobody. To recognize a Samba user, the user must be added to the file smbpasswd. If LDAP is used for authentication, the users can be stored in the LDAP database. To add a user to the smbpasswd, that user must exist as a Linux user. Therefore, to add a Samba user, the Linux user must be created first.

Authentication and credentials of a user are two separate issues. A user can be authenticated to any user in the universe and Samba in its flexibility allows this. The authentication, however, does not carry any credentials. So that the authentication has some credentials, an authenticated Samba user must exist as a Linux/BSD user. The reason is because the Samba server will be accessing files from a Linux/BSD operating system that requires the credentials of a user.

Therefore when planning Samba servers, remember that user accounts must be maintained on the Linux/BSD server. The synchronization of the two accounts should be maintained using scripts. For those readers willing to venture into a Linux/BSD domain credentials solution, Network Information Service (NIS(+)) and Pluggable Authentication Modules (PAM)should be investigated on your own. As a point to remember even on Windows, a share requires a user registered on the local computer or domain.

Managing Users and Groups on Linux/BSD

When manipulating users, you can use a GUI tool such as *KDE User Manager* as shown in Figure 6.15. (You can explore this option on your own, if interested.)

The approach used in this book, however, is to add a user via the command line. You can use the command line to write scripts that will add users to both the Linux operating system and to the Samba server.

A user is added using the adduser command, which when executed without any command-line options allows a user to be added interactively:

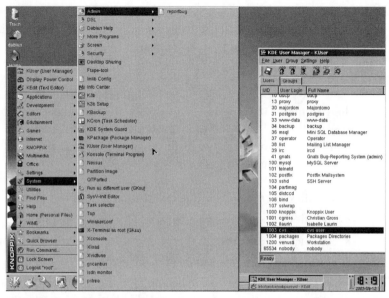

FIGURE 6.15 KDE User Manager.

```
root@pluto:~# adduser
Enter a username to add: sgross
Adding user sgross...
Adding new group sgross (1007).
Adding new user sgross (1007) with group sgross.
Creating home directory /home/sgross.
Copying files from /etc/skel
Enter new UNIX password:
Retype new UNIX password:
passwd: password updated successfully
Changing the user information for sgross
Enter the new value, or press ENTER for the default
        Full Name []: Simon Gross
        Room Number []:
        Work Phone []:
        Home Phone []:
        Other []:
Is the information correct? [y/n] y
root@pluto:~#
```

The command adduser will ask for a Unix password twice, and then for the personal details (Full Name, Room Number, Work Phone, Home Phone, and Other). Finally, it asks for verification that all the information is correct. When it's a Linux user, the home directory is created under the directory /home. For the user sgross, the home directory is /home/sgross. The home directory is important to know about because it is used to store user settings that are referenced by other applications.

You can add a user using solely command-line options:

```
useradd -m -s /bin/bash -d /home/whome -p hello whome
```

The command useradd is used instead of adduser because it is simpler and does not go through any interactive questions if the data is not provided from command-line options. Shown in the example useradd command are the minimum command-line options as explained here:

-m: Specifies to create the home directory if it does not exist.

-s: Specifies the shell (e.g., Bash) to use for the logged in user.

-d: Specifies the directory that represents the home directory of the user.

-p: Specifies the password to use for the user.

whome: The name of the user to be added. If the user already exists, then an error will indicate that the user cannot be added again.

After a user has been added, that user can be deleted using the following command:

```
deluser --remove-home whome
```

The command deluser removes the user from the system. The command-line options are used as described by the following list. Note that two options have been added for explanation purposes.

--remove-home: Removes the home directory of the user.

--remove-all-files: Removes all the files including the home directory owned by the user. Using the --remove-all-files option implies the option --remove-home.

--backup: Before removing the user, back up the contents of the user's home directory in the form of a compressed archive in the /home directory.

whome: The identifier of the user to remove.

An added user needs to be assigned security rights by associating the user with groups. To add a group the following command is used:

```
groupadd mygroup
```

To add a group is simple, in that the command `groupadd` at the minimum expects one command-line argument, which is the name of the group. A group is deleted using the following command:

```
groupdel mygroup
```

The command `groupdel` is used to delete a group and expects a single command-line option that is the name of the group.

To add a user to a group the following command is executed:

```
addgroup whome mygroup
```

The command `addgroup` has two command-line options. The first option `whome` is the name of the user to add to the group `mygroup`, which is the second command-line option.

Linux Security Model

Linux security and rights are based on the traditional Unix security model. Windows (NT, 2000, or XP) security is based on an access control list (ACL). An ACL allows the user to manage individual security flags on every object. This type of security allows for more fine-tuning, but sometimes it makes the security model more complicated than it needs to be. Linux security can use ACLs also if the hard disks are formatted to use the xfs filesystem.

In Linux security, there is the user root, which can do anything it wants. The other users exist, but their rights are limited.

NOTE

The previous sentence explains everything about Linux security. The root is akin to the Windows Administrator account. A root can do whatever it wants regardless of how you set the security bits of the individual files, directories, and processes. This means if hackers gain access to the root account, they can bring down the entire system. However, Linux systems have adapted so that gaining access to the root account has been restricted to only specific situations.

There are three levels of security:

owner: When a user creates an object, that user is the owner. The owner of an object is typically the user that created the object.

group: Defines an entity that contains multiple users. There can only be one group per object.

everybody: This is everybody else and could be considered as a guest in Windows security terms.

For each security level, there are three types of accesses:

read: Allows reading of the object.

write: Allows writing of the object.

execute: Allows executing of the object.

The security level is combined with an access right to define the security privileges of an object, such as a file or directory.

Assigning File Owners and Groups

Each file and directory is assigned three levels of security. To set the security, often it is necessary to properly assign the owner of a file and the group to which the file is a part of. The group assigned to a file does not need to include the owner of the file. To assign the owner of a file, the following command is executed:

```
chown whome filename.txt
```

The command `chown` requires at the minimum two command-line options, where the first option `cgross` is the new name of the owner and the second option is the name of the file or directory. The command `chown` can also be used to reassign the owning group of a file or directory. Following is an example command of how to assign the group of a filename:

```
chown :mygroup filename.txt
```

In the example command, the first option is distinguished as a group by the colon in front of the identifier `mygroup`. It is possible to change both the owner and the group simultaneously shown by the following command:

```
chown whome:mygroup filename.txt
```

Modifying Security Privileges

To modify security descriptors of a file, the following command is executed:

```
chmod a+x hello.sh
```

The command `chmod` has two command-line options: `a+x` and the name of the file. The command-line option `a+x` is a bit cryptic; it assigns execute access to all security levels. A security privilege is the combination of security level and access. The command-line option is a sequential combination of three parts. The first part, which is the letter a stands for all and defines the security level. The second part is the plus sign that says to add the access level defined in the third part to the security level defined in the first part. Instead of the plus sign, the minus sign could have been used, which means to remove the access level from the security level. The last part is the letter x, which is the access level.

The possible characters that can be used for each of the three parts are defined as follows. (Note that each of the letters can be add side by side, e.g., part one could be gou.)

First part: g - group, o - others "everyone else," u - user "owner," a - a simple letter that is the same as gou.

Second part: - - take these rights away, + - add these rights, = - assign these rights ignoring whatever has been assigned so far.

Third part: l - lock the object during access, r - allow read, s - set user or group ID, t - set the sticky bit, w - allow write, x - allow execution of a file.

There is another way of specifying the read, write, and execute bits of a file that involves the use of octal numbers. Usually this format is used in configuration files and should be remembered even though it is extremely nonadministrator friendly. For example, instead of using letters, octal numbers can be used:

```
chmod 111 hello.sh
```

The first command-line option 111 is an octal that specifies the rights of the owner, group, and others. Notice that the octal is three digits long and there are three different levels of security privileges. The leftmost digit represents the owner rights, the middle digit represents group rights, and the rightmost digit represents others' rights. The values that each digit can take are best illustrated using Table 6.10.

Using the table to decipher the octal value of 777, it means read, write, and execute access for the owner, group, and others.

Some special values can be prefixed to the octal value as described in the following list:

4000: Sets the user ID on execution of file.

2000: Sets the group ID on execution of the file.

1000: Sets the link permission to directories or sets the save text attribute for files.

TABLE 6.10 Octal Value and Associated Letter-Based Rights and Descriptions

Octal Value	Letter Equivalent	Description
1	x	Execute-only access
2	w	Write-only access
4	r	Read-only access
5	rx	Read and execute access
6	rw	Read and write access
7	rwx	Read, write, and execute access

Putting It All Together

To make file-based security work, a scenario has to be outlined. Let's say that the previously defined smb.conf configuration file is used with the user accounts cgross and nobody. The user account cgross is a member of the group mygroup. The security policy that is to be created is that anybody in the group mygroup can read, write, and create files and directories. Other authenticated users and anonymous users can only read files.

The security of a Samba share depends on the security of the directory being shared. The directory /home/temp is assigned the security descriptors defined as follows:

```
chmod u=rwx,g=rwx,o=rx /home/temp
```

The directory has the security descriptor defined as follows:

u: The owner of the directory is allowed to read, write, and execute in the directory /home/temp.

g: The group assigned to the directory is allowed to read, write, and execute in the directory /home/temp.

o: Others are allowed to read and execute in the directory /home/temp. Setting the execute bit is important because otherwise others cannot read the contents of the directory.

After the security descriptors have been set, the owner and group have to be set using the following command:

```
chown operator:mygroup /home/temp
```

The owner of the directory is operator, but the group is mygroup. Effectively this means that only the root or operator user can change or delete the directory /home/temp. This is useful because it will stop accidents from happening on a computer. However, child directories of the directory /home/temp can still be deleted and manipulated by anyone who is a member of the mygroup group.

To add a Linux user as an authenticated Samba user to the Samba password file, the following command is executed:

TABLE 6.11 Key, Value, and Description of Values for smb.conf File

Key	Value	Description
comment	Group Directory	A string identifier that describes the purpose of the share.
path	/home /shared	A string identifier that references a path that will be shared on the network.
public	no	A yes/no value key that is used to indicate whether a password is needed to access the share. This key is the same as the key guest ok. The value of no says that share must have an associated user and password. An unauthenticated guest user cannot access the share.
browseable	no	A yes/no value key that is used to define whether the share will appear when the server is being browsed using File Explorer or the command net view. The value of no indicates that no browsing is allowed because the global share should only be known to a closed group of people. This means to access the share, the name of the share has to be known. $\rightarrow$

Key	Value	Description
printable	no	A yes/no value key that is used to indicate whether the share is a printer share. The no value is used because the global share is not a printer.
write list	@%S	A string of comma-separated identifiers that define which users can write files and directories to the share. @%S is a macro to define the write list, which is everyone who is in the group mygroup. More about macros is explained in the section "Technique: Using Macros."
valid users	@%S	A string of comma-separated identifiers that defines which users can access the share. The letters @%S are explained in the key write list.
invalid users	root	A string of comma-separated identifiers that defines which users cannot access the share. Specifying the root user is a safety measure that ensures no hacker can attempt to override the security profile.
force group	%S	An identifier that specifies the group that the user accessing the share will assume. The letters %S is a macro and indicates that all authenticated users will get the group token mygroup.
force create mode	0764	Sets the security bits whenever a new file is created. The value of 0664 says that the owner can read, write, and execute; the group can read, and write; and others can only read the file.
force directory mode	2775	Sets the security bits whenever a new directory is created. The value of 2775 says that the owner and group can read, write, and execute while others can only read and execute. The prefixed number 2 means that the group ID bit will be set when a file or directory is executed.

```
#smbpasswd -a cgross
New SMB password:
Retype new SMB password:
Added user steve.
```

The command smbpasswd has two command-line options: -a to add a user and cgross as the user to add. If the file smbpasswd does not exist, it will be created, and a message will indicate that the file has been created. The password given is not the Linux user password, but the password that will allow Samba to authenticate a user to represent a given Linux user.

Having set both the security bits and the ownership of the directory, the security of the directory has been defined even though the Samba share test is a public share that everyone can get access to. In this example scenario, Samba manages the authentication of the user, and Linux manages the files and directories that can be manipulated.

Technique: Managing a Closed Group Global Share

Creating a public share with Linux managing the security brings together a good way of managing files and directories. There are many situations when instead of allowing public shares, a share will only be used in a closed circle of users that belong to a single group. In that case, you need to ensure that files and directories have a consistent security and ownership policy. Samba can be given instructions on how to create, manipulate, and manage files and directories. Samba allows the definition of a security policy. Following is a smb.conf configuration file that is a good way of defining global share:

```
[groupdrive]
    comment = Group Directory
    path=/home/shared
    public = no
    browseable = no
    printable = no
    write list = @%S
    valid users = @%S
    invalid users = root
    force group = %S
    force create mode = 0664
    force directory mode = 2775
```

The different key values and reason for setting that value is explained in Table 6.11. Note some key explanations are abbreviated because they have been explained earlier in Table 6.10.

The Samba share `mygroup` will not be visible to the browser list of the network, but can be connected to by the client computer if the share is known. The exact specifications of the user become useful when an attached client creates a file or directory. Shown in the following text block are the listing details of a newly created directory and file:

```
root@pluto:/home/temp2# ls -l
total 4
drwxrwsr-x   2 cgross    mygroup     4096 Sep 14 21:15 mydir
-rwxrw-r--   1 cgross    mygroup        0 Sep 14 21:15 doc.txt
root@pluto:/home/temp2/something#
```

Notice how the ownership of the file `doc.txt` and directory `mydir` belongs to the person `cgross` who was authorized to access the share, but the group is `mygroup`. Having the group set to `mygroup` ensures that everybody who can access the share is part of `mygroup` and can access every file and directory present in the share. When using the generic file sharing shown in the section "Technique: Sharing Files Using File-Based Security," there could be files and directories inaccessible to some people.

The directory security of the shared directory `/home/shared` is assigned the security descriptors:

```
chown operator:mygroup /home/shared
```

You may be tempted to mix Windows ACLs with Linux security descriptors, but you shouldn't. The group share as it was set up is designed to pose the least amount of administrative headaches. Samba can become confused when attempting to mix and match security descriptors. If security is extremely important because of the nature of the environment, you should investigate the xfs Linux filesystem, which supports ACLs and makes it simpler to mix Windows with Linux security.

Technique: Using Macros to Create Dynamic Shares

When a `%S` option is used within the `smb.conf` file, a macro is defined. In the previous `smb.conf` file, which used the `%S` option, the macro was used to force a group identifier as valid users and writers to a share. Macros in Samba configuration files are nice and easy ways of defining generic items without having to specifically define everything. The following list defines all the possible macros that can be used in a Samba configuration file:

%a: The type of operating system that the client machine is running. Using this macro is not a reliable indicator of architecture and should not generally be used.

%d: The process ID of the current Samba server process.

%G: The primary group of the user specified by the macro %U.

%h: The hostname of the system that Samba is running on.

%I: The IP address of the client machine.

%L: The NetBIOS name of the Samba server machine.

%m: The NetBIOS name of the client machine.

%M: The DNS name of the client machine in lowercase.

%N: The name of the NIS directory server.

%R: The core protocol used when the client and Samba server communicate.

%T: The current date and time.

%U: The name of the user sent by the client computer to the Samba server.

%v: The Samba version.

Other macros are available, but those macros can only be used in the context of a share and are defined as follows:

%g: The name of the primary group of the user %u.

%H: The home directory of a logged in user.

%P: The root directory of the currently defined share.

%S: The name of the current share.

%u: The username of the current user accessing the current share in terms of the Linux operating system.

The power of the macros is that they allow the dynamic definition of shares and usernames. Using the %s macro made it possible to dynamically associate a share name with a Linux group. The name of the group could have been copied, but the advantage is that an administrator could copy and paste the share configuration and only have to change the share name.

Another way of creating a closed share for each group is to use the following groups share smb.conf configuration file fragment that defines a group-based share.

```
[%G]
    comment = %G global share
    path = /home/shared/%G
    public = no
```

```
browseable = yes
printable = no
read only = no
write list = @%S
valid users = @%S
invalid users = root
force group = %S
force create mode = 0664
force directory mode = 2775
```

For the configuration file fragment, the way that the share properties are declared is similar to previous smb.conf definitions. What is different is the property path and share itself. The share is %G and says that when a user browses the server, display a share that has the same name as the primary group that the user belongs to. Remember when the user browses a server, a username is associated with the browsing. The rights associated with the share are based on the group being exposed as discussed in the "Technique: Sharing Files Using File-Based Security."

Another type of share is the sharing of a personal home directory, shown in the following user share smb.conf configuration file fragment:

```
[homes]
    comment = %U home directory
    path = /home/%U
    browseable = yes
    writeable = no
    valid users = %U, @%G
    write list = %U
    create mask = 0750
    directory mask = 0750
```

The share homes is a special-purpose share that exposes the share name of the user and the share homes. Notice how the macro %U is used to enforce a Samba security policy where only the user can write to the directory. Also notice how the macros %U and @%G are used to allow others to read the contents of the directory.

In all the configuration examples, the group is used to allow access or allow writing to a share. The important tip is that all the Samba examples rely on the Linux security model when managing Samba security. This means that the administrator is highly advised to devise a group and user Linux security policy.

Technique: Adding a Samba Server to an Existing Domain

All the `smb.conf` configuration file examples illustrated thus far assume that the Linux Samba server is a sole server on the network and not part of a domain. Samba can act like a PDC or can be part of a Windows domain. In this section, the technique of adding a Samba server to the domain is covered. From a security point of view, adding a server to an already existing domain makes Samba security simpler because the `smbpasswd` command does not have to be used. Delegating Samba security to another server still requires adding Linux security, and essentially it means that the shares do not change.

The global section changes in the `smb.conf` configuration file as shown here:

```
[global]
        comment = Samba %v
        workgroup = NOTEBOOK
        netbios name = PLUTO
        password server = *
        encrypt passwords = yes
        map to guest = bad user
        guest account = nobody
        security = domain
```

The new keys added are explained in Table 6.12.

TABLE 6.12 Key Descriptions Necessary to Add a Server to a Domain

Key	Description
`workgroup`	The workgroup identifier has already been explained previously, but when a Samba server is made part of another domain, the domain identifier must refer to the domain name.
`password server`	A string identifier that references the name of the PDC and potential Backup Domain Controller (BDCs). It is important to ensure that the names of the PDCs and BDCs are added to the hosts file or to the DNS.

$\rightarrow$

Key	Description
security	A string identifier that defines the client authentication used when accessing shares. The identifier can be one of the following values:
	share: The password to access the share is given in the share configuration section. This is similar to Windows 95/98 shares.
	user: Each user has to be authenticated before accessing the server. After authentication, the user is given the rights to access shares.
	server: Identical to a user client authentication except that the user is authenticated by another server.
	domain: The server is part of a domain and the user is authenticated by a PDC, which could be a Windows or Samba server.

To add the computer to the domain managed by the PDC, the following command is executed:

```
net rpc join --server=venus --user=Administrator%mypassword
```

The command-line application net requires four parameters. The first parameter defines the mode of access of the PDC, which for the scope of this book is mode rpc. The mode rpc is used to address servers using Windows NT4 or Windows 2000 protocols. The second parameter join is the action, which means to add the computer to the domain. The third parameter --server defines the server, which is used to add the computer where the command is being executed. It is important to make sure that the server is the PDC and is added to the DNS resolution table. Otherwise, name resolution errors will be generated. The last parameter --user is a username and password of a user that is authorized to add a computer to the domain.

TIP

Depending on the configuration of the DNS server, the PDC server may not be added to the name resolution of the PDC server. The simplest test is to execute net rpc --server=venus *and see whether a name resolution error occurs. If an error occurs, the simplest solution is to add the IP and name of the PDC server to the* /etc/hosts *file shown as follows.*

```
127.0.0.1       pluto localhost
venus
```

It is possible to use Active Directory Kerberos security. However, that requires knowing about Kerberos and how it works on Linux, which is beyond the scope of this book.

If a local Linux user account does not exist on the Samba server to be accessed, but does exist on the domain, you can add the user automatically by using the smb.conf *configuration defined as follows:*

```
[global]
    add user script = /usr/sbin/useradd -d /dev/null
-g 100 -s /bin/false -M %u
```

Technique: Resolving Network Servers Using WINS

Often a Windows domain exists on multiple subnets. Broadcasting on multiple subnets is not possible with Windows file sharing and it is necessary to install a Windows Internet Naming Server (WINS). A WINS is like a DNS server except it is for a network of Windows machines. When multiple subnets exist, it is necessary to add a WINS so that two Windows computers on different subnets can see each other. A Samba server can act as a WINS, and it is easy to configure as shown by the following smb.conf configuration file fragment:

```
[global]
        wins support = yes
```

The only addition to make to the global section of the configuration file is the addition of the key wins support with a value of yes. For all the Windows and Samba computers, the WINS must be added as an entry in the network configuration. For a Samba server, the following smb.conf configuration file fragment shows how to add a WINS reference:

```
[global]
        wins server = 192.168.1.240
```

The key wins server has an IP address that is the WINS.

When properly configured, a WINS will stop the constant chatter of Windows computers asking about each other. It is important that all Windows computers refer a WINS. If a Samba server is the WINS server, then do not add the wins server key because this is not a valid configuration.

To ensure that the Samba WINS is kept as the master browser, the following smb.conf keys should be added:

```
[global]
        local master = yes
        preferred master = yes
        os level = 66
```

For the smb.conf fragment, the keys local master and preferred master are used to set the local Samba server as master browser, which makes sure that no other server attempts to override the local server when keeping name information. The key os level is used when multiple browser masters are attempting to figure out who should be the master. A higher level such as 66 means that the local machine should be the highest level and hence master browser. It is important that no other Samba server use a higher level.

Technique: Defining a Primary Domain Controller (PDC)

Samba can be the PDC of a domain. When defining a Samba server as a PDC, often it is assumed other tasks such as WINS and timeserver are also managed. The following text block is an example smb.conf configuration file that is complete and fulfills many roles:

```
[global]
        netbios name = PLUTO
        workgroup = DOM-DEVSPACE
        passdb backend = smbpasswd,guest
        os level = 66
        preferred master = yes
        domain master = yes
        local master = yes
        wins support = yes
        security = user
        encrypt passwords = yes
        domain logons = yes
        logon path = \\%L\profiles\%u
        logon drive = H:
        logon home = \\PLUTO\%u
        logon script = logon.cmd
        time server = yes

[netlogon]
        path=/var/lib/samba/netlogon
        read only = yes
        write list = ntadmin

[profiles]
        path = /var/lib/samba/profiles
```

```
        read only = no
        create mask = 0600
        directory mask = 0700

[homes]
        comment = %u home directory
        browsable = no
        read only = no
```

In the illustrated smb.conf, there are four sections: global, netlogon, profiles, and homes. The global and homes sections have been explained. The netlogon share is the location where a login script can be executed. The section profiles is required to store the profiles of the individual users. Refer to the "Profile and Logon Scripts" section in Chapter 5 to get a better insight on the purpose and usefulness of the profiles and netlogon shares. Both of these shares are required and need not contain any data. For example, for the profiles share, if the profile of a user does not exist the first time you log on, an error stating that the profile information could not be retrieved will be generated. Ignoring that error, the profiles will be created when the user exits the session.

The new or modified keys in the PDC configuration file are explained in Table 6.13.

TABLE 6.13 Key Descriptions for the Samba PDC Server

Key	Description
netbios name	A string identifier that identifies the name of the server to the Windows network. In a PDC context, it is important to have such a reference to avoid mixups.
workgroup	The workgroup identifier references the domain that will be managed by the Samba server.
password server	A string identifier that references the name of the PDC and potential BDCs. It is important to ensure that the names of the PDCs and BDCs are added to the host's file or to the DNS.
passdb backend	A list of string identifiers separated by commas. Each identifier represents a way of checking the credentials of a user. In the example, the identifier smbpasswd checks the credentials using the smbpasswd mechanism. The smbpasswd mechanism has been used in all the Samba examples. For all possible identifiers, check the Samba documentation.

$\rightarrow$

Key	Description
domain logons	A yes/no key value that causes the Samba server to process domain logs. Because the Samba server will serve as a PDC, the correct setting is yes.
logon path	A string identifier that references the location where a domain user can reference their profile. It is important to not specify a generic share, but the exact location where a user can read and write their profile.
logon drive	A string identifier that is the home directory drive letter.
logon home	A string identifier that is the network home directory bound to the drive letter specified by the key logon drive when the user logs in.
logon script	A string identifier that sets the script to run when the user logs in. The path is relative to the share netlogon.
time server	A yes/no key value that allows the Samba server to advertise itself to the Windows network as a time server.

Rebooting the computer with the PDC `smb.conf` configuration file, the Windows network will have a working PDC server. After the Samba server has been started, any client can access the PDC server and make itself a part of the domain. Only one small detail still needs to be clarified. When a computer attempts to connect to the PDC and register itself as part of the domain, the connecting computer has to be associated with a Linux user account. For example, if the computer with the NetBIOS name athena wants to be part of the domain, the following command has to be executed:

```
useradd -g 100 -d /dev/null -c "Athena notebook" -s /bin/false athena$
```

The command useradd adds a user athena$ that has very little rights as per the command-line options -d and -s. Notice, however, that the NetBIOS name of the computer is appended with a $ sign. This is a specific notation and is necessary. The password is then locked as shown by the following command:

```
passwd -l athena$
```

The computer account needs to be activated in the smbpasswd password file shown as follows:

```
smbpasswd -a -m athena$
```

Notice the additional command-line option -m, which is used to indicate that the account to be added is a machine account. Now the computer with the Net-BIOS name athena can be added to the domain. The other task is to make sure that the root account is active in the smbpasswd file because, otherwise, the computer cannot be added. In contrast to Windows domains, the administrator account administrator is the account root and the command is executed as follows:

```
smbpasswd -a root
```

After having executed all the commands, the Windows client or Samba server can be added to the domain managed by the Samba PDC server.

Technique: More Advanced Techniques

All the techniques shown in this book to manage a Samba server are the basics that will work in a short period of time. The Samba server is a very sophisticated piece of software that can do many other things. For example, it is possible to use LDAP to authenticate the usernames and passwords. The best source on how to implement other topics is the document Samba-HOWTO-Collection.pdf, which is found in the Samba sources as defined earlier in Table 6.5. It's more important, however, to keep things simple by using techniques described in this book. The administrator writes scripts to automate all operations, such as automatic user account creation and the security descriptors.

SUMMARY

The purpose of this chapter is to explain how to use OpenLDAP to keep user identification information, and Samba as a file server. LDAP is an underutilized protocol that is very effective for storing individual data such as e-mail address, city, name, and so on. If your infrastructure depends on Open Source software, then using an LDAP server for user authentication is an excellent central solution. However, it should be noted that LDAP should not be used for general user authentication for the Windows operating system because the OpenLDAP server is not designed for such a task.

Samba is a project that can be used to create a file server or PDC on the network. Using Samba, the Linux operating system fits into a primary Windows-based network. Samba makes it easy to manage file shares and Windows users.

User authentication and user data belongs in either one of these repositories and not other repositories, unless there is a good reason. Too often many administrators have some users authenticated in one place, and then others in another place. This causes people to be sloppy with passwords and makes it difficult to administer large number of applications and users.

7 Managing Data Stores

ABOUT THIS CHAPTER

The focus of this chapter is to illustrate how to use MySQL to store data in a relational database. Relational data is not a filesystem, because relational data is less granular. A relational database stores its data using tables and records that can be indexed for quicker retrieval.

MySQL is the only project covered in this chapter. There are other relational databases, but in the Open Source domain, MySQL is extremely successful and popular. Additionally MySQL works well on Windows, which not all relational databases do.

Not covered in great detail is the Structured Query Language (SQL). It is not that SQL is not important, but SQL is more geared toward the database administrator. A database administrator has a different role than a system administrator, who is more focused on keeping the database server running from a process point of view; they handle topics such as database installation, deployment, management of the table types, and backups.

PROJECT: MYSQL

MySQL has become one of the most popular and widely supported Open Source databases in the world. With each release, MySQL improves and implements more features. Originally MySQL was intended to be a server that managed a number of Indexed Sequential Access Method (ISAM) routines from another database mSQL.

However, those routines were not fast enough and not portable enough, so a new database was created.

MySQL has grown in popularity and has become a robust and fast relational database that works. It is available on many platforms, including Windows. One of the benefits of using MySQL on Windows is that the Windows administrators get a native Windows application that works well. A corporation called MySQL AB headquartered in Sweden currently supports MySQL, however, the company has developers and subsidiaries all over the world.

NOTE

Often on the MySQL site and other related sites, there are references to buying commercial licenses. Quickly reading the license conditions might lead you to think that a license must be purchased whenever MySQL and InnoDB are used in a commercial setting. MySQL and InnoDB are licensed as a GPL product, which means that anyone can use MySQL without any costs. However, when you create a product that you will charge money for or it is distributed outside of the corporation and it depends on MySQL, then you will need to purchase a non-GPL licensed product. You might be interested in purchasing the very good commercial support for MySQL in a 24x7 mission critical setting.

Table 7.1 contains reference information about the MySQL project.

TABLE 7.1 Reference Information for MySQL

Item	Description
Home page	*http://www.mysql.com*, downloads page *http://www.mysql.com/downloads/index.html*
Installation	MySQL can be installed using an installer program or unzipped to a directory using the compressed archive.
Version	Latest stable released version is 4.1, but at the time of this writing 5.0 is available.
Dependencies	MySQL has no dependencies when using the precompiled binaries.

$\longrightarrow$

Item	Description
Documentation	The documentation available at the MySQL home page is fairly extensive and can be used to figure out how to use MySQL. The SQL language is generally not explained at the MySQL site. It is highly recommended to purchase a SQL language book because details like running queries and manipulations are covered in more detail. The documentation is available at *http://www.mysql .com/doc/en/index.html*.
Mailing Lists	Many mailing lists are available at the MySQL Web site at *http://lists.mysql.com/*. Of specific interest to the administrator are the following mailing lists: `MySQL General Questions`: A mailing list that can be used to ask both MySQL and SQL-specific questions and general administrative issues. `MySQL on Win32`: A mailing list specifically geared toward the Windows administrator. Note that the questions on this mailing list can be general, but usually are geared toward a specific Windows platform question. `MySQL Control Center`: A mailing list for the MySQL Control Center, which is used to administer the MySQL database. This book focuses on using this tool for administrative issues. `MySQL ODBC`: A mailing list used to ask questions about the MySQL ODBC (Open Database Connectivity) driver. `MySQL Bugs`: An optional mailing list used to follow the bugs found in MySQL. Following this list is a good idea to know what bugs are found so that when users run into them an answer can be given quickly.
Impatient Installation Time Required	Download time: 19-22 MB download depending on the MySQL distribution selected. Installation time: 5-10 minutes depending on the speed of the computer.

$\rightarrow$

Item	Description
Firewall Port	3306 (TCP)
DVD Location	The latest stable binaries are located in the directory `/packages/mysql`.

Additional Notes

At the time of this writing, version 4.1 was in beta and the development of version 5.0 was started. MySQL is a commercial company that sells an Open Source database and is fairly successful, which means that MySQL is a safe bet when using it on a Windows network. The big new feature in Version 5.0 is the support for stored procedures based on the SQL-99 specification. The following are currently supported in version 4.1:

ANSI SQL: Supported are a broad number of ANSI SQL-99 commands. Also supported are some alternate databases.

Cross-platform: MySQL is available on multiple platforms such as Linux, Windows, FreeBSD, IBM™ AIX®, Mac™ OSX HP-UX, QNX™, Novell™ NetWare™, SCO OpenUnix, SGI™ Irix™, and Dec OSF™.

Multiple storage engines: It is possible to store MySQL relational data using multiple data formats depending on the requirements of the project. For example, storing data in the ISAM format instead of the InnoDB format is faster, but the cost are transactions and row locking.

Transactions: When data is added, manipulated, or deleted from the database, Transactions allows certain tasks to be undone.

Multiple security systems: Database security can be managed using either the integrated security systems or added on security such as Secure Sockets Layer (SSL).

Query caching: Caches previously executed queries when they are repeatedly called increasing query performance.

Replication: Databases can be replicated using a master and slave configuration.

Full-text indexing and searching: Blob fields that contain arbitrary text pieces can be individually indexed and searched mimicking search engine functionality.

Features to be added in the version 5.0 release:

Multiple simultaneous character support: MySQL currently allows the definition of a database to use a single character encoding set, e.g., Unicode. This feature allows the addition of multiple character encodings in the same database.

Expanded support for subqueries: More support for subqueries, which are queries within queries.

Geometrical data support: Support for a specific datatype used for spatial data such as geographic data.

Stored procedures and triggers: Support of standard ANSI SQL trigger and stored procedure language. Currently MySQL can be extended using either Perl or a C program.

Views: Gives the ability to define a specific query as a view, which is similar in characteristics as a table.

Impatient Installation

The MySQL application is distributed in two different forms: self-installing executable or ZIP file archive. For an administrator, either one can be used, but the impatient installation will focus on using the ZIP archive. The time required installing the self-installing executable or ZIP file archive is not significant. The only advantage that the self-installing executable has is the included uninstall application.

Removing an Old Install

If a MySQL installation already exists, it has to be removed before doing a new installation or upgrade. The data associated with the old MySQL installation should not be deleted, but can be kept. If this is your first time installing MySQL, the removal of the old installation instructions are not very relevant. However, remember that these instructions exist because you will need to sometime upgrade your installation and then these instructions must be followed.

When upgrading a MySQL database, it is important to back up the original database before performing an upgrade. The process of dumping and reading in a MySQL database is explained in more detail in the section "Technique: Backing Up and Dumping a Database."

When a MySQL server has been installed, it will most likely be installed as a service, which needs to be stopped and removed by using the commands defined as follows:

```
./mysqladmin -u root shutdown
./mysqld-max-nt —remove
```

The commands stops the MySQL service and then removes the service from the Windows Services list. It is expected that the commands are executed on the machine that will be upgraded, in a Cygwin BASH console, and in the directory [MySQL installation]/bin. The command also assumes that the MySQL server installed is represented by the command mysqld-max-nt, which might not be the case. More details about the different server types are explained in the section "Installing MySQL."

The MySQL installation can be removed by deleting the old installation. Note that the data can be deleted because you should have backed it up and hence it will need to be reloaded again.

Downloading the Archives

Downloading the MySQL distribution is a bit more complicated because of the sheer number of downloads available. All the MySQL downloads are available at the Web page at *http://www.mysql.com/downloads/index.html*. On that page, the available downloads are grouped into specific download types such as database server, Application Programming Interfaces (APIs), and so on. The types that you need to know about are defined in the following sections. After you choose the types you want, copy the downloaded MySQL archive to the installation directory, which could be the C drive or some other directory. Unzip the MySQL archive using the following command:

```
unzip mysql-[version number].zip
```

It is preferable to unzip the MySQL archive in the root of the C drive because that is the default that MySQL expects. However, using another directory does not complicate the installation of MySQL significantly.

The downloaded archive for the MySQL Control Center is also a ZIP file except that it contains an installation script. It is best to unzip the MySQL Control Center ZIP archive in its own subdirectory such as `c:/temp/mysqlcc` using the `unzip` command. The ODBC driver is distributed as an installable windows executable. To install the ODBC driver, the application is executed like any other Windows application would be installed.

Following are the types to choose from for the download.

MySQL Database Server and Standard Clients

This references the different versions of the MySQL database that can be downloaded. The first download is the Production Release version, which is also the stable build and generally recommended for production settings. The other downloads are either old versions or new beta/alpha builds.

Graphical Clients

This defines a couple of applications used to graphically interact with the MySQL database. There are multiple applications including some new ones developed by MySQL AB. As a Windows administrator, most likely you will want to download the MySQL Control Center application because it allows management of MySQL servers using a GUI tool and has an integrated SQL editor. The MySQL Administrator tool is also available, which happens to be an excellent tool for monitoring and managing MySQL databases. The advantage of using the MySQL Administrator tool is its capability to monitor the different MySQL servers. For the scope of this book, the MySQL Control Center application is used, but you should consider multiple tools because not all tools solve all problems.

Application Programming Interfaces

This references a number of toolkits used for a specific programming language or environment used to access the MySQL database. In the simplest case, the ODBC driver should be downloaded because most toolkits can use the ODBC driver. For efficiency, a specific toolkit driver should be used and is dependent on the program being managed.

Installing MySQL

When the MySQL archive has been expanded, the root directory of MySQL becomes the path [installation directory]/mysql. If the path is c:/mysql, then MySQL is ready to run. If the path is something else, however, then a configuration file has to be created that defines where MySQL and its datafiles are located.

When using the unzip program from the Cygwin toolkit, the files unzipped will not have execute access associated with it. For example, all the files in the directory [installation directory]/mysql/bin *cannot be executed even though they are executable files. Attempting to execute the files will generate an error* Access denied. *Also included are DLLs that will be loaded by an application. This sort of behavior may seem incredibly frustrating, but it is added for a reason. Allowing any sort of file to be executed means that potentially a hacker could get access to a computer. To get around this problem, use the* chmod *program and assign execute rights to only those that should get it. Or use the Security tab to assign the execute properties. If you do not want to go through this trouble, then you will need to find a Windows native unzip program, such as the 7-Zip Open Source file manager in Chapter 5.*

If the MySQL database has been expanded to the default location, it is always a good idea to know about the MySQL configuration file. The MySQL configuration file must be used if the MySQL installation is not in the default location. The purpose of the MySQL configuration file is to determine the initial defaults of how the MySQL server should execute. The following text is an example my.cnf MySQL configuration file:

```
[mysqld]
basedir=C:/bin/mysql
datadir=C:/bin/mysql/data
```

The example text can either be saved to a file called c:/my.cnf or to the directory [WINDOWS INSTALLATION/my.ini. The name of the file can be either one, but there should only be one. The .ini version is preferred because there is always a Windows installation directory, and Windows might not be installed on the C drive. The my.cnf keys are defined as follows:

basedir: Defines the root directory of the MySQL application. This directory is used by MySQL when executing programs and not for data.

datadir: Defines the root directory for the MySQL data, which would be the tables and other database data.

To start the MySQL server application and create the initial databases, the following command is executed:

```
$ ./mysqld-max-nt --console
InnoDB: The first specified data file .\ibdata1 did not exist:
InnoDB: a new database to be created!
030929 17:14:05  InnoDB: Setting file .\ibdata1 size to 10 MB
InnoDB: Database physically writes the file full: wait...
030929 17:14:07  InnoDB: Log file .\ib_logfile0 did not exist:
new to be created
InnoDB: Setting log file .\ib_logfile0 size to 5 MB
InnoDB: Database physically writes the file full: wait...
030929 17:14:08  InnoDB: Log file .\ib_logfile1 did not exist:
new to be created
InnoDB: Setting log file .\ib_logfile1 size to 5 MB
InnoDB: Database physically writes the file full: wait...
InnoDB: Doublewrite buffer not found: creating new
InnoDB: Doublewrite buffer created
InnoDB: Creating foreign key constraint system tables
InnoDB: Foreign key constraint system tables created
030929 17:14:14  InnoDB: Started
c:\bin\mysql\bin\mysqld-max-nt.exe: ready for connections.
Version: '4.1.0-alpha-max'  socket: ' '  port: 3306
```

The generated output shows that the initial database is created and initialized. It is advisable to use this approach because if there are errors, it is easy to see where the problems are and fix them before registering MySQL as a Windows Service.

To shut down the MySQL server process, a second console is started and the following command is executed:

```
./mysqladmin -u root shutdown
```

When either of the commands to start or stop MySQL are executed, it is assumed that the commands are executed in the directory [MySQL Installation Directory]/bin.

Installing the MySQL Service

In a production scenario, you shouldn't run MySQL server from the console. To register MySQL as a service, the following command is executed:

```
$ ./mysqld-max-nt --install
Service successfully installed.
```

If the command executes unsuccessfully, it is probably because the service has already been registered. To unregister MySQL, the following command is executed:

```
$ ./mysqld-max-nt --remove
Service successfully removed.
```

The command removes the application from the Windows Service list; using the --install option, the MySQL service can be added to the Windows Service list. Figure 7.1 shows the added MySQL service to the Windows Service list. When the computer reboots or when the administrator accesses the service list, it is possible to execute MySQL without having to resort to the command line.

Do not use the service for the impatient install, but use the console to start and manage the MySQL service. For those that are not acquainted with MySQL, it will be easier to diagnose any errors that might occur.

CAUTION

Installing the MySQL Control Center

The expanded MySQL Control Center archive contains three files: Setup.ini, mysqlcc.msi, and Setup.exe. The file Setup.exe bootstraps the file mysqlcc.msi, which is a Windows Installer program. Because this tool is specifically geared for the administrator, there are no deployment considerations so clicking on the file Setup.exe and installing the MySQL Control Center application is adequate.

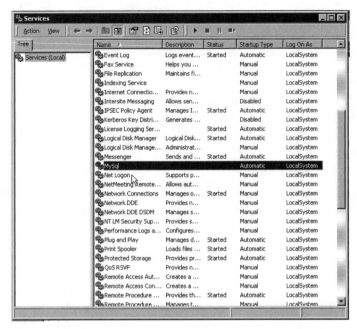

FIGURE 7.1 MySQL service shown in the Windows Service list.

The MySQL Control Center application needs to be installed because all techniques described in this book use this tool.

Installing the ODBC Connector

The ODBC Connector application is installed by double-clicking on the downloaded ODBC Connector Windows Installer. You don't need to change any of the configuration items; just click through the individual dialog boxes and install the application.

Deployment: MySQL Server

The impatient installation used to install MySQL is adequate to use in a deployment scenario. Of course, it goes without saying that the routines would be scripted using a BASH script. More problematic is the deployment of data within the MySQL database. The simplest and best solution to deploy the data is to dump it using the associated MySQL utilities. The advantage of this approach is that it is safe to export data and add it to another database regardless of version and platform. More details about dumping and reading a database are given in this chapter in the "Technique: Backing Up and Dumping" section.

Deployment: MySQL APIs

Deploying the individual APIs such as the ODBC connector is a more complicated scenario because the various connectors do not have deployment-friendly installers. The installers need to be distributed using manual deployment techniques, which are not exactly administrator friendly. The exceptions to the rules are the Java and .NET MySQL drivers, which can be deployed alongside an individual application. These drivers are files that can be referenced by the application and hence do not require a complex setup script.

Technique: Managing the MySQL Service

The administrator will want to run MySQL server as a service because it is the only logical production solution. However, there are issues that need further explanation when running MySQL as a service.

Resolving Security Problems

Attempting to run the MySQL service as described in the "Impatient Installation" section of MySQL will most likely cause an error to be generated. When running MySQL from the console, MySQL was in the context of a user. The automatically generated files are then attached to that user. This means when running as a service, the file `[MySQL Installation][datadir/ibdata1]` has the incorrect security privileges. Figure 7.2 shows the security privileges of the InnoDB database file.

In Figure 7.2 at the top of the figure is an editor with the output of the error that is generated when the MySQL service cannot be started. Cross-referencing the

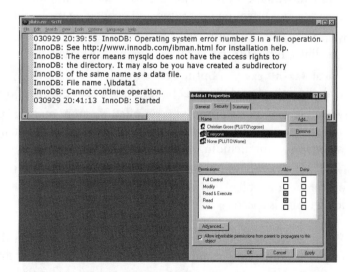

FIGURE 7.2 Security privileges for the InnoDB database file.

error with the MySQL Web site reveals that the error is due to permissions, which are shown in the ibdata1 Properties dialog box. The Security listbox shows three entries with the Everyone entry highlighted. The problem is that Everyone does not have Modify or Write access and hence will generate an error. Put more accurately, the user System, which is the default user for a service, does not have Modify or Write access. The solution is to either change the security descriptors of the file, or have the MySQL service execute under a different user account. The decision is left to you, but be aware that there are security issues that need to be resolved.

The error shown in Figure 7.2 is stored in the file [datadir]/*.err. *Whenever something goes wrong, inspect any of the* *.err *files because they will contain the causes of the error. This is because services do not have the capability to generate content to the console.*

Starting the Right Service

When installing MySQL as a service, the program mysqld-max-nt.exe was used as the MySQL server application to process MySQL requests. Looking within the MySQL bin directory, there are many more executables with a similar name. Each executable is a specially compiled version of MySQL that has certain features and are defined as follows:

mysqld.exe: A compiled version of MySQL that includes all features such as symbolic links, InnoDB, and Berkley Database (BDB) with full debug symbols and memory allocation checking. This version is not intended for production scenarios, but intended for testing and debugging problems.

mysqld-max.exe: An optimized, compiled version of MySQL that includes symbolic links, InnoDB, and Database Driver (DBD) tables.

mysqld-max-nt.exe: An optimized, compiled version of MySQL that includes symbolic links, InnoDB, DBD tables, and named pipe support.

mysqld-nt.exe: An optimized, compiled version of MySQL that supports named pipes and has no support for transactional tables such as InnoDB. The advantage of not including transactional tables is speed.

mysql-opt.exe: An optimized, compiled version of MySQL that has no support for transaction tables such as InnoDB. The advantage of not including transactional tables is speed.

Which service is used to start MySQL depends entirely on the context of the problem. The impatient installation used the version that included all features for simplicity. However, depending on the context, a different version might be necessary. A context could be the requirement to use named pipes or to ignore transactions. Named pipes will be discussed in the next section, but not using transactional tables makes for a faster database, albeit the cost is transactions. Transactions are very often useful in enterprise applications.

Using Named Pipes

Named pipes are useful when the client and server are on the same machine. It is expensive to open a TCP/IP socket and exchange data when everything transpires on the same machine. An optimization is to use named pipes. When communicating between computers, the simplest is to use TCP/IP sockets. To enable named pipes, the compiled version of MySQL with named pipes enabled has to be used, and then named pipes have to be enabled by changing the `my.cnf` MySQL configuration file to something similar to the following:

```
[mysqld]
enable-named-pipe
basedir=C:/bin/mysql
datadir=C:/bin/mysql/data
```

The entry `enable-named-pipe` is added to enable named pipes. To use named pipes on a local machine, the reference used is a period as shown in Figure 7.3 for the ODBC Connector configuration.

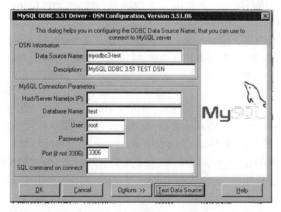

FIGURE 7.3 ODBC connection configuration shown to use named pipes.

In the MySQL ODBC 3.51 Driver dialog box, the text box Host/Server Name (or IP) has been replaced with a period, which tells the driver to use named pipes. Even though there is a value for the text box Port (if not 3306) the value will be ignored.

When the Server Crashes

Suppose the MySQL server works as normal and then on a moment's notice, the MySQL server process crashes. The cause of the crash is unknown, but the crash can be duplicated because the conditions leading to the crash can be duplicated. If a crash cannot be duplicated, only further crashes can indicate what the problem could be. The debugging-enabled version of MySQL can trace its calls and provide a context of why MySQL is crashing. The following command shows how to start a debug-enabled version of MySQL:

```
./mysqld --debug --console
```

The MySQL program `mysqld.exe` is used because it includes debugging support. The command is executed from the command line because the MySQL service has already been registered as being another executable. The command-line option –debug is used to enable tracing, which generates the file `c:/mysqld.trace`. Within that file should be details on why a crash occurred. If the details are not comprehensible to you, post the part of the error to the MySQL mailing list for further help. The trace log is important because only with the trace log can the cause of the crash be determined.

The debug-enabled version of MySQL does not include support of named pipes, which can make testing problematic if you are using named pipes. Therefore, before using the debug version, perform the same tests using TCP/IP connections to see whether the problem does not lie with the named pipe support. The other option is to compile a custom version of MySQL with named pipe support enabled. It is also important to disable named pipes in the configuration file; otherwise, an error will be generated.

The `--debug` command-line option that is used when starting the MySQL server application essentially traces everything. The MySQL server with debugging enabled uses the DBUG debugging package that contains a number of options. After the command-line option `--debug` can be a number of flags and modifiers as shown here. (Even though the example is split onto multiple lines, the example represents a single command-line option.)

```
./mysqld
--debug=d,info,error,query,general,where:O,c:/temp/mysqld.trace
--console
```

The change to the `--debug` command-line option creates two command sequences separated by the colon character. The letters d and O relate to the kind of command-line option modifier. The letter d is used to provide additional debug options, which in the case of the command will trace the messages that relate to info, error, query, general, and where. The letter O defines the location of the trace file, which in the case of the command is c:/temp/mysqld.trace.

In a generic sense, debug command-line options and modifiers can be specified as follows:

```
./mysqld --debug=option,modifier,modifier:option,modifier:option
```

The double colon separates each option and a comma separates each modifier. Following is a list of available options. (Note many of these options are only usable by programmers who understand the sources of MySQL.)

d (administrator): Used to output the messages associate with a specific macro. Within the MySQL sources, there are a number of DBUG_x message types, and each modifier logs a specific message type. When this flag is not specified, all messages are logged. The important ones are shown in the previous example debug command line, but there are more such as test, loop, my, safe, and so on. For low-level details about MySQL, the my modifier is useful as it logs low-level MySQL messages. Otherwise, the message types are more useful for programmers. Those options useful for the administrator will be marked with the word administrator. More details about processing a log file are given after this list.

D: The amount of delay in units of tenths of a second to add after each logging output. Be wary of using this message as doing a full log will massively slow down MySQL.

f: This option limits tracing to the method functions defined by the modifiers. This option can be used to trace specific MySQL code blocks to find specific causes of a crash.

F: An option used to identify the source filename for each generated log entry.

i (administrator): An option used to identify the process or thread ID for each generated log entry. When testing the output, knowing which thread is processing the request might establish whether there is a state problem.

g: Enables MySQL profiling, where the individual associated modifiers are the functions to profile. The profile information will be generated in the file dbug-mon.out.

L: An option used to identify the source file line number for each generated log entry.

n: An option used to generate the current nesting depth of each function.

N: This option is used to line number each line of output.

o: The output is redirected to a file where the modifier specifies the name of the file.

o (**administrator**): The output is redirected to a file, where each call flushes the data to the file and the modifier specifies the name of the file. This option is slower, but safer in contrast to the o option. This option should be used so that the log file is saved to a standard location.

p: This option limits debugger output to a specified process ID.

P: For this option, each line of output is associated with a process ID.

r: When the output generates a new state, the previous state is not inherited.

s: Outputs messages used for tracking down memory leaks in MySQL.

t (**administrator**): This option, which is enabled by default, enables the generation of function calls and exit macros. Using this output, it is possible to figure out a call stack, which can then be submitted to the MySQL team for potential further investigation.

When a trace file is generated, it appears similar to the following text block:

```
T@1      : <_mymalloc
T@1      : info: c:\bin\mysql\bin\mysqld.exe
Ver 4.1.0-alpha-max-debug for Win95/Win98 on i32
T@1      : >unireg_init
T@1      : | >calc_daynr
T@1      : | | exit: year: 2003  month: 9  day: 30 -> daynr: 731853
T@1      : | <calc_daynr
T@1      : <unireg_init
T@1      : >init_errmessage
T@1      : | >read_texts
T@1      : | | >fn_format
T@1      : | | | enter: name: errmsg.sys
dir: C:\bin\mysql\share\english\  extension:   flag: 4
T@1      : | | | >dirname_part
T@1      : | | | | enter: 'errmsg.sys'
T@1      : | | | <dirname_part
T@1      : | | | >unpack_dirname
T@1      : | | | | >dirname_part
T@1      : | | | | | enter: 'C:\bin\mysql\share\english\'
T@1      : | | | | <dirname_part
```

Essentially every debug message is output to the log file. In trace output, each line starts with a letter and a number, which identifies that a thread (T) with a particular identifier is generating the line of output. After the double colon are message details.

If the message starts with the > character, then a function is being called where the function name is the identifier after the > character. If the message starts with a < character, then the function is being exited. The horizontal bars are used to indicate the location of the message being generated. For example, in trace output the line with the two horizontal bars followed by the exit identifier is used to indicate that the message is being generated in the context of the function calc_daynr. Whenever the identifiers exit and enter are being output, the associated data calling the function and leaving the function are output.

The administrator does not need to know the details of all the calling sequences. The administrator needs to use the trace logs to figure out what went wrong. For example in a crash, the cause of the error needs to be found. After the error has been located, the administrator needs to retrace the steps of MySQL and figure out what caused the error. The best approach is not to open the entire file and attempt to figure it out, but use the command grep and then search the trace log for an error. An example trace file that has been searched by grep is as follows:

```
$ grep --line-number --context=3 'error' mysqld.trace
174-T@1     : <_mymalloc
175-T@1     : >my_setwd
176-T@1     : | my: dir: 'C:\bin\mysql\datasdfsdf\'  MyFlags 16
177:T@1     : | >my_error
178-T@1     : | | my: nr: 17  MyFlags: 36  errno: 2
179:T@1     : | <my_error
180-T@1     : | >my_message_no_curses
181-T@1     : | | enter: message:
Can't change dir to 'C:\bin\mysql\datasdfsdf\' (Errcode: 2)
182-T@1     : | <my_message_no_curses
183-T@1     : <my_setwd
184-T@1     : >unireg_abort
185:T@1     : | >sql_print_error
186:T@1     : | | error: Aborting
187-
188:T@1     : | <sql_print_error
189-T@1     : | exit: clean_up
190-T@1     : | >free_root
191-T@1     : | | enter: root: 7cc9e0  flags: 0
—
281-T@1     : | | <_myfree
282-T@1     : | | >hash_free
283-T@1     : | | <hash_free
284:T@1     : | | >sql_print_error
285:T@1     : | | | error: c:\bin\mysql\bin\mysqld.exe:
Shutdown Complete
286-
287:T@1     : | | <sql_print_error
288-T@1     : | | >_myfree
289-T@1     : | | | enter: ptr: b76dc8
290-T@1     : | | <_myfree
```

The grep command is used with the command-line option --context to display all the places where an error has occurred and the three lines before and after the error. The --context command-line option is good to use because it gives an idea of the trace lines near the error.

Looking at the trace output that has been filtered by grep, there are two things that come to mind. First the error is that MySQL cannot change to the directory specified in the configuration file. That in fact is the cause of the MySQL server "crash." The second thing to notice is that while the search was intended for explicit error identifiers, the function my_error was found in the search. This is a good search find because it means that MySQL is outputting the error. Using the --line-numbers option with the command grep makes it possible for you to pinpoint where in the log file the error occurred and then attempt to figure out in detail what went wrong.

The search techniques using grep are just a beginning on finding out the cause of a problem. Depending on the cause of the crash, you might have to use grep in different variations. However, regardless of the crash, grep should be used to search the trace file because just using a text editor and scrolling through the file contents is like searching for a needle in a haystack.

TIP

Startup and Command-Line Options

Consider the my.cnf configuration file with the identifier enable-named-pipes. The MySQL documentation constantly mentions that to enable named pipes, the MySQL command-line option --enable-named-pipes should be used. This means that there are two ways to specify the same configuration, and both ways of enabling named pipes is fine. When a command-line option is added to the configuration file, MySQL recognizes the option as a command-line option and treats it as such.

The reason for using the command line instead of the configuration file is to enable multiple MySQL server instances to run concurrently on the same computer. For example, by using the command line, you can specify a data directory location as another running instance could be reading the directory from a configuration file. Following is a list of the most common configuration items that you will most likely use from the command line:

ansi: An option without any value that forces the use of ANSI SQL and not the dialect of MySQL, which is ANSI SQL and some extra bits.

big-tables: An option without any value that stores big result sets as temporary files on the hard disk. This could be the result of a select statement that joins several tables together and returns a very large result set. If the result set is too large, an error stating that the table is too big will be generated, so using this option will write a file and not generate the error. However, performance will be degraded.

bind-address: An option with a string value that references an IP that MySQL will bind to when the server process starts.

flush: An option without any value that saves the data to a hard disk in between SQL commands.

language: An option with a value that specifies the language that will be sent to the client. For example, setting a value of german means all messages that the client sees are in german. The value must be in lowercase. The message value can also be a full path to a directory containing the messages. An example of the German messages is in the directory [MySQL Installation]/share/german.

max_connections: An option with a numeric value that identifies the maximum user connections that can be made to the MySQL server database.

max_user_connections: An option with a numeric value that identifies the maximum number of concurrent connections per user that can be made to the MySQL server database.

port: An option with a numeric value that identifies the TCP/IP port that the MySQL server will listen to.

safe-mode: An option without any value that is used in a testing context to not load and use some database optimizations.

skip-bdb: An option without any value that is used to skip the initialization of the BDB database system. Using this option improves the speed of MySQL.

skip-innodb: An option without any value that is used to skip the initialization of the InnoDB system. Using this option improves the speed of MySQL.

skip-networking: An option without any value that is used to not make available a TCP/IP port for remote networking. For MySQL to have any sort of functionality, the named pipes option must be enabled.

table_cache: An option with a numeric value that indicates the number of tables that will be held open by MySQL. When MySQL opens a table, that reference to the table will be held in memory. When a table is opened and the number of open tables equals the size of the cache, then the least used table is discarded and the new table is opened. If all tables are in use, an error is generated. The default value of table_cache is 64 and should be 1024 or 2048 and not in the millions range.

thread_cache_size: An option with a numeric value that indicates the number of threads that will be kept in the cache. If client connections are quickly made and dropped, then the thread number should be higher than when a client keeps a connection to the MySQL server. The default thread cache size is 32, but could be higher and depends on the number of concurrent users. The exact number depends on the difference in connections and variable threads. More about environment variables is discussed in the section "Technique: Using the MySQL Control Center."

`thread_concurrency`: An option with a numeric value that gives an indication to the system on how threads the system should run concurrently. The ideal number is a calculation where the number of CPUs is multiplied by two.

`thread_stack`: An option with a numeric value that defines how much of a stack to give each thread that is executing. An ideal starting value would be 64 KB.

`tmpdir`: An option with a string value that defines the directory where temporary files will be stored. This option is useful when the temporary files should be stored in a different directory.

`tmp_table_size`: An option with a numeric value that when exceeded will convert temporarily created tables in memory into files on the hard disk. This option relates back to when a query is made and multiple tables are joined. If multiple joins result in a very large data set, it is better to save the results to a temporary file than to have the MySQL server process run out of memory.

`wait_timeout`: An option with a numeric value that determines the number of seconds a client connection can be idle before being disconnected by the server. It is important that this number not be less than automatic disconnects set on the client side because that could cause transactions to be aborted. Or setting this value to short might slow down the system because the ODBC layer on Windows can pool ODBC connections for faster connect times. The advice is to be wary and think about what the client connections are doing.

The options explained are only a few of the options that can be used to tune and tweak the MySQL database server. The simplest way to know about the latest available options is to execute the following command.

```
./mysqld --help
```

The command-line option `--help` will output the available options and command-line switches. Then if an option is of interest to you and not mentioned in this book, do a search of that switch in the MySQL mailing lists or on Google.

The MySQL server can have its variables tweaked using the SQL set command while the MySQL server is executing.

TIP

Technique: Using the MySQL Control Center

When MySQL is installed, you can use the default administrator tool `mysqladmin.exe`. `mysqladmin.exe` is an acceptable tool for some things, such as shutting down the server, which can also be accomplished from the command line using the following command:

```
net stop mysql
```

For managing a farm of servers, a better tool is the MySQL Control Center. The MySQL Control Center application is nothing more than a colorful GUI that communicates to the MySQL server using SQL commands much like `mysqladmin.exe` would. The difference is that the MySQL Control Center has a more intuitive user interface than `mysqladmin.exe` does.

Connecting to a Database

The MySQL Control Center is a better tool because it allows the administrator to view and manipulate the individual MySQL servers using a GUI. Generally GUIs are not that useful when managing servers because GUIs require human interaction. The MySQL Control Center has the capability to run SQL scripts, making it a good compromise between flexibility and ease of use. In MySQL terms, automation is written using the SQL programming language. Figure 7.4 shows a sample snapshot of the MySQL Control Center when it is first started and is not connected to any database.

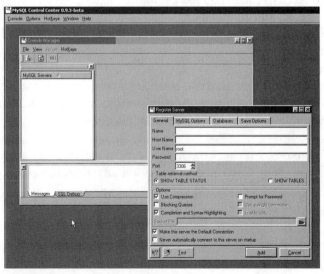

FIGURE 7.4 Initial window layout when starting the MySQL Control Center for the first time.

To connect to a database, the Register Server dialog box in Figure 7.4 is used to define the details of the connection string used to connect to the MySQL database. Before using this application, it is important to have a MySQL server instance running on some computer because otherwise the MySQL Control Center will fail. For the simplest case, fill in the text boxes explained as follows:

Name: An identifier displayed in the MySQL Control Center server listbox. Use a name that makes it easy to remember which server is being manipulated.

Host Name: The name of the host, which could be an IP address or a friendlier DNS name.

User Name: The name of the user that will log on to the server, which most commonly will be root as you are the administrator.

Password: The password associated with the **User Name**, which after the impatient installation is still nothing and should be left blank. The "Technique: Managing Users and Security" section shows how to change the password.

After the text boxes have been filled in, click the Test button to make sure the connection works. If the connection is successful or an error occurs, the output is generated in the Messages window at the bottom of the Console Manager window as shown in Figure 7.4. If the connection is successful, click the Add button and the Console Manager window will contain an entry for the server.

In the Console Manager window, there will only be a single entry in the MySQL Servers listbox with a little red dot, which means that a connection has not yet been established. To make a connection to the MySQL server, double-click on the listbox entry and expand all the nodes by double-clicking to load the data from the server to the client. By default, the MySQL Control Center will not load all the information and only does so on as needed basis. Figure 7.5 shows a listbox with all possible elements expanded.

In Figure 7.5, each MySQL server has three major functionalities that can be managed: Databases, Server Administration, and User Administration. The three major functionalities are explained as follows:

Databases: Manages the individual databases with data and tables contained within them. This includes the system databases stored in the database mysql.

Server Administration: Manages the MySQL server process, including the attributes defined in the previous "Technique: Managing the MySQL Service" section. The administrator can read the statistics of the database, know the states of the various flags, and understand the pulse of the MySQL database.

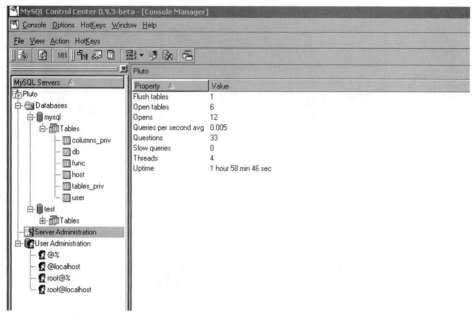

FIGURE 7.5 The MySQL Control Center showing all available properties for a database.

User Administration: Manages the individual users on the database and allows the administrator to manage passwords and rights.

When using the MySQL Control Center, the application behaves very much like a MMC snap-in. The MySQL Control Center is not a MMC snap-in, but supports the notion of context-sensitive clicks and context menus. For example, clicking on a database allows an administrator to manage the properties associated with a database. The downside is that it's very easy to damage a database if you are not careful.

Refining How Things Are Displayed

When connecting to the database, the default settings were used, but you can connect to the database using custom attributes on how the administrator interacts with the database. To edit the connection settings used to connect to the server, select the server from the MySQL Servers listbox and right-click as shown in Figure 7.6.

When you click the Edit menu item, the window changes as shown in Figure 7.7.

The definitions and preferred settings of the individual fields are as follows (fields we've already discussed are not listed):

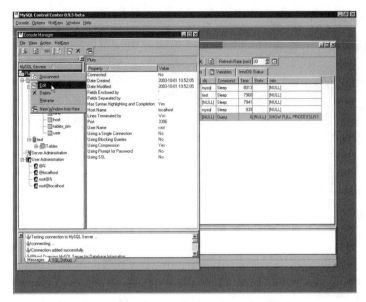

FIGURE 7.6 Right-click Edit to edit the properties of the MySQL Control Center element.

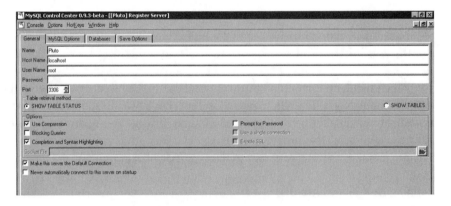

FIGURE 7.7 Connection properties for the MySQL Control Center.

Port: The port used to connect to the MySQL server instance, which must equal the port number given by the MySQL Server users.

Table Retrieval Method: There are two ways to inspecting tables: SHOW TABLE STATUS and SHOW TABLES. The default is to use SHOW TABLE STATUS, which provides a more comprehensive output of the nature of the tables. The default value should be kept.

Use Compression: Indicates that the communications between the MySQL Control Center and MySQL server should be compressed. The default is to compress communications and should be kept as a default.

Blocking Queries: Instead of using asynchronous communications for queries, the queries are executed and the MySQL Control Center waits for the query to end. For long queries, this could cause the application to hang, and therefore should not be set.

Completion and Syntax Highlighting: With the MySQL Control Center, you can execute SQL commands in the SQL window. By using this option, those SQL commands will highlight SQL commands and be friendlier for editing purposes. The default is to enable and it should be kept set.

Prompt for Password: This option causes the MySQL Control Center to ask for a password whenever the administrator attempts to connect to the server. Depending on the security policy, it is a good option to set, even though the default is not to prompt for a password.

Make This Server the Default Connection: This option causes the server being managed to be the default server that will be connected to. There is no real advantage or disadvantage to this option and it can be set or unset.

Never Automatically Connect to This Server on Startup: When the MySQL Control Center starts, a connection to the individual servers will be automatically made. This is not a good idea when managing servers where the server may or may not be available. The default is to connect, but a preferred approach is to set the checkbox so that a server is connected to it manually.

The Register Server dialog box has three tabs: MySQL Options, Databases, and Save Options. All these tabs contain functionality that can be used to customize the characteristics of the MySQL Control Center application. Many of these options are not that important to tweak because the defaults are acceptable and most likely you will not edit any of the values. Following is an explanation of the functionality for each of the tabs:

MySQL Options: This tab contains settings that define how the connection to MySQL is established. You can set the parameters such as connection timeout, communication packet sizes, and query sizes. These settings may need tweaking if the administrator is using either a slow network or unreliable network.

Database: This tab allows the administrator to determine which databases are displayed in the output. This is useful if the administrator wants to create views of a server and only have specific databases loaded for specific purposes.

Save Options: The options on this tab are related to the SQL entry window; they should not be edited because they are default values for best operation.

Server Administration

The Server Administrator element is in the MySQL Servers list box. You can click this element to display the current statistics of the MySQL server. If you double-click the same element, the Administration Panel appears. Both the current statistics and the Administration Panel are shown in Figure 7.8.

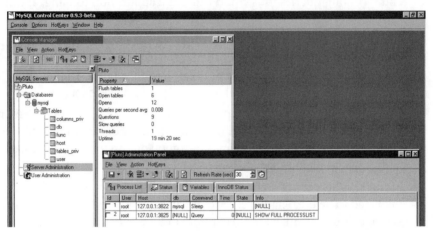

FIGURE 7.8 The MySQL Control Center showing administration content.

In Figure 7.8, the Console Manager contains a listbox with a number properties and values. Each of these properties has an associated value that can be used to see the vital statistics on the execution of MySQL.

To know what the MySQL server is telling you, it is important to know all the MySQL server configuration options that are available. Some of them have already been discussed and more will be discussed in this chapter.

For example, the property Open Tables has a value of 6, and going back to the configuration item `table_cache`, the value should not be near to the maximum value. The value of `table_cache` can be found the window Administration Panel on the Variables tab, but let's not shift focus for the moment. The default value for `table_cache` is 64, which means that the number of open tables is not near the maximum value allowed in the cache. This is generally good because it means that a table can automatically be opened without having to go to the hard disk. If the property Open Tables were constantly near the value of 64, however, then a potential optimization would be to increase the `table_cache`, although this operation will require the use of more resources.

The single best optimization for a machine hosting a relational database is to have as much RAM as possible with a very fast IO subsystem.

TIP

Going back to Figure 7.8, the Administration Panel has a number of tabs. This window appears when the Server Administrator element is double-clicked. In the Administration Panel, not much can be managed, but it's an important window because the tabs Status, Variables, and InnoDB Status display all the MySQL configuration items and status in a simple, easy-to-read location.

For example, clicking on the Variables tab displays many of the configuration variables discussed in the "Startup and Command-line Options" section. It is not possible to edit the values of the variables, as that still has to be done manually on the command line or in the MySQL configuration file. The Status tab contains the status of the execution of the MySQL server process. The InnoDB Status tab contains the status of the InnoDB databases.

Technique: Querying a Database

When administrating a MySQL database, most of the SQL queries will be entered using the SQL Query Window as shown in Figure 7.9.

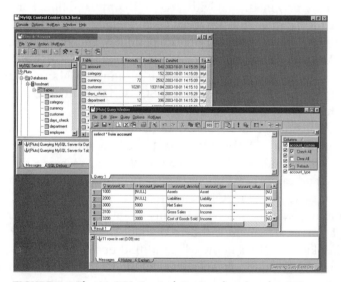

FIGURE 7.9 The MySQL Control Center showing the SQL Query Window.

In Figure 7.9 the Query Window is used to query a database. It appears when you select a database, and then click on the SQL toolbar item in the Console Manager window. In Figure 7.9, the `foodmart` database will be queried. The Query Window in Figure 7.9 shows that a single query `select * from account` has been typed in. To run the query, you click the exclamation point toolbar button in the Query Window. The output is generated as a data grid in the query result, which is the middle window in the Query Window.

By using the SQL editor, you can run multiple queries and generate some results that can then be saved as a result set. The editor also allows you to manually add a row or edit a single field in a result set. To edit, you simply select the field in the query result window and wait until the edit cursor appears.

TIP

The best use for the SQL editor is to run queries to see the state of the data within a table. It is also very useful when making small edit changes or scripts that need to be run on occasion. The SQL editor is not useful when the SQL script has been created and is used to automate a process. Essentially use the SQL editor as an editor to create the automation.

Technique: Automating Queries Using Scripts

Having said that the MySQL Control Center will be used for most editing functions, there are limitations to the SQL editor. The problem with the SQL editor is that it is extremely inefficient with large SQL command files. For example, imagine dumping the database into a large SQL command file. Loading that file for execution into the SQL editor will dramatically slow your computer. For example, loading a 22 MB SQL command file for execution requires about a gigabyte of memory. The SQL editor is also not very useful when running SQL scripts periodically. SQL scripts are like BASH scripts except that SQL scripts contain a number of SQL commands that manipulate the data in a database.

In production scenarios, SQL commands need to be executed without the intervention of a GUI. The program mysql.exe is used to run SQL commands much like the Query Window. The advantage of the mysql.exe program is that it is console based and can process or generate data in a host of ways. The most common use of mysql.exe is to run SQL scripts that recreate full databases.

For example, imagine having to run a script every day that retrieves some state. The SQL select statement is shown as follows. Note that this book assumes that you either know SQL or know where to find out more about SQL (e.g., MySQL documentation). This book is geared at administrators who might have to do some SQL, but care more about managing the database and let somebody else run the SQL commands to manipulate the data.

```
use foodmart;
select account_id, account_description from account;
```

In the example script, the first line is required because of the nature of using the program mysql.exe. When the program mysql.exe executes the example script, it knows which MySQL server to connect to, but does not know which database to use. The command use specifies the database that will be used when executing the queries.

Not using the use command will get a No Database Selected error. The line thereafter is the select command that returns all the records within the table account.

To run the script that selects a data set from the command line, the following command is executed:

```
$ c:/bin/mysql/bin/mysql --host=pluto --user=root
--password= < simple.sql
account_id      account_description
1000    Assets
2000    Liabilities
3000    Net Sales
3100    Gross Sales
3200    Cost of Goods Sold
4000    Total Expense
4100    General & Administration
4200    Information Systems
4300    Marketing
4400    Lease
5000    Net Income
```

The command mysql.exe has some command-line parameters and the SQL script is fed to the mysql.exe program using the input stream. Using both command-line options and the input stream is common when executing SQL scripts. The generated output is a tabular formatted table that has the column names as headings. That output could be piped to another program or to another file for further processing as is customary in BASH scripting.

The command-line options used are part of the subset that are explained as follows:

batch: An option that has no value and generates the resulting data in tabular format, where spaces between the fields are separated using tabs and each line represents a row of data.

host: An option with a value that represents the name of the server as DNS or IP address where the SQL commands will be executed on.

html: An option that has no value and generates the resulting data in an HTML page format, which could be piped to a file.

line-numbers: An option that has no value and generates line numbers when an error occurs in the SQL script.

password: An option that has a value and is the password used in conjunction with the user to identify the client to the server.

pipe: An option that has no value and is used to connect to the server using named pipes.

port: An option that has a numeric value and is used to identify the port used to connect to the server.

unbuffered: An option that has no value and is used to flush the buffer after every query.

table: An option that has no value and is used to output the data in table format.

user: An option with a value that represents the username used to access the MySQL server process.

xml: An option that has no value and is used to generate the result set as XML data. This is useful when the data is to be further processed with other XML tools such as Extensible Stylesheet Language Transformation (XSLT).

The power of the mysql.exe program is its capability to generate data in a format other than tabular space-delimited data. For example, by using mysql.exe you can generate an XML formatted file that contains reference information used by other programs. The mysql.exe program can also be used to add data to the database because the SQL script can execute any SQL script.

The options specified in the previous list can be added to the MySQL configuration file as shown in the "Startup and Command-Line Options" section. The difference, however, is that the options are added to a client section of the my.cnf configuration file as follows:

```
[client]
xml
host=pluto
user=root
password=
```

Then instead of using a large number of command-line options, the command line only requires an input stream as follows:

```
$ c:/bin/mysql/bin/mysql < simple.sql
```

Technique: Creating a Database

A database is created in MySQL using either a SQL command or using the MySQL Control Center. Following is the SQL command to create the database mydatabase:

```
create database mydatabase;
```

Following is the SQL command to delete the database mydatabase:

```
drop database mydatabase;
```

To create a database by using the MySQL Control Center, select the server, right-click, and then choose the Databases folder under the server identifier as shown in Figure 7.10.

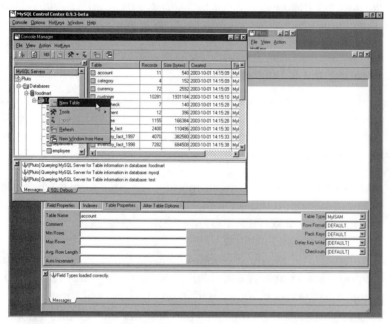

FIGURE 7.10 Creating a database in the MySQL Control Center.

Click the New Database menu item to open a dialog box that asks for the name of the database. You then type in the database name and click on the OK button. The Databases folder will then contain the newly created database.

To delete the newly created database, select the database name, right-click, and then choose Drop Database as shown in Figure 7.11.

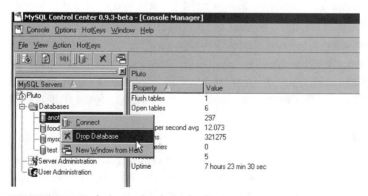

FIGURE 7.11 Deleting a database in the MySQL Control Center.

TIP

In all SQL scripts, there should be a use [database identifier] *command so that the SQL commands have a database to work with. Not using this command will generate an error. Be wary of SQL scripts that delete databases and create them haphazardly because it is very easy to delete something that should not be deleted. As a precaution, back up the database before deleting it.*

Technique: Creating and Managing Tables

After a database has been created, you can add tables that will be used to store data. In most relational databases, there is only one table format. MySQL has multiple table formats and each one has a definite purpose and reason for existence. MySQL supports the following table formats:

MyISAM: This is the most commonly used table format when the table does not have to support transactions. The advantages of the MyISAM table type are that it is the most versatile and supports many extra features the MySQL offers such as text search facilities.

InnoDB: This is the most commonly used table format when the table has to support transactions. The InnoDB table format is geared toward traditional relational database operations used in enterprise applications.

HEAP: This table format is not a database per say, because it does not support persistence. The HEAP table format stores all its data in memory and when the database is stopped, the data disappears and must be added again. An in-memory database is very useful when creating data that is more often read than written, and that must be accessed as quickly as possible using a relational format.

BDB: This table format is similar to the InnoDB table format except that the underlying storage mechanism is the Sleepycat™ Berkeley DB format. Using this table format, you can exchange data directly with the Sleepycat database system. The InnoDB table format is preferred for transactions.

ISAM: This table format is the precursor to the MyISAM table format and should not be used in new projects.

MERGE: This table format is not a format, but a collection of multiple MyISAM tables to be presented as one table to the end user. You can use the MERGE table format to combine multiple MyISAM files as one file.

Creating a Table

When creating tables for the MySQL server, many options can be used to optimize access to the table. For a simple database not used by many clients, using the SQL command CREATE TABLE is good enough. However, for higher traffic production systems where many queries and updates are made, some additional attributes have to be added. You can add those attributes and tables in general using the MySQL language, but that's not the only way. The MySQL Control Center is ideally suited to managing tables. The MySQL Control Center can even be used to generate the scripts to recreate the tables that it manipulates.

To create a new table in the MySQL Control Center, select the Tables folder, right-click, and select New Table as shown in Figure 7.12.

FIGURE 7.12 Creating a new table.

A new window appears allowing you to edit the characteristics of the table. Figure 7.13 shows a table being edited.

FIGURE 7.13 The MySQL Control Center used to edit a table.

The Editing Table 'account' in Database Foodmart window shows everything necessary to define a table in MySQL. The grid table in the middle of the window contains all the fields that define the table.

A field is defined by three major parts: Field Name, Allow Null, and Data Type. The Field Name is a case insensitive unique name that represents the field in the table. Allow Null is only of consequence when adding new records. When checked, it means that a new record can be added without specifying a value for the field. The Data Type references the type of data that can be stored in the field and is one of the following types:

bigint: A numeric value that can range from −9223372036854775808 to 9223372036854775807 and uses an 8-byte space.

bit: A type that is a synonym for tinyint.

blob: A binary type that allows storage of a maximum 65,535 (2^16 - 1) bytes.

bool: A type that is a synonym for tinyint.

char: A string type of fixed length. For example, char(32) identifies a string of 32 characters in length, where the character type is determined by the database. A char buffer can have a length between 1 and 255 characters. It is important to note that if the field is 32 characters long, then all data is 32 characters long and will be padded with spaces. This can have a dramatic effect in a client application.

date: A type that identifies a date in the form of YYYY-MM-DD in numeric form. For example, 2003-01-01 would be January 1st, 2003.

datetime: A type that identifies a date and time in the form YYYY-MM-DD 00:00:00 and the time is represented in 24H format.

decimal: A numeric type that identifies a number with a width and precision. The width defines the total number of digits and the precision defines how many digits after the decimal point. It is important to realize that a decimal value is stored in a character buffer where each digit represents one character. This means it is not possible to use standard mathematics on the individual numbers.

double: A double-precision floating type number that can range from −1.7976931348623157E+308 to −2.2250738585072014E-308. An option is to add the display width as an example double(10,5), which means to store the number with 10 digits and 5 digits after the decimal point. If the double type is prefixed with the identifier unsigned, then negative values are not allowed.

enum: A type that can only contain predefined types. For example enum ('red', 'green', 'blue') defines a field that can only contain the string buffers red, green, blue, or NULL. The field can be addressed by an index or by the string itself. In the color example, there would be the indices,0 (NULL),

1(red), 2(green), and 3(blue). An enum can reference 65,536 different values. Using the MySQL Control Center, the enum's values are declared in the field value text box.

float: A single-precision floating type number that can range from 1.175494351E-38 to 3.402823466E+38. An option is to add the display width as in example double(10,5), which means to store the number with 10 digits and 5 digits after the decimal point. If the double type is prefixed with the identifier unsigned, then negative values are not allowed.

int: A numeric type that can range in value from −2147483648 to 2147483647 and uses 4 bytes space. If the double type is prefixed with the identifier unsigned, then negative values are not allowed.

integer: A type that is a synonym for int.

longblob: A binary type that allows storage of maximum 4294967295 (2^32 - 1) bytes. Note that many of the table types do not have the capability to store the full length of the field.

longtext: A text type that allows storage of maximum 4294967295 (2^32 - 1) characters. Note that many of the table types do not have the capability to store the full length of the field.

mediumblob: A binary type that allows storage of maximum 16777215 (2^24 - 1) bytes.

mediumint: A numeric type that can range in value from −8388608 to 8388607 and uses 3 bytes space.

mediumtext: A text type that allows storage of maximum 16777215 (2^24 - 1) characters.

numeric: A type that is a synonym for decimal.

real: A type that is a synonym for double.

set: Similar to an enum with the difference that a set defines each value uniquely at the bit level. For example, the first value has a binary value of 0001, the second 0010, and so on. This means it is possible to use binary operators to uniquely combine multiple values. For example, the binary number 0011 means that the field references both the first and second value. Each set can only uniquely identify 64 different values.

smallint: A numeric type that can range in value from −32768 to 32767 and uses 2 bytes space.

time: A time type that is displayed as HH:MM:SS, where the time is 24H format.

timestamp: A time type that is automatically updated whenever a SQL insert or update is executed on a specific field. It is possible to manually set the value, but that is discouraged. The timestamp can be declared one of the ways as shown in Table 7.2.

TABLE 7.2 Timestamp Declaration Possibilities

Declaration	Display Format
timestamp(14)	YYYYMMDDHHMMSS
timestamp(12)	YYMMDDHHMMSS
timestamp(10)	YYMMDDHHMM
timestamp(8)	YYYYMMDD
timestamp(6)	YYMMDD
timestamp(4)	YYMM
timestamp(2)	YY

tinyint: A numeric type that ranges in value from −128 to 127 and uses 1 byte space.

text: A text type that allows storage of maximum 65535 (2^{16} - 1) characters.

tinyblob: A binary type that allows storage of maximum 255 (2^8 - 1) bytes.

tinytext: A text type that allows storage of maximum 255 (2^8 - 1) characters.

varchar: A text type like char, except that the buffer that is stored and that a shorter in length buffer than the declared value will not be padded.

year: A numeric type that can be either two digits or four digits long and is used to define a year.

Going back to Figure 7.13 near the bottom of the Editing window are four tabs that are used to define the properties of the table. Figure 7.14 shows the Field Properties tab as it contains the definitions to the individual field types.

In Figure 7.14, some of the fields are enabled and others are disabled depending on the datatype selected for a specific field. In generic terms, each of the items in Figure 7.14 are explained as follows:

Length: For datatypes that can have a maximum length, this text box is used to identify the maximum length of the field.

Default: Defines a default value that is assigned to a record field when the insert field value is not specified.

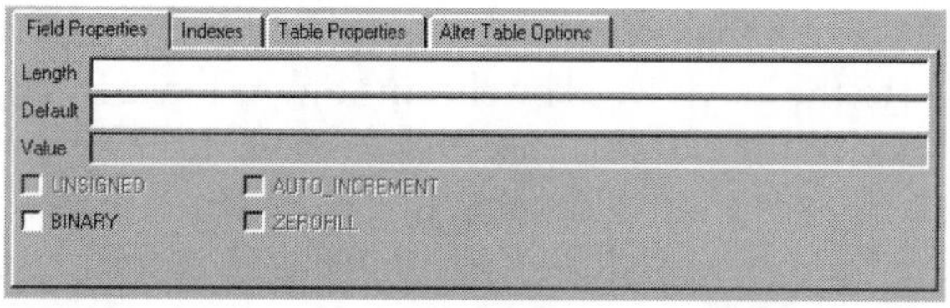

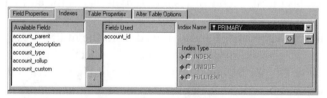

FIGURE 7.14 The Field Properties tab displaying properties that can be edited for a specific field type.

`Value:` Used to define values for `enums` and `sets`.

`UNSIGNED:` Used to define a numeric field type as unsigned, which means that the field value cannot contain a negative value.

`BINARY:` Used to define a field type as containing binary data and will not be translated to text. This is useful when you want to store data such as an image, as images are binary only.

`AUTO_INCREMENT:` Used to define a field as generating "unique" identifiers. For example, you might add a record to a database and want to uniquely identify the record using some number. Autoincrementing a numeric value means giving each record a unique value based on a counter managed by MySQL.

`ZEROFILL:` When a record is added and there is no value, then the entire field will be filled with zeros, which would set the value to zero and not undefined.

Every table can have associated with it one or multiple indices. Using an index makes it quicker to find data and dramatically speeds up a query. However, part of the speed up depends on whether or not an index is used in the context of the SQL `select` statement. Shown in Figure 7.15 is the tab to edit the indices of the table.

FIGURE 7.15 The Indexes tab displaying the indices associated with a table.

In Figure 7.15 there are two listboxes: Available Fields and Fields Used. All the identifiers represented in both listboxes represent all the fields of the table. When a new table is created, there will be no identifiers in the Fields Used listbox. This means that all data associated with a table will not be indexed, so when performing a search, the query has to manually go through each field and figure out if the constraints are satisfied. Using this approach results in slow queries.

Figure 7.15 shows that when you select a field from the Available Fields listbox, it can be added to the Fields Used by clicking on the top arrow button that is between the two listboxes. In the extreme case, to search using every field, all the fields could be transferred to Fields Used. However, that would introduce other problems. When a field is indexed, any newly added entry that has an index must be added to a sorted structure. When all fields are indexed, there is a longer entry insertion and deletion time. Indexing all fields requires every field to be added to an index and is expensive for very large index files. Therefore, when creating an index, only add the fields that will be used in actual queries. Leave the other fields nonindexed.

Every table has a primary index, which is called PRIMARY as shown by the Index Name combo-box on the right side of Figure 7.15. The primary index is used implicitly when searching a table. When creating a primary index, you should carefully select the correct fields to index. All fields that are part of the PRIMARY index must be unique and not have null values.

It is possible to creating additional indices that are explicitly used in a query. In Figure 7.15, to create an index, you click the plus sign button. A dialog box appears asking for the identifier of the index. You should use a unique name and then click OK. The unique index is added to the Index Name combo box. For custom indices, it is possible to define the type of index, which can be selected by the Index Type group box. Each of the types are explained as follows:

INDEX: Each field in the index will be sorted and there can be multiple fields with the same value.

UNIQUE: Each field that is added to an index must have a unique value and that there cannot be any values with the same identifiers.

FULLTEXT: The fields added to the index are added using a search engine type index. This means each word is indexed instead of the entire field as a whole.

The fields can be added and removed from the index as explained for the primary index. The minus sign button deletes the selected index.

The Table Properties tab shown in earlier in Figure 7.13 is used to modify the overall table characteristics and give hints. Some hints include record size. Figure 7.16 shows the details of the Table Properties tab.

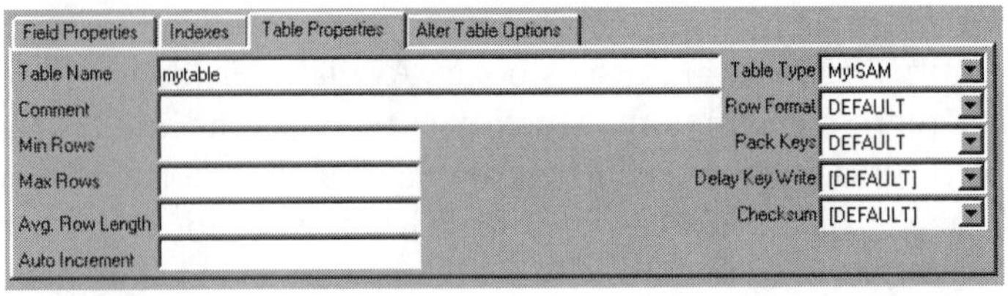

FIGURE 7.16 The Table Properties tab showing the properties of a table.

In Figure 7.16, the text boxes and combo-boxes are defined as follows:

Table Name: Identifies the name of the table.

Comment: Associates a comment with the table.

Min Rows: A value that represents the planned minimum number of rows that will be stored in the table. This value is an optimization.

Max Rows: A value that represents the planned maximum number of rows that will be stored in the table. This value is an optimization.

Avg. Row Length: A value that represents the average number of bytes that a row will occupy. This optimization is needed when using blob or text type fields. In those situations, the upper limits of the blob or text would result in a huge database, and therefore requires an indication of potentially how big a record of data will be.

Auto Increment: The value for the table to start incrementing the autoincrement values. Note that a table should only have one autoincrement field.

Table Type: Specifies the format used to store the data in the table format. It must be one of the types discussed in the "Technique: Creating and Managing Tables" section.

Row Format: This option defines how a record of data is stored in a table. For example, if a table contained three fields of 32-byte characters, then a row size of 96 can be precalculated. This is known as a FIXED row format. If the field is a blob or text, however, the exact dimensions of the row cannot be precalculated unless a hint is given, and hence the record must be stored as DYNAMIC. The other option is COMPRESSED, which compresses the data within the record. These different formats only apply to the MyISAM table format.

Pack Keys: This option when activated compresses the index files, and should be used when the data is read more often than written. When the index is compressed, writing to the compressed file is more expensive than reading from the index. By default, strings are compressed whether or not the Pack Keys option is set.

Delay Key Write: This option when activated will update key data when the table is closed.

Checksum: This option when activated will write checksums for every record that is generated. Using checksums is useful when a database has become corrupted or when it is desirable to not have a database become corrupted. Data warehousing is a good example of where checksums should be used.

The Alter Table Options tab shown earlier in Figure 7.13 is used to define which column is used to order the table when no ordering is specified.

After a table has been created using the MySQL Control Center, it can be saved and will become part of the database. Saved tables can be reverse engineered by the MySQL Control Center and a SQL create table command can be created. In the Tables folder, you can select a table, right-click, choose Tools, and Show Create as shown in Figure 7.17.

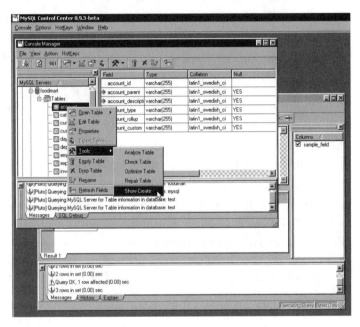

FIGURE 7.17 Using the MySQL Control Center to show the create table SQL command.

When you click Show Create, another dialog box appears that contains a list-box of all tables available in the database. The table you selected and right-clicked is highlighted. Click on the Execute button to open a SQL editor window with the MySQL create table statement that can be used to create the table from a SQL script. The script can then be saved for recreating the table in another database.

Managing a MyISAM Table

The default table format used by MySQL is the MyISAM format. The MyISAM table format does not include transactions when data is saved or manipulated. The advantage of the MyISAM format is its flexibility. MyISAM is well suited for one type of applications. Enterprise applications are well defined and have generally fixed-length fields, so they are not well suited for the MyISAM table format. The

MyISAM table format is ideally suited for other applications such as those found on the Internet that have extended field lengths and do not fit in a single mold.

When a MyISAM table is created, three different files represent a single table. For example, if a table `mytable` was created in database `mydatabase`, then as a subdirectory of the option `datadir`, there will be three files: `mydatabase/mytable.frm`, `mydatabase/mytable.MYD`, and `mydatabase/mytable.MYI`. The notation used by MySQL is to store the table datafiles under a directory named after the database. The file extensions are explained as follows:

frm: A file that contains the descriptors of the table in terms of columns and attributes.

MYD: A file that contains the data as made up by the individual records of the table.

MYI: A file that contains the index data from the table datafile.

When the data of the MyISAM table is stored, there are three formats defined as follows:

Static (fixed length): The static table is used as default when there are no `varchar`, `blob`, or `text` types used in the table declaration. The result is that a static table is very fast, easy to cache, and can be easy to rebuild after a crash because all fields are fixed length. The downside to using the `char` datatype is that it is fixed length and has space padded. The client might have to constantly trim the buffer before appending to a string. Forcing the client to constantly manipulate the data before using it might lose the advantage gained by saving to fixed-length strings.

Dynamic: The dynamic table is a bit more complicated because each record is stored with a piece of header information indicating how long the record is. All text or binary data is saved as chunks in the database that might not be contiguous. This can and will lead to database fragmentation. Because of the unknown record length after a crash, it is more complicated to determine where the data is, and potentially can result in the deletion of many records.

Compressed: This table format compresses the data so that a database can very easily fit into small places. It is slower than all the other formats. To create a compressed table, the table can be defined as compressed, or be compressed using the tool `myisampack`.

The one big advantage of the MyISAM table format is its capability to easily deal with large text fields. For example, imagine creating a mailbox backend with MySQL. Using the MyISAM table format, you can easily store all the user's e-mail in a relational table.

The only downside is that a database crash could potentially corrupt the database. In that case, the table will most likely contain inconsistent data, which could cause further crashes. To verify the state of a table, the table file is checked explicitly using the program myisamchk.exe as shown here. (Note it is assumed when running myisamchk.exe that the MySQL server process is not running.)

```
$ ./myisamchk.exe c:/bin/mysql/data/foodmart/account.MYI
Checking MyISAM file: c:/bin/mysql/data/foodmart/account.MYI
Data records:       11   Deleted blocks:        0
- check file-size
- check key delete-chain
- check record delete-chain
- check index reference
- check data record references index: 1
- check data record references index: 2
- check data record references index: 3
- check record links
```

The program myisamchk.exe is passed an index file via a command-line option; this index file is used to reference a specific table. The myisamchk.exe program will then check and verify if everything is okay. So additional command-line options are as follows (all the command-line options have no attributes or parameters):

--extend-check: An option that does an in-depth error check on a table.

--sort-index: An option that sorts the index blocks.

--analyze: An option that analyzes the index keys to make some joins faster.

--verbose: An option to be very descriptive in the output of the analysis of the MyISAM file.

The example use of myisamchk.exe only checks a table. To repair a table the command-line option --recover is used in conjunction with the following additional options:

--backup: An option that makes a backup of the file before fixing up the table.

--force: An option that forces the overwriting of any files.

--extend-check: An option that does an in-depth repair of the table being investigated.

--safe-recover: An option that is slower and repairs some things that would normally be considered nonrepairable.

When using MyISAM, a few options can be added to the configuration file that relate specifically to the MyISAM:

log-isam: A configuration item with a string value that references a filename. The purpose of the option is to log all MyISAM table changes.

concurrent-insert: A configuration item with no value that allows a concurrent insert. Concurrent inserts make it possible to allow multiple people to add to the table increasing performance.

Managing an InnoDB Table

The InnoDB table format is geared toward enterprise applications. By default, InnoDB tables support transactions and row locking. While running backups, InnoDB allows clients to lock records, make changes, and then undo those changes using the rollback command. The biggest difference between the InnoDB file format and the MyISAM file format is that the InnoDB does not have a number of files distributed depending on the database and table names. The InnoDB file format is an encapsulated file format where the data is stored in a set of files.

CAUTION

The MyISAM file format is very flexible and can be backed up by manipulating the files directly. The InnoDB file format cannot be manipulated directly. The only way of interacting with InnoDB tables is to use SQL tools to manipulate the data.

When MySQL starts, an InnoDB database is created automatically. That database could be used to store tables and data. InnoDB database files need to be configured properly and optimized. Following are some default InnoDB configuration settings that are added to the my.cnf configuration file:

```
[mysqld]
basedir=C:/bin/mysql
datadir=C:/bin/mysql/data

innodb_data_home_dir = C:/bin/mysql/innodb-data
innodb_data_file_path = ibdata1:100M:autoextend:max:8000M

innodb_log_group_home_dir = C:/bin/mysql/innodb-log
innodb_log_arch_dir = c:/bin/mysql/innodb-log
innodb_log_files_in_group=3
innodb_buffer_pool_size=50M
innodb_additional_mem_pool_size=10M
innodb_log_file_size=10M
innodb_log_buffer_size=8M
innodb_file_io_threads=4
```

```
innodb_lock_wait_timeout=50
innodb_flush_log_at_trx_commit=1
```

In the `my.cnf` configuration file, there are three sections: original database definitions, InnoDB database file locations, and InnoDB settings. The InnoDB database locations are defined by the configuration items `innodb_data_home_dir` and `innodb_data_file_path`. The item `innodb_data_home_dir` defines the root location where all InnoDB database files will be located. For the `my.cnf` configuration file, that meant the directory `c:/bin/mysql/innodb-data` would hold all files. In a production scenario that might be okay, as long as the directory being referenced had mounted drives as shown in Chapter 2. If the drives were mounted to different drive letters, then the item `innodb_data_home_dir` needs to be added to the configuration file, but not reference any directory. That gives the InnoDB subsystem an indicator that all database files will be referenced using an absolute path.

The other item `innodb_data_file_path` defines the different locations for the InnoDB database files. The database files defined are relative to the option `innodb_data_home_dir`. Each database file is referenced using a notation:

```
innodb_data_file_path = [db description];[db description]
```

The `db description` is a description of an InnoDB database file that is used by the MySQL server. Multiple databases can be defined, which are separated by a semicolon. The database description is shown as follows:

```
[path to InnoDB file]:
[initial size of InnoDB file]:[autoextend]:[max]:
[maximum size of database]
```

In the database description, only the `path to InnoDB file` and `initial size of InnoDB file` are required options. The other options are optional. The `path to the InnoDB file` defines a filename that will contain the InnoDB data. MySQL will create the file, but not create the path to the file so it is important to create the paths ahead of time. The `initial size of the InnoDB file` defines the beginning size of the database. This number depends entirely on how big the database will be. The database numbers are appended with either an `M` for megabytes, or `G` for gigabytes.

The other options are not necessary, but should be defined. The keyword `autoextend` is used to automatically grow the database in increments whenever more database space is required. The keyword `max` and option `maximum size of database` are two options that should be added so that the database does not grow beyond control. If the keyword `max` and size is not specified, then the database will grow until there is no room left on the hard disk.

The other InnoDB items defined in the `my.cnf` configuration file are defined as follows:

innodb_additional_mem_pool_size: A numeric value that defines how much memory is used to store data dictionary information and other internal structures. The default definition of 10 MB is good to start with. If it's not enough, warnings are written into the MySQL error log.

innodb_buffer_pool_size: A numeric value that defines how much memory will be used to store InnoDB data such as records and indices. This single item needs to be properly configured and optimized. The correct value depends entirely on how many applications are running concurrently and how much RAM a computer has. In the simplest situation, start with 50% of the computer's RAM and start increasing percentages. You'll know that you have used too much RAM when the computer starts wildly thrashing on the hard disk as the operating system is constantly paging the leftover RAM to and from the hard disk. Having a large amount of RAM significantly increases the performance of the database.

innodb_file_io_threads: The number of concurrent threads used to manage the IO of the InnoDB. The true value depends on the number of users, which for a Windows system should start at 4 and potentially be increased to 8 or 10.

innodb_flush_log_at_trx_commit: This numeric value should normally have a value of 1 to indicate that the database should always flush the logs after a transaction has completed thus ensuring the survivability of the database if anything crashes.

innodb_lock_wait_timeout: This numeric value determines how long InnoDB should wait before it detects a deadlock in seconds. If a deadlock is detected, then the transaction is automatically rolled back.

innodb_log_buffer_size: This numeric value determines the amount of RAM needed for storing the transaction log in memory. A value between 1 MB and 8 MB should be sufficient. If transactions tend to be long, in that they contain many SQL statements, then a bigger log buffer will save IO traffic as the log data can remain in memory.

innodb_log_file_size: This numeric value determines the size of the log files on the hard disk. A log file is used to manage the InnoDB transactions. Having larger log files means that more transaction data can be stored making it more robust in case of a crash. A larger log file means also longer recovery times if a crash does occur.

innodb_log_files_in_group: This numeric value determines the number of log files that InnoDB uses when writing the log data. The ideal number is 3.

Technique: Managing Users and Security

Up to this point there has been only one user, root, and root does not have a password. This is not a good approach in managing a database. All users should have passwords and should have their rights restricted so that a user will not damage the database. MySQL has three levels of security: access to the server, access to a database, and rights for a table.

All the users and their rights are stored in the table user, which is a system table located in database mysql. It is possible to manage all the security descriptors by simply modifying the table user. The following SQL command shows how to add a user:

```
insert into user values (
    'localhost', 'cgross', PASSWORD( 'mypassword'),
    'Y','Y','Y','Y','Y','Y','Y','Y','Y','Y','Y','Y','Y','Y');
```

It is assumed that the SQL command is executed in the context of the mysql database. The first value localhost identifies the location where the user may log in. It is possible to restrict access to certain tables depending on the location where the user logs in. This is a good security feature and allows the administrator to define workstations that are trusted. The second value cgross is the username. The third value mypassword is the password for the username. However, the password cannot be stored in clear text format and is hash encrypted using the function PASSWORD. The series of Y characters represents the rights that the user cgross has.

A user can also be added to the database using the SQL statements grant and revoke, which are friendlier to use. The following command uses the SQL grant statement to add a user's privileges with the same data as in the previous code snippet:

```
grant all privileges on *.* to cgross@localhost identified
by 'mypassword' with grant option;
```

In this code snippet, the username and host are replaced using a single identifier separated by the @ character. The password does not need to be manually hash encrypted because the grant statement will take care of that automatically. The series of Y characters is replaced with the keywords all privileges that allows the user to do whatever he likes on the database. The keywords with grant option allows the user that is being created to add or remove users. In a production scenario, that should not be the norm when adding users because only an administrator or database administrator should be allowed to add or remove users.

The privileges that can be assigned are defined as follows:

alter: Allows a user to execute the SQL command `alter table`.

create: Allows a user to execute the SQL command `create table`.

create temporary tables: Allows a user to execute the SQL command `create temporary table`.

delete: Allows a user to execute the SQL command `delete`.

drop: Allows a user to execute the SQL command `drop table`.

execute: Allows a user to run stored procedures, which are a part of MySQL 7.0.

file: Allows a user to execute the SQL commands `select … into outfile` or `load data infile`.

index: Allows a user to execute the SQL commands `create index` or `drop index`.

insert: Allows a user to execute the SQL command `insert`.

lock tables: Allows a user to execute the SQL command `lock tables` on the tables that the user can run the SQL command `select`.

process: Allows a user to execute the SQL command `show full processlist`.

references: Reserved for the future.

reload: Allows a user to execute the SQL command `flush`.

replication client: Allows the client to ask where the replication slaves are.

replication slave: Necessary for the slave to read the binary log on the master necessary for replication.

select: Allows a user to execute the SQL command `select`.

show databases: Allows a user to execute the SQL command `show databases`.

shutdown: Allows a user to run the `mysqladmin shutdown` command to shut down the MySQL process.

super: Allows a user to connect to the server even if the maximum connection count has been reached.

update: Allows a user to execute the SQL command `update`.

usage: A synonym for no privileges meaning that the user has no rights.

The rights and privileges can be assigned on four different levels: global, database, table, and column. For example, the following SQL command shows how to assign privileges to a set of columns in a table:

```
GRANT select (more,something) ON test.junk TO tom@"%"
        IDENTIFIED BY 'some_pass';
```

The SQL command can be translated as follows. Create a user tom that can access the MySQL server from any client as described by the % character. The user tom has the password some_pass and cannot add or remove user or privileges. The user tom can perform a select from the table junk and columns more and something in the database test.

The SQL command is an example of adding a very specific set of rights and privileges on a specific set of columns in a table in a database. To add varying levels of security depending on the column, table, and database, multiple grant statements have to be executed. Of course, another strategy is to grant all rights and then revoke the rights on an as-needed basis.

To revoke a privilege the following SQL command is executed:

```
REVOKE select (more,something) ON test.junk FROM tom@"%"
```

The command REVOKE is used to remove a right from a specific user. The notation used to identify a right is virtually identical to the command GRANT. Notice, however, instead of the keyword TO, the keyword FROM is used. If a right is removed that the user did not have in the first place, MySQL will generate an error.

In all the privilege examples, the user was specified using a percentage character for the hostname. The percentage sign represents a wildcard allowing a client to log in from anywhere to access the server. If the hostname were replaced with localhost, then the client rights and privileges would be with respect to whenever the user logs in locally. The percentage sign can be combined with other text to represent a specific domain or address range shown as follows:

```
tom@'192.168.1.%'
tom@'%.domain.com'
```

Notice that a quote surrounds any text that includes the wildcard character because this is part of the MySQL coding convention. Not including the quote will generate an error. Another wildcard character is the asterisk, which is used when specifying a database name or table name.

You can manage users using the MySQL Control Center. To add a user, right-click User Administration and choose New User from the menu that appears as shown in Figure 7.18.

The MySQL Control Center - Add User window appears (see Figure 7.19).

We've already discussed the three text boxes in this window, so now let's discuss the listboxes.

The Allow Access To listbox to the right represents the part of the grant statement that is after the on part of the statement. Essentially this listbox allows an administrator to define which databases and tables that the user can have access to.

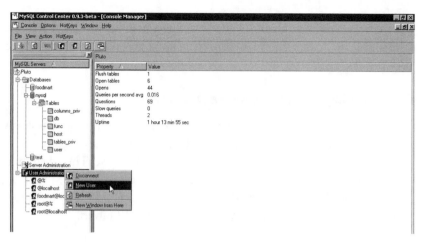

FIGURE 7.18 Using the MySQL Control Center to add a user.

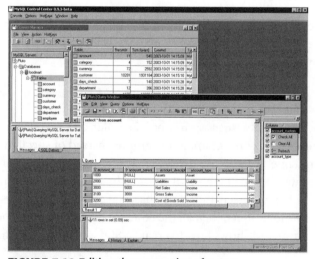

FIGURE 7.19 Editing the properties of a user.

For example, selecting a database in this list means that a user has access to all tables of the database. Selecting the item Global Privileges means that a user can access all databases and tables.

The Privileges listbox on the left defines the privileges that are associated with the individual tables and databases. The Privileges listbox can be confusing because by default any table or database selected will result in the assignment of all privileges of the selected table or database. The usual approach is for the administrator to select a table and define the associated privileges. For large databases with many tables, this can be tedious and probably should be scripted. Checking the All

Privileges checkbox gives a user all privileges just like the grant statement all privileges. The With GRANT Option checkbox gives the user the with grant option
of the grant statement.

Technique: Backing Up and Dumping a Database

You can back up and dump a database in many ways, but the safest way is to use the
dump and load utilities from MySQL. These utilities generate a number of SQL
script files that can then be used to generate a database. The advantage of using this
approach is that an administrator could dump a database, tweak the SQL statements, and then load a new database. For example, the administrator might want
to move the data from MyISAM tables to InnoDB tables.

By using SQL scripts, the administrator could use sed *to generate SQL scripts that
can be used to create databases for other relational database servers.*

The utility mysqldump.exe is used to generate a SQL script that can be used to
recreate the database. In the simplest case, the program mysqldump.exe can be used
as follows:

```
$ ./mysqldump.exe --user=root --password= sampledb account
```

The program mysqldump.exe has a similar command-line option structure, as
does the mysql.exe program. For example, instead of specifying the options on the
command line, you can use the my.cnf configuration file. Specified after the options
are the databases, or tables that need to be dumped. When the command is executed, the table account in the database sampledb is output to the console. If there
are no table identifiers, then all the tables of the database will be generated. The following command shows how to create a SQL script file for multiple databases:

```
$ ./mysqldump.exe --databases mysql sampledb > script.sql
```

The command assumes that the username, password, and host information is
stored in the my.cnf configuration file. The option --databases expects after it a list
of databases to generate the SQL scripts for. If you want to generate the SQL scripts
for all databases, then the command-line option --all-databases is used. In the example command for multiple databases, the generated output is stored in the file
script.sql. Following is a partial listing of the options available for the program
mysqldump.exe:

--add-drop-table: Before a new table is created in the script, the old one is dropped. Note that this option will cause all the old data, if it exists, to be deleted.

--add-locks: Add table locks around the SQL command insert statements.

--compatible: An option that is associated with one of the following values: mysql323, mysql40, postgresql, oracle, mssql, db2, no_key_options, no_table_options, and no_field_options. This option allows the generation of scripts that is compatible with another database such as Oracle or SQL Server. The options that start with a no remove all the specialized options, such as table type, which are associated with SQL commands and specific to MySQL only.

--complete-inserts: Uses a complete SQL insert command.

--extended-inserts: Uses the new faster extended SQL insert command.

--flush-logs: Before starting the dump, a flush is issued. The flush automatically writes all the data that should be written. This option is useful for getting a consistent database dump.

--force: Continue the database dumping process even if an error occurs.

--lock-tables: Before dumping the database, lock all the tables for read-only access. This option is very important when it is necessary to get a consistent database dump.

--single-transaction: Dump all the database tables in a single transaction. This option and the –lock-tables option solve the same problem, except that they are mutually exclusive of each other.

--result-file: Dump the result into the file defined by the option, instead of the console text.

After the data has been saved to a hard disk, it can be recreated using the mysql.exe program as shown in the "Technique: Automating Queries Using Scripts" section.

The database dump is used to get a consistent database state at a certain point in time. The database dump is also the best way to do a database backup. There is a proper way of doing a database backup, because the entire process should be able to recover from a crash. Database backups are done periodically, e.g., every day, week, two weeks, or month. The cycle depends entirely on the environment. Between backups, data will be added and manipulated, which will not be part of the backup. If the tables become corrupted during some processing, it would be useful to be able to recreate the complete database with minimal data loss.

A meaningful backup strategy involves using a binary log file. The binary log file contains all the updates of the database that are executed. Log files can be used to recover from database crashes. The updates are regardless of table types. To add a binary log file, the configuration file is updated to something like this:

```
[mysqld]
basedir=C:/bin/mysql
datadir=C:/bin/mysql/data
log-bin=c:/bin/mysql/data/bin-logfile.log
log-bin-index=c:/bin/mysql/data/index-bin-logfile.indx
binlog-do-db=sampledb
binlog-ignore-db=test
```

The new configuration items are `log-bin`, `log-bin-index`, `binlog-do-db`, and `binlog-ignore-db`. When MySQL starts, the `log-bin` directive tells MySQL to create a binary log file as specified by the filename and path. The log file `bin-logfile.log` has an extension, which is removed and replaced with a numeric identifier. To keep track of the different log files, the configuration `log-bin-index` is used to create an index file. The `log-bin-index` option is optional and does not need to be specified. The option `binlog-do-db` references a database that should be logged, and the option `binlog-ignore-db` references the databases that should be ignored and not logged. To specify multiple databases to log or ignore, multiple `binlog-do-db` or `biblog-ignore-db` options are used.

The binary logs contain the instructions that can be used in conjunction with the SQL scripts to recreate a database. The binary logs are used by the replication system and hence when doing both replication and database backup, log files cannot be ignored. More about replication will be discussed in the next section "Technique: Replicating a Database." The binary log stores the instructions in binary format and a special program is needed to extract the programs. The following text block shows how to generate a SQL script from a log file.

```
$ ./mysqlbinlog.exe c:/bin/mysql/data/bin-logfile.000002
# at 4
#031005 10:46:26 server id 1   log_pos 4
Query    thread_id=4     exec_time=1      error_code=0

use test;
SET TIMESTAMP=1065343586;
insert into mytable(field1,field2) values ("hello", "another");
```

In the generated SQL, there are several commented lines indicating how the SQL command was executed, followed by three SQL command lines. The SQL instruction use test defines the database that is used, which is necessary as the log file could contain SQL commands for different databases. The SQL instruction SET TIMESTAMP is used to assign the time when the data is manipulated. This way if the data is recreated, the timestamps will reflect when the data was actually manipulated. The last line of the generated SQL is the manipulation carried out on the database. Notice in generated SQL that the binary log filename is bin-log-file.000002 and not the my.cnf log filename extensions .log because there might be multiple log files.

Considering scripts and binary log files, the correct way to perform a backup is to follow these steps:

1. Lock the tables using the MySQL SQL command FLUSH TABLES WITH READ LOCK. This SQL command is a combination command that locks the tables and flushes the data. This will lock the tables for read-only access and ensure that nobody can add or manipulate data while the backup is executing. Leaving read-only access means that clients could still access the database and perform queries.
2. Perform a backup using the program mysqldump.exe. This action will generate the SQL scripts necessary for recreating a database.
3. Flush the log files and start a new log file using the MySQL SQL command flush logs. This command starts a new log file with a new number. The old log file can then be backed up for safe keeping, if so desired, or it can be deleted. Default should be to delete the log file, because the dump will contain the latest state.
4. Unlock the tables using the MySQL SQL command unlock tables. This action allows full execute actions on the database and is in production mode again.

The backup procedure outlined is a generic one that will work regardless of the table type and the structure of the database. It is the safest bet and should be used. However, having said that, there are optimizations that are beyond the scope of this book shown in the MySQL documentation.

The purpose of the binary logs is to recover between database dumps. For example, if a computer crashes, a fairly recent database image can be created by using the binary log files and database dumps. Using the binary log files also reduces the frequency of needing to do a full database dump.

CAUTION

Locking the table might seem like overkill because it is possible to dump while the database server is running. Locking the tables forces the business processes to complete and not continue with another step. That way, for example, a database will not have a partially completed mortgage application. Locking a table will ensure that the mortgage application will be in the database or not be in the database.

Technique: Replicating a Database

To increase the performance of a single MySQL server database, you can connect multiple MySQL server databases together in a master-slave configuration. This sort of configuration can even be used to perform as a backup mechanism. Imagine having a very large database that ranges in gigabytes and is used 24×7. Doing a backup that takes 10 minutes might not be acceptable. The solution is to create a slave that copies the data from the master and as such becomes the "backup." The slave could then be subjected to regular backups. Using a multipoint MySQL server database configuration also makes MySQL more robust because there are multiple places where the MySQL data is hosted.

Learning how to install MySQL server is important. Just as important is how to install MySQL in a multipoint configuration. MySQL is well suited to be replicated across multiple servers, meaning to increase performance instead of buying a very big computer box, it is possible to buy multiple smaller computer boxes.

TIP

Replication is useful and is not difficult to activate. However, replication is also one of the most difficult things to keep consistent. Replication must be done with an attention to details and methodology. The methodology explained in this book might not correlate with other documentation, but is geared toward safety. With safety, there is consistency and less chance of doing something wrong.

CAUTION

When using MySQL replication, there are host of ways of configuring the databases, but the most common configurations are shown in Figure 7.20 and 7.21.

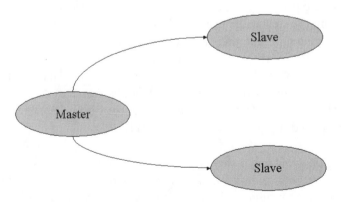

FIGURE 7.20 Master-Slave configuration.

In Figure 7.20 the Master-Slave configuration is used to copy data from the master to the slave in a one-way fashion. The slave only gets data changes. In Figure 7.21 there is a Multi-Master-Slave configuration in which each server is both master and slave. The advantage of this approach is that any server can be updated and the rest of the servers will automatically receive those changes. The disadvantage to this approach is that a client should never update two servers with data. For example, if a load balancer for one request used one server and then was bounced to another server for another request, then the replication might not have copied the data. The application would attempt to query data that does not exist, and might even add it again. Following is a list of items that work or do not work in a replicated database structure:

- The column types and descriptors AUTO_INCREMENT, LAST_INSERT_ID(), and TIMESTAMP replicate properly.
- The function RAND() does not replicate properly and should be replaced with RAND(some_value).
- Update queries that use user variables are not safe in Version 4.0.
- The MySQL SQL command flush is not stored in the binary logs and hence not replicated.
- Users are replicated when the MySQL database is replicated. This may be a desired or not desired feature.
- If a slave crashes, then the replication may have problems because the slave might not have closed everything properly. It is safe to stop a slave cleanly and let the slave continue where it left off.

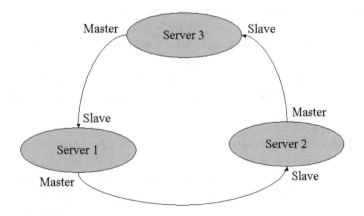

FIGURE 7.21 Multi-Master-Slave configuration.

Activating Master-Slave Replication

To activate replication, the master needs to do two things: activate the binary logging mechanism and identify itself with a unique identifier. A typical `my.cnf` configuration file for a master is shown as follows:

```
[mysqld]
basedir=C:/bin/mysql
datadir=C:/bin/mysql/data
log-bin=c:/bin/mysql/data/bin-logfile.log
server-id=1
```

The only unknown option is `server-id`. The option `server-id` is a unique identifier used to identify the server. When setting up replication systems, each server must have its own unique identifier regardless of whether it is a slave or a master.

Following is a sample `my.cnf` configuration file used by the slave:

```
[mysqld]
basedir=C:/bin/mysql
datadir=C:/bin/mysql/data
master-host=pluto
master-user=repl
master-password=mypassword
master-port=3306
server-id=2
```

The slave has more configuration items. In the slave, the configuration items relate to the hostname, user, password, and port used to access the master server. Replication in MySQL is efficient because the slave does most of the work. The slave reads the binary log of the server and executes the instructions contained within the log on the slave.

When setting up a master, there is the additional step of adding a user that a slave can use for replication. Following is the typical `grant` statement used for the user `repl`:

```
GRANT REPLICATION SLAVE ON *.* TO repl@"%" IDENTIFIED BY 'mypassword';
```

The user `repl` should either have a wildcard as hostname or the identifier of the slave that will be accessing the master. If there are multiple slaves, there should be multiple host identifiers. The privilege `replication slave` allows the slave to access the log files.

Adding Slaves

With MySQL, adding a slave and then synchronizing the data is more complicated. The problem is not the synchronization of a single database server, but the dynamic addition of multiple slaves. For example, imagine having a configuration running and then adding another slave dynamically. The question is how to synchronize the master data with the slave. There is no simple answer to this problem and in a future version of MySQL, replication will be able to dynamically add a slave without any problem.

Adding slaves requires some understanding of the details of synchronization. The problem with adding slaves is not the addition of a single slave, but the adding of slaves when there are already other slaves. Replication works because the slaves read the binary log file and based on that information, execute some SQL commands. On the slave side, a cursor is kept on which location the slave has read to. The files created on the client side are stored in the `datadir` directory. The files have the extension `.info` and/or have the identifier `relay` in the filename. If those files are deleted or the MySQL command `reset slave` is executed, the slave will not know the position of the slave. As a result, the slave will reread the binary log file and execute the commands again.

Remember, the master is in control of the data that is replicated and the slave is responsible for reading that data. To control the replication, the slave is responsible for getting periodic updates and the master is responsible for keeping that data available. When using replication, it is important that the binary log files be managed carefully.

The best approach to replication and the adding of slaves is to use the simplest and safest way. The method just described might not be fast. The problem with multiple slaves is when to know to capture the state and when to know to capture the log file output.

The safest approach for adding a slave is to manage the backup of the master in an orderly manner. The purpose of the master backup is not to back up the master, but to create a predictable state that can be used to add new slaves. In the context of a replicated MySQL server network, follow these steps to manage the backup for a master server:

1. Define a time when there is minimal activity on the server and inform everyone of those times. This time could be once a month, once every two months, or even once every six months.
2. Lock the tables using the MySQL SQL command FLUSH TABLES WITH READ LOCK. This SQL command is a combination command that locks the tables

and flushes the data. This locks the tables for read-only access and ensures that nobody can add or manipulate data while the backup is executing. Leaving read-only access means that clients could still access the database and perform queries.

3. Ensure that all slaves have been updated to the current stage, because otherwise consistency problems will result.

4. Perform a backup using the program `mysqldump.exe`. This action generates the SQL scripts necessary for recreating a database.

5. Flush the log files and start a new log file using the MySQL SQL command `flush logs` and then reset the logs using the command `reset master`. This rotates and resets the logs so that when a new slave is added, the old log data will not be used to synchronize the master and the slave.

6. Unlock the tables using the MySQL SQL command `unlock tables`. This action allows full execute actions on the database and is in production mode again.

When using replication, the log files need to be rotated regularly, because otherwise a log file might get too large and adding a new slave will take too long. Following is a `my.cnf` configuration file that a master server should have that will rotate the logs and assign a maximum cache size:

```
[mysqld]
log-bin=c:/bin/mysql/data/bin-logfile.log
max_binlog_size=50M
max_binlog_cache_size=10M
basedir=C:/bin/mysql
datadir=C:/bin/mysql/data
server-id=1
```

The binary log files are rotated by the configuration item `max_binlog_size`, which says when the binary log exceeds 50 MB, a new binary log will be created. The configuration item `max_binlog_cache_size` is used to cache the amount of memory used to buffer queries.

To add a slave to the network, perform the following steps:

1. Run the SQL scripts on the slave to add the data that defines some state on the master.

2. Stop the slave server.

3. Add the configuration items of the sample `my.cnf` configuration file for the slave to set up the slave.

4. Start the slave server.

5. Let the slave server run its synchronization routines.

Running a Multi-Master-Slave Network

Running a Multi-Master-Slave network is simple as long as all servers produce a binary log that can be used to update other servers. The only additional configuration item to add on all servers involved is the my.cnf configuration file item (other configuration items have been removed for abbreviation):

```
[mysqld]
log-slave-updates
```

The configuration log-slave-updates informs that the MySQL server in question will be used in a potential daisy chain as illustrated earlier in Figure 7.20.

The problem of running MySQL in a Multi-Master-Slave network is not the network, because MySQL runs very efficiently in such a network. The problem is figuring out how to add nodes in the network and how to recover from crashes. A network of MySQL servers daisy-chained together is dynamic and always changing. There is no one consistent state as there could always be updates somewhere in the daisy chain. The only solution is to create a network structure similar to Figure 7.22

In Figure 7.22, the network of servers has a slave server attached to Server 2. The purpose of the server slave is to back up all the data from Server 2 and provide a database snapshot. To create a snapshot, follow these steps:

1. Define a time when there is minimal activity on the network and inform everyone of those times. This time could be once a month, once every two months, or even once every six months.

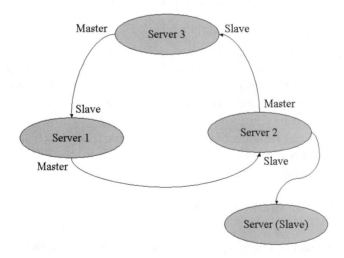

FIGURE 7.22 Multi-Master-Slave configuration with backup server.

2. Lock the tables on all servers using the MySQL SQL command FLUSH TA-BLES WITH READ LOCK.

3. Let the network settle down and run all its updates, which in an active running network would probably be only 1-5 minutes.

4. For all the servers on the network, flush the log files and start a new log file using the MySQL SQL command flush logs. Reset the logs using the command reset master.

5. Unlock the tables using the MySQL SQL command unlock tables. This action allows full execute actions on the database and is in production mode again.

6. For the external slave server, run the command stop slave, and then reset slave.

7. Perform a backup on the external slave server using the program mysql-dump.exe. This action generates the SQL scripts necessary for recreating a database.

To add a server to the daisy network of servers, follow these steps:

1. Run the SQL scripts on the server that will be added to the daisy network.
2. Add the replication user to the server to be added.
3. Stop the server to be added.
4. Add the configuration items: log-slave-updates, basedir, datadir, log-bin, and server-id. Make sure that the server to be added references some parts of the daisy chain.
5. Start the server to be added.
6. Reconfigure the daisy-chained servers to include the new server.

Setting up a replication network and creating a backup plan is not that complicated using MySQL. The plan of action requires keeping SQL script and binary log files to recreate a complete database. Every now and then, the SQL script needs to be updated and the binary log files trimmed by locking the system for updating. You can get away without doing that by doing a hot copy, but the problem is that consistency might be compromised depending on the nature of the data. For example, a search engine that updates constantly might be okay with a few inconsistent records. However, a financial application must be 100% consistent and therefore chances should not be taken.

Some Configuration Tweaks for Replication

When replicating data, there are configuration tweaks in what data is copied and how it is copied. The following options can be added to the configuration file:

`replicate-do-table`: An option that has a value identifying the table to replicate in the `database.table` notation. To specify multiple tables, the option is used multiple times.

`replicate-do-db`: An option that has a value identifying the database that is replicated. To specify multiple databases, the option is used multiple times.

`replicate-ignore-db`: An option that has a value identifying the database that is ignored during replication. To specify multiple databases, the option is used multiple times.

`replicate-ignore-table`: An option that has a value identifying the table to ignore in replication in the `database.table` notation. To specify multiple tables, the option is used multiple times.

`replicate-rewrite-db`: An option that is used to replicate the contents of a source database into a destination database as shown. An example is `src_database->dest_database`.

`replicate-wild-do-table`: An option that has a value identifying the table(s) to replicate, much like the option `replicate-do-table`. The difference is that the table can be specified using wildcards such as `database%.table%`.

`replicate-wild-ignore-table`: An option that has a value identifying the table(s) to ignore in replication, much like the option `replicate-ignore-table`. The difference is that the table can be specified using wildcards such as `database%.table%`.

`skip-slave-start`: This option delays the starting of the slave replication server. When the configuration file includes a slave configuration, the slave is automatically started when the server starts. Using this option, the slave is started when the SQL command `start slave` is executed.

Technique: Performance Tuning and Profiling

You can use many different tweaks to configure MySQL to perform better in one situation or another. The exact tweaks are beyond the scope of this book because there are simply too many. However, we've included references to the tweaks that you can find in the MySQL Reference Manual:

4.4.6.10 Table Optimization: Shows how to defragment a MyISAM table.

4.47 Setting Up a Table Maintenance Program: Shows how to keep MyISAM tables tuned and optimal.

4.7.6 Show Syntax: Illustrates how to retrieve various statistics about the currently running database.

4.10.7 Replication FAQ: Lists FAQs about some MySQL replication issues.

4.10.8 Troubleshooting Replication: Describes how to solve some of the more complicated replication problems.

5 MySQL Optimization: Discusses how to optimize MySQL tables and databases (we recommend you read the entire chapter).

6.8 MySQL Full-text Search: Shows how to fully use the full text query search engine available in MySQL.

Appendix A Problems and Common Errors: Illustrates some solutions to common problems and errors.

You can also search for help at Google (*http://www.google.com*) and Dejanews (*http://www.dejanews.com*). In both search engines, whenever searching for a solution type in the query MySQL and the problem.

SUMMARY

Data storage is an extremely important topic in any architecture. MySQL database is an example of a good piece of Open Source software that works well. MySQL is also one of the most popular Open Source databases. Many Open Source applications on the Internet rely on MySQL or work best with MySQL.

This chapter focused on the most important issues related to MySQL and how an administrator could properly configure it. Tuning and tweaking a database can be a full time job and book to itself; however, this book is a good starting point.

8 Generating Web Content

ABOUT THIS CHAPTER

The focus of this chapter is to illustrate how to use one of the most important pieces of software on the Internet, the Apache Web server. HTTP has become one of the most important protocols and the Apache Web server is the most popular Web server.

The success of Apache is its capability to be used on a wide array of operating systems and with a wide array of third-party solutions. Other Web servers are available, of course, and in specific contexts, these other servers are useful and important.

The topics covered in this chapter include the following:

Installation and Configuration: Apache can be installed and managed from the perspective of a Windows administrator.

Managing Modules: Modules are pieces of code that are loaded at runtime by the Apache server. Apache itself is not a very powerful Web server; modules make Apache powerful. The flexibility of Apache and its capability to integrate a wide array of third-party solutions makes Apache a dominant Web server.

Virtual Hosting: The details of how to host multiple Web sites on a single computer are covered. Hosting multiple Web sites is useful when a company has different Web sites for different purposes.

Activating SSL: SSL was covered in Chapter 3, but it is possible to use SSL natively within Apache. If SSL is necessary for performance reasons, the native SSL support in Apache should be used.

439

Sharing Using WebDAV: Samba and Windows share files using a specific protocol. WebDAV is a similar protocol and intended for sharing files on the Internet. The details of using Apache and Windows to share files using the WebDAV protocol are outlined.

PROJECT: APACHE HTTPD

Apache Web server is primarily an HTTP server used to serve HTML content. Apache server is an evolution of the original National Center for Supercomputing Applications (NCSA) Web server. In the early years of HTTP programming, an HTTP server called the NCSA HTTP server was developed at the NCSA. As time passed, another team created a set of patches to modify the original NCSA sources. The patches improved the NCSA HTTP server and provided extra capabilities. Soon the patches became so numerous that people started referring to the patched server as "a patchy server." At this point the "patchy server" became a new HTTP server called Apache server. Apache's quality, flexibility, and availability of sources separated it from the rest of the field (at the time it was a novelty that the sources were available). Around the time of Apache's inception in 1995, Open Source was beginning to be coined as an expression.

As of this writing, Apache has a 62% market share of currently running Web servers (*http://www.netcraft.co.uk*), but the statistics are debatable. Proponents in the debate say that in terms of the Secure HTTP (HTTPS) (typically e-commerce) protocol, the statistics are not so lopsided in favor of Apache Web server. Although this is correct, it is misleading because these types of sites use commercial products, which are based on the Apache source code base.

Apache works for three major reasons:

Open Source: Apache is not owned by anyone; rather, it is the intellectual property of the Apache Software Foundation (ASF). It's available in source code format, so anyone can download the sources, modify them, and distribute the changes in binary or source code format. Apache works because its license scheme is very liberal and allows users to do whatever they please with the sources. The only real restrictions are that you cannot call Apache your own development, and if you release a product using Apache sources, you must reference Apache somewhere in your application or documentation.

Flexibility: Apache works anywhere and at any time. The Internet has introduced the concept of 24x7 operations where a Web site needs constant availability to be accessed by anyone on the Internet anywhere and anytime. Apache fulfilled this requirement and hence has been used extensively at large Internet Service Providers (ISPs).

Third-Party Support: There is a huge amount of third-party support for Apache. Literally thousands of third-party modules can do whatever the client requires. The administrator just needs to find the third-party application and then integrate it into the infrastructure.

Table 8.1 contains reference information about the Apache HTTPD project.

TABLE 8.1 Reference Information for Apache HTTPD

Item	*Description*
Home page	*http://httpd.apache.org/*, and potentially the main Apache site at *http://www.apache.org*
Version	At the time of this writing, there are two released versions: 2.x and 1.3.x. For the scope of this book, the only Apache server that is of interest to a Windows administrator is version 2.x. The 1.3.x version works well on Unix platforms and is not optimized for the Windows platform.
Installation	The Apache HTTP application can be installed as a Microsoft Installer application.
Dependencies	Apache HTTPD has no dependencies when installed using the provided binaries. If SSL is going to be used with the Web server, then the OpenSSL, and `mod_ssl` binaries are needed. If Database Management (DBM) authentication databases are going to be used, the Perl interpreter from ActiveState needs to be downloaded.
Documentation	The documentation for the Apache 2.x installation is provided at *http://httpd.apache.org/docs-2.0/*. The documentation is good when you have a basic understanding of how the Web server works, but for a beginner, it can be a bit daunting.

$\longrightarrow$

Item	Description
Mailing Lists	Many mailing lists are available at the Apache Web site because there are so many projects. For the Apache HTTPD server, the main mailing list page is at *http://httpd.apache.org/lists.html*. For many problems, it is highly recommended that the developer consult the mailing list archives. Most likely the question has already been asked and answered.
Impatient Installation Time Required	Download size: 3-6 MB depending on whether the msi installer (smaller) or the executable installer (larger) are installed. Installation time: 5-10 minutes.
Firewall Port	80 (TCP), but the port can be defined to whatever the administrator wants it to be. For SSL connections, the default port should be 443.
DVD Location	`/packages/Apache` contains both the Windows installer package and the source code packages.

Impatient Installation

In binary format, the Apache HTTPD server is only distributed as a Windows Installer application that can be executed using a mouse double-click.

Downloading the Apache Server HTTPD Archive

Downloading the Apache Server HTTPD archive is not complicated. The *http://httpd.apache.org/download.cgi* site has a reference to a mirrored site containing the Apache HTTPD distribution. Choose the *Win32 Binary (MSI Installer)* link located under the heading Apache 2.x. The other versions should not be downloaded because they are either Unix distributions or older Windows distributions.

Installing Apache

After the Apache HTTPD archive has been downloaded, double-click the downloaded file and the Windows Installer starts the Installation Wizard dialog box as shown in Figure 8.1.

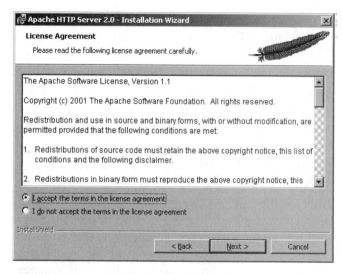

FIGURE 8.1 Initial Apache HTTP installation dialog box.

The License Agreement dialog box has the I Accept the Terms in the License Agreement radio button preselected by default. Click the Next button to accept the license terms. The Read This First dialog box appears that includes information about the HTTP server, and where the latest version can be downloaded. Click the Next button to open the Server Information dialog box shown in Figure 8.2.

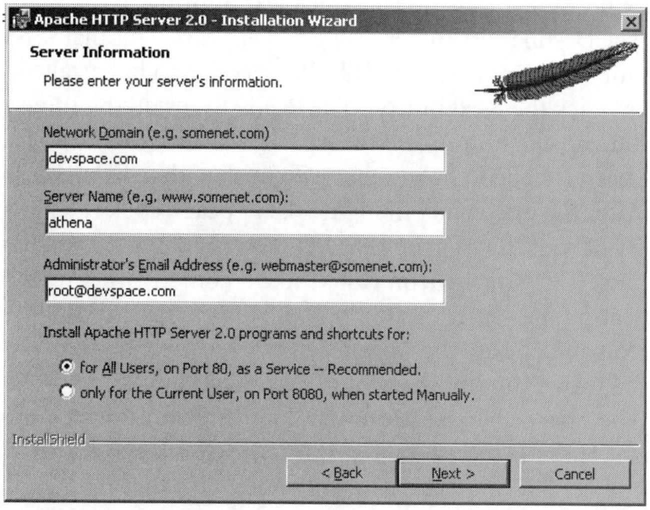

FIGURE 8.2 Apache HTTPD Server Information dialog box.

In Figure 8.2 the dialog box asks for some basic information about general operating conditions. The text boxes and radio buttons are explained as follows:

Network Domain: Identifies the domain in which the server will operate.

Server Name: Identifies the name of the server in DNS terms and not Windows server name terms.

Administrator's Email Address: Identifies the e-mail address of an administrator that will receive e-mails for problems.

For All Users...: Installs Apache as a service ready to receive request on the port 80, which is the default port.

Only for the Current User...: Installs Apache to run as a console application that is started manually and listens to port 8080. The reason for port 8080 is due to Unix security rights. For a user to start a service that can listen to any port number below 1024, the user must have root privileges. On Windows this does not matter, so the best option is to install Apache for All Users.

When installing Apache on port 80, remember to remove IIS, switch ports of IIS, or not have IIS running. If IIS is running, Apache, IIS, or another Web server will generate errors and not serve content properly.

After all the items in Figure 8.2 have been properly filled, click the Next button. The Setup Type dialog box appears with two possible options to install: Typical and Custom. The default installation is Typical, which is good for an impatient installation. The Custom option would be chosen if you intend to compile Apache modules. Choose Typical and click the Next button.

The Destination Folder dialog box appears. This dialog box is used to choose the directory where the Apache HTTPD server is to be installed. The default should be fine, so click the Next button. The Ready to Install the Program dialog box appears. Click the Install button and the Apache HTTPD files will be installed. After the files have been installed, the installer will finish with a dialog box as shown in Figure 8.3.

After the dialog box in Figure 8.3 appears, click the Finish button.

By default the Apache HTTPD server is copied, and the service is installed and running. The Apache icon (looks like a comet with a feather) with a green arrow (indicating the server is running) will appear in the Windows tray. Right-click on the icon and choose the Apache Service Monitor from the menu that appears. Figure 8.4 shows the Apache Monitor application.

The Apache Service Monitor allows an administrator to start and stop the local Apache HTTPD server. You can click the Connect button to manage a collection of Apache HTTPD services. The only operation that the Apache Service Monitor allows is the starting, stopping, and restarting of the Apache HTTPD server.

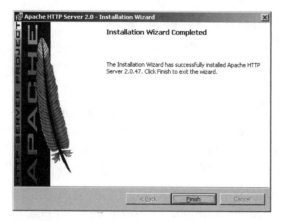

FIGURE 8.3 Dialog box that appears after Apache HTTPD has finished installation.

Figure 8.4 shows a Web browser with the *http://localhost/* URL. The resulting page is the default home page. It's best to change the home page, but the impatient installation is complete and the Web server is running.

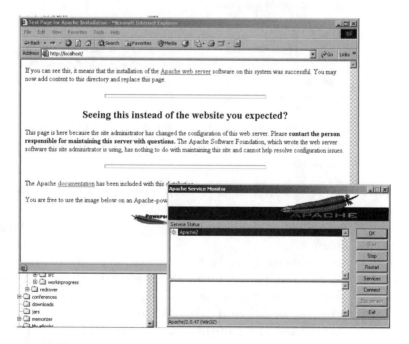

FIGURE 8.4 Apache Service Monitor application and browser showing the default home page.

Deployment: Apache HTTPD Server and Modules

Deploying the Apache HTTPD server after it has been installed using the Microsoft installation program is simple. Assuming that the Apache HTTPD server has been installed using the Windows Installer, follow these steps to create a compressed archive:

1. Open a console window and change the directory to the Apache bin home directory [c:/program files/Apache Group/Apache2/bin].
2. Run the program ./Apache.exe -k stop to stop the Apache service.
3. Zip up the directory c:/program files/Apache Group/ to an archive.

The Apache HTTPD archive can be manually installed using a script to whichever destination location. Follow these steps to use the script to fully install the Apache server:

1. Unzip the Apache HTTPD archive into a destination archive.
2. Change the directory to [Apache installation]/bin.
3. Run the program ./Apache.exe -k install to install the Apache service.
4. Modify the ServerRoot key in the following registry script. (Note registry scripts are saved as files with the extensions .reg and can be executed like an executable program).

```
[HKEY_LOCAL_MACHINE\SOFTWARE\Apache Group]
[HKEY_LOCAL_MACHINE\SOFTWARE\Apache Group\Apache]
[HKEY_LOCAL_MACHINE\SOFTWARE\Apache Group\Apache\2.0.47]
"ServerRoot"="c:\\program files\\Apache Group\\Apache2"
"Shared"=dword:00000001
```

5. Run the registry script to add the Apache home path.
6. In the file [Apache installation]/conf/httpd.conf, modify the following variables:

ServerRoot: Should point to the root directory as specified by the Server-Root key in the registry script.
ServerAdmin: Make sure that the e-mail address of the Webmaster is still correct.
DocumentRoot: Should point to the root directory of the documents, which in the default case is the htdocs directory underneath the variable Server-Root. In a production setting, it does not need to be a subdirectory, but could be an entirely different location.
ServerName: Make sure that the DNS server name is still valid.
Directory: There should be a directory entry with the old htdocs directory specified. Above the directory element is a comment saying that the value should be identical to the variable DocumentRoot.

When adjusting paths, use common sense. For example, in the configuration files there are multiple Directory *and* Alias *entries that will point to the incorrect locations. Fix them up based on the new locations. Ideally the administrator should create a templated script that would generate a site-specific* httpd.conf *file.*

When creating an Apache HTTPD deployment, most likely it will include modules and other pieces of functionality. The best deployment model is to create a running installation with all the modules and files. Then based on the running installation, create a compressed archive and write the scripts that tweak the configuration files to reflect the new installation. Even simpler, keep the installation paths identical and use a mirroring tool such as Unison described in Chapter 5. Then when the main site changes, Unison will propagate the changes throughout the entire network.

Technique: Managing the Configuration File

To do any type of operation with Apache, the configuration file has to be properly defined. The Apache HTTPD server is best described as an application that delegates requests based on its configuration. The Apache HTTPD server has become an extremely modular and flexible Internet Server Application Framework. The server could be used as a mail server or even a FTP server if modules are written to implement those types of servers. The configuration file makes the Apache HTTPD server what it is.

There is no simple three-line configuration file. To understand the Apache configuration file, it is necessary to understand a fully running Apache configuration file. There are major sections in an Apache HTTPD configuration file that do specific things. Each configuration file has the following major blocks:

Main Initialization: The main initialization section defines the main characteristics of the Apache HTTPD server. Defined are the root location of the server (ServerRoot), timeouts (Timeout), modules loaded (LoadModule), and who the server administrator is (ServerAdmin).

Directory Configuration: The directory configuration sections are dispersed throughout the configuration file and are usually defined by the identifiers directory.

Miscellaneous Other Stuff: All the other sections are identifiers used to define a specific characteristic of the server such as a URL's alias (AliasMatch) or languages (AddLanguage).

The configuration file format is a leftover from the original NCSA Web server, and is a mixture of XML tags with key value pairs. It is best to think of the format style as the Apache HTTPD file format.

Whenever Apache HTTPD server starts, it knows nothing regarding its environment and execution context, so the first task is to find the execution files and data. The execution context is typically stored in the configuration file. With a well-written configuration file, it is possible to separate the Apache executables and data. This allows an administrator to upgrade an Apache HTTPD installation without having to modify the Web site documents.

Locating the Root Directory

The configuration file is either specified in the registry or on the command line. In the impatient installation, the configuration file location is deduced from the registry variable ServerRoot. The deduction results in appending the buffer conf/httpd.conf to the ServerRoot variable.

The other way is to specify the ServerRoot variable on the command line when starting Apache:

```
./Apache.exe -d c:/bin/Apache2
```

Instead of specifying the ServerRoot variable, you can specify the configuration file itself and let the ServerRoot environment variable be defined within the configuration file. Following is an example of loading the Apache HTTPD configuration directly:

```
./Apache.exe -f c:/bin/Apache2/conf/httpd.conf
```

When Apache initializes and starts, it is allowed to have a different ServerRoot defined. This makes it possible to separate the executable modules from the configuration modules and runtime modules. This approach is more complicated, but is very useful when managing servers with a large number of Web sites.

At a minimum when the Apache starts, a document root from where all document requests are fulfilled is required. The directive DocumentRoot provides a root directory. Most content will be generated from the root directory, although it is not the only directory from which content can be served. You can use aliases and virtual definitions to define content in other directories. The main purpose of the DocumentRoot item is to provide a default location to find content.

Listening on an IP Address and Port

To serve content, the IP address, port, and identifier should be specified within the configuration file:

```
Listen 80
Listen 192.168.1.1:8080
ServerName athena:80
```

The directive Listen is used to identify which ports and IP addresses the server will listen on. There are two instances of Listen, which say to listen to requests on port 80 and to listen on the IP address 192.168.1.1 and port 80. The IP addresses that Apache listens on must be an IP address from the local computer multihomed network configuration. There can be as many Listen items as required. The directive ServerName is an identifier used by Apache to identify the server to the client.

The directive ServerName is not a required feature and Apache will attempt to deduce the identifier if the item does not exist. Not including the item can be a potential problem spot if you use virtual hosting or redirection.

The Listen *command supports IPv6 by specifying the IP part in square brackets* Listen [fe80::a00:20ff:fea7:ccea]:80. *Apache is IPv6 aware and if required, you should read the Apache documentation for further details.*

Faster Connections Using Persistent Connections

Persistent connections are useful because they enable a client to make multiple requests using a single HTTP connection. Overall, persistent connections are faster because the client does not have to establish a connection for every request. The default settings generated in the configuration file by the Apache installation program are adequate for general operating conditions. Following are some default settings used in the configuration file:

```
KeepAlive On
MaxKeepAliveRequests 100
KeepAliveTimeout 15
```

The three settings relate to each other. The item KeepAlive with the value of On indicates that persistent connections should be used. The item MaxKeepAliveRequests with a value of 100 means that the client can make 100 requests on the same connection before the connection is closed forcibly by the server. After the connection has been closed forcibly, a new persistent connection is started if the client makes another request. The item KeepAliveTimeout with a value of 15 seconds means that the server will keep a persistent connection available for 15 seconds before forcibly closing the persistent connection.

At first glance, the default settings seem odd in that a persistent connection is only kept for 15 seconds, which does not seem like a very long time. The strategy goes back to the original invention of the Web. The problem of the original HTTP 1.0 protocol was that making an HTTP connection was expensive, and when requesting a page with many items, there would be many requests. Between those page requests, nothing would be happening on the server; whereas processing a page request generated spikes in Web server loads.

Persistent connections solved the spiking problem. So consider the case where a persistent connection is kept around for an hour or two. In that scenario, persistent connections introduce other problems as they can cause timeout errors if dial-up connections, firewalls, or NATs are used. Therefore, long-term persistent connections introduce more problems than they solve. Going back to the original problem, a persistent connection should exist when an HTML page is loaded with many items on the page. After the HTML page has been loaded, a persistent connection is no longer needed. The persistent connection could be dropped, which frees the resources associated with the HTTP server and the resources of all devices that are connected between the client and the server.

You should keep the default persistent connection settings. Otherwise, the HTTPD server might run out of resources keeping inactive connections alive. Each persistent connection ties up one thread, which means one connection is inactive and one thread is doing nothing.

Technique: Stopping the Apache Process

When Apache is installed on a Windows computer, the Apache HTTPD server process can be started as either a service or as a console application. Stopping the Apache HTTPD server process while running as a service is not a problem. The problem is when the Apache HTTPD server process is executed in the context of a console window. The documentation states to use the command stop or shutdown as shown in Figure 8.5.

Figure 8.5 shows that if Apache is running as a console application attempting to stop it using the documented ways will not stop the console application. This is because Apache is attempting to stop the service that is not executing.

The only way to stop the Apache console is to kill it. The Ctrl+C keyboard escape sequence should not be used because, by default, Apache starts multiple processes and killing the main console process will not kill the other processes. The other option is to kill the entire console window, but that only works if Apache was started in a Windows batch command console. Killing the console when using Cygwin or another type of shell will have the same effect as using Ctrl+C. The other option is to use the Task Manager and individually kill the Apache processes. The best solution, however, is to use the following script:

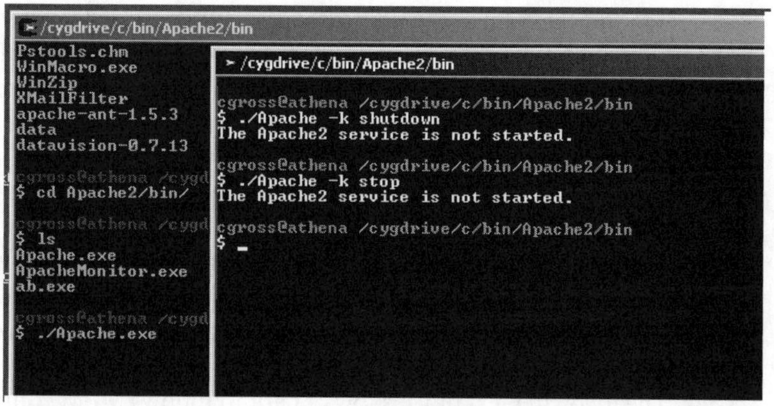

FIGURE 8.5 Attempting to stop the Apache console application using Apache.

```
#!/bin/bash
pslist | grep 'Apache ' | awk '{print $2}' > /tmp/pids.txt
exec 3<&0
exec < /tmp/pids.txt
while read line
do
    pskill $line
done
exec <&3
exec 3<&-
rm /tmp/pids.txt
```

In the script, a list of all running processes is created using the command pslist. Note that pslist is part of the Systools from Sysinternals (*http://www.sysinternals.com*). The result set is searched using grep for the Apache processes. Notice that the search term Apache has a space after it. Not having the space will cause the ApacheMonitor.exe application to be killed. Then the grep results are fed into awk to retrieve the process IDs, which are then saved in the file pids.txt. The file pids.txt is loaded and manually iterated. Each iteration contains the process ID of an Apache process that needs to be killed using the command pskill. Finally the file pids.txt is deleted. Having run this script, all the Apache processes will be killed.

Technique: Multi-Processing Modules (MPM) Tuning

In the past, the Apache HTTPD server versions for the Windows platform were not optimally tuned and tended to be slower than the Unix counterpart versions. This was because the Apache HTTPD server of old was best tuned for the Unix platform. Apache Version 2.x changed dramatically because the concept of a Multi-Processing Module (MPM) was introduced. Essentially an MPM abstracts the operating system into an Apache *micro-kernel*. The job of the micro-kernel is to provide Apache services best tuned for the platform. The MPM is specific to the platform. The administrator would tune the MPM to get the best performance on the operating system used by the Apache HTTPD server process.

The Windows MPM is very simple and does not have many different configuration options. Essentially the Windows MPM consists of two processes: controller and worker. The controller process makes sure that if the worker process dies, then a new worker process is started. The threads in the worker process manage the actual processing. The following text block shows a basic Windows MPM configuration:

```
<IfModule mpm_winnt.c>
    ThreadsPerChild 250
    MaxRequestsPerChild 100
</IfModule>
```

The directives ThreadsPerChild and MaxRequestsPerChild are contained within the IfModule directive. The purpose of the IfModule directive is to contain items that may or may not apply with a given Apache configuration. More about this will be discussed in the next section "Technique: Block Defined Configuration Files for Dynamic Configuration." Different MPM directives are explained as follows:

ListenBacklog: The associated value specifies the maximum number of clients that can wait in a queue before being processed. A queue will be formed when the maximum thread count has been reached and all the threads are busy processing other requests.

MaxRequestsPerChild: The associated value specifies the maximum requests that the child process will handle before exiting. The default configuration file will have an associated value of zero meaning that the child process, or in the case of Windows, the worker process will never exit. The advantage of having the process exit is that any memory leaks of resources will be returned to the machine. Apache HTTPD server does not have any leaks because it uses resource management techniques. However, a module might have leaks. The default is to use the value zero; however, if there are resource leaks, use a value that gives optimum server performance.

ThreadLimit: This associated value specifies the maximum number of threads that can be created in the context of a child process. For the Windows MPM, this value should be equal to the value of ThreadsPerChild because otherwise resources will be wasted. It is simpler to ignore this directive entirely and use ThreadsPerChild.

`ThreadsPerChild`: Specifies the number of threads created by the child process initially and throughout the life of the work process. In the case of the Windows MPM where there is only one worker process, the number should be set high so that the Web server can process all requests.

Directives such as `MinSpareServers`, `MaxSpareServers`, *and* `StartServers` *do not apply to the Windows MPM and will generate a configuration parse error.*

Technique: Block Defined Configuration Files for Dynamic Configuration

In a typical computer infrastructure, some servers may be executing on one platform and another server will be executing on another platform. There could even be installation differences for servers on the same platform. Maybe some servers will not have database access and others will have LDAP access. In all these scenarios, a unique configuration file must be created. This can be extremely tedious and potentially a source of configuration errors. The Apache HTTPD server configuration file can define blocks of configuration entries that are processed under certain circumstances.

Defining a configuration block was shown in the MPM configuration example. The directives `IfModule` and `IfDefine` can be used to define a block that can contain other directives. When using `IfModule`, the administrator is asking the Apache system if a specific module has either been compiled into the Apache server, or loaded using the directive `LoadModule`. To know which modules have been compiled into the Apache HTTPD server, the following command is executed:

```
$ ./Apache -l
Compiled in modules:
  core.c
  mod_win32.c
  mpm_winnt.c
  http_core.c
  mod_so.c
```

Cross-referencing output with the `IfModule` directive in the MPM configuration example, the module `mpm_winnt.c` is available. The syntax of the `IfModule` is similar to an XML tag definition; the value following the identifier `IfModule` is the name of the module. Going back to the example MPM configuration, in plain English the configuration is saying: if the module `mpm_winnt.c` is compiled or dynamically loaded then make the contained block part of the overall configuration.

Loading Modules Dynamically

For the Windows platform, by default there are multiple modules such as `mod_win32.c` and `mod_so.c`. There are more modules that are not shown because the

Windows Apache HTTPD server relies on loading modules dynamically. Following is an example dynamic module configuration:

```
LoadModule setenvif_module modules/mod_setenvif.so

<IfModule mod_setenvif.c>
Listen 8080
</IfModule>
```

The configuration example shows how to load a module dynamically using the LoadModule command. The first value setenvif_module is the name of the module structure that is exposed by the module. The identifier of the module structure is not based on any specific programmatic logic, so it can be chosen by the whim of the developer. With most modules, there is a naming pattern such as [module identifier]_module. If you're unsure of the pattern, ask the developer of the module for specifics. The value after the module identifier is the path to the module to be loaded. In the case of dynamic module configuration, the module uses a relative path, as there is no drive letter specification. The relative path is converted to an absolute path by concatenating with the path value in the directive ServerRoot.

If the administrator cannot find a developer for the module identifier, or needs an immediate answer, and the sources to Apache HTTPD server are available, then the grep command can be used. Following is an example where grep is used to find the module identifier of an Apache HTTPD included module:

```
$ grep --recursive --include=*.c 'AP_MODULE_DECLARE_DATA' *
aaa/mod_access.c:module AP_MODULE_DECLARE_DATA access_module;
aaa/mod_access.c:module AP_MODULE_DECLARE_DATA access_module =
aaa/mod_auth.c:module AP_MODULE_DECLARE_DATA auth_module;
aaa/mod_auth.c:module AP_MODULE_DECLARE_DATA auth_module =
aaa/mod_auth_anon.c:module AP_MODULE_DECLARE_DATA auth_anon_module;
aaa/mod_auth_anon.c:module AP_MODULE_DECLARE_DATA auth_anon_module =
aaa/mod_auth_dbm.c:module AP_MODULE_DECLARE_DATA auth_dbm_module;
aaa/mod_auth_dbm.c:module AP_MODULE_DECLARE_DATA auth_dbm_module =
```

The command grep is used to search directories recursively because of the addition of the command-line option –recursive. The problem is that the last command-line option applies on the directory name and not the filename. When using grep to search within a directory, the last command option is a filename filter. The --include option filters the filename identifiers that will be searched. The grep results are the Apache HTTPD module declarations. The module identifier is found by looking for the identifier AP_MODULE_DECLARE_DATA and then the next identifier is the module identifier.

IfModule *Details*

After the module has been loaded using static compilation or using a dynamic module, the directive IfModule can be used to define a block of directives that can be processed. The directive IfModule can be embedded within another IfModule or other blocks. However, under no circumstances can blocks overlap as the following text block:

```
<IfModule mod_setenvif.c>
<IfDefine something>
</IfModule>
</IfDefine>
```

In the example text block, the syntax is not correct, because the IfDefine item ends outside the boundary of the IfModule item. This will cause a parse error. It is possible to embed the IfDefine item within the IfModule item.

The IfModule item expects the name of the file that contains the module identifier as the value. This is either given to you by the developer or found by using the grep command to search the sources.

For the IfModule, it is also possible to define the negative, which means if a module is not available, activate a block shown as follows:

```
<IfModule !mod_setenvif.c>
sfdsdfsdf
</IfModule>
```

The exclamation character before the mod_setenvif identifier performs a negation operation.

The notation of the LoadModule *and* IfModule *identifiers is not user friendly and the only way to learn the different module identifiers and filenames is through experience. If your company develops its own modules, then the Apache naming convention should be followed for consistency purposes.*

IfDefine *Details*

The IfDefine directive is used to define a block that is activated from the command line. Following is a define block configuration example:

```
<IfDefine mydefinition>
Listen 8080
</IfDefine>
```

The identifier `mydefinition` is defining the port that the Apache HTTPD server will listen on. To activate the port, the `Apache.exe` server is started with the command-line option `mydefinition`:

```
./Apache.exe -D mydefinition
```

The command-line option `-D` and associated value `mydefinition` will activate the following block:

```
<IfDefine mydefinition>
Listen 8080
</IfDefine>
```

Using command-line option definitions works well when starting Apache from the console. Starting Apache as a service makes passing command-line arguments more complicated. To add a command-line option to the service, the best approach is to edit the registry setting as shown in Figure 8.6.

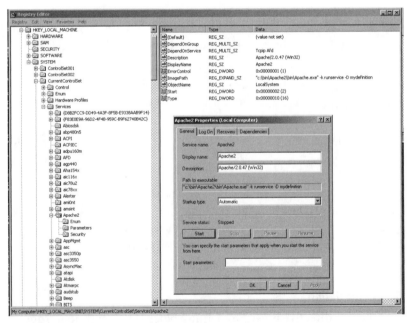

FIGURE 8.6 Adding command-line options to the Apache HTTPD service.

From Figure 8.6, the Apache HTTPD service is located under the registry key `HKEY_LOCAL_MACHINE\SYSTEM\CurrentControlSet\Services\Apache2`. The registry value `ImagePath` is edited to something similar to Figure 8.6. It is possible to edit the start parameters in the text box of the Apache2 Properties dialog box in Figure 8.6. The problem with this approach is that the settings are not persistent.

To activate a block based on nonexistence of a definition, the exclamation mark is added to the IfDefine directive:

```
<IfDefine !mydefinition>
Listen 8080
</IfDefine>
```

Technique: Cross-Referencing Directives with Modules

All directives have an associated module. The module might be part of the Apache HTTPD core or it might be loaded dynamically. In any respect, using a directive without the module loading will cause problems. For example, if the Apache HTTPD process generates an error about an unknown configuration directive, then most likely the associated module is not loaded. The problem with this approach is that associating the directive with the module is not obvious. The simplest solution is to check the documentation located at *http://httpd.apache.org/docs-2.0/mod/ directives.html.*

The Web page attempts to define all the directives that are part of the Apache HTTPD server. Find the directive, click on the link, and you are transported to a page that contains the name of the module that needs to be added to the configuration file. Most likely that module is already added to the configuration file, but commented out. To add the module, make sure to use the LoadModule notation defined by the earlier "Loading Modules Dynamically" section.

Technique: Defining URLs

When the default installation of the Apache HTTPD is executed, the default Web page with the text "Seeing this instead of the Web site you expected?" appears. The installation has hidden under the covers many references and directories that relate to a large number of directory directives. Each has a purpose and the best way is to start with the simplest.

Defining the Base URL

When starting the Web server, the administrator wants to by default lock everything down, thus not allowing a user to add executable content or content that can be processed. In the default mode, the server knows nothing. To give the server some content to understand, the directive DocumentRoot is defined as follows:

```
DocumentRoot "C:/data/htdocs"
```

The DocumentRoot directive defines the root directory where content can be served. Using this configuration, all URLs would reference content from within the document directory or some subdirectory of the document directory. If the module mod_dir.so were not loaded, then an explicit URL defining the file to be loaded would have to be explicitly defined. For example, the URL *http://localhost/* would retrieve something similar to Figure 8.7.

Figure 8.7 shows a directory listing because the URL does not define any specific document and the Apache server process has no idea what to do as a default action. You can load a specific HTML document by clicking on the appropriate link in Figure 8.7.

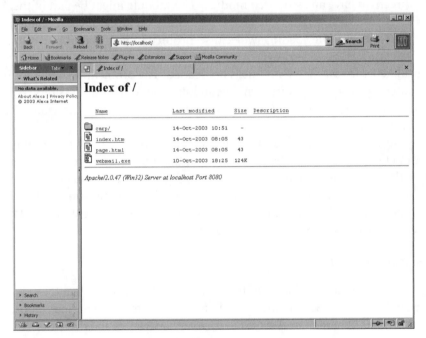

FIGURE 8.7 Directory listing shown in browser.

Default Page Served

When making a request such as the URL *http://localhost*, there is no request for a page. In HTTP speak, the directory contents of the root folder are requested. However, the reality is that some page will appear because the Web server has a notion of a default page to serve. Following is a configuration entry that shows how to define the default page:

```
DirectoryIndex index.html index.html.var
```

The directive `DirectoryIndex` is a way of indicating which file should be served to a client when a default page is requested. Relating this back to the original URL *http://localhost*, the server would cross-reference the root URL with the root directory. Knowing the location of the root directory, the default files are searched, where the first file to find is `index.html`. If the file `index.html` does not exist, then the file `index.html.var` is searched for. If the file `index.html.var` also does not exist, then a generic directory listing of the root directory is given, as earlier shown in Figure 8.7.

Let's say you installed a module that processed a file using some special processing such as PHP. You would then need to add the `index.php` to the directive `Directo-ryIndex` so that PHP index files are automatically processed. Otherwise, a generic directory listing would result. Note that the order of the documents to be searched is important. If `index.php` is appended as the last value in `DirectoryIndex`, then if `index.html` exists, it would be loaded before `index.php`.

If the module `mod_dir.so` is dynamically loaded and the `DirectoryIndex` directive is not specified, then a default of `index.html` is assumed when doing a directory listing.

Defining Virtual Directories

A virtual directory is an URL location that is not a subdirectory of the `DocumentRoot`. For example, for the URL `http://localhost/virtual`, the identifier `virtual` is an URL location that can be redefined. The client does not know or care whether the identifier is virtual; only the configuration file knows whether the identifier is virtual. An example of a virtual directory definition is shown as follows:

```
Alias /virtual "C:/bin/Apache2/docs3"
```

When the URL contains the identifier `/virtual`, the URL represents a subdirectory from the server URL. The client could also have issued the URLs as `/virtual/an-other/level` or even `/virtual/`. Using the different URLs would not matter because each of the URLs start with the identifier `/virtual`. Regardless of the name, the identifier represents a buffer used by Apache HTTPD to decipher an URL. If the identifier is found, it is replaced with the directory value. The URL `/virtual/index.html` is converted into the filename `c:/bin/Apache2/docs3/index.html`.

When a trailing / is appended to the identifier, e.g., `/virtual/`, it requires that the client URL has to include the trailing slash; otherwise, an error will be generated.

Another way of defining an alias is to use a regular expression and the directive `AliasMatch`:

```
AliasMatch ^/virtual/(.*)   "C:/bin/Apache2/docs3$1"
```

The identifier `^/virtual/(.*)` is a regular expression that is matched to the URL sent by the client. If the regular expression is matched, then the variable `$1` is replaced in the directory identifier with the found identifier in the regular expressions. The data found by the `(.*)` is replaced with the variable `$1`.

Using regular expressions makes for a very powerful URL resolution technique, but that technique is more computationally expensive than using the simple Alias directive.

To define an alias as having script execution privileges, the directive `ScriptAlias` is used and shown as follows:

```
ScriptAlias /cgi-bin/ "C:/bin/Apache2/cgi-bin/"
```

The `ScriptAlias` directive works identically to the `Alias` directive except that the directory referenced can include executable content. There is an associated `ScriptAliasMatch` directive that behaves like the `AliasMatch` directive except that it is used for executable content.

Specifying Rights

When managing the different aliases and document roots with its subdirectories, it is important to assign rights to the different locations. The rights determine the kinds of actions and who can carry them out. Whenever the alias is a directory, a `Directory` directive is added to a configuration file:

```
<Directory "C:/bin/Apache2/docs3">
    Options Indexes FollowSymLinks
    Order deny,allow
    Deny from all
    Allow from all
    AllowOverride All
</Directory>
```

The `Directory` directive defines a block in the configuration file where the directives within are specific to the context of the `Directory` directive. The directives `Options`, `Order`, `Deny`, `Allow`, and `AllowOverride` only apply to the `Directory` block that they were defined in. The `Directory` directive applies to the directory `c:/bin/Apache2/docs3`, which also happens to be the identifier of the directive.

Directory directives and URL directives are based on inheritance, which means that the state of document access is unknown because the previous configuration is based on some directory that may refer to the root directory or may refer to a virtual URL directory. The directory hierarchy for the directory `c:/bin/Apache2/docs3` as seen by Apache HTTPD is as shown as follows:

```
/
c:/
c:/bin
c:/bin/Apache2
c:/bin/Apache2/docs3
```

The root of all listings is the `/`, which is a special notation on the Windows platform to define the root of all root directories. After the `/` character, a drive letter appears, which in this case is the drive letter `c`. Then based on the directory, the next significant directory is `c:/bin`, and the process continues. In configuration terms, it means something defined at the `/` level will apply to the directory `c:/bin/Apache2`. If a configuration were to define something at the directory `c:/bin/Apache2/docs3`, then the directory `c:/bin/Apache2/docs` would not see the definition. An example definition of two different directory levels is shown as follows:

```
<Directory />
    Options None
    AllowOverride None
</Directory>

<Directory "c:/bin/Apache2">
    Options Indexes
</Directory>
```

The root directory `/` has used the value `None` twice, which means that everything is essentially not available and has locked down the Apache HTTPD server. Then the `Directory` directive for the directory `c:/bin/Apache2` has assigned the `Options` directive a value of `Indexes`. The result is that the directory and subdirectories of the `c:/bin/Apache2` directory will have its `Options` value as `Indexes` and `AllowOverride` will still have an associated value of `None`.

For reference purposes, the definition of the directory `/` used in the example configuration file should also be the definition that you use in your configuration file. It is safest and does not allow anyone without access to the configuration file to manipulate the Apache HTTPD settings.

Within each directory definition, the `Options` directive can be set. The purpose of the `Options` directive is to set the available options within a specific directory. `Options` relate to what a server can do with the content. In the previous example configuration, the `Options` directive for the root directory / is very restrictive as it allows only document retrieval. In most cases, a more Web browser-friendly configuration is warranted. The following options are available:

All: All options are made available except for `MultiViews`.

ExecCGI: Permits the execution of CGI scripts (`mod_cgi.so`). However, just setting this option will not automatically execute CGI scripts.

FollowSymLinks: Permits the Apache HTTPD process to follow symbolic links within the current directory. Because Windows does not support this option in the filesystem, it is not all that useful and can be ignored.

Includes: Permits the execution of server side includes (`mod_include.so`).

IncludesNOEXEC: Permits the use of server side includes, except the server side tag `#exec` to run a CGI script or command is not included. The exception is if the CGI script resides within a `ScriptAlias` directory.

Indexes: Permits the generation of a directory listing when a directory is issued and a default document does not exist. This option should not be enabled, because it might be a potential security hole. A hacker could look at what files exist on your server and use it to exploit given security bugs.

MultiViews: Permits the notion of generated content based on content negotiation (`mod_negotiation`).

SymLinksIfOwnerMatch: Permits the Apache HTTPD process to follow symbolic links for a target file where the user ID of the user is the same as the owner ID of the file. This option is not useful in a Windows context and can be ignored.

Options can be applied and removed by using the + and - characters as shown in the following configuration fragment:

```
<Directory "c:/bin/Apache2">
    Options Indexes
    AllowOverride None
</Directory>

<Directory "c:/bin/Apache2/docs">
    Options -Indexes +Includes
</Directory>
```

The second `Directory` directive removes the `Indexes` option and adds the `Includes` option.

Merging within a configuration file has already been discussed, but there are some finer points when using the Options directive. Consider the following configuration fragment:

```
<Directory "c:/bin/Apache2">
    Options Indexes
</Directory>

<Directory "c:/bin/Apache2/docs">
    Options Includes
</Directory>
```

At first impression, it appears that the Options available for the directory c:/bin/Apache2/docs are Includes and Indexes. However, this is not the case because the Includes value does not have a + character. The Options directive for the directory c:/bin/Apache2/docs is saying its value replaces all other Options directive values. To perform a merge, the + character has to be used.

It is a good habit to use the + and - characters when using Option *directives as there will be the least amount of surprises.*

The blocks defined within the Directory block allow a large amount of fine-tuning. The problem with this approach is that the Apache HTTPD server will need to be restarted. This can be done gracefully using the following command:

```
./apache -k restart
```

If the Web server is hosting a large number of users, then doing a graceful restart very often is not a good idea. Ideally the administrator wants to hand off some of the rights to the user of the directory. Apache HTTPD server allows this in the form of an .htaccess file. The filename can be explicitly defined using the AccessFileName shown as follows:

```
AccessFileName .htaccess
```

On the Windows platform, the access filename should be changed from .htaccess *to something like* file.htaccess *because Windows Explorer does not allow a user to name a file with no filename and only an extension.*

Within the .htaccess file can be all directives that could be added to the Directory block. The directory where the .htaccess file is located is the directory and subdirectories to which the directives within the .htaccess file apply.

To allow the .htaccess file to apply its configuration directives, the httpd.conf file must allow it and is shown as follows:

```
<Directory "c:/bin/Apache2">
    AllowOverride All
</Directory>

<Files ~ "^\.ht">
    Order allow,deny
    Deny from all
</Files>
```

The AllowOverride directive allows subdirectories of the directory c:/bin/ Apache2 to use .htaccess files that can change whatever is required. Those changes are with respect to the directory where the .htaccess file is located. The Files directive is something that is usually added to ensure that nobody can view the contents of the .htaccess file from a Web browser.

The directive AllowOverride has the following options:

All: Combines all the available options.

AuthConfig: Allows the use of authorization directives.

FileInfo: Allows the use of directives that control the content document types.

Indexes: Allows the use of directives that control the directory indexing.

Limit: Allows the use of directives that control client access.

Options: Allows the use of directives that control specific directory features.

If the name of the .htaccess file is renamed using the AccessFileName directive, then the Files directive regular expression needs to be changed as well. More about the Files directive is given in the next section "Managing File Access."

The contents of an .htaccess will appear similar to the following:

```
Options +ExecCGI
```

Notice that there is no Directory block encapsulating the Options directive.

Managing File Access

Files can be controlled by Apache just like Apache controls directories. It is possible to use the Files directive within an .htaccess file or within a Directory block. It then means that all the files that match the identifier will have a block of directives applied to it.

The main reason it is necessary to control access to files is that some files are sensitive and should not be manipulated by a browser. For example, the directive file .htaccess should not be visible to Web browsers. Defining a `Files` directive ensures that all `.htaccess` files are kept invisible, even though the directory directives indicate otherwise.

The other directive `FilesMatch` uses a regular expression to match the filename, but works identically to the directive `Files`. Use regular expressions if you want to match multiple files.

Restricting Access to Directories, Actions, and Files

When the configuration file allows the definition of an `.htaccess` file, the configuration file was updated with the directives `Order`, `Allow`, and `Deny`. The purpose of these directives is to restrict what the client can browse. The directives can be used in the context of a `Directory`, `Location`, `Files`, or `FilesMatch` directive. To understand the structure of the access directives, consider the following configuration fragment:

```
<Files ~ "^\.ht">
    Order Allow,Deny
    Deny from all
    Allow from all
</Files>
```

The directive `Order` has two values separated by a comma. The first value is `Allow` and the second is `Deny`. The order of these values could be reversed, but that would mean something else. In terms of the previous code snippet, the meaning of the `Order` is that if the client matches a `Deny` directive or does not match an `Allow` directive, then access is denied. It seems the configuration is contradictory because the client matches both the `Deny` and the `Allow` directive. However, because the rule matches the `Deny` directive and that has priority, access is denied.

To allow access to the resource, the `Order` directive's values have to be flipped similar to the following configuration fragment:

```
Order Deny,Allow
Deny from all
Allow from all
```

As far as the ordering goes for the `Deny` and `Allow` values of the `Order` directive, the rule is that if the client matches the `Allow` directive and does not match the `Deny` directive, then access is granted. The default is to grant access and the priority is on the `Allow` directive, so access is granted.

In any of the examples, there can be multiple lines of either the `Deny` or the `Allow` directive. The values after the identifier can be from one of the following:

all: The identifier `all` specifies that any client host identifier is selected.

domain-name: The `domain-name` identifier can be a specific name of the client host, such as www.devspace.com, or it can be a partial domain name such as de-vspace.com. Using the domain name means that a reverse DNS has to be made, which could take a moment or two to figure out.

IP address: The IP address could be a full IP address or a partial IP address. For example, a full IP address would be 192.168.1.1, whereas a partial IP address would be 192.168. The partial IP address would attempt to match entire classes of IP addresses.

Network/Netmask address: The IP address approach is fine if entire classes can be filtered. For a fine-tuned approach, the network address is combined with a netmask. For example:

```
192.168.1.0/255.255.255.0
```

Environment variable: This is a clever approach in that access is granted or denied if an environment variable exists. For example, access might be granted on the basis of the browser type to get customized HTML content:

```
SetEnvIf User-Agent ^KnockKnock/2.0 let_me_in
<Directory /docroot>
    Order Deny,Allow
    Deny from all
    Allow from env=let_me_in
</Directory>
```

Another way to control access to a resource is to add the `Limit` directive within a `Directory` or other type of block. The `Limit` directive can control what kinds of HTTP actions the client can execute. Following is an example of using a `Limit` directive:

```
<Limit POST>
    Order Allow,Deny
    Deny from all
</Limit>
```

The `Limit` directive applies to the HTTP POST command and says that nobody can execute it. All the other HTTP commands can be executed. The problem with this approach is that it has to specify which HTTP commands can be executed in which context.

Another way to specify executing rights is to use the command `LimitExcept`, which means all the other HTTP commands have the restrictions except the ones listed. An example is shown as follows:

```
<LimitExcept GET>
    Order Allow,Deny
    Deny from all
</Limit>
```

The limitations do not apply to the HTTP command GET, but to the other HTTP commands. The list of possible HTTP commands are GET, POST, PUT, DELETE, CONNECT, OPTIONS, PATCH, PROPFIND, PROPPATCH, MKCOL, COPY, MOVE, LOCK, and UNLOCK.

The LimitExcept *directive is easier to use to fine-tune a lockdown of an Apache HTTP server.*

Technique: Running CGI Programs and Modules

The default for a Web server is to serve static content, however, you can also generate dynamic content. The two types of dynamic content are CGI generated and Apache HTTPD module generated. Loading Apache HTTPD modules has been outlined in the section "Loading Modules Dynamically." Some of the modules are activated using specific configuration commands, but others such as mod_cgi.so require activation.

When modules are activated using handlers, these modules react to a request. Other modules such as mod_alias.so are filter-like handlers. Consider this example. The client sends an HTTP request to an Apache HTTPD server at *http://server/ documents/something.html.* From previous sections, you learned how to convert a virtual directory into an actual directory and file on the hard disk, but we haven't shown you the undercover details.

Apache has many different handlers and filters to manage the HTTP request process. There are handlers to create a request structure, translate the URL to a filename, fix up the request, check the access, authenticate the checker, and so on. Many of the modules, such as mod_alias.so, hook into those handlers. After the individual handlers have been processed, a configuration file-based handler processes the request and generates some data. The administrator does not have to be concerned with the details of the Apache HTTPD handlers because it is a module implementation detail. An administrator can introduce a filter that will process either the input content or the output content. For example, a filter might remove some tags or clean up the content before sending it to the client.

CGI is a handler that translates a request for a file into a request that executes the file. The executed file generates some content that is piped to the Apache HTTPD server, and then it is piped to the client.

Running CGI Scripts

The simplest way to run a CGI script is to associate the cgi extension with the cgi handler as shown in the following configuration file fragment:

```
AddHandler cgi-script .exe
```

The fragment uses the AddHandler directive to associate the identifier cgi-script with any file that has the exe extension. The identifier cgi-script is a sort of magic descriptor that is associated with the request whenever a URL with a file-name with the exe extension is requested. When the mod_cgi.so sees the cgi-script identifier, the module takes control of the HTTP request and processes the request. The administrator does not know from inspecting the module the name of the identifier used to associate the handler with the HTTP request. The identifier can be found in the documentation, but is not available from a self-describing program.

The AddHandler directive can be put into the configuration file, or it can be made part of a Directory block or even an .htaccess file.

Another way to run a CGI script is to use the ScriptAlias directive shown as follows:

```
ScriptAlias /cgi-bin/ "C:/bin/Apache2/cgi-bin/"
<Directory "C:/bin/Apache2/cgi-bin">
    AllowOverride None
    Options None
    Order allow,deny
    Allow from all
</Directory>
```

Notice how the Options directive did not include ExecCGI because it was implied by the ScriptAlias directive. The ExecCGI value is necessary when the AddHandler directive is used within a Directory block.

To get acquainted with the Apache handler identifiers, inspect the default Apache HTTPD configuration file and look for the AddHandler *and* SetHandler *directives.*

Using Locations

Another way to use handlers is to define a virtual directory where the handler will respond to every request. This means instead of serving static content, the handler will process the request and generate some kind of content. These kinds of handlers are not dependent on the files residing on the hard disk. These kinds of handlers rely on a data store that they define. An example of this kind of handler is the server status. The server status does not need to interact with the hard disk as it generates the statistics from the Apache HTTPD server. The following configuration file fragment shows how to activate the server status module:

```
LoadModule status_module modules/mod_status.so

<Location /server-status>
    SetHandler server-status
    Order deny,allow
    Deny from all
    Allow from devspace.com
</Location>
```

To to use the server-status handler, the module mod_status.so has to be loaded because, by default, it is not loaded. The Location directive references a virtual directory that represents the URL to access the server status. The server-status handler is called whenever a URL starts with the identifier /server-status. If there are extra virtual directories references appended, the handler is still called and the handler determines whether or not to process the extra virtual directories. Within the Location block, it is also possible to add other directives that are normally found in a Directory block.

Note that the directives Directory, Location, *and* Files *have matching directives that end with the identifier* Match, *e.g.,* DirectoryMatch, FilesMatch, *and* LocationMatch. *The difference with the identifier* Match *is that the values used to match are regular expressions.*

Technique: Logging Requests

Apache HTTPD server performs two types of logging: error logging and access logging. *Error logging* is the logging of messages related to the operation of the server. *Access logging* is the logging of which clients access which content on the server. The format of the error log is predefined, and the format of the access logs are free text, which is defined within the configuration file.

Error Logging

The error log is activated using the ErrorLog directive shown as follows:

```
ErrorLog logs/error.log
LogLevel warn
```

The ErrorLog directive has a value that defines the name of the log file where the messages will be logged. In the case of the example error log, the activation log filename is relative to the ServerRoot directive. The LogLevel directive specifies which Apache HTTPD messages are logged. The different levels are defined as follows:

emerg: The highest level of error that indicates a system that has become unusable; Apache HTTPD server will exit immediately.

alert: A lower level of error that indicates the system is having problems and the administrator must take action.

crit: An error level that indicates the system is having critical problems that the system will most likely have to cope with; however, an administrator will have to fix the problem.

error: An error level that indicates the system is having problems and most likely will not function correctly even though things seem okay. The administrator should look at what is going on and potentially intervene.

warn: A message level that indicates the system does not like something in particular, but can continue trying or moving on. However it does need the attention of the administrator at some point in time.

notice: A message level that does not indicate any type of error, but indicates the system is taking a specific course of action for some reason. The system considers this course of action as part of a normal process; however, the administrator should look at the log to see if something else is causing this course of action.

info: A message level that indicates the system is doing something and the administrator is being informed of that action.

debug: A message level that is very verbose and should only be used when attempting to debug a problem or action. It is generally used to figure difficult misbehaviors of the system.

When a specific error level is chosen, all the higher levels are also output. For example, if the error level crit is chosen, then all the messages for the levels crit, alert, and emerg are output.

Access Logging

Access logging is the process of logging the requests that the client makes. This form of logging is the most flexible and can be tuned for the needs of the administrator. To log, two things need to be defined: log format and the file that contains the log format. The log format is the data generated when creating a single entry in the log file. An example of defining a log file format and file is shown as follows:

```
LogFormat "%h %l %u %t \"%r\" %>s %b" common
CustomLog logs/access.log common
```

The LogFormat directive has two parameters: escape string and log format identifier. The escape string is a buffer enclosed by a set of quotes that contains a number of tokens representing a piece of information that is replaced when the log entry is generated. For example, the %h represents the remote hostname. The log format identifier is a unique identifier used by the CustomLog directive to define the format of the log file that is being saved to. The idea is that the administrator can create as many different log files as required to monitor what content is retrieved and who is retrieving the content.

The escape string can be compromised by the following tokens:

%%: Generates a percent sign.

%a: Generates the remote IP address.

%A: Generates the local IP address, which is useful when the Apache HTTPD server is multihome with multiple network cards.

%b: Generates the number of bytes sent excluding the HTTP headers using the Common Log Format (CLF) format where a – is used to represent a 0 when no bytes are sent.

%B: Generates the number of bytes sent excluding the HTTP headers, which is useful when counting the number of bytes that are transferred over a period of time.

%{mycookie}C: Generates the contents of the cookie specified in-between the curly brackets. This is useful when it is desired to track a cookie session, which could represent a user or application context.

%D: Generates the amount of time taken to serve the request in microseconds. This is useful when it is desired to profile an in-production application.

%{envvar}e: Generates the contents of the environment variable of the executing Apache HTTPD child process.

%f: Generates the name of the file that is being retrieved in the request, if possible.

%h: Generates the remote host identifier.

%H: Generates the request protocol.

%{header-request}i: Generates the contents of the HTTP header value that was part of the request.

%I: Generates the bytes received, including the request headers. To use this escape sequence, the module mod_logio.so must be loaded.

%l: Generates the remote log name, but for the Windows platform this is not relevant.

%m: Generates the HTTP request method (e.g., GET, POST, and so on).

%{module}n: Generates the contents of the note from the module specified by the module identifier.

%{header-reply}o: Generates the contents of the response HTTP header value that was part of the reply.

%O: Generates the bytes sent, including headers. To use this escape sequence, the module mod_logio.so must be loaded.

%p: Generates the port of the server processing the request.

%P: Generates the process ID of the child that processed the request. In the context of Apache HTTPD running on the Windows platform, this ID is not very relevant as there is only one Apache HTTPD process.

%{identifier}P: Generates the process ID or thread ID of the child that serviced the request. The identifier can be replaced with either pid or tid. For the Windows platform, only the tid identifier is useful.

%q: Generates the query string of the request, if it exists; otherwise, an empty string is generated.

%r: Generates the first line of the HTTP request.

%s: Generates the resulting HTTP status request. For most common scenarios, the notation to use is %>s, which includes the redirected status codes.

%[{format}]t: Generates the time when the request was made. The format identifier can either be left off or added. If the format identifier is added, the format is the same as the strftime C function:

```
[day/month/year:hour:minute:second zone]

day = 2*digit

month = 3*letter

year = 4*digit

hour = 2*digit

minute = 2*digit

second = 2*digit

zone = (`+' | `-') 4*digit
```

%T: Generates the time to service the request in seconds.

%u: Generates the name of the authenticated user if the authorization information exists.

%U: Generates the URL path sent in the request, including the query string information if it exists.

%v: Generates the server name according to the `ServerName` directive.

%V: Generates the server name according to the `UseCanonicalName` directive.

%X: Generates the connection status when the request and response connection are completed. An `X` indicates that the connection aborted, `+` indicates that the connection may be kept alive, and `-` indicates that the connection is closed.

Using Webalizer to Process Log Files

The purpose of generating a log is to figure out who is accessing the site and when. One of the most popular Web analyzer programs is called *Webalizer*, although there are plenty of other packages. To find one that suits your needs, visit the Web site *http://www.freshmeat.net* and browse to the topic *Topic::Internet::Log Analysis*. For the scope of this book, the package *Webalizer* is shown because it is quick to install and easy to use.

In the default mode, Apache already generates the log file in CLF, which is required by Webalizer. You can also use the combined log file format. Following is an example configuration directive shows both the CLF and combine log formats:

```
LogFormat "%h %l %u %t \"%r\" %>s %b \"%{Referer}i\" \"
%{User-Agent}i\" " combined
LogFormat "%h %l %u %f %t \"%r\" %>s %b" common
```

The log format used is up to you. You can even log multiple files for specific attributes. Table 8.2 contains the reference information for the Webalizer project.

Installation of the Webalizer program is accomplished by unzipping the contents of the ZIP archive into a precreated directory. Note that the ZIP archive does not create an installation directory and expands the contents of the file into the current directory.

After the ZIP file archive has been expanded, the program `webalizer.exe` can be executed as follows:

```
$../webalizer.exe y:/Apache2/logs/access.log
Webalizer V2.01-10 (CYGWIN_NT-5.0 1.3.10(0.51/3/2)) English
Using logfile y:/Apache2/logs/access.log (CLF)
Creating output in current directory
Hostname for reports is 'ATHENA'
History file not found
Generated report for October 2003
Generating summary report
Saving history information
9540 records in 4.18 seconds, 2284/sec
```

TABLE 8.2 Reference Information for Webalizer

Item	Description
Home page	*http://www.mrunix.net/webalizer/*
Installation	The Webalizer program is distributed for the Windows platform as a ZIP archive file. Contained within the ZIP file is an executable that can be immediately executed.
Dependencies	None.
Documentation	The ZIP archive file contains an HTML page that describes the command-line arguments in a simple to read and easy to understand format.
Mailing Lists	There does not seem to be a mailing list with the Webalizer program, but at the Web site is a FAQ reference that could potentially solve your problems.
Impatient Installation Time Required	Download size: 794 KB Installation time: 1-2 minutes
DVD Location	`/packages/Apache/Webalizer`

After Webalizer has completed processing the logs, a number of HTML pages are generated that span the time period in the log file. These HTML pages can be viewed using a HTML browser.

Rotating the HTTPD Logs

Consider running Apache HTTPD for years at a time, and during that time not having stopped the Apache HTTPD server process once. During that entire time, the log files will not be rotated, but just increase incrementally. This could be a problem because as the file increases in size, the time to append to the file may take longer.

You need to be able to rotate the log files. In the simplest case, the process involves stopping Apache HTTPD for a very short period and then restarting it again. The following command shows how to stop, rotate the logs, and start the server:

```
./Apache.exe -k stop
mv ../logs/*.log c:/some/other/place
./Apache.exe -k start
```

The command mv is used to move the log files to another directory. The commands could be run every day, week, or month.

The purpose of shutting down the Apache HTTPD process is to provide a way of resetting the log files. While the Apache HTTPD process is running, it is possible to copy the log files. The reason for shutting down the server is to not lose log records. If it's okay to lose some records, then the files can be copied ahead of time, and during the shutdown the log files are deleted.

Another way to rotate the logs is to use the pipe command within the Custom-Log directive. The pipe can be used to move data from one program to another. Using the pipe in a log causes Apache to write the log entry to the pipe, which can then be managed by some other process. Following is a configuration file fragment that shows how to pipe the log content to the program rotatelogs.exe:

```
CustomLog "|C:/bin/Apache2/bin/rotatelogs.exe
c:/bin/access.log 86400" common
```

The pipe character is before the drive letter C, which indicates that the log entry should be piped. The path reference after the pipe character is the program that will read the pipe data. The options after the program reference relate to the program rotatelogs.exe. Finally the common identifier references the log format that will be logged.

The program rotatelogs.exe is provided by the Apache HTTPD package and is able to rotate the logs. The program rotatelogs.exe can change log filenames when a file reaches a specific size or if a specific amount of time has passed. In the log file configuration file fragment, the first command-line option c:/bin/access.log is the name of the file that will be used for the log data. Note that the log filename will be appended with some characters to make the filename unique. If rotatelogs.exe did not do this, the old log file would be overwritten by the current log file.

The second command-line option 86400 references the amount of time in seconds that will pass before the log is rotated. Following is a list of numbers that corresponds to the number of seconds that transpire in a specific time period.

Day (24 hours): 86400
Week: 604800
Month (30 days): 259200
Year: 31449600

The second command-line option could also refer to the maximum size of the log file before it is to be rotated. The number has to be appended with the letter M to indicate megabytes. For example 10M means if the log file reaches 10 megabytes, then it is replaced with a new log file.

Another twist in using the pipe is to pipe directly to a MySQL database. Alternatively, if you don't want to pipe directly into a MySQL database, a batch process will periodically convert the log file into SQL data.

Logging to a file, and then converting the data into a batch process has the advantage of not slowing down the Apache HTTPD server. There is no limit on the kind of data that can be added, because essentially any data that can be generated by the LogFormat directive can be added. The format of the log entry is the important part. Following is a simple example of the important elements when generating a log file:

```
LogFormat "\"%h\",\"%{Referer}i\" " sqlformat
```

If the LogFormat is processed, then the log file might contain an entry that resembles the following:

```
"127.0.0.1","/something.html"
```

Notice in the log file entry that the two values are enclosed by a set of quotes, and a comma separates each quoted buffer. This technique is not used by default in the CLF format, nor the combined log file format. It is required when adding the data to a SQL database because the quotes and commas separate the fields when they are added to a table. The following MySQL SQL command shows how to add the log file to the MySQL database:

```
LOAD DATA INFILE 'c:/bin/Apache2/logs/access.log' INTO TABLE
table_name FIELDS TERMINATED BY ',' OPTIONALLY ENCLOSED BY '"'
ESCAPED BY '\\'
```

The SQL command executes within a SQL editor (e.g., mysql.exe) and loads the data into a relational table. The command LOAD DATA will load the data from a file, and define the individual fields enclosed by a double quote and separated by a comma. It is possible to use a space as separator, but that could introduce problems, as the UserAgent HTTP header variable will have spaces. The format defined in the preceding code snippet is the safest and will work.

Another format that could be used by the LogFormat directive is to generate a series of SQL INSERT commands. The SQL INSERT command would be used in the context of a script. Following is an example configuration file directive that shows how to do this:

```
LogFormat "INSERT INTO table_name (remote_ip, remote_log_name,
remote_user, server_name, request_uri, request_date, request_status,
 request_bytes_sent, request_content_type, request_referer,
request_user_agent) VALUES ('%a', '%l', '%u', '%v', '%U%q',
'%{%Y%m%d%H%M%S}t', '%>s', '%B', '%{Content-Type}o', '%{Referer}i',
'%{User-Agent}i' );" mysql
```

Notice in the configuration directive that the log file entry format is a SQL INSERT command. In fact, if so desired the log file entry could be any programming language as only text can be used for further processing. To pipe the log command to the database, the following configuration file directive is used:

```
CustomLog "|mysql.exe --user=somebody --password={password} logs" mysql
```

The configuration file directive CustomLog executes the command mysql.exe and then pipes the content to the database. The only downside to using this technique is that the password is available for all to see, because the command-line arguments are available when a process listing is done. In this case, it might be better to save the password in a configuration file as shown in the "Technique: Automating Queries Using Scripts" section in Chapter 7. If the user that is used to add the log data has limited rights, when a security breach occurs the worst case is that the log files might be damaged.

The SQL command CREATE TABLE used for adding the log file data is shown as follows:

```
(URL: http://www.phpbuilder.com/mail/php-db/2003032/0254.php)
CREATE TABLE `access_log_archive` (
  `id` int(11) NOT NULL auto_increment,
  `remote_ip` varchar(15) NOT NULL default '',
  `remote_host` varchar(255) NOT NULL default '',
  `remote_domain` varchar(10) NOT NULL default '',
  `remote_log_name` varchar(20) NOT NULL default '',
  `remote_user` varchar(20) NOT NULL default '',
  `server_name` varchar(255) NOT NULL default '',
  `request_uri` varchar(255) NOT NULL default '',
  `request_date` datetime NOT NULL default '0000-00-00 00:00:00',
  `request_status` int(11) NOT NULL default '0',
  `request_bytes_sent` int(11) NOT NULL default '0',
```

```
`request_content_type` varchar(50) NOT NULL default '',
`request_referer` varchar(255) NOT NULL default '',
`request_user_agent` varchar(255) NOT NULL default '',
PRIMARY KEY (`id`),
) TYPE=MyISAM COMMENT='Apache Logging Table'
```

When using SQL commands in the LogFormat *directive and piping the data to the database, remember to add the semicolon after the SQL command. Not adding the semicolon will cause the data not to be added while the* mysql.exe *program waits for further commands.*

Technique: Virtual Hosting

Virtual hosting in the context of Apache HTTPD is the capability to host multiple Web sites on the same server. There are essentially two ways to do this, via IP-based or name-based virtual hosting. IP-based virtual hosting means that a Web server has multiple IP addresses attached to the computer and each address is used for a domain. Name-based virtual hosting is when a computer has a single IP address, but multiple name-based domains (e.g., *www.mycompany.com* and *files.mycompany.com*).

IP-based Hosting

When setting up a computer with multiple IP addresses, there are two ways to set up the Apache HTTPD server process. The first way involves using two Apache HTTPD instances where each instance listens to its assigned IP address. The second way is to use the virtual hosting capabilities within Apache HTTPD.

Partitioning a Web site into two different Apache HTTPD instances is the safest installation from a stability, robustness, and simplicity point of view. The magic in running multiple Apache HTTPD instances is to define the correct Listen directive as shown earlier in the "Listening on an IP Address and Port" section. The problem with this approach is that it is not suitable on a Windows platform because it's difficult to run multiple services beside each other. You can run one Apache instance as a service and the other as a console program, but that's not an optimal configuration.

The best way to implement a multihomed infrastructure is to use one configuration file and allocate the IPs within the configuration. The problem with this approach is that the administrator needs to keep a close view of what is configured; otherwise, problems might arise. It is important to define the Listen directives properly in the following configuration file fragments. (Note the fragments are for a computer that has two IP network addresses, 192.168.1.33 and 192.168.1.35.)

```
Listen *:80

Listen 192.168.1.33:80
Listen 192.168.1.35:8080
```

The fragments represent two different examples, where the empty line between the `Listen` directive separates the two directives. For the first fragment, all the available IP addresses are bound to the port 80, whereas for the second fragment, one IP was bound to one port and the other IP to another port. Either case is acceptable because all the IP addresses were configured.

After the IP addresses have been assigned, Apache HTTPD will serve the same content on the IPs and their associated ports. The following directives defines the content of the "default" Web server:

```
ServerName athena:80
DocumentRoot "C:/bin/Apache2/htdocs"
```

The directives `ServerName` and `DocumentRoot` define the defaults. These defaults should reference some kind of minimal Web site.

The task of the virtual host definition is to provide a specialization on all the listening IP addresses or ports. It does not matter which port or IP address is specialized, as Apache does not recognize the concept of a default network adaptor or IP address. It is recommended to specialize all the IPs and not leave a default Web site. The following configuration file fragment shows how to specialize the IP address `192.168.1.35`:

```
NameVirtualHost 192.168.1.35:8080

<VirtualHost 192.168.1.35:8080>
    ServerAdmin webmaster@example.com
    DocumentRoot C:/bin/Apache2/docs/virtual
    ErrorLog logs/example.com-error_log
    CustomLog logs/example.com-access_log common
</VirtualHost>
```

The directive `NameVirtualHost` is an identifier that identifies an IP address and port that will be used in a virtual hosting context. After the IP address `192.168.1.35` has been identified, it can then be used in a `VirtualHost` directive block. Notice the usage of the port `8080` in both the `NameVirtualHost` and `VirtualHost` context. If the port number is not specified, then the default of port `80` is assumed. Looking at the previous configuration file fragment, however, there is no association of the Port `80` with the IP address `192.168.1.35`. This would mean that the virtual host would be available, but not accessible.

Within the `VirtualHost` directive block can be any settings that relate to the location of a document such as the `DocumentRoot ErrorLog`, or `CustomLog` directives. The `VirtualHost` directive block is in essence another configuration file that is embedded within the main configuration file.

Name-based Hosting

Name-based hosting can be used with either one or multiple IP addresses. What changes with using name-based hosting is that within each `VirtualHost` directive, the `ServerName` directive has to be defined. The purpose of defining the `ServerName` directive is to distinguish requests between different servers. For example, consider the DNS addresses defined as follows:

```
192.168.1.33    test.devspace.com
192.168.1.33    test2.devspace.com
192.168.1.35    www.devspace.com
```

The servers `test` and `test2` both map to the same IP addresses. Using IP-based virtual hosting, when the client makes a request to either DNS address, it would have received the same content. Using the following `NameVirtualHost` directives, it is possible to distinguish between the two servers. (Note that the `VirtualHost` directives have been abbreviated for clarity.)

```
NameVirtualHost 192.168.1.33:80
NameVirtualHost 192.168.1.35:80

<VirtualHost 192.168.1.33:80>
    DocumentRoot C:/bin/Apache2/docs2
    ServerName test2.devspace.com
</VirtualHost>

<VirtualHost 192.168.1.33:80>
    DocumentRoot C:/bin/Apache2/docs3
    ServerName test.devspace.com
</VirtualHost>
```

The `NameVirtualHost` directives have been declared for all the IP addresses and ports that will be exposed. Even though the default port of 80 is implied, it is a good practice to add it for clarity and maintainability purposes. The `VirtualHost` directives in the example are identical, which is acceptable because two separate configuration blocks are defined. The difference is in the `ServerName` and `DocumentRoot` directives. The `ServerName` directives have to reference the servers that are registered in the DNS table.

One server is missing from the virtual host directives: *www.devspace.com*, which was implied when virtual hosting was not used. Remember from a previous statement that when using virtual hosting, everything should be declared explicitly. The correct configuration is shown as follows:

```
NameVirtualHost 192.168.1.33:80
NameVirtualHost 192.168.1.35:80

<VirtualHost 192.168.1.33:80>
    DocumentRoot C:/bin/Apache2/docs2
    ServerName test2.devspace.com
</VirtualHost>

<VirtualHost 192.168.1.33:80>
    DocumentRoot C:/bin/Apache2/docs3
    ServerName test.devspace.com
</VirtualHost>

<VirtualHost 192.168.1.35:80>
    DocumentRoot C:/bin/Apache2/htdocs
    ServerName www.devspace.com
</VirtualHost>
```

The previous configuration file fragment covers all bases and combines named-based virtual hosting with IP-based virtual hosting.

If the computer you are using has only one IP address, then the NameVirtualHost, VirtualHost *directive values can be replaced with an asterisk (*). However, do not use that notation when the computer has multiple IP addresses as it increases the likelihood that you will make a mistake.*

Defining Directories and Locations in a Virtual Host

Now that we've defined the concept of virtual directories, it is necessary to make the virtual directories do something. When virtual hosts are used, they can be complemented using configuration items specific to the virtual host. The problem, however, is that if the local server has many virtual hosts, the configuration file can become unmanageable. A way to manage the complexity is to use the Include directive as follows. The Include directive can include wildcards to load multiple files at once. Following is an example of using the Include directive:

```
Include conf/vhost.conf
```

In the example a relative path is used, which means that the path is relative to the ServerRoot directive. It is possible to use an absolute path if desired.

Considering the structure of the configuration in a big picture sense, each virtual host would be included in its own configuration file. The main server configuration would be separated from the domain configuration. This means in the httpd.conf, there should be no directives such as Directory, ScriptAlias, Alias, Location, and so on. The directives that should be in the httpd.conf file only relate to the overall configuration of the Apache HTTPD server process, such as ServerRoot, Listen, and so on.

Within a virtual host, you can define a Directory or Location directive:

```
<VirtualHost 192.168.1.33:80>
    DocumentRoot C:/bin/Apache2/docs2
    ServerName test2.devspace.com
    <Location /server-info>
        SetHandler server-info
        Order deny,allow
        Deny from all
        Allow from all
    </Location>
    <Directory "C:/bin/Apache2/htdocs">
        Options Indexes FollowSymLinks
        AllowOverride All
        Order allow,deny
        Allow from all
    </Directory>
    Alias /icons/ "C:/bin/Apache2/icons/"
    <Directory "C:/bin/Apache2/icons">
        Options Indexes MultiViews
        AllowOverride None
        Order allow,deny
        Allow from all
    </Directory>
</VirtualHost>
```

The individual Location, Directory, and Alias directive blocks will not be explained as they have been explained previously in this section. It is only necessary to show that they can be added to a VirtualHost block with respect to the parent block.

The power of this local block definition is that it is possible for two different domains to point to the same Web site content, but have different accessibility options. For example, you have a Web site that has an IP address that connects to the Internet and an IP address that connects to the local network. For the Internet, the Order and Allow directives can be tuned to only allow access to certain public pages.

Whereas for the local network IP address, the Order and Allow directives can be tuned to allow access to all pages.

As stated previously, when using virtual hosting, use the Include *directive to modularize the configuration file. An Apache HTTPD configuration file can very quickly become large and unmanageable, so structure the configuration properly from the first day.*

Technique: Serving Content in Multiple Languages and Formats

Apache HTTPD makes it possible to serve HTML content that is based on a language or a format. For example, an HTTP client will typically send the language in the HTTP header that it expects to receive content:

```
Accept-Language: en-gb
```

The language that is being accepted by the client is English (en) from Great Britain (gb). There are other language encodings such as fr for French, en for American English, and so on. The different language encodings are added using the AddLanguage directive, which already exist for most languages in the default httpd.conf configuration file. Following is an example configuration file fragment that adds supports:

```
AddLanguage da .dk
AddLanguage en .en
AddLanguage et .et
AddLanguage fr .fr
AddLanguage de .de
AddLanguage pt-br .pt-br
AddLanguage ltz .ltz
AddLanguage zh-CN .zh-cn
AddLanguage hr .hr
```

The AddLanguage directive has two options: the language and the extension associated with the language. In the example of the browser that is asking for a British English document, and cross-referencing the example configuration file fragment, there is no match for a British English document. A closest match would be attempted and then the en identifier would be used. The notation of using two two-letter identifiers is a standard where the first identifier is the main language, and the second is the dialect of the language. For example pt-br represents the language Portuguese and the dialect Brazilian.

After the individual languages have been identified, a priority of the languages needs to be defined. Using a priority, Apache HTTPD will calculate which language to send to the client when there is no perfect language match. The following configuration directive uses the `LanguagePriority` directive to assign the priorities:

```
LanguagePriority en da nl et fr de el it ja ko no pl pt pt-br
ltz ca es sv tw
```

The example `LanguagePriority` directive illustrated is the default that is generated by Apache. To enable the use of multiple languages on HTML files, the directory has to be enabled by setting the `MultiViews` value as shown in the following configuration file directive:

```
<Directory "C:/bin/Apache2/htdocs">
    Options MultiViews Indexes FollowSymLinks
</Directory>
```

The `Options` directive has to have an explicit addition of the value `MultiViews` to enable the choosing of multiple languages.

Serving Static Content

If the content is static, adding the language identifier to the end of the filename represents the different languages. For example if the document to be retrieved is `my-document.html`, then the English version of the document is `mydocument.html.en`, and the German version is `mydocument.html.de`. The built-in content negotiation will translate the name `mydocument.html` to the correct language document, which could be either `.de` or `.en`. If the language document does not exist, then the priority of the document that is retrieved is based on the `LanguagePriority` directive.

The resolution of a document to a language-specific document only works for the files that have a URL extension of html *or* htm. *This means that the HTML content has to be static.*

Serving Dynamic Content

Using the language extension technique is useful if the multilingual content is represented as a number of static Web pages. There are other situations when it is desirable to negotiate the content type. For example, a Web site might need to send a GIF image file instead of a JPEG image file. Using dynamic content negotiation, an administrator can redirect content dependent on headers of the HTTP request. The following example shows a directive that activates dynamic content negotiation:

```
LoadModule negotiation_module modules/mod_negotiation.so
AddHandler type-map var
```

The module `mod_negotiation` implements the content negotiation and the handler `type-map` is associated with any file that has the extension `var`. When a request is made for the file with the `var` extension, the negotiation handler will load the file, read the entries, and then perform a redirection to a URI defined within the file. The logic of which URI to choose is based on the HTTP headers of the client. Following shows an example `index.html.var` file that will perform a redirection:

```
URI: index.html.de
Content-language: de
Content-type: text/html

URI: index.html.el
Content-language: el
Content-type: text/html
```

The file is structured similar to an HTTP header in that there are key value pairs, such as the key `URI` and the value `index.html.de`. Each key value pair is grouped into a block, and each block is separated from the other block by an empty line. The keys within a block, other than the key `URI` define a set of conditions that must be met by the client. If the conditions are met then the `URI` value is the URL that the client will receive.

In the example `index.html.var`, the first and second blocks have two keys: `Content-language` and `Content-type`. Both of the keys define a condition that has been met. In the first block, the key `Content-language` has the value of `de` and will match a client HTTP header `Accept-language` with a starting value of `de`. The second key `Content-type` in the first block will match a client HTTP header `Accept` and one of the values should be `text/html`. In reality, the HTTP header often includes the `*/*` value indicating that the client will accept all types of content. After a block is matched, the `URI` is used to generate the new content and it can reference any `URI` that exists on the server, including CGI, PHP, Perl, or any other dynamic type of data. The `URI` cannot reference another server.

Dynamic Content Details

When creating the blocks in the `.var` file, the following keys can be used for comparison purposes:

Content-Encoding: Defines the encoding of the file, which has been added using the directive `AddEncoding`.

Content-Language: Defines the encoding language of the file.

Content-Length: Defines the content length of the buffer, which if not used is set to the length of the buffer.

Content-Type: Defines the Multipurpose Internet Mail Extensions (MIME) encoding of the data.

The Content-Type key can be used to determine which kind of file to send. Consider the scenario where a server would prefer to send an image in one format instead of the other due to image size or clarity. To know which image to send, the Accept HTTP header from the client is inspected for content types that are accepted. Following is the Accept HTTP header from the Mozilla browser:

```
Accept=text/xml,application/xml,application/xhtml+xml,text/html;
q=0.9,text/plain;q=0.8,image/png,image/jpeg,image/gif;
q=0.2,*/*;q=0.1
```

Following is the Accept HTTP header from Internet Explorer:

```
Accept=image/gif, image/x-xbitmap, image/jpeg, image/pjpeg,
application/vnd.ms-powerpoint, application/vnd.ms-excel,
application/msword, application/x-shockwave-flash, */*
```

The reason for showing the same header from Mozilla and Internet Explorer is to show which formats are preferred to others. Internet Explorer accepts most image types as indicated by image/[image type] MIME types. In contrast, Mozilla accepts most image types except for the image/gif type, which has an additional descriptor. The additional descriptor q=0.2 is a rating of the accepted type.

The accepted data types can be encoded with a rating. By default when there is no rating, the rating value is 1.0. The rating value is a ranking that is combined with a server rating to determine which content is sent to the client. Just looking at the client-side headers, Mozilla prefers the PNG and JPEG image types to GIF image types.

The */* encoding from the client's perspective has a rating of 1.0, but in reality, Apache HTTPD considers the */* encoding as 0.1. The reason is that if specific types are preferred, then the */* encoding is the default value, which indicates that if no specific types are available, send whatever there is.

On the server side, a .var file can contain ratings as shown in the following example:

```
URI: pic.jpeg
Content-type: image/jpeg; qs=0.8

URI: pic.gif
Content-type: image/gif; qs=0.5
```

In the example, the server side prefers to send a JPEG image file because the qs (also known as q) rating is higher than the GIF image file. Which file is sent to the client depends on the decision that Apache HTTPD makes. Apache HTTPD will combine the client-side rating with the server-side rating using a multiplication. The result of the multiplication is compared to the rest of the accepted content types and the highest overall rating URI is sent.

Technique: Custom Error Pages

When a document that is being requested does not exist, an HTTP error is generated. Figure 8.8 shows an example HTTP 404 error for a document that does not exist.

FIGURE 8.8 HTTP 404 error for a document that is not found.

The resulting HTML page that is generated doesn't look very friendly. Using the ErrorDocument directive, the error page can be improved. Following is an improved HTML document that will be shown when a document does not exist:

```
<html><body>Dude, the page does not exist</body></html>
```

The following directive shows how to use the ErrorDocument directive to reference the HTML document:

```
ErrorDocument 404 /errors/404error.html
```

The ErrorDocument directive has two options: 404 and /errors/404error.html. The 404 option is the HTTP error code that is being associated with a document. The /errors/404error.html is a URL or text buffer that is output when the HTTP error occurs. The URL can reference another server or a local URL.

Technique: Activating SSL

Chapter 4 showed how to use STunnel to provide SSL facilities for a HTTP server. Apache has its own SSL facilities based on OpenSSL. The disadvantage of using mod_ssl is that you will have to download the sources of both OpenSSL and mod_ssl and then compile them. By default, the binary Windows distribution does not contain any SSL libraries.

Compiling SSL

The module mod_ssl is part of the Apache sources and can be compiled with either Visual C++ 6.0 or Visual Studio .NET C++. mod_ssl is located in the directory [httpd-sources-directory]/modules/ssl. When the Apache HTTPD project is loaded using Visual Studio, it is the mod_ssl project. If you decide to compile the mod_ssl sources, then the OpenSSL sources are installed under the directory [httpd-sources-directory]/srclib. The OpenSSL directory also has to be renamed to openssl and not have any version identifiers.

When mod_ssl is compiled in the link phase, it will look for libraries in the directory [httpd-sources-directory]/srclib/openssl/out32dll. The problem is that the libraries do not exist in that directory, but in a subdirectory that could be named either debug or release. To solve the linkage problem, copy the contents of either the release or debug subdirectories to the library search directory. After mod_ssl and OpenSSL have been compiled, the files SSLeay32.dll, libeay32.dll, and mod_ssl.so need to be copied to the Apache modules subdirectory.

Configuring SSL

SSL is activated on a server by loading the module as shown by the following directive:

```
LoadModule ssl_module modules/mod_ssl.so
```

Adding the directive and then running Apache HTTPD with the default configuration file will generate an error saying that the file ssl.conf does not exist. The reason has to do with a configuration directive item near the end of the default configuration file that looks similar to the following:

```
<IfModule mod_ssl.c>
    Include conf/ssl.conf
</IfModule>
```

When Apache HTTPD loads the SSL module, it activates the Include command that loads the file ssl.conf. The error arises because the file ssl.conf does not exist and has never been discussed previously. The idea with the ssl.conf file is to put the SSL configuration information into another file.

If you have not yet read the "Project: OpenSSL and STunnel" section in Chapter 4, do so now because the concepts learned there will be used for the rest of this section.

Following is an example ssl.conf configuration file:

```
Listen 443
AddType application/x-x509-ca-cert .crt
AddType application/x-pkcs7-crl    .crl
SSLCertificateFile
"C:/Program Files/Apache Group/Apache2/conf/certs/user.crt"
SSLCertificateKeyFile
"C:/Program Files/Apache Group/Apache2/conf/certs/user.key"
SSLPassPhraseDialog  builtin
SSLSessionCache          dbm:logs/ssl_scache
SSLSessionCacheTimeout  300
SSLMutex  default
SSLRandomSeed startup builtin
SSLRandomSeed connect builtin
SSLEngine on
SSLProtocol all
SSLCipherSuite HIGH:MEDIUM
SSLOptions +StdEnvVars
```

In the ssl.conf configuration file, there are some new and some old options. The directive Listen is used to force HTTPD to listen for a connection on the default SSL port 443. Note that just by loading mod_ssl and activating a listener on port 443 is not enough to use the SSL protocol. The key AddType is added twice to define the SSL certificates.

The key SSLCertificateFile and SSLCertificateKeyFile are the public key and private key for the server, respectively. The public and private keys are created using the OpenSSL program shown in Chapter 4. You should use an Internet-based or local-based signing authority to sign the public key.

In many cases the administrator will want to protect the private key with a passphrase. The problem is that when the Apache HTTPD server starts to use the private key, a passphrase is required. The directive SSLPassPhraseDialog is used to define how that passphrase will activate an interaction between the administrator and the Apache HTTPD process. The value builtin means that a console window will open and the administrator can manually enter the passphrase.

The other option for the SSLPassPhraseDialog is to use a program that will fetch the passphrase and then output it to the standard output. An example command value is exec:runapp.sh. The script runapp.sh can access a database, an encrypted file, or whatever the administrator wants. runapp.sh will be executed and passed two parameters: servername:port and RSA (or DSA).

The directives SSLSessionCache and SSLSessionCacheTimeout relate to keeping a cache of SSL sessions. SSL sessions are already cached, but on a process level and not an interprocess level. Browsers will launch multiple requests, and on Linux/FreeBSD operating systems, different processes may process each request. The problem is that each process will be hosting each own local SSL cache and the client will receive multiple SSL cache tokens. The solution is to create an interprocess SSL session cache using the directives SSLSessionCache and SSLSessionCacheTimout. However, because Windows processes all requests from one process, it is not necessary to define an interprocess SSL session cache.

The directive SSLMutex is used to define a synchronization mechanism when mod_ssl needs to perform global operations. The value default is best because it allows the operating system to choose which is the best mechanism. This is especially notable on the Windows platform as most locking mechanisms are designed for Linux/FreeBSD operating systems.

The directive SSLRandomSeed is used to define a seed for the random values used to perform secret key encryptions. There should be multiple entries to create the maximum amount of randomness. This is important because many years earlier, the premier browser was not careful with its random values. The result is that the secret key could be figured out and all SSL encryptions became vulnerable.

The directive SSLEngine with value on indicates that the SSL engine is to be activated and used to process SSL requests.

The directives SSLProcotol and SSLCipherSuite keys are similar and are used to define the communications between the client and the server. The directive SSL-Procotol is used to activate a specific version of the SSL protocol, which can be one of the following:

SSLv2: Original SSL protocol as developed by Netscape Corporation.

SSLv3: Successor SSL protocol to SSLv2 that is the current Internet standard used by all browsers.

TLSv1: Successor SSL protocol layer called Transport Layer Security (TLS) and current not supported by the popular browsers.

All: This is a shortcut of specifying that all protocols will be activated and served by the Apache HTTPD daemon.

The values for the SSL protocol key can be prepended with a plus or minus sign to indicate additive or subtractive behavior. For example, the SSLProtocol directive activates all protocols except the TLSv1 protocol:

```
SSLProtocol all -TLSv1
```

The directive SSLCipherSuite specifies the SSL negotiation algorithms that are used. The value HIGH:MEDIUM means that first strong encryption is used and then medium encryption. The difference between strong encryption and medium encryption is the length of the key. If anything, this key is one of the most complex keys. The reason for the complexity is that every aspect of the SSL communications can be defined.

The SSL communication has the following phases: key exchange, authentication, and content encryption. For each phase, a specific encryption algorithm can be specified. For example, the administrator could specify to use the RSA algorithm for the key exchange. However, the details of which algorithm to use in which phase is beyond the scope of this book as it is very detailed information. For this information, read the documentation provided by Apache at *http://httpd.apache.org/docs-2.0/ mod/mod_ssl.html#sslciphersuite*.

What is not beyond the scope of this book are the aliases that can be used to specify a set of algorithms defined by the following list:

SSLv2: Specifies all SSL version 2 encryption algorithms.

SSLv3: Specifies all SSL version 3 encryption algorithms.

TLSv1: Specifies all TLS version 1 encryption algorithms.

EXP: Specifies the usage of all export grade encryption algorithms, which means short key lengths.

EXPORT40: Specifies the usage of 40-bit key length encryption algorithms. This is not an acceptable key length, but is legacy due to earlier export restrictions.

EXPORT56: Specifies the usage of 56-bit key length encryption algorithms. This is not an acceptable key length, but is legacy due to earlier export restrictions.

LOW: Specifies a low strength encryption algorithm that does not include the export encryption algorithms.

MEDIUM: Specifies the use of the 128-bit encryption algorithms, which is an acceptable length.

HIGH: Specifies the use of strong encryption algorithms, which includes the Triple Data Encryption Standard (DES) encryption algorithm.

For the SSLCipherSuite directive, the individual identifiers can be added and subtracted as shown in the example ssl.conf file and configuration item SSLOptions. The directive SSLOptions in is used to establish the environment variables that can be used when executing CGI type applications.

Using SSL in a Production Setting

If the previously defined ssl.conf configuration file and the default httpd.conf file were used by an executing Apache HTTPD server, there would be no more non-SSL connections available. For example, trying to issue the URL results in a message box similar to Figure 8.9.

FIGURE 8.9 Bad Request error.

It would seem that by adding the SSL configuration, the HTTPD server has become unable to process regular HTTP requests on port 80. The fact of the matter is that the HTTPD server has been forced to serve all requests using the SSL protocol. In the ssl.conf configuration file, the directive SSLEngine with value on means that all connections will be processed as SSL connections. Consider the context of the SSLEngine directive declaration and it is obvious the key has been declared globally.

The proper solution to using SSL is to consider the entire HTTPD server as having multiple domains where there exists an open domain and an SSL domain. Each domain is implemented using virtual hosting. The concept of virtual hosting has been discussed previously in this chapter ("Technique: Virtual Hosting").

Shown as follows is an abbreviated configuration example to illustrate how to create the two domains:

```
<VirtualHost 192.168.1.33:80>
    SSLEngine off
</VirtualHost>
<VirtualHost 192.168.1.33:443>
    SSLEngine on
    SSLProtocol all
    SSLCipherSuite HIGH:MEDIUM
    SSLOptions +StdEnvVars
</VirtualHost>
```

There are two virtual hosts: one on port 80 and one on port 443. The virtual host on port 80 has a directive SSLEngine with value off meaning not to use SSL. The other virtual host has for the directive SSLEngine the value of on. Notice also for the virtual host where SSL is active, the directives SSLProtocol, SSLCipherSuite, and SSLOptions have been defined. Using the virtual host approach, you can define custom SSL connections that are either based on the virtual host or a directory within the virtual host.

SSL is not that complicated to activate. What can become complex is that SSL will generally require that the administrator activate virtual hosting. Therefore it is absolutely important that the administrator be organized about the Apache HTTPD configuration files.

Technique: Authentication

In many Web applications, the authentication of the user is managed by the Web application. HTTP has built-in authentication techniques that are supported by most browsers. Granted some authentication routines are clear text, but using SSL can encrypt the authentication.

Apache HTTPD supports user authentication in multiple ways. The default mechanism uses internal algorithms. You can also use the user database from the Windows domain or users from an LDAP database.

Regardless of which authentication technique is used, a directory or virtual host requires directives that indicate that a valid user is required. Also required are the proper settings if the authentication directives are to being managed by a custom user setting. Following is the correct value for the AllowOverride directive that allows user authentication:

```
AllowOverride AuthConfig
```

Authenticating Using Passwords

The simplest way to authenticate a user is to create a password file. When a user accesses a protected directory, the Apache HTTPD server will issue a request to the client for username and password, and typically the client displays a dialog box to the user. To create a password file, use the following command:

```
htpasswd -c passwords someuser
```

The command `htpasswd` is used to create Apache HTTPD password files. The first command-line option `-c` is used to create a password file, which is necessary for the first time. The second command-line option `passwords` is the filename where the password is being stored. The last command-line option `someuser` is the username. When the command in `htpassd` executes, the user is prompted for a password, and then prompted to confirm the password. After execution of the command, a file `passwords` is created with contents similar to the following:

```
someuser:$apr1$bV/.....$S8gF5Cp6m9li.5j62ucIm1
```

The `htpasswd` command has the following command-line options that can be combined:

-c: This option is used to create a new file. If the file already exists, it will be overwritten.

-n: This option does not update the file, but writes the results of the actions to the standard output.

-m: This option forces the use of the MD5 hash encryption algorithm, which is the default.

-d: This option forces the using of the CRYPT hash encryption algorithm. On the Windows platform, this will default to the MD5 algorithm.

-p: This option saves the password in clear text in the password file. This option is not recommended.

-s: This option forces the use of the SHA hash encryption algorithm, which is longer and is more resistant to brute force attacks than MD5.

-b: Instead of prompting for the password interactively, the password is retrieved from the command line. If the password is specified on the command line, then the password follows the username.

-D: This option deletes the user from the specified password file.

To require authentication in the root directory, the authentication directives are added to the configuration file and will appear similar to the following. (Note that the configuration file has been abbreviated for clarity purposes.)

```
<Directory "C:/Program Files/Apache Group/Apache2/htdocs">
    AllowOverride AuthConfig
    AuthType Basic
    AuthName "Root directory requires password"
    AuthUserFile "C:/Program Files/Apache Group/Apache2/conf/passwords"
    Require user someuser
</Directory>
```

The four new directives are explained as follows:

AuthType: This directive specifies how the authentication information will be sent from the client to the server. There are two possible options: Basic,\ and Digest. When using Basic Authentication, the password information is sent from the client to the server in an encoded clear text format. When using Digest Authentication, the password information is sent from the client to the server in hash-encrypted format. Digest mode means that the user does not require an SSL connection. The downside is that not all authentication modules support Digest mode.

AuthName: This directive specifies the message that will be displayed in the dialog box. The message should be something that explains the domain and why it is restricted.

AuthUserFile: This directive specifies the password file where the users and passwords are stored.

Require: This directive is used to specify who, when authenticated, can access the protected resource. The option user specifies that any following identifier is a user that can access the protected resource.

When using authentication, the best strategy for maximum flexibility is to use .htaccess *files.*

Configuring Group Access

Specifying each user that can access a protected zone in a Web site is a tedious process and would require constant updates of the configuration file. It is possible to create groups and specify groups that have access to a protected zone. Following is an example configuration file fragment that shows how to manage access at a group level:

```
AuthType Basic
AuthName "Restricted Files"
AuthUserFile "C:/Program Files/Apache Group/Apache2/conf/passwords"
AuthGroupFile "C:/Program Files/Apache Group/Apache2/conf/groups"
Require group mygroup
```

When authenticating at a group level, the directive `AuthGroupFile` has been added. The value of the directive references a file that has multiple lines specifying which users belong to which group. The directive `AuthUserFile` needs to be present as it provides the users that the group file manages. The directive `Require`, instead of referencing individual users, references the identifier `group` and the groups that can access the protected resource. Following is an example group configuration file:

```
mygroup: someuser
```

Authenticating Using DBM

Using flat files to authenticate for larger Web sites does have its performance problems. For a performance enhancement, the Berkley Database Manager (DBM) can be used. The configuration is not that different from a flat file, except that the references to the username and password files have changed.

To use DBM databases, the `mod_auth_dbm` has to be loaded as shown by the following configuration file directive:

```
LoadModule auth_dbm_module modules/mod_auth_dbm.so
```

After the module has been loaded, the following configuration file fragment is used to use a DBM database:

```
AuthType Basic
AuthName "Restricted Files"
AuthDBMUserFile "C:/Program Files/Apache Group/Apache2/conf/info"
AuthDBMGroupFile "C:/Program Files/Apache Group/Apache2/conf/info"
Require group mygroup
```

In the configuration file fragment, there is only one major change in that the directives that reference the flat files have been changed to use directives that include the letters DBM. The difference with the DBM file format is that a utility has to be used to manage the users, passwords, and groups.

Distributed with the Apache distribution is the file `dbmmange.pl`, which is a Perl script that can be used to manage the DBM database. To use the file, a Perl interpreter has to be installed. The interpreter distributed with Cygwin should not be used because the interpreter relies on Cygwin and the Apache distribution is a native Windows application. The best interpreter to install is from ActiveState available at the URL *http://www.activestate.com/Products/ActivePerl/*. After Perl has been installed, you need to use CPAN (choose ActivePerl -> Perl Package Manager menu item) to install the `Crypt::PasswdMD5` module. Shown in Figure 8.10 is the installation of the module.

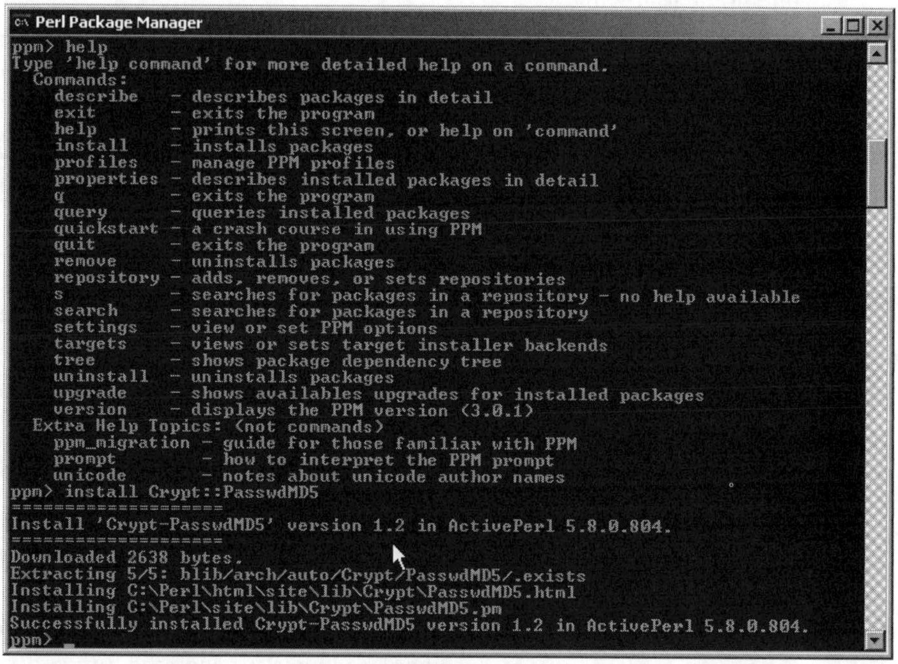

FIGURE 8.10 Installation of the CPAN module.

After the module has been installed, it is possible to run the `dbmmange.pl` script and add a user:

```
$ perl "c:\Program Files\Apache Group\Apache2\bin\dbmmanage.pl"
something.dbm add someuser mypassword mygroup
User someuser added with password encrypted to
password:mygroup using md5
```

The `dbmanage.pl` script is run directly using the Perl interpreter. It is possible to simply type in the `dbmmange.pl` script into the console if the Perl interpreter is installed properly as per the extension directions in Chapter 2. The command-line options after the script identifier are passed to the script. The script has the command-line option notation shown as follows:

```
dbmmanage.pl [database] [command] [user] [password] [group] [comment]
```

Each of the options are explained as follows:

database: This option specifies the database that is being manipulated.

command: This option specifies the command that will be executed and can be one of the following:

add: Adds an entry for the specified user. If the user already exists, then console-specified fields will overwrite the already existing fields. The password should already be encrypted.

adduser: Like the command add, except the password is asked at the command line.

check: Asks for a password and if the user specified exists, verifies that the passwords match.

delete: Deletes the user from the database.

import: Imports from the standard input user:password entries where each entry is one line.

update: Functions like the adduser command, except the user must already exist.

view: Displays the entire contents of the database.

user: This option identifies the name of the user.

password: This option identifies the password associated with the user. The password must be in encrypted format, which can be encrypted by using the htpasswd utility, and the data is sent to standard output.

group: This option specifies the groups that the user belongs to. A user may belong to multiple groups by specifying each group separated by a comma.

Authenticating Using LDAP

Another way to authenticate is to use an LDAP server. The LDAP server would contain the user entries much like the flat file and the DBM interface. To use an LDAP server for authentication, the LDAP module has to be loaded using the following configuration file directive:

```
LoadModule auth_ldap_module modules/mod_auth_ldap.so
LoadModule ldap_module modules/util_ldap.so
```

The LDAP functionality is stored in two modules: mod_auth_ldap.so and util_ldap.so. The module util_ldap.so contains helper functions used to manage the LDAP cache. The module mod_auth_ldap.so performs LDAP-based authentication.

The LDAP module documentation talks about requiring the Netscape, OpenLDAP, iPlanet, or Netscape LDAP libraries. For the Windows platform, none of these libraries are needed. The default compilation is against the Windows LDAP headers provided by the Active Directory. These libraries are provided by default for Windows 2000 and later. Earlier operating systems need to install the Active Directory distribution. If you plan on compiling the LDAP modules, however, make sure to install the Windows Platform SDK.

The caching strategy employed by the modules is meant to minimize traffic to the LDAP server. If possible, the modules will cache the data. This requires that most of the LDAP data should be read-mostly and be updated externally very rarely.

There are two types of caches used: the search and bind cache and the operation cache. The *search and bind cache* is required by a user to connect to the LDAP server to perform a query. The *operations cache* is used to perform comparison operations when the LDAP server is queried.

In the global section of the Apache HTTPD configuration file, the LDAP configuration file directives are added as follows

```
LDAPSharedCacheSize 200000
LDAPCacheEntries 1024
LDAPCacheTTL 600
LDAPOpCacheEntries 1024
LDAPOpCacheTTL 600
```

The directives used are explained as follows:

LDAPSharedCacheSize: This directive specifies the overall cache size in bytes. The default is 100 KB.

LDAPCacheEntries: This directive specifies the number of search and bind entries in the cache. The default size is 1,024 entries. Assigning a value of 0 disables the cache.

LDAPCacheTTL: This directive specifies the number of seconds a search and bind entry will exist in the cache. The default time to live is 600 seconds.

LDAPOpCacheEntries: This directive specifies the number of comparison entries that will be kept in the cache. The default size is 1,024. Assigning a value of 0 disables the cache.

LDAPOpCacheTTL: This directive specifies the number of seconds a comparison entry will exist in the cache. The default time to live is 600 seconds.

You are not required to use the cache; it is purely optional and should be tested in a Windows installation. Remember, Windows has only one process so the cache performance will be different than on Linux/FreeBSD systems. There is no best rule of thumb of which settings to use for the cache as each installation is different. However, if you use caching, remember that the amount of RAM a computer has is very important.

To protect a resource using LDAP authentication, the authentication directives are a bit different in that there is no reference to any files. The file references are replaced with LDAP directory references shown as follows. (Note the configuration information has been abbreviated for clarity purposes.)

```
<Directory "C:/Program Files/Apache Group/Apache2/htdocs">
    AllowOverride AuthConfig
    AuthType Basic
    AuthName "Restricted Files"
    AuthLDAPEnabled on
    AuthLDAPURL ldap://192.168.1.240/dc=contacts,dc=devspace,dc=com?cn
    AuthLDAPAuthoritative on
    require valid-user
</Directory>
```

The directives AuthType and AuthName are still required because they set the parameters of how the Apache HTTPD server interacts with the HTTP client. However, the directive AuthType can only be Basic and not Digest. For security purposes, therefore, an SSL connection is required.

The directive AuthLDAPEnabled is like the SSLEngine directive in that LDAP can be enabled for individual directories and locations. The directive AuthLDAPAuthoritative is used either to enable or disable other authentication mechanisms. If the value is on, then no other authentication techniques can be used. A value of off allows other applications to authenticate if the LDAP module fails.

The directive AuthLDAPURL specifies the URL that will be used to authenticate the user. The URL is broken in several blocks described as follows:

ldap: Specifies the protocol to use to communicate to the LDAP server. It is possible to use LDAPS for secure SSL communications.

192.168.1.240: Specifies either the DNS or IP address of the LDAP server.

dc=contacts,dc=devspace,dc=com: Specifies the root DN of the LDAP query.

cn: Specifies comparison attribute to use when checking the identity of the user. Not shown are two additional operators (e.g., ldap://server:port/?attribute ?scope?filter) that can be used to define a scope and filter. The scope identifies the context of the search, which is either one or sub. A search of one means to search in the current LDAP directory. A search of sub means to search the child LDAP directories. The filter is a valid LDAP filter as defined in Chapter 6.

It is simple to write the directives in the configuration file and then prepare the LDAP server to accept the requests. What is not so obvious is what the individual pieces do and why LDAP authentication works.

LDAP users should exist in an LDAP directory. For example, in example configuration item `AuthLDAPURL`, all the users will be existing in the LDAP directory `dc=contacts,dc=devspace,dc=com`. The choice of the directory is whatever the administrator wants it to be. It is possible to create multiple LDAP directories to represent multiple domains and contexts. For example, some directories could be shared by multiple applications.

Each user in the LDAP directory must be at a minimum an LDAP object `person`. An LDAP `person` has the attributes `dn`, `objectclass`, `telephoneNumber`, `userPassword`, `description`, `seeAlso`, and `sn`. When the user accesses the Web server, the value after the `cn` attribute is cross-referenced with the HTTP user.

So, for example, if the user in the HTTP dialog box is `someuser`, then an LDAP object with a `cn` of `someuser` must exist. The HTTP dialog box also expects the user to add a password. The password is compared to the LDAP object `userPassword`. If the two passwords match, then the user is considered authenticated with the username of `someuser`.

The directive `require` is a bit different from before because it does not reference either a user or a group. The identifier `valid-user` means that any user that has been authenticated by the LDAP server can access the resource. It is still possible to use the user identifier directive:

```
require user someuser
```

The only difference with using the user identifier is that the users specified must be part of the query. The `cn` attribute is queried and therefore an LDAP object with attribute `cn` and value of `someuser` must exist.

Groups can also be used in an LDAP server, except that the group is stored in the LDAP database as shown by the following LDIF file:

```
dn: cn=mygroup, dc=devspace,dc=com
objectClass: groupOfUniqueNames
uniqueMember: cn=someuser,dc=contacts,dc=devspace,dc=com
uniqueMember: cn=anotheruser,dc=contacts,dc=devspace,dc=com
```

The LDIF formatted text creates an object `groupOfUniqueNames` that only contains names. The name of the group is represented by the `cn` attribute with a value of `mygroup`. The `uniqueMember` attributes identifies individual users in the LDAP database that are part of the group.

The following configuration file directive shows how to reference the group in the main HTTPD configuration file:

```
require group "cn=mygroup, dc=devspace, dc=com"
```

Using the LDAP module will allow the administrator to validate against a specific distinguished name:

```
require dn "cn=someuser,dc=contacts,dc=devspace,dc=com"
```

When using the distinguished name to grant access, the default is to do a string comparison on the distinguished name of the user who was authenticated and the distinguished name defined by the require directive. If the attribute AuthLDAPCompareDNoServer is enabled, then a proper LDAP comparison is performed. This sort of comparison is consistent, but slower. With a proper adjusted cache, the comparison performance can be improved.

When mod_auth_ldap accesses the LDAP server, it does so using an anonymous connection. If the LDAP server has security implemented and does not allow anonymous connections, then it is necessary to assign a user and password. The following configuration file directives shows how the directives AuthLDAPBindDN and AuthLDAPBindPassword can be used to access and LDAP server:

```
AuthLDAPDBindDN  "cn=Manager, dc=devspace,dc=com"
AuthLDAPBindPassword "hello.world"
```

The problem with putting the user and password in a configuration file is that it is a potential security hole. Ideally, the LDAP server should allow anonymous connections from predetermined servers. However, if the Apache HTTPD configuration is properly secured, then putting the password in clear text into the configuration file might be partially acceptable.

Technique: Providing a User Home Access

Many times on a Web site, there is URL notation that contains a tilde character such as *http://server/~someuser/*. The purpose of the tilde is to define a home directory. To load the user directory the following directive is used:

```
LoadModule userdir_module modules/mod_userdir.so
```

The user directory is defined by using the directive UserDir as shown in the following example:

```
UserDir "My Documents/My Web site"
```

The directive says that the user directory is a subdirectory underneath the user's home directory. For example, if the URL *http://localhost/~someuser* were issued and `someuser` was a Windows user, then the home directory of the user is `c:/Documents and Settings/someuser/My Documents/My Website`. For the Windows platforms, as long as the `UserDir` directive is not an absolute path, the home directory is always the Windows home directory.

If the directory is absolute, the user is appended to the absolute directory. For example, if the absolute directory is `c:\websites\personal`, then for `someuser` the home directory is `c:\websites\personal\someuser`.

Technique: User Tracking

One of the jobs of the administrator is to manage the log files to see what the Web site users are clicking on. The standard logs do not provide for tracking the user to see which links are clicked and which things are inspected. It is possible to track a user using the `mod_usertrack`, which is loaded using the following directive:

```
LoadModule usertrack_module modules/mod_usertrack.so
```

To enable tracking, cookies are sent to the client and then processed by the server. Following are the configuration file directives that are used to enable user tracking:

```
CookieTracking on
CookieStyle Cookie2
CookieName cookietracking
CookieExpires "1 years 1 weeks 1 months 1 hours 1 minutes 1 seconds"
CookieDomain .devspace.com
```

The directives are explained as follows:

CookieTracking: This directive is either `on` or `off`. You can enable tracking for some virtual directories and not others. The advantage of selectively switching tracking on and off is that it enables the administrator to track individual areas of the Web site.

CookieStyle: This directive specifies the format of the cookie and is one of the following values (the cookie format relates to how the date, and so on appear):

Netscape: The original cookie format as specified by Netscape. This format has been deprecated and should be avoided if possible.

Cookie | RFC2109: The next version cookie format.

Cookie2 | RFC2965: The current version cookie format and should be used.

CookieName: This directive is the identifier of the cookie that is sent to the client.

CookieExpires: This directive defines when the cookie expires. Shown in the previous cookie configuration example are all the possible terms that can be used with associated numbers. Of course, because the number 1 is used, the plural form of the individual periods is required.

CookieDomain: This directive identifies the domain for which the cookie applies. It is important to realize that when defining the domain it is a domain and not an individual server. For example, www.devspace.com is not a domain, but a reference to an individual server. The correct value is .devspace.com; be sure not to forget the period in front of the domain.

To track the cookies, a log file has to be defined for the user. Following is the configuration file directive that shows how to define a log file that tracks all the generated cookies:

```
CustomLog logs/usertrack.log "%{cookie}n %r %t"
```

The tag %{cookie}n will output in the log files each of the cookies generated in the user tracking module.

Technique: URL Rewriting

In all the techniques presented, the user or Web site designer knows the URLs that they are manipulating or using. As time passes, Web sites will change and URLs that worked at one time will cease to work. The module mod_rewrite is intended to help manage changing URLs.

This book does not attempt to provide all answers regarding URL rewriting because of the flexibility of mod_rewrite. This book attempts to provide the fundamentals so that you can better understand the Apache documentation at *http://httpd.apache.org/docs-2.0/misc/rewriteguide.html* and *http://httpd.apache.org/ docs-2.0/mod/mod_rewrite.html*. The problem with the Apache documentation is that it quickly becomes very complicated.

The module is loaded using the following configuration file directive:

```
LoadModule rewrite_module modules/mod_rewrite.so
```

Moved Documents

The simplest use for mod_rewrite is to shorten very long URLs. For example, imagine having stored some data in a directory that is nested deeply. Following is an example use of the RewriteRule directive to a URL:

```
RewriteEngine on
RewriteRule ^/simpler$ /manual/mod
```

The directive `RewriteEngine` activates the module `mod_rewrite` in the defined context. The action is in the directive `RewriteRule` that has two parts. The first part `^/simpler$` is the regular expression that is matched. If the match is successful, then the matched part is replaced with the second part `/manual/mod`.

For example, if the URL is *http://localhost/simpler*, it will be replaced with *http://localhost/manual/mod* in the browser. However, if the URL is *http://localhost/simpler/page.html*, an error will result because there is no match. The way that the rule is written means that only complete identifiers will be matched.

The fixed URL approach can be used to fix the problem of trailing slashes, e.g., http://localhost/location *should be* http://localhost/location/. *The solution involves matching the identifier without the slash and then redirecting to the identifier with a slash.*

Adding Rewrites to `.htaccess` *Files*

Adding rewrite rules to the Apache HTTPD configuration file is simple. Consider the situation where the Web site may change regularly. Doing a constant update of the Apache HTTPD configuration file is not a good idea. The usual solution is to use `.htaccess` files. The advantage of this approach is that the user who manages the Web site can manage the redirections without bothering the administrator. Note that the rules that apply to the `.htaccess` files also apply to virtual hosts and directory directives.

The following configuration file directives show a modified set of rewrite rules:

```
RewriteEngine on
RewriteBase /
RewriteRule ^simpler$ manual/mod
```

The added directive is `RewriteBase`, which provides a base for the regular expressions. The value `/` means that the `.htaccess` file is stored in the root directory, and all rules are relative to the root directory. The directive `RewriteRule` has been modified to not include the leading slash because it is provided by the directive `RewriteBase`.

You can navigate directories when using `.htaccess` files shown as follows:

```
RewriteEngine on
RewriteBase /sub-directory
RewriteRule ^simpler$ ../manual/mod
```

The second part to the directive `RewriteRule` includes the double dot to indicate moving up the virtual directory structure and then down to the directory `/manual/mod`.

Wildcard Matching

In the initial example of defining a rewrite rule, the moved document matches a specific document and not the URLs that contain the moved document. For example, the problem was that was that the URL *http://localhost/simpler* was moved, and will be matched, but the URL *http://localhost/simpler/core.html* will not be matched, even though it has moved as well. The solution to this problem is to use wildcard matching as follows:

```
RewriteEngine on
RewriteBase /
RewriteRule ^simpler/([a-z]*.[a-z]*$) ../manual/mod/$1
```

The directive `RewriteRule` has some rules afterwards that match whatever the user might type in. If the user typed in the URL *http://localhost/simpler/core.html*, then the text *core.html* will be matched and substituted in the second part for the text *$1*.

Running the rewritten rule will most likely result in something similar to Figure 8.11.

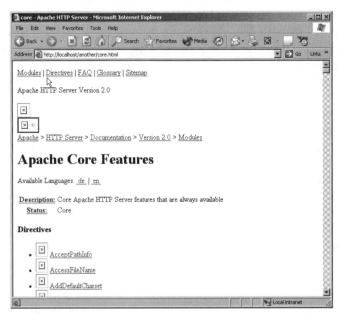

FIGURE 8.11 Redirected view of HTML page.

In Figure 8.11, the contents of the HTML are correct, but the HTML page contains a large number of broken image links. The reason for the broken image links and broken links in general is because the redirected HTML page was only redirected internally on the Apache HTTPD server. The client does not know that the content is redirected from some other location. As a result when it cross-references the other locations for the images, the wrong location is figured out.

The solution to the broken link problem is to instruct mod_rewrite to send an HTTP redirection as shown as follows:

```
RewriteEngine on
RewriteBase /
RewriteRule ^simpler/([a-z]*.[a-z]*$) ../manual/mod/$1 [R]
```

The directive RewriteRule has an additional flag [R] that instructs the client to perform a HTTP redirect.

The example of matching a generic URL can be simplified by using the notation (.*), which says to match whatever.

TIP

The directive RewriteRule has more flags that are comma separated and the ones relevant for the scope of this book are as follows:

R=code: Forces an HTTP redirect that will force the client to reassign its base URL used for link calculations. The default HTTP 302 code is sent, but optionally a different response code in the range 300-400 can be sent.

F: If the rule matches, sends back a forbidden request indicating that the URL cannot be accessed.

G: The HTTP 410 response code is sent to the client indicating that the document has disappeared and no longer exists.

L: The URL rewriting process is one where the URL can infinitely be rewritten if the regular expression is written incorrectly. If the rule is matched, this flag stops URL rewriting processing and causes mod_rewrite to continue processing the HTTP request.

N: The URL rewriting process is started again from the beginning if the regular expression is matched.

C: The current rule is chained with the next rule. This means if the current rule is matched, then the next rule will be processed for a potential match. However, if the current rule does not match, then the next rule is skipped. Note that next rule means the next rule in the configuration file.

NC: The match pattern is case insensitive.

S=num: If the current rule matches, then the next set of rules is skipped per the variable num.

Matching Conditions

The preceding rules just presented the idea of a URL rewrite engine. Let's consider what this means by looking at the following set of configuration file directives:

```
RewriteEngine on
RewriteBase /another
RewriteRule more /manual/mod/core.html [R]
RewriteRule something more
```

There are two RewriteRule directives. Let's say the user sends the HTTP request *http://localhost/another/something* to the URL rewrite engine. When the rules are combined with the request, the URL rewrite engine iterates the rule set three times. In the first iteration, the request will be altered from /another/something to /another/more. In the second iteration, the request will be altered from /another/more to /manual/mod/core.html. A third iteration is made and because no rules fire, the rule rewriting stops.

Because of the iterative nature of URL rewriting, it is very easy to write rewrites that will cause mod_rewrite to become either very slow or loop infinitely. Therefore, be careful and, if necessary, do some performance checking.

In all the examples, the rules have a single condition, which is the first part of the RewriteRule directive. You can use the directive RewriteCond to assign additional preconditions before a rule can be fired.

Essentially the HTTP conditions are based on variables already present in the HTTP request, e.g., HTTP_USER_AGENT. Those variables can be used to form a condition before a rule is fired. The following directives show how to convert a port 80 request to a new server request:

```
RewriteCond %{SERVER_PORT} !^80$
RewriteRule ^/(.*) http://newserver:%{SERVER_PORT}/$1  [L,R]
```

The directive RewriteCond has two parts. The first part %{SERVER_PORT} is the variable to test. The second part !^80$ is the regular expression to match. The condition is saying that if the value of the variable SERVER_PORT matches 80, then test the immediately following rule. The immediate rule simply matches against everything.

The second part of the rule is a bit more complicated in that it sends the client to an entirely new server, but uses the port that was used to call it. The addition of the variable %{SERVER_PORT} is superfluous, but was added to show that variables can be used to generate the URL of the redirection. Notice the flags L and R to indicate a final URL rewrite match and full HTTP redirection.

Following is a list of variables that can be used in a condition:

HTTP header: HTTP_ACCEPT, HTTP_COOKIE, HTTP_FORWARDED, HTTP_HOST, HTTP_PROXY_CONNECTION, HTTP_REFERER, and HTTP_USER_AGENT.

mod_rewrite: API_VERSION, IS_SUBREQ, REQUEST_FILENAME, REQUEST_URI, and THE_REQUEST.

Request variables: AUTH_TYPE, PATH_INFO, QUERY_STRING, REMOTE_ADDR, REMOTE_HOST, REMOTE_IDENT, REQUEST_METHOD, REMOTE_USER, and SCRIPT_FILENAME.

Server variables: DOCUMENT_ROOT, SERVER_ADDR, SERVER_ADMIN, SERVER_NAME, SERVER_PORT, SERVER_PROTOCOL, and SERVER_SOFTWARE.

System variables: TIME, TIME_DAY, TIME_HOUR, TIME_MIN, TIME_MON, TIME_SEC, TIME_WDAY, and TIME_YEAR.

The second part of the condition can be a regular expression or it can include other types of conditions such as a test to see if the item is a file as shown in the following example:

```
RewriteCond %{REQUEST_FILENAME}        !-f
RewriteCond %{REQUEST_FILENAME}        !-d
```

The example conditions test to make sure that variable REQUEST_FILENAME is not a file (!-f) or a directory (!-d). This condition could be used to test when content becomes missing. If content is missing, then the user can be redirected to another Web site.

Technique: Installing PHP

One of the most common programming languages used in conjunction with Apache is PHP (original called Personal Home Page Tools, but now referred to as PHP Hypertext Processor). PHP is an extension used extensively and is a full topic on its own for programmers. However, for the administrator, there are only a couple issues: installing PHP and adding extensions. Table 8.3 provides the reference information for PHP.

The PHP distribution to choose for installation is the bigger one, because it contains most of the extensions that you will want to use. The bigger distribution does not contain an installer, so you have to do everything either manually or by using scripts.

TABLE 8.3 Reference Information for PHP

Item	Description
Home page	Main Web site *http://www.php.net/*.
Version	At the time of this writing, the current version is 5.0.3.
Installation	The PHP toolkit is distributed in two forms: self-installing application and binary ZIP file.
Dependencies	The only major dependency PHP has, and even that has been removed, is a Web server. PHP is used most often in conjunction with Apache, but PHP will work with other Web servers.
Documentation	The documentation for PHP is provided at the main Web site at *http://www.php.net/docs.php*. The documentation for PHP has been translated into many different languages.
Mailing Lists	Many mailing lists are available at *http://www.php.net/ mailing-lists.php*. For the administrator the mailing lists `Announcements`, `Windows PHP`, and `Installation issues and problems` are of most interest.
Impatient Installation Time Required	Download size: 1 to 7 MB depending on the distribution chosen. Installation time: 10-15 minutes.
DVD Location	`/packages/Apache` contains both the Windows installer package and the source code packages.

After the distribution has been downloaded, expand it into a directory. The expanded archive creates a subdirectory php-[version number]. You can use PHP as a CGI (Common Gateway Interface) application or as an Apache module. For performance reasons, the Apache module is the preferred solution.

From the root of the expanded PHP subdirectory, copy the file php.ini-dist to the Windows system root directory and rename it as php.ini. The php.ini file is bootstraps the location of the PHP interpreter. In most cases, this will mean c:\windows, c:\winnt or c:\winnt40.

Within the `php.ini` file, the entries defined as follows need to reflect the PHP installation directory and root directory of Apache:

```
doc_root = "C:\Program Files\Apache Group\Apache2\htdocs"
extension_dir = ".;C:\bin\php-5.0.0\extensions"
```

The entry `doc_root` should to point to the same directory that the root directory in the Apache HTTPD server points to. If the Apache HTTPD server is multi-hosted, then choose a directory that provides the root directory for the server. The entry `extension_dir` points to the directory containing all the DLLs that start with the identifier `php_`. For the entries, separating the individual paths with a semicolon can specify multiple paths.

To let the Apache server or any other server find the PHP and extension DLLs, the following paths have to be added to the PATH environment variable: `[php-in-stallation]/dlls`, `[php-installation]/extensions`, and `[php-installation]/sapi`. The purposes of the PHP subdirectories are defined as follows:

cli: This directory contains the command-line interpreter used for command-line scripting.

dlls: This directory contains all the support DLLs required for running the PHP interpreter. These files could be copied to the Windows system directory, or more appropriately, the directory is added to the path.

extensions: This directory contains the extension DLLs for the PHP interpreter. If you are going to add your own extensions, this directory is the place where you add the DLLs.

openssl: This directory references the support files for OpenSSL support, however, as earlier chapters showed, the OpenSSL directories will be added to the path.

sapi: This directory contains the support DLLs used by the individual Web servers such as Apache.

In the root directory of the PHP subdirectory, there is a file called `php4ts.dll` that must either be copied to the Windows system directory or copied to the PHP subdirectory `sapi`. The preferred directory is `sapi`, but be sure to add the `sapi` directory to the Windows path.

The module is loaded using the following configuration file directive:

```
LoadModule php5_module "c:/bin/php-5.0.0/sapi/php4apache2.dll"
```

To use PHP pages, the extension `.php` is registered in the Apache configuration file shown as follows:

```
AddModule mod_php5.c
AddType application/x-httpd-php .php
```

After the three Apache HTTPD directives have been added, it is possible to use the PHP interpreter.

The only outstanding task remaining is the maintenance of PHP extensions. A PHP extension is added to the `extensions` subdirectory. Then in the `php.ini` file, the following extension entry is added:

```
extension=php_bz2.dll
```

There is an extension entry for each and every extension that is to be loaded into the PHP interpreter workspace.

Technique: Sharing Files Using WebDAV

Files are created, deleted, manipulated, updated, and so on by users. A file is a fundamental concept of a computer. Files were discussed in Chapter 6, but only with respect to an intranet. To share files across the Internet, a common practice is to use WebDAV (Web Distributed Authoring and Versioning protocol). The WebDAV protocol is an Internet standard that has native support within the Windows operating system in the form of Web folders. The Apache HTTPD server supports Web-DAV using the `mod_dav` module.

The WebDAV functionality is implemented using two modules: `mod_dav` and `mod_dav_fs`. The module `mod_dav` is responsible for the WebDAV interface and supports both Class 1 and Class 2 method calls. The current implementation of `mod_dav` does not support versioning. Versioning is provided by a utility such as SubVersion (*http://subversion.tigris.org*). The purpose of the module `mod_dav_fs` is to provide a filesystem that the module `mod_dav` can operate on. The `mod_dav` module interfaces with a filesystem using an Apache WebDAV module interface. The module `mod_dav_fs` exposes a provider, which happens to interact with the filesystem. For reference purposes, a developer could develop a provider that interacts with a database.

When the Apache HTTPD server process loads both modules, WebDAV is activated, and can be used to upload, download, create directories, or delete directories. By default, both modules are distributed with the Apache-provided Windows Installer. For reference information regarding the WebDAV modules, refer to the Apache HTTPD reference information in Table 8.1 shown earlier.

To activate WebDAV, the modules have to be loaded in the Apache configuration file shown as follows:

```
LoadModule dav_module modules/mod_dav.so
LoadModule dav_fs_module modules/mod_dav_fs.so
```

The modules loaded should already exist in the default configuration file, but are commented out. You will need to uncomment them. Then in the configuration file, a reference to the WebDAV lock database is made:

```
DavLockDB "c:/bin/Apache2/var/DavLock"
```

The directive `DavLockDB` is required by module `mod_dav_fs` for file-locking purposes.

To enable a directory to use WebDAV, the directive `Dav` is used as shown in the following configuration file fragment:

```
<Directory "C:/bin/Apache2/htdocs">
    Dav On
</Directory>
```

The directive `Dav` is assigned a value of `On` indicating that the directory referenced can be manipulated using the WebDAV protocol. Sharing WebDAV without any security is not a good idea because as the WebDAV share is defined, it is by default a public share, which can be manipulated by anyone. Ideally, an administrator would use authentication and SSL as discussed previously.

If the root of a directory is enabled for WebDAV, then all child directories will automatically be WebDAV-enabled regardless of the configuration.

The WebDAV user that is used to add, delete, or manipulate files on the remote server is the same user that executes the Apache HTTPD server process.

After activating WebDAV, there are some additional notes on some best practices regarding the WebDAV modules. The directive `LimitXMLRequestBody` can be used to enable a maximum size of the client request shown as follows. The value is in units in terms of bytes.

```
LimitXMLRequestBody 10000
```

The reason for using the directive `LimitXMLRequestBody` is so that clients do not by accident send too large XML packets. Note that the directive `LimitRequestBody` has no effect on regulating the size of the HTTP packet with respect to the WebDAV interface.

The directive `DavDepthInfinity`, which does not need to be specified, helps stop Denial of Service (DoS) attacks. The directive disables the capability to perform a property find on very large repositories. The problem of doing a property search is that it can take a more resources, thus disabling the activity of other clients.

Retrieving the Sources and Contents

Part of the problem with manipulating scripts in WebDAV is that sometimes the generated content is manipulated and not the actual contents. This results in the problem that a Web site developer cannot update a file because the file is being executed when it is retrieved. For example, consider when WebDAV does a GET of a PHP script. WebDAV doesn't receive the file, but instead it receives the generated contents of the file. Following is a configuration that enables the source code editing of PHP scripts:

```
Alias /sources "C:/bin/Apache2/htdocs"
<Location /sources>
    DAV On
    ForceType text/plain
</Location>
```

The directive Alias is used to define a reference to a URL directory that is created virtually. The virtual URL directory is then referenced within a Location directive block. The directive DAV will activate the WebDAV interface. The directive ForceType is the trick that stops the scripts from being processed because it overrides any AddHandler directive. When a document is referenced within the Location block, the handler type will be forced and not let any module manage the content type.

Using Web Folders

One of the simplest ways to connect to a WebDAV server is to use Web Folders available within Windows. Web Folders are an enhancement provided by Internet Explorer that make it possible to connect to a WebDAV server and expose the contents within Windows Explorer.

A Web Folder is added using the Add Network Place wizard as shown in Figure 8.12.

In Figure 8.12, the Add Network Place wizard icon is located in the right window pane of Windows Explorer. To start the wizard, double-click this icon and a dialog box similar to Figure 8.13 appears.

The Add Network Place Wizard dialog box in Figure 8.13 has a single text box that references the URL of the WebDAV server. In the initial WebDav configuration example where the identifier Dav was assigned a value of on within a Directory identifier, the URL used to access the WebDav server would be *http://localhost/*. If a Location identifier is used to activate WebDav as shown in the previous configuration

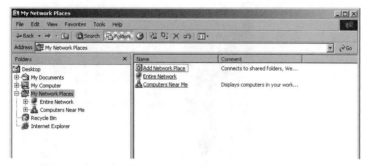

FIGURE 8.12 Location of the Add Network Place wizard.

FIGURE 8.13 Initial wizard dialog box.

example, the URL would be *http://localhost/sources*. Both examples assume that the client is on the local machine.

After the URL has been entered, click the Next button can be pressed to open the next dialog box in the wizard as shown in Figure 8.14.

The single text box is used to identify the name of the WebDAV resource in the Windows Explorer. The default name used is the name of the server, but it should be changed to something more intuitive.

After giving the WebDAV resource an identifier, click the Next button to open a Windows Explorer window. The files shown in the window represent the files on the server. Within the Windows Explorer window will be a shortcut to the Web-DAV resource as shown in Figure 8.15.

FIGURE 8.14 Identification of the shared network resource.

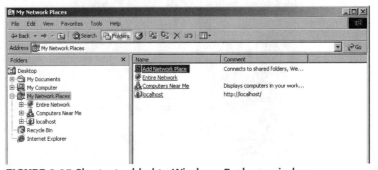

FIGURE 8.15 Shortcut added to Windows Explorer window.

In Figure 8.15, the shortcut to the WebDAV localhost resource is added. It is important to realize that the shortcut to the WebDAV resource is just that—a shortcut. The shortcut can be copied to a local place on the hard disk and can be manipulated by the Windows Explorer and any application that uses the Windows shell. The shortcut becomes problematic when a console or script program wants to manipulate the remote resource. The console program or script simply sees a file that is a shortcut.

SUMMARY

There are many Web servers on this planet, but Apache HTTPD is one of the most popular and most versatile. The Apache HTTP Web server is and can be considered its own application server. This chapter attempted to show what is possible and not possible, but it should also be apparent how flexible Apache HTTPD is. Remember that you probably won't use all the techniques presented in this chapter because most scenarios do not require such sophistication.

9 Processing E-mail

ABOUT THIS CHAPTER

The focus of this chapter is to introduce how to manage Internet-based e-mail, which means how to use Simple Mail Transfer Protocol (SMTP) and Post Office Protocol (POP3). E-mail and HTML are the killer applications of the Internet. More people now have e-mail accounts than ever before, making e-mail addresses as prevalent as telephone numbers.

The popularity of e-mail has given rise to a big problem: spam. Anyone with an e-mail account knows what spam is. Many people complain about how insecure e-mail protocols are and want e-mail to be like it used to be when there was no spam and things were wonderful. In those days, however, each ISP had its own e-mail technology and sending e-mails was a real pain. Today, e-mail is seamless and very popular. With popularity, comes abuse that is not caused by the protocol, but by the people using the e-mail accounts and by administrators who are too trusting.

By enforcing an *e-mail policy*, the amount of spam can be dramatically reduced. Although an e-mail policy is not a silver bullet solution, the implementation of a number of processes will improve the overall e-mail process. This chapter will introduce some e-mail policy software and introduce an e-mail processing strategy.

Specifically, the following projects will be covered in this chapter:

XMail server: In the Open Source community, mail servers such as SendMail, QMail, and Postfix are extremely popular. These industrial-strength mail servers are intended for ISPs with literally thousands off e-mails arriving daily. XMail server is intended for people who have a large number of users, but do not want the headaches of configuring SendMail, QMail, or Postfix. XMail

517

server is also industrial strength, but geared toward corporations that want to manage their own e-mail. Illustrated in this chapter are the details of managing POP3 and SMTP servers used to process e-mail, including topics such as user and domain management, and preprocessing and postprocessing of e-mails.

ASSP: Spam has become a big problem in the industry. Although there is no single solution to spam, measures can be implemented to slow it down and make it ineffective. The open source ASSP (Anti-Spam SMTP Proxy) project is an example spam filter that is very effective in controlling spam and reducing the count of unwanted e-mails. Other projects, such as SpamBayes and Spamassassin, are very good, but are not as easy to use as ASSP. ASSP is essentially install and then train as you go along, which makes it simple and effective.

E-mailRelay: Interrupting the flow of e-mail is playing with fire because it can cause e-mails to bounce. Many mailing lists when they encounter a bounced e-mail address will require the individual to resubscribe, which is a pain for the user and the domain because it causes large amounts of unnecessary e-mail. E-mailRelay solves the interruption problem by acting as a router. E-mailRelay makes it possible to capture e-mails, and then relay them using a script or E-mailRelay itself.

AN E-MAIL STRATEGY

Administrators who manage e-mail servers with thousands of accounts agree that e-mail is a project that never ends and there is always something to do or tweak. The reason is because e-mail has become a technology that we rely on and use in different forms. People send and receive many e-mails for business and personal reasons. Organizing e-mail is like organizing documents, in that the organization rules work well for 10 or 20 files, but falls apart when dealing with more files. When you sort your hundreds of documents, you are constantly using one strategy or another. Managing files on a hard disk is another example of a project that never ends.

For example, some e-mail clients can organize e-mails according to search criteria. That works well as long as the user does not receive large amounts of mailing list e-mails, because that can confuse the e-mail client. Also problematic and confusing for the client is spam. The result is that e-mail is complex and requires an effective management strategy.

Figure 9.1 illustrates a potential e-mail strategy that can be used on Windows using Linux/FreeBSD tools.

Figure 9.1 shows several named tools: Exim, Procmail, Spamassassin, UW-POP, and UW-IMAP. The tool Exim is a Message Transfer Agent (MTA). The role of the MTA is to listen to the SMTP port and transfer any content captured to a

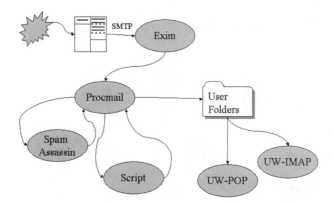

FIGURE 9.1 E-mail architecture using Linux/FreeBSD.

local directory in the form of a file. The MTA architecture has a very long history that comes from the traditional Unix architecture. The application Exim can execute rules to process the incoming e-mail and then store it in the appropriate folder.

Leaving the discussion of Procmail for the moment, the item User Folders in Figure 9.1 needs further discussion. Each user on a computer has a home directory, which on Windows would be c:\Documents and Settings\[username]. A directory is created as a subdirectory within the user's home directory that serves as a folder that contains all the e-mails a user receives. An e-mail client then reads the e-mails that reside in the directory. Alternatively, an application such as UW-POP or UW-IMAP reads the home directory and lets an e-mail client use POP or IMAP to read the e-mails. Another strategy is not to use POP or IMAP, but use a file copying method to synchronize the mail directories between two computers. Originally that was the strategy used by Unix, but the problem with that strategy is that it assumes a computer is always connected to the Internet. The resulting solution was to develop POP and let a client manage the details of manipulating the e-mail messages.

Going back to Figure 9.1 and the Procmail tool, the e-mail message is sent from the MTA to Procmail, which is a Local Delivery Agent (LDA). The purpose of the LDA is to sort, classify, and process e-mails. For example, filters in an e-mail client could be processed using the LDA. The LDA processes the e-mails and then sorts them in the local user's e-mail folders. The LDA executes the Spamassassin application to filter out spam e-mails, and runs another script to perform some other type of actions if necessary.

The Linux/FreeBSD strategy used to manage e-mails is acceptable, but not a traditional way to process e-mails on a Windows computer. The difference on Windows is that instead of using e-mail folders, the common denominator is SMTP as shown in Figure 9.2.

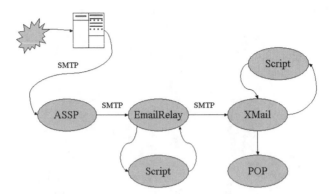

FIGURE 9.2 SMTP-based e-mail architecture.

In Figure 9.2, the architecture is similar to Figure 9.1 in that there is an overall processing flow. The tools and protocol used are different. The tools ASSP, E-Mail-Relay, and XMail are SMTP engines that capture and process e-mail messages. ASSP is a spam filter, E-mailRelay is an e-mail processor, and XMail is the e-mail server.

The individual tools are chained together using SMTP because it is simpler to manage on an overall e-mail architecture. Granted it is possible to use individual tools as scripts in the XMail server, but that could potentially complicate the setup of the XMail server. Each application serves a specific task. For example, ASSP is used to manage spam using a specialized spam-detection algorithm. The administrator to control spam would only have to manage ASSP. If necessary, the administrator could either replace or take down spam detection and allow normal e-mail traffic to resume without any downtime.

E-mail is complicated because there are process flows, for example, spam, mailing list, automated response, e-mail folder sorting, and so on. In Figure 9.2 the e-mail is managed using SMTP and not POP. The thinking is that e-mail should be sorted and categorized in the user's folder on XMail, and also as the user retrieves the e-mail. The advantage is that a user could reroute their e-mail to another server, and because the e-mail is already sorted, spam and mailing list data would not be sent to the other server.

Another potential architecture is shown in Figure 9.3.

In Figure 9.3, the User Folders have shifted slightly and are manipulated by the E-mailRelay program directly. The reason for this is that the User Folders are used by application UW-IMAP to provide IMAP services. In an e-mail flow scheme, those users that access their e-mail using IMAP would not have the e-mail sent to the XMail application, because XMail only provides POP services.

In the architectures shown in Figure 9.1, 9.2, and 9.3, the overall objective is to create an e-mail policy that slices and dices e-mail and delivers it to the correct

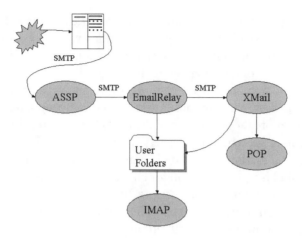

FIGURE 9.3 SMTP-based e-mail architecture that includes IMAP.

person. Although it is possible to do everything using one application, that can be problematic because it creates a single point of failure. The applications ASSP and E-mailRelay provide a first line of defense against spam and e-mail attacks.

At this point, it is necessary to step back and think about e-mail. The big e-mail problem is controlling the flow and accessing old e-mails. The classical approach to accessing old e-mails is to create an archive using e-mail folders and then search the folders. Searching e-mails in an archive that extends a year or more is very compli-cated and not feasible. A better approach is to treat the e-mail archive problem as a search engine problem, and use the e-mail client as a temporary storage mechanism used to interact with SMTP, POP, and IMAP.

The structure of this chapter is to outline the XMail server application because XMail is the center of the entire e-mail infrastructure and is used to provide the in-dividual users. We'll also discuss ASSP and E-mailRelay.

PROJECT: XMAIL SERVER

The project XMail server has managed to create a very robust and versatile server without setting the world aflame. A loyal following of people use it constantly, pro-vide feedback, and help in its development. It is an open source project where both the Windows platforms and Linux/BSD platforms have been important. XMail server works as well on the Windows platform as it does on the Linux/BSD platform.

On the Linux/BSD platforms, mail is managed by an orchestration of programs working together. For example, there are programs to receive e-mail, programs to process e-mail, and programs to allow a user to retrieve e-mail. The orchestration has shown to work well for very large installations processing millions of e-mails daily. Classically, the orchestration is managed using scripting languages that are very specific to the programs managing the e-mail.

XMail server combines the program orchestration into a single program. This is the classical approach used by most Windows e-mail programs. However, XMail server does not ignore the advantages of the Linux/BSD approach as it allows orchestration of e-mails. The orchestration is very similar to Linux/BSD and includes the creation of scripts that can be inserted at different stages in the e-mail-processing flow.

Overall XMail is a great solution for an administrator who is willing to spend a little time to manage e-mail using scripts. In return, the administrator can create mailing lists, custom response e-mail replies, and workflow applications, as well as manage spam. An administrator with one application and a few scripts can keep the e-mail for a domain under control. Table 9.1 contains reference information about the XMail server project.

TABLE 9.1 Reference Information for XMail Server

Item	*Description*
Home page	*http://www.xmailserver.org/*
Version	At the time of this writing, the released version is 1.21.
Installation	The XMail server distribution is distributed as a ZIP file archive that needs to be expanded manually.
Dependencies	The XMail server distribution has no dependencies. However, to make it simple to administer XMail server, you should use a GUI-based administration tool.
Documentation	The documentation is a single, comprehensive HTML file.
Mailing Lists	The two mailing lists for XMail server are `xmail` and `xmail-announce`. The `xmail` mailing list is for those using XMail. The `xmail-announce` mailing list is for XMail server announcements. The administrator is advised to subscribe to both.

$\longrightarrow$

Item	Description
Impatient Installation Time Required	Download size: 0.5 MB Installation time: 5-35 minutes depending on the settings that need to be made.
Firewall Port	25 (TCP) SMTP, 110 (TCP) POP, 6107 (TCP) Control Port. All the port definitions can be redefined, but note redefining the ports can have the side effect that mail will not be delivered or picked up.
DVD Location	/packages/xmail contains the ZIP file archive and all the installable modules.

Impatient Installation and Deployment

When installing XMail server, an impatient installation and full deployment are the same thing. There are no quick ways to install XMail server. The installation is not that complicated, but it does require some manual intervention or some automation scripts.

The XMail archive can be downloaded directly from the XMail server home page at *http://www.xmailserver.org*. The generated HTML XMail Download page contains links to the appropriate version, which is either Linux or NT/2K (Windows) binaries. The Windows binary zipped archive is downloaded and then expanded into the subdirectory that will be used to execute XMail server.

XMail Directory Structure

When the XMail server archive is expanded, there will be the subdirectory xmail-[version number]. Within that subdirectory are a number of files and a subdirectory mailroot. The files in the xmail-[version number] subdirectory need to be copied to the subdirectory [xmail-version number]/mailroot/bin.

It may seem odd to have to copy some files from one location in the archive to another. This is done on purpose so that a site only has to update the binaries when doing an upgrade. The binaries are located in the root subdirectory xmail-[version number].

NOTE

TIP

When upgrading an existing XMail server installation, it is extremely important to read all the change log file (`xmail-[version number]/changelog.html`*). Often there may be changes in the change log that require immediate attention when upgrading an installation.*

The subdirectory `mailroot` is the root directory of the XMail server application. In theory, everything in the `mailroot` subdirectory could be copied to another location on the hard disk. For the initial installation purposes, it is not important to know what the individual subdirectories of the `mailroot` directory do. The only important fact is that the files within the `mailroot` directory are the configuration files used by the XMail server application.

Installing as a Service and Setting Bootstrap Parameters

XMail server can be installed as a service so that when the computer is restarted, the XMail server application will automatically start. The XMail server application is installed as a service using the following command:

```
XMail.exe --install-auto
```

The option `--install-auto` starts XMail automatically when the server is rebooted. Alternately, if the option `--install` is used, then XMail will be installed as a service that needs to be started manually when a computer is rebooted.

NOTE

If you have installed IIS, then most likely the SMTP relay service will be installed and running. It must be disabled before running XMail because XMail has its own SMTP service and will conflict with the Microsoft SMTP relay service. Running both concurrently is not recommended because the Microsoft SMTP server is primarily a relay server.

When XMail starts as a service, you won't know where XMail is installed, because it has no default location. XMail bootstraps itself with configuration information that is read from the Windows registry. Following is a registry script that is used to bootstrap XMail:

```
Windows Registry Editor Version 5.00
[HKEY_LOCAL_MACHINE\SOFTWARE\GNU\XMail]
"MAIL_ROOT"="C:\\bin\\xmail-1.17\\MailRoot"
"MAIL_CMD_LINE"="-Pl -Sl -Ql -Cl -Ll -Md -Yi 6000"
```

In the registry script, there are two registry key values: `MAIL_ROOT` and `MAIL_CMD_LINE`. The registry key value `MAIL_ROOT` defines the root directory of the XMail server application. The root directory of XMail is typically the directory

that contains all the configuration files (end with .tab). The registry key value
MAIL_CMD_LINE represents the command-line arguments that are used to initialize
the XMail server application. The purposes of the individual command-line options are explained in detail in the XMail documentation and in the "Technique:
Changing a Port, Logging Requests, Performance Tuning, and Controlling Relay"
section later in this chapter.

Within the mailroot subdirectory, edit the server.tab file by modifying the
following keys:

```
"RootDomain"        "devspace.com"
"SmtpServerDomain"  "devspace.com"
"POP3Domain"        "devspace.com"
"HeloDomain"        "devspace.com"
"PostMaster"        "root@devspace.com"
"ErrorsAdmin"       "root@devspace.com"
"RemoveSpoolErrors"      "0"
"MaxMTAOps" "16"
"ReceivedHdrType"   "0"
"FetchHdrTags"      "+X-Deliver-To,+Received,To,Cc"
"DefaultSmtpPerms" "MRZ"
```

Each key and associated value is surrounded by a set of double quotes and then
the buffer is separated by spaces. The individual keys are defined as follows:

RootDomain: Defines the primary domain for the server.

SmtpServerDomain: Defines the e-mail domain that is used in Extended SMTP
(ESTMP) to support Challenge Respond Authentication Mechanism – Message Digest 5 (CRAM-MD5) authentication.

POP3Domain: Defines the default domain for POP3 client connections.

HeloDomain: Defines the domain that is used when a client connects to the
server and the domain identifier is exchanged.

PostMaster: Defines the e-mail address of the postmaster that manages the e-
mail server.

ErrorsAdmin: Defines the e-mail address where notification messages are sent
when a message had delivery or processing errors.

RemoveSpoolErrors: Specifies whether an e-mail that has problems is removed or
whether the value is stored in the frozen directory. A value of "0" means not to
remove the spool errors, whereas "1" means to remove the problematic e-mails.

ReceiveHdrType: Specifies the verbosity of the received message headers that are
generated, which can be one of the following: 0 standard (client IP shown and

server IP not), 1 verbose (client IP shown and server IP shown), 2 strict (no IP shown), 3 same as 0 (but the client IP is not shown if the client can authenticate itself), and 4 same as 1 (but the client IP is not shown if the client can authenticate itself).

`FetchHdrTags`: Defines the list of header tags that are extracted when XMail retrieves e-mail remotely. When XMail retrieves e-mail remotely, the addresses in the e-mail are extracted from the e-mail headers specified by the `FetchHdrTags`. The individual headers are comma separated without a space, and from the example `server.tab` file, the default values are shown. More about this key will be discussed later in this chapter.

`DefaultSmtpPerms`: Defines the list of permissions that are assigned when users want to relay SMTP e-mail. More about this is discussed later in this chapter. the SMTP relay must be restricted; otherwise, spammers will use the e-mail server to relay thousands of messages.

After the `server.tab` file has been saved, you can start the XMail service using the Windows service control panel. When the XMail service has started, you can send and receive e-mail, but because the server is in a very rudimentary stage, it is extremely vulnerable. The next step is to properly configure XMail server and add some e-mail accounts.

Logging On to XMail Server

One of the most complicated parts of XMail is configuration. There are three ways to configure XMail: easy, somewhat complicated, and complicated. The easy way to configure XMail is to use a configuration tool such as XMail PHP Administration Interface (XPAI). The somewhat complicated procedure is to use a command-line utility or library. The complicated way is to manipulate the configuration files themselves. You cannot configure XMail entirely using the easy way. The level of complexity of the configuration depends entirely on the task that is being solved. This book, when possible, attempts to show both a programmatic approach and a click-and-run GUI approach.

For the click-and-run GUI approach, the application XPAI is used. XPAI is a Web-based XMail administration utility based on PHP. The reference information for XPAI is shown in Table 9.2.

When the XPAI archive is unzipped, the subdirectory `xpai` is created. The subdirectory `xpai` can be copied as a subdirectory of the Web server, or if the Apache Web server is used, an alias is defined as follows:

```
alias /xpai  "c:/my/installation/directory"
```

TABLE 9.2 Reference Information for the XPAI Application

Item	Description
Home page	*http://www.akxak.de/xpai/*
Version	At the time of this writing, the released version is 1.15.
Installation	The XPAI application is an archive that is expanded and the files are installed as a PHP application.
Dependencies	The XPAI application is a PHP application and is dependent on PHP being installed on either Apache, Microsoft Internet Information Server (IIS), or some other Web server.
Documentation	The documentation is scant, and requires knowledge about the XMail configuration files. This means it is essential to read the XMail documentation and understand how XMail works. It is not essential to know the contents of the configuration files and which files to edit to achieve a desired result.
Mailing Lists	There are no mailing lists, but the author can be contacted directly from the Web site.
Impatient Installation Time Required	Download size: 0.5 MB Installation time: 5-35 minutes depending on the settings that need to be made.
Firewall Port	80 (TCP) or whatever port the HTTP server is using.
DVD Location	`/packages/xmail/xpai` contains the ZIP file archive.

To let the XPAI application know which XMail server to manage, some settings in `[xpai-installation]/config.php` need to be changed. Following is a list of variables that need to be changed:

$_SESSION['ip'] = "IP": The value `IP` needs to be changed to reflect where the XMail server is installed.

$_SESSION['xpai_user'] = "administrator": The value `administrator` needs to be change with an administrator identifier stored in the `ctrlaccounts.tab` file.

$_SESSION['xpai_pwd'] = "password": The value `password` needs to be changed to the password associated with the administrator identifier.

Regardless of how the XPAI archive is referenced, after the application has been installed in the Web server, it can be called by issuing the URL *http://localhost/xpai/index.php*. The resulting HTML page will appear similar to Figure 9.4.

FIGURE 9.4 Initial XPAI administration logon screen.

In Figure 9.4 the User Name and Password text boxes refer to XMail control accounts used to allow administrators to log on to XMail remotely and manipulate the XMail configuration.

Configuration applications for XMail can be useful, but only for some configuration issues, namely e-mail domains and the users in the domains. The rest, such as assigning root account, relay control, and so on, must be carried out manually.

An administrator account is added manually to the file `ctrlaccounts.tab`:

```
"admin"    "170004094b161015150a1711"
```

Each line in the `ctrlaccounts.tab` file represents a username and password combination. The username and password are enclosed in quotes and separated by four spaces. The password shown is not the actual password, but an encoded encrypted buffer created by the application `xmcrypt.exe`. The buffer is created using the following command line:

```
cgross@pluto /cygdrive/c/bin/mailroot/bin
$ ./xmcrypt.exe password
15041616120a1701
```

The command `xmcrypt` accepts a single command-line parameter that represents the password to be encoded and encrypted. The `xmcrypt` command uses one-way hash encoding. The result is output to the console and is copied as the password in the `ctrlaccounts.tab` file. After the `ctrlaccounts.tab` file has been updated and the XMail server is restarted, you can log on using XPAI. After logging on, the result should appear similar to Figure 9.5.

FIGURE 9.5 Successfully logged on administrator.

A successfully logged on administrator as shown in Figure 9.5 has the ability to manage domains, users, and XMail server settings.

Technique: Controlling Relay

One of the most important tasks with an e-mail server is to control the SMTP relay. The SMTP by default allows automatic relaying by third parties. Spammers like to use open relays to relay their spam because when using different senders, the receiver cannot pinpoint the source of the spam.

Do not underestimate the ramifications of leaving an SMTP relay open. An SMTP relay must exist to relay e-mail to your domain or for your users to send e-mail to other domains. You don't want to allow just anyone to send e-mail from your relay. If it does happen, then your IP address will be put on a black list, meaning that many domains might reject your e-mail because it is a known spammers SMTP relay.

Setting Up the `Server.tab` File

Several places in the different configuration files can be used to control how e-mail is relayed. The first entry that must be modified is the key `DefaultSmtpPerms`, which controls the e-mail relaying permissions. The purpose of the `DefaultSmtpPerms` key was shown in the `server.tab` file. The individual settings are explained as follows:

M: This letter allows any e-mail to be relayed. This setting may seem hazardous, but not setting it is even more hazardous because no e-mail, regardless from whom and destination, will be relayed. This means e-mail destined for the server will not be received. If the letter is present, then anybody can relay e-mail to a local domain.

R: This letter allows a user to relay e-mail. Even if the letter exists, it does not mean that the SMTP relay is open for all to use. The presence of this letter allows a user to be authenticated when relaying e-mail not intended for the local server.

V: This letter allows a client program to verify the existence of a user. It should be noted that the verify command is a security hole because it allows a hacker to retrieve a list of valid e-mail users that can be spammed to.

T: This letter allows the local server to act like a backup server. Imagine the situation where a domain is based on an Internet connection that is not always available. In that case, the backup e-mail server will receive all the mails missed by the main server. When the main server is available on the Internet, it will issue an ETERN command to the backup server and download all the missed e-mails.

z: This letter allows the setting of a maximum e-mail size that can be relayed by any individual user.

For the server.tab file, the recommended SMTP default flag for the key DefaultSmtpPerms is MRZ.

Setting Up Trusted Users

When the server.tab file is properly set up to allow relaying to outside e-mail servers, the only users that can relay e-mail are those that are recognized by the e-mail server. The users recognized are part of a domain managed by XMail server.

There is a bit of a catch with respect to trusted users and users that are part of a domain. In the simplest case, a user is added to a domain. For example, a domain could be mycompany.com, and a user that is part of the domain could be alex. Putting the two together creates the e-mail address alex@mycompany.com. Then when retrieving POP e-mail, the user could either be alex or alex@mycompany.com. For relaying SMTP e-mail, the authentication requires the full e-mail address as a user.

When installing an XMail server, the individual users can be referenced in the POP e-mail using two different notations. You should use the full notation, which is the e-mail address, because there will be no confusion if multiple domains have the same user identifier.

If a user wants to use the XMail server as a relay but does not have a user account, then a user can be added to the file smtpfwd.tab as follows:

```
"someuser" "apassword" "MR"
```

Each line of the smtpfwd.tab file represents a user (someuser), the user's password (apassword), and the rights (MR) the user has with respect to relaying e-mail. The rights are the same rights associated with the key DefaultSmtpPerms. The number of entries in this file should be kept at a minimum because the username and password are stored in clear text and thus present a potential security hole.

Setting Up Trusted or Untrusted Hosts

If the administrator wants to run automated e-mail programs, for example Web-based feedback forms, then using authentication might not be possible. Authentication might not be possible because it would require adding a username and password to the application and could be a potential security hole. The solution that XMail offers is the capability to define hosts that can relay mail without having to provide authentication. The information is stored in the following `smtprelay.tab` file example:

```
"192.168.1.0"  "255.255.255.0"
"10.4.0.0"     "255.255.255.0"
"10.3.0.0"     "255.255.255.0"
```

Each line of the `smtprelay.tab` file represents a subnet (e.g., 192.168.1.0) and mask (e.g., 255.255.255.0). Using the first line as an example, a C subnet is being specified, so any address that is in the range 192.168.1.0, and 192.168.1.254 can relay e-mail.

There is also the inverse in that some hosts are entirely untrusted. spammers will keep sending out e-mail and sometimes those hosts cannot be trusted. By using the file `spammers.tab`, it is possible to define hosts that are not allowed to connect to the server and relay e-mail. Following is an example `spammers.tab` file:

```
"212.113.1.0"    "255.255.255.0"
```

Each line of the `spammers.tab` file represents a subnet and mask range. It is also possible to specify a spammer using an e-mail address that is stored in the file `spam-address.tab`. Following is an example of the `spam-address.tab` file:

```
"*@adomain.com"
```

Each line of the `spam-address.tab` file represents an e-mail address that will be filtered and considered spam. In the case of the example file, the asterisk is a wildcard character that defines that all e-mails from the domain `adomain.com` will be filtered.

Filtering spam e-mail based on the e-mail address is very dangerous, as spammers have resorted to changing their e-mail addresses and hijacking legitimate e-mail addresses.

CAUTION

Technique: Configuring the XMail Server Programmatically

The XPAI application makes it simple to configure XMail using the GUI. However, the GUI is not useful if the administrator wants to automate certain routines. To configure XMail programmatically, a script could manipulate the individual configuration files, or the XMail admin protocol can be used. The XMail admin protocol is the preferred technique and involves using networking APIs.

The XMail admin protocol is text based and, if necessary, an administrator could use the Telnet application to perform XMail configuration tasks as illustrated in the following Telnet session example:

```
$ telnet pluto 6017
Trying 192.168.1.2...
Connected to pluto.
Escape character is '^]'.
+00000 <1075722056.2404@192.168.1.240> XMail 1.21
(Win32/Ix86) CTRL Server; Mon, 2 Feb 2004 12:40:56 +0100
"admin" "password"
+00000 OK
"userlist"       "mydomain.com"
+00100 OK
"devspace.com"   "someuser"    "apassword"       "U"
"devspace.com"   "anotheruser"        "password.2" "U"
"."
```

In the example Telnet session, Telnet connects to port 6017, which is the default XMail admin protocol port. XMail server responds with a +0000 <1075… as a server greeting. The client would need to respond with an administrator account (admin) and password (password). The administrator identifier used is from the ctrlaccounts.tab file. The format of the administrator identifier is a double quote-enclosed buffer separated by spaces.

If the administrator identifier is valid, then XMail responds with a +00000 OK response. The Telnet client then needs to type in some command. In the example Telnet session, the command is userlist for the domain mydomain.com. The command userlist retrieves all users associated with a particular domain. All the commands are listed in the XMail documentation (*http://www.xmailserver.org/Readme.html*) section "XMail Admin Protocol." If the command can be processed, XMail will respond with a leading +00100 OK to indicate success and that data is following. The date is generated as lines of quote-encapsulated buffers. To indicate that the data has been finished, a "." buffer is sent.

The Telnet approach is acceptable if the administrator needs to get something done quickly and has no other access to a particular XMail server instance. For BASH or Batch-type scripts, XMail provides a command-line tool called Ctrl-Clnt.exe. Following is an example using CtrlClnt.exe to list the individual users of a domain:

```
$ CtrlClnt -u admin -p password -s 192.168.1.2 userlist mydomain.com
"devspace.com"   "someuser"    "apassword"       "U"
"devspace.com"   "anotheruser"        "password.2" "U"
```

The options `-u`, `-p`, and `-s` are used to identify the administrator identifier, password, and XMail server, respectively. The command `userlist` and domain `mydomain.com` are specified without using quotes. That is okay because XMail will automatically add the quotes. The only time quotes are necessary is if a buffer contains a space.

For scripts, the `CtrlClnt.exe` application is perfectly acceptable. However, using scripts is not acceptable if the scripts are exposed as CGI applications. Scripts exposed as CGI scripts are security loopholes. Therefore, the better choice is to use a programming language such as Python. The approach taken in this book is to create a Python module that wraps the XMail admin protocol. The Python wrapper class is found on the DVD in the directory `/packages/xmail/PyXMail`. By using the Python wrapper class, you can create scripts for command-line use or CGI use. Following is an example that uses the Python wrapper classes to list the users of a domain:

```
xmc = PyXMail.XMailController( 'admin', 'password', '192.168.1.2')
if xmc.connect() == True :
    print xmc.domainlist()
    xmc.disconnect()
```

The class `PyXMail.XMailController` is created and the administrator identifier, password, and XMail server are passed in the constructor. The method `connect` is called to log in and initialize the client. If a connection is successful, then methods can be called that are used to manipulate the XMail server configuration. An example method is `domainlist` to retrieve all the domains managed by the XMail server. Finally, when all configuration operations have been executed, the method `disconnect` is called to terminate the connection to the XMail server.

Technique: Adding a Domain

In XMail, managing domains means managing e-mail domains such as `dev-space.com`, which would be part of the e-mail address `osswin@devspace.com`.

XMail server can manage as many domains as required. However, no e-mails will be sent to XMail server if the DNS Mailing Exchange (MX) record is not assigned for a particular domain. To assign the MX record, read the documentation of the DNS server as it is a topic beyond the scope of this book.

Manual Configuration

The domains in XMail are stored in two locations: `domains.tab` and individual directories. Following is an example `domains.tab` file where each line contains a single identifier that represents a domain:

```
"xmailserver.test"
"devspace.com"
```

Each domain in the `domains.tab` file will have an associated subdirectory underneath the `xmail-[version number]/mailroot/domains` directory. If a domain is deleted from the `domains.tab` file because of a domain deletion, the domain subdirectory is not deleted. This is done to make sure that if any still waiting user e-mails have not been picked up, the administrator can manually move them.

Configuration Using XPAI

When using XPAI, domains are managed and a new domain can be added. Figure 9.6 shows how to use XPAI to create a new domain.

FIGURE 9.6 HTML page used to add and manage domains.

The Web page in Figure 9.6 is generated when you are logged in as administrator and click the Manage Mail Domains menu item. To add a new domain, click the Create New Domain link. Another Web page will be generated asking for the domain name and postmaster password as shown in Figure 9.7.

The first text box is used to define the domain name. An example domain is `mydomain.com`, or `local.mydomain.com`. The other two text boxes are used to define the password of the postmaster account. The postmaster account is created by default by

FIGURE 9.7 HTML page used to add a new domain.

XPAI and is used to route all e-mails when they do not have an account or contain potential errors. The Spamassassin checkbox is used to associate each user in the domain with the Spamassassin spam-filtering program. We recommend that you don't use Spamassassin because it is more complicated to set up and get running on the Windows platform. Later in this chapter, we'll outline another spam program.

Configuration Using Python

Adding a domain using the Python class wrapper involves calling the `adddomain` method:

```
xmc = XMailController( 'admin', 'apassword', '192.168.1.2')
if xmc.connect() == True :
    try :
        print xmc.adddomain( 'domain.com')
    except XMailError, err:
        print err
    xmc.disconnect()
```

The method `adddomain` has one parameter that represents the domain to be added.

Technique: Adding a User to a Domain

For each domain, there are users that can receive e-mail. With XMail, there are two types of users: regular users and mailing list users. A *regular user* is a user that can send and receive e-mails. *Mailing list users* are in a group that receives broadcast e-mails usually geared to a specific topic.

Manual Configuration

When configuring individual users like the domain, there is a central mail account file and a subdirectory. All users are stored in the following example `mailusers.tab` file:

```
"devspace.com"    "user"    "1d08040c09"    1    "user"    "U"
"devspace.com"    "me"      "461a0a153e4w"   2    "me"      "U"
```

For the file `mailusers.tab`, each line represents the individual users. The meaning of the individual fields are explained as follows:

devspace.com: Defines the domain for which the user will receive e-mails. The domain identifier must be an already existing domain handled by XMail.

user: Defines the user identifier that e-mail can be sent to. For example, if an e-mail address is `user@devspace.com`, then the user identifier is user.

1d08040c09: Defines the password of the user used to relay e-mails or pick up the e-mail using POP3. The password identifier is generated using the XMCrypt utility as shown when generating the admin password example.

1: Defines a unique identifier, which cannot be zero.

user: Defines the identifier of the subdirectory where the user's incoming e-mails will be stored.

U: An identifier that can either have the value U for user or M for a mailing list account.

The way e-mail is stored in XMail is a bit tricky. The identifier used to identify the subdirectory where e-mail for an individual is stored is a subdirectory of the domain subdirectory. For example, the user `user@devspace.com` e-mail directory is `xmail-[version number]/mailroot/domains/devspace.com/user`.

In the user's subdirectory are other subdirectories. The naming of the subdirectories depends entirely on the technique used to store the e-mails. There are two different delivery methods: Maildir and mailbox. For both formats, the individual e-mails are stored as individual files for performance and stability purposes. The Maildir format is based on the creation of three subdirectories underneath the user's directory: new, cur, and temp. The purpose of these subdirectories relates to how the individual e-mails are processed. It is possible for another mail user agent (MUA) to operate on the files when using the Maildir format. The mailbox format has only a single subdirectory and all the incoming e-mails are stored in that directory.

The Maildir format is the default format on Unix and mailbox is the default format on Windows. The following command-line options for the XMail server determines which mail format to use:

-MM: Runs XMail server to use the Maildir format.

-Mm: Runs XMail server to use the mailbox format.

When editing the users or the domains manually, XMail server must be restarted to become aware of the changes. It is better to use XPAI or the Python XMail admin protocol wrapper to manipulate the user and domain database.

Configuration Using XPAI

Adding a user using XPAI is a two-step process. The first step is to select the domain where the user will be added. The second step is to add the user to the currently managed domain. Figure 9.8 shows the page used to edit a domain and make it the managed domain.

FIGURE 9.8 Page used to manage a domain by clicking on the domain properties link.

After you select a domain to manage, the XPAI menu on the left side of the screen shows Selected Domain: (and the name of the domain) about halfway down the menu. To add an individual user, click the Manage Users link and the XPAI HTML page changes as shown in Figure 9.9.

FIGURE 9.9 Page used to manage and add users to a domain.

Click the Add New User link to open the Create New User in Domain page as shown in Figure 9.10.

The User Name text box identifies the user to be added. By default, the user identifier will also be the subdirectory identifier. The two text boxes for the User Password are used to enter the password associated with the user. The User Type is assigned by selecting one of the three radio buttons. The default user type is User, which means a regular user. The other types relate to a mailing list and how it works. The type Mailing List means that anyone, even those who are not on the mailing list, can post something. This type of mailing list should be avoided because it is an open invitation for spammers. The type Mailing List (Closed) means that only those who are registered on the mailing list are allowed to potentially post. It is a potential post because when a user is added, the ability to post or only receive e-mail is defined. The checkbox for Spamassassin should be ignored because it is

FIGURE 9.10 Page showing how to define the properties associated with a user.

only useful on the Linux/BSD platforms. After all the values have been set, you can click the Submit button. At that point, the user is added and can receive and send e-mails or distributed e-mails.

Configuration Using Python

Adding a user to the domain involves using the Python class wrapper and calling the method adduser as shown in the following example:

```
xmc = XMailController( 'admin', 'apassword', '192.168.1.2')
if xmc.connect() == True :
   try :
      print xmc.adduser( 'domain', 'user', 'password', 'U')
   except XMailError, err:
      print err
   xmc.disconnect()
```

The method adduser has four parameters: domain, user, password, and U. The first parameter domain is the domain that the user will be added to. The second parameter user is the username identifier. The third parameter password is the password in clear text. The fourth parameter U specifies the user as a normal user account. The other variation of the fourth parameter is the letter M, which specifies the user as a mailing list user account.

Managing the User's Configuration File

For every user that XMail manages, there is an associated `user.tab` file. The `user.tab` file contains items that describe the user, and variables that override global default values. The values are defined using a quote-enclosed set of buffers separated by spaces. Following is a list of possible `user.tab` file items:

`RealName`: Identifies a full descriptive username.

`HomePage`: Identifies the home page of the user.

`MaxMBSize`: Specifies the maximum size that the mailbox can be in kilobytes. If the limit is exceeded, the user cannot receive any additional e-mail.

`CloseML`: Specifies whether or not the mailing list is open to subscribed users only. This only applies to e-mail accounts that are mailing lists.

`ListSender`: Identifies the mailing list administrator that is sent with every e-mail.

`SmtpPerms`: Specifies the permissions that are used when the user sends e-mail. For more details about this key, see the earlier "Technique: Controlling Relay" section.

`ReceiveEnable`: Specifies whether the e-mail account can receive e-mails. A value of 1 means the user can receive e-mails, whereas a value of 0 means the user cannot receive e-mails.

`PopEnable`: Specifies whether the e-mail account can fetch e-mails using POP3. A value of 1 means the user can use POP3, whereas a value of 0 means the user cannot use POP3.

`UseReplyTo`: Specifies whether the mailing list account is set as `Reply To:`. If the value is 1, then a `Reply To:` e-mail field header is generated so that whenever an e-mail client clicks Reply, the mailing list account is set to default. The `From:` field is set to the e-mail address of the original creator of the e-mail. If the value is set to 0, then the `Reply To:` field header is not generated and all replies are sent to the original creator of the e-mail.

`MaxMessageSize`: Defines the maximum size of an individual message that the user can relay via the server.

`DisableEmitAuthUser`: Specifies whether to send the `X-Auth-User` e-mail header for authenticated users. A value of 0 means that emission is enabled, and a value of 1 means that emission is disabled.

Technique: Assigning User Filters and Properties

By adding a domain and a user and setting up the MX record properly, you create a working e-mail server. The user can pick up and send their e-mail. An administrator, however, needs to create scripts that can control how the server processes e-mail. When an e-mail arrives or is sent, XMail server can filter the e-mail on a domain or user basis.

The individual scripts can be edited using the XMail admin protocol, but because only user filters can be edited, it does not make sense to use the XMail admin protocol. Using the XMail Admin protocol for file editing is a tedious process.

SMTP Message Filters

When an e-mail is sent to the XMail server, it is received and then can be acted upon. There are two types of filters: prefilters and domain filters.

Prefilter Filter

A *prefilter* will filter a message before any further processing is undertaken. The prefilter is useful when you want to determine the validity of the overall e-mail message and the source of the e-mail message.

The filters are added to the files `filters.pre-data.tab` and `filters.post-data.tab`. The `filters.pre-data.tab` file is executed after the SMTP client has sent the DATA tag, and the server has not responded. Essentially, at this stage, the SMTP client and server will have exchanged an identifier stating whom the e-mail message is from, and to whom the e-mail message is being sent. A filter program could then stop any further communications. Adding this filter is useful when stopping spammers who send e-mail without valid data.

The `filters.post-data.tab` is executed when the SMTP connection has sent all the data. However, the final server DATA message has not been sent. At this point, the filter program could run a spam or virus checker and modify or reject the message.

For either file, each line represents a command as follows:

```
"c:\Python22\python.exe" "c:\bin\mailroot\scripts\smtpfilter.py"
"@@FILE"
```

The double quote-enclosed and space-separated buffers represent a command to be executed. The first buffer represents an executable that is executed. Because the filter scripts are all Python-based, the first buffer is the Python interpreter. The second buffer is the Python script that is to be executed. The buffers thereafter are all command-line parameters that the Python script will process.

The example command file has a special notation for a command-line option. The double ampersand represents an escape sequence to replace the buffer with the contents of an XMail variable. The different XMail variables available in this context are defined as follows:

@@FILE: Identifies the filename of the e-mail message that has been temporarily written to the hard disk located in the XMail spool subdirectory.

@@LOCALADDR: Identifies the local IP address and port that has received the e-mail.

@@REMOTEADDR: Identifies the remote IP address and port of the e-mail server that is sending the e-mail.

@@USERAUTH: Name of authenticated user, if the user is authenticated; otherwise, a "`-`" is generated.

When the script is being executed, XMail expects a return code. The return code is used by XMail to determine what to do with the e-mail message. A script could delete or modify an e-mail. Following are a list of return codes that can be used:

3: Reject the e-mail message.

16: Stop any further filter message processing.

Domain Filters

A script can also filter an e-mail for a domain or a user. The filters are added to the files `filters.in.tab` and `filters.out.tab`, which are located in the `mailroot` directory. Each of these files contains directives to activate filters based on some conditions. Following is an example of how to define a filter that will process e-mails as they are received:

```
"*" "*" "0.0.0.0/0" "0.0.0.0/0" "domain-filter.tab"
```

There are five double quote-enclosed space-separated buffers. The first four buffers are used to define a condition that when matched will cause the fifth buffer, which represents an execution file, to be called. This format is powerful because rule sets can be defined to execute different scripts in different contexts. For example, one set of scripts are executed for e-mail from trusted senders; another set of scripts are executed for the rest of users.

Following is an example rule that replaces the individual buffers with an identifier that represents the purpose of the buffer:

```
"sender"  "recipient"  "remote-address"  "local-address"  "filename"
```

The purpose of each item is explained as follows:

sender: Identifies the sender of an e-mail based on the sender e-mail addresses present in the e-mail being received. The asterisk (`*`) is used as a wildcard. A single asterisk results in matching all senders. It is possible to identify a domain by adding the asterisk before the ampersand sign, such as `*@mydomain.com`.

`recipient`: Identifies the receiver of an e-mail based on the receiver e-mail addresses presents in the e-mail being received. The wildcard selection rules are identical to the `sender` buffer.

`remote-address`: Identifies an IP address and associated subnet of a sender, which is matched to the actual IP of the e-mail server sending the e-mail.

`local-address`: Identifies an IP address and associated subnet of a receiver, which is matched to the actual IP of the e-mail server receiving the e-mail address. This part of the rule is only useful if the server where XMail is running is multihomed.

`filename`: Identifies the name of a file that contains multiple commands to be executed when the `sender`, `recipient`, `remote-address`, and `local-address` are matched.

The previously defined example rule will match every e-mail that is received by the e-mail server. When a rule is matched, the file identified by the `filename` is loaded and read. Each line within the file represents the command line of an application that is executed. The file that contains the commands must exist in `[xmail-version number]/mailroot/filters`. Following is an example command file:

```
"c:\Python22\python.exe" "c:\bin\mailroot\scripts\test.py"
"@@FILE"
```

The double quote-enclosed and space-separated buffers represent a command to be executed. The first buffer represents an executable that is executed. Because the filter scripts are all Python based, the first buffer is the Python interpreter. The second buffer is the Python script that is to be executed. The buffers thereafter are all command-line parameters that the Python script will process.

The example command file has a special notation for a command-line option. The double ampersand represents an escape sequence to replace the buffer with the contents of an XMail variable. The different XMail variables are defined as follows:

`@@FILE`: Identifies the filename of the e-mail message that has been temporarily written to the hard disk located in the XMail spool subdirectory.

`@@FROM`: Identifies the sender of the e-mail address.

`@@LOCALADDR`: Identifies the local IP address and port that has received the e-mail.

`@@MSGID`: Identifies the unique message ID assigned by XMail to the incoming e-mail message.

@@MSGREF: Identifies the reference SMTP message ID.

@@RCPT: Identifies the receiver of the e-mail message.

@@REMOTEADDR: Identifies the remote IP address and port of the e-mail server that is sending the e-mail.

@@RFROM: Identifies the sender of the e-mail address with any aliases resolved, if possible.

@@RRCPT: Identifies the real receiver of the e-mail with an alias being resolved to the true e-mail address if possible.

The file `filters.out.tab` has the same structure as the `filters.in.tab` file. The difference is that instead of filtering incoming e-mails, outgoing e-mails are filtered.

When the script is being executed, XMail expects a return code. The return code is used by XMail to determine what to do with the e-mail message. A script can delete an or modify an e-mail. Following are a list of return codes that can be used:

0: Success, everything is okay and XMail should continue processing `filters.in.tab` or `filters.out.tab`.

4: The e-mail message is rejected, not frozen, and no notification is sent to the user. Essentially the e-mail disappears and no record of having it ever appear is recorded.

5: The message is rejected and depending on the `server.tab` key `RemoveSpool-Error` value, the e-mail message is either deleted or frozen. There is no notice of rejection sent to the user. When an e-mail is frozen, it is kept in the spool and moved to the frozen messages directory. An administrator could then manually investigate which frozen e-mails should be reprocessed or deleted. XPAI can be used to manage frozen e-mails.

6: The message is rejected and XMail deletes or freezes the e-mail message. A notification of the message being rejected is sent to sender of the e-mail.

7: The message has been modified and the XMail server reloads the e-mail message to process the changes.

16: By default, the XMail server processes all matched rules in the files `filters.in.tab` and `filters.out.tab`. Returning an exit code of 16 tells XMail server to stop processing any further rules. This is very useful when using rules for trusted and untrusted senders.

The return codes 0, 4, 5, 6, and 7 are base return codes that determine the state of the e-mail message. The return code 16 is used to stop processing rules and is a special exit code that can be returned in addition to the base return codes. The way to return multiple return codes is to add them. For example, if a message has been modified and no further rules should be applied, then the return codes 7 and 16 should be added to generate the return code of 23.

User Filters

Users can have their e-mail account associated with filter files similar to the domain filters. The difference with a user filter file is that the e-mail message can never be rejected. The e-mail message can be modified and used to generate another message. Creating user filters is useful when creating automatic reply messages when a user is on vacation. Another difference with user filters is that they are time restricted. That means a script must execute within a specific period.

A user filter is defined in the file `mailproc.tab` that is stored in the local subdirectory of the user as defined in the "Technique: Adding a User to a Domain" section. The file `mailproc.tab` file contains several lines that represent actions to be taken when an e-mail arrives for the specific user. An example `mailproc.tab` file is shown as follows:

```
"redirect" "user@domain.com"
"mailbox"
"external" "0" "3000" "c:\Python23\python.exe"
        "c:\bin\mailroot\scripts\test.py" "@@FILE"
```

The buffers `redirect`, `mailbox`, and `external` are all commands that manipulate the e-mail that has arrived to a particular user. The buffers on the same line after the command relate to the command itself. The following commands are available:

`external`: A command that allows the execution of a script in the same manner as shown in the "Domain Filters" section. The second buffer "0" defines the priority of the script when it is executed, where 0 is normal, -1 lower priority, and +1 higher priority. The third buffer "3000" defines the timeout in milliseconds that XMail should wait before continuing to process the `mailproc.tab` file. The timeout is only necessary when using the `@@FILE` identifier as a parameter for a script. The fourth and following parameters are identical to the parameters as explained in the "Domain Filters" section.

`lredirect`: A command that redirects the e-mail to the person identified by the second parameter, which in the case of the preceding code snippet is user@domain.com. The difference with the `lredirect` command in contrast to the `redirect` command is that the receiver user@domain.com sees the message as being sent from the mailbox doing the redirection and not the original sender.

`mailbox`: A command that redirects the e-mail to the local mailbox so that the end user can pick it up using POP3. If the `mailproc.tab` file is not present, then this command is assumed. If the file `mailproc.tab` is present and the mailbox command does not exist, then there will be no e-mail stored locally.

`redirect`: A command that redirects the e-mail to the person identified by the second parameter, which in the case of the example `mailproc.tab` file is `user@domain.com`.

`smtprelay`: A command that redirects the e-mail to the e-mail server specified by the second parameter. Using `smtprelay` is like redirecting an e-mail, except that the e-mail is directly sent to a specific server. This is useful when the e-mail server where the e-mail is being sent is not the server referenced by the DNS MX record.

Technique: Using Scripting and Local E-mails to Implement Autoresponders

One of the things that people would want is the ability to define an autoresponder that responds to the sender when an e-mail is received. By default XMail does not have an autoreply mechanism. By using filter scripts, it's easy to add a reply. A user can add a reply script as a user filter and then it reacts to every e-mail. The catch, however, is that asking a user to add a reply script is a very demanding task and not generally recommended.

The purpose of this section is not the reply script, but to show how an administrator can add script architecture to react to specific commands such as generating a reply script.

Defining a Command Account

A reply script is added to the user filter file using the `external` command. Again, the problem of adding the script is that a normal user would have no idea what to do. Having a normal user phone the administrator is also a problem in that it would be very tedious for both the administrator and user. The solution used in this book is to create a command account that accepts via e-mail commands to manipulate the reply buffer. You could also use a Web page, but that is left as an extra exercise for you.

The command account is a generic account that is used as a filter to receive commands from users of the local domain. The command account has an empty `mailproc.tab` file because the no one will receive the e-mails sent to it so they should not be stored. The only reason to have a `mailbox` command entry in the `mailproc.tab` file is for command-tracking purposes.

The command account is associated with an entry in the domain filter file `filters.in.tab` as follows:

```
"*" "*" "0.0.0.0/0" "0.0.0.0/0" "domain-filter.tab"
*@mydomain.com command@mydomain.com "192.168.1.0/256"
     "0.0.0.0/0" "domain-commands.tab"
```

The second line explicitly filters for the `command` account of the domain `mydo-main.com`. The second line says to execute the file `domain-commands.tab` if the sender is part of the `mydomain.com`, sends mail to the account `command`, and is on the local network `192.168.1.0`. Filtering based on the sender and network address ensures that only local users will ever send commands that influence the settings of the individual users on the domain `mydomain.com`. Not using the filtering provided by XMail would mean having to introduce a username and password mechanism, which is more work. On a very large intranet, a username and password mechanism may still be required.

Processing E-mail for the Command Account

Within the file `domain-commands.tab` are the programs used to process any e-mail intended for the domain. There could be commands to process reply requests, mailing list requests, or information requests, such as a file on a hard disk. The idea is that the account is used to process e-mails in an automated manner. The following illustrates an example `domain-commands.tab` file:

```
"c:\python23\python.exe"  "c:\bin\mailroot\scripts\commands.py"
    "@@FILE" "c:\bin\mailroot\scripts" "@@FROM" "@@RCPT"
```

The `commands.py` Python script is executed, which will process the contents of an e-mail. The first, third, and fourth command-line options are XMail escape characters. The second command-line option is a hardcoded parameter that defines the root directory of the scripts. This is necessary because the `command.py` script will copy files and call up other files.

Following is an example e-mail message body that is sent to the `command` account and is used to activate the automatic reply message:

```
action: reply
=====
Thanks for sending me email, but I am away at the moment
and will be back soon.
```

The command to activate the automatic reply message is the identifier `action`, with the value of `reply`. The five equals signs all in one line are used to define a break. Everything that follows the break is a custom buffer used to define an e-mail response. The file `commands.py` needs to extract the command identifier `reply` and the custom response as a buffer.

The implementation of the `commands.py` file is shown as follows:

```
#!c:/Python24/python.exe

import sys, string, os, shutil, xreadlines

writeFlag = False
command = 0
fileobject = open( sys.argv[ 1])
replyFile = None
for line in fileobject :
    if string.find( line, 'action') != -1 :
        foundcommand = string.strip( line[ 7:])
        if foundcommand == "reply" :
          command = 100
          dirbuffer = '%s/local/%s' % (sys.argv[ 2], sys.argv[ 3])
          filebuffer = '%s/reply.txt' % dirbuffer
          try :
              replyFile = open( filebuffer, 'w')
          except Exception, inst :
             os.makedirs( dirbuffer)
             replyFile = open( filebuffer, 'w')
          srcfilename = '%s/server/reply.sh' % sys.argv[ 2]
          shutils.copyfile( srcfilename, dirbuffer)
    elif string.find( line, '=====') != -1 :
        writeFlag = True
        continue
    if writeFlag == True :
        if command == 100 :
          replyFile.write( line)

if writeFlag == True :
    replyFile.close()

fileobject.close()
sys.exit( 0)
```

The e-mail message is opened using the open command and retrieves the first
command-line argument using the method sys.argv[1]. Then the individual lines
are read in loop using the xreadlines.xreadlines method. A command is found
using the method string.find, which tests to see if the variable line contains the
identifier action.

After the identifier `action` has been found, the nature of the exact command is extracted and any extra spaces are stripped. Then another condition is used to test which command is being executed. The identifier `reply` references the exact command to define a reply for a specific user. The Python code within the conditional `foundcommand` block relates to copying a file from a generic location to specific user location.

To read the custom response buffer separated by the five equals signs, the `writeFlag` is used. If the five equals signs are found, then every e-mail line thereafter is part of the buffer that should be used for the custom response.

Processing User Commands Automatically

The `commands.py` file copies a file from a neutral location to the location of the XMail user's local subdirectory. The idea behind this strategy is to have the user filter automatically process commands by checking for files in a subdirectory. If no files exist, then no commands need to be processed. The advantage of this approach is that the user's filter file `mailproc.tab` doesn't need to be updated by the `commands.py` script.

The following text block shows the contents of the user's `mailproc.tab` file:

```
"mailbox"
"external" "0" "3000" "c:\cygwin\bin\bash.exe"
    "c:\bin\mailroot\scripts\localauto.sh"
    "c:\bin\mailroot\scripts\local\test" "@@FILE"
    "@@FROM" "@@RCPT"
```

The external command executes the shell interpreter `bash.exe` and executes the script `localauto.sh`. The first command-line option is the path where the user scripts that need to be executed are located. The second, third, and fourth command-line options are standard XMail escape identifiers.

The script `localauto.sh` is written in BASH to show that it is possible to use BASH in an XMail context, and that it is simpler to dynamically execute scripts using BASH. Following are the details for the script `localauto.sh`:

```
#!c:/cygwin/bin/bash.exe
cd "$1"
for filename in *
do
    `$1/$filename $*`
done
```

The script does two things. First it changes the directory to the local working directory. Second, it executes all the files found in the local directory . If there are no files, nothing will happen. If the e-mail is sent, a reply script executes and returns a reply e-mail.

For all the listings in this chapter, the first line with #! characters have referenced actual executable applications used to interpret the execution of the command. The first line is extremely important when BASH scripts execute other scripts because otherwise an execution error will be generated.

Sending Local E-mail

When the reply script executes, it needs to send e-mail locally, as a user filter has no mechanism built in to send a reply. XMail in the binary distribution has a program called sendmail.exe, which when executed, locally drops an e-mail into the XMail spool for sending purposes. Following is an example script that shows how to generate a response e-mail:

```
XMAIL_ROOT=c:/bin/mailroot

tmpfile=$(mcookie)
tmppath="$1/$tmpfile.tmp"
responsefile="$1/local/$4/reply.txt"

echo -n Date: > $tmppath
date --rfc >> $tmppath
echo X-Mailer:Auto-Reply 1.0 >> $tmppath
echo To:$3 >> $tmppath
echo "Subject: Auto Reply" >> $tmppath
echo >> $tmppath
cat  $responsefile >> $tmppath

$XMAIL_ROOT/bin/sendmail -t -F$3 < $tmppath

rm $tmppath
```

The command mcookie is used to generate a temporary filename to store the contents of the e-mail that will be generated as a response. The temporary filename is stored in the variable tmppath. An e-mail that is sent by the XMail sendmail.exe application only needs a few header elements and a body. The resulting generated e-mail has four header elements: Date, X-Mailer, To, and Subject. The header of the e-mail is separated from the body by an empty carriage return and line file. The body of the e-mail is the reply response file.

If an autoreply is active, whenever anyone sends an e-mail to the command account, the following file is generated:

```
Date:Fri, 13 Feb 2004 22:24:26 +0100
X-Mailer: Auto-Reply 1.0
To:chg@devspace.com
Subject:Auto Reply

Thanks for sending me email, but I am away at the moment and
will be back soon.
```

After the e-mail has been generated, it is sent using the `sendmail.exe` command. After the command has been executed, the generated e-mail is added to the outgoing spooler. The application `sendmail.exe` supports the following command-line options:

-f: Sets the sender of the e-mail address.

-F: Sets the extended sender of the e-mail message.

-t: Extracts the recipients of the e-mail address

--input-file: Loads the message from a file instead of the standard input, but expects the message to be in Request For Comment (RFC) format.

--xinput-file: Loads the message from a file instead of the standard input, but expects the message to be in XMail format. The XMail format has some additional headers, and is the default format when XMail processes e-mail.

--rcpt-file: Defines the file where the recipients of the e-mail are listed. This command-line option is used in combination with the -t command-line option.

XMail Mail Format

Whenever a script processes an e-mail, the script will see the e-mail in the XMail file format. Following is an example e-mail message in XMail format (some parts have been abbreviated for clarity purposes):

```
192.168.1.2:2969;192.168.1.2:225;Fri, 13 Feb 2004 22:24:23 +0100
dom.com
S24415
MAIL FROM:<user@dom.com> BODY=8BITMIME
RCPT TO:<test@dom.com>
<<MAIL-DATA>>
Received: from neptune.local (192.168.1.241:2969)
    by devspace.com with [XMail 1.21 (Win32/Ix86) ESMTP Server]
    id <S24415> for <test@dom.com> from <chg@dom.com>;
    Fri, 13 Feb 2004 22:24:23 +0100
Received: FROM localhost ([127.0.0.1]) BY neptune.local
```

```
WITH ESMTP ; Fri, 13 Feb 2004 22:28:07 +0100
From: "user" <user@dom.com>
To: test@dom.com
Subject: Test
Date: Fri, 13 Feb 2004 22:28:06 +0100
Content-Type: text/plain; charset=iso-8859-1
X-Mailer: Some application

Test
```

The first five lines are the XMail-specific settings. For e-mail processing purposes, these lines cannot be deleted. If the script is a domain filter that the lines can be modified, but XMail must be notified by sending the appropriate return code. The e-mail message is after the buffer <<MAIL-DATA>>. The e-mail header data can be modified, but should only be modified if the XMail-specific settings are modified. The message body can be modified without much concern; in the case of the example code, the message body is the text Test.

A listing of tools that can be used with XMail server appears at the Web site http://www.xmailserver.org. Specifically the tools econv or rbuild can be used to convert the e-mail from XMail to RFC and vice versa.

TIP

Technique: Mail Scanning, Verified Responder, and Other Tasks

XMail provides many services, however, many administrators will want to extend the functionality using scripts. Although the individual scripts are beyond the scope of this book, you can find the tools at *http://www.xmailserver.org*. It is highly advised that the XMail user look at these add-ons for additional scripts to perform operations such as scanning e-mail for viruses or executable attachments.

This book does not delve into the details of implementing a scanner for viruses or attachments because ASSP does that automatically and is recommended.

TIP

Technique: Managing Mailing Lists

Mailing lists are effective communication mechanisms used to broadcast information to many readers. The included mailing list functionality in XMail manages mailing lists, but does not automatically allow a user to subscribe or unsubscribe from the mailing list. To automate this, you use a command e-mail account to process mailing list requests.

Manual Configuration

An account is a mailing list account when the user is marked with an `M` in the `mailusers.tab` file as follows:

```
"dom.com" "testml" "1100161108094b5c5c" 15 "testml" "M"
```

A mailing list account is created with a password, but the password is not required because e-mails will not be stored on the server. The e-mail account `testml` will be located as a subdirectory below the domain `dom.com` subdirectory. The user subdirectory has to contain two files: `user.tab` and `mlusers.tab`.

The details of the `user.tab` file were discussed in the "Managing the User's Configuration File" section. Specifically for the mailing list, the variables `ClosedML`, `SmtpPerms`, and `MaxMBSize` should be set. Otherwise, the mailing list will be susceptible to spammers.

The file `mlusers.tab` contains several lines that reference the users that make up the mailing list. Following is an example `mlusers.tab` file:

```
user@dom.com    "RW"
another@dom.com    "R"
```

There are two users in the mailing list: `user@dom.com` and `another@dom.com`. The e-mail address `user@dom.com` has associated `RW` letters allowing both posting and receiving of e-mails. The e-mail address `another@dom.com` has an associated `R` allowing the user to only receive e-mails.

Configuration Using XPAI

A mailing list account can be added using XPAI, except that there are two steps. The first step is to create the account using the steps outlined by the "Technique: Adding a User to a Domain" section. The difference is that the Mailing List or Mailing List (Closed) radio button should be chosen on the Create New User in Domain page (refer to Figure 9.10).

After the user has been added to the domain, the mailing list subscribers are adding by selecting the user (as shown previously in Figure 9.9) and then editing the user's properties. After a mailing list user has been selected in the menu, you can use the Manage Mailing List Users link to add individual e-mail readers. Figure 9.11 shows the Web page to use to add a user to a mailing list.

This Web page can also be used to delete users from the mailing list.

FIGURE 9.11 Web page showing how to add users to a mailing list.

Configuration Using Python

A mailing list user account is added using the add user code sample, except instead of the fourth parameter being a U it is an M. To add mailing list e-mail addresses, the following code is used:

```
xmc = XMailController( 'admin', 'apassword', '192.168.1.2')
if xmc.connect() == True :
    try :
        print xmc.addmluser( 'domain', 'user', 'addr', 'R')
    except XMailError, err:
        print err
    xmc.disconnect()
```

The method `addmluser` has four parameters: `domain`, `user`, `addr`, and `R`. The parameters `domain` and `user` relate to the mailing list account and domain. The parameter `addr` is the e-mail address that is to be added to the mailing list. The parameter `R` relates to the permissions of the user being added to the mailing list, which can either be `R` or `RW`.

Technique: Routing and Managing Domains and Aliases

XMail is very powerful in that e-mails can be easily routed if the user or domain does not exist. For example, if an e-mail arrives for someotheruser@domain.com, an e-mail alias can be used that routes the e-mail to a user that the system knows about. Alternatively, if the domain does not exist, the e-mail can be rerouted to another domain.

Adding an Alias

A user can define an alias that XMail exposes as an e-mail account, but e-mail addressed to the alias will be routed to the user. For example an alias exposed that is rerouted to the e-mail account user allows someone else to send e-mail to the address exposed@domain.com. Aliases are specific to a user in a domain.

All user aliases are added to the file aliases.tab as follows:

```
"xmailserver.test"  "root"  "xmailuser"
"xmailserver.test"  "postmaster"  "xmailuser"
```

For the file aliases.tab, each line represents an alias definition and requires three buffers. The first buffer xmailserver.test defines the domain where the alias will be defined. The second buffer root is the alias that is defined for the domain. The third and last buffer xmailuser is the actual account that will process the e-mail received by the alias root.

An alias can be added using the XPAI application and using the Python class. The following example shows how to add an alias using Python:

```
xmc = XMailController( 'admin', 'apassword', '192.168.1.2')
if xmc.connect() == True :
    try :
        print xmc.addalias( 'domain', 'alias', 'account')
    except XMailError, err:
        print err
    xmc.disconnect()
```

The method addalias has three parameters, which are defined in the same order as the configuration file aliases.tab.

Slowing Down Spam Using Aliases

Using an alias is a great way to control spam. Most people assume that if you are given one e-mail address then you can only use that single e-mail address. You can literally define millions of e-mail addresses by using aliases. This is useful when you want to control who sends you e-mail and in which context.

The common problem in controlling spam is that some legitimate e-mail is considered spam. For example, if you buy books from Amazon.com, you'll probably receive many spam e-mails that hijack Amazon and send out e-mail that contains references to Amazon or another legitimate business. A spam application will have problems distinguishing the true Amazon.com e-mails from the spammed e-mail.

The solution is to use an alias when communicating with Amazon. That alias could be Amazon@domain.com, or it could be some other combination of words. Never should the alias be a combination of your private e-mail address and the identifier Amazon. That sort of combination makes it easy for a spammer to deduce your private e-mail address.

To separate the true Amazon e-mails from the fake Amazon e-mails, the sender and receiver of the e-mails must match. For example, if Amazon sends you an e-mail, then filtering on e-mail with the Amazon domain will result in a positive match. Any other e-mails need to go through the spam filter.

TIP

From the previous paragraph, we're not saying that companies are responsible for spam. The reference is based on a previous incidence that occurred with the developer of the alias spam solution. He created e-mail aliases for each company that he dealt with. Then one alias that belonged to a reputable company (not Amazon) received a large number of spams because the company was hacked or someone internally sold the e-mail database. The point is that spammers employ less than reputable techniques.

The best strategy for dispersing aliases is to create a Web site where users of a domain can dynamically create their own aliases. That way a user will know their own aliases and manage them. Also note that this strategy is a starting point for managing the spam problem.

Adding a User Alias

Another way of handling a user's alias is to add the user as a command alias. The user alias described in the previous sections used the XMail built-in mechanism. Essentially the built-in mechanism is an SMTP relay to a specific user account. A command alias is like a user filter file, in that e-mails could be rerouted, preprocessed, or use any other external command. It is important to realize that when a command alias is used, there is no e-mail account that the e-mails will be sent to.

For example, if an e-mail was sent to commandalias@domain.com, and the user commandalias did not exist as an alias or user account, then to add a command alias a file with the name commandalias.tab has to be stored in the directory [xmail-version number]/mailroot/cmdaliases/domain.com. The contents of the commandalias.tab file can be anything that is described in the "User Filters" section. The only command that is not supported is mailbox because there is no default mailbox.

If a script uses the @@FILE *escape identifier, the file cannot be edited and should be treated as read only.*

Adding a Domain Alias

A domain alias is very similar to a user alias, except that a domain alias is used to process e-mails for domains not managed by XMail server. For example, if an e-mail arrives destined for the e-mail address user@sub.domain.com, and sub.domain.com is not managed by XMail server, custom domain mail processing will start.

XMail will look in decreasing importance order for the files sub.domain.com.tab, .domain.com.tab, .com.tab, and .tab within the directory [xmail-version number] /mailroot/custdomains. The individual files are structured the same way as described in the "User Filters" section. The only command that is not supported is mailbox because there is no default mailbox.

If a script uses the @@FILE *escape identifier, the file cannot be edited and should be treated as read only.*

Technique: Changing a Port, Logging Requests, Performance Tuning, and Controlling Relay

Many of the characteristics of how XMail executes are managed by command-line options. There are roughly two dozen command-line options, which are grouped in different sections for simplicity purposes.

Each section is identified by a server: XMail Core, POP, SMTP, SMail, PSync, Finger, Ctrl, and LMail. Each server serves a specific functionality, which for the administrator is beyond the scope of this book. The only servers that are not obvious and need explaining are SMTP and SMail. The SMTP server receives an external e-mail; SMail is responsible for redirecting the e-mail locally or remotely. The following sections illustrate how to manage tasks.

Changing Port Identifier

There are three main ports to manage: SMTP, POP3, and the XMail administration port (Ctrl). The command-line options to change the ports are:

- -Pp port for POP3.
- -PI ip:[port] binds the POP3 server to a specific IP address and port.
- -Sp port for SMTP.
- -SI ip[:port] binds the SMTP server to a specific IP address and port.
- -Cp port for the Ctrl port.

Logging Requests

For each server, it is possible to log the actions that each server performs. It is *highly* recommended that you activate logging so that the servers can be monitored for hacker and spammer attacks. The command-line options to log are:

- -Md (optional) activates verbose mode.
- -Pl enables POP3 logging.
- -Sl enables SMTP logging.
- -Ql enables SMAIL logging.
- -Yl enables POP3 account synchronization logging.
- -Cl enables XMail administration protocol logging.
- -Ll enables local mail logging.

Performance Tuning

To manage performance, XMail offers the possibility to manage how threads perform tasks, define the packet size, and handle queue processing. The command-line options to manage performance are:

- -MR bytes sets the size of the socket receive buffer.
- -MS bytes sets the size of the socket send buffer.
- -MD ndirs sets the number of subdirectories allocated for DNS cache files.
- -PX nthreads sets the number of threads that manage POP3 connections.
- -St timeout sets the SMTP session timeout.
- -SX nthreads sets the maximum number of threads for the SMTP server.
- -Se nsecs sets the timeout in seconds for POP3 authentication before SMTP.
- -Qn nthreads sets the number of mailer threads.
- -Qt timeout sets the timeout in seconds for filter commands that are not subject to a timeout.
- -Yt nthreads sets the number of POP3 synchronization threads.
- -Ct timeout sets the XMail administration protocol timeout.
- -CX nthreads sets the number of threads for the XMail administration protocol.
- -Ln nthreads sets the number of local mailer threads.
- -Lt timeout sets the sleep timeout in seconds for the local mailer threads.

Controlling Relay

There are multiple command-line options that control how e-mails are relayed to other servers. These options are used to manage resources so that an e-mail server will run optimally. The command-line options to control relaying are:

- -Sr maxrcpts controls the maximum number of recipients for a single SMTP message that can also be used to control spam.
- -Qt timeout sets the timeout in seconds before an e-mail relay retry is attempted.
- -Qi ratio sets the ratio of when a message reschedule occurs where numbers greater than zero and increasing cause a longer more even delivery attempt.
- -Qr nretries sets the number of times an e-mail relay is attempted.

Controlling POP3 Access

When accessing the POP3 server, it is possible to tune the timeout values and access times. The command-line options to control POP3 access are:

- -Pt timeout sets the POP3 session timeout in seconds if no commands are received.
- -Pw timeout sets the delay timeout when a POP3 login fails with each successive failure doubled.
- -Ph hangs the connection in response to a bad login.

Technique: Synchronizing with a POP3 Account

An extremely powerful technique for departments within companies, small home offices, or small corporations is the ability to synchronize local XMail accounts with remote accounts. Many companies need 100% uptime with an e-mail server and will maintain their e-mail domain on another server. However, an e-mail server on another domain will not have the features that are desired by the users. Using XMail server, it is possible to contact the other server and download the e-mails to the local account.

Manual Configuration

When XMail synchronizes external POP3 accounts, the reference information is stored in the pop3links.tab file. Following is an example pop3links.tab file:

```
"dom.com" "user" "pop.mail.yahoo.com" "user33"
    "160a17171c4b1611041100" "CLR"
"dom.com" "another" "bk.dom.com" "some" "16150a060e"
    "CLR"
```

For a pop3links.tab file, each line represents a single external POP3 link. Taking as an example the first line, each enclosed buffer is explained as follows:

dom.com: Represents the local domain that will receive the external e-mail. The domain must exist. If the domain does not exist, or you want the e-mail to be spooled, then an @ must precede the domain identifier (e.g., @dom.com). When the e-mail is spooled in such a fashion, there either needs to be a domain or a domain alias that will process the e-mail. If a question mark (e.g., `?.local`) is used instead, then the domain is appended to the incoming domain. For example, if the incoming e-mail is addressed to `some@dom.com`, then the spooled e-mail address is `some@dom.com.local`.

`user`: Identifies the user that will receive the e-mail if the domain is hosted on the local machine. If an e-mail is retrieved, it is sent without spooling to the account `user@dom.com`. However, if the domain is prefixed with an `@` character, then the e-mail is spooled to the `user@dom.com`. Finally, if the domain is prefixed with the `?` character, then the e-mail is spooled based on the `To`, `CC`, or `BCC` users concatenated with the domain `dom.com`. For example, for the first line in the code snippet preceding this list, it would be spooled to `user33@dom.com`. Note that the `user33` is only an example, and the e-mails downloaded may reference other e-mail addresses.

`pop.mail.yahoo.com`: Defines the external POP3 server where the external e-mails are located.

`user33`: Defines the username used to log on to the POP3 server.

`160a17171c4b1611041100`: Defines the password used to log on to the external POP3 server. The password text is encrypted with the application `XMCrypt.exe`.

`CLR`: Defines the technique used to authenticate the user against the POP3 server. `CLR` indicates that the password is sent via clear text to the POP3 server. `APOP` is the other authentication mechanism that does not send the password in clear text format, but fewer servers support the `APOP` technique.

The POP3 synchronization by default occurs every 120 seconds, which may be too quick for some servers. Using the `-Yi interval`, where interval is a time in seconds, command-line option, it is possible to set the synchronization to whatever time delay is required.

Configuration Using XPAI

To define an external POP3 link, an administrator has to manage both a domain and a specific user within the domain. After a user has been selected, the Manage Pop3 Links link will appear as a menu item. Figure 9.12 shows the page after the Manage Pop3 Links link is clicked.

If Figure 9.12 contained any external POP3 links, they would appear as HTML links, which can be selected and edited. To add a new external POP3 link, click the HTML link Add New POP3 Link. The page changes to appear like Figure 9.13.

Multiple text boxes are used to edit the characteristics of the POP3 server. The text box names are self-explanatory, for example, the Servername text box references the server where the external POP3 e-mails are hosted.

FIGURE 9.12 Page showing available external POP3 links.

FIGURE 9.13 Page allowing you to edit the external POP3 link.

TIP

XPAI only allows you to define an external POP3 link that is a direct import of e-mails. You cannot define an external link that includes the characters @ and & as described in the previous section.

Configuration Using Python

An external POP3 link is added using the following Python code:

```
xmc = XMailController( 'admin', 'apassword', '192.168.1.2')
if xmc.connect() == True :
    try :
        print xmc.addPOP3Link( 'domain', 'user', 'extern-server',
            'extern-username', 'extern-password', 'authtype')
    except XMailError, err:
        print err
    xmc.disconnect()
```

The method addPOP3Link has six parameters: domain, user, extern-server, extern-username, extern-password, and authtype. The parameters domain and user relate to the mailing list account and domain. You can use the @ and & characters to define more complicated processing actions. The parameters extern-server, extern-username, extern-password, and authtype relate to the external POP3 server where the e-mail is stored. The parameter authtype is the authentication mechanism to use, which can either be CLR or APOP.

Technique: Custom Authentication

Using XMail, you can implement custom authentication. For example instead of using the internal authentication provided by XMail, the user's authentication details are stored in an LDAP database. It is important to realize that XMail will still require the user to be created because details of the user are stored within XMail.

The user can be authenticated for two separate protocols: SMTP and POP3. In terms of SMTP, the authentication is only used when relaying e-mails across XMail. When using POP3 custom authentication, it is a bit more complicated because the external programs can also manipulate the user when XMail manipulates its user.

SMTP Custom Authentication

The default SMTP authentication mechanism uses clear text and the SMTP standard login. Using custom authentication, you can take advantage of the SMTP Authentication Extensions (RFC 2554).

So, for example, imagine trying to authenticate users for the domain domain.com. A file entitled domain.com.tab is stored in the directory [xmail-version number]/mailroot/userauth/smtp. The naming of the file follows the same rules as the domain filters (see the "Adding a Domain Alias" section), which means the file could be entitled com.tab or .tab. Within the domain.com.tab file are lines that represent the individual users and how they can be authenticated. Following is an example authentication file:

```
"plain"     "foouser"    "foopasswd"
"login"     "foouser"    "foopasswd"
"cram-md5"   "foouser"    "foopasswd"
```

Each line of the authentication file has three buffers. The first buffer is the type of authentication used, which can be plain, login, or cram-md5. The authentication techniques login or cram-md5 are SMTP extensions set in the e-mail client. The second buffer is the username, and the third buffer is the password in clear text format.

There is another option to use an external program in the same fashion as using external programs for the user or domain filters. Following is a declaration of the external command for an SMTP authentication file:

```
"external" "auth-name" "secret" "prog-path" "args" ".."
```

The individual buffers are explained as follows:

"external": This is a command.

"auth-name": This defines the authentication type used to validate the username and password. The authentication identifier must match the identifier that the client sends from the client to the server.

"secret": Identifies the secret phrase used with the program.

"prog-path": This defines the path of the program to execute.

"args": This buffer can be defined multiple times similar to user and domain filters, but with different escape sequences: @@CHALL specifies the server challenge string, @@SECRT specifies the secret, and @@RFILE specifies the output response file.

When an external program is executed, the program should write its response to the @@RFILE response file. Not doing so will cause the user authentication to fail.

POP3 Authentication

POP3 authentication is different from SMTP in that there are multiple operations and not just authentication. Consider adding a user to the XMail database. To keep the external user database current, commands can be added that will automatically add, authenticate, edit, or even delete a domain or user.

Custom authentication files for POP3 are stored in the directory [xmail-version number]/mailroot/userauth/pop3. POP3 authentication files are based on the domain, and follow the same naming conventions as the SMTP authentication.

The following listing shows a sample POP3 authentication file that illustrates all commands used to maintain a user database on an LDAP server. Some of the commands should look familiar from Chapter 6. The other commands are hand-coded scripts that perform the desired actions.

```
"userauth" "ldap-auth" "-u" "@@USER" "-d" "@@DOMAIN"
"useradd" "ldap-add" "-u" "@@USER" "-d" "@@DOMAIN"
     "-p" "@@PASSWD" "-P" "@@PATH"
"useredit" "ldap-add" "-u" "@@USER" "-d" "@@DOMAIN"
     "-p" "@@PASSWD" "-P" "@@PATH"
"userdel" "ldap-del" "-u" "@@USER" "-d" "@@DOMAIN"
"domaindrop" "ldap-domdrop" "-d" "@@DOMAIN"
```

The individual lines of the listing represent an action. The first buffer is the action, which can be one of the following: `userauth` to authenticate a user, `useradd` to add a user, `useredit` to edit the user details, `userdel` to delete a user, and `domaindrop` to drop the domain from the external database.

The second buffer and thereafter are the programs to execute and their associated command-line parameters. The POP3 authentication file has four escape identifiers: `@@USER` identifies the user, `@@DOMAIN` identifies the domain that is associated with the user, `@@PASSWD` is the password associated with the user, `@@PATH` identifies the path of the user.

PROJECT: ASSP

Spam is a problem that has spawned multiple strategies to control it. Some people think the solution is to use the law or to use a scheme that will cost money that will make it prohibitive to send spam. Although good ideas, they aren't the necessary solution; however, the idea of legal ramifications for sending unsolicited spam is a start.

Understanding the Spam Problem

The spam problem is similar to the bank robbery problems that were prevalent in the Old West in the United States in its early history. Instead of being safe depositories for money, more often than not banks became victims of robberies. At that time, it would seem that putting your money in a bank was a bad idea. However, sheriffs were hired and laws were enacted, so that today no one thinks twice about putting money into a bank. Banks are still robbed, but safes are much harder to crack and security guards are usually present. The point is that banks in conjunction with the law made it harder to steal money. Banks took safeguards to make sure the money is not stolen.

The same strategy has to be taken with spam because a new e-mail solution will not solve the problems. A new e-mail solution will temporarily slow down spam, but as soon as spammers discover how to circumvent the solution, it will be exploited. As an example of the cleverness of spammers and hackers, consider the following. Many companies attempt to stop automated HTTP bots by creating application forms that require a user to spell out the letters visible in a graphic into a text box. Because the letters are twisted it is virtually impossible to have a computer figure out what the letters are. The spammers and hackers were not deterred, however, so they created a solution where the same image was presented on another Web site for analysis. This solution sounds simple, but requires spammers to hire people, which increases their costs. The solution was not to hire people, but to make people do it voluntarily by using free pornography as a way of deciphering the content.

The reality is that to stop spam and viruses, the administrator must keep constant vigil. To keep the network free of problems, the administrator should use a number of tools in combination. Like a bank that relies on video cameras, hardened steel, and security guards to stop potential bank robbers.

Solution: ASSP

One way to control spam is to use a Bayesian filter. A *Bayesian filter* is an application that can scan an e-mail and determine whether it is spam. The English mathematician Thomas Bayes developed the theory of probability inference and developed the idea of a Bayesian filter. A Bayesian filter does this by looking for spam-identifying words in subject lines, headers, or the e-mail body. If those words exist in a specific combination, then a Bayesian filter will recognize the e-mail as spam or having a degree of spaminess.

ASSP employs two major spam-fighting techniques: white lists and a Bayesian filter. The white lists are also known as circles of trust. The idea is that you will trust e-mail from certain people and hence know that they do not send spam. Therefore, those e-mail addresses are not subjected to spam filtering and are sent directly to the recipient. That direct sending could be a potential spam exploit, but it requires the spam sender to know who is sending another person e-mail. Lacking that knowledge, the spam sender is shooting into the dark and guessing the identity of a potential e-mail user could be. Table 9.3 contains the reference information for the ASSP project.

TIP

ASSP will only work as well as the administrator who is managing the application. To a large degree, ASSP takes care of itself, but it does require periodic tuning and tweaking.

TABLE 9.3 Reference Information for ASSP

Item	Description
Home page	*http://assp.sourceforge.net/*
Version	At the time of this writing, the released version is 1.0.12.
Installation	The ASSP application is distribution as an archive file that is expanded into an already created subdirectory.
Dependencies	ASSP is a Perl application that is dependent on Perl being installed. To run the application as a service, either XYNTService is required or the Perl service component.
Documentation	The documentation is slightly disorganized, but very detailed, so with a bit of time and effort, you can find a solution to an individual problem. The documentation is located at *http://assp.sourceforge.net/fom/cache/1.html.* You should read the documentation to understand the details of ASSP.
Mailing Lists	The mailing list is found on the home page of the ASSP Web site in the menu.
Impatient Installation Time Required	Download size: 0.5 MB Installation time: 5-35 minutes depending on how long it takes to tune the Bayesian filter.
Firewall Port	25 (TCP) or whatever port the SMTP server is using.
DVD Location	`/packages/xmail/assp` contains the ZIP file archive.

Impatient Installation and Deployment

When installing ASSP, an impatient installation and deployment is the same thing. The installation of ASSP can be a bit tricky because there are multiple steps that will cause e-mails to be lost if they are not performed correctly. However, if the installation instructions are followed correctly, there will be no problems and things will work straight out of the box.

The first and most important aspect is to make sure that a working Perl installation is on the computer where ASSP is to be installed. It is recommended to use ActiveState's (*http://www.activestate.com*) Perl distribution, as it is a simple and straightforward installation. After Perl has been installed, you can install ASSP. ASSP is distributed as an archive, which is expanded into a created subdirectory. For example, the ASSP archive could be expanded into the subdirectory `c:\bin\assp`.

After the archive has been expanded, add the directories `[assp-installation]/spam`, `[assp-installation]/notspam`, `[assp-installation]/errors`, `[assp-installation]/errors/spam`, and `[assp-installation]/errors/notspam`. These directories can be empty, but are necessary for the proper operation of ASSP.

After that, the application is complete and can be executed from the ASSP installation directory using the following command line:

```
perl assp.pl
```

If there are no errors, the application will execute without problems. To run the application as a service, the simplest is to use XYNTService. The following listing shows a sample XYNTService configuration entry (global entry details have been omitted for clarity):

```
[Process0]
CommandLine = perl assp.pl c:\bin\assp
WorkingDir = c:\bin\assp
PauseStart = 1000
PauseEnd = 1000
UserInterface = No
Restart = Yes
```

The key `CommandLine`, which represents the command line, references the ASSP directory in absolute terms, and the working directory is the ASSP binary directory.

The next important task is to figure out how to configure ASSP. The simplest way to configure ASSP is to use the included Web server, which is accessed by using the URL *http://localhost:55555* (assuming ASSP is running on the local computer). The resulting page (see Figure 9.14) explains itself so you don't need a help file.

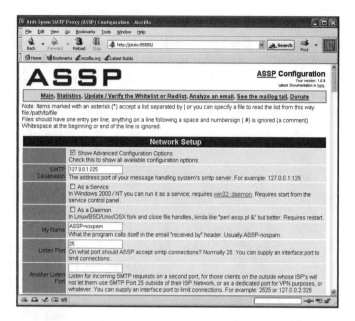

FIGURE 9.14 ASSP home configuration page.

In Figure 9.14, check the Show Advanced Configuration Options checkbox. Scroll to the bottom of the page and click on the Apply Changes button. The page reloads and shows additional options. Keep the advanced settings active as the various techniques will reference variables that are only visible in the advanced mode.

Technique: Rebuilding a Spam Database

ASSP is primarily a spam filter, so ASSP requires a database of e-mails that are both spam and not spam. It is a common misconception that ASSP only requires e-mails that are spam to build a good database. ASSP requires an equal representation of e-mails that are spam and are not spam to generate a balanced database that will identify e-mails properly.

In the initial phase, ASSP will most likely not mark e-mails properly because most administrators have a hard time finding 10,000 e-mails where half are spam. Using e-mails from another domain does not help because a spam database is domain specific due to the nature of the e-mails that individuals receive.

TIP

Expect at least a week for the ASSP filtering process to work correctly. Also do not expect perfect results. ASSP helps quite a bit, but it isn't perfect. Messages will be marked as spam when they should not, and spam will get through. Spammers are moving targets and they will attempt to get past your filters with all means possible.

Before a spam database can be rebuilt, prototype e-mails have to be present in their respective directories: [assp-installation]/spam for spam e-mails and [assp-installation]/notspam for regular e-mails. At a minimum, there should be at least 400 e-mails in either directory. Less than 400 will give skewed results. After the e-mails have been stored, you can rebuild/build the spam database using the following command (the command is executed in the directory where ASSP is installed):

```
perl rebuildspamdb.pl
```

Depending on the number of e-mails and the resources of the computer, building the database can vary between a few seconds and a few hours.

When rebuilding the spam database, do so on a machine that is not in production use. The ASSP rebuild process hogs resources and could potentially cause "resources are not available" problems for an extended period. Either mirror the ASSP directory or use a network share to access the ASSP directory and then execute the rebuild *command.*

The spam database needs to be rebuilt periodically. The exact frequency depends on the volume of e-mail, but if you receive approximately 100 e-mails a day, then once a week should be fine. The more e-mails per day, the more often the spam database needs to be rebuilt, with the minimum frequency being once a day.

ASSP keeps statistics that can be called up from the Statistics link at the top of the ASSP administration page. To see the overall statistics for most ASSP servers, you can click the Here link in the lower-middle page of the ASSP statistics page. By default, ASSP sends the local statistics to the parent server for overall statistic aggregation. Note that no private information is transmitted. You should allow your statistics to be sent as it shows a support for the ASSP project.

Technique: Building a Ring of Trust

A ring of security in ASSP is created using a white list and red list. A *white list* is a list of e-mail addresses from people who are considered part of your ring of trust. For example, if you receive e-mail from a spouse or friend, doing a spam check on that e-mail is a waste of resources. When the e-mail address of the spouse or friend is added to the white list, no Bayesian filtering occurs and the e-mail is sent to the e-mail server.

When a user is on the white list, any e-mail that the user sends is checked for other e-mail addresses that are automatically added to the white list. That means other users can send you e-mails without being checked for spam. Although this sounds like everybody will eventually be added to the white list thus nullifying the Bayesian filter and letting spam through, it does not happen. The reason it does not happen is because, by default, people have a closed communications circle of people they trust. Also implemented is the concept of timeouts. If a white list user does not send e-mail within a specific time period, then that user will be removed. A whitelisted user needs to be a user who sends you e-mails on a regular basis.

A red list is different in that users cannot add users to a white list. Redlisted users are users that you generally trust, but do not know if you should trust who they send e-mails to.

Following are a number of settings that can be altered on the ASSP administration page to configure the white list and red list. (The format of the text box contents is not described in this book and is very clearly defined in the ASSP administration page. Distributed with the ASSP documentation is an introduction to Perl regular expressions.)

Blacklisted Domains: This text box contains a list of domains that are considered spam and all e-mails from the domains are blocked. Generally speaking this text box should only be used for problematic domains. Examples include domains that keep sending e-mails, even though they are not desired and attempts to gently stop them failed. If used as a general blocking mechanism the updating will become an administrative chore.

Expression to Identify Redlisted Mail: This text box contains a Perl regular expression that will attempt to match an e-mail header and then consider that e-mail as red listed. The e-mail addresses will not be added to either the red list or white list.

Keep Whitelisted Spam: This checkbox will cause whitelisted e-mails that were marked as spam to be kept. This occurs when a user who you trust sends you e-mail for the first time, and the Bayesian filter marks it as spam. The user would then add the e-mail address to the white list; however, the e-mail is still in the spam collection. This is a problem because it could skew your Bayesian filter score, so by default ASSP will clean up whitelisted e-mails marked as spam. By checking the checkbox, you are saying "Even though the sender is white listed, the e-mail is still representative of spam e-mail." That decision might or might not be good, and depends entirely on the sort of e-mails that are being sent.

Max Whitelist Days: This text box contains a value that represents the number of days an e-mail address should be kept in the white list. If an e-mail address is not used within that time frame, then it is removed and needs to be added to the white list again.

Only Local or Authenticated Users Contribute to the Whitelist: This checkbox option changes the default operation from white list users being able to add to the white list, to only authenticated and local users. In effect it turns already added white-listed e-mail addresses to a sort of red list for external users. In a large corporation, it is a good idea to set this option so people will create a smaller circle of trust and it ensures that e-mails that have to get through will get through.

Only the Envelope-Sender Is Added/Compared to Whitelist: This checkbox option only allows the addition of the sender to contribute to the white list. The normal operation is to extract the e-mail headers FROM, SENDER, REPLY-TO, ER-RORS-TO, and LIST-*. If one of those headers contains a white-listed e-mail address, then the other e-mail address are whitelisted as well. It is important to realize that mailing list addresses should be red listed and not whitelisted. Often people will use public e-mail addresses that are known to other spammers and hence could be a potential spam loophole. This checkbox should not be set.

Reject All But Whitelisted Mail: This option only allows whitelisted e-mails to get through without being marked as spam. It is not advised to set this checkbox as it could introduce more problems that it would solve.

Whitelisted Domains: This text box defines all the domains that are part of the white list, and they do not expire. It is advisable to set this text box to domain addresses that your mail server has sporadic, but regular communications with. That way all those e-mails will never be marked as spam and the user does not have to constantly update the whitelist.

As an extra bit of information, anyone whose e-mail address is defined in the Spam-Lover Addresses text box will automatically contribute to the white list in his or her outgoing emails.

Technique: Additional Processing Techniques to Determine Spam Level

By default, e-mail is defined as spam if the Bayesian filter processes the e-mail and determines the rating to be a higher level than allowed. ASSP is very flexible, however, in that it allows an administrator to define other rules that indicate whether an e-mail is spam. For example, not allowing attachments with specific extensions is also useful in blocking spam e-mails that contain viruses.

Following are a number of settings that can be altered on the ASSP administration page to influence whether an e-mail is considered spam. (The format of the text box contents is not described in this book, but is clearly defined in the ASSP administration page. Distributed with the ASSP documentation is an introduction to Perl regular expressions.)

Block Executable Content: This checkbox is set by default and blocks all extensions defined in the List of Blocked Extension Files text box. Keep this checkbox checked to ensure that attachments that end with an incorrect extension are blocked. This is especially useful if the client is on a Windows platform. The default setting in Windows Explorer is not to show the extension for registered types, and people mistake executable content for graphical content. Checking this checkbox automatically blocks this type of content ensuring that a user cannot inadvertently activate such a virus.

Block Whitelisted Exe Attachments Too: This checkbox is set by default and blocks all attachments defined.

Disable Good Hosts Antispam: This checkbox is set by default and disables the use of the good hosts file. The good hosts file contains a number of host identifiers where spam is not sent. However, that approach can be problematic as the server might become compromised and allow a flood of spam.

Expression to Identify Non-Spam: This text box contains a regular expression that is used to identify e-mails that are not spam. The regular expression is executed on both the e-mail headers and body. If a match occurs, then the e-mail is not considered spam. This text box should be used when certain e-mails have "secret" tokens to identify that they are not spam.

Expression to Identify Spam: This text box contains a regular expression that is used to identify e-mails that are spam. The regular expression is executed on both the e-mail headers and body. If a match occurs, then the e-mail is not considered spam. This text box should be used when certain e-mails arrive in high frequency, such as the Blaster virus e-mail. This text box is useful to implement immediate actions.

Expression to Identify No-processing Mail: This text box contains a regular expression that is used to identify e-mails that will not be processed. Although this text box seems similar to the Expression to Identify Non-Spam text box, it is not the same. The e-mail is not processed, not added to the not-spam collection, and no redirection or other operations occur.

List of Blocked Extension Files: This text box contains a list of extensions that should be blocked. The extensions are the types defined in the MIME-encoded buffer that is present within the e-mail. The default value in the text box will catch most viruses that have a tendency to execute some application.

Technique: Managing Processed E-mails

When an e-mail arrives and is processed, a spam rating is given. From there, an administrator can decided what to do with the e-mail. There are multiple strategies: blocking the e-mails that are spam, sending an error, or just tagging the e-mail. Many administrators block spam e-mails and do not let them reach the user. That is an incorrect strategy. Although it might save the user time from having to go through the spam, often the server filters the e-mail due to its spam rating, but the e-mail was actually not spam. The information loss will be blamed on the administrator. The better solution is to tag the e-mail as spam and then let the user figure out what to do with the e-mail. Often, it is possible to set up a filter in the client software.

Following are a number of settings related to managing processed e-mails that can be altered on the ASSP administration page. (The format of the text box contents is not described in this book and is clearly defined in the ASSP administration page. Distributed with the ASSP documentation is an introduction to Perl regular expressions.)

Add Spam Header: This checkbox adds the e-mail header X-Assp-Spam: YES if the e-mail proves to be spam. The end client application can use the presence of this header to filter spam e-mails into a specific folder location.

Add Spam Probability Header: This checkbox adds the e-mail header X-Assp-Spam-Prob: [value] to the e-mail. The value can vary between 0 and +1 where a value above 0.65 is spam. The ASSP documentation specifies a value of 0.6, but the Perl source code uses 0.65. The end client application can read the presence and value of this header to determine the spaminess of the e-mail and take further actions.

Address to CC All Spam: This text box CCs the spam to an e-mail address that can be used to validate the e-mails. If spam e-mail is being blocked and not forwarded to the user, it is important to have a track record for the spam. For example, the spam could be sent to an e-mail address that is archived and can be searched when some e-mails are missed.

Block Outgoing Spam-Prob Header: This checkbox, which is set by default, suppresses the generation of the spam headers when outgoing e-mail is filtered. The setting should be left as is.

Prepend Spam Subject: This text box prefixes the contents of the text box with any e-mail that is considered spam. This action only occurs for addresses in the Spam Lovers Addresses list or if the Debug checkbox is set.

Spam Addresses: This text box contains a list of e-mail addresses that are spam-only e-mail addresses. One of the challenges of managing the spam database is keeping up with the newest versions of spam. Often the strategy is to create an e-mail address that is put into the public Internet domain and does nothing more than receive spam. Adding this e-mail to the spam Addresses text box will automatically update spam collection, which updates the spam database and makes your ASSP application more effective.

Spam-Lover Addresses: This text box contains a list of e-mail addresses, domain addresses, or users that will accept e-mails marked as spam. By default, ASSP will block all e-mails that are marked as spam. An e-mail address that is a Spam-Lover will receive the e-mail, but with associated e-mail header and title modifications. The default setting should be to accept spam for all local domains and let the client mail programs manage the filtering.

Unprocessed Addresses: This text box contains a list of e-mail addresses, domain addresses, or users that will receive their e-mails without being processed for spam. These e-mails pass directly through ASSP and are sent to the destination server.

User Subject as Maillog Names: This checkbox renames the e-mails to the subject title of the e-mail instead of numeric identifiers. It is recommended when manually trimming the spam database to know which e-mails to move directories.

After you have become accustomed to your ASSP application and are able to interact with it using just the Web interface or e-mail interface, then you will need to deactivate User Subject as Maillog Names. This is because the spam database will then begin to delete and add newer versions of spam and not spam e-mails. To move an old database to numeric identifiers, use the command line `perl move2num.pl -r`.

Technique: Managing and Allowing Relaying

By default, ASSP will be used as a frontend SMTP server to the real SMTP server. This means that the e-mail is first processed by SMTP before being sent to an SMTP server such as XMail. You can run both ASSP and XMail or another SMTP server on the same computer. In those scenarios, it is only necessary to remap the SMTP port of the SMTP server. If the SMTP server were XMail, then the "Technique: Changing a Port, Logging Requests, Performance Tuning, and Controlling Relay" section needs to be read on remapping the SMTP port.

Regardless whether the ASSP and SMTP server are on the same machine, the ASSP server takes the role of the SMTP server. This means e-mail from the Internet need to be routed over the ASSP server. The local e-mail clients can route the e-mail over the ASSP server or the SMTP server for external relay. However, if the client wants to update the ASSP database, then it must route its e-mail via ASSP.

Following are a number of settings that can be altered on the ASSP administration page to define how e-mail messages are relayed. (The format of the text box contents is not described in this book, but is clearly defined in the ASSP administration page. Distributed with the ASSP documentation is an introduction to Perl regular expressions.)

Accept All Mail: This text box defines a number of IP addresses that allows relaying of e-mails to externally defined domains. An externally defined e-mail is not defined in the Local Domains text box or in the Local Domains File text box.

Local Domains: This text box defines e-mail domains that will be processed by the local SMTP server. You must set the value of this text box; otherwise, relay errors will occur.

Local Domains File: This text box defines a file that contains the local domains handled. If the number of local domains cannot easily fit into the Local Domains text box, or the local domains change constantly, using a file is more convenient and efficient.

Listen Port: This text box defines the SMTP listening port, which is port 25. However, the ASSP server could be a server in a relay chain and then listening to another port might be a better idea.

Relay Host: This text box defines the host that will relay external e-mails. If you use XMail, then XMail could be used as the smart relay host. However, even if ASSP allows external relaying of e-mail, the smart host may not. The administrator needs to be aware of the two levels of relay control. An example relay host can include IP address or server name and port.

Relay Host File: This text box defines a filename that contains a list of IPs that can relay e-mail. This file serves the same purpose as the Accept All Mail text box.

Relay Port: This text box identifies the port that the mail server should connect to for relaying external data.

SMTP Destination: This text contains the IP address and potentially the port of the destination SMTP server that will process the e-mail and send it to the appropriate user.

Technique: Adding, Deleting, and Modifying White Lists or Spam Databases

One of the last techniques that an administrator needs to know about is how an administrator or user can interact with ASSP. Generally ASSP is a transparent process that the user does not need to know about. The only time the user needs to know about ASSP is when a user wants to update the white list or reclassify an e-mail that has been considered as spam or as regular e-mail.

Following are a number of settings that can be altered on the ASSP administration page to define how the administer and user can interact with ASSP. (The format of the text box contents is not described in this book, but is very clearly defined in the ASSP administration page. Distributed with the ASSP documentation is an introduction to Perl regular expressions.)

Add to Whitelist Address: The contents of the text box describe a username that is used to receive e-mails that should be added to the white list. The username is combined with the contents of the Local Domains text box to get a full address. For example, if the Local Domains text box shows domain.com, then to add white list data, the e-mail address is assp-white@domain.com.

Allow Admin Connections From: This text box specifies a list of IP addresses that can access the Web interface of ASSP.

Enable Email Interface: This checkbox is used to enable the e-mail interface, which allows the sending of e-mails to ASSP to reclassify them as spam, not-spam, or white list additions.

From Address for Email: This text box is used when ASSP sends e-mails or reports to a user and identifies the source of the e-mail. Typically a user will assign this e-mail address to something like postmaster@domain.com.

My Name: This text box is used to identify the ASSP server in the relay logs, or when connecting to another SMTP server.

Report not-Spam Address: The contents of the text box describe a username that is used to receive e-mails that have been marked as spam and should be added to the not-spam collection. The username is combined with the contents of the Local Domains text box to get a full address. For example, if the Local Domains text box contains domain.com, then to add white list data, the e-mail address is assp-notspam@domain.com.

Report Spam Address: The contents of the text box describe a username that is used to receive e-mails that have been marked as not-spam and should be added to the spam collection. The username is combined with the contents of the Local Domains text box to get a full address. For example, if the Local Domains text box contains domain.com, then to add white list data, the e-mail address is assp-spam@domain.com.

Web Admin Password: This text box identifies the password used when attempting to access the ASSP server using an HTML browser. When confronted with the HTTP authentication dialog box, there is no need to add a username. However, most browsers will not remember a password if there is no user associated with a password, so any user identifier can be used. The user identifier is never read by ASSP and therefore no problems occur.

Web Admin Port: This text box identifies the port of the ASSP administrative Web site. For example, the default is 5555, which means to access the main ASSP administrative page the URL *http://[ASSP-HOSTNAME]:55555* is executed.

TIP

You can manipulate the white list or red list from the HTML browser. To do so, load the ASSP administrative page and then click on the Update/Verify the Whitelist or Redlist link found near the top of the page. From there, instructions will show you how to add, remove, verify, or view the users and lists.

PROJECT: E-MAILRELAY

ASSP is a sort of e-mail relay, except that the relay is specifically intended to root out spam. The project E-mailRelay is a relay as well, except its role is to control how e-mail is relayed and when it is relayed.

For example, imagine having a notebook and wanting to send e-mail to the Internet. Yet instead of having the e-mail waiting in the outbox, it can be sent directly. E-mailRelay will capture the e-mail and then send it when there is an Internet connection.

Another example is the problem of spammers testing the validity of e-mail accounts. Using E-mailRelay and user authentication, it is possible to see how often a server probes; if a threshold is exceeded, all e-mail contact is immediately broken. E-mailRelay can also be used to presort, preprocess, or postprocess e-mails.

The objective of E-mailRelay is to give an administrator some type of global control of all e-mails that are sent and received externally. E-mailRelay is a purely optional application, but for those that need it, it is a blessing because it solves the outlined problems elegantly and allows the integration of scripts. The administrator does not have to resort to programming, but can use scripting techniques in either BASH or Python. Table 9.4 is the reference information for E-mailRelay.

TABLE 9.4 Reference Information for E-mailRelay

Item	Description
Home page	*http://emailrelay.sourceforge.net/*
Version	At the time of this writing, the released version is 1.3.1.
Installation	The E-mailRelay application is distributed as an archive file that is expanded into an already created subdirectory.

$\longrightarrow$

Item	Description
Dependencies	The E-mailRelay application is a C++ application that needs the C runtime to be installed, which in most cases is already the case. To run the application as a service, XYNTService is required.
Documentation	The documentation is acceptable, but it does require a bit of time to get adjusted to it. All the documentation needed is distributed with the binary distribution in the [Email Relay Installation]/doc directory. The documentation is either a series of HTML pages or text pages.
Mailing Lists	There is no mailing list, but the author of email-relay has an e-mail contact on the main Web site that can be used for support issues.
Impatient Installation Time Required	Download size: 0.7 MB. Installation time: 5 minutes.
Firewall Port	25 (TCP) or whatever port the SMTP server is using.
DVD Location	/packages/xmail/emailrelay contains the ZIP file archive.

Impatient Installation and Deployment

When installing E-mailRelay, an impatient installation and deployment is the same installation. The installation of E-mailRelay is extremely simple in that it only needs to be expanded into an already precreated subdirectory such as emailrelay.

To start the emailrelay.exe application, it's important to get the command-line arguments correct. E-mailRelay does not use a configuration file and relies solely on command-line options for its configuration. Following is an example E-mailRelay XYNTService configuration:

```
[Process0]
CommandLine = emailrelay.exe [arguments]
WorkingDir = c:\bin\emailrelay
PauseStart = 1000
PauseEnd = 1000
UserInterface = Yes
Restart = No
```

The command-line options that are used to configure E-mailRelay are based on context. Therefore, the most efficient way of explaining and understanding E-mailRelay is to know the individual techniques.

E-mailRelay should not be considered in the same context as ASSP. This means if E-mailRelay is used to filter external e-mails that arrive at the local domain, then E-mailRelay should not also be used for external relaying. The reason is because E-mailRelay should be used in as simple a context as possible; otherwise, the administrator might make an error and cause an open relay or cause bounced e-mails.

Technique: Using E-mailRelay as a Proxy

When using E-mailRelay as a proxy, E-mailRelay does nothing but accept e-mail and then send it to another server. Following is the simplest command-line option that will relay e-mail from a local sender to a remote server:

```
emailrelay --as-proxy server:225 --spool-dir c:\bin\data\spool
```

The command-line option --as-proxy dictates that E-mailRelay will proxy received e-mails to the remote server server:225. The identifier server is the name or IP address of the host that is running a SMTP server (ASSP or XMail). The numeric value 225 is the port of the destination SMTP server. The command-line option --spool-dir and value c:\bin\data\spool defines the location where an e-mail will be temporarily stored before being relayed to the destination server.

In the default case, E-mailRelay will not accept an e-mail that originates from an external e-mail address. If an attempt is made to relay, a relay error will result. To allow external clients to connect, which means anyone not executing on the local machine, the following command is executed:

```
emailrelay --as-proxy server:225 --remote-clients
--spool-dir c:\bin\data\spool
```

The command-line option --remote-clients will allow remote clients to connect and relays any e-mail received.

Be very careful about using the --remote-clients *option because it will override any security settings that may exist on the e-mail server. Consider that XMail server allows automatic e-mail relaying if the e-mail connection is local. Because E-mailRelay is put into the middle of the relaying, XMail will see all connections as local and thus will allow all e-mails to be relayed. The solution is to require authentication always whenever e-mails are sent externally.*

Technique: Using E-mailRelay as a Spooler

To run E-mailRelay as a spooler, there are two parts: client and server. The server accepts the e-mail and stores it in a spooler. Then the client reads the spool and forwards the e-mail to a relay server. The following command shows how to start E-mailRelay in Server Spool mode:

```
emailrelay --as-server --spool-dir c:\bin\data\spool
```

When E-mailRelay receives an e-mail, it is stored in the spool directory. The e-mail that is received is stored as a file with the extension content. The content of the file is the e-mail message with e-mail headers. The other file that is generated has the extension envelope. The contents of the file are a number of headers used as a quick reference for routing the e-mail.

If a script were to manipulate the headers, then they must be manipulated on both the envelope and content file. Not doing so will potentially confuse E-mailRelay.

To forward the stored e-mails in the spool and run E-mailRelay as a spooling server, the following command is executed:

```
emailrelay --as-client server:smtp --spool-dir c:\bin\data\spool
```

The command-line option --as-client forces E-mailRelay to read the spooled e-mails and then forward them to the host server using the smtp port (25). After all the e-mails have been processed, E-mailRelay will exit.

Technique: Assigning Logging, Port Definition, and Other Settings

E-mailRelay can be tweaked to have other runtime characteristics:

Changing listing port identifier: The command-line option --port and associated identifier is used to define a listening port other than port 25.

Logging: The command-line option `--log` is used to enable logging. On Windows, the logging messages are sent to the Windows Event Log. The log messages are sent both to the standard out and the Windows Event Log. To surpress sending log messages to the Windows Event Log, the command-line option `--no-syslog` is used. To generate more extensive logging messages, the option `--verbose` is used.

Activating an administration port: The command-line option `--admin` with port identifier represents the port that can be used to perform remote administration while E-mailRelay is running. The administrator would use Telnet to access the administrative port.

Technique: Using E-mailRelay as a Filter

One of the reasons for using E-mailRelay in proxy mode is to filter e-mails for global purposes. E-mailRelay only allows the definition of one script to execute on the command line with an example command line shown as follows:

```
emailrelay --as-proxy server:225
--filter "c:\cygwin\bin\bash.exe c:\bin\emailrelay\scripts\filter.sh"
--spool-dir c:\bin\data\spool
```

The command-line option `--filter` is used to define a script or program that is executed whenever an e-mail arrives. The BASH script is executed because, by default, a process does not know what to do with the `sh` extension. When specifying the program as the execution of a scripting engine and a script, both buffers are enclosed by double quotes so that they appear as one command-line parameter.

The script that is executed has one associated command-line parameter, which is the path of the file. The script could load that file, manipulate it, and store the file back on the disk. E-mailRelay does not keep an internal state and will reload the file. If the script decides to abort processing, the script should delete the e-mail, and return an exit code 100 to indicate to E-mailRelay that the e-mail no longer exists. Otherwise, an exit of 0 will indicate success and forward the e-mail or keep it in the spooler. If a value other than 0 is returned, it is expected that the script output some kind of error text enclosed by << and >> characters on the standard output. That text is return to the e-mail client to indicate why the e-mail caused an error.

If the script wants to generate more e-mails that should be sent, e.g., begin a broadcast, then the script could create further e-mails. The solution is to create an e-mail such as in the XMail `sendmail.exe` example, and make sure that the `--poll` command-line option is used. E-mailRelay will then periodically poll the spool directory and send any e-mails that it might find. This is an easy way to send e-mails without having to use a specialized SMTP client library.

When deleting and adding new e-mails to the spool buffer, it is important to re-member that a script needs to either delete or add the .content *file in addition to the* .envelope *file.*

Technique: Using E-mailRelay for User Authentication

The other very valuable use of E-mailRelay is as a user authentication tool. By ver-ifying who is sending e-mails from what IP addresses and adding filters, the ad-ministrator can block mass spams and viruses before they get out of control and make an e-mail server unable to respond due to the flood of e-mails.

The following command line shows how to specify a user authentication filter:

```
emailrelay --as-proxy server:225
--verifier "c:\cygwin\bin\bash.exe
c:\bin\emailrelay\scripts\userauth.sh"
--spool-dir c:\bin\data\spool
```

The userauth.sh script will be called with up to eight command-line arguments that are defined as follows, in the order that they appear on the command line:

Email address: Specifies the e-mail address where the e-mail is being sent.

User: Specifies the user identifier of the destination e-mail address, which would be everything before the @ sign.

Domain: Specifies the domain identifier of the destination e-mail address, which would be everything after the @ sign.

Local server: Specifies the identifier of the local server, which is only of inter-est if the server is multihomed.

Sender email address: Specifies the e-mail address of the user sending the e-mail.

Connecting IP: Specifies the immediate IP address of the server connected to the E-mailRelay and is sending the e-mail.

Authentication mechanism: An optional identifier that defines the authentica-tion mechanism.

Authentication name: An optional identifier that defines the authentication name or the fourth field from the authentication secrets file.

The script after having performed the authentication must output two lines of text and return code. The lines of text are potentially used to identify why the error occurred. An exit error code of 0 indicates that the user is a valid local user. An exit code of 1 indicates that the user is valid, but not on the local domain. Any exit code greater than 1 indicates an error and means that the e-mail should be rejected.

SUMMARY

This chapter introduced how e-mail is managed using a host of tools. Three tools in particular were shown: Xmail, ASSP, and E-mailRelay. Each tool is used to address a specific problem that is part of an e-mail solution. Xmail could be used on its own and scripts could be used to implement all the missing functionality. Regardless, to manage e-mail, scripts must be written. Using scripts, the administrator can fine-tune their e-mail workflow.

10 Productivity Applications

ABOUT THIS CHAPTER

The focus of this chapter is to illustrate the two projects: Mozilla and OpenOffice. On a typical computer desktop, there are a number of standard applications, such as a word processor, spreadsheet, and e-mail client that are called productivity software. There are other utilities used to compress files or copy files from one computer to another, and those were covered in other chapters. In this chapter, the focus is on productivity software and how an administrator or a power user can take advantage of that software.

For the administrator, the main interest with respect to productivity software is whether it will work. One of the most popular pieces of productivity software is Microsoft Office, which is popular because it works extremely well. Other productivity suites are Lotus™ Smart Suite™ or Corel® WordPerfect® Office. However, some companies may want for one reason or another to switch to something like OpenOffice and Mozilla. Often the question is whether the user will lose any functionality or whether it will make the user's life more complicated. The answer is that it depends.

Open Office is an application suite that seems similar to other productivity suites, but in use, you'll see many differences. Initially these differences seem insurmountable and could frustrate some users; however, they are simply differences, not disadvantages. For example, the autocomplete feature in Open Office takes some getting used to, but after you get used to it, you can't live without it—especially when writing technical documentation such as this book as long complicated words are autocompleted. Users just need to get used to the new environment.

The following projects will be covered:

Comparison: The most important topic before even discussing OpenOffice and Mozilla is how well the applications will work. The beginning of the chapter outlines what works and does not work so that you can make a good estimate of the advantages and disadvantages in their specific context.

OpenOffice: OpenOffice is an Open Source productivity suite that includes a spreadsheet and word processor among other applications. The details of how to use those applications is not discussed; instead, we discuss the details that relate to an administrator, namely managing document templates, dictionaries, and macros.

Mozilla: Mozilla is an Internet productivity suite that includes an e-mail client, newsreader, and Web browser. The details of using those applications are not discussed; instead, we discuss the details that relate to managing a Mozilla installation, defining security policies, and plug-ins.

ARE MOZILLA AND OPENOFFICE USABLE?

Many would like to switch to OpenOffice or Mozilla, but the question is whether it's even possible? This section attempts to answer that question. The answer to the question of conversion is a yes if you are willing to think a bit differently.

OpenOffice Issues

Following are the main issues related to an OpenOffice conversion:

Applications: OpenOffice contains the following applications: word processor, spreadsheet, HTML editor, presentation applications, and drawing application. Mini applications, for example, are an equation editor, database explorer, label editor, form editor, report generator, and business card editor. Missing applications such as a database or e-mail client are available using other applications such as MySQL or Mozilla.

Cross-platform Support: OpenOffice is available on most platforms including Windows, OSX, and most Unix flavors. An administrator can easily deploy OpenOffice in a heterogeneous environment that includes terminal servers and PCs.

Document formats: Many people consider document formats to be one of the biggest issues related to switching to OpenOffice. This argument is only partially valid. Many documents are relatively simple and do not contain complex formatting nor any macros. These documents can be converted with about 90% correctness, whereas the rest of the problems are formatting issues. These formatting issues are similar to viewing documents rendered by different browsers with no loss of data.

Extensibility and macros: All the productivity packages in the market have very different extensibility models. It is very difficult to port or convert logic from one package to OpenOffice. The only real solution is to figure out what was attempted in the original logic and then rewrite that logic for OpenOffice. OpenOffice supports three major programming paradigms: OpenBasic, C++, and Java. Writing macros using C++ or Java is beyond the scope of this book, however OpenBasic is covered here. The administrator who is interested in integrating OpenOffice into an overall workflow architecture should learn OpenBasic.

Installation and deployment issues: Deploying OpenOffice in comparison to other productivity software is about the same level of complexity. A standard installation is relatively simple. The only problem is that OpenOffice (1.1 and lower levels) has to be installed for every user on a single computer. This can be tedious because it means to install OpenOffice for every user in either a new location or the same location, which overwrites the old installation.

Language support: OpenOffice is available in more than 20 different languages. The exact list of languages supported is readily available on the OpenOffice Web sites.

Standards: OpenOffice has the advantage in that it supports many standard file formats such as Word documents, RTF, XML, HTML, Text, dBASE®, and PDF (export). OpenOffice fits well into a multiformat infrastructure.

Document and text styles: An OpenOffice document can have styles attached with it much like a style can be attached to Microsoft Word. To a large degree, styles are portable across document formats. When using a multiproductivity suite infrastructure, a common denominator is found by defining basic styles. For example, bullets have formatting issues because multiple productivity applications interpret them differently. Using a common style ensures that document portability problems are kept to a minimum.

User experience: OpenOffice in contrast to other productivity suites has a different user experience. Many even consider the OpenOffice user experience annoying, but it's actually just different. For example, OpenOffice has automatic word completion based on the first few letters typed. For the novice, this feature can be distracting. After the user learns this feature, it becomes a time saver.

OpenOffice Recommendations

OpenOffice can be used effectively in many settings, as long as the administrator under promises and over delivers. The problem with OpenOffice is the first impression it gives, which should be understated so that after users use OpenOffice, they will become amazed at how useful the applications are.

Mozilla Issues

The other productivity application is Mozilla, which is primarily a browser and e-mail application. Following are the main issues related to a Mozilla conversion:

Applications: Mozilla contains the following main applications: Web browser, Mail and Newsgroup manager, and HTML Composer. Mini applications available for Mozilla are IRC chat, Calendar, FTP downloader, and others available from the companion Mozilla Web site.

Cross-platform support: Mozilla is available on a large number of platforms and devices, including Windows, OSX, and most Unix flavors. An administrator can easily deploy Mozilla in a heterogeneous environment that includes terminal servers and PCs.

Document formats: An e-mail program in a Windows platform context is typically not considered to have a document format. In fact, there are many document formats. E-mail is stored in the standard mailbox format allowing an administrator to move e-mails to different platforms. Contacts and calendar information can be stored in standard vCard and iCal formats. Importing and exporting e-mails is very simple and it is possible to import most proprietary e-mail formats.

Extensibility and macros: All the productivity packages in the market have very different extensibility models. Porting or converting logic from one package to Mozilla is difficult. The only real solution is to figure out what was attempted in the original logic and then rewrite that logic for Mozilla. Mozilla is extended using XML User Interface Language (XUL), which is an XML-based programming environment that combines JavaScript and GUI components. To write components for Mozilla, either the Java or C++ programming languages are used to create XPCOM components.

Installation and deployment issues: Deploying Mozilla is simple and straightforward after a distribution has been created. Mozilla can use many plug-ins, but you need to install other applications to make those plug-ins work.

Language support: Mozilla is available in a large number of languages, including individual dialects of a language. It is also important to realize that Mozilla will work extremely well with other languages if only a specific language package is installed. Mozilla is truly global and you should not have a problem finding a specific language.

Standards: Mozilla adheres to all open standards applicable to the individual applications such as HTML, XHTML, POP3, IMAP, SMTP, iCal, and so on. There should be no concern that Mozilla does not adhere to the standards.

User experience: Mozilla has no disadvantages in this area. Some things are different, but overall the learning curve is not large. A problem might arise if you make extensive use of the Microsoft Exchange message server. Mozilla only supports standards such as POP3, SMTP, and IMAP. Mozilla does not support the groupware options available in Microsoft Outlook. Mozilla supports views, automatic spam recognition, and HTML composer capabilities.

Mozilla Recommendations

Mozilla is a tool that can be used without too many complications as long as the administrator is not using Exchange. If users are using Exchange, they will need to adjust their architecture. For example, instead of using traditional calendaring, they could use presence software (also known as Instant Messaging) to schedule meetings and contact individuals.

PROJECT: OPENOFFICE

OpenOffice is an application that originally was developed by a company called Star Corporation based in Germany. At that time, OpenOffice was called StarOffice™ and was available for purchase as a productivity suite. Then Sun Microsystems™ purchased Star Corporation and integrated StarOffice into its product line. A short while thereafter, Sun decided to open source StarOffice and called it OpenOffice.

StarOffice still exists as an individual product and is part of the Java Desktop System (JDS) sold by Sun. JDS is an easy-to-use operating system (Linux) that includes productivity software in a low-cost package. StarOffice features some applications that are not available in OpenOffice, such as an integrated database. However, it's easy to integrate a database such as MySQL into OpenOffice and the SQL client tools have not been removed.

OpenOffice includes the following applications:

Calc: Spreadsheet application.

Draw: Drawing application that can be used to create flowcharts and other diagrams.

Impress: Presentation application.

Writer: Word processing application that can edit HTML documents.

Contained in Table 10.1 is the reference information for OpenOffice.

For the administrator or power user that will be automating OpenOffice, it is absolutely imperative that all the available documentation from the OpenOffice Web site is downloaded. Also be sure to download the OpenOffice SDK because it contains documentation about the OpenOffice document model.

TABLE 10.1 Reference Information for OpenOffice

Item	Description
Home page	*http://www.openoffice.org/*
Version	At the time of this writing, the released version is 1.1.4, and beta of 2.0. Recommendation is to use 2.0.
Installation	The OpenOffice distribution is distributed as a ZIP archive that when expanded creates a directory that contains many files, including the installation program.
Dependencies	The OpenOffice program has no absolute dependencies, but if add-ons were used, then the Java Runtime needs to be installed.
Documentation	The documentation of OpenOffice is very good and recommended.
Mailing Lists	There are many mailing lists for OpenOffice, which are offered as newsgroups using GMANE. For the administrator, the following lists are of interest: users, announce, discuss, and releases.
Impatient Installation Time Required	Download size: 65 MB
	Installation time: 5-15 minutes depending on the settings that need to be made. Depending on the speed of the Internet connection, the download of OpenOffice might be longer.
DVD Location	/packages/openoffice contains the ZIP file.

Impatient Installation

The OpenOffice distribution is downloaded from the OpenOffice Web site. Depending on the needs of the user, either the 1.1.x or 2.x version can be downloaded. Although you can run both versions side by side, you shouldn't because of unnecessary complexities. The user can download a particular ZIP archive for a specific language. If your company uses multiple languages, then each language must be downloaded. Note that downloading one language does not impede a user from editing a document written in another language. For example, downloading the English edition of OpenOffice involves downloading English dictionaries. If German documents need to be edited, then the German dictionaries need to be downloaded and installed as well.

After the ZIP archive has been downloaded, it is expanded, and a subdirectory similar to the name OOo_1.1.4_Win32Intel_install is created (the subdirectory example is for a version 1.1.x distribution). Within the subdirectory are a large number of files and, in particular, the file setup.exe. The file setup.exe is the file used to install OpenOffice. Also created is the file SETUP_GUIDE.pdf that can be read by the administrator to help install OpenOffice.

It is expected in the future that OpenOffice will be distributed on the Windows platform as a Windows Installer archive without using setup.exe.

To install OpenOffice, double-click the setup.exe file. The installation program starts and asks several questions, which can be left in default mode. Click Next and the installer attempts to find a Java installation. For a simple installation, Java is not necessary. If a Java installation is not found, the following items will not function: XSLT transformations, Java Database Connectivity (JDBC), applets, form generators, accessibility, and Java APIs used by OpenOffice extensions.

If OpenOffice has been installed without Java, you can install Java afterwards. The order of events is to install the Java Runtime Environment (JRE), and then run the program jvmsetup.exe *in the directory* [OpenOffice Installation Directory]/program.

After the OpenOffice installation has completed, the user can use OpenOffice to edit documents or spreadsheets. If the installed version is earlier than 1.1.2, the settings for the user and the application are stored in the OpenOffice installation directory. This means a user will see any change another user makes.

OpenOffice 2.0 solves the installation problem in that OpenOffice 2.0 can be installed on the computer for multiple users. It makes sense to install OpenOffice 2.0 if the administrator makes extensive use of OpenOffice automation. The OpenOffice 2.0 scripting model is much simpler to use and comprehend.

Deployment

A deployment of OpenOffice is similar to the impatient installation, except the installation is executed in a different context. When doing an OpenOffice deployment, you'll usually want to use the network installation and a response file. A network installation allows an administrator to have common read-only files and private read/write files.

OpenOffice 2.0 uses the network server installation, but combines the two deployment steps into one with some extras. Therefore, if the administrator wants to use OpenOffice 1.1.x and be able to use one installation, then a deployment installation should be chosen.

A multiuser installation could be considered as a network installation in that there are two installation steps. The first installation step is to install OpenOffice to a standard location that will be referenced by all users of OpenOffice. That standard location could be a local computer location or a network location. The second installation step is to perform a workstation installation.

The details of executing either setup installations are not described in this book because the `setup_guide.pdf` file that is part of the OpenOffice distribution is very detailed.

Directory Details

For deployment, OpenOffice has to be installed to a standard location such as `c:\Program Files\[OpenOffice]`. Another installation location could be a shared network driver; however, that network driver should be connected to a high-speed network.

After the installation has completed, it is considered a server installation. From the server installation, a local per-user installation is performed. The `setup.exe` file used to install the local per-user installation is located in a subdirectory of the server install. If OpenOffice were installed in `c:\Program Files\[OpenOffice]`, then the `setup.exe` program would be located in the directory `c:\Program Files\[OpenOffice]\program\`. Running that `setup.exe` version will start a different installation that can be used to either create a full local installation or a partial local user installation. If the server installation is located on the local computer, then a partial installation should be accomplished. When the server installation is on a remote server, then a full installation should be carried out. The reasons for each has to do with resource management and making better use of the hard disk and network.

When doing a two-step installation, a main user installation exists and the per-user installation creates a set of local user directories. For example, if OpenOffice were installed in the directory c:\Program Files\[OpenOffice], then there would be four subdirectories: help, program, share, and user described as follows:

help: Contains programs and files related to the OpenOffice help.

program: Contains the main programs and libraries related to the OpenOffice program. Contained within the directory and of interest to the administrator are the configuration files used when OpenOffice executes.

share: Contains the shared files used by all users of the OpenOffice program. These files could be templates, macros, or stylesheets.

user: Contains the private files used by a specific user. Like the share subdirectory, this subdirectory contains files that relate to templates, macros, and stylesheets. When installing a single-user version, this subdirectory is used. However, when installing a server and local installation, this subdirectory is stored underneath the Application Data directory, e.g., c:\My Documents\[user]\Application Data\[OpenOffice].

Configuration Details

Within the OpenOffice program subdirectory, a number of configuration files are used. Each of the configuration files uses a configuration format similar to the Windows .ini file in that there are sections that have a number of child key value pairs.

Even though it appears that the OpenOffice configuration files are editable, it is a complicated process. Any change, even though it might point to the same directory location, can cause errors. You can experiment, but you're left to your own devices when attempting to figure out what works and does not work. However, some details are presented so that you can become acquainted with where things are stored. You also shouldn't copy OpenOffice from one directory to another directly. OpenOffice is not relocatable and development actions have been taken to fix that problem.

The root configuration file bootstrap.ini is used to initialize the OpenOffice execution environment. Some keys of interest are defined as follows:

BaseInstallation: This key specifies the location where all the OpenOffice program files are stored. The default value is $ORIGIN/... The variable $ORIGIN is defined by OpenOffice and is used to indicate the location from which the initial soffice.exe program is executed. The default value should not be changed as it could cause problems.

UserInstallation: This key specifies the location where the user settings of the OpenOffice information are kept. In the default case, the information is kept in the subdirectory user. This is not useful when there are multiple users using the same configuration. To make the installation multiuser aware, change this value to $SYSUSERCONFIG/[OpenOffice]. The variable [OpenOffice] could be the subdirectory OpenOffice or OpenOffice with an appended version number. The variable $SYSUSERCONFIG when it is expanded will reference the directory c:\Documents and Settings\[user]\Application Data.

InstallMode: This key specifies which mode is used by OpenOffice. The value can either be STANDALONE for a local installation, or NETWORK for a multi-user installation.

The other configuration files are similar to bootstrap.ini in structure except that they are used to bootstrap other subsystems that belong to OpenOffice:

configmgr.ini: This is the core configuration file that references the other configuration files such as the bootstrap.ini or the Universal Network Objects (UNO) subsystem.

pythonloader.ini: A configuration file used to define the location of the Python subsystem, which for OpenOffice 1.1.x and OpenOffice 2.x is Python 2.2.x. You can replace the Python runtime with another runtime, but don't use a lower version Python runtime than 2.2.x.

pyuno.ini: A configuration file that defines some core definitions of how types are mapped from the UNO layer to the Python bindings.

setup.ini: A configuration file that defines the UNO services and location of the Java class files used by OpenOffice.

soffice.ini: A configuration file that seems to do very little other than define whether a logo is displayed when OpenOffice is started.

uno.ini: A configuration file that defines the location where the individual UNO libraries will be found, and the associated data types.

Technique: Other Languages and Dictionaries

OpenOffice supports many languages and dictionaries in different languages. All the support for the grammar, spelling, and hyphenation is from the Lingucomponent Project (*http://lingucomponent.openoffice.org/index.html*). The Lingucomponent Project was created because StarOffice, the parent project of OpenOffice, could not open source the existing dictionaries and other language aids. The aim of the Lingucomponent Project is to provide an infrastructure where anybody can download or create their own dictionaries, grammar checkers, thesauruses or hyphenation checkers.

There are two ways to install a dictionary: manual and automatic. In the automatic installation, an OpenOffice macro is used to download and configure additional macros.

Installing a Dictionary Manually

When manually installing a dictionary, all files are stored in the directory `[OpenOffice]/share/dict/ooo`. There are two main file extensions: `.aff` and `.dic`. The `.dic` extension is associated with a hyphenation checker, dictionary, or thesaurus. Each of these files use the ispell file format, which is an open source dictionary format. Creating your own dictionary is beyond the scope of this book, but the OpenOfficeLingucomponent Project has more details if you want to create your own dictionary.

When downloading a dictionary from the OpenOffice Web site, typically the dictionary, thesaurus, or hyphenation dictionary will be distributed as a ZIP archive. Contained within the ZIP archive will be a file that has an identifier based on a naming convention. The naming convention is based on the language and dialect. For example, English is defined as EN, and a dialect such as Canadian is CA, or American is US. Putting the two identifiers together, a filename like `en_us.dic` would be created to uniquely identify an American English dictionary.

The subdirectory that contains the dictionary files also contains the file `dictionary.1st`. The purpose of the `dictionary.1st` file is to provide a reference point for the dictionary files. Following is an example `dictionary.1st` file:

```
HYPH de DE hyph_de_DE
DICT en GB en_GB
DICT en US en_US
HYPH en US hyph_en_US
THES en US th_en_US
```

Each line represents a dictionary definition. The first identifier of a line can be a HYPH for hyphenation dictionary, DICT for dictionary, or THES for thesaurus. The second identifier is the language, the third identifier is the dialect of the language, and the fourth identifier is the filename of the file.

So if for example you were to download the Canadian English dictionary, the addition to the `dictionary.1st` would be the following line:

```
DICT en CA en_CA
```

After the dictionary has been added, it can be used for reference purposes in the document.

Installing a Dictionary Automatically

The automatic install process performs all the same steps as a manual installation. The automatic installation document is downloaded from *http://lingucomponent. openoffice.org/dictpack.html*. On the downloaded page at the top of the available files to download list is a file described as *DicOOo Macro* with the filename DicOOo.sxw. After downloading the file DicOOo.sxw, start it automatically by double-clicking on it. A message box will probably appear asking if it is acceptable to execute the contained macros. Click Run and the resulting document should appear similar to Figure 10.1.

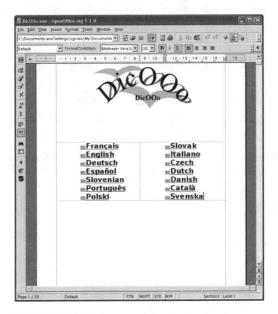

FIGURE 10.1 Dictionary document allowing a user to choose which dictionaries to download.

In the dialog box asking whether or not to run the contained macros, there is a checkbox that can be used to add the path of the document as a secure path. In this example of the dictionary download document, most likely you will not want to add the path to the secure path. A secure path is considered as trusted and the macro execution dialog box will not appear.

The languages defined in Figure 10.1 have nothing to do with the dictionaries that can be downloaded. The languages refer to the language of the dialog boxes that will be displayed when downloading the dictionaries. For example purposes, the English language link in Figure 10.1 is chosen. The document will scroll down to the English language section as shown in Figure 10.2.

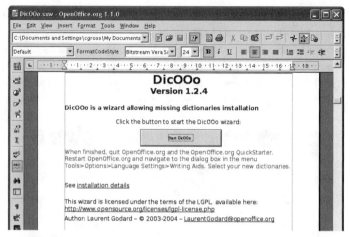

FIGURE 10.2 Dictionary wizard displaying the download options for the available dictionaries.

In Figure 10.2 the document wizard has a single button to click to start the dictionary download wizard. The other links on the document relate to details on how to install the packages and reference the license used to distribute the package. Click the Start DicOOo button to open the dialog box shown in Figure 10.3.

In Figure 10.3, there are several different installation strategies: offline, current user, and administrative. When choosing offline mode, it is assumed that all the dictionaries, thesauruses, and hyphenation libraries have already been downloaded. The offline mode is useful in a corporate network scenario where all users are downloading their own libraries. If the offline mode is checked, then a Select a

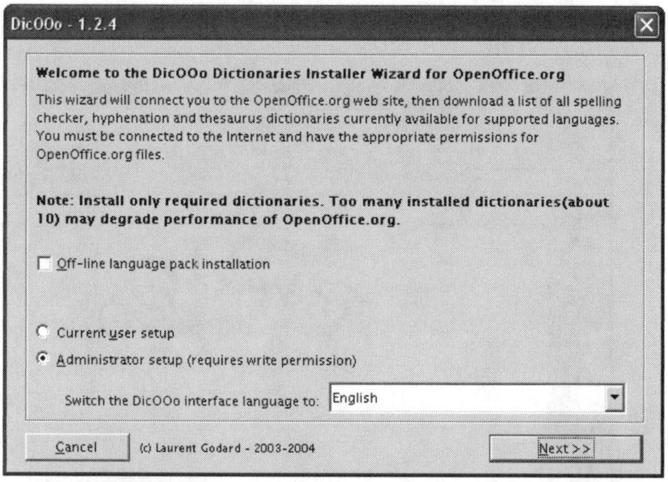

FIGURE 10.3 Dictionary wizard displaying the general options for installing the dictionaries.

Language Pack text box appears. Beside the text box is a Browse button that allows you to select a language pack. A language pack is downloaded from the same download page as the Dic0Oo.sxw is downloaded. Language packs tend be organized in major languages such as English, which will include individual dialects such as Canadian, British, or American English. For illustration purposes, click the online download variant and click Next to open the dialog box shown in Figure 10.4.

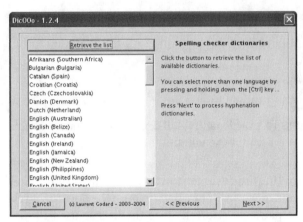

FIGURE 10.4 Dictionary wizard displaying available dictionaries.

The available dictionaries that can be installed appear in the main listbox. Note that when doing an online installation, the listbox is initially empty and you must click the Retrieve the List button. After you click the button, the available dictionaries list is downloaded. Choose the dictionaries to download by selecting one or more from the list. Click Next to open the dialog box shown in Figure 10.5.

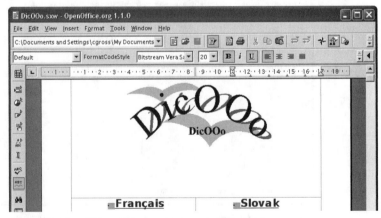

FIGURE 10.5 Dictionary wizard displaying available hyphenation dictionaries.

The dictionary wizard is not only intended for dictionaries, but is also used for downloading a thesaurus or a hyphenation library. Figure 10.5 is used to specify all the hyphenation dictionaries that should be downloaded using the same selection process used in Figure 10.4. After all the hyphenation dictionaries have been selected, click the Next to open Thesaurus Dictionaries dialog box as shown in Figure 10.6.

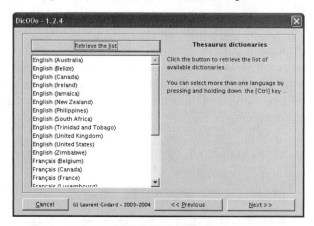

FIGURE 10.6 Dictionary wizard displaying available thesauruses.

Figure 10.6 is used to specify all the thesauruses that should be downloaded using the same selection process as used in Figure 10.4. After all the thesauri have been selected, click Next to open the dialog box shown in Figure 10.7.

In Figure 10.7, the checkbox by default is checked so that the installation does not overwrite dictionaries that are already installed. When you click the Next button, the individual language files are downloaded and installed. After everything has been installed, a dialog box appears indicating that the install was successful. It is important that OpenOffice is completely restarted so that the newly installed libraries are available.

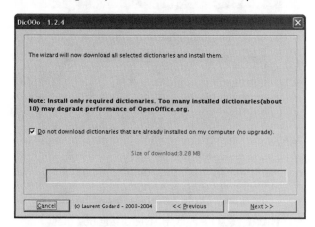

FIGURE 10.7 Dictionary wizard before performing downloading of files and indicating download size.

Using a Specific Language in a Document

The language can be defined to be applied for a full document, paragraph, or for a selected text. To apply a language for a full document, choose Tools -> Options to open the Options - Language Settings - Languages dialog box as shown in Figure 10.8.

In the Options dialog box, the item Language Settings - Languages is selected. The dialog box displays the default languages used, which in Figure 10.8 happened to be English with the dialect American. This means whenever a new document is created, an American English dictionary, hyphenation, and thesaurus is assumed. Changing the combo box changes the default language, unless the For the Current Document Only checkbox is set. If the checkbox is set, then the language for the current document is changed, but the default language will remain as before.

To change the language used for a specific paragraph, the cursor must be in the paragraph that needs to be altered. Then, right-click and choose Edit Paragraph Style from the menu to open the Paragraph Style dialog box shown in Figure 10.9.

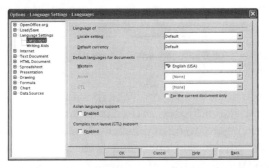

FIGURE 10.8 Options dialog box used to choose the language for the document.

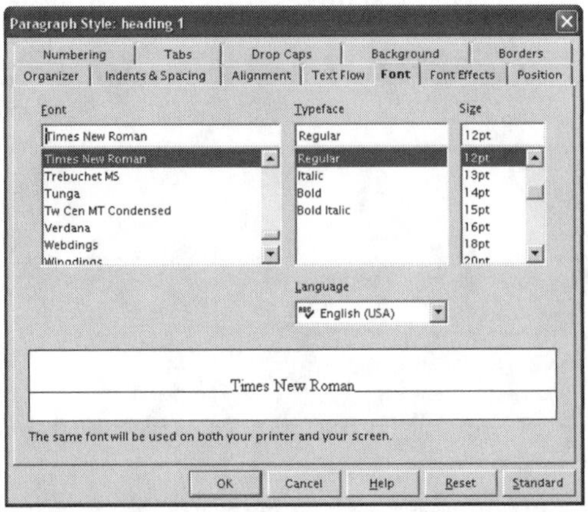

FIGURE 10.9 Paragraph Style dialog box that allows selection of language.

In Figure 10.9, the Font tab contains a Language combo box that can be used to select the language that should be applied to the paragraph.

To select the language for a selected text block, right-click on the selected text block. Choose Character from the menu that appears to open the dialog box and tab shown previously in Figure 10.9. Like Figure 10.9, the language is selected from the combo box.

The techniques described used OpenOffice Writer as an example, but the same dialog boxes apply to the different OpenOffice applications.

Technique: Managing Document Templates

One of the objectives when creating standardized content is to define a set of styles that people should use. By default, all documents have associated styles. There are default styles shipped with OpenOffice. Document styles make it possible to format entire sections using a notation that can be updated dynamically. A document style is similar to a stylesheet for HTML documents. Styles are applied to a document, and the document is stored as a template. The template is then used as a base document for others to create content.

Managing Styles

OpenOffice has the notion of five different style groupings: character, paragraph, frame, page, and numbering. The difference between the different style groupings is scope. For example, defining a paragraph style makes changes to an entire paragraph. That logic may seem obvious, but sometimes users attempt to define a single style for both individual characters and a paragraph. Each of the styles are defined as follows:

Character: Any style defined in character scope will apply to the text selected or to the text beside the cursor.

Paragraph: Any style applied in paragraph scope will apply to the paragraph where the cursor is located.

Frame: A style that is applied in frame scope relates to text within a boxed area called a frame. Consider a frame like a picture that has been embedded into a document. The difference is that a frame contains text and not just a picture.

Page: A style that is page scope relates to items added to individual pages such as footnotes or page count numbers.

Numbering: A style that is of numbering scope relates items that are numbered and list related.

Individual styles can be applied to a document using the style list dialog box, which can be made visible by pressing the F11 key or selecting the menu item Format → Stylelist. The dialog box appears as shown in Figure 10.10.

FIGURE 10.10 Style list dialog box showing the available styles for the Paragraph style grouping.

You use the style list dialog box to format text according to an available style. The style list is also a place to modify an existing style or create a new style based on the selected style. To create a new style or modify a style, you select the style from the style list dialog box, right-click, and choose New or Modify (the same dialog box appears regardless of which option you choose) as shown in Figure 10.11.

Regardless in what grouping a style is being defined there are some common attributes. In Figure 10.11, each style is given a name as defined in the Name text box.

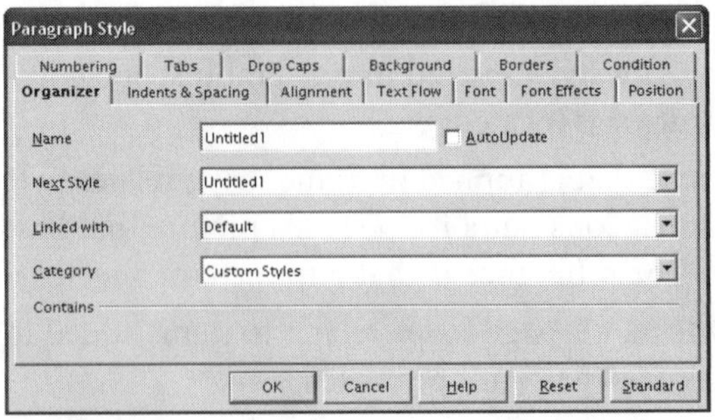

FIGURE 10.11 Dialog box showing paragraph style attributes.

Each style is also linked to another style for base attribute values as defined by the Linked With combo box. Linking is useful because a hierarchy of styles can be defined. In the example given in Figure 10.11, the base style definition is the Default style. If nothing is changed in any of the tabs of the dialog box, then the new style is a direct inheritance of the Default style. This results in the ramification that if any changes in the Default style are made, those changes are propagated to the new style definition.

The styles described thus far all relate to OpenOffice writer, but each OpenOffice application has its own style groupings. For example, OpenOffice Calc has cell and page style groupings. Regardless of which OpenOffice application is used, the definition of a style within a particular grouping has some common dialog box tabs. The individual tabs in Figure 10.11 are the individual attributes that can be used to define a particular style in a grouping. OpenOffice has standard tabs used in different style groups and they are defined as follows. Note that the number of tabs that OpenOffice has to define the different styles is very large, so just consider the following a reference to get an idea of what can and cannot be configured:

Alignment: Configures how the text will be arranged in a text block such as a paragraph. Text alignment examples include justified or right aligned.

Area: Defines how a graphical object will be filled, which could be a color, hatching, or graphical image.

Background: Configures the background look of a text block, such as coloring or if a graphic is used. Adding a background is useful when paragraphs are meant to be highlighted without having to have the text added to a graphic. OpenOffice automatically realigns the background coloring or graphic if the text block dimensions change.

Borders: If the Background tab configured the rectangular area contained by a text block, then the Borders tab configures the border around the rectangular area. You can configure whether a box is drawn, the thickness of the box, the box shadow, and the color of either the box or shadow. Using the Borders tab it is possible to define the spacing that text has with respect to the rectangular area the text occupies.

Bullets: Defines the bullet style of a numbering type format such as bullets in Writer or presentation points in Impress.

Cell Protection: Defines whether a cell of a spreadsheet can be manipulated or made read only. Using this style attribute is important when creating spreadsheets that implement formulas and some numbers of the formulas need to be protected from editing. Note that a cell becomes protected when the spreadsheet is explicitly protected.

Columns: Defines the column structure of a style in a text block. An example of a multiple column structure is a newspaper.

Connector: Defines how the individual lines that join multiple graphical objects are represented.

Dimensioning: Configures how a dimensional graphical object is drawn. A dimensional graphical element is typically used by Draw to indicate a dimension such as length, width, or height.

Drop Caps: Configures how the first letter or letters or word of a paragraph appears.

Font: Configures the font attributes such as font, size, typeface, and language.

Footer: Defines the footer information of a page such as if a footer exists and the dimensions of the header block.

Footnote: Configures the footnote block of a page.

Font Effects: Configures font-related effects such as underlining, font color, shadowing, outlining, or blinking.

Graphics: Defines how specific attributes are graphically represented, for example, when bullets use graphical image representations.

Header: Defines the header information of a page such as if a header exists and the dimensions of the header block.

Indents & Spacing: Configures the spacing of the text within a text block. Defined can be whether or not single spacing or double spacing is used, and indentation of the first and last line of text in the text block.

Line: Applies a certain style to lines drawn as graphical objects.

Macro: Enables a style designer to associate macros with specific events such as when a user clicks on text block.

Numbers: Configures the formatting of a number and defines attributes such as the number of decimal places and leading zeros.

Numbering: Defines how items will be numbered.

Numbering Style: Defines the numbering style of a numbering type format such as numbered bullets in Writer or presentation points in Impress.

Options: Defines some miscellaneous options related to the style and varies in the different style groupings.

Organizer: Configures the overall information about the style such as identifier and which base style relates to the style.

Outline: Defines a formatting style used when creating formatted outlines used in a table of contents or in document section headings.

Page: Configures the page structure such as page dimensions and how the page is printed (e.g., landscape or portrait).

Position: Configures the positioning of the text such as the rotation, spacing, and subscript or superscript.

Shadowing: Configures how a graphical object will be shadowed.

Sheet: Configures the page structure of a spreadsheet in terms of how pages that make up a spreadsheet will be printed, and what elements of the spreadsheet are printed.

Text: Configures how text will be located on a graphical object. This tab is different from the Position tab in that the orientation of text within a graphical object is defined. Usually a text block is defined as a rectangular area that can be made to look like a rectangular graphical object. It is important to realize the rectangular area is not a graphical object.

Text Animation: Configures the text animation when animation is activated for a graphical document or a presentation.

Text Flow: Configures the hyphenation or breaks of the text within a text block. You can define when hyphenation occurs and how words are broken up, including paragraph breaks.

Tabs: Configures location of unique tabs in a text block. This is useful when creating lists or table-like structures.

Transparency: Configures the transparency of an object. The transparency is used to create a layered effect when combining multiple graphical objects on top of another.

Type: Configures the type of frame block in terms of width, height, and positioning on the page.

Wrap: Configures the spacing of text that wraps around a text frame block.

OpenOffice allows an administrator to fine-tune how a document is constructed, displayed, and printed. An advantage of the style list is that there is no macro programming required. The administrator is well advised to take some time to learn all the style features when defining styles.

When a style has been defined, it can be utilized in the document by picking the newly defined style from the style list dialog box shown previously in Figure 10.10. There is a potential problem in that when defining multiple styles, the style list listbox can become too crowded and the user is constantly scrolling the listbox. In the earlier Figure 10.11, when defining a new style there is the option to define the Category of the style. In most cases, the Custom Styles value will be used. In Figure 10.10, it is possible to filter according to the category using the combo box at the bottom of the style list dialog box.

Managing Templates

After a set of styles has been defined, it can be used to form the basis of a template. A *template* is nothing more than a document that contains some macros, styles, and information that is used to create a new document. In effect, it is like opening up a reference document and then saving the document under a new name. The template automatically creates a new document using the new document naming convention.

A template is created by saving the document as a template in the Save As dialog box. If the document is created using Writer, then using the Save As dialog box the template document is saved as the file type OpenOffice.org 1.0 Document Template (.stw). There are no additional steps required to create a template. Most template documents have a t in the extension. For example, a Write document is saved as .sxw, and a template for Write is .stw, where the x is replaced with a t.

To make use of a template, the template has to be loaded by the OpenOffice application. When creating a new document instead of loading an explicit OpenOffice application, a template is loaded using the menu item From Template. The Templates dialog box shown in Figure 10.12 appears.

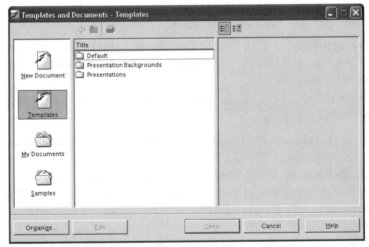

FIGURE 10.12 Template dialog box used to choose a template to load.

The templates dialog box in Figure 10.12 can be used to load templates located in the default position or somewhere within the My Documents subdirectories. To add templates to the default templates listbox Title as shown in Figure 10.12, templates can either be copied manually or managed using the Template Management dialog box.

A user manages the templates using the Template Management dialog box (see Figure 10.13) that is activated by choosing Templates -> Organize. (Note this works from any OpenOffice application.)

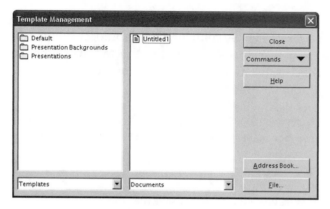

FIGURE 10.13 Dialog box used to manage templates.

Comparing the lefthand listbox of Figure 10.13 and the listbox of Figure 10.12, it should be apparent that they are identical. This is intentional because the dialog box in Figure 10.12 is read-only access to the template folders, and the dialog box in Figure 10.13 is used to edit the template folders.

Template folders in Figure 10.13 are added by right-clicking the lefthand list-box in Figure 10.13 to open the menu shown in Figure 10.14.

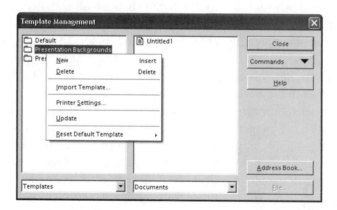

FIGURE 10.14 Template Management dialog box showing shortcut menu.

To create a new folder, click the New menu item. A folder labeled Untitled is created, and even though it is not apparent, the label can be edited to whatever value is desired by typing on the keyboard. After the label has been edited, it cannot be changed.

There is a way to change the label value by editing the underlying configuration file Hierarchy.xcu. The file configuration file is located in the directory /user/registry/data/org/openoffice/ucb and the directory will either be a location within the OpenOffice installation or Application Data directories. Following is an example excerpt from the Hiearchy.xcu file:

```
<node oor:name="OOPS%20an%20error" oor:op="replace">
    <prop oor:name="TargetURL" oor:type="xs:string">
        <value/>
    </prop>
    <prop oor:name="Title" oor:type="xs:string">
        <value>OOPS an error</value>
    </prop>
    <prop oor:name="Type" oor:type="xs:int">
        <value>1</value>
    </prop>
</node>
```

The XML node node is part of a generic structure that creates a folder structure. To update a label, there are two changes to make. The first change is to update the attribute oor:name. If the identifier contains spaces, they must be replaced with an escape identifier %20. The second change to make is to update the node prop and value of OOPS an error. To complete the changes, all instances of OpenOffice including the quick launcher have to be exited.

You can also manually add templates and folders by simply copying the templates to the /user/templates directory. Then the next time OpenOffice starts, the configuration files will be updated and the Templates and Documents dialog box shown earlier in Figure 10.12 will contain the new templates.

The other requirement for some deployments is the ability to define a default template. When an OpenOffice applications starts, an empty document is created based on the default template. The default template is assigned by selecting a document from the Template Management dialog box shown previously in Figure 10.13. After a document has been selected, right-click and a menu similar to Figure 10.14 appears. This time, choose Set As Default Template.The other menu item Reset Default Template is used to reset the default template to the OpenOffice internally defined default template.

In a deployment scenario, assigning the default template using a GUI is not effective because it is labor intensive and prone to errors. You can define a default template by manipulating the Setup.xcu configuration file located in the directory /user/registry/data/org/openoffice. The Setup.xcu file contains a number of XML nodes that define a number of factories used when a new document is created. An abbreviation is shown as follows.

```
<node oor:name="com.sun.star.text.TextDocument">
    <prop oor:name="ooSetupFactoryWindowAttributes"
     oor:type="xs:string">
        <value>327,283,1015,709;1;</value>
    </prop>
    <prop oor:name="ooSetupFactoryTemplateFile"
     oor:type="xs:string">

<value>file:///C:/Documents%20and%20Settings/cgross/Application%20Data/
OpenOffice.org680/user/template/testdefault.stw</value>
    </prop>
</node>
```

The XML node `node` with attribute `oor:name` defines default attributes for the
`com.sun.star.text.TextDocument`, which is the Write application. To define a default template to load the XML node `prop` with the `oor:name` attribute value, `ooSe-`
`tupFactoryTemplateFile` defines the default template. The document is defined as a
URL, which in the case of `file:///` `identifier` is a file on a hard disk.

Technique: Creating and Binding a Macro

Styles and templates are used to define custom content on a document, spreadsheet, or presentation. To create workflow applications, automation and forms
have to be created that are supported by OpenOffice. To automate OpenOffice,
scripts or programs can be created using programming languages such as OpenBasic, Java, C++, or Python. Creating automation programs using Java or C++ is a
complicated process and beyond the scope of this book. Creating automation
scripts using OpenBasic is essentially the simplest.

Creating a Simple Macro

This book was written using OpenOffice Write and the content was created using
formatting rules prescribed by the publisher of this book. One example of a special
formatting rule is the use of Courier fonts to indicate a code segment. Converting
some selected text into Courier font is a three-step process.

1. Create a style that represents the code formatting. Because the coding style
   is straightforward, it's also possible to convert the text directly to Courier
   font. However, the downside to that strategy is that it would not be possible at a later time to change the characteristics of how code segments are
   generated.
2. Create a macro that converts the selected text into the code style.
3. Attach the macro to a toolbar, or menu item, or keyboard shortcut.

To create a code style, be sure to read the previous technique, which described all the details about styles and templates. To create a macro, the administrator could write the script as an OpenBasic or Python script. The simplest method, however, is to record a macro, which generates an OpenBasic script.

To record a macro, choose Tools → Macros → Record Macro to open a dialog box with a single Stop Recording button. OpenOffice begins at that moment to record every event. OpenOffice is recording OpenOffice events and not mouse movements. So, for example, if a font is converted to bold, the macro recorder will record the conversion to bold and not the keystrokes or mouseclicks. After the actions for the macro have been completed, click the Stop Recording button and the Macro dialog box appears as shown in Figure 10.15.

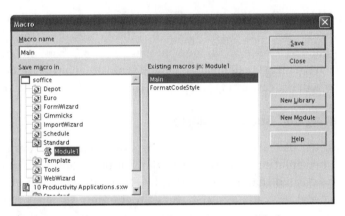

FIGURE 10.15 Dialog box used to assign a recorded macro to an OpenBasic module.

In Figure 10.15, the dialog box is used to associate the recorded macro with a module. It is possible to overwrite an already existing macro or create a new macro using the dialog box. The default is to associate the recorded macro with the Main function in the Module1 module of the Standard library. To associate the recorded macro with another macro, you type the name of the macro in the Macro Name text box. To save the macro, click the Save button.

The Save Macro In listbox contains a listing of libraries and modules that are available. The libraries and modules are grouped into two blocks: soffice, and in the case of Figure 10.15, 10 Productivity Applications.sxw. soffice is a global block that when manipulated affects every OpenOffice user on the local machine. The 10 Productivity Applications.sxw block when manipulated is specific to the document being edited only. Clicking the New Library button creates a new library that can contain multiple modules. Clicking the New Module button creates a new module that can contain multiple functions.

Click the Save button to close the Macro dialog box and return control to OpenOffice Write. To view the macro, choose Tools → Macros → Macro and the Macro dialog box appears. The main difference is that now additional buttons are available to add and delete the item selected in either of the listboxes of the dialog box. Select the macro that was added and then click the Edit button to open the window shown in Figure 10.16.

FIGURE 10.16 OpenOffice macro editor used to write OpenBasic functions.

In Figure 10.16, the macro `NewFormat` recorded the steps that involved converting a selected text into the text style `Code`. As the macro definition stands, it is usable, but because it is not bound to any GUI element, the macro `NewFormat` is not used for anything.

Binding a Macro to a Menu

You can bind a macro to a GUI event in several ways: by using the toolbar, keyboard shortcut, or menu item.

Unlike other productivity applications, a macro must be created when you want to apply a specific text style to a block of text using a GUI event such as a toolbar.

Regardless of which GUI event is defined, the Configuration dialog box is used. Open this dialog box by choosing Tools → Configure (see Figure 10.17).

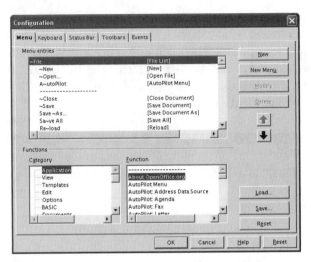

FIGURE 10.17 Dialog box used to define a binding.

The Configuration dialog box has several tabs that are used to bind some OpenOffice functionality to a GUI element. The Menu tab can be used to bind a macro to a menu item. The Menu Entries listbox contains all menu items used in the particular OpenOffice application. Scrolling up and down the list shows all the menu items, and the indent of an individual item represents the menu level. In Figure 10.17, the item ~File is a top-level menu and ~New is subitem within the ~File menu. Any item that includes a number of dashes is a menu separator.

To add a menu within the menu anywhere, click the New Menu button. Two menu items are created: Menu, and a menu separator that is a sublevel item of the Menu item. To create a new menu item based on some functionality, click the New button. The functionality depends on the value selected in the Function listbox. The level of the added functionality item is the same as the selected item in the Menu Entries listbox.

The Category listbox of Figure 10.17 is a way of grouping functionalities that are displayed in the Function listbox. By selecting a value in the Category listbox, the available functionalities are generated in the Function listbox. To assign a macro to a menu item, scroll to the bottom of the Category listbox so that the items OpenOffice.org BASIC Macros is shown, and the item after that. The item after is not named because it is a concatenation of the document identifier and the text BASIC Macros. In front of each menu item a plus sign in a box represents that the menu item can be double-clicked and expanded to expose the available libraries and modules. By selecting an individual module and library, the function names will be loaded into the Function listbox.

To update the functionality of an individual menu item, select the functionality from the Function listbox, select the menu item from the Menu Entries listbox, and click the Modify button. The menu item then reflects the new functionality. Clicking the Delete button deletes the item selected in the Menu Entries listbox.

Editing a menu using the dialog box is acceptable for an initial structure update, but not for fine-tuning and tweaking the menu. In fact, it's essentially impossible to update the text identifier used in the menu. To tweak and tune the menu structure, you need to update the underlying XML files. The name of the file depends on the version of OpenOffice used. In either version, the location is somewhere underneath the OpenOffice installation directory. Then within either `share/config/soffice.cfg` or `user/config/soffice.cfg` will be either the files `[OpenOffice application]` `menubar.xml` or `[OpenOffice application]/menubar/menubar.xml`.

In either case, the XML file will contain content similar to the following:

```
<menu:menubar
    xmlns:menu="http://openoffice.org/2001/menu"
    menu:id="menubar">
    <menu:menu menu:id="slot:5510" menu:label="~File">
        <menu:menupopup>
            <menu:menu menu:id="slot:3" menu:label="Menu">
                <menu:menuitem
    menu:id="macro:///Standard.Module1.FormatCodeStyle()"
    menu:label="Inline Code Format"/>
                <menu:menuitem menu:id="slot:5501"
                  menu:helpid="5501" menu:label="Open File"/>
        </menu:menupopup>
    </menu:menu>
</menu:menu>
```

The example illustrates a menu definition used for OpenOffice 1.1.x, whereas OpenOffice 2.x versions tend to use more descriptive terms when describing the `menu:id` attribute.

To avoid errors in the menu configuration file, the `menu:id` *values should not be changed; instead, they should be generated using the Configuration dialog box. For simplicity purposes, the administrator could just randomly add all the needed items somewhere in the menu and then organize the menu configuration file for organization and descriptive identifiers.*

The XML attribute `menu:id` with a value of `macro:///...` is the same in either OpenOffice 1.1.x or 2.x and is used to denote a reference to a macro. The attribute `menu:label` can and should be edited because it represents the descriptive text that the user will read to understand what the menu item does.

Binding a Macro to a Keyboard Sequence

To bind a macro to a keyboard sequence, the Keyboard tab on the Macro dialog box is used as shown in Figure 10.18.

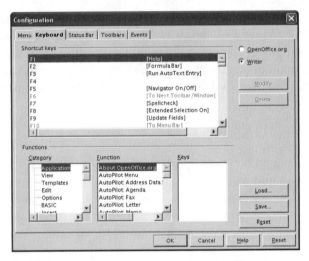

FIGURE 10.18 Dialog box used to define a keyboard sequence binding.

The Shortcut Keys listbox contains all the available keyboard sequences. If the keyboard sequence has been assigned, then a functionality will be assigned, such as the Help functionality that is assigned to the key F1. If no functionality is assigned, then a blank will appear in the list as is the case for the F4 key. The OpenOffice.org radio button is used to define keyboard sequences that are globally defined. The Writer radio button is used to define keyboard sequences specific to the Open Office Writer application.

To modify or delete a keyboard sequence, select the sequence from the Shortcut Keys listbox. If an entry is selected and the Modify and Delete buttons remain disabled, then that definition is system defined.

To assign a keyboard sequence, select the appropriate items in the Category and Function listboxes in the same way as shown in the "Binding a Macro to a Menu" section. If a function has already been assigned to a keyboard sequence, it is displayed in the Keys listbox. The purpose of doing that is to make it simpler to figure out if a function has already been assigned.

To edit the keyboard sequence binding configuration file, look at /user/config/soffice.cfg directory. The directory may either be local to the user if a network installation is performed or within the OpenOffice installation directory. Within the directory is a file that contains the identifier keybinding (e.g., writerkeybinding.xml) and represents the key sequence binding configuration file. Within the configuration file are a number of XML nodes that describe the key sequence bindings.

Binding a Macro to a Toolbar

To bind a macro to a toolbar, you use the Toolbars tab on the Macro dialog box shown in Figure 10.19.

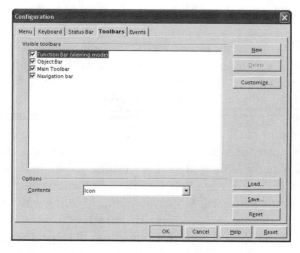

FIGURE 10.19 Dialog box used to define a new toolbar.

The Toolbars tab is used to add and delete toolbars. In the Visible Toolbars listbox, the checkbox is used to display or hide the toolbar. A check means that the toolbar is visible. The Customize button is used to modify the contents of the toolbars in the Visible Toolbars listbox. The Contents combo box is used to define what is displayed in the toolbar (for example, text or the icon if available). You should keep the default, Icon, as an icon tends to require less space.

Clicking the Customize button will open the Customizing Toolbars dialog box as shown in Figure 10.20.

When the Customize Toolbars dialog box is activated, the Toolbars combo box will not show the toolbar that was selected in the Configuration dialog box of Figure 10.19. The user must select the toolbar to manipulate, which in Figure 10.20 is a custom defined toolbar.

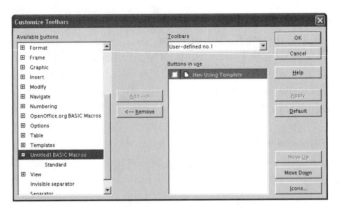

FIGURE 10.20 Dialog box used to manipulate a toolbar.

To add buttons to the toolbar, select the functionality from the Available Buttons listbox. Expand the items OpenOffice.org BASIC Macros and Untitled1 BASIC Macros to select the appropriate macro function. To add the functionality, click the Add button and the item will be added to the Buttons in Use listbox.

The Move Up and Move Down buttons are used to move the item to the beginning or ending of the toolbar. Newly added macros in the Buttons in Use listbox will not have an associated icon. To associate an icon, select the macro identifier and then click on the Icons button. The Customize Buttons dialog box appears containing icons that are used to define an item on the toolbar.

To edit the keyboard sequence binding configuration file, look at the /user/config/soffice.cfg directory. The directory may either be local to the user if a network installation is performed or within the OpenOffice installation directory. Within the directory is a file that contains the identifier toolbox (e.g., userdeftoolbox1.xml; ignore the file toolboxlayout.xml as that file contains the references to all toolbars), which represents the toolbar configuration file. Within the configuration file are a number of XML nodes that describe the individual toolbar buttons.

Technique: Analyzing the Document Structure

Every OpenOffice document uses XML as the underlying data structure. Opening a typical OpenOffice document using some text editor will make the administrator not believe that OpenOffice is using XML. As an optimization, OpenOffice stores all its data in a compressed ZIP archive. To see the contents of the ZIP archive, open an OpenOffice document using some ZIP archive processor and extract all the files.

When extracting OpenOffice documents using a ZIP file archive program, make sure to precreate a subdirectory; otherwise, all the directories and files will be extracted into the current directory.

TIP

OpenOffice XML Document Structure

The following listing is a sample document extraction and the structure that it represents (note that directories are represented by a plus sign):

```
+Basic
  +ExampleLibrary
    script-lb.xml
    Module1.xml
  +Standard
    script-lb.xml
  script-lc.xml
+Dialogs
  +ExampleLibrary
    dialog-lb.xml
  +Standard
    dialog-lb.xml
  dialog-lc.xml
+META-INF
  manifest.xml
content.xml
meta.xml
mimetypes
settings.xml
styles.xml
```

The definition of each of the files and its associated directory is as follows where the individual items are sorted using a top down approach:

`content.xml`: Contains the raw document contents, which are not dependent on any specific OpenOffice application. All OpenOffice applications have the potential capability to generate the same content. The individual XML namespaces make each content unique.

`meta.xml`: Defines the meta information that is associated with the document. The meta information is typically the same information stored in the Document Properties dialog box (choose File → Properties).

`styles.xml`: Defines extra styles used specifically only within the document. For example, when defining a template the styles will be stored in the `styles.xml` document.

`settings.xml`: Defines information that is not directly related to the document, but related to the settings used for the document when OpenOffice edits the document.

`mimetype`: Contains the various defined mime-types used by the document.

Basic: A directory that contains all the OpenOffice Basic macros associated with the document. If the document references a global macro, then that macro is found in the directory [OpenOffice installation]/share/basic. Both the global and local macro directory structures are identical.

Dialogs: A directory that contains all OpenOffice Basic dialog boxes and formulas used.

script-lc.xml: A configuration file that contains references to the libraries defined in the document.

ExampleLibrary, Standard: Directories that define a higher-level library definition.

script-lb.xml: A configuration file that contains all references to the modules defined within the library directory.

Module1.xml: A module definition file that contains a number of functions. The functions are defined using OpenOffice Basic and defined as an XML node of escaped text.

dialog-lb.xml: A configuration file that contains references to all dialog boxes and formulas defined in the document. The individual dialog boxes and formulas are represented using an XML structure within an XML document.

mainfest.xml: A configuration file that defines the mime type of the individual documents contained within the OpenOffice document structure.

Each of the XML files has an associated Document Type Definitions (DTD) definition file. All the DTD definition files used in OpenOffice are defined in the directory [OpenOfficeinstallation]/share/dtd. The administrator or user shouldn't actually edit the files, but use them when defining their own documents.

The administrator can easily create document and template structures because OpenOffice saves all its files using XML. The administrator should consider using the XML structure as a way of converting between one format and another. For example, some XSLT transformation pages can be used to generate PDF or PostScript.

Using OpenOffice-Built XML Transformations

As OpenOffice documents are XML based, there exists functionality within OpenOffice to transform other XML documents. OpenOffice calls this transformation *XML filtering*. Using XML filtering, you can import or export XML documents to or from OpenOffice. For example, a default filter exists to import or export the DocBook file format.

To use the XML filters, choose Tools → XML Filter Settings to open the XML Filter Settings dialog box as shown in Figure 10.21.

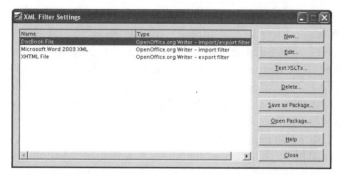

FIGURE 10.21 Dialog box used to define and test XSLT filters.

The dialog box in Figure 10.21 shows that you can import Microsoft Word 2003 XML files, and export XHTML files. To define a new set of XML import export filters, click the New button and the XML Filter: New Filter dialog box appears as shown in Figure 10.22.

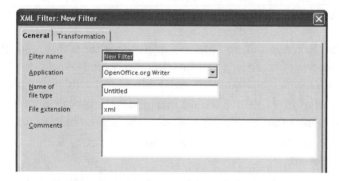

FIGURE 10.22 Dialog box used to define a new XML filter.

The dialog box in Figure 10.22 allows the user to define a new XML filter and associate it within the OpenOffice application. Click on the Transformation tab to expose parameters used to import or export an XML document. You can define the DTD, XSLT documents for exporting, XSLT documents for importing, and a default template that is assigned when importing a document. After you've defined the individual parameters, click OK to create a new XML filter.

To use the newly created XML filter, a user has to simply open a document or export a document. When either of these operations are performed, a dialog box appears in which the user can find the newly defined XML filter in the File Types combo box. It is important that the data in the General tab of Figure 10.21 are properly filled out as the file operations dialog box uses those values.

Figure 10.21 shows the Test XSLTs button that can be used to test XSLT documents. It is good to use that functionality when the XSLT document has already been coded and debugged. This raises the question of how to code and debug an XSLT filter. This solution is a two-step process. The first step is to read the XML file format OpenOffice documentation found at *http://xml.openoffice.org*. The documentation is fairly hefty at nearly 600 pages long. However, to write a good filter, the author has to be aware of the different elements and therefore should at least skim the entire 600 pages. The second step is to invest in an XSLT development environment. Although it's possible to use a simple editor to code an XSLT sheet, trying to debug that sheet and fix errors is a lesson in futility. XSLT can be very hard to debug when the script becomes complicated and OpenOffice filter can become complicated.

Technique: Using Auto Pilots

A very powerful feature within OpenOffice is the Auto Pilot. The individual Auto Pilots are accessed by choosing File → Auto Pilot. An Auto Pilot is a script that acts as a wizard and can perform some generic operation. The individual Auto Pilots are defined as follows:

Letter, **Fax**, **Agenda**, and **Memo**: Multistep wizards that guide the user through the process of creating a custom letter, fax, agenda, and memo that can include custom logos, text alignment, and addresses of sender and receiver.

Presentation: Multistep wizard that guides the user through the process of creating a presentation that can contain custom presentation templates, and so on.

Web Page: Wizard used to create an HTML page with a specific layout and background.

Form: Wizard that generates a form page that is bound to a database table. The created form will access the database using live database techniques.

Report: Multistep wizard that generates a report page that is bound to a database table. The wizard can be used organize and sort the data in the report. The created report will access the database using live database techniques.

Document Converter: Multistep wizard used to convert a group of documents into another format. This Auto Pilot is especially useful when it is necessary to convert a large number of documents from one productivity application to another.

Euro Converter: Wizard used to batch convert a number of documents that contain currencies in a European currency that has been replaced by the Euro. The conversion rates used are the standard rates issued by the European Central Bank.

StarOffice 5.2 Database Import: Wizard used to access and convert data stored in a StarBase 5.2 database. The wizard will not in any way change the original database.

Address Data Source: Multistep wizard used to import address book data into OpenOffice. The OpenOffice applications use the address functionality from Mozilla.

For the administrator, one of the most useful Auto Pilots is the mass conversion of document types. OpenOffice can read and write documents in multiple formats, and OpenOffice can use other formats as default storage formats. However, by doing a mass conversion, there will be fewer future problems.

Technique: Writing Automation Scripts Using OpenOffice Basic or Python

In the "Technique: Creating and Binding a Macro" section, you saw how to create a simple macro and then bind it to a GUI. That section also pointed out that it's possible to create an automation script in different programming languages. For the scope of this book, we'll explain only the macro programming languages Python and OpenOffice Basic.

Following are the disadvantages and advantages of each language.

OpenOffice Basic pros:
- Easy to program
- Seamless integration into OpenOffice
- Full debugging and development support

OpenOffice Basic cons:
- Requires learning the OpenOffice Basic programming language
- Uses a programming language that is not object oriented and could result in convoluted solutions

Python pros:
- Straightforward object-oriented language
- As simple as OpenOffice Basic when manipulating the UNO object model
- Has a wide variety of editors and libraries

Python cons:
- Not as simple as OpenOffice when attempting to integrate as a full solution
- Not as simple as OpenOffice Basic
- Debugging of solutions is more complicated, if possible at all

Overall, however, the language used depends on the sophistication of the people programming the various solutions. If the people writing the code tend to be programmers who have business knowledge, then Python might be a better solution. If the people writing the code tend to be business people who have programming knowledge, then OpenOffice Basic is the better solution. If complete integration to the GUI and the most flexibility is required, then OpenOffice Basic is a better solution. Using OpenOffice Basic as the programming environment does have the ramification that all solutions written are very specific to OpenOffice and porting the application to another productivity suite is next to impossible. At least with Python a semiportable layer could be written. Success with the semiportable layer is not guaranteed, however.

Understanding the UNO Object Model

Regardless of the programming language used, you need to understand the UNO object model. The UNO object model has the same overall structure in each programming language; however, the individual details are different. For example, in Python it is possible to use attributes and properties whereas that might not be possible in Java or C++. The UNO object model is not documented in the standard OpenOffice documentation, but is documented in the OpenOffice SDK.

One of the biggest issues with developing for OpenOffice is its documentation. The problem of the documentation is not that it's not thorough enough, but that it's not very user-friendly. A casual scriptwriter when reading the documentation will become very concerned at the complexity of OpenOffice. For example, the standard documentation with the OpenOffice SDK tends to be focused on the C++ or Java programmer. A programmer that does not program in C++ or Java will then essentially have to read through a large number of methods and properties that have nothing to do with the language being used.

The reason a programmer of OpenOffice will want to read or at least skim some of the SDK documentation is because it is the reference. With respect to documentation, a better approach is to open a browser and surf to *http://development .openoffice.org/*. This site is the main place where developers can find information they need to write their script and macros.

Scroll down to the Write Scripts and Macros section on the page. The URLs in that section reference other documents that can be used to figure out how to write scripts and macros for OpenOffice. In particular, look at the introductory documentation entitled StarOffice Software Basic Programmers Guide, and OpenOffice Macro Document by Andrew Pitonyak. If you intend to write any type of macros to automate OpenOffice, then it is very important to read the mentioned documents.

You should download the OpenOffice SDK to access a number of examples and documentation that goes beyond the basic knowledge. The OpenOffice SDK can be downloaded at the same URL where OpenOffice was downloaded. The

OpenOffice SDK is distributed as an archive that when expanded will create the `OpenOffice SDK` subdirectory.

Within the OpenOffice subdirectory is the `docs` directory and within that directory is the `DevelopersGuide` subdirectory. Within the `DevelopersGuide` subdirectory is the `DevelopersGuide.pdf` file that outlines the UNO object model and OpenOffice architecture. The `DevelopersGuide.pdf` is not very OpenOffice Basic nor Python friendly. The documentation tends to focus on the needs of the C++ or Java programmer.

The OpenOffice SDK documentation is roughly 1,000 pages long. Although you could read all 1,000 pages, we suggest you focus on the following chapters:

Chapter 2: The entire chapter should be read. The focus of the chapter is to introduce how UNO works.

Chapter 3: The entire chapter should be read with focus on the language that pertains to you.

Chapter 4: Read this chapter if the developers are creating C++ or Java or components. The focus of this chapter is on the architecture and deployment of those types of components.

Chapter 5: Only the parts that relate to OpenOffice Basic or Python should be read.

Chapter 6: The entire chapter should be read as it provides an understanding of the overall OpenOffice architecture.

Chapter 7 - 13: These chapters deal with the particulars of the individual OpenOffice application's object structure and therefore should only be read as needed.

If Chapters 7–13 of the OpenOffice SDK documentation are too complex, you can use the HTML-generated object model documentation. The root HTML page can be found at the location `[OpenOffice SDK Installation]/docs/common/ref/com/sun/star/module-ix.html`.

When writing an OpenOffice script, each script (regardless of the language) has a certain structure. Essentially each script can be split up into three parts. The first part deals with retrieving the context of the OpenOffice application. The idea behind retrieving a context is to provide a root object that can then be used to retrieve other objects such as text objects. The second part of a script deals with creating a command within a program structure. The last part is used to execute the command within the OpenOffice context.

The first part of the script could be further divided into two different types. There is the automation type of script, which does not integrate into the Open Office and is used solely to drive OpenOffice. An example of an automation type of script is running a batch process to generate a report or perform some calculations. Automation scripts do not even need to execute on the same machine where OpenOffice office is executing. OpenOffice automation scripts are also the easiest to debug.

The other type of script is is used to integrate into OpenOffice to provide some functionality that OpenOffice does not provide. For example, this type of script was created in the "Technique: Creating and Binding a Macro" section earlier in this chapter. These types of scripts are much more complicated to debug if they're not written in OpenOffice Basic.

When an OpenOffice script retrieves a context, the script is asking for service. A service within OpenOffice represents a piece of functionality in an OpenOffice application. In a programming context, a service represents some kind of programmatic interface. The keyword service is used because there are two ways of accessing the programmatic interface.

The traditional way of accessing a service is to define an interface with the series of methods and properties. A service that is represented by an interface could also be used to query for another interface for some other functionality.

The other way of accessing a service is to use a dispatch helper. The idea behind a dispatch helper is that the scriptwriter will populate some type of object with a series of properties and values. The populated object will then be passed to a dispatch helper that will process the data per the URL given to the dispatch helper.

Writing Macros Using OpenOffice Basic Recorder

Writing macros and scripts using OpenOffice Basic Recorder is the simplest and quickest approach. By being able to record a macro, OpenOffice provides a basic infrastructure on which other macros could be created. The macro recorder uses the dispatch helper construct to automate OpenOffice documents.

If you plan on using OpenOffice Basic as the basis for all scripts, then the Record Macro feature will become an indispensable part of your script development. The advantage of using the Record feature is that it is very simple to write sophisticated scripts that perform some type of automation. For example, multiple scripts can be strung together to perform some larger task.

Refer to Figure 10.16 where the generated code is as follows:

```
sub FormatCodeStyle
    rem - Part 1
    document   = ThisComponent.CurrentController.Frame
    dispatcher = createUnoService(
        "com.sun.star.frame.DispatchHelper")
```

```
rem - Part 2
dim args1(1) as new com.sun.star.beans.PropertyValue
args1(0).Name = "Template"
args1(0).Value = "Code Inline"
args1(1).Name = "Family"
args1(1).Value = 1

rem - Part 3
dispatcher.executeDispatch(document,
    ".uno:StyleApply", "", 0, args1())
end sub
```

The generated code and has been split into the three different parts of a script as defined earlier. The first part of the script creates an object called the dispatch helper as defined by the variable `dispatcher`. The second part of the script creates a bean object that contains some values that represent a change in the structure of some text. In the case of the preceding code snippet, the change is the redefinition of the text to the style `Code Inline`. The last part of the script applies the style to the document using the dispatcher.

The method `executeDispatch` has five parameters. The first parameter `document` represents the object that will be operated on. The second parameter `.uno:StyleApply` represents the URI that will be executed. The best way to understand the URI is to consider the dispatch infrastructure as a way of sending a message from a script to the new office application.

The `.uno` URI method values are documented either by reading the StarOffice 6.0 Administration Guide or by reading the OpenOffice command reference document. The command reference document is found by surfing to the OpenOffice Web site and searching for the document using the terms "command URL." Both of these techniques are neither the most efficient nor the simplest. The simplest way is just to record a macro and then modify the source code that is generated.

Writing OpenOffice Basic Macros Using the OpenOffice UNO Object Model

The other approach to use when writing OpenOffice Basic macros is to use the UNO object model. This approach is more complicated because it requires that the programmer understand the UNO object model. The advantage of this approach is that the code could be more easily read and understood. If this approach is used, it is absolutely vital that the programmer reads the introductory documentation.

Within the introductory documentation are some pointers to the UNO object model. For example, within the StarOffice Basic documentation, there is simple code on how to select text and then delete it or replace it with some other text. This approach is ideal if the administrator wants to invest time to automate OpenOffice.

More details about this approach will not be covered here as the introductory documentation does a much better job.

Writing Macros Using Python

For those people that want to create more sophisticated OpenOffice automation applications that depend on some type of external data such as a database or enterprise application, using Python is a better approach. If OpenOffice is fully installed, the *pyUno bridge* is also installed. The pyUno bridge allows a Python developer to use the OpenOffice API. There are two approaches to using the pyUno bridge. The first approach is to use sockets to connect to OpenOffice; the second approach is to create a UNO component.

When using sockets to communicate to OpenOffice, OpenOffice must be started to accept sockets connections. The following example shows how to start OpenOffice to accept sockets connections:

```
soffice "-accept=socket;port=2002;urp;"
```

The argument -accept will start a socket connection on a specific port, which in the case of the example would be 2002. The port number can be whatever the administrator wants it to be. OpenOffice will then start as a normal application and wait for a client to connect. Before executing this code, it's important that all OpenOffice instances are killed, including the OpenOffice quick start application.

Following is an example Python script that connects to the OpenOffice instance, creates a document, and populates the document with the text "hello world":

```
import uno

# Part 1
context = uno.getComponentContext()
resolver = context.ServiceManager.createInstanceWithContext(
    "com.sun.star.bridge.UnoUrlResolver", context )
ctx = resolver.resolve(
  "uno:socket,host=localhost,port=2002;urp;StarOffice.ComponentContext"
)
smgr = ctx.ServiceManager

# Part 2
desktop = smgr.createInstanceWithContext(
    "com.sun.star.frame.Desktop",ctx)
model = desktop.getCurrentComponent()
text = model.Text
cursor = text.createTextCursor()
```

```
text.insertString( cursor, "Hello World", 0 )

#Part 3
ctx.ServiceManager
```

In the script, the module Uno is imported. The module Uno contains code that bootstraps the UNO object model. In part one, a connection is created between the Python script and the OpenOffice instance. As explained previously, the first part is to create context.

The second part creates a service or interface instance. Note that the interface instance that is created is the class com.sun.star.frame.Desktop. The details of the methods and properties exposed by the class com.sun.star.frame.Desktop are available in the documentation [OpenOffice SDK Installation]/docs/common/ref/com/sun/star/module-ix.html.

The third part is the method call used to make sure that the commands are flushed to do your Office instance.

What is not so obvious in part two is the fact that the variable model.text references a document. The reason the script knows a document is being edited is because in the earlier code when OpenOffice starts, a text document is created. To start an empty spreadsheet document, the following command is executed:

```
soffice -calc "-accept=socket;port=2002;urp;"
```

Following is a list of available document options.

-writer: Empty writer document.

-calc: Empty calc document.

-draw: Empty draw document.

-impress: Empty impress document.

-math: Empty math document.

-global: Empty global document.

-web: Empty HTML document.

When writing your own automation scripts, the focus will be on part two. The code contained within part two will reference the UNO object model. As shown in the preceding code snippet, the script will reference to text document, create a cursor, and then insert text.

To run the Python script, the Python interpreter from OpenOffice has to be used. The OpenOffice Python interpreter is located in the subdirectory [OpenOffice installation]/program. This is because the Python interpreter distributed with OpenOffice has all the necessary Python modules distributed with it.

To integrate a Python component, it has to be written as a UNO component. A Python UNO component implements a specific method and registers itself as a package within the OpenOffice application. Following is an example Python UNO component:

```
import uno
import unohelper

from com.sun.star.task import XJobExecutor

class HelloWorldJob( unohelper.Base, XJobExecutor ):
    def _ _init_ _( self, ctx ):
        self.ctx = ctx

    def trigger( self, args ):
        # Part 1
        desktop =
self.ctx.ServiceManager.createInstanceWithContext(
            "com.sun.star.frame.Desktop", self.ctx )

        # Part 2
        model = desktop.getCurrentComponent()
        text = model.Text
        cursor = text.createTextCursor()

        # Part 3
        text.insertString( cursor, "Hello World", 0 )

# Part 4
g_ImplementationHelper = unohelper.ImplementationHelper()
g_ImplementationHelper.addImplementation( \
        HelloWorldJob,
        "org.openoffice.comp.pyuno.demo.HelloWorld",
        ("com.sun.star.task.Job",),)
```

There are four parts to a Python UNO component. The first three parts are identical in nature to the three parts we have discussed previously. The three parts are not an independent piece of quote, but are part of the trigger method. The trigger method is a required method used by the Python UNO bridge to execute code. The trigger method is part of the HelloWorldJob class that derives from the classes unohelper.Base and XJobExecutor. The definitions of the class HelloWorldJob, the inheritance from the classes, and the definition of the method `trigger`, are default pieces of code that will be implemented for each UNO component. What will vary is the implementation of the `trigger` method.

Part four is some global code used to define the UNO component. The method `addImplementation` has three parameters. The first parameter `HelloWorldJob` represents the constructor that will be executed to instantiate an object. The second parameter `org.openoffice.comp.pyuno.demo.HelloWorld` represents the implementation class. This value is cross-referenced with the package deployment file. The last parameter `com.sun.star.task.Job` is used to define the type of service.

To register the UNO component, a deployment file has to be defined. The exact syntax of the deployment file is described in the OpenOffice SDK documentation specifically in the file `DevelopersGuide.pdf` in section 4.7.3 Add-Ons. Following is an example descriptor file for a Python UNO component:

```xml
<?xml version="1.0" encoding="UTF-8"?>
<oor:node xmlns:oor="http://openoffice.org/2001/registry"
 xmlns:xs="http://www.w3.org/2001/XMLSchema"
 oor:name="Addons" oor:package="org.openoffice.Office">
<node oor:name="AddonUI">
 <node oor:name="AddonMenu">
  <node
   oor:name="org.openoffice.comp.pyuno.demo.HelloWorld"
   oor:op="replace">
   <prop oor:name="URL" oor:type="xs:string">
     <value>
service:org.openoffice.comp.pyuno.demo.HelloWorld?insert
     </value>
   </prop>
   <prop oor:name="ImageIdentifier" oor:type="xs:string">
    <value>private:image/3216</value>
   </prop>
   <prop oor:name="Title" oor:type="xs:string">
    <value xml:lang="en-US">Insert Hello World</value>
   </prop>
  </node>
 </node>
</node>
</oor:node>
```

The deployment file is defined as an XML file. Specifically, this deployment file adds the Python UNO component as a menu item. The actor attributtes with values `AddonUI` and `AddonMenu` are standard values used to define a specific menu location. The attribute `oor:name` with value `org.openoffice.comp.pyuno.demo.HelloWorld` cross-references the Python UNO component. Each of the XML `prop` nodes represents an individual property that is used in the deployment package. For example in the preceding code listing the title and the icon associated with the deployment package are defined.

Both the Python UNO component and deployment file are saved to files on hard disk and then added to a ZIP archive. OpenOffice uses the ZIP archive format as the default compression algorithm. To deploy the package, the following command is executed (note that all OpenOffice instances need to be exited):

```
pkgchk.exe ziparchive.zip
```

The command `pkgchk.exe` is found in the OpenOffice `program` subdirectory. The command `pkgchk.exe` is the package management utility that deploys a ZIP archive. If successful, no errors will be reported. The expanded ZIP archive can be found in the `[OpenOffice installation]/share/uno_packages` subdirectory.

When the OpenOffice Writer application is started, the UNO component will be added to the menu as shown in Figure 10.23.

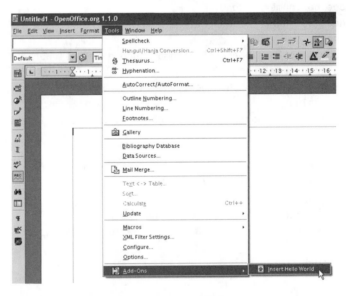

FIGURE 10.23   Menu illustrating added UNO component.

Final Tips for Writing Macros

OpenOffice is a sophisticated productivity suite. Creating stylesheets templates and simple macros using the recording macro functionality are all straightforward and easy to comprehend. Even easier to comprehend then most productivity suites is the ability to edit the raw OpenOffice documents. Large amounts of automation can be performed without having to resort to more sophisticated macros.

When it is necessary to write OpenOffice macros in a more sophisticated style, this book only scratches the surface because writing sophisticated OpenOffice macros requires a book of its own. Therefore, there's a specific technique that references the various pieces of freely available macro documentation.

If you want to pursue a strategy for writing workflow applications using Open-Office, you'll need to spend at least two to four weeks just getting acquainted with the OpenOffice environment. The suggestion is not meant to scare off a potential Open-Office macro developer. The suggestion is meant to indicate that writing Open-Office macros is possible, although it requires some investment in time. After that time has been invested, writing macros for OpenOffice will not seem that complicated.

Technique: Creating Database Bindings in OpenOffice

OpenOffice does not contain a database application. OpenOffice does contain the bindings necessary to bind in an OpenOffice application to a database. A variety of bindings can be used such as ODBC or JDBC. For the context of this book, a possible combination could be using OpenOffice to access data on a MySQL database.

To create a database binding, open the Database Explorer by clicking the Data Sources toolbar button (see the cursor in Figure 10.24). A window appears as shown in Figure 10.24.

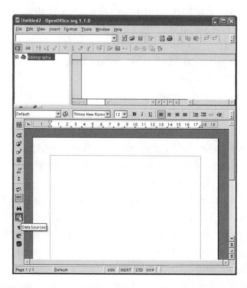

FIGURE 10.24 OpenOffice Write application showing the Database Explorer window.

In the Database Explorer window, you can create queries and manage data. Those queries or tables can then be integrated into documents, such as reports or spreadsheet data mining. All OpenOffice applications use the Database Explorer as a reference point for data.

To add a new data source, choose Tools → Data Sources, which opens the Data Source Administration dialog box shown in Figure 10.25.

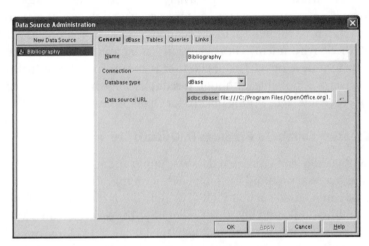

FIGURE 10.25 Dialog box used to manage database connections.

The Data Source Administration dialog box is split into two sections. The listbox on the lefthand side contains all the database connections. When a database collection is selected, then the properties associated with the connection are shown in the tabs on the righthand side the dialog box. To create a new data source, click the New Data Source button.

The General tab is used to define the database connection. The database connection is made up of two parts: database type and data source URL. The database type is the binding technology used when OpenOffice communicates to the database. There are various technologies available, such as MySQL, ODBC, or JDBC. After one of these database technologies has been selected in the combo box, the data source URL is specific to the database type.

When selecting the database, type the second tab in Figure 10.25 changes its name. In Figure 10.25, for example, the database type is dBase, and hence the tab name is dBase. If the database type is changed to ODBC, then the second tab identifier will change to ODBC. The second tab is used to further refine the connection settings for the binding technology.

The tabs Tables, Queries, and Links are used to define what database and resources the database connection will present to the OpenOffice applications. The values can be defined in those tabs or additional items can be defined in the database resource window as shown previously in Figure 10.24.

After all the values have been assigned, click OK. To precreate database connections, the XML formatted file `DataAccess.xcu` needs to be modified. The file is located in the subdirectory `[OpenOffice]/user/registry/data/org/openoffice/Office`. Another solution is for the administrator to use OpenOffice to precreate all the database connections. The modified `DataAccess.xcu` file would then be copied to each OpenOffice deployment.

PROJECT: MOZILLA

The Mozilla Internet application suite has had a checkered past. Originally, Mozilla was the Netscape Internet application suite. With the demise of the Netscape Corporation, it was decided to open source the client applications. The Netscape Internet application suite was very large and the code base was hard to maintain. The only option the Mozilla organization had was to rewrite the Netscape Internet application suite.

The Mozilla Internet application suite rewrite took a long time, which caused a lot of doubt. Many people thought that the Web browser wars were over. Many people thought that there would be no Web browser diversity. When Mozilla Internet application suite 1.0 was released, things started to change as people started to take notice of Mozilla. With each revision, Mozilla has grown stronger.

Now Mozilla can be considered a mature product and implements many interesting and new features. The Mozilla Internet application suite contains the following applications:

Web Browser: An application used to surf the Web.

Composer: An application used to compose HTML pages.

Mail and Newsgroups: An application used to process e-mail and messages from newsgroups.

Address Book: An application used to manage contact information.

IRC Chat: An application used for IRC, which is a real-time chat system.

Calendar: An application used to manage a calendar. This application is not installed by default and must be downloaded from the Mozilla Web site.

The Mozilla Internet application suite has been split into independent applications as follows:

Firefox: An application used to surf the Web.

Thunderbird: An application used to process e-mail and messages from newsgroups.

The Mozilla Internet application suite and the applications Firefox and Thunderbird use the same base components. For example, Firefox and the Mozilla Web browser both use the Gecko rendering engine. What is different between Firefox and the Mozilla Web browser are some of the GUI elements and some of the configuration settings. The idea behind Firefox and Thunderbird is to allow an administrator only to install only the necessary functionality.

With the release of Mozilla 1.6, components such as Shockwave, Java, and Flash have become trivial to install. What is encouraging is that with the Mozilla and Firefox releases, many Web sites have created HTML-compliant content making it easier to surf with Mozilla and Firefox. Contained in Table 10.2 is the reference information for Mozilla, Firefox, and Thunderbird applications.

The focus of this chapter is on the Mozilla Internet application suite. At the time of this writing, many are focused on the individual tools Firefox and Thunderbird. All these applications use an identical configuration structure, so if you plan to use e-mail and Thunderbird, the Mozilla e-mail options are identical.

TABLE 10.2 Reference Information for Mozilla, Firefox, and Thunderbird

Item	Description
Home page	*http://www.mozilla.org/*
Version	At the time of this writing, the released version of Mozilla is 1.8, Firefox 1.0, and Thunderbird 1.0.
Installation	Mozilla is distributed as both a self-installing executable and a zipped archive. Which version is downloaded depends on the deployment used. The other applications Firefox and Thunderbird have similar distribution packages.
Dependencies	The Mozilla or Firefox Web browsers require for most scenarios the Shockwave, Flash, and Java applications. The additional applications need to be installed after Mozilla or Firefox have been installed.

$\rightarrow$

(Table 10.2 Continued)

Documentation	The Mozilla Internet application suite from a user's perspective is fairly intuitive. There is introductory documentation on how to use the individual applications at *http://www.mozilla.org/support/*.
Mailing Lists	Many mailing lists exist for Mozilla covering different aspects of how to use or develop for Mozilla. All the mailing lists are described at the URL *http://www.mozilla.org/community/developer-forums.html*. The administrator would be interested in the mailing lists `announce` and `general`.
Impatient Installation Time Required	Download size: Mozilla 11 MB, Firefox 6.2 MB, Thunderbird 6 MB Installation time: 5-15 minutes depending on the options on the settings that need to be made.
DVD Location	`/packages/mozilla` contains packages for all applications.

Impatient Installation

The impatient installation of the Mozilla Internet application suite, Thunderbird, or Firefox is very simple. The user simply downloads the self-installing executable, and then the executes the executable. The default settings for all the dialog boxes can be used, and clicking the Next and Finish buttons will result in a fully installed application. The Mozilla Internet application suite installer is fully Windows compliant (e.g., includes a proper uninstall).

Deployment

Deploying the Mozilla Internet application suite, Thunderbird, or Firefox is almost as simple as using the self-installing executable. In a deployment scenario, the ZIP archive of Mozilla Internet application suite, Thunderbird, or Firefox is downloaded. After the ZIP archive has been downloaded, the archive is expanded and the application is considered deployed. The remaining settings are automatically created when the application is executed for the first time.

TIP

It would seem that Mozilla Internet application suite, Thunderbird, and Firefox are extremely easy to install and deploy. What is not obvious is that none of the applications are as easy to relocate. The installation and deployment covered relate only to those conditions where a fresh installation and no user settings are involved.

Technique: Relocating an Installation

Relocating a Mozilla installation is not complicated as long a few rules are followed. Mozilla can fix itself when problems are encountered. This is good because it allows an administrator to make changes to redirect Mozilla, and Mozilla will take care of the rest. The administrator needs to understand how Mozilla finds things. Mozilla performs two search steps: loading the registry data and loading the profile.

Manipulating the Registry

The registry data is not the same as the Windows registry, but is a Mozilla-specific registry that functions very similar to the Windows registry. Mozilla created its own registry because the Mozilla solution is cross-platform and cross-application capable. When Mozilla starts, the registry file is loaded from the location `c:\My Docu-ments\[user]\Application Data\Mozilla\registry.dat`. Within the file `registry.dat` is a profile key that references the profile directory that contains a user's data.

The `registry.dat` file could be converted into XML with the help of a utility (`readMozProfile.pl`) found at *http://www.alain.knaff.lu/howto/MozillaCustomization/find.html*. In XML form, the individual registry keys can be manipulated. Another utility (`writeMozProfile.pl`) found at the same Web site can be used to convert the XML into a registry file.

When creating deployment files, a more efficient process is to create a base profile and then deploy that version. The URL *http://www.alain.knaff.lu/howto/MozillaCustomization/cgi/readMoz.cgi* references a page that can create a base profile with a user-specific profile path. You should use that page to create a base profile that is then converted into XML, manipulated, and converted back to a registry. The reason is because the base profile does not contain extra registry keys or values that could potentially confuse an installation. Following is an abbreviated registry file that has been converted into XML:

```
<opt>
  <name>/</name>
  <down>0xa8</down>
  <type>1</type>
  <dir>
    <name>Users</name>
    <down>0x0</down>
```

```
    <type>1</type>
    <dir>
        <atom>
            <value>C:\DOCUMENTS AND SETTINGS\Testuser\APPLICATION
DATA\Mozilla\Profiles\default\nv56xqoq.slt</value>
            <name>directory</name>
            <down>0x0</down>
            <type>17</type>
        </atom>
    </dir>
  </dir>
</opt>
```

The structure of the XML file is based on dir XML nodes being embedded in one another. The dir XML node represents an individual level in a registry directory structure. The descriptors of the level are given by the XML nodes name, down, and type. Registry key values are stored as embedded values within an atom XML node. The value XML node references the directory where a Mozilla profile is stored. By changing the value to another directory, Mozilla will load the profile from the other directory. When relocating a Mozilla installation, this is the only registry value that needs to be changed. After the XML file has been manipulated it is changed back into a registry file and stored in the location c:\My Documents\[user]\Application Data\ Mozilla\.

Manipulating the Files in the Profile Directory

In the profile directory are all the files used to control Mozilla. The most important of the files is pref.js. The file prefs.js is a JavaScript file used to dynamically load all the settings associated with a user. There is a possibility to define some settings in the user.js file, which is stored in the same directory prefs.js. Any setting written in the user.js file overrides the prefs.js value. However, there is a problem in that if any setting changes are made, then they are written into the prefs.js file and not user.js file. This means potential changes or deletions require deletion in two places. It is recommended not to use the user.js file as it could confuse the Mozilla application.

When inspecting the prefs.js file, the individual fields will be fairly obvious for the administrator. What is not obvious is where the individual values within the prefs.js are defined. The problem is that there is no central definition of the prefs.js file. This means the administrator needs to search the Mozilla Web site, Internet, and mailing lists. If an answer has not been found then the question needs to be posted to a Mozilla mailing list.

The content of the prefs.js file is similar to the following abbreviated sample:

```
user_pref("browser.tabs.warnOnClose", false);
user_pref("dom.disable_open_during_load", true);
```

The examples are only two possible values, but they show the general gist of how a `prefs.js` file is structured. There are a number of lines that call the function `user_pref`. The function `user_pref` has two parameters that are key value pairs. The first parameter is the key, and the second parameter is the associated value. To change a preference value, the Mozilla Internet application suite is completely exited, the value is changed, and then Mozilla can be started. Remember that Mozilla on exiting the last instance of a Mozilla application will write the `prefs.js` file. Mozilla while executing does not reread or reload the `prefs.js` or `user.js` files.

If this book nor the mailing lists address your problems, a possible solution is to search using the phrase "Mozilla Prefs." There are multiple pages that show some hidden tips and tricks and potentially one of those pages may answer a question.

The rest of the techniques presented in this book will reference when possible using the configuration files and not the GUI. In some cases, it is possible to accomplish the same preference using a GUI dialog box or setting.

Technique: Managing Security Policies

One of the major problems on the Internet is a script kiddy. A *script kiddy* is a hacker that uses scripting to write viruses, Trojan e-mails, or other mischievous things. The script kiddy will typically write scripts using programming languages such as JavaScript, which is supported by the Mozilla Internet application suite. Although the e-mail client in Mozilla is not at risk, the browser can be.

One way of controlling the risk is to use security policies. Security policies in Mozilla control the access of an individual script when it is executed. Following is an example security policy that does not allow a script to open another browser window, which is a common action performed by pop-up scripts.:

```
user_pref("capability.policy.default.Window.open", "noAccess");
```

The security policy is assigned using the function `user_pref` within the `prefs.js` file, with the appropriate key value pair. The security policy key has a special notation and is made up of multiple parts separated by a period. Using the keywords `capability.policy` indicates a security policy. The first identifier after the security policy is a policy identifier, where `default` is a reserved case that applies by default to all URLs.

When a script is downloaded or executed, the original location of the script is a URL that Mozilla will use to resolve to a specific security policy. If there is no specific security policy, then the default case is used.

The identifiers after the security policy identifier references a class (`Window`) and method (`open`) or property that a script can access. The `noAccess` value shown in the preceding code snippet means that a script cannot execute the class method `Window.open`.

The overall idea when defining security policies is to restrict access to individual scripts, individual classes, and their associated methods and properties. For flexibility, Mozilla allows the definition of security policies associated with individual URLS.

Security policies can only be managed from the `prefs.js` *file.*

Following is a security policy created for *http://www.devspace.com*:

```
user_pref("capability.policy.default.Window.open", "noAccess");
user_pref("capability.policy.policynames", "trusted")
user_pref("capability.policy.trusted.sites",
"http://www.devspace.com");
user_pref("capability.policy.trusted.Window.open", "allAccess");
```

The key `cabilitity.policy.policynames` is used to add another security policy `home`. After the `home` security policy has been defined, URLs can be associated with it using the key `capability.policy.home.sites`. The values of the key are a number of URLs separated by a space, but in this example, `http://www.devspace.com` is the only URL.

The strategy that has been used is to deny access by default to the class method `Window.open`, but allow access to the class method for specific URLs. Another strategy would be to allow access to a class method and deny access for specific URLs. The choice of which strategy to follow is left to the administrator.

There are three different access levels that can be assigned to a class method or property:

noAccess: The executing script is denied access to the class method.

sameOrigin: The executing script is allowed access to any URL as long as the URL is part of the same domain as the domain of the executing script. For example, the URL *http://site.domain.com/document/index.html* will match to all documents to the domain URL *http://site.domain.com*. The script programmer can shorten the domain to match by assigning the class property `document.domain`.

allAccess: The executing script is allowed access to any URL and any class method or property.

When writing security policies, essentially all class methods and properties can be assigned. The problem assigning a class method or property is to know the underlying object identifier. For example, to assign a policy to a link, it is not possible to just reference the link object or a link instance. The class identifier used by Mozilla to implement the link has to be used. The class identifier is not the same as the JavaScript identifier. To find the class identifier, the following code is executed:

```
javascript:alert( window.toString.apply( document.links[0]))
```

The command is executed in the Web Browser URL text box. When you press the Enter key, a dialog box appears because the protocol identifier `javascript` is used to execute a JavaScript script that follows the colon. The function `alert` is used to create a dialog box.

To display the class identifier of the link implementation, the `toString` method is called, which by default returns the class identifier. In the case of the link object (`document.links[0]`), the implementation to the `toString` method returns a URL. To use the default `toString` method implementation, the additional method call `window.toString.apply` is used.

The classes that make up the Mozilla object model are not only populated with methods, but also contain properties such as `background` or `leftmargin`. When a policy is assigned to the property name, then both read and write access have the same policies. To specifically define a policy to read or write to a property, a get or set identifier is used as shown in the following example:

```
user_pref("capability.policy.default.HTMLAnchorElement.name.get",
"allAccess");
user_pref("capability.policy.default.HTMLAnchorElement.name.set",
"noAccess");
```

In the example, read access to the `name` property of a link (`HTMLAnchorElement`) is granted, but it is not possible to write to the `name` property.

TIP

Often properties can be accessed in different ways. One way is to access the property directly, and another way is through a collection. If a security policy is assigned to only the direct property access, then a script could still do whatever it wanted using the collection. Therefore, when defining policies make sure to consider all the different options.

Technique: Managing Accounts and Folders

E-mail accounts can be managed using the GUI, which is the fastest way to create an account or define the properties of the account. For deployment purposes, using the GUI is not the most effective because it would require each user to create his own settings, which is a support nightmare.

The best way to manage a deployment is to manage the `prefs.js` file for each user. The individual accounts within the `prefs.js` file are not individual blocks, but modularized definition blocks. Each protocol, POP3, SMTP, and NNTP, are split into definition blocks. The blocks are defined using identifiers similar to the preceding code snippet.

To illustrate how an account is defined, the following definitions are the sample settings that will be translated into `prefs.js` settings:

```
POP3 account: user
SMTP account: user@domain.com
POP Server Identifier: pop.domain.com
SMTP Server Identifier: smtp.domain.com
```

The way that Mozilla converts the settings in the preceding code to user preferences in the `prefs.js` is not entirely logical from a user perspective, but it is entirely logical from a programmer's perspective. Mozilla divides an e-mail account into subfunctionalities such as identities and servers. A server is a server in the abstract sense and could reference a set of folders, an e-mail protocol account, or even a news protocol account. For the sample settings, there are two Mozilla accounts: one account represents the sample settings and the other account represents the local folders. The local folders are used by a user to store all e-mails for all accounts, as there can be multiple e-mail or news accounts.

Following are the function calls stored in `prefs.js` of the sample settings:

```
user_pref("mail.account.account1.identities", "id1");
user_pref("mail.account.account1.server", "server1");
user_pref("mail.account.account2.server", "server2");
user_pref("mail.accountmanager.accounts", "account1,account2");
user_pref("mail.accountmanager.defaultaccount", "account1");
user_pref("mail.accountmanager.localfoldersserver", "server2");
```

The identifiers `id1`, `server1`, `server2`, `account1`, and `account2` are used to reference structures that make up various accounts. The identifier `id1` defines an identity used when creating e-mails or news messages. An identity includes attributes such as signature, where e-mails are sent to, or where messages are stored. The identifiers `server1` and `server2` identify servers where e-mails, news messages, or local message data is stored. The identifiers `account1` and `account2` identify constructs that combine an identity with a server to create an account at the user level. Not all user accounts have both an identity and server as some servers, such as local folders, do not need an identity.

The default notation used by Mozilla is to use the identifiers `id`, `account`, and `server` and then append the appropriate numeric identifier. The administrator does not need to do this as long as the other naming convention wires the correct account with the correct server and identity.

The property `defaultaccount` is set to the default account that is used when creating new messages or executing default actions. The property `localfoldersserver` is used to define the common folders, which can be used for storage.

A sample identity is defined as follows:

```
user_pref("mail.identity.id1.attach_signature", true);
user_pref("mail.identity.id1.doBcc", true);
user_pref("mail.identity.id1.doBccList", "another@domain.com");
user_pref("mail.identity.id1.draft_folder",
    "mailbox://user@pop.domain.com/Drafts");
user_pref("mail.identity.id1.drafts_folder_picker_mode", "0");
user_pref("mail.identity.id1.escapedVCard", "");
user_pref("mail.identity.id1.fcc_folder",
    "mailbox://user@pop.domain.com/Sent");
user_pref("mail.identity.id1.fcc_folder_picker_mode", "0");
user_pref("mail.identity.id1.fullName", "Some User");
user_pref("mail.identity.id1.organization", "");
user_pref("mail.identity.id1.reply_to", "");
user_pref("mail.identity.id1.sig_file",
  "C:\\Documents and Settings\\user\\My Documents\\DefaultQuote.txt");
user_pref("mail.identity.id1.sig_file-relv",
    "[ProfD]../ DefaultQuote.txt");
user_pref("mail.identity.id1.smtpServer", "smtp1");
user_pref("mail.identity.id1.stationery_folder",
    "mailbox://user@pop.domain.com/Templates");
user_pref("mail.identity.id1.tmpl_folder_picker_mode", "0");
user_pref("mail.identity.id1.useremail", "user@domain.com");
user_pref("mail.identity.id1.valid", true);
```

The identity is defined by the use of the identifier id1. Each property defined is with respect to the identity id1. The identity references multiple properties that reference values for a server. For example, the `draft_folder` property references the value `mailbox://user@pop.domain.com/Drafts`. The identifier mailbox means that a file is being referenced and is mailbox formatted. The identifier `user@pop.domain.com` means that there is a server where the property username is user and the hostname is `pop.domain.com`. The identifier Drafts is the name of a mailbox that will be used for the property `draft_folder`, which is used to save e-mails by the user for later processing or later sending.

The format of the mailbox notation leads the administrator to believe that the username and hostname properties are used in the server settings to reference the

TIP

actual servers. The deduction is only half correct. If the user changes the identifier's username *or* hostname, *the changed values are stored in the properties* realuser-name *and* realhostname. *The original values are left and at that point only used for cross-reference purposes.*

The SMTP server used to send any e-mails is referenced by the property smtpServer. The value smtp1 is used as a property like id1.

The properties for server1 are shown as follows:

```
user_pref("mail.server.server1.directory",
"C:\\DOCUMENTS AND SETTINGS\\USER\\APPLICATION
DATA\\Mozilla\\Profiles\\default\\00te08pr.slt\\Mail\\pop.domain.com");
user_pref(vmail.server.server1.directory-rel",
    "[ProfD]Mail/pop.domain.com");
user_pref("mail.server.server1.download_on_biff", true);
user_pref("mail.server.server1.hostname", "pop.domain.com");
user_pref("mail.server.server1.leave_on_server", false);
user_pref("mail.server.server1.login_at_startup", true);
user_pref("mail.server.server1.name", "user@domain.com");
user_pref("mail.server.server1.type", "pop3");
user_pref("mail.server.server1.userName", "user");
```

There are two types of settings: directory location of the local e-mail folders, and settings for the server account. The property type defines the type of account, which is pop3. The property name is the identifier displayed in the e-mail client folder listbox, which is typically on the left side of the e-mail client. Unique is also the use of the unique escape text identifier [ProfD], which is the path of the profile directory. Wherever the escape identifier appears, the profile directory is substituted. The password for the account is not stored in the prefs.js file and is managed separately by Mozilla. As you know, it is not a good idea to write passwords in a configuration file.

To send e-mails, an SMTP server has to be defined by referencing the SMTP identifier smtp1 that was defined in the sample identity. Mozilla can use and define multiple SMTP servers. Following is an example of defining multiple SMTP servers:

```
user_pref("mail.smtpservers", "smtp1");
user_pref("mail.smtp.defaultserver", "smtp1");
user_pref("mail.smtpserver.smtp1.auth_method", 0);
user_pref("mail.smtpserver.smtp1.hostname", "smtp.domain.com");
user_pref("mail.smtpserver.smtp1.port", 25);
user_pref("mail.smtpserver.smtp1.try_ssl", 0);
user_pref("mail.smtpserver.smtp1.username", "");
```

The SMTP servers are defined like the different accounts defined the sample identity. The smtp1 identifier has parameters associated with it that are used to relay e-mails. It is possible to use a username and password combination, but the password is not stored in the prefs.js file.

Not all details regarding e-mail and news accounts have been covered. We covered enough material so that you could figure out how the account structure works and what the important details are. The practical way to deploy e-mail or news accounts is to create a prototype using the Mozilla GUI, and then tweak the resulting prefs.js *file for each user. That way the administrator does not have to worry about the proper structure, and can use the generated* prefs.js *file as a template.*

Technique: Using the Spam Filters

Mozilla has built within it a spam filter. As shown in Chapter 9, the ASSP application and Mozilla use a Bayesian filter to detect spam. Mozilla will classify an e-mail as spam as the e-mail is downloaded and stored in the inbox of the e-mail account.

Managing Spam from the GUI

By default the spam filter is not turned on, and can be activated from the Mozilla e-mail client by choosing Tools → Import. The Junk Mail Controls dialog box appears as shown in Figure 10.26.

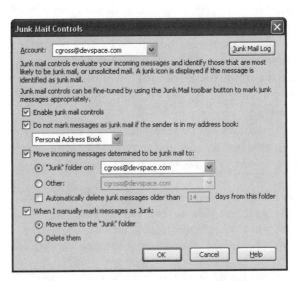

FIGURE 10.26 Dialog box used to manage e-mail spam filtering.

The Enable Junk Mail Controls checkbox is used to activate or deactivate spam filtering. If the checkbox to enable junk mail is deactivated, then the other checkboxes and radio buttons will be disabled. When the other checkboxes and radio buttons are enabled, the characteristics of the spam filtering are defined.

The Do Not Mark Messages As... checkbox is used to define a white list of e-mails that will not be subjected to any spam filtering. When white lists are enabled, the e-mail addresses used to define the white list are either from the personal address book, or from the e-mail addresses that are collected. Collected e-mail addresses are those e-mail addresses that arrive in your inbox. Of course this approach can be a bit self-defeating as some of those e-mail addresses might be spam e-mail addresses. The default, which should not be changed, is to use the personal address book.

The Move Incoming Messages Determined... checkbox is used to define an action when an e-mail is determined to be spam. The default is to move the e-mail considered as spam to the Junk folder. The checkbox When I Manually Mark Messages... checkbox is used to define a behavior when an e-mail is manually marked as spam. The default behavior is to move the e-mail to the Junk folder.

When the changes have been made in the GUI, the prefs.js file will be updated for the appropriate server. The following listing contains the preferences needed to activate spam detection:

```
user_pref("mail.server.server1.moveOnSpam", true);
user_pref("mail.server.server1.spamActionTargetAccount",
    "mailbox://user@pop.domain.com");
user_pref("mail.server.server1.spamActionTargetFolder",
    "mailbox://user@pop.domain.com/Junk");
user_pref("mail.server.server1.spamLevel", 100);
```

The settings are fairly obvious and can be related back to the definitions in the GUI. The only nonobvious property is spamLevel, which is by default set to 100, and should not be altered. When the spamLevel property is set or does not exist in the prefs.js file, then spam filtering is activated. The only additional catch is that if the spamLevel property does not exist and none of the other three spam properties (moveOnSpam, spamActionTargetAccount, and spamActionTargetFolder) exist, then spam filtering is not activated. The logic is a bit convoluted. To deactivate spam filtering, the property spamLevel is set to 0 or none of the spam properties exist in the prefs.js file.

When spam filtering is activated, Mozilla does a fairly adequate job even though Mozilla was not taught what spam e-mail was. Both ASSP and Mozilla use Bayesian filtering, which requires that they be taught the differences by using e-mail that is acceptable and e-mail that is spam. Distributed with Mozilla is the file training.dat that contains an initial training data set.

When spam filtering is activated, then e-mail marked as spam will appear similar to Figure 10.27.

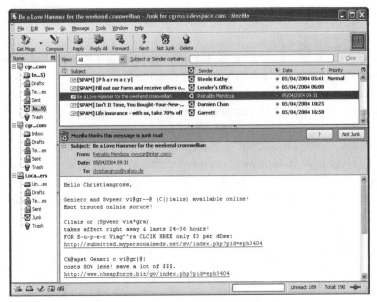

FIGURE 10.27 Mozilla showing e-mail marked as spam.

Spam-marked e-mails appear with a recycling box beside the sender e-mail address. When the spam-marked e-mail is selected, the window highlights that Mozilla considers the e-mail as junk e-mail. It is safe to click on a spam-marked e-mail because Mozilla automatically removes remote display and download rights associated with the e-mail. If the e-mail still shows an image, it is because the image was downloaded with the e-mail. However, under no circumstance will Mozilla execute any application such as Java.

Mozilla is not perfect when detecting spam, and will miss or mark e-mails as spam. Therefore, it is absolutely vital that e-mails are marked correctly. As an e-mail is marked correctly, the `training.dat` file is updated. An administrator would be smart to create folders for spam and nonspam e-mail. Then for both folders, choose Tools → Run Junk Mail Controls on Folder. The spam filters will mark all the e-mails as either spam or not spam. For e-mails marked as spam in the nonspam folder, the e-mail is reclassified as nonspam, and vice versa for the spam folder. E-mail is marked as spam by clicking in the recycle bin icon column.

After the training has been completed, the administrator can deploy the `training.dat` file for all users. This does introduce an additional problem in that users might train their own spam filters, which are always overwritten when a new `training.dat` file is created. Ideally the solution is to send incorrectly classified e-mails to a nonspam and spam account, which is managed by the administrator. The administrator downloads the e-mails for each account and uses those e-mails for a newer version of the `training.dat` file.

Technique: Installing and Managing Plug-ins such as Java or Flash

A plug-in is an added piece of functionality that makes Mozilla be able to process Java or Flash content. Plug-ins go beyond the basic HTML paradigm and make it possible to create interactive and dynamic applications. There are many plug-ins that can be used to process many types of content.

Mozilla by default does not ship with many plug-ins and users are expected to install their own. When installing plug-ins, a deployment can be complicated because many plug-ins require other applications to be installed. For example, the Java plug-in requires that the Java runtime be installed.

When attempting to install a new plug-in, the first step is to surf to *http://plugindoc .mozdev.org. or https://addons.update.mozilla.org/*. The Web sites *plugindoc.mozdev.org* and *https://addons.update.mozilla.org/* are central repositories for information regarding plug-ins and the Mozilla Internet application suite, including Firefox. References to multiple platforms are included on these sites; of interest to the administrator are the Windows links. The necessary links to automatically install the most important plug-ins are found at *https://addons.update.mozilla.org/plugins/*.

To know which plug-ins are installed, choose Help → About Plug-ins, and a page similar to Figure 10.28 appears.

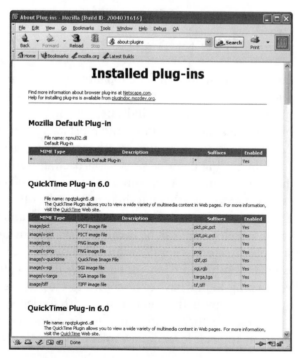

FIGURE 10.28 Mozilla showing installed plug-ins.

The page shows the name of the plug-in and the MIME types associated with the plug-in. In most cases, the plug-ins are installed in the directory [Mozilla Installation]/Mozilla/plugins. Contained within the plugins directory are a number of shared libraries and other files that are used to execute dynamic content. For deployment purposes, an administrator simply needs to copy a plug-in into the plugins directory as Mozilla will automatically pick up the plug-in and load it.

Scanning for a plug-in is more complicated than just searching the plugins directory. The plugins directory method was discussed first because it is the simplest and should be used for most deployment purposes. Mozilla can search multiple places for a plug-in, such as the paths defined by the environment variable MOZ_PLUGIN_PATH.

Example Plug-in Detection and Installation for Java Plug-ins

Another strategy used by Mozilla is to search the most common places where plug-ins may reside. For example, the Java plug-in somehow is magically loaded even though the Java plug-in shared library NPJava13.dll is not in any directory that Mozilla has a reference to. The solution used by Mozilla is to search the hard disk in the most common places when instructed to. The global preferences file [Mozilla Installation]/Mozilla/defaults/prefs/winpref.js has instructions to find plug-ins of a certain type. Following are some sample settings that are used to start a search process:

```
pref( "plugin.scan.SunJRE", "1.3");
pref( "plugin.scan.Acrobat", "5.0");
```

The function pref is similar in functionality to user_pref, but pref assigns a global preference for all users. The key plugin.scan.SunJRE activates the Java runtime scan routines and the value 1.3 indicates to find at least a Java 1.3 runtime. There are more plug-in scanning routines and most have been activated in the winpref.js file. Mozilla does not attempt to search for the plug-in at startup, but when it is requested. When using the winpref.js approach, the administrator needs to ensure that the Java runtime or Acrobat has been properly deployed.

Another strategy is to copy the plug-in files from the other application such as Java into the plugins subdirectory. The Java plug-in is an interesting example of how complicated a deployment can be because a Java deployment involves multiple files in multiple directories. For demonstration purposes, if the first line of the example winpref.js is commented out, then to have the Java plug-in recognized as a plug-in, the Java plug-in files have to be copied to the plugins directory. The way to do that would be to copy all the files that start with the letters NP in the [Java Installation]/jre/bin directory to the plugins directory. Then when Mozilla is started and when an applet is loaded, Java will be automatically be started.

Example Plug-in Detection and Installation for Flash Plug-ins

The Flash plug-in example shows where the entire plug-in is contained within the `plugins` directory. From the Web site *https://addons.update.mozilla.org/plugins/*, there is a link to the Flash installer. You can double-click on the link and install the plug-in. If you then inspect the `plugins` directory, the file `NPSWF32.dll` appears, which represents the Flash plug-in. The Flash plug-in is self contained because the application Dependency Walker does not show a reference to another external shared library. Shown in Figure 10.29 is Dependency Walker that has loaded the `NPSWF32.dll` shared library.

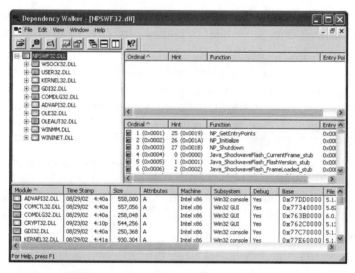

FIGURE 10.29 Dependency Walker showing the dependencies for `NPSWF32.dll`.

In Figure 10.29, the upper lefthand window creates a directory tree of shared libraries that the shared library `NPSWF32.dll` depends on. You can investigate each reference to determine whether the library is a system or application reference. If a reference happens to be an application reference, then the you need to make plans to deploy the application reference. If all references are system references, then the administrator could do a direct copy for deployment.

One of the most annoying dialog boxes appears when a plug-in is not installed or not installed properly. The default action is to pop up a dialog box and ask to download the plug-in. The problem with this strategy is that it very often does not work and further aggravates the user. To stop this dialog box from appearing, the plug-in `npnul32.dll` *is deleted from the plug-ins directory.*

Technique: Relocating User Profiles

When a user's computer is reinstalled, the user will want her old bookmarks and e-mail accounts. The administrator is responsible for transferring the appropriate files. In the simplest scenario, the contents of the entire profile path could be copied. However, the cache, cookies, and other potentially unnecessary files would also be copied.

When relocating a user profile, the best strategy is to copy a default empty profile, and then overwrite certain files with user-specific settings. Following are the directories that make up a typical profile:

`cache`, `cache.trash`: Two directories that are used to store visited documents. These directories should not be copied with directories from a user profile.

`chrome`: A directory that contains UI customizations (`userChrome.css` and `userContent.css`). The UI customizations are useful if an individual user needs larger fonts due to a physical impairment or computer device. By default there are no user customizations, so the contents of the `chrome` directory do not need to be copied. The `chrome` directory is not intended for deploying themes, but user-specific UI alterations.

`mail`: A directory that contains the various e-mail mailboxes and servers. Most likely this directory is copied for each user, as it contains the e-mails for each user. The exception is if the administrator in the `prefs.js` file references remote e-mail mailboxes and servers.

`news`: A directory that contains newsgroup information such as subscribed newsgroups and messages. This directory should be copied for each user.

Following are the files that make up a typical profile:

`[numeric identifier].s`: Stores the individual username and passwords for all e-mail accounts, HTML forms, and newsgroups. This file can be deleted or reset, but then it would require that the user reenter the passwords again. In a deployment scenario, deploying this file is purely optional for the administrator. The administrator could edit the file and only deploy those passwords necessary to carry out a user's daily task. It is not possible to precreate this file, as the individual texts are hash encoded.

`abook.mab`: Stores the user's addresses and contact information. When relocating a user, this file should be copied. A complementary strategy would be to store the addresses in a centrally managed LDAP database, which Mozilla can communicate with. LDAP should be used when the administrator wants central control and consistency in the contact information. The address book is in text format and it seems logical, but it isn't. Therefore although it is possible to relocate the address book file, it isn't easily possible to precreate or manipulate the address book file. This file should be relocated so that collected e-mail addresses that have been moved into this file will help autocomplete e-mail addresses.

`bookmarks.html`: Stores the user's bookmarks in HTML format. The file is in text format and can be relocated, precreated, and manipulated. The format of the file is relatively simple and the attributes added by Mozilla can be easily recreated. The attribute ID that is part of the A HTML element is a unique identifier that an administrator can randomly generate, as there is no reference to the ID in another configuration file.

`cert8.db`, `key3.db`, `secmod.db`: A set of files used by Mozilla to store certificates, security modules, and keys. These files should not be relocated and can be safely deleted. Mozilla will automatically recreate these files.

`cookies.txt`: Contains in plain text the various cookies a user uses. The heading of the file says not to edit this file, but administrators can edit the file if they take care to exactly follow the format. This file can be relocated and should be filtered when relocated to only contain those cookies needed. This file should not be precreated;, if necessary, it can also be tweaked by the cookie manager before relocation.

`cookperm.txt`: Determines which sites can set cookies or cannot set cookies. This file can be edited and relocated. For control purposes, the administrator should manage the relocation of this file.

`downloads.rdf`: Contains all the past downloads. This file should not be relocated and can be safely ignored or deleted.

`history.dat`: Contains the past history of pages visited and should not be relocated or manipulated. If deleted, Mozilla will automatically recreate the file.

`history.mab`: Contains collected addresses from incoming e-mails. This file should not be manipulated, but should be relocated because when a user types in an e-mail address, autocompletion partially relies on this file.

`localstore.rdf`: Stores the orientation and location of the windows. This file can be deleted and does not need to be relocated.

`mailviews.dat`: Stores how Mail and News items are displayed. This file does not need be relocated and should not be deleted.

`mimetypes.rdf`: Contains reference information for helper applications used to process content. This file can be relocated and edited manually. The format is described in the file, but the Mozilla editor can edit the MIME types. To access the MIME editor, choose Edit → Preferences and a dialog box similar to Figure 10.30 appears.

In Figure 10.30, the preferences editor is found under the tree node Navigator → Helper Applications. A helper application is defined by associating a file extension or

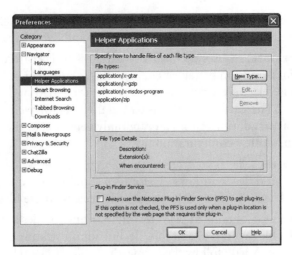

FIGURE 10.30 Preferences dialog box used to define helper applications.

MIME type with an action such as saving to the disk or running an application. Helper applications are not plug-ins, and should be used when there is no alternative plug-in.

panacea.dat: A cache for the mail folders and layout of the individual windows. This file should not be relocated, nor generated.

panels.rdf: Defines the side panels that are shown when the F9 button is pressed. Some applications install themselves as side panels and the administrator can relocate this file, as long as the associated applications are relocated as well. If this file is deleted, Mozilla automatically recreates a default file.

parent.lock: Created and managed by Mozilla to lock a profile so that it is not started twice.

prefs.bak: The backup prefs.js file.

prefs.js: The main preferences file that can and is relocated. The paths referenced within the file need to be modified or relocated as well.

search.rdf: Stores the search engines used in Mozilla. Customizations can be performed, and the file can be relocated if customizations are present. If the file is deleted, it will be automatically recreated.

training.dat: The Bayesian training file. This file should not be deleted, but it can be relocated.

XUL.mfl: Mozilla creates and controls this file to cache the UI elements. This file is not to be relocated and should generally not be deleted.

A few times it was indicated not to precreate a file. The exception to that is when the file is precreated by Mozilla and tweaked by the administrator. You should avoid precreating a file from scratch and not basing it on what Mozilla created.

Technique: Using Profiles

It is possible to use multiple profiles with Mozilla. The default scenario is to use a single profile for each user, which is the simplest solution in most cases. Multiple profiles cause multiple profile directories to be created, and each profile has its own prefs.js file.

A new profile is created from the GUI. When Mozilla is installed, the Profile Manager menu item is created. You click on that link and a dialog box similar to Figure 10.31 appears.

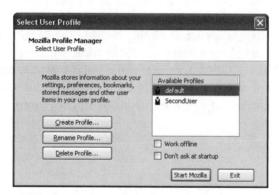

FIGURE 10.31 Dialog box used to manage user profiles.

The dialog box in Figure 10.31 does not by default appear when there is only a single profile assigned for the user. The dialog box can be used to create, delete, or rename profiles, and it can be used to start Mozilla with a particular profile. If there are multiple profiles, then the dialog box will appear every time. To stop the dialog from appearing, select the Don't Ask at Startup checkbox; the profile you select become the default profile to be loaded.

From an implementation point of view, multiple profiles are defined in the registry.dat file as separate directories. The administrator could manage the separate profiles by manually editing the registry.dat file using the readMozProfile.pl and writeMozProfile.pl scripts. To get an idea of how multiple profiles are structured, you should use the User Profile Manager dialog box to create a template. The individual profiles are exactly the same as explained in this chapter.

To have Mozilla load a particular profile, the command-line argument -p is used:

```
Mozilla.exe -p SecondUser
```

The profile SecondUser is the profile identifier from Figure 10.31. The administrator would then create shortcuts for each of the profiles to be loaded.

SUMMARY

This chapter introduced two productivity applications: OpenOffice and Mozilla. The chapter started out with the advantages and disadvantages of each suite. OpenOffice can be used in your corporation if you are willing to invest a bit of time as an administrator. The administrator needs to prepare the environment and create templates or macros so that a switch to OpenOffice will be painless. With a proper environment, any user can use OpenOffice without much effort.

With Mozilla, the switch is simple because the Mozilla Internet Application suite has matured to become an excellent application. The e-mail and Web browser clients are fabulous. Overall, however, the point is that Open Source works with productivity applications. The user and administrator can control their futures and tune the applications to suit their needs. It might require a bit of time, but it's worth the effort.

Appendix

A

About the DVD

This DVD contains all of the software mentioned in the book "Open Source For Windows Administrators."

To be able to run the software you will need about 1 gigabyte of free hard disk space, minimum Intel Pentium 2 processor (or comparable x86 clone), and 128 MB of RAM. The software is intended for a Windows operating system (minimum Windows 98; Windows 2000, Windows XP, or Windows Server 2003). You must have a DVD drive to run the disc.

The individual URLs from which the software or sources can be downloaded are indicated in the book or within the archive files.

DIRECTORIES

cygwin (*http://sources.redhat.com/cygwin/*): Contains all of the files to install the Cygwin LINUX compatible layer.

extras: Contains extras mentioned only in passing within the book.

extras/msys (*http://www.mingw.org*): Contains the files for the MinGW distribution, which is similar to Cygwin. MinGW is different than Cygwin in that it attempts to use Windows Native API. MinGW contains a bash shell and many UNIX utilities.

extras/vim (*http://www.vim.org*): Contains the files for a Windows native VI implementation, which does not use the console.

packages: Contains all of the packages mentioned in the book.

packages/7-Zip (*http://www.7-zip.org*): Contains 7-zip application, which is a console and gui based application used for archiving files.

packages/Apache (*http://www.apache.org*): Contains the Apache HTTPD application, which is used as a Web Server.

packages/Apache/php (*http://www.php.net*): Contains the PHP application, which is used in the context of the Apache Web Server application.

packages/Apache/webalizer (*http://www.mrunix.net/webalizer/*): Contains the Webalizer application, which is used to generate statistics of who is accessing a website.

packages/knoppix (*http://www.knoppix.net*): Contains the Knoppix ISO image that can be burned to a CD, and then used to boot the Knoppix Linux Operating System. You will need software to convert the iso image into a bootable CD.

packages/LDAP (*http://www.openldap.org*): Contains the source code for the Open LDAP server.

packages/mozilla (*http://www.mozilla.org*): Contains the Mozilla, Firefox, and Thunderbird applications that are used to surf the Web, and process email.

packages/mysql (*http://www.mysql.com*): Contains the MySQL database packages.

packages/openoffice (*http://www.openoffice.org*): Contains the OpenOffice application that contains a word processor, spreadsheet, presentation package, etc.

packages/pks (*http://pks.sourceforge.net*): Contains the Public Key Server used to manage Public keys.

packages/python (*http://www.python.org, http://starship.python.net/crew/ mhammond/win32/Downloads.html*): Contains the Python runtime applications from the Python.org and the Python Win32 Extensions.

packages/Shell/links: Contains a file that references multiple websites that could be useful for the reader when writing Shell, Awk, or Batch scripts.

packages/TWEAK (*http://thegoldenear.org/tweak/*): Contains the TWEAK application used to tweak the Windows Operating system.

packages/unison (*http://www.cis.upenn.edu/~bcpierce/unison/*): Contains the UNISON file synchronization program.

packages/vnc (*http://ultravnc.sourceforge.net*): Contains the UltraVNC application used to remote control another Windows server.

packages/xmail (*http://www.xmailserver.org*): Contains the XMail email server application.

packages/xmail/assp *http://assp.sourceforge.net*): Contains the ASSP Anti-SPAM filter application. (Requires PERL Runtime from Active State, http://www.activestate.com).

packages/xmail/emailrelay (*http://emailrelay.sourceforge.net*): Contains the EmailRelay application used to relay emails.

packages/xmail/xpai (*http://www.akxak.de/xpai/*): Contains the XPAI XMAIL administration package, which requires both Apache and PHP (Both packages are part of this DVD).

packages/xmail/PyXMail (*http://www.opensoftwareservices.biz/Menu/services/ software*): Contains an archive that contains a Python source file used to manage an XMail server.

packages/XYNTService: Contains the XYNTService application sources, which need to be compiled. Otherwisea compiled XYNTService application is part of the XYSystem.zip distribution.

figures: This folder contains all of the images from the text, organized in folders by chapter. There is no folder for Chapter 1, since this chapter has no images.

Software License

GNU GENERAL PUBLIC LICENSE

GNU General Public License
Version 2, June 1991
Copyright (C) 1989, 1991 Free Software Foundation, Inc.
675 Mass Ave, Cambridge, MA 02139, USA

Everyone is permitted to copy and distribute verbatim copies of this license document, but changing it is not allowed.

Preamble

The licenses for most software are designed to take away your freedom to share and change it. By contrast, the GNU General Public License is intended to guarantee your freedom to share and change free software—to make sure the software is free for all its users. This General Public License applies to most of the Free Software Foundation's software and to any other program whose authors commit to using it. (Some other Free Software Foundation software is covered by the GNU Library General Public License instead.) You can apply it to your programs, too.

When we speak of free software, we are referring to freedom, not price. Our General Public Licenses are designed to make sure that you have the freedom to distribute copies of free software (and charge for this service if you wish), that you receive source code or can get it if you want it, that you can change the software or use pieces of it in new free programs; and that you know you can do these things.

To protect your rights, we need to make restrictions that forbid anyone to deny you these rights or to ask you to surrender the rights. These restrictions translate to certain responsibilities for you if you distribute copies of the software, or if you modify it.

For example, if you distribute copies of such a program, whether gratis or for a fee, you must give the recipients all the rights that you have. You must make sure that they, too, receive or can get the source code. And you must show them these terms so they know their rights.

We protect your rights with two steps: (1) copyright the software, and (2) offer you this license which gives you legal permission to copy, distribute and/or modify the software.

Also, for each author's protection and ours, we want to make certain that everyone understands that there is no warranty for this free software. If the software is modified by someone else and passed on, we want its recipients to know that what they have is not the original, so that any problems introduced by others will not reflect on the original authors' reputations.

Finally, any free program is threatened constantly by software patents. We wish to avoid the danger that redistributors of a free program will individually obtain patent licenses, in effect making the program proprietary. To prevent this, we have made it clear that any patent must be licensed for everyone's free use or not licensed at all.

The precise terms and conditions for copying, distribution and modification follow.

GNU GENERAL PUBLIC LICENSE
TERMS AND CONDITIONS FOR COPYING, DISTRIBUTION AND MODIFICATION

0. This License applies to any program or other work which contains a notice placed by the copyright holder saying it may be distributed under the terms of this General Public License. The "Program," below, refers to any such program or work, and a "work based on the Program" means either the Program or any derivative work under copyright law: that is to say, a work containing the Program or a portion of it, either verbatim or with modifications and/or translated into another language. (Hereinafter, translation is included without limitation in the term "modification.") Each licensee is addressed as "you."

Activities other than copying, distribution and modification are not covered by this License; they are outside its scope. The act of running the Program is not restricted, and the output from the Program is covered only if its contents constitute a work based on the Program (independent of having been made by running the Program). Whether that is true depends on what the Program does.

1. You may copy and distribute verbatim copies of the Program source code as you receive it, in any medium, provided that you conspicuously and appropriately publish on each copy an appropriate copyright notice and disclaimer of warranty; keep intact all the notices that refer to this License and to the absence of any warranty; and give any other recipients of the Program a copy of this License along with the Program.

You may charge a fee for the physical act of transferring a copy, and you may at your option offer warranty protection in exchange for a fee.

2. You may modify your copy or copies of the Program or any portion of it, thus forming a work based on the Program, and copy and distribute such modifications or work under the terms of Section 1 above, provided that you also meet all of these conditions:

a) You must cause the modified files to carry prominent notices stating that you changed the files and the date of any change.

b) You must cause any work that you distribute or publish, that in whole or in part contains or is derived from the Program or any part thereof, to be licensed as a whole at no charge to all third parties under the terms of this License.

c) If the modified program normally reads commands interactively when run, you must cause it, when started running for such interactive use in the most ordinary way, to print or display an announcement including an appropriate copyright notice and a notice that there is no warranty (or else, saying that you provide a warranty) and that users may redistribute the program under these conditions, and telling the user how to view a copy of this License. (Exception: if the Program itself is interactive but does not normally print such an announcement, your work based on the Program is not required to print an announcement.)

These requirements apply to the modified work as a whole. If identifiable sections of that work are not derived from the Program, and can be reasonably considered independent and separate works in themselves, then this License, and its terms, do not apply to those sections when you distribute them as separate works. But when you distribute the same sections as part of a whole which is a work based on the Program, the distribution of the whole must be on the terms of this License, whose permissions for other licensees extend to the entire whole, and thus to each and every part regardless of who wrote it.

Thus, it is not the intent of this section to claim rights or contest your rights to work written entirely by you; rather, the intent is to exercise the right to control the distribution of derivative or collective works based on the Program.

In addition, mere aggregation of another work not based on the Program with the Program (or with a work based on the Program) on a volume of a storage or distribution medium does not bring the other work under the scope of this License.

3. You may copy and distribute the Program (or a work based on it, under Section 2) in object code or executable form under the terms of Sections 1 and 2 above provided that you also do one of the following:

>   a) Accompany it with the complete corresponding machine-readable source code, which must be distributed under the terms of Sections 1 and 2 above on a medium customarily used for software interchange; or,

>   b) Accompany it with a written offer, valid for at least three years, to give any third party, for a charge no more than your cost of physically performing source distribution, a complete machine-readable copy of the corresponding source code, to be distributed under the terms of Sections 1 and 2 above on a medium customarily used for software interchange; or,

>   c) Accompany it with the information you received as to the offer to distribute corresponding source code. (This alternative is allowed only for noncommercial distribution and only if you received the program in object code or executable form with such an offer, in accord with Subsection b above.)

The source code for a work means the preferred form of the work for making modifications to it. For an executable work, complete source code means all the source code for all modules it contains, plus any associated interface definition files, plus the scripts used to control compilation and installation of the executable. However, as a special exception, the source code distributed need not include anything that is normally distributed (in either source or binary form) with the major components (compiler, kernel, and so on) of the operating system on which the executable runs, unless that component itself accompanies the executable.

If distribution of executable or object code is made by offering access to copy from a designated place, then offering equivalent access to copy the source code from the same place counts as distribution of the source code, even though third parties are not compelled to copy the source along with the object code.

4. You may not copy, modify, sublicense, or distribute the Program except as expressly provided under this License. Any attempt otherwise to copy, modify, sublicense or distribute the Program is void, and will automatically terminate your rights under this License. However, parties who have received copies, or rights, from you under this License will not have their licenses terminated so long as such parties remain in full compliance.

5. You are not required to accept this License, since you have not signed it. However, nothing else grants you permission to modify or distribute the Program or its derivative works. These actions are prohibited by law if you do not accept this License. Therefore, by modifying or distributing the Program (or any work based on the Program), you indicate your acceptance of this License to do so, and all its terms and conditions for copying, distributing or modifying the Program or works based on it.

6. Each time you redistribute the Program (or any work based on the Program), the recipient automatically receives a license from the original licensor to copy, distribute or modify the Program subject to these terms and conditions. You may not impose any further restrictions on the recipients' exercise of the rights granted herein. You are not responsible for enforcing compliance by third parties to this License.

7. If, as a consequence of a court judgment or allegation of patent infringement or for any other reason (not limited to patent issues), conditions are imposed on you (whether by court order, agreement or otherwise) that contradict the conditions of this License, they do not excuse you from the conditions of this License. If you cannot distribute so as to satisfy simultaneously your obligations under this License and any other pertinent obligations, then, as a consequence, you may not distribute the Program at all. For example, if a patent license would not permit royalty-free redistribution of the Program by all those who receive copies directly or indirectly through you, then the only way you could satisfy both it and this License would be to refrain entirely from distribution of the Program.

If any portion of this section is held invalid or unenforceable under any particular circumstance, the balance of the section is intended to apply and the section as a whole is intended to apply in other circumstances.

It is not the purpose of this section to induce you to infringe any patents or other property right claims or to contest validity of any such claims; this section has the sole purpose of protecting the integrity of the free software distribution system, which is implemented by public license practices. Many people have made generous contributions to the wide range of software distributed through that system in reliance on consistent application of that system; it is up to the author/donor to decide if he or she is willing to distribute software through any other system and a licensee cannot impose that choice.

This section is intended to make thoroughly clear what is believed to be a consequence of the rest of this License.

8. If the distribution and/or use of the Program is restricted in certain countries either by patents or by copyrighted interfaces, the original copyright holder who places the Program under this License may add an explicit geographical distribution limitation excluding those countries, so that distribution is permitted only in or among countries not thus excluded. In such case, this License incorporates the limitation as if written in the body of this License.

9. The Free Software Foundation may publish revised and/or new versions of the General Public License from time to time. Such new versions will be similar in spirit to the present version, but may differ in detail to address new problems or concerns.

Each version is given a distinguishing version number. If the Program specifies a version number of this License which applies to it and "any later version," you have the option of following the terms and conditions either of that version or of any later version published by the Free Software Foundation. If the Program does not specify a version number of this License, you may choose any version ever published by the Free Software Foundation.

10. If you wish to incorporate parts of the Program into other free programs whose distribution conditions are different, write to the author to ask for permission. For software which is copyrighted by the Free Software Foundation, write to the Free Software Foundation; we sometimes make exceptions for this. Our decision will be guided by the two goals of preserving the free status of all derivatives of our free software and of promoting the sharing and reuse of software generally.

NO WARRANTY

11. BECAUSE THE PROGRAM IS LICENSED FREE OF CHARGE, THERE IS NO WARRANTY FOR THE PROGRAM, TO THE EXTENT PERMITTED BY APPLICABLE LAW. EXCEPT WHEN OTHERWISE STATED IN WRITING THE COPYRIGHT HOLDERS AND/OR OTHER PARTIES PROVIDE THE PROGRAM "AS IS" WITHOUT WARRANTY OF ANY KIND, EITHER EXPRESSED OR IMPLIED, INCLUDING, BUT NOT LIMITED TO, THE IMPLIED WARRANTIES OF MERCHANTABILITY AND FITNESS FOR A PARTICULAR PURPOSE. THE ENTIRE RISK AS TO THE QUALITY AND PERFORMANCE OF THE PROGRAM IS WITH YOU. SHOULD THE PROGRAM PROVE DEFECTIVE, YOU ASSUME THE COST OF ALL NECESSARY SERVICING, REPAIR OR CORRECTION.

12. IN NO EVENT UNLESS REQUIRED BY APPLICABLE LAW OR AGREED TO IN WRITING WILL ANY COPYRIGHT HOLDER, OR ANY OTHER PARTY WHO MAY MODIFY AND/OR REDISTRIBUTE THE PROGRAM AS PERMITTED ABOVE, BE LIABLE TO YOU FOR DAMAGES, INCLUDING ANY GENERAL, SPECIAL, INCIDENTAL OR CONSEQUENTIAL DAMAGES ARISING OUT OF THE USE OR INABILITY TO USE THE PROGRAM (INCLUDING BUT NOT LIMITED TO LOSS OF DATA OR DATA BEING RENDERED INACCURATE OR LOSSES SUSTAINED BY YOU OR THIRD PARTIES OR A FAILURE OF THE PROGRAM TO OPERATE WITH ANY OTHER PROGRAMS), EVEN IF SUCH HOLDER OR OTHER PARTY HAS BEEN ADVISED OF THE POSSIBILITY OF SUCH DAMAGES.

END OF TERMS AND CONDITIONS

Appendix: How to Apply These Terms to Your New Programs

If you develop a new program, and you want it to be of the greatest possible use to the public, the best way to achieve this is to make it free software which everyone can redistribute and change under these terms.

To do so, attach the following notices to the program. It is safest to attach them to the start of each source file to most effectively convey the exclusion of warranty; and each file should have at least the "copyright" line and a pointer to where the full notice is found.

> one line to give the program's name and a brief idea of what it does.
> Copyright © 19yy name of author

This program is free software; you can redistribute it and/or modify it under the terms of the GNU General Public License as published by the Free Software Foundation; either version 2 of the License, or (at your option) any later version.

This program is distributed in the hope that it will be useful, but WITHOUT ANY WARRANTY; without even the implied warranty of MERCHANTABILITY or FITNESS FOR A PARTICULAR PURPOSE. See the GNU General Public License for more details.

You should have received a copy of the GNU General Public License along with this program; if not, write to the Free Software Foundation, Inc., 675 Mass Ave, Cambridge, MA 02139, USA.

Also add information on how to contact you by electronic and paper mail.

If the program is interactive, make it output a short notice like this when it starts in an interactive mode:

Gnomovision version 69, Copyright © 19yy name of author
Gnomovision comes with ABSOLUTELY NO WARRANTY; for details type 'show w'.

This is free software, and you are welcome to redistribute it under certain conditions; type 'show c' for details.

The hypothetical commands 'show w' and 'show c' should show the appropriate parts of the General Public License. Of course, the commands you use may be called something other than 'show w' and 'show c'; they could even be mouse-clicks or menu items—whatever suits your program.

You should also get your employer (if you work as a programmer) or your school, if any, to sign a "copyright disclaimer" for the program, if necessary. Here is a sample; alter the names:

Yoyodyne, Inc., hereby disclaims all copyright interest in the program 'Gnomovision' (which makes passes at compilers) written by James Hacker.

signature of Ty Coon, 1 April 1989
Ty Coon, President of Vice

This General Public License does not permit incorporating your program into proprietary programs. If your program is a subroutine library, you may consider it more useful to permit linking proprietary applications with the library. If this is what you want to do, use the GNU Library General Public License instead of this License.

Index